Critical Race Theory THE CUTTING EDGE

Critical Race Theory

THE CUTTING EDGE

Edited by
Richard Delgado

TEMPLE UNIVERSITY PRESS PHILADELPHIA

Temple University Press, Philadelphia 19122
Copyright © 1995 by Temple University. All rights reserved
Published 1995

☉ The paper used in this publication meets the minimum
requirements of American National Standard for Information
Sciences—Permanence of Paper for Printed Library Materials,
ANSI Z39.48-1984

Printed in the United States of America

Text design by Arlene Putterman

Library of Congress Cataloging-in-Publication Data

Critical race theory : the cutting edge / edited by Richard
Delgado.
        p.   cm.
    Includes bibliographical references and index.
    ISBN 1-56639-347-7. — ISBN 1-56639-348-5 (pbk.)
    1. Race relations—Philosophy. 2. Assimilation
(Sociology). 3. Racism. 4. Racism in language.
I. Delgado, Richard.
HT1521.C75   1995
305.8—dc20
                                95-16203

Contents

Acknowledgments

I AM grateful for the assistance and cooperation of the many Conference of Critical Race Theory members who contributed their work and encouragement. I am particularly indebted to the members of the 1993 workshop, where the idea for this reader was born. Jean Stefancic and Bonnie Kae Grover contributed suggestions, technical assistance, and editing ideas. My thanks to Doris Braendel and Temple University Press for their professionalism and skill. Marge Brunner, Cindy Carter, Kay Wilkie, Anne Guthrie, and Vanessa Smith prepared the manuscript with intelligence and precision.

Introduction

THIS book collects the best of a new generation of writing about civil rights—the cutting edge of Critical Race Theory, or CRT. Here you will find the ironic, challenging Chronicles of Derrick Bell, the evocative autobiographical essays of Patricia Williams, the implacable assault on traditional civil rights strategies of Girardeau Spann. You will read James Gordon's astonishing historical argument that the first Justice Harlan (author of the dissent in *Plessy v. Ferguson*) had a black brother. You will read about the movies' dominant gaze from Margaret Russell, about "microaggressions"—those stunning, ambiguous assaults on the dignity and self-regard of people of color—from the pen of law professor Peggy Davis. You will read about interracial crime, the black community's relation to its own youthful offenders, and whether a black man can get a fair trial from a white jury. In an essay that rivals the best of Tom Wolfe, you will read Trina Grillo and Stephanie Wildman's demonstration of how white people, even ones of good will, twist discussions concerning race so that the conversation becomes about themselves. You will read about the atrocities of federal Indian law, minority women who wear their hair in braids (and live to tell the tale), race as masks, the role of guns and self-defense in the black community, and what it is like to be a black female professor teaching law at a major law school. You will read Thomas Ross's and Mary Dudziak's brilliant examinations of the "dominant narratives" of the law.

This book is for the reader who wishes to learn about Critical Race Theory, a dynamic, eclectic, and growing movement in the law, and about the young writers, many but by no means all of color, who have been challenging racial orthodoxy, shaking up the legal academy, questioning comfortable liberal premises, and leading the search for new ways of thinking about our nation's most intractable, and insoluble, problem—race.

Critical Race Theory sprang up in the mid-1970s with the early work of Derrick Bell (an African American) and Alan Freeman (a white), both of whom were deeply distressed over the slow pace of racial reform in the United States. It seemed to them—and they were quickly joined by others—that the civil rights movement of the 1960s had stalled, that, indeed, many of its gains were being rolled back. New approaches were needed to understand and come to grips with the more subtle, but just as deeply entrenched, varieties of racism that characterize our times. Old approaches—filing amicus briefs, marching, coining new litigation strategies, writing articles in legal and popular journals exhorting our fellow citizens to exercise moral leadership in the search for racial justice—were yielding smaller and smaller returns. As Freeman once put it, if you are up a tree and a flood is coming, sometimes you have to climb down before finding shelter in a taller, safer one.

Out of this felt need came Critical Race Theory, now a body of more than three hundred leading law review articles and perhaps a dozen books, most of which are noted or excerpted in this volume. The movement has predecessors—Critical Legal Studies, to which it owes a great debt, feminism, and Continental social and political philosophy. It derives its inspiration from the American civil rights tradition, including Martin Luther King, W.E.B. Du Bois, Rosa Parks, and Cesar Chavez, and from nationalist movements, including Malcolm X and the Panthers. Although its intellectual origins go back much further, as a self-conscious entity the movement began organizing in 1989, holding its first working session shortly thereafter. This book grew out of the fifth annual workshop, held at Mills College, Oakland, California, in June 1993, at which time the organization decided to put its energies into producing a reader.

CRT begins with a number of basic insights. One is that racism is normal, not aberrant, in American society. Because racism is an ingrained feature of our landscape, it looks ordinary and natural to persons in the culture. Formal equal opportunity—rules and laws that insist on treating blacks and whites (for example) alike—can thus remedy only the more extreme and shocking sorts of injustice, the ones that do stand out. Formal equality can do little about the business-as-usual forms of racism that people of color confront every day and that account for much misery, alienation, and despair.

Critical Race Theory's challenge to racial oppression and the status quo sometimes takes the form of storytelling, in which writers analyze the myths, presuppositions, and received wisdoms that make up the common culture about race and that invariably render blacks and other minorities one-down. Starting from the premise that a culture constructs social reality in ways that promote its own self-interest (or that of elite groups), these scholars set out to construct a different reality. Our social world, with its rules, practices, and assignments of prestige and power, is not fixed; rather, we construct it with words, stories, and silence. But we need not acquiesce in arrangements that are unfair and one-sided. By writing and speaking against them, we may hope to contribute to a better, fairer world.

A third premise underlying much of Critical Race Theory is interest-convergence. Developed by Derrick Bell, this idea holds that white elites will tolerate or encourage racial advances for blacks only when they also promote white self-interest. Other Criticalists question whether civil rights law is designed to benefit blacks, and even suggest that it is really a homeostatic mechanism that ensures that racial progress occurs at just the right pace: change that is too rapid would be unsettling to society at large; change that is too slow could prove destabilizing. Many question whether white judges are likely to propel racial change, raising the possibility that nonjudicial avenues may prove more promising. A number of writers employ Critical tools to address such classic civil rights issues as federal Indian law, remedies for racist speech and hate-motivated crime, and women's reproductive liberty.

In addition to exploring new approaches to racial justice, Criticalists have been trying out new forms of writing and thought. Many Critical writers are post-moderns, who believe that form and substance are closely connected. Accordingly, they have been using biography and autobiography, stories and counter-stories to expose the false necessity and unintentional irony of much current civil rights law and scholarship. Others have been experimenting with humor, satire, and narrative analysis to reveal the circular, self-serving nature of particular legal doctrines or rules. Most mainstream scholars embrace universalism over particularity, abstract principles and the "rule of law" over perspectivism (an approach characterized by an emphasis on concrete personal experience). Clashing with this more traditional view, Critical Race Theory writers emphasize the opposite, in what has been termed the "call to context." For CRT scholars, general laws may be appropriate in some areas (such as, perhaps, trusts and estates, or highway speed limits). But political and moral discourse is not one of them. Normative discourse (as civil rights is) is highly fact sensitive—adding even one new fact can change intuition radically. For example, imagine a youth convicted of a serious crime. One's first response may be to urge severe punishment. But add one fact—he was seen laughing as he walked away from the scene—and one's intuition changes: even more serious punishment now seems appropriate. But add another fact—he is mentally impaired, or was abused as a child—and now leniency seems in order. Because civil rights is more like the latter case than the former (highway law), universal, neutral principles like formal equality can be more of a hindrance than a help in the search for racial justice. For this reason, many CRT writers urge attention to the details of minorities' lives as a foundation for our national civil rights strategy.

Each of the prime Critical themes just mentioned—the call for context, critique of liberalism, insistence that racism is ordinary not exceptional, and the notion that traditional civil rights law has been more valuable to whites than to blacks—and others as well, have come in for criticism. Some mainstream critics challenge the use of stories and parables, warning that they can be used to mislead as easily as ordinary analysis can. Others charge that the race-Crits are too negative—that the despairing images of racial progress and regress that they put forward leave too little room for hope. A number of the critics appear in this volume, particularly in Part X, along with the Crits' responses. Ultimately, the reader will have to decide for herself or himself whether our system of civil rights law needs a complete overhaul, as the CRT writers argue, or just a minor tune-up—and if the former, whether the race-Crits' suggestions are good places to start. It is with the hope that the fifty closely edited selections by the *enfants terribles* (and *éminences gris*) of the left can help the reader make this decision that Temple University Press offers this book.

A NOTE about the selections that make up this volume. We chose articles that were original, readable, and that collectively illustrated a number of themes we deemed characteristic of Critical Race Theory. Space considerations prevented us from including many excellent works—these are generally mentioned in the

Notes or Suggested Readings. Most of the articles that appear here have been edited for readability, and the number of footnotes has been radically pruned. Readers desiring to peruse the complete works will find their citations at the bottom of each article-opening page.

A few authors declined to participate. In particular, three articles that played important parts in the early development of Critical Race Theory could not be included. All of these influential pieces are mentioned in the relevant Suggested Readings. Each spurred additional scholarly articles that extended and explored their ideas, many of which are included in this book. The three articles are significant for their role in the formation of Critical theory, however, and warrant separate treatment here. In 1987, Professor Mari Matsuda of Georgetown University attended a "summit meeting" of the Conference of Critical Legal Studies in Los Angeles, California, which was called in order to discuss, for the first time in an extended way, issues of relevance to the minority community. Several of the presentations were later printed in a special edition of *Harvard Civil Rights-Civil Liberties Law Review* entitled "Minority Critique of CLS." These articles included Professor Matsuda's "Looking to the Bottom" (cited fully in the Suggested Readings for Part X). The article praised the theories and critiques of writers in the CLS movement, but nevertheless urged that their work could be improved by the practice of looking to the stories and viewpoints of persons of color who have experienced racism. She theorized that this technique of "looking to the bottom" can enhance jurisprudential method, and in particular that it justifies a reparations-oriented approach to racial justice.

In an article also published in 1987, Professor Charles Lawrence of Georgetown Law School argued that much discrimination is unconscious, that is, not accompanied by the actor's intent to harm or disadvantage a particular black victim. Yet, legal doctrine for the most part requires demonstration of intent. In "The Id, the Ego, and Equal Protection" (cited fully in the Suggested Readings for Part IV), Lawrence urged that the Supreme Court's approach in *Washington v. Davis* (a major case on "intent versus effects") is inadequate to deal with racism that is implicit, or latent, rather than express. He proposed a new "cultural meaning" test, according to which courts would look to cultural symbols to decide whether an act's meaning is racially discriminatory. The article constituted an important, early use of social science to expose the deficiencies of legal doctrine.

Finally, in "Race, Reform, and Retrenchment," published in 1988 (cited fully in the Suggested Readings for Part I), CRT co-founder Kimberlé Crenshaw critiqued the conservative right's and the liberal left's approaches to antidiscrimination law. Echoing the work of others, she argued that "color blind" race-reform law, espoused by the conservative right, can make only modest inroads into institutionalized racism. But she also pointed out that the left's harsh criticism of such measures ignores the benefits they can provide, while downplaying the role racism plays in legitimizing oppression. Her article constituted an early, and influential, attempt to delineate the differences between Critical and non-Critical approaches to racial justice.

CRITIQUE OF LIBERALISM

VIRTUALLY all of Critical Race thought is marked by deep discontent with liberalism, a system of civil rights litigation and activism characterized by incrementalism, faith in the legal system, and hope for progress, among other things. Indeed, virtually every essay in this book can be seen as an effort to go beyond the legacy of mainstream civil rights thought to something better.

Part I begins with two chapters written in a storytelling vein. Derrick Bell's arresting "racial realist" tale asks the reader to imagine a Space Trader offer to sacrifice all American blacks. This is followed by Michael Olivas's reflections on his own ethnic history, as well as that of Native Americans and Chinese Americans; he draws the sobering conclusion that Bell's frightening trade has indeed happened many times in U.S. history. Part I ends with Girardeau Spann's remorseless indictment of the U.S. legal system, particularly the Supreme Court, for failing to safeguard the rights of minorities. He urges that communities of color abandon their near reflexive practice of taking racial grievances to courts and instead pursue ordinary, interest-based "pure politics"—mass mobilization, election of local officials, and requests directed to the legislative and executive branches of government. The reader interested in going further may wish to consult the demanding, but original, critiques of the current electoral system by Lani Guinier, a number of which are listed in the Suggested Readings for Part I.

1 Racial Realism—After We're Gone: Prudent Speculations on America in a Post-Racial Epoch

DERRICK BELL

I T I S time—as a currently popular colloquialism puts it—to "Get Real" about race and the persistence of racism in America. The very visible social and economic progress made by some African Americans can no longer obscure the increasingly dismal demographics that reflect the status of most of those whose forebears in this country were slaves. Statistics on poverty, unemployment, and income support the growing concern that the slow racial advances of the 1960s and 1970s have ended, and retrogression is well under way.

Perhaps Thomas Jefferson had it right after all. When musing on the future of Africans in this country, he expressed the view that blacks should be free, but he was certain that "the two races, equally free, cannot live in the same government."[1] Jefferson suspected that blacks, whether originally a distinct race, or made distinct by time and circumstances, are "inferior to the whites in the endowments both of body and mind."[2] Such differences prompted Jefferson to warn that "[i]f the legal barriers between the races were torn down, but no provision made for their separation, 'convulsions' would ensue, which would 'probably never end but in the extermination of the one or the other race.' "[3]

Jefferson's views were widely shared. In his summary of how the Constitution's framers came to include recognition and protection of human slavery in a document that was committed to the protection of individual liberties, Professor Staughton Lynd wrote: "Even the most liberal of the Founding Fathers were unable to imagine a society in which whites and Negroes would live together as fellow-citizens. Honor and intellectual consistency drove them to favor abolition; personal distaste, to fear it."[4]

In our era, the premier precedent of *Brown v. Board of Education* promised to be the twentieth century's Emancipation Proclamation. Both policies, however, served to advance the nation's foreign policy interests more than they provided actual aid to blacks. Nevertheless, both actions inspired blacks to push for long-denied freedoms. Alas, the late Alexander Bickel's dire prediction has proven cor-

34 ST. LOUIS U. L.J. 393 (1990). Originally published in the St. Louis University Law Journal. Reprinted by permission.

rect. He warned that the *Brown* decision would not be reversed but "[could] be headed for—dread word—irrelevance."[5]

Given the current tenuous status of African Americans, the desperate condition of those on the bottom, and the growing resentment of the successes realized by those who are making gains despite the odds, one wonders how this country would respond to a crisis in which the sacrifice of the most basic rights of blacks would result in the accrual of substantial benefits to all whites? This primary issue is explored in a fictional story that could prove to be prophetic.

The Chronicle of the Space Traders

The first surprise was not their arrival—they had sent radio messages weeks before advising that they would land 1,000 space ships along the Atlantic coast on January 1, 2000. The surprise was the space ships themselves. Unlike the Star Wars variety, the great vessels, each the size of an aircraft carrier, resembled the square-shaped landing craft used to transport troops to beachhead invasion sites during World War II.

The great ships entered the earth's atmosphere in a spectacular fiery display that was visible throughout the western hemisphere. After an impressive, cross-continental "fly by," they landed in the waters just off the Atlantic coast. The lowered bows of the mammoth ships exposed cavernous holds that were huge, dark, and impenetrable.

Then came the second surprise. The welcoming delegation of government officials and members of the media covering the event could hear and understand the crew as they disembarked. They spoke English and sounded like the former President Ronald Reagan, whose recorded voice, in fact, they had dubbed into their computerized language translation system. The visitors, however, were invisible—at least they could not be seen by whites who were present or by television viewers to the special coverage that, despite howls of protest, had preempted football bowl games. American blacks were able to see them all too well. "They look like old South sheriffs, mean and ugly," some said. They were, according to others, "more like slave drivers and overseers." Particularly frantic reports claimed, "The visitors are dressed in white sheets and hoods like the Ku Klux Klan." In whatever guise they saw them, blacks all agreed that the visitors embodied the personification of racist evil.

The space visitors cut short the long-winded welcoming speeches, expressed no interest in parades and banquets, and made clear that their long journey was undertaken for one purpose, and one purpose only: trade. Here was the third surprise. The visitors had brought materials that they knew the United States needed desperately: gold to bail out the almost bankrupt federal, state, and local governments; special chemicals that would sanitize the almost uninhabitable environment; and a totally safe nuclear engine with fuel to relieve the nation's swiftly diminishing fossil fuel resources.

In return, the visitors wanted only one thing. This demand created more of a shock than a surprise. The visitors wanted to take back to their home star all African Americans (defined as all citizens whose birth certificates listed them as black). The proposition instantly reduced the welcoming delegation to a humbling disarray. The visitors seemed to expect this reaction. After emphasizing that acceptance of their offer was entirely voluntary and would not be coerced, they withdrew to their ships. The Traders promised to give the nation a period of sixteen days to respond. The decision would be due on January 17, the national holiday commemorating Dr. Martin Luther King, Jr.'s birthday.

The Space Traders' proposition immediately dominated the country's attention. The President called the Congress into special session, and governors did the same for state legislatures that were not then meeting. Blacks were outraged. Individuals and their leaders cried in unison, "You have not seen them. Why don't you just say no?" Although for many whites the trade posed an embarrassing question, the Space Traders' offer proved to be an irresistible temptation. Decades of conservative, laissez-faire capitalism had taken their toll. The nation that had funded the reconstruction of the free world a half-century ago following World War II was now in a very difficult state. Massive debt had debilitated all functioning. The environment was in shambles, and crude oil and coal resources were almost exhausted.

In addition, the race problem had greatly worsened in the last decade. A relatively small group of blacks had survived the retrogression of civil rights protection that marked the 1990s. Perhaps twenty percent managed to make good in the increasingly technologically oriented society. But more than one-half of the group had sunk to an unacknowledged outcast status. They were confined in former inner-city areas that had been divorced from their political boundaries. High walls surrounded these areas, and entrance and exit were carefully controlled. No one even dreamed anymore that this mass of blacks and dark-complexioned Hispanics would ever "overcome."

Supposedly, United States officials tried in secret negotiations to get the Space Traders to exchange only those blacks locked in the inner cities, but the visitors made it clear that this was an all-or-nothing offer. During these talks, the Space Traders warned that they would withdraw their proposition unless the United States halted the flight of the growing numbers of blacks who—fearing the worst—were fleeing the country. In response, executive orders were issued and implemented, barring blacks from leaving the country until the Space Traders' proposition was fully debated and resolved. "It is your patriotic duty," blacks were told, "to allow this great issue to be resolved through the democratic process and in accordance with the rule of law."

Blacks and their white supporters challenged these procedures in the courts, but their suits were dismissed as "political questions" that must be determined by co-equal branches of government. Even so, forces that supported the proposition took seriously blacks' charges that if the nation accepted the Space Traders' proposition it would violate the Constitution's most basic protections. Acting swiftly, supporters began the necessary steps to convene a constitutional con-vention. In ten days of feverish work, the quickly assembled convention drafted and, by a substantial majority, passed an amendment that declared:

> *Every citizen is subject at the call of Congress to selection for special service for periods necessary to protect domestic interests and international needs.*

The amendment was scheduled for ratification by the states in a national referendum. If ratified, the amendment would validate previously drafted legis-lation that would induct all blacks into special service for transportation under the terms of the Space Traders' offer. In the brief but intense pre–election day campaign, pro-ratification groups' major argument had an appeal that surprised even those who made it. Their message was straightforward:

> *The framers intended America to be a white country. The evidence of their in-tentions is present in the original Constitution. After more than 137 years of good faith efforts to build a healthy, stable interracial nation, we have concluded that our survival today—as the framers did in the beginning—requires that we sacri-fice the rights of blacks in order to protect and further the interests of whites. The framers' example must be our guide. Patriotism and not pity must govern our de-cision. We should ratify the amendment and accept the Space Traders' proposi-tion.*

To their credit, many whites worked hard to defeat the amendment. Never-theless, given the usual fate of minority rights when subjected to referenda or initiatives, the outcome was never really in doubt. The final vote tally confirmed the predictions. By a vote of seventy percent in favor—thirty percent opposed—Americans accepted the Space Traders' proposition. Expecting this result, gov-ernment agencies had secretly made preparations to facilitate the transfer. Some blacks escaped, and many thousands lost their lives in futile efforts to resist the joint federal and state police teams responsible for the roundup, cataloguing, and transportation of blacks to the coast.

The dawn of the last Martin Luther King holiday that the nation would ever observe illuminated an extraordinary sight. The Space Traders had drawn their strange ships right up to the beaches, discharged their cargoes of gold, minerals, and machinery, and began loading long lines of silent black people. At the Traders' direction, the inductees were stripped of all but a single undergarment. Heads bowed, arms linked by chains, black people left the new world as their forebears had arrived.

And just as the forced importation of those African ancestors had made the nation's wealth and productivity possible, so their forced exodus saved the coun-try from the need to pay the price of its greed-based excess. There might be other unforeseen costs of the trade, but, like their colonial predecessors, Americans facing the twenty-first century were willing to avoid those problems as long as possible.

Discussion

It is not a futile exercise to try to imagine what the country would be like in the days and weeks after the last space ship swooshed off and disappeared into deep space—beyond the reach of our most advanced electronic tracking equipment. How, one might ask, would the nation bear the guilt for its decision? Certainly, many white Americans would feel badly about the trade and the sacrifice of humans for economic well-being. But the country has a 200-year history of treating black lives as property. Genocide is an ugly, but no less accurate, description of what the nation did, and continues to do, to the American Indian. Ignoring the Treaty of Guadalupe Hidalgo was only the first of many betrayals by whites toward Americans of Spanish descent. At the time of writing, Japanese Americans who suffered detention during World War II and lost hard-earned property and status were still awaiting payment of the small compensation approved, but not yet funded, by Congress. The country manages to carry on despite the burden of guilt that these injustices impose against our own people. In all likelihood, the country would manage the Space Trader deal despite recriminations, rationalizations, and remorse. Quite soon, moreover, the nation could become preoccupied with problems of social unrest based on class rather than race.

The trade would solve the budget deficit, provide an unlimited energy source, and restore an unhealthy environment. The new resources, however, would not automatically correct the growing income disparities between blacks and whites as reflected in the growing income gap between upper and lower income families in the nation as a whole. According to the Center on Budget and Policy Priorities: "In 1985, 1986 and 1987, the poorest fifth of American families received only 4.6 percent of the national family income. . . ."[6] The poorest two-fifths of American families received 15.4 percent of the national family income in 1986 and 1987.[7] In contrast, "the richest fifth of all families received 43.7 percent of the national family income in 1986 and 1987, the highest percentage on record."[8] The top two-fifths of all families' share was 67.8 percent, which broke another record.[9] The poorest two-fifths of American families received a smaller share of the national family income in 1986 and 1987 than in any other year since the Census Bureau began collecting data in 1947.[10] Meanwhile, the richest two-fifths of American families received a larger share of the national income in 1987 than in any year since 1947.[11]

These statistics are shocking, but they are certainly not a secret. Even more shocking than the serious disparities in income is the relative silence of whites about economic gaps that should constitute a major political issue. Certainly, it is a matter of far more importance to voters than the need either to protect the American flag from "desecration" by protesters or to keep the "Willie Hortons" of the world from obtaining prison furloughs. Why the low level of interest about so critical a pocketbook issue? Why is there no political price to pay when our government bails out big businesses like savings and loans, Chrysler, Lockheed, and even New York City for mistakes, mismanagement, and thinly veiled theft that are the corporations' fault? Why is there no public outrage when thousands of farmers go under due to changes in economic conditions that are not their fault? Why does government remain on the sidelines as millions of factory workers lose their livelihood because of owners' greed—not the workers' fault? Why is there no hue and cry at a tax structure that rewards builders who darken the skies with gigantic, expensive condominiums for the rich while the working class spend up to one-half of their minimum-wage incomes for marginal housing, and as our poor live on the streets?

The reasons are likely numerous and complex. One substantial factor, however, seems to be the unstated understanding by the mass of whites that they will accept large disparities in economic opportunity in comparison to other whites as long as they have a priority over blacks and other people of color for access to those opportunities. On any number of occasions in American history, whites have acquiesced in—when they were not pressuring for—policy decisions that subordinated the rights of blacks in order to further some other interest. One might well ask, what do the masses of working class and poor whites gain from this continued sacrifice of black rights that justifies such acquiescence when so often the policies limit whites' opportunities as well as those of blacks?

The answer is as unavoidable as it is disturbing. Even those whites who lack wealth and power are sustained in their sense of racial superiority by policy decisions that sacrifice black rights. The subordination of blacks seems to reassure whites of an unspoken, but no less certain, property right in their "whiteness." This right is recognized by courts and society as all property rights are upheld under a government created and sustained primarily for that purpose. With blacks gone, the property right in "whiteness" goes with them. How long will the masses of whites remain silent about their puny share of the nation's wealth?

The film *Resurgence* shows a poor southern white, mired in poverty, who nevertheless declares: "Every morning I wake up and thank God I'm white." But after we're gone, we can be fairly sure, this individual will not shout, "Thank God, I'm poor." What will he and millions like him shout when the reality of his real status hits him? How will the nation's leaders respond to discontent that has been building for so long and that has been so skillfully misdirected toward a group no longer here? It will be too late to call off the trade—too late to bring back African Americans to fill their traditional role. Indeed, even without an extraterrestrial trade mission, the hour is growing late for expecting that black people will always keep the hope of racial equality alive. For millions in what is now designated the underclass, that hope has already died in the devastation of their lives. The cost of this devastation is not limited to the ghetto. As manifestations of self-hate and despair turn to rage and retaliation against the oppressors, those costs will rise dramatically and frightfully.

When I ask audiences how Americans would vote on the Space Traders' offer, rather substantial majorities express the view that the offer would be accepted. That is a present day measure of an almost certain future decision—one that will be required whether or not we have trade-oriented visitors from outer space. The century-long cycles of racial progress and reform cannot continue, and should not. Those subordinated on the basis of color cannot continue forever in this status, and will not. Politics, the courts, and self-help have failed or proved to be inadequate. Perhaps the prospect of black people removed from the American landscape will bring a necessary reassessment of who has suffered most from our subordination.

NOTES

1. Quoted in Staughton Lynd, *Slavery and the Founding Fathers, in* BLACK HISTORY 115, 129 (M. Drimmer ed., 1968) (citations omitted).

2. ROBINSON, SLAVERY IN THE STRUCTURE OF AMERICAN POLITICS, 1765–1820, at 91 (1971) (quoting NOTES ON THE STATE OF VIRGINIA (Abernethy ed., 1964)).

3. *Id.* at 90.

4. Lynd, *supra* note 1, at 129.

5. ALEXANDER BICKEL, THE SUPREME COURT AND THE IDEA OF PROGRESS 151 (1978).

6. CENTER ON BUDGET AND POLICY PRIORITIES, STILL FAR FROM THE DREAM: RECENT DEVELOPMENTS IN BLACK INCOME, EMPLOYMENT AND POVERTY 21 (Oct. 1988).

7. *Id.*

8. *Id.* at 22.

9. *Id.*

10. *Id.* at 21.

11. *Id.* at 22.

2 The Chronicles, My Grandfather's Stories, and Immigration Law: The Slave Traders Chronicle as Racial History

MICHAEL A. OLIVAS

THE funny thing about stories is that everyone has one. My grandfather had them, with plenty to spare. When I was very young, he would regale me with stories, usually about politics, baseball, and honor. These were his themes, the subject matter he carved out for himself and his grandchildren. As the oldest grandson and his first godchild, I held a special place of responsibility and affection. In Mexican families, this patrimony handed to young boys is one remnant of older times that is fading, like the use of Spanish in the home, posadas at Christmas, or the deference accorded all elders.

In Sabino Olivas' world, there were three verities, ones that he adhered to his entire life: political and personal loyalties are paramount; children should work hard and respect their elders; and people should conduct their lives with honor. Of course, each of these themes had a canon of stories designed, like parables, to illustrate the larger theme, and, like the Bible, to be interlocking, cross referenced, and synoptic. That is, they could be embellished in the retelling, but they had to conform to the general themes of loyalty, hard work, and honor.

Several examples will illustrate the overarching theoretical construction of my grandfather's worldview and show how, for him, everything was connected, and profound. Like other folklorists and storytellers, he employed mythic heroes or imbued people he knew with heroic dimensions. This is an important part of capturing the imagination of young children, for the mythopoeic technique overemphasizes characteristics and allows listeners to fill in the gaps by actively inviting them to rewrite the story and remember it in their own terms. As a result, as my family grew (I am the oldest of ten), I would hear these taproot stories retold both by my grandfather to the other kids and by my brothers and sisters to others. The core of the story would be intact, transformed by the teller's accumulated sense of the story line and its application.

34 ST. LOUIS L.J. 425 (1990). Originally published in the St. Louis University Law Journal. Reprinted by permission.

One of the earliest stories was about New Mexico's United States Senator Bronson Cutting, and how he had died in a plane crash after attempting to help Northern New Mexico Hispanics regain land snatched from them by greedy developers. Growing up near Tierra Amarilla, New Mexico, as he did, my grandfather was heir to a longstanding oral tradition of defining one's status by land ownership. To this day, land ownership in Northern New Mexico is a tangle of aboriginal Indian rights, Spanish land grants, Anglo and Mexican greed, treaties, and developer domination. Most outsiders (that is, anyone south of Santa Fe) know this issue only by having seen *The Milagro Beanfield War*, the Robert Redford movie based on John Nichols' book. But my grandfather's story was that sinister forces had somehow tampered with Senator Cutting's plane because he was a man of the people, aligned against wealthy interests. Senator Cutting, I was led to believe as I anchored the story with my own points of reference, was more like Jimmy Stewart in *Mr. Smith Goes to Washington* than like the Claude Rains character, who would lie to get his own greedy way.

Of course, as I grew older, I learned that the true story was not exactly as my grandfather had told it. Land ownership in New Mexico is complicated; the Senator had his faults; and my grandfather ran afoul of Cutting's political enemy, Senator Dennis Chavez. But the story still held its sway over me.

His other favorite story, which included a strong admonition to me, was about how he and other Hispanics had been treated in Texas on their way to World War I. A trainload of soldiers from Arizona and Northern New Mexico, predominantly of Mexican origin (both New Mexico and Arizona had only recently become states), were going to training camp in Ft. Hays, Kansas. Their train stopped in a town near Amarillo, Texas, and all the men poured out to eat at a restaurant, one that catered to train travelers. But only to some. A sign prominently proclaimed, "No coloreds or Mexicans allowed," and word spread among them that this admissions policy was taken seriously.

My grandfather, who until this time had never been outside the Territory or the State of New Mexico (after 1912), was not used to this kind of indignity. After all, he was from a state where Hispanics and Indians constituted a majority of the population, especially in the North, and it was his first face-to-face encounter with racism, Texas style. Shamefacedly, the New Mexicans ate the food that Anglo soldiers bought and brought to the train, but he never forgot the humiliation and anger he felt that day. Sixty-five years later, when he told me this story, he remembered clearly how most of the men died in France or elsewhere in Europe, defending a country that never fully accorded them their rights.

The longer, fuller version, replete with wonderful details of how at training camp they had ridden sawhorses with saddles, always ended with the anthem, "Ten cuidado con los Tejanos, porque son todos desgraciados y no tienen verguenza" (Be careful with Texans because they are all sons-of-bitches and have no shame). To be a *sin verguenza*—shameless, or without honor—was my grandfather's cruelest condemnation, reserved for faithless husbands, reprobates, lying grandchildren, and Anglo Texans.

These stories, which always had admonitions about honorable behavior, always had a moral to them, with implications for grandchildren. Thus, I was admonished to vote Democrat (because of FDR and the Catholic JFK), to support the National League (because the Brooklyn Dodgers had first hired Black players and because the relocated Los Angeles Dodgers had a farm team in Albuquerque), and to honor my elders (for example, by using the more formal *usted* instead of the informal *tu*).

People react to Derrick Bell and his storytelling in predictably diverse ways. People of color, particularly progressive minority scholars, have been drawn to his work. The old guard has been predictably scornful, as in Lino Graglia's dyspeptic assessment: "There can be no sin for which reading Professor Derrick Bell is not, for me, adequate punishment. . . . [The Chronicles are] wails of embittered, hate-filled self-pity. . . ."[1]

My objection, if that is the proper word, to the *Chronicle of the Space Traders* is not that it is too fantastic or unlikely to occur, but rather the opposite: This scenario has occurred, and more than once in our nation's history. Not only have Blacks been enslaved, as the *Chronicle* sorrowfully notes, but other racial groups have been conquered and removed, imported for their labor and not allowed to participate in the society they built, or expelled when their labor was no longer considered necessary.

Consider the immigration history and political economy of three groups whose United States history predates the prophecy for the year 2000: Cherokee removal and the Trail of Tears; Chinese laborers and the Chinese Exclusion Laws; and Mexicans in the Bracero Program and Operation Wetback. These three racial groups share different histories of conquest, exploitation, and legal disadvantage; but even a brief summary of their treatment in United States law shows commonalities of racial animus, legal infirmity, and majority domination of legal institutions guised as "political questions."[2] I could have also chosen the national origins or labor histories of other Indian tribes, the Filipinos, the Native Hawaiians, the Japanese, the Guamese, the Puerto Ricans, or the Vietnamese, in other words, the distinct racial groups whose conquest, colonization, enslavement, or immigration histories mark them as candidates for the Space Traders' evil exchange.

Cherokee Removal and the Trail of Tears

Although the Cherokees were, in the early 1800s, the largest tribe in what was the Southeastern United States, genocidal wars, abrogated treaties, and Anglo land settlement practices had reduced them to 15,000 by 1838, predominantly in Georgia, Tennessee, North Carolina, and Alabama.[3] During the 1838–1839 forced march to the "Indian Territory" of what is now Oklahoma, a quarter of the Cherokees died on the "Trail of Tears," the long march of the Cherokees, Seminoles, Creeks, Choctaws, and Chickasaw. Gold had been discovered on Indian land in Georgia. The newly confederated states of the United

States did not want sovereign Indian nations coexisting in their jurisdiction; and President Andrew Jackson, engaged in a bitter struggle with Chief Justice John Marshall, saw the removal of the Indians as a means to his own political ends.

Not only were the tribes removed from their ancestral homelands, guaranteed to them by treaties, at forced gunpoint, but there were other elements that fore-shadowed Bell's *Chronicles*. The Cherokees had sought to integrate themselves into their conquerors' social and legal systems; they engaged as sovereigns to ne-gotiate formally and lawfully their place in the United States polity; and they lit-igated their grievances in Federal courts to no avail. Like the fictional Blacks in the *Chronicles*, they too appealed to the kindness of strangers. One authoritative account of this shameful occasion noted:

> [M]any Cherokees continued to hold to their hope even while soldiers drove them from their homes into the stockades and on to the Trail of Tears. Some refused to believe that the American people would allow this to happen. Until the very end, the Cherokees spoke out supporting their rights to resist removal and to continue to live in the ancestral homelands.[4]

In order to coexist with their conquerors, the Cherokees had adopted Anglo ways, developing their own alphabet, bilingual (English-Cherokee) newspapers, a court system, and a written constitution.[5] They entered into a series of treaties that ceded dominion to the United States, but that preserved a substantial mea-sure of self determination and autonomy.[6] Beginning in 1802 with the Georgia Compact, however, white landowners and officials variously entered into and re-pudiated treaties and other agreements with Indian tribes.[7] By 1830, the Indian Removal Act had been passed by Congress,[8] and the stage was set for *Cherokee Nation v. Georgia*[9] and *Worcester v. Georgia*.[10] In *Cherokee Nation*, Justice Mar-shall held that the Cherokee were a "domestic dependent nation[,]" and thus the Supreme Court did not have original jurisdiction; he invited another "proper case with proper parties" to determine the "mere question of right."[sic].[11]

The "proper party" presented itself the following year, in *Worcester v. Geor-gia*, and Chief Justice Marshall held for the Cherokees. Marshall found that each Indian tribe was

> a distinct community, occupying its own territory, with boundaries accurately described, in which the laws of a state can have no force, and which the citizens of [a state] have no right to enter, but with the assent of the [Indians] themselves, or in conformity with treaties, and with the acts of Congress.[12]

Despite this first clarification of Indian sovereignty and the early example of pre-emption, the state of Georgia refused to obey the Court's order, and President Jackson refused to enforce the Cherokees' victory. Georgia, contemptuous of the Court's authority, in what it contended was its own affairs, did not even argue its side before the Court.

The Cherokees' victory was Pyrrhic, for even their supporters, such as Daniel Webster, turned their attention away from enforcement of *Worcester* to the Nullification Crisis, which threatened the very existence of the Union.[13] The case of *Worcester* was resolved by a pardon, technically mooting the Cherokees' victory.[14] The "greater good" of the Union thus sacrificed Cherokee rights at the altar of political expediency, foreshadowing Blacks' sacrifice during the Civil War, Japanese rights sacrificed during World War II, Mexicans' rights sacrificed during Operation Wetback, and Black rights extinguished in the year 2000 for the Space Traders.

Chinese Exclusion

No racial group has been singled out for separate, racist treatment in United States immigration law more than have the Chinese. A full political analysis of immigration treaties, statutes, cases, and practices reveals an unapologetic, variegated racial character that today distinctly disadvantages Latin Americans. But peculiar racial antipathy has been specifically reserved for Asians, particularly the Chinese. While Chinese laborers were not enslaved in exactly the same fashion that Blacks had been, they were imported under a series of formal and informal labor contracting devices. These were designed to provide cheap, exploitable raw labor for the United States railroad industry, a labor force that would have few legal or social rights. Immigration law developments in the 1800s, particularly the last third of the century, were dominated by racial devices employed to control the Chinese laborers and deny them formal rights. These formal legal devices included treaties, statutes, and cases.

Anti-Chinese animus was particularly virulent in California, where a series of substantive and petty nuisance state ordinances were aimed at the Chinese. These ordinances provided for arbitrary inspections of Chinese laundries,[15] special tax levies,[16] inspections and admission regulations for aliens entering California ports,[17] mandated grooming standards for prisoners that prohibited pigtails,[18] and a variety of other regulations designed to harass and discriminate against the laborers.[19] Many of these statutes were enacted in defiance of the preemptive role of the federal government in immigration policymaking, and would not have survived the United States–China Burlingame Treaty, adopted in 1868.

Although many of these statutes were struck down and Reconstruction legislation was worded to specify certain protections to immigrants, by 1880 the Burlingame Treaty had been amended to restrict the immigration of Chinese laborers.[20] Congress enacted the Chinese Exclusion Act in 1882,[21] and even harsher legislation in 1884.[22] By 1888, Congress reached the point of no return. Another, harsher act was passed which virtually prohibited Chinese from entering or reentering the United States,[23] while the Burlingame Treaty was altered again, ratcheting even further the mechanisms aimed at the Chinese.

In a series of important cases, the United States Supreme Court refused to strike down these federal laws and treaties, on political question grounds. In one of these cases, the Court stated:

The power of exclusion of foreigners being an incident of sovereignty belonging to the government of the United States, as a part of those sovereign powers delegated by the Constitution, the right to its exercise at any time when, in the judgment of the government, the interests of the country require it, cannot be granted away or restrained on behalf of any one. . . . If there be any just ground of complaint on the part of China [or the Chinese immigrants], it must be made to the political department of our government, which is alone competent to act upon the subject.[24]

Although the aliens, like the Cherokees before them, prevailed in some of the most egregious instances, the racist tide had undeniably turned. In 1892, Congress extended the amended Burlingame Treaty for an additional ten years, and added a provision for removing, through deportation, those Chinese who had managed to dodge the earlier bullets.[25] An extraordinary provision suspended deportation for those Chinese laborers who could qualify (through a special hardship exemption) and could furnish "one credible white witness" on their behalf.[26]

In 1893, this proviso was tested by the luckless Fong Yue Ting, who foolishly produced only another Chinese witness to stay his own deportation. The United States Supreme Court upheld his expulsion, on political question grounds.[27] The majority opinion speculated that the Chinese would not be truthful, noting that Chinese testimony in similar situations "was attended with great embarrassment, from the suspicious nature, in many instances, of the testimony offered to establish the residence of the parties, arising from the loose notions entertained by the witness of the obligations of an oath."[28] As my grandfather would have said, they obviously had no shame and were probably *sin verguenzas*.

Congress enacted additional extensions of the Chinese exclusion statutes and treaties until 1943. When the immigration laws began to become more codified, each iteration formally included specific reference to the dreaded and unpopular Chinese. Thus, the Immigration Acts of 1917, 1921, and 1924 all contain references that single out this group. If the Space Traders had landed in the late 1800s or early 1900s and demanded the Chinese in exchange for gold, antitoxins, and other considerations, there is little doubt but that the States, Congress, and the United States Supreme Court would have acquiesced.

Mexicans, the Bracero Program, and Operation Wetback

Nineteenth century Chinese labor history in the United States is one of building railroads; that of Mexicans and Mexican Americans is agricultural labor, picking perishable crops. In the Southwestern and Western United States, Mexicans picked half of the cotton and nearly 75 percent of the fruits and vegetables by the 1920s. By 1930, half of the sugar beet workers were Mexican, and 80 percent of the farmhands in Southern California were Mexican. As fields became increasingly mechanized, it was Anglo workers who rode the machines, consigning Mexicans to stoop-labor and hand cultivation. One observer noted: "The consensus of opinion of ranchers large and small . . . is that only the small minority of Mexicans are fitted for these types of labor [i.e., mechanized agricultural jobs] at the present time."[29]

Most crucial to the agricultural growers was the need for a reserve labor pool of workers who could be imported for their work, displaced when not needed, and kept in subordinate status so they could not afford to organize collectively or protest their conditions. Mexicans filled this bill perfectly, especially in the early twentieth century Southwest, where Mexican poverty and the Revolution forced rural Mexicans to come to the United States for work. This migration was facilitated by United States growers' agents, who recruited widely in Mexican villages, by the building of railroads (by Mexicans, not Chinese) from the interior of Mexico to El Paso, and by labor shortages in the United States during World War I.

Another means of controlling the spigot of Mexican farm workers was the use of immigration laws. Early labor restrictions through federal immigration law (and state law, as in California) had been aimed at Chinese workers, as outlined in the previous section. When agricultural interests pressured Congress to allow Mexican temporary workers during 1917–1921, the head tax (then set at $8.00), literacy requirements, public charge provisions, and Alien Contract Labor Law provisions were waived. By 1929, with a surplus of "native" United States workers facing the Depression, the supply of Mexicans was turned off by reimposing the immigration requirements.

While United States nativists were pointing to the evils and inferiority of Southern European immigrants, Mexicans were characterized as a docile, exploitable, deportable labor force. As one commentator noted:

> Mexican laborers, by accepting these undesirable tasks, enabled [Southwestern] agriculture and industry to flourish, thereby creating effective opportunities for [white] American workers in the higher job levels. . . . The representatives of [United States] economic interests showed the basic reason for their support of Mexican immigration[;] employers of the Southwest favored unlimited Mexican immigration because it provided them with a source of cheap labor which would be exploited to the fullest possible extent.[30]

To effectuate control over the Southern border, the Border Patrol was created in 1924, while the Department of Labor and the Immigration Bureau began a procedure in 1925 to regulate Mexican immigration by restricting the flow to workers already employed or promised positions.

During the Depression, two means were used to control Mexican workers: mass deportations and repatriations. Los Angeles was targeted for massive deportations for persons with Spanish-sounding names or Mexican features who could not produce formal papers, and over 80,000 Mexicans were deported from 1929–1935.[31] Many of these persons had the legal right to be in the country, or had been born citizens but simply could not prove their status; of course, many of these workers had been eagerly sought for perishable crops. In addition, over one-half million Mexicans were also "voluntarily" repatriated by choosing to go to Mexico rather than remain in the United States, possibly subject to formal deportation.

By 1940, the cycle had turned: labor shortages and World War II had created the need for more agricultural workers, and growers convinced the United States government to enter into a large scale contract-labor scheme, the Bracero Program. Originally begun in 1942 under an Executive Order, the program brokered laborers under contracts between the United States and Mexico.[32] Between 1942 and 1951, over one-half million "braceros" were hired under the program. Public funds were used to seek and register workers in Mexico who, after their labor had been performed, were returned to Mexico until the crops were ready to be picked again. This program was cynically employed to create a reserve pool of temporary laborers who had few rights and no vesting of equities.

By 1946, the circulation of bracero labor, both in its certification and its deportation mechanism, had become hopelessly confused. It became impossible to separate Mexican Americans from deportable Mexicans. Many United States citizens were mistakenly "repatriated" to Mexico, including men with Mexican features who had never been to Mexico.[33] Thus, a system of "drying out wetbacks" was instituted. This modest legalization process gave some Mexican braceros an opportunity to regularize their immigration status and remain in the United States while they worked as braceros.

In 1950, under these various mechanisms, 20,000 new braceros were certified, 97,000 agricultural workers were dehydrated, and 480,000 old braceros were deported back to Mexico. In 1954, over one million braceros were deported under the terms of "Operation Wetback," a "Special Mobile Force" of the Border Patrol. The program included massive roundups and deportations, factory and field raids, a relentless media campaign designed to characterize the mop-up operation as a national security necessity, and a tightening up of the border to deter undocumented immigration.

Conclusion and My Grandfather's Memories

In two of his books based on folktales from Tierra Amarilla, New Mexico, the writer Sabine Ulibarri has re-created the Hispano-Indian world of rural, northern New Mexico. In *Cuentos de Tierra Amarilla (Tales from Tierra Amarilla)*,[34] he collects a variety of wonderful tales, rooted in this isolated town that time has not changed, even today. My grandfather enjoyed this book, which I read to him in his final years, 1981 and 1982. But his favorite (and mine) was Ulibarri's masterwork, *Mi Abuela Fumaba Puros (My Grandmother Smoked Puros* [Cigars]),[35] in which an old woman lights cigars in her house to remind her of her dead husband.

My grandfather loved this story, not only because it was by his more famous *tocayo*, but because it was at once outlandish ("mujeres en Nuevo Mexico no fumaban puros"—that is, women in New Mexico did not smoke cigars) and yet very real. Smells were very real to him, evocative of earlier events and cuentos, the way that tea and madeleines unlocked Proust's prodigious memory.[36] Biscochitos evoked holidays, and empanadas Christmas. Had he outlived my grandmother, he would have had mementos in the house, perhaps prune pies or apricot jam.

My grandfather's world, with the exception of his World War I sortie in Texas and abroad, was small but not narrow. He lived by a code of behavior, one he passed to his more fortunate children (only one of whom still lives in New Mexico—my father) and grandchildren (most of whom no longer live in New Mexico). But for me, no longer in New Mexico, reading Derrick Bell's Chronicles is like talking to my grandfather or reading Sabine Ulibarri; the stories are at once outlandish, yet very real.

Folklore and corridos have always held a powerful place in Mexican society. Fiction has always held a powerful place in the human experience, and the Chronicles will inform racial jurisprudence and civil rights scholarship in the United States in ways not yet evident. Critical minority renderings of United States racial history, immigration practices, and labor economy can have equally compelling results, however, recounting what actually happened in all the sordid details. If Derrick Bell's work forces us to engage these unsavory practices, he will have performed an even greater service than that already attributed to him in this forum and elsewhere. He will have caused us to examine our grandfathers' stories and lives.

It is 1990. As a deterrent to Central American refugees and as "bait" to attract their families already in the United States, the INS began in the 1980s to incarcerate undocumented adults and unaccompanied minors in border camps.[37] One, near Brownsville, Texas, was once used as a United States Department of Agriculture pesticide storage facility.[38] The INS has defied court orders to improve conditions in the camps,[39] and by 1990 hundreds of alien children were being held without health, educational, or legal services.[40] Haitian boat persons were being interdicted at sea, given "hearings" on the boats, and repatriated to Haiti; by 1990, only six of 20,000 interdicted Haitians had been granted asylum.[41] The INS had begun a media campaign to justify its extraordinary practices on land and on sea. The cycle of United States immigration history continued, and all was ready for the Space Traders.

NOTES

1. Graglia, Book Review, 5 CONST. COMM. 436, 437 (1988) (reviewing D. BELL, AND WE ARE NOT SAVED: THE ELUSIVE QUEST FOR RACIAL JUSTICE (1987)).
2. *See, e.g.,* Derrick Bell, *After We're Gone: Prudent Speculations on America in a Post-Racial Epoch,* 34 ST. LOUIS U. L.J. 393, 399 (1989) ("Blacks and

their white supporters challenged these procedures in the courts, but their suits were dismissed as 'political questions' that must be determined by co-equal branches of government.").

3. *See* Strickland & Strickland, *The Court and the Trail of Tears*, SUPREME COURT HISTORICAL SOCIETY 1979 YEARBOOK 20 (1978).

My grandfather had many stories about Indians, mostly about how they had been bilked out of their land and tricked by Anglos. His familiarity with Native Americans was with the various Pueblo peoples, whose lands are predominantly in Northern New Mexico, as well as Navajos and Apaches (Mescalero and Jicarilla). I clearly remember him taking me and my brothers to the Santa Fe Plaza (the "end of the Santa Fe trail") and showing us a plaque in the Plaza commemorating the commercial triumphs over the "savage" Indians.[sic] Years later, someone scratched out the offensive adjective and the State felt compelled to erect another, smaller sign next to the plaque, explaining that the choice of words was a sign of earlier, less-sophisticated times, and that no insult was really intended.

My grandfather, for one, never intended insult, and would have approved of the scratching. He taught us that Indians were good people, excellent artists (he would point to the Indian women selling their jewelry on the sidewalks in front of the Palace of the Governors), and generally preyed upon by the world-at-large. Interestingly, he held a very strong devotion both to Mary, La Senora de Guadalupe, the Mexican-Indian veneration, and to Mary, La Conquistadora, the New Mexican–Spanish veneration representing the Conquest over the Indians. My grandparents' house had vigil lights, pictures, and figurines in both Hispanic traditions, and the incongruity never occurred to me then. In addition to the Plaza walks, he would take us as he tended the gravesite of his daughter who had died as a baby. The cemetery plot was a couple of hundred yards from an Indian school and church (St. Catherine's), where he would often choose to pray for his daughter. In any event, my grandfather was, for his day, generous toward and supportive of Indians.

4. Swindler, *Politics as Law: The Cherokee Cases*, 3 AM. INDIAN L. REV. 7 (1975); *see also* Strickland & Strickland, *supra* note 3, at 22 (recounting history of bitter disagreements over role of Supreme Court).

5. *See* Strickland & Strickland, *supra* note 3, at 22; *see also* M. WARDELL, A POLITICAL HISTORY OF THE CHEROKEE NATION (1938, reprinted in 1977).

6. *See, e.g.,* Strickland & Strickland, *supra* note 3, at 21; R. Strickland, *From Clan to Court: Development of Cherokee Law*, 31 TENN. HIST. Q. 316 (1972).

7. *See generally* WARDELL, *supra* note 5; Strickland & Strickland, *supra* note 3, at 20–22.

8. Indian Removal Act, 4 Stat. 411 (1830).

9. 30 U.S. (5 Pet.) 178 (1831). Richard Peters, the official Supreme Court reporter at that time, gathered all the arguments, briefs, and opinions into a single volume, THE CASE OF THE CHEROKEE NATION AGAINST THE STATE OF GEORGIA (1831) (cited in Strickland & Strickland, *supra* note 3, at n.19).

10. 31 U.S. (6 Pet.) 515 (1832).

11. 30 U.S. (5 Pet.) at 181 (1831).

12. 31 U.S. (6 Pet.) 515, 560 (1832).

13. In November, 1832, South Carolina attempted to secede and "nullify" its membership in the Union. President Jackson issued his Nullification Proclamation, insisting that states could not secede. Faced with this crisis, even staunch Indian supporters rushed to Jackson's side in favor of the Union. *See, e.g.,* Joseph C. Burke, *The Cherokee Cases: A Study in Law, Politics, and Morality,* 21 STAN. L. REV. 500 (1969); Strickland & Strickland, *supra* note 3, at 28–29.

14. *See* G. JAHODA, THE TRAIL OF TEARS 1813–1855 (1975) (Georgia officials anticipated Jackson's non-enforcement); *see also* Strickland, *supra* note 6, at 326.

15. *See* Yick Wo v. Hopkins, 118 U.S. 356 (1886) (invalidating city health ordinance applied only to Chinese).

16. *See* Ling Sing v. Washburn, 20 Cal. 534 (1862) (striking down "capitation" tax on Chinese). *See generally* Ronald Takaki, *Strangers From a Different Shore* (1988) (discussing immigration and labor history of Asians).

17. *See* Chy Lung v. Freeman, 92 U.S. 175 (1875) (striking down California Commissioner of immigration's authority to admit aliens); People v. Downer, 7 Cal. 170 (1857) (striking down state tax on Chinese arrivals).

18. *See* Ho Ah Kow v. Nunan, 5 Sawyer 552 (C.D. Cal. 1879).

19. McClain, *The Chinese Struggle for Civil Rights in Nineteenth Century America: The First Phase, 1850–1870,* 72 CAL. L. REV. 529 (1984). For a review of recent evidence that Asians remain discriminated against, despite high statistical achievement, see *Asian and Pacific Americans: Behind the Myths,* CHANGE, November/December 1989 (special issue).

20. *See* 22 Stat. 826 (1880) (revising 1868 treaty to suspend Chinese immigration).

21. 22 Stat. 58 (1882) (suspending Chinese immigration for ten years and establishing Chinese certificate requirement).

22. *See* 23 Stat. 115 (1884) (making certificate mandatory for Chinese entry into U. S.).

23. *See* 25 Stat. 476 (1884) (rescinding right of Chinese to re-enter U.S., even if they had entry certificates; stipulating "punishment to master of vessel unlawfully bringing Chinamen [sic]").

24. Chae Chan Ping v. United States, 130 U.S. 581, 609 (1889) ("The Chinese Exclusion Case").

25. *See* 27 Stat. 25 (1892).

26. *See* Fong Yue Ting v. United States, 149 U.S. 698 (1893).

27. *See id.* at 731.

28. *Id.* at 730 (citing Chae Chan Ping v. United States, 130 U.S. 581, 598 (1889)).

29. P. TAYLOR, MEXICAN LABOR IN THE UNITED STATES IMPERIAL VALLEY 42 (1928).

30. *See, e.g.,* R. DIVINE, AMERICAN IMMIGRATION POLICY, 1924–1952, at 58, 59 (1957).

31. *See* A. HOFFMAN, UNWANTED MEXICAN AMERICANS IN THE GREAT DEPRESSION: REPATRIATION PRESSURES, 1929–1939, at 126 (1974); A. Hoffman, *Mexican Repatriation Statistics: Some Suggested Alternatives to Carey McWilliams,* 1972 W. Hist. Q. 391.

32. *See, e.g.*, J. R. GARCIA, OPERATION WETBACK: THE MASS DEPORTATION OF MEXICAN UNDOCUMENTED WORKERS IN 1954, at 18–69 (1980).

33. *See* MARIO BARRERA, *Race and Class in the Southwest: A Theory of Racial Inequality* 104–07 (1979).

34. S. ULIBARRI, CUENTOS DE TIERRA AMARILLA (1971). Sabine Ulibarri, also a native of Tierra Amarilla, told me he had known of my grandfather because the town was small and because their names were so similar. My grandfather, who never met Ulibarri (who was 20 years younger), called him his *tocayo* (namesake).

35. S. ULIBARRI, MI ABUELA FUMABA PUROS (1977).

36. *See* M. PROUST, REMEMBRANCE OF THINGS PAST (rev. ed. 1981).

37. *See, e.g.*, U.S. COMMITTEE FOR REFUGEES, REFUGEES AT OUR BORDERS: THE U.S. RESPONSE TO ASYLUM SEEKERS (1989) (critical report on detention policies in South Texas); ABA COORDINATING COMMITTEE ON IMMIGRATION LAW, LIVES ON THE LINE: SEEKING ASYLUM IN SOUTH TEXAS (1989) (critical report on legal services available to detainees in South Texas).

38. Author's observation during a personal visit to South Texas in the summer of 1989; also based on discussions with El Proyecto Libertad attorney (private immigration legal assistance program), Madison, Wisconsin, October, 1989.

39. *See* Orantes-Hernandez v. Meese, 685 F. Supp. 1488 (D. Cal. 1988) (INS officials must not only refrain from placing obstacles in way of communication between detainees and their attorneys, but are obligated to affirmatively provide detainees with legal assistance); Orantes-Hernandez v. Thornburgh, No. 82–1107 (D. Cal. 1989) (INS not in compliance with earlier court order). *See also* Ramos v. Thornburgh, No. TY89–42-CA (E.D. Tex. 1989) (requiring INS to treat Salvadoran asylum claims as "having established a substantial likelihood of success on the merits," when INS had characterized claims as "frivolous").

40. *See, e.g.*, U.S. COMMITTEE FOR REFUGEES, *supra* note 37; ABA COORDINATING COMMITTEE, *supra* note 37.

41. *See* U.S. COMMITTEE FOR REFUGEES, *supra* note 37, at 12–13.

3   Pure Politics

GIRARDEAU A. SPANN

T H E present Supreme Court has been noticeably unreceptive to legal claims asserted by racial minorities. Although it is always possible to articulate nonracial motives for the Court's civil rights decisions, the popular perception is that a politically conservative majority wishing to cut back on the protection minority interests received at majority expense now dominates the Supreme Court. In reviewing the work of the Court during a recent term, *United States Law Week* reported that "[a] series of civil rights decisions by a conservative majority of the U.S. Supreme Court [made] it easier to challenge affirmative action programs and more difficult to establish claims of employment discrimination.[1] *U.S. Law Week* went on to cite seven decisions handed down that term that adversely affected minority interests.

During the term in question, the Court invalidated a minority set-aside program for government contractors and imposed the heavy burden of proving past discrimination as a prerequisite to the use of affirmative action remedies; permitted an affirmative action consent decree to be attacked collaterally by white workers who had chosen not to intervene in the Title VII action giving rise to the consent decree despite their knowledge that the Title VII action was pending; increased the burden of proof imposed on minorities who assert Title VII claims by requiring minority employees both to focus their challenges on specific rather than aggregate employment practices and to disprove employer assertions of legitimate job relatedness; adopted a narrow interpretation of the Reconstruction civil rights statute now codified in 42 U.S.C. section 1981, holding that the statute did not prohibit racial harassment of minority employees by their employers; held that discrimination claims filed against municipalities under 42 U.S.C. section 1981 could not be based upon a theory of respondeat superior; held that the statute of limitations for Title VII challenges to discriminatory seniority systems began to run when a seniority system was first adopted rather than when its discriminatory impact later materialized in the form of subsequent seniority-based demotions; and held that attorney's fees for a prevailing plaintiff in a Title VII case could not be assessed against a union that intervened in order to defend the discriminatory practice being challenged.

88 MICH. L. REV. 1971 (1990). Originally published in the Michigan Law Review. Reprinted by permission.

For the time being, at least, Supreme Court adjudication appears to offer little hope for minorities seeking to protect their legal interests from either public or private disregard. The Court has responded to a conservative shift in majoritarian attitudes about race discrimination by subtly incorporating contemporary attitudes into the constitutional and statutory provisions that govern discrimination claims. One could argue, of course, that what we are witnessing is the proper operation of a complex and sophisticated governmental process—that, consistent with a refined understanding of its constitutional function, the Court is exhibiting a proper sensitivity to the evolving content of our fundamental social values. By the same token, the same social sensitivity that once permitted the Court to condemn segregation and permit miscegenation might be argued now to compel the Court to retard the rate at which minority gains can be extracted from an increasingly disgruntled majority. The problem, however, is that judicial review is not supposed to work that way.

Under the traditional model of judicial review, the Court is supposed to be above the inevitable shifts that occur in the prevailing political climate. Exercising the skills of reasoned deliberation, within the constraints of principled adjudication, the Supreme Court is expected to protect minority rights from predictable majoritarian efforts at exploitation. What eludes consensus, however, is an assessment of just how far the actual performance of the Court diverges from the ideal of the traditional model, and just how much significance that divergence ought to command. This chapter postulates that the discrepancy between actual and model Supreme Court performance is so great as to erase any qualitative difference between Supreme Court adjudication and ordinary politics.

Supreme Court adjudication is characterized most strongly by the existence of loosely constrained judicial discretion. This discretion may well render the Court incapable of withstanding in any sustained manner the majoritarian forces that govern representative politics. Indeed, far from serving the countermajoritarian function envisioned by the traditional model of judicial review, the Supreme Court can better be understood as serving the veiled majoritarian function of promoting popular preferences at the expense of minority interests.

Veiled Majoritarianism

Close examination suggests that the countermajoritarian assumption of the traditional model cannot be valid. Because justices are socialized by the same majority that determines their fitness for judicial office, they will arrive at the bench already inculcated with majoritarian values that will influence the manner in which they exercise their judicial discretion. Accordingly, unless judicial discretion can be reduced to acceptably low levels, justices can be expected to rule in ways that facilitate rather than inhibit majoritarian efforts to advance majority interests, even at minority expense. None of the safeguards relied upon by the traditional model, however, can satisfactorily control judicial discretion.

The formal safeguards of life tenure and salary protection, which are designed to insulate the judiciary from external political pressure, simply cannot guard against the majoritarianism inherent in a judge's own assimilation of dominant social values. Moreover, the operational safeguard of principled adjudication has not proved capable of significantly reducing judicial discretion. In many instances, the governing substantive principles of law themselves incorporate majoritarian values in a way that leaves the Court with no choice but to acquiesce in majoritarian desires. In other instances, the guidance available to the Court in selecting among potentially governing principles simply is insufficient to prevent the need for recourse to judicial discretion in making the selection. In still other instances, the ambiguities that inhere in a governing principle even after it has been selected require recourse to the socialized values of the justices. As a result, when the Court is called upon to protect minority interests, it may merely be participating in the sacrifice of those interests to majority desires.

Supreme Court justices are themselves majoritarian, in the sense that they have been socialized by the dominant culture. As a result, they have internalized the basic values and assumptions of that culture, including the beliefs and predispositions that can cause the majority to discount minority interests.[2] Indeed, a justice's sympathy toward majoritarian values is thoroughly tested by the appointment and confirmation process, which is specifically designed to eliminate any candidate whose political inclinations are not sufficiently centrist for the majoritarian branches to feel comfortable with that candidate's likely judicial performance. As a statistical matter, therefore, a Supreme Court justice is more likely to share the majority's views about proper resolution of a given social issue than to possess any other view on that issue. Moreover, to the extent that the justice has been socialized to share majoritarian prejudices, he or she may not even be consciously aware of the nature of those prejudices, or the degree to which they influence the exercise of the justice's discretion.[3] Whatever factors cause majority undervaluation of minority interests, justices socialized by the dominant culture will have been influenced by them too. Accordingly, justices will come to the task of protecting minority interests possessed by the very predispositions that they are asked to guard against.

Because judges will have personal attitudes and values significantly similar to those of the majority, judicial review cannot be expected to protect minority interests unless something in the judicial process guards against the influence of majoritarian preferences. The traditional model of judicial review assumes that the formal safeguards of life tenure and salary protection, as well as the operative safeguards attendant to the process of principled adjudication, can accomplish this task. Contrary to this assumption, however, neither set of safeguards is likely to be effective.

Although the instrumental value of the formal safeguards is questionable, the symbolic value of those safeguards may prompt a justice to resist majoritarian influences. Life tenure and salary protection, however, are directed at the problem of majoritarian pressures exerted by other branches of government. Accordingly, they may not prompt a justice to guard against his or her own majoritarian attitudes and values. Even if they do, however, and even if a justice makes strenuous efforts to compensate for his or her known prejudices, the justice will still be vulnerable to those biases and predispositions that continue to operate at a subconscious level—the level at which most noninvidious discrimination is likely to occur. As a result, the formal safeguards of life tenure and salary protection, enhanced by any symbolic importance they may have, are simply inapposite to the problem of majoritarian-influenced judicial values. A justice cannot be impartial simply by trying; majoritarian influences are too effective for such efforts to be more than marginally successful. If the countermajoritarian assumption of the traditional model is to hold, it will have to be through the constraints imposed upon judicial discretion by the process of principled adjudication.

However well the constraint of principled adjudication should work in theory, it simply has not worked well in practice. The Supreme Court often adopts legal principles that expressly incorporate majoritarian preferences into their meanings, and thereby provide no safeguard whatsoever from majoritarian desires. Perhaps the most celebrated example is the Court's ruling in *Garcia v. San Antonio Metropolitan Transit Authority*,[4] which held that the constitutional principle of federalism contained no judicially enforceable standards; the majoritarian branches themselves were responsible for defining the meaning of the constitutional standard. Although that approach to constitutional enforcement might make some sense in the context of federalism, where the Senate arguably is capable of securing political protection for federalism interests, the Court has issued similar rulings in the context of race discrimination, where the very premise of the traditional model is that racial minorities do not possess the power to protect their interests in the political process. In *McCleskey v. Kemp*,[5] the Court rejected equal protection and eighth amendment challenges to the imposition of capital punishment under a Georgia statute where statistical evidence indicated that black murder convicts were more than four times as likely to receive the death penalty if their victims were white than if their victims were black. In rejecting the eighth amendment challenge, the Court held that the governing constitutional standard was to be given operative meaning through reference to the preferences of the state legislature and the defendant's jury. Both the legislature and the jury are majoritarian institutions. As a result, the Court's incorporation of the preferences of those institutions into the meaning of the constitutional standard had the ironic effect of constitutionalizing the level of discrimination that exists in the society at large.[6] In this sense, the Court seems actually to have promoted rather than prevented majoritarian exploitation of minority interests.

When a legal principle does have content that is not derived from the majoritarian branches of government, the ambiguities encountered in both identifying and applying that principle eliminate any meaningful constraint on judicial discretion. In a case of first impression, selection of the governing legal principle is necessarily an act of unconstrained judicial discretion because the Court has no precedent to which it may turn for guidance.[7] The Supreme Court's history in choosing between intent and effects principles in discrimination suits illustrates the problem. One could rationally prefer either principle. The basic argument in favor of focusing on intent is that a prohibition on innocently motivated, neutral actions that simply happen to have a racially disparate impact would unduly restrict the ability of governmental decisionmakers to use precise and efficient classifications that are directly responsive to the merits of the regulatory problems with which they are confronted. The major drawback of focusing on intent is that evidence of intentional discrimination often is difficult or impossible to secure, thereby permitting acts of intentional discrimination to escape invalidation by masquerading as acts of neutral policymaking. The basic argument in favor of focusing on effects is that harmful effects are harmful regardless of the intent with which they are produced; the major drawback is that such a focus would require governmental decisionmakers explicitly to consider race as a factor in formulating social policy, thereby contravening the very principle of racial neutrality embodied in our antidiscrimination laws.

In *Washington v. Davis*,[8] the Supreme Court held that the applicable principle for equal protection clause purposes is the intent principle.[9] Five years earlier, however, in *Griggs v. Duke Power Co.*,[10] the Court had expressly rejected the intent principle for Title VII purposes, finding that the desire of Congress to reach discriminatory effects as well as discriminatory intent was "plain from the language of the statute."[11] How did the Court know that the intent principle governed discrimination claims asserted under the equal protection clause while the effects principle governed claims asserted under Title VII? Although one might initially suspect that the drafters of the two provisions must have had different intents, no evidence supports such a suspicion. The drafters of the fourteenth amendment appear to have left no hint of their views concerning which principle should apply to equal protection claims—at least the *Washington v. Davis* Court cited no such evidence in support of its "intent" decision. And contrary to the Court's assurance in *Griggs*, nothing in the language or legislative history of Title VII compels the adoption of an "effects" test for statutory claims of discrimination. The two decisions can be reconciled only on policy grounds. But the policy advantages and disadvantages associated with each principle seem equally present in both cases. There is no obvious reason to suppose that the presence or absence or relative weight of these policy considerations should vary with the constitutional or statutory nature of the underlying cause of action, and the Court offered no nonobvious reason why this should be the case.

Not only was the Court's discretion in making an initial selection between the intent and effects principles unconstrained, but after having made that initial selection the Court deemed itself free to change its mind when confronted with a mildly different factual setting. The Court's most recent decision on the issue seems to defy all notions of consistency and constraint. In *Wards Cove Packing Co. v. Atonio*,[12] the Court held—consistent with *Griggs*—that the effects principle governed Title VII challenges to the discriminatory use of subjective employment criteria, but the Court also imposed a standard of proof—consistent with *Washington v. Davis*—that may well be more difficult to meet than the burden of proving discriminatory intent. The Court's effortless vacillation between intent and effects principles reveals the absence of any meaningful constraint upon judicial discretion that operates at the principle selection stage. Even if the Court were constrained in its selection of governing principles, however, it would remain largely unconstrained when called upon to apply the principle that had been selected.

In theory, once a governing principle is identified, the principle reduces the danger of judicial majoritarianism because the principle rather than judicial discretion generates the adjudicatory result. This theory, however, cannot work for two reasons. First, in order to be generally acceptable, a legal principle must be stated at a high enough level of abstraction to permit interest groups with divergent preferences to believe that their objectives can be secured by the principle. This level of abstraction both precludes meaningful constraint and requires an act of discretion to give the principles operative meaning. Second, the contemporary nature of legal analysis makes it unrealistic to expect that even a precise principle can generate only one, consistent result. Since the advent of legal realism and its demonstration of the linguistic and conceptual imprecision of legal principles, legal analysis has tended to consist of functional or policy analysis.[13] However, because we are ambivalent about most of the social policies that we espouse, that ambivalence can cause a single principle to generate inconsistent outcomes.

The problem can be illustrated by considering the dilemma posed by the state action principle. The Supreme Court has held that the fourteenth amendment prohibits official acts of racial discrimination but that it does not reach acts of private discrimination.[14] The apparent purpose in drawing this distinction is to isolate a sphere of personal autonomy in which private parties are free to exercise their associational preferences free from state intervention, but to preclude the state itself from expressing a preference for one race over another. In *Corrigan v. Buckley*,[15] the Court held that a racially restrictive covenant in a white property owner's deed could be legally enforced by the state without offending the constitutional prohibition on official discrimination. Presumably, the Court viewed the state as a neutral actor making its legal enforcement machinery equally available to all citizens without regard to their private associational preferences, thereby advancing the purposes of the state action principle. Then, in *Shelley v. Kraemer*,[16] the Court changed its mind and held that judicial enforcement of racially restrictive covenants was unconstitutional, because such enforcement facilitated private acts of discrimination and thereby undermined the goal of official neutrality. In essence, the *Shelley* Court inverted the perceived connection between the state action principle and its underlying policy objectives that had originally been established in *Corrigan*. The problem of determining which is the correct application of the state action principle is simply insoluble. Because state acquiescence can always be recharacterized as state action, the meaning of the state action principle can only amount to a matter of perspective, which inevitably will be colored in particular contexts by our ambivalent social views concerning the competing policy considerations on which the principle rests. For present purposes, however, it is sufficient to note that even after a legal principle has been selected, vast amounts of loosely constrained judicial discretion may still be needed in order to apply it.

Majoritarian preferences reside in the socialized attitudes and values of Supreme Court justices, and they find expression in the exercise of judicial discretion. Although a justice may be prompted by the formal safeguards of life tenure and salary protection consciously to guard against majoritarian influences, such efforts cannot be effective against the unconscious operation of those influences. Moreover, the operational safeguard of principled adjudication cannot guard effectively against majoritarianism because many legal principles incorporate majoritarian preferences into their meanings. In addition, the ambiguity inherent in both the selection and application of governing principles is too great to permit the principles to serve as meaningful constraints on the exercise of judicial discretion. Rather than protecting minority interests from majoritarian abrogation, as envisioned by the traditional model of judicial review, the Supreme Court appears actually to serve the function of advancing majority interests at minority expense, while operating behind the veil of countermajoritarian adjudication. Assuming that the traditional model has in fact failed, racial minorities must consider novel strategies to deal with the essentially majoritarian nature of the Court.

Race and Positive Politics

In light of the failure of countermajoritarianism, minorities could rationally choose to forgo reliance on judicial review altogether and concentrate their efforts to advance minority interests on the overtly political branches of government. The Framers had faith in the ability of pluralist politics to protect the minority interests with which they were concerned. The political branches have historically done more than the Supreme Court to advance minority interests, while the predominant role of the Court, consistent with its veiled majoritarian design, has been to retard the rate at which minority claims of entitlement could prevail at the expense of majority interests.

In a contest between competing societal interests that is ultimately to be judged by political considerations, minorities might well prefer to compete in an arena that is openly political, rather than one from which political concerns nominally have been excluded. In an overtly political process, minority interests will receive whatever degree of deference their innate strength can command, subject only to limitations in the bargaining and organizational skills of minority politicians. In a positive sense, therefore, the overt political process is pure. Outcomes are determined by counting votes, with no need to consider the reasons for which those votes were cast. The process purports to be nothing more than what it is—a pluralistic mechanism for generating binding results. Although rhetorical principles may accompany the solicitation of political support, the principles themselves are inconsequential. No one cares much about their content, and their meaning is measured only by the extent to which their rhetorical invocation proves to be effective.

For racial minorities, the overt political process has two attractions. First, the political process is definitionally immune from distortion because it has essentially no rules that can be violated. In the film *Butch Cassidy and the Sundance Kid*, Butch Cassidy prevailed in a knife fight over one of his adversaries by exploiting the absence of formal rules. Butch first suggested that he and his adversary needed to clarify the rules of the knife fight. As the adversary—put off-guard by Butch's suggestion—protested that there were no such things as "rules" in a knife fight, Butch kicked the adversary very hard in a very sensitive part of his anatomy. With this one action, Butch was able both to establish the truth of the proposition being asserted by his adversary and to capitalize on that proposition in order to win the fight.

As a positive matter, the pure political process is nothing more than the process of casting and counting votes. Outcomes cannot be right or wrong, nor can they be just or unjust. They are simply the outcomes that the process produces. Although outcomes may be determined by how the issues are framed, how support for those issues is secured, and even by who is permitted to vote, minorities should not be distracted by considerations relating to whether the process is operating fairly. The process simply works the way it works. What minorities should focus on is how best to maximize their influence in that process. Minority participation in pluralist politics can, of course, take the form of voting, running for office, or making campaign contributions, but it is not limited to those forms of involvement. Minority participation can also take the form of demonstrations, boycotts, and riots. Although such activities may be independently illegal, for purposes of positive politics their significance is limited to their potential for increasing or decreasing political strength. This is not to say that no rules at all govern the positive political process. Operative rules determine which strategies will increase and which will decrease political power. However, the operative rules are not only too complex and contingent to permit them to be articulated accurately, but those rules need never be articulated, because the selective responsiveness of the political process itself will promote adherence to those rules without regard to the accuracy of their formal expression. The process of positive politics—like a knife fight—cannot be distorted because it has no formal rules. In addition, the operative rules that do govern the process tend to be self-enforcing.[17]

The second attraction of the overt political process is that it permits minorities to assume ultimate responsibility for their own interests. There are, of course, inherent limits on the political strength of any interest group. Within those limits, however, positive politics gives minorities themselves control over the degree to which minority interests are advanced. Minorities determine how important it is for minorities to engage in political activity; minorities determine how much political activity is appropriate; and minorities decide what minority priorities should be in selecting among competing political objectives. Positive politics gives minorities both the credit for minority advances and the blame for minority failures. By thus promoting minority self-determination, positive politics elevates minority dignity and self-esteem in a way that is likely to be of more long-term significance than minority success in advancing any particular interest.

Minority Frustrations in the Supreme Court

The influence that pluralist theory predicts minorities will have in the majoritarian political process has been borne out empirically. Minorities have not only secured significant concessions from the representative branches, but those branches have typically done more than the Supreme Court to advance minority interests. In fact, the Supreme Court's civil rights performance has historically been so disappointing that it lends little, if any, support to the traditional model of judicial review. Rather, the Court's decisions serve more as a refutation than a validation of countermajoritarian judicial capacity.

Minority interests in the United States have typically been advanced through the political process. The most obvious example is the manumission of black slaves. Slavery itself was a political creation that the majoritarian Framers chose to accord some degree of constitutional protection.[18] At the time the Constitution was ratified, slavery was a very contentious issue that the Framers anticipated would continue to be the focus of future political attention.[19] That attention gradually resulted in total emancipation. First, some northern states enacted legislation that abolished slavery within their jurisdictions. Then, Congress enacted federal legislation prohibiting slavery in most of the new territory acquired through the Louisiana Purchase. Next, in 1863, after the outbreak of the Civil War, President Lincoln issued the Emancipation Proclamation, which abolished slavery in the southern states. Finally, in 1865, after the end of the Civil War, Congress adopted and the states ratified the thirteenth amendment, abolishing slavery throughout the United States. Manumission illustrates that even the interests of completely disenfranchised minorities will be advanced through the political process when they correspond to the perceived interests of the majority.

Manumission also illustrates that the political process can be much more advantageous to racial minorities than the judicial process. When the Supreme Court was given the opportunity to limit slavery six years before the Emancipation Proclamation in the infamous *Dred Scott* case,[20] it declined to do so, issuing an opinion so demeaning to blacks that it reads like a parody of Supreme Court insensitivity to minority interests. In rejecting the claim of free status asserted by a slave who had been taken by his owner to a free state, then to a part the Louisiana Territory where slavery had been prohibited, and then brought back to the owner's original slave state, Chief Justice Taney's opinion made two assertions that are remarkable coming from a purportedly countermajoritarian institution. First, the opinion asserted that the Court lacked jurisdiction over the suit because the subhuman character of the black plaintiff deprived him of the capacity for citizenship required to invoke the Court's diversity jurisdiction.[21] Second, even though the Court lacked jurisdiction, the opinion declared that the provision of the Missouri Compromise statute prohibiting slavery in the Louisiana Territory was unconstitutional because it deprived slave owners of a property interest in their slaves.[22] The first assertion is remarkable because it evidences an unmistakably strong attitudinal predisposition that would seem to be disqualifying for an institution charged with safeguarding minority interests. Considering the range of political positions concerning slavery that existed at the time, the subhuman position adopted by the Court seems to have been the most disadvantageous to blacks.[23] The second assertion is remarkable because it reveals that this subhuman-property predisposition of the Court was so strong that the Court felt itself obligated to invalidate a majoritarian enactment limiting the spread of slavery. It is even more remarkable because the Court relied upon the need to defer to majoritarian policymakers as a justification for its jurisdictional holding.[24] Indeed, most of the judicial encounters with slavery that occurred prior to the Civil War resulted in judicial invalidation of majoritarian efforts to limit slavery. *Dred Scott* was the second Supreme Court decision to invalidate a congressional enactment on constitutional grounds; *Marbury v. Madison*[25]—a case in which the Supreme Court refused to enforce a legal right to receive a judicial commission—was the first. *Dred Scott*, therefore, can be seen as continuing the Supreme Court tradition established in *Marbury* of sacrificing the interests of those that the Court is charged with protecting in order to advance ulterior political objectives.

The major advances that racial minorities have made since manumission have also come from the representative branches. The fourteenth amendment overruled *Dred Scott* by granting citizenship to blacks, and it provided constitutional validation for the Reconstruction civil rights statutes now codified in sections 1981, 1982, and 1983 of title 42 of the United States Code. After a post-Reconstruction lapse in congressional responsiveness to minority interests, congressional civil rights activity increased in the mid–twentieth century. The Civil Rights Acts of 1957 and 1960 created federal remedies for voting discrimination. The omnibus Civil Rights Act of 1964 prohibited various types of public and private discrimination. Among its most significant provisions are Title II, which prohibits discrimination in public accommodations, Title IV, which authorizes the Attorney General to maintain school desegregation suits, Title VI, which prohibits segregation in schools receiving federal funds, and Title VII, which prohibits discrimination in employment. The Voting Rights Acts of 1965, 1970, and 1975 substantially enhanced the federal safeguards against voting discrimination contained in the 1957 and 1960 Acts by suspending literacy tests for voter registration and by requiring Attorney General preclearance of apportionment changes that might be used to dilute minority voting strength. The Fair Housing Act of 1968 contains provisions that prohibit discrimination in the sale or rental of housing and imposes increased federal criminal sanctions for the violation of individual civil rights. The Public Works Employment Act of 1977 contained minority set-aside provisions requiring that ten percent of the funds given to state and local governments for construction purposes had to be used to secure goods or services supplied by minority-owned enterprises.

The Supreme Court has greeted majoritarian efforts to advance minority interests with a mixed response. On occasion those efforts have been validated, as when the Court upheld the federal minority set-aside program established by the 1977 Public Works Employment Act in *Fullilove v. Klutznick*.[26] Sometimes the Court has shown even more sensitivity to minority interests than the representative branch whose action the Court validated. For example, in holding that the Reconstruction statutes reached private as well as official government conduct, the Court may well have gone beyond the actual intent of the Reconstruction Congress in its solicitude for minority interests.[27] On other occasions, majoritarian efforts to advance minority interests have met with marked judicial hostility, as they did in *Dred Scott*. For example, although the Court upheld the federal minority set-aside program in *Fullilove*, recently it invalidated a similar municipal program in *City of Richmond v. J. A. Croson Co.*[28] And although it recently reaffirmed the applicability of the Reconstruction statutes to private action, it simultaneously redefined the substantive scope of prohibited discrimination in a way that excluded much discrimination that did not constitute state action. Like the representative branches, the Supreme Court has not been uniform or consistent in its deference to minority interests. Rather, the Court, too, has made concessions to minority interests when the overall political climate has been conducive to such concessions.

I have argued that a rational minority response to the veiled majoritarian nature of the Supreme Court would be to abandon efforts to influence the Court and to concentrate minority political activities on the representative branches, because minorities are more likely to secure concessions from an overtly political branch of government than from one whose political dimensions are covert. I have also argued that comparison of the historical performances of the representative branches and the Supreme Court provides empirical support for this theory, because the representative branches have done more than the Court to advance minority interests. One might object to this asserted preference for the representative branches by arguing that if the actions of each branch are ultimately determined by majoritarian political preferences, it should not matter which branch minorities choose as the focus of their political efforts. Therein lies the dilemma.

NOTES

1. *Review of Supreme Court's Term: Labor and Employment Law*, 58 U.S.L.W. 3065 (Aug. 8, 1989).

2. In the present context, the term "majoritarian" is an idealization. As a

literal matter, a Supreme Court justice is no more likely to reflect the views of the actual majority than is a president, a senator, or a member of the House of Representatives. The "majority" that matters for present purposes is that segment of the electorate having the inclination and resources to influence representative politics. The disenfranchisement of so many individuals from the political process may ultimately render our operative vision of democratic government unappealing. The present thesis, however, expresses a type of skepticism about the utility of judicial review that persists even if the assumptions of representative democracy are accepted as true.

3. *See* C. Lawrence, *The Id, the Ego, and Equal Protection: Reckoning with Unconscious Racism*, 39 STAN. L. REV. 317 (1987).

4. 469 U.S. 528 (1985).

5. 481 U.S. 279 (1987).

6. One way to conceptualize the decision is that the Court permitted whites to have the increased deterrent and retributive benefits of a capital punishment statute even though the costs associated with those benefits (concomitantly lower deterrence and retribution, as well as higher execution rates) were disproportionately imposed upon blacks. Presumably, it is precisely such undervaluation of minority interests that the traditional model was designed to prevent. For a general discussion of the *McCleskey* decision addressing this and other aspects of the case, see R. Kennedy, McCleskey v. Kemp: *Race, Capital Punishment, and the Supreme Court*, 101 HARV. L. REV. 1388, 1390–95 (1988).

7. In all cases other than ones of first impression, the act of principle selection really amounts to an act of principle application—the difficulties of which are discussed below. The only way that the selection of a governing principle can be constrained is by some other principle that controls the selection process. As a result, selection of the immediate principle, if not arbitrary, necessarily entails application of the metaprinciple.

8. 426 U.S. 229 (1976).

9. 426 U.S. at 238–48. The holding of *Davis* has been reaffirmed in a number of cases, including Village of Arlington Heights v. Metropolitan Hous. Dev. Corp., 429 U.S. 252, 264–65 (1977), Personnel Administrator of Mass. v. Feeney, 442 U.S. 256, 272 (1977), and Hunter v. Underwood, 471 U.S. 222, 227–28 (1985).

10. 401 U.S. 424 (1971).

11. 401 U.S. at 429.

12. 109 S. Ct. 2115 (1989).

13. This development is discussed at greater length in G. WHITE, TORT LAW IN AMERICA 63–75 (1980).

14. The Civil Rights Cases, 109 U.S. 3, 14–15 (1883).

15. 271 U.S. 323 (1926) (dismissing appeal for want of substantial federal question).

16. 334 U.S. 1 (1948).

17. There are, of course, competing conceptions of the political process under which the process is more principled than it is under mine. Because those conceptions postulate adherence to principle, however, they share the same weaknesses that are inherent in a principled model of judicial review. The value of politics as I have conceptualized it here is that it escapes the need to depend upon principle for its proper operation.

Nevertheless, I do not wish to overstate the degree to which pure politics needs to be a self-regulating endeavor. Bribery, ballot box stuffing, and vote miscounting could be considered forms of misconduct that require external regulation—although strong arguments could be made that even these abuses are subject to correction by the political process itself. Nor do I wish to obscure the fact that differential access to the political process can drastically affect political outcomes. Rather, the present argument is that, despite these potential abuses, the political process may still be preferable to policymaking processes involving the Supreme Court.

I also realize that some advocates of political pluralism hold the political process in high regard, according its outcomes the imprimatur of democratic legitimacy. The advantages of positive politics on which I am focusing, however, do not rest upon normative claims of external validity.

18. The Constitution contains three provisions that are directly addressed to slavery. Article I, § 9, prohibits Congress from terminating the importation of new slaves until 1808, and authorizes the imposition of a federal tax on imported slaves. U.S. CONST. art. I, § 9, cl. 1. Article I, § 2, apportions legislative representation in the House of Representatives on the basis of state population, counting each slave as three-fifths of a person for apportionment purposes. U.S. CONST. art. I, § 2, cl. 3 (1788, amended 1868). Article IV, § 2, prohibits one state from according free status to a slave who has escaped to that state from another state. U.S. CONST. art. IV, § 2, cl. 3 (1788, superseded 1865). *See* G. STONE ET AL., CONSTITUTIONAL LAW 472 (2d ed. 1991).

19. *See, e.g.,* U.S. CONST. art. I, § 9 (prohibiting congressional termination of slave trade until 1808); *see* G. STONE, *supra* note 18, at 472–73.

20. Dred Scott v. Sandford, 60 U.S. (19 How.) 393 (1857).

21. The opinion states:

> The words "people of the United States" and "citizens" are synonymous terms, and mean the same thing. . . . The question before us is, whether [blacks are] a portion of this people . . . . We think they are not and that they are not included, and were not intended to be included, under the word "citizens" in the Constitution, and can therefore claim none of the rights and privileges which that instrument provides for and secures to citizens of the United States. On the contrary, they were at that time considered as a subordinate and inferior class of beings, who had been subjugated by the dominant race, and, whether emancipated or not, yet remained subject to their authority, and had no rights or privileges but such as those who held the power and the Government might choose to grant them. . . .
>
>   It is difficult at this day to realize the state of public opinion in relation to that unfortunate race, which prevailed in the civilized and enlightened portions of the world at the time of the Declaration of Independence, and when the Constitution of the United States was framed and adopted. But the public history of every European nation displays it in a manner too plain to be mistaken.
>
>   They had for more than a century before been regarded as beings of an inferior order, and altogether unfit to associate with the white race, either in social or political relations; and so far inferior, that they had no rights which the white man was bound to respect; and that the negro might justly and lawfully be reduced to slavery for his benefit.

60 U.S. (19 How.) at 404–05, 407.

22. The opinion states:

[The] right of property in a slave is distinctly and expressly affirmed in the Constitution. The right to traffic in it, like an ordinary article of merchandise and property, was guaranteed to the citizens of the United States, in every State that might desire it, for twenty years. And the Government in express terms is pledged to protect it in all future time, if the slave escapes from his owner. This is done in plain words—too plain to be misunderstood. And no word can be found in the Constitution which gives Congress a greater power over slave property, or which entitles property of that kind to less protection than property of any other description. The only power conferred is the power coupled with the duty of guarding and protecting the owner in his rights.

60 U.S. (19 How.) at 451–52.

23. Although Chief Justice Taney professed to be reporting the views of the Framers rather than his own concerning the status of blacks (see 60 U.S. (19 How.) at 404–05, 407), the tone of Taney's opinion belies any suggestion that Taney himself did not share those views. *See supra*. Although slavery has existed in numerous societies and cultures, the brand of slavery that existed in the American South developed to the highest degree a slaveholder ideology under which the honor of the slaveholder was directly dependent upon the degradation of the slave. *See* O. PATTERSON, SLAVERY AND SOCIAL DEATH 94–97 (1982).

24. In justifying its conclusion that the subhuman character of blacks made them incapable in the eyes of the Framers of acquiring the citizenship necessary to give the Court jurisdiction, the opinion states: "It is not the province of the court to decide upon the justice or injustice, the policy or impolicy, of these laws. The decision of that question belonged to the political or lawmaking power . . . ." 60 U.S. (19 How.) at 405. It is more than a little ironic that the Court found itself to lack jurisdiction to entertain suits filed by those whose interests it was required to protect under the traditional model.

Although one might argue that Chief Justice Taney was deferring to the majoritarian Framers rather than to the majoritarian Congress that enacted the Missouri Compromise, arguments of this type pose insoluble analytical difficulties. Where the Framers did not specifically provide otherwise, they likely desired congressional preferences to govern resolution of future issues that would arise concerning slavery. The Framers, however, may have specifically "provided otherwise" by including in the Constitution the protections for private property on which Chief Justice Taney relied to invalidate the Missouri Compromise prohibition on slavery. It is precisely this sort of analytical difficulty that the first part of this chapter argues can be resolved only through recourse to the personal preferences of individual judges.

25. 5 U.S. (1 Cranch) 137 (1803).

26. 448 U.S. 448 (1980).

27. *See* Patterson v. McLean Credit Union, 109 S. Ct. 2363 (1989); Runyon v. McCrary, 427 U.S. 160 (1976); Jones v. Alfred H. Mayer Co., 392 U.S. 409 (1968); *cf.* The Civil Rights Cases, 109 U.S. 3 (1883); The Slaughter-House Cases, 83 U.S. (16 Wall.) 36 (1873).

28. 109 S. Ct. 706 (1989).

From the Editor:
Issues and Comments

W O U L D America accept the Space Traders' horrid offer? And if all blacks were to go off to the unknown (but dire) fate Bell implies, who would be next—and what would the consequences be for the rivalry between classes? Is Olivas right in stating that the United States has regularly and with few qualms traded groups of color for material gain of elite groups? Is Spann right in asserting that the judiciary is no longer a sensible place to take complaints of racial injustice—and if so, what *is* the solution for a black or Latino aggrieved by racism? If judges will not listen (is it true they rarely will?), who will?

You may wish to reconsider your answers after examining Parts III (revisionist history of civil rights progress), VIII (on cultural nationalism), and X (on criticism of CRT and self-analysis). An expanded, book-length version of Spann's critique is noted in the Suggested Readings, immediately following. See also the two books by Derrick Bell listed there, and the recent, much praised volume by Patricia Williams.

Suggested Readings

Bell, Derrick A., Jr., Brown v. Board of Education *and the Interest-Convergence Dilemma*, 93 HARV. L. REV. 518 (1980).

BELL, DERRICK A., JR., FACES AT THE BOTTOM OF THE WELL: THE PERMANENCE OF RACISM (1992).

BELL, DERRICK A., JR., RACE, RACISM, AND AMERICAN LAW (3d ed. 1992).

Bell, Derrick A., Jr., *Racial Realism*, 24 CONN. L. REV. 363 (1992).

Bell, Derrick A., Jr., *Serving Two Masters: Integration Ideals and Client Interests in School Desegregation Litigation*, 85 YALE L.J. 470 (1976).

Calmore, John O., *Critical Race Theory, Archie Shepp, and Fire Music: Securing an Authentic Intellectual Life in a Multicultural World*, 65 S. CAL. L. REV. 2129 (1992).

Crenshaw, Kimberlé Williams, *Race, Reform, and Retrenchment: Transformation and Legitimation in Antidiscrimination Law*, 101 HARV. L. REV. 1331 (1988).

Delgado, Richard, *Campus Antiracism Rules: Constitutional Narratives in Collision*, 85 NW. U. L. REV. 343 (1991).

Delgado, Richard, *Shadowboxing: An Essay on Power*, 77 CORNELL L. REV. 813 (1992).

Freeman, Alan D., *Legitimizing Racial Discrimination Through Antidiscrimination Law: A Critical Review of Supreme Court Doctrine*, 62 MINN. L. REV. 1049 (1978).

Gotanda, Neil, *A Critique of "Our Constitution Is Color-Blind,"* 44 STAN. L. REV. 1 (1991).

Greene, Linda S., *Multiculturalism as a Metaphor*, 41 DEPAUL L. REV. 1173 (1992).

Guinier, Lani, *The Triumph of Tokenism: The Voting Rights Act and the Theory of Black Electoral Success*, 89 MICH. L. REV. 1077 (1991); *No Two Seats: The Elusive Quest for Political Equality*, 77 VA. L. REV. 1413 (1991).

Kennedy, Duncan, *A Cultural Pluralist Case for Affirmative Action in Legal Academia*, 1990 DUKE L.J. 705.

Matsuda, Mari J., *Liberal Jurisprudence and Abstracted Visions of Human Nature: A Feminist Critique of Rawls' Theory of Justice*, 16 N.M. L. REV. 613 (1986).

SPANN, GIRARDEAU, RACE AGAINST THE COURT (1993).

WILLIAMS, PATRICIA J., THE ALCHEMY OF RACE AND RIGHTS (1991).

PART II

STORYTELLING, COUNTER-STORYTELLING, AND "NAMING ONE'S OWN REALITY"

A M O N G the most characteristic approaches in the Critical Race Theory genre are storytelling, counterstorytelling, and analysis of narrative. Thomas Ross brings sensitivity and skill to the task of exposing the varying narratives of race and racism that interweave in the Supreme Court opinions in an important recent decision, *Richmond v. J. A. Croson Company*. Gerald Torres and Kathryn Milun show, through analysis of a recent Indian law case, how the law can prevent a people from expressing their own voice and worldview by imposing rigid categories and ways of speaking. Margaret Russell examines how a recent film, *Soul Man*, makes light of affirmative action and the predicament of minorities by super-imposing a "dominant gaze," in a manner reminiscent of early minstrel shows. Richard Delgado demonstrates how the same event can be retold differently, and that oppositional storytelling can alter how we construct legal reality. Next, Derrick Bell, dean and originator of the modern storytelling movement, analyzes the way in which society has constructed the idea of whiteness as a superior status conferring broad-based entitlements. He shows the costs of that construction, both to whites and blacks, and offers suggestions concerning what we might do to mitigate those costs. And consummate storyteller Patricia Williams weaves several stories—about finding an apartment, about learning of her own slave origins, and about her law school experience at Harvard—to show how many minority lawyers cling to *rights* while white lawyers in the Critical Legal Studies left are quick to throw them away.

SECTION ONE
THEORIZING ABOUT NARRATIVES

4   The Richmond Narratives

THOMAS ROSS

T H I S is a story of the "Richmond narratives."

In *City of Richmond v. J. A. Croson Co.*,[1] a majority of the Supreme Court struck down a Richmond ordinance that set aside thirty percent of the subcontracting work on city construction jobs for minority firms. The majority concluded that the ordinance denied the white contractors "equal protection of the laws." Justice Marshall, dissenting, characterized the *Richmond* decision as "a deliberate and giant step backward in [the] Court's affirmative action jurisprudence."[2]

The *Richmond* decision is not just another chapter in the Court's evolving affirmative action jurisprudence. The decision is a source of powerful, and potentially disturbing, insights. The *Richmond* opinions, the "Richmond narratives," tell stories. These stories reveal much, and not just about the decision in *Richmond*. They reveal, with special clarity, the deeper nature of our struggle to move to a world where discrimination on the basis of race truly has no place, no purpose, no logic.

Judicial Opinions as Narrative

To think of and read judicial opinions as narratives is dangerous business. In doing so, one can miss or obscure the essential lesson taught by Robert Cover—the violence of the word.[3] Although other stories can be put to violent ends—such as the persistent myth of the Jewish conspiracy—judicial opinions embody violence in a special way. Opinions that tell a story of the choice to send a boy to execution, to take children away from their father and mother, to obliterate living communities, are vividly connected with violence. But the power of Cover's lesson was that he taught us to see the violence of law everywhere, even in apparently mundane judicial choices.[4] After all, what empowers a judge to command that one person shall pay damages to another person, what accounts for the surface formality and peace of the courtroom battlefield, and why do persons accept with apparent peace deeply felt injustice, every day in every courtroom in this country? It is the violence of the word.

"Law talk," in its various forms, usually suppresses this connection with violence. Law talk is rational and calm, even dispassionate. Judicial opinions are generally well-controlled pieces of apparently rational discourse. Even in dissent, judges ultimately seem to take on the sense of detachment and cool rationality that is part of the ascribed cultural role of judges.

Reading opinions as narratives can become another way of suppressing the violence of these texts. If reading opinions as narratives obscures that point, it is a pernicious endeavor. I hope instead to read opinions as narratives as a way of illuminating the idea of law as composed essentially of choices made for and against people, and imposed through violence.

The Richmond Narratives

The constitutionality of affirmative action has been perhaps the most divisive and difficult question of contemporary constitutional jurisprudence. Affirmative action demands the paradoxical solution of first taking account of race in order to get to a world where it is not taken into account. Legal scholars have recounted this struggle elsewhere. For our purposes it is sufficient to note that prior to *Richmond* the Court's affirmative action jurisprudence had been characterized by acrimonious talk and little clear consensus. In this regard, the Richmond narratives carried on their historical legacy.

In *Richmond*, the Court struck down the city of Richmond's Minority Business Utilization Plan.[5] The plan required that prime contractors who were awarded city construction contracts had to subcontract at least thirty percent of the dollar amount of each contract to "minority business enterprises." A "minority business enterprise" was defined as any business at least fifty-one percent owned or controlled by "[c]itizens of the United States who are Blacks, Spanish-speaking, Orientals, Indians, Eskimos, or Aleuts." A majority of the Court concluded that this particular affirmative action measure violated the fourteenth amendment's equal protection clause.

The *Richmond* case spawned six opinions—six potential narratives. Each narrative is rich. Yet, the most powerful, complex, and important narratives are the concurring opinion by Justice Scalia[6] and the dissenting opinion by Justice Marshall.[7] Scalia and Marshall occupied the Court's most extreme positions on the issue of affirmative action; Scalia opposed and Marshall in support. Scalia and Marshall's disagreement by itself suggests that their opinions merit special scrutiny. Nonetheless, this analysis focuses on a different feature of Scalia's and Marshall's opinions.

Scalia's opinion as narrative is on the surface an impoverished and abstract story. The facts of the *Richmond* case are recounted in snippets. Moreover,

Scalia never speaks concretely about any case or context. The opinion, in terms of what it says, is mostly abstract principles drawn from precedents that Scalia strung together with no recounting of the cases, or principles drawn from an unexplored historical context. These abstract principles seem to drive Scalia to his choice.

Marshall's narrative is altogether different. Marshall tells not only the stories of the particular dispute, but also the stories of the city of Richmond, as the capital of the Confederacy, the place of "apartheid," the city with a "disgraceful history." While Scalia sets forth some facts and Marshall asserts abstract principles, the overall texture of the two narratives is markedly distinct.

Scalia and Marshall are not simply engaged in a struggle for the future meaning of equal protection and the possibility of affirmative action programs. These two storytellers have chosen forms of narrative that reveal the essential form of their respective ideologies. They have thereby demonstrated a connection between narrative and ideology spilling beyond the particular questions of affirmative action. Scalia's and Marshall's opinions are, in that sense, two of our most important stories.

Narrative and Ideology

Seeing judicial opinions as narratives and then linking that conception to ideology is, in one sense, a simple matter. A judge chooses to tell the reader one thing and not another. For example, in *Richmond*, Justice Marshall chooses to tell the reader the story of Richmond's resistance to school desegregation.[8] Justice Scalia chooses not to speak of Richmond's school desegregation at all.[9] Justice O'Connor mentions it only as an instance of Marshall's irrelevancies.[10] Each Justice told a different version of that story, or no version at all. Each choice connects, in at least a rhetorical way, with each Justice's ideology of affirmative action. Telling, or not telling, the reader that this is a city with a "disgraceful history" of race relations is a rhetorical move connected to ideology. Other examples of this sort of connection between the particular form of judicial narrative crafted and the ideology of its crafter abound.

There is, however, a different and special sort of connection between narrative and ideology that one can discern in the Court's affirmative action opinions. One can distinguish the narrative form most commonly used by those Justices who seek to limit or stop affirmative action from the narrative form used by Justice Marshall—the most important voice on the Court for affirmative action. This distinction in narrative form reveals the ideology of the narrator and thus demonstrates the special connection between narrative and ideology.

The various opinions both for and against affirmative action have much in common. Yet, there are discernible tendencies and emphases which divide the opinions. The text of the opinions limiting affirmative action is mostly abstract. Except for the formal recitation of facts at the beginning of a majority or plurality opinion, the Justices reason mostly by reference to abstract principles. The Justices draw these principles from rhetorical journeys back to the period of the Reconstruction amendments or to precedents. These are "rhetorical journeys" in the sense that the opinions speak hardly at all of a precedent's facts or to its historical context. The point is to derive very quickly some abstract principle which then forms part of a syllogistic argument for the choice made.

One of the central abstract principles is "symmetry." Equal protection, it is said, demands symmetry. A law drawn on racial lines favoring whites is the same as one drawn to favor blacks. Turn about is not fair play. There is only one level of scrutiny—and on and on. The principle of symmetry tells us that once we know that a law is drawn on racial lines, we know what we must do. We walk up to the law with the same presumptions, suspicions, and level of scrutiny, regardless of the race advantaged and regardless of the concrete circumstances surrounding the law.[11]

Another important abstraction is that of innocence. Those who seek to limit or stop affirmative action say the white "victims" of affirmative action are "innocent."[12] The mere existence of an affirmative action program tells us that there are innocent white victims. In this vocabulary, the white person is innocent so long as he has not committed an act of particular and proven racial discrimination in connection with the job or other interest at stake. This definition of innocence puts aside the more subtle questions that can be asked of the position of any white person in our culture, questions that turn on the obvious advantage that we and our predecessors have enjoyed by the oppression of others.

Everywhere in these sorts of opinions (narratives) are abstract principles and choices that are compelled by syllogisms composed of these abstract principles. Almost nowhere in these opinions do Justices tell the richer stories of the people and places of the case, or the stories of the historical context. Justice Marshall's opinions are the exception. He tells the richer story, talking about places and people.[13] For Marshall, history is a source of stories, rather than simply abstract principles.[14] Innocence seems a more complex thing for him. His opinions, although built around legal structures, seek to move the reader as much through empathy as the cool compulsion of the syllogism.

To these observations one might say: "But of course." It is simply a matter of rhetorical strategy. Abstraction works rhetorically for Scalia. Narrative works better for Marshall. But why would that be so? And is it so? Certainly one could construct a rhetorically respectable opinion for affirmative action built mostly on abstractions, and one could build an opinion against affirmative action with richly told stories.

The opinions of Scalia and Marshall in *Richmond* exemplify the two forms of narrative which run through the contemporary Court's affirmative action cases. Working through these two opinions will illuminate the connection between narrative and ideology—a connection that is not one of absolute necessity, nor one of mere rhetorical strategy.

SCALIA AND THE WHITE IMAGINATION

Scalia's opinion is, in structure and purpose, straightforward. He has constructed a series of arguments, each related to his central thesis that affirmative action must be severely circumscribed. "In my view there is only one circumstance in which the states may act by race 'to undo the effects of past discrimination': where that is necessary to eliminate their own maintenance of a system of unlawful racial classification."[15]

In form and language the opinion seems ordinary. Virtually every paragraph is littered with cites to other cases. The rhetorical format is one of reliance on abstract principles, derived from precedents and the lessons of history. All in all, it is an opinion familiar in its structure and language.

Nonetheless, Scalia's opinion, however ordinary in form and apparently abstract, has a special vividness and concrete quality that emerges in the process of reading. In the first paragraph Scalia quotes Alexander Bickel: "[D]iscrimination on the basis of race is illegal, immoral, unconstitutional, inherently wrong, and destructive of democratic society."[16] Scalia quickly follows with the language from Harlan's dissent in *Plessy* stating that "our Constitution is color-blind." By linking the Bickel and Harlan quotes, Scalia begins the process of constructing the important argument of symmetry. But as the opinion continues, the Bickel quote has another significance. It is the beginning of a continuing metaphor, the metaphor of the bad seed, or implicitly, the metaphor of affirmative action as a cancer. Several paragraphs later, Scalia speaks of the special danger of "oppression" from political "factions" (blacks) in "small political units" (Richmond, Virginia).[17] Subsequently, Scalia speaks the words that offer the reader a powerful sense of vividness. "The prophesy [of oppression] . . . came to fruition in Richmond in the enactment of a set aside clearly and directly beneficial to the dominant political group, which happens also to be the dominant racial group."[18]

To understand the vividness of Scalia's extended metaphor, one must recall Bickel's lesson and ask what it is that makes affirmative action "destructive" to society. To say that a particular kind of law will "destroy" us is an abstraction waiting to be made real and vivid in the reading. The abstraction can become vivid for the white reader by imagining the oppression that white people might suffer at the hands of black people. When and where blacks are the dominant racial group, they will oppress whites, unless whites act to stop them. Affirmative action is thus the seed that will destroy whites. It is the means by which whites might be oppressed in those places where whites are racially outnumbered. In the city of Richmond, the dangerous seed of affirmative action came to fruition.

Scalia draws out this metaphor by language which seems abstract, formal, and quite ordinary. The vividness is provided by the reader. This provided meaning is a product of both the reader's individual imagination and the cultural influences shared by a white audience. Individual imagination may lead the reader to imagined stories of personal disadvantage in the name of affirmative action ("I did not get the appointment because I am a white male"), or perhaps a brute image of the white man's fear of the black man ("I left the building late last night and a black man followed me, asking for money"). Individual imagination as part of the process of reading Scalia's opinion will take different readers to different imaginings. Any particular reader, white or black, may have imaginings different from mine.

Nonetheless, one can suppose that throughout the white audience there will be a large measure of consonance in the readings. In some way the white reader will experience associations: connecting ideas of "difference" and "dominance," "victims" and "revenge," or other nonpictorial imaginings that produce precisely the sense of unease and fear that make Scalias metaphor vivid and powerful.

The metaphor of destruction takes an even more evocative turn when Scalia amplifies it by the use of the metaphor of fire.[19] "When we depart from [the principle that racial discrimination is destructive of our society] we play with fire, and much more than an occasional DeFunis, Johnson, or Croson burns."[20] The fear of black insurrection is part of the unbroken history of the white man's imagination. To live in a society with people whose great grandparents we enslaved and who are themselves the subjects of continuing humiliation must give us our own versions of the white slave master's nightmares. When and where we have been dominant, we have abused our power. What could we imagine when Scalia tells us that the prophecy of oppression came to fruition in Richmond? When Scalia speaks of the black person "even[ing] the score,"[21] we can fill out the story for ourselves.

The last, single-sentence paragraph of Scalia's opinion is a perfect composite of the abstract and vivid: "Since I believe that the appellee here had a constitutional right to have its bid succeed or fail under a decisionmaking process uninfected with racial bias, I concur in the judgment of the Court."[22] This sentence is abstract in several senses. First, it speaks of no names or places. It is universal in its ostensible implications. Second, the central and implicit assumption in this declaration is that once the bias of the ordinance is removed no other racial bias will exist. This assumption has compelling plausibility in an abstract conception of place and time. It becomes problematic in its real place and time. We would not realistically suppose that the public contracting process in Richmond, Virginia, or anywhere in America, would be wholly uninfected by racial bias once it is cleansed of the taint of affirmative action.

The last sentence's proclamation of the "infection" of racial bias connects the white reader to the metaphor of affirmative action as the seed of our destruction. That metaphor, in turn, can take us again to the imaginings of oppression and revenge at the hands of black citizens. Scalia demands of his readers that they become more than mere readers—he demands that they become storytellers as well—and we do.

MARSHALL AND STORIES OF RACISM

Marshall's dissenting opinion is in many respects quite ordinary. It is littered with string cites, and is, in part, built around an abstract decisional model. His model is two-pronged, requiring that the affirmative action ordinance pursue "important governmental objectives" and that the chosen means be "substantially related" to those objectives.[23] He appears to build the bulk of his text around these formal inquiries.

Nonetheless, on closer consideration, Marshall's opinion is much more than simply an argument built around a model. As Scalia's opinion, in its reading, is much more than a series of abstract principles constituting a syllogistic argument, Marshall's opinion gets thicker and more complex in its reading.

The central and powerful distinction between Marshall's and Scalia's narratives is the distinction between the narrative invited and the narrative given. Scalia's narrative in its abstractions and metaphors invites the reader to embellish with his narratives and imaginings, to make the abstract concrete, to provide meaning to the metaphors. Marshall's opinion, on the other hand, gives the reader narratives. It names and talks of persons and places. For Marshall, history is a source of other stories more than a repository of abstract principles. Marshall is a storyteller in a very different way.

Every storyteller knows that stories have beginnings and endings and that readers often pay special attention to those places in the narrative. A reader of the Richmond narratives encounters the ending of Scalia's story juxtaposed with the beginning of Marshall's story. As the echoes of Scalia's infection of affirmative action fades, Marshall begins thus: "It is a welcome symbol of racial progress when the former capital of the Confederacy acts forthrightly to confront the effects of racial discrimination in its midst."[24] In that first sentence, Marshall introduces a story he will not merely invite, but will also tell—the story of Richmond's "disgraceful history" of race relations.[25]

Marshall tells of the "Richmond experience," an experience of "the deliberate diminution of black residents' voting rights, resistance to school desegregation, and publicly sanctioned housing discrimination."[26] Marshall speaks of the attempt to annex white suburbs to avoid the specter of a black majority in the city,[27] and uses the word "apartheid."[28]

O'Connor dismisses and Scalia speaks only implicitly to this story of Richmond's history. The Justices thus dispute whether the story of Richmond's history is legally relevant. For Marshall, however, as the spokesperson for affirmative action, it is a special and powerful narrative. Here Marshall is talking to the same audience as Scalia—the white audience. Marshall tells the white audience a story that is likely to be neither part of their actual personal experience nor part of their culture's repertoire of stories. He asks the white reader to hear this story and to empathize. It is a struggle for the reader, and one that may, for some, never succeed. Still, if Marshall fails to tell this story and other stories like it, the white reader is unlikely to tell this narrative on his own. Marshall cannot merely invite narratives from this audience. He must provide them. From these told narratives, and the imaginings and narratives of the reader, there is the hope of the essential empathy from which a person can act beyond self-interest.

Marshall rejects the argument for symmetry by defining the difference between "governmental actions that themselves are racist, and governmental actions that seek to remedy the effects of prior racism" or, perhaps more evocatively, between "remedial classifications" and "the most brute and repugnant forms of state-sponsored racism."[29] Although this part of the opinion is closer to Scalia's narrative-invited style, the narratives that Marshall invites here are those more likely told by the white reader. For example, "state-sponsored racism" is a powerful set of words invoking imaginings in the reader, of whatever race, of the institutions of slavery and apartheid which scar our history.

Marshall tells another story of racism. He tells the story of the racism that may be discerned in O'Connor's opinion, among others. He focuses on O'Connor's references to the dominant racial group in Richmond, and the specter of simple racial politics.[30] Marshall argues that cities under the leadership of members of a racial minority may often be cities with much to remedy. He reminds us that this is certainly true of Richmond. Thus, Marshall argues, one should assume that the political leaders of Richmond acted with sincere remedial goals in mind and not simple racial politics. This measured objection contrasts sharply with his final reaction to O'Connor's argument on simple racial politics.

> The majority's view that remedial measures undertaken by municipalities with black leadership must face a stiffer test of Equal Protection Clause scrutiny than remedial measures undertaken by municipalities with white leadership implies a lack of political maturity on the part of this Nation's elected minority officials that is totally unwarranted. Such insulting judgments have no place in constitutional jurisprudence.[31]

At this moment, Marshall invites the white reader to imagine the hurt and insult of racism.

Marshall's charge that O'Connor and others have expressed "insulting judgments" about black elected officials is a story of racism on the Court. As such, it is a powerful move and an especially evocative moment for the reader. Marshall's charge is, in a sense, inviting a narrative about the Justices. As the white reader struggles to understand the deeper meaning of Marshall's charge, he experiences discomfort. Marshall reveals the unthinkable notion that the Justices themselves harbor racist assumptions and attitudes. Yet, this almost unthinkable notion is surely true—just as I harbor such assumptions and attitudes. For some readers, this may be the most powerful story Marshall has told.

Thus Scalia and Marshall tell different narratives. Scalia invites the reader to make his abstractions and metaphors concrete and vivid. Marshall tells stories in explicit detail, stories with details not likely to be provided by his audience. Marshall's stories quite obviously do not necessarily persuade the white reader. But his stories make possible the essential move for any white reader who might embrace affirmative action—the move to empathy. Only if we can join, in some imperfect way, in the feelings and circumstances of the beneficiaries of affirmative action can we accept the role of those disadvantaged by affirmative action. Although Marshall makes our acceptance *possible* through his stories, whether it happens depends on the narratives we tell ourselves.

NOTES

1. 109 S. Ct. 706 (1989).

2. *Id.* at 740 (Marshall, J., dissenting).

3. *See* Robert Cover, *Violence and the Word*, 95 YALE L.J. 1601, 1609 (1986) (discussing the violence inherent in judicial opinions and other legal interpretations).

4. "The judges deal pain and death. That is not all that they do. Perhaps that is not what they usually do. But they do deal death, and pain. . . . In this they are different from poets, from critics, from artists." *Id.* at 1609.

5. *See* City of Richmond v. J. A. Croson Co., 109 S. Ct. 706, 730 (1989) (plurality opinion).

6. *See id.* at 735–39 (Scalia, J., concurring).

7. *See id.* at 739–57 (Marshall, J., dissenting).

8. *See id.* at 748.

9. *See id.* at 735–39 (Scalia, J., concurring).

10. "The 'evidence' relied upon by the dissent, the history of school desegregation in Richmond and numerous congressional reports, does little to define the scope of any injury to minority contractors in Richmond or the necessary remedy." *Id.* at 727 (plurality opinion).

11. Regents of the Univ. of Cal. v. Bakke, 438 U.S. 265, 291 (1978) ("Racial and ethnic distinctions of any sort are inherently suspect and thus call for the most exacting judicial examination.").

12. *See, e.g.,* Justice Powell's reference to "legal remedies that work against innocent people." [*Wygant*, 476 U.S. at 276;] *see also* Thomas Ross, *Innocence and Affirmative Action*, 43 VAND. L. REV. 297 (1990) (discussing the power and danger of the "rhetoric of innocence" in affirmative action).

13.

The majority's perfunctory dismissal of the testimony of Richmond's appointed and elected leaders is also deeply disturbing. These officials—including councilmembers, a former mayor, and the present city manager—asserted that race discrimination in area contracting had been widespread, and that the set-aside ordinance was a sincere and necessary attempt to eradicate the effects of discrimination.

City of Richmond v. J. A. Croson Co., 109 S. Ct. 706, 747 (1989) (Marshall, J., dissenting).

14.

Had the majority paused for a moment on the facts of the Richmond experience, it would have discovered that the city's leadership is deeply familiar with what racial discrimination is. The members of the Richmond City Council have spent long years witnessing multifarious acts of discrimination, including, but not limited to, the deliberate diminution of black residents' voting rights, resistance to school desegregation, and publicly sanctioned housing discrimination. Numerous decisions of federal courts chronicle this disgraceful recent history.

Id. at 748 (citations omitted).

15. *Id.* at 737 (Scalia, J., concurring).

16. *Id.* at 735 (quoting ALEXANDER BICKEL, THE MORALITY OF CONSENT 133 (1975)).

17. *Richmond,* 109 S. Ct. at 737 (Scalia, J., concurring).

18. *Id.*

19. *See id.* at 736–39. Scalia has used the "bad seed" metaphor in his academic writing to describe affirmative action. *See* Antonin Scalia, *The Disease as Cure,* 1979 WASH. U. L.Q. 147, 157.

20. *See Richmond,* 109 S. Ct. at 739 (Scalia, J., concurring).

21. *Id.* at 739 (Scalia, J., concurring).

22. *Id.*

23. *See Richmond,* 109 S. Ct. at 739–57 (Marshall, J., dissenting).

24. *Id.* (Marshall, J., dissenting).

25. *Id.* at 739–43.

26. *Id.* at 748.

27. *See id.* at 748.

28. *Id.*

29. *Id.* at 752.

30. *See id.* at 753.

31. *Id.* at 754–55.

5 Translating *Yonnondio* by Precedent and Evidence: The Mashpee Indian Case

GERALD TORRES and KATHRYN MILUN

T H E telling of stories holds an important role in the work of courts. Within a society, there are specific places where most of the activities making up social life within that society simultaneously are represented, contested, and inverted. Courts are such places. Like mirrors, they reflect where we are, from a space where we are not. Law, the mechanism through which courts carry out this mirroring function, has a curious way of recording a culture's practices of telling and listening to its stories. Such stories enter legal discourse in an illustrative, even exemplary, fashion.

"Yonnondio"—the address, the salutation—became a medium through which contending Indian and European cultures interacted. The evolving meaning of this salutation reflected changing relations of power as the Indians' early contact with European explorers themselves evolved into contact with the states represented by those explorers. Likewise, the land claim suits filed by various Tribes during the 1970s[1] served as a channel through which some Indians attempted to communicate with the state—this time, through the medium of courts. In order for the state to hear their claims, however, these Indians were forced to speak in a formalized idiom of the language of the state—the idiom of legal discourse. Consider one such land claim suit, *Mashpee Tribe v. Town of Mashpee*,[2] and the formalized address that it incorporated. What happens, we ask, when such claims receive a legal hearing? We suggest that first they must be translated by means of examples that law can follow (precedent) and examples that law can hear (evidence).

We should suspect that the legal coding through which such translation is conducted highlights a problem inherent in the post-modern condition—the confrontation between irreconcilable systems of meaning produced by two contending cultures. The post-modern condition is a crisis of faith in the grand stories that have justified our history and legitimized our knowledge.[3] The very idea of what we can know is unstable. The crisis in the law that emerged with the Legal Realists and the attempts to reconstitute formalism—as the basis for survival of the "rule of law"—also reflect our post-modern condition. In the case of the

1990 DUKE L.J. 625. Originally published in the Duke Law Journal. Reprinted by permission.

Mashpee, the systems of meaning are irreconcilable: The politics of historical domination reduced the Mashpee to having to petition their "guardian" to allow them to exist, and the history of that domination has determined in large measure the ways the Mashpee must structure their petitions. The conflict between these systems of meaning—that of the Mashpee and that of the state—is really the question of how we can "know" which history is most "true."

Yet the difficulty facing the Mashpee in this case is not just that they cannot find the proper language with which to tell their story or capture the essence of the examples that would prove their claims. The problem with conflicting systems of meaning is that there is a history and social practice reflected and contained within the language chosen. To require a particular way of telling a story not only strips away nuances of meaning but also elevates a particular version of events to a non-contingent status. More than that, however, when particular versions of events are rendered unintelligible, the corresponding counter-examples that those versions represent lose their legitimacy. Those examples come unglued from both the cultural structure that grounds them and the legal structure that would validate them. The existence of untranslatable examples renders unreadable the entire code of which they are a part, while simultaneously legitimizing the resulting ignorance.

"Ignorant," of course, merely means uninformed. The central problem is whether the limitations of the legal idiom permit one party truly to inform the other, or conversely, whether the dimension of power hidden in the idiomatic structure of legal storytelling forecloses one version in favor of another.

> [W]hen you are powerless, you don't just speak differently. A lot, you don't speak. Your speech is not just differently articulated, it is silenced. Eliminated, gone. You aren't just deprived of a language with which to articulate your distinctiveness, although you are; you are deprived of a life out of which articulation might come.[4]

What constitutes proof and what constitutes authority; what are the pragmatics of "legal" storytelling? Pragmatics in this context might be analyzed best in terms of a game. Any game must have rules to determine what is an acceptable move, but the rules do not determine all available moves. Although the total content of acceptable moves is not predetermined, the universe of potentially permissible moves is limited necessarily by the structure of the game. All language, but especially technical language, is a kind of game. What are the rules that govern discourse in the legal idiom? What kind of knowledge is transmitted?

By highlighting the peculiar nature of legal discourse and comparing it to other ways of telling and reading the Mashpee's history, we can explore and make concrete the roles of power and politics in legal rationality. The *Mashpee* case is especially well suited to this investigation because it casts so starkly the problem of law as an artifact of culture and power.

Looking Back at Indians and Indians
Looking Back: The Case

In 1976 in *Mashpee Tribe v. Town of Mashpee*, the Indian community at Mashpee on Cape Cod sued to recover tribal lands alienated from them
over the last two centuries in violation of the Indian Non-Intercourse Act of
1790.[5] The Non-Intercourse Act prohibits the transfer of Indian tribal land to non-
Indians without approval of the federal government. The Tribe claimed its land
had been taken from it, between 1834 and 1870, without the required federal consent. According to the Mashpee, the Commonwealth of Massachusetts had permitted the land to be sold to non-Indians and had transferred common Indian
lands to the Town of Mashpee. The defendant, Town of Mashpee, answered by
denying that the plaintiffs, Mashpee, were a Tribe. Therefore, they were outside
the protection of the Non-Intercourse Act and were without standing to sue.

As a result, the Mashpee first had to prove that they were indeed a "Tribe."
A forty-day trial then ensued on that threshold issue. The Mashpee were required
to demonstrate their tribal existence in accordance with a definition adopted by
the United States Supreme Court at the turn of the century in *Montoya v. United
States:* "By a 'tribe' we understand a body of Indians of the same or a similar race,
united in a community under one leadership or government, and inhabiting a particular though sometimes ill-defined territory."[6] This is a very narrow and particular definition. As Judge Skinner, who presided over the trial of the Mashpee's
claim, explained in his instructions to the jury: "Now, what is the level of the
burden of proof? I've said these matters need not be determined in terms of cos-
mic proof. The plaintiff has the burden of proving . . . if the [Mashpee] were a
tribe."

Judge Skinner agreed to allow expert testimony from various social scientists
regarding the definition of "Indian Tribe." By the closing days of the trial, however, the judge had become frustrated with the lack of consensus as to a definition:

> I am seriously considering striking all of the definitions given by all of the experts
> of a Tribe and all of their opinions as to whether or not the inhabitants of Mash-
> pee at any time could constitute a Tribe. I let it all in on the theory that there was
> a professionally accepted definition of Tribe within these various disciplines.
>
> It is becoming more and more apparent that each definition is highly subjec-
> tive and idiosyncratic and generated for a particular purpose not necessarily hav-
> ing anything to do with the Non-Intercourse Act of 1790.

In the end, Judge Skinner instructed the jury that the Mashpee had to meet the
requirements of *Montoya*—rooted in notions of racial purity, authoritarian leadership, and consistent territorial occupancy—in order to establish their tribal
identity, despite the fact that *Montoya* itself did not address the Non-Intercourse
Act.

The case providing the key definition, *Montoya*, involved a company whose livestock had been taken by a group of Indians. The company sued the United States and the Tribe to which the group allegedly belonged under the Indian Depredation Act. This Act provided compensation to persons whose property was destroyed by Indians belonging to a Tribe. The theory underlying tribal liability is that the Tribe should be responsible for the actions of its members. The issue in *Montoya* was whether the wrong-doers were still part of the Tribe. The court found they were not.

Beyond reflecting archaic notions of tribal existence in general, the *Montoya* requirements incorporated specific perceptions regarding race, leadership, community, and territory that were entirely alien to Mashpee culture. The testimony revealed the *Montoya* criteria as generalized ethnological categories that failed to capture the specifics of what it means to belong to the Mashpee people. Because of this disjunction between the ethno-legal categories and the Mashpee's lived experience, the Tribe's testimony and evidence never quite "signified" within the idiom established by the precedent. After forty days of testimony, the jury came up with the following "irrational" decision: The Mashpee were not a Tribe in 1790, were a Tribe in 1834 and 1842, but again were not a Tribe in 1869 and 1870. Based on the jury's findings, the trial court dismissed the Mashpee's claim.

The Baked and the Half-Baked

Whether the Mashpee are legally a Tribe is, of course, only half the question. That the Mashpee existed as a recognized people occupying a recognizable territory for well over three hundred years is a well-documented fact.[7] In order to ascertain the meaning of that existence, however, an observer must ask not only what categories are used to describe it but also whether the categories adopted by the observer carry the same meaning to the observed.

The earliest structure used for communal Mashpee functions—a colonial-style building that came to be known as "the Old Meetinghouse"—was built in 1684. The meetinghouse was built by a white man, Shearjashub Bourne, as a place where the Mashpee could conduct their Christian worship. Shearjashub's father, Richard Bourne, had preached to the Mashpee and oversaw their conversion to Christianity almost a generation earlier. The Bourne family's early interest in the Mashpee later proved propitious. The elder Bourne arranged for a deed to be issued to the Mashpee to "protect" their interest in the land they occupied. Confirmation of this deed by the General Court of Plymouth Colony in 1671 served as the foundation for including "Mashpee Plantation" within the protection of the Massachusetts Bay Colony. As part of the Colony, the Mashpee were assured that their spiritual interests, as defined by their Christian overseers, as well as their temporal interests would receive official attention. However, the impact of introducing the symbology of property deeds into the Mashpee's cultural structure reverberates to this day. Whether the introduction of European notions of private ownership into Mashpee society can be separated from either the protection the colonial overseers claim actually was intended or the Mashpee's ultimate undoing is, of course, central to the meaning of "ownership."

Colonial oversight quickly became a burden. In 1760, the Mashpee appealed directly to King George III for relief from their British overlords. In 1763, their petition was granted. The "Mashpee Plantation" received a new legal designation, granting the "proprietors the right to elect their own overseers."[8] This change in the Tribe's relationship with its newly arrived white neighbors did not last long, however. With the coming of the Colonies' war against England and the founding of the Commonwealth of Massachusetts, all previous protections of Mashpee land predicated on British rule quickly were repealed, and the Tribe was subjected to a new set of overseers with even more onerous authority than its colonial lords had held. The new protectors were granted "oppressive powers over the inhabitants, including the right to lease their lands, to sell timber from their forests, and to hire out their children to labor."[9]

During this time the Mashpee were on their way toward becoming the melange of "racial types" that ultimately would bring about their legal demise two hundred years later. Colonists had taken Mashpee wives, many of whom were widows whose husbands had died fighting against the British. The Wampanoags, another southern Massachusetts Tribe that suffered terrible defeat in wars with the European colonists, had retreated and had been taken in by the Mashpee. Hessian soldiers had intermarried with the Mashpee. Runaway slaves took refuge with and married Mashpee Indians. The Mashpee became members of a "mixed" race, and the names some of the Mashpee carried reflected this mixture. What was clear to the Mashpee, if not to outside observers, was that this mixing did not dilute their tribal status because they did not define themselves according to racial type, but rather by membership in their community. In an essay on the Mashpee in *The Predicament of Culture*,[10] one authority explained that despite the racial mixing that had historically occurred in the Mashpee community, since the Mashpee did not measure tribal membership according to "blood" Indian identity remained paramount. In fact, the openness to outsiders who wished to become part of the tribal community was part of the community values that contributed to tribal identity. The Mashpee were being penalized for maintaining their aboriginal traditions because they did not conform to the prevailing "racial" definition of community and society.

In 1833, a series of events began that culminated in the partial restoration of traditional Mashpee "rights." William Apes, an Indian preacher who claimed to be descended from King Philip, a Wampanoag chief, stirred the Mashpee to petition their overseers and the Governor of Massachusetts for relief from the depredation visited upon them. What offended Apes was the appropriation of the Mashpee's worshipping ground by white Christians. In response to the imposition of a white Christian minister on their congregation, they had abandoned the meetinghouse in favor of an outdoor service conducted by a fellow Indian. The petition Apes helped draft began, "we, as a Tribe, will rule ourselves, and have the right to do so, for all men are born free and equal, says the Constitution of the country."[11] What is particularly important about this challenge is that it asserted independence within the context of the laws of the commonwealth of Massachusetts. The Massachusetts Governor rejected this appeal, and the Mashpee's attempt at unilateral enforcement of their claims resulted in the arrest and conviction of Apes.

The appeal of Apes' conviction, however, produced a partial restoration of the Tribe's right of self-governance and full restoration of its right to religious self-determination, for the Tribe was returned to its meetinghouse. When the white former minister tried to intervene, he was removed forcibly and a new lock was installed on the meetinghouse doors. By 1840, the Mashpee's right to worship was secured.

Control of the land remained a critical issue for the Mashpee. By late in the 17th century, the area surrounding the homes and land of the "South Sea Indians" had been consolidated and organized into a permanent Indian plantation. The Mashpee's relationship to this land, however, remained legally problematic for the Commonwealth. In 1842, Massachusetts determined that the land was to be divided among individual Mashpee Tribe members, but their power over it was closely circumscribed; they could sell it only to other members of the Tribe. The "plantation" could tax the land, but the land could not be taken for nonpayment of those taxes. In 1859, a measure was proposed to permit the Mashpee to sell land to outsiders and to make the Mashpee "full citizens" of the commonwealth. This proposal was rejected by the Tribe's governing council. In 1870, however, the Mashpee were "granted" rights to alienate their property as "full-fledged citizens" and their land was organized by fiat into the town of Mashpee.[12]

It was the land that had moved out of Indian control, eleven thousand acres of undeveloped land estimated to be worth fifty million dollars, that the Mashpee Wampanoag Tribal Council sued to reclaim in 1976. Some of the land had been lost in the intervening years, and more was in danger of being lost or reduced to non-exclusive occupancy. The Council based its claim on the 1790 Non-Intercourse Act,[13] which prohibits the alienation of Indian lands[14] without federal approval. The Non-Intercourse Act applies to transactions between Indians and non-Indians, and, despite its inherent paternalism, serves to protect tribal integrity.

The Non-Intercourse Act applied only if the Mashpee had retained their "tribal identity" (defined, however, by the white man's rules of the game) from the mid-17th century until they filed their land claim action in 1976. In order to fall within the scope of the Act's protection, the Mashpee had to prove first that they were indeed a "Tribe" and that their status as such had not changed throughout this period. If the Mashpee were no longer a "Tribe" (or if they never had constituted a "Tribe" in the first place), the protection provided by the Non-Intercourse Act evaporated. If, however, the Indians retained their tribal status, then the transactions that resulted in the loss of their village were invalid. At the very heart of the dispute was whether the Mashpee were "legally" a people and thus entitled to legal protection.[15]

Many of the facts underlying the Mashpee's suit were not disputed. What the parties fought about was the *meaning* of "what happened." Seen from the perspective of the Mashpee, the facts that defined the Indians as a Tribe also invalidated the transactions divesting them of their lands. From the perspective of the property owners in the Town, however, those same acts proved that the Mashpee no longer existed as a separate people. How, then, is an appropriate perspective to be chosen? As told by the defendants, the Mashpee's story was one about "a small, mixed community fighting for equality and citizenship while abandoning, by choice or coercion, most of its aboriginal heritage."[16]

Using the same evidence, the plaintiffs told a very different story. It was the story of cultural survival: "[T]he residents of Mashpee had managed to keep alive a core of Indian identity over three centuries against enormous odds. They had done so in supple, sometimes surreptitious ways, always attempting to control, not reject, outside influences."[17] Which of the two conflicting perspectives is the "proper" one from which to assess the facts underlying the Mashpee's claim?

NOTES

1. *See generally* P. BRODEUR, RESTITUTION: THE LAND CLAIMS OF THE MASHPEE, PASSAMAQUODDY, AND PENOBSCOT INDIANS OF NEW ENGLAND (1985). During the late 1960s and early 1970s, several Indian tribes pursued legal actions aimed at reclaiming land alienated from them by various means during the 16th, 17th, 18th, and 19th centuries: the Passamaquoddy and Penobscot in Maine; the Gay Head Wampanoag in Massachusetts; the Narragansett in Rhode Island; the Western Pequot, Schaghticot, and Mohegan in Connecticut; the Oneida, Cayuga, and St. Regis Mohawk in New York; the Catawba in South Carolina; the Chitimacha in Louisiana; and the Mashpee of Cape Cod in Massachusetts, to name a few.

2. 447 F. Supp. 940 (D. Mass. 1978), *aff'd sub nom.* Mashpee Tribe v. New Seabury Corp., 592 F.2d 575 (1st Cir.), *cert. denied*, 444 U.S. 866 (1979).

3. *See* J. F. LYOTARD, THE POSTMODERN CONDITION: A REPORT ON KNOWLEDGE (G. Bennington & B. Massumi trans. 1984) (The crisis of modernity is examined as a lack of belief in the grand narratives which legitimized the modern social order, for example liberalism and Marxism.).

4. C. MACKINNON, FEMINISM UNMODIFIED: DISCOURSES ON LIFE AND LAW 39 (1987) (articulation of feminism as a critique of the gendered system of social hierarchy and social power).

5. 25 U.S.C. § 177 (1988) (derived from Act of June 30, 1834, ch. 161, § 12, 4 Stat. 730). This Act provides: "No purchase, grant, lease, or other conveyance of lands, . . . from any Indian nation or tribe of Indians, shall be of any validity in law or equity, unless the same be made by treaty or convention entered into pursuant to the Constitution." *Id.* The original language read: "That no person shall be permitted to carry on any trade or intercourse with the Indian tribes, without a license for that purpose under the hand and seal of the superintendent of the department. . . ." Act of July 22, 1790, ch. 33, § 1, 1 Stat. 137.

6. Montoya v. United States, 180 U.S. 261, 266 (1901).

7. Paul Brodeur notes:

Mashpee was never really settled in any formal sense of the word. It was simply inhabited by the Wampanoags and their Nauset relatives, whose ancestors had been coming there to fish for herring and to gather clams and oysters since the earliest aboriginal times, and whose descendants currently represent, with the exception of the Penobscots and the Passamaquoddies of Maine, the largest body of Indians in New England.

P. Brodeur, *supra* note 1, at 7–9; *see also* J. CLIFFORD, THE PREDICAMENT OF CULTURE: TWENTIETH-CENTURY ETHNOGRAPHY, LITERATURE, AND ART 289 (1988) ("[The Mashpee] did have a place and a reputation. For centuries Mashpee had been recognized as an Indian town. Its boundaries had not changed since 1665, when the land was formally deeded to a group called the South Sea Indians by the neighboring leaders Tookonchasun and Weepquish."].

The irony of this "documentation" is that either as journalism or as anthropology it recounts a telling that is not documentation for purposes of the dispute.

8. Brodeur, *supra* note 1, at 15.

9. *Id.*

10. J. CLIFFORD, *supra* note 7, at 306–07.

11. P. BRODEUR, *supra* note 1, at 17.

12. *Id.* at 19–20.

13. 25 U.S.C. § 177 (1988); *see* P. Brodeur, *supra* (quoting the relevant provisions of the Act).

14. Under the Non-Intercourse Act, protected "Indian lands" are the lands a Tribe claims title to on the basis of prior possession or ownership. *See* 25 U.S.C. § 194 (1988). Section 194 provides:

In all trials about the right of property in which an Indian may be a party on one side, and a white person on the other, the burden of proof shall rest upon the white person, whenever the Indian shall make out a presumption of title in himself from the fact of previous possession or ownership.

15. *See* 25 U.S.C. § 177 (1988) (referring to "Indian nation" and "tribe of Indians" as those covered by statute).

16. J. CLIFFORD, *supra* note 7, at 302.

17. *Id.*

6 Race and the Dominant Gaze: Narratives of Law and Inequality in Popular Film

MARGARET M. RUSSELL

Cinematic Narrative and Racial Injustice

In *Birth of a Nation* (Epoch Pictures, 1915), frequently cited as a milestone in the history of American motion pictures, D. W. Griffith offered his vision of race relations in the United States. Originally entitled *The Clansman* (from the popular novel of the same name), the film portrays a South ravaged by the Civil War, corrupted by Reconstruction, and eventually redeemed by the birth of the Ku Klux Klan. *Birth of a Nation*'s bluntly white supremacist message is conveyed through a narrative chronicling the effect of the Civil War on the South Carolina plantation of the Cameron family. As the silent film begins, subtitles extol the virtues of the Camerons' tranquil way of life which "is to be no more." Benevolent masters are served by loyal slaves who contentedly pick cotton, perform domestic chores, and otherwise aim to please. By war's end, this felicitous social order has degenerated into lawlessness. The newly emancipated roam the streets and terrorize the white community; anarchic hordes take over the polls, disenfranchise white voters, and seize control of the Congress. Griffith's first Black legislators are contemptible, priapean fools; swigging from whiskey bottles and gnawing on fried chicken legs, they conduct their first legislative session with shoes off and legs splayed carelessly across their desks. The film depicts emancipation as destructive of the private sphere as well; freedmen lust after Southern belles and communities fall prey to "ruin, devastation, rapine, and pillage." The saga climaxes with a dramatic, victorious ride to the rescue by the Klan, which defeats the Black rebels and restores civilization.

Birth of a Nation was advertised upon its release as a film that would "work audiences into a frenzy . . . it will make you hate." The "you" to whom this exhortation was addressed, of course, was not a neutral or universal "You," but a specifically targeted one: the white viewer threatened by integration and fearful of Black insurgency. Through his carefully constructed fusion of unprecedented technical wizardry and degrading racial stereotypes, Griffith sought to convince this audience that his was the "true" story of the old South and that white domination was necessary for their survival. To a great extent, he succeeded: The

15 LEGAL STUD. F. 243 (1991). Originally published in Legal Studies Forum. Reprinted by permission.

film's enormous popularity fueled the growing influence of the Klan, and *Birth of a Nation* remains to this day one of the highest-grossing box office successes in Hollywood history. Thus, it continues to be important not only as an individual aesthetic statement or arcane historical artifact, but as a popular work which has profoundly affected both popular discourse and events concerning race relations in the United States.

In this latter respect—as a text about race, dominance, and the American social/legal order—*Birth of a Nation* exemplifies what I would call the "dominant gaze": the tendency of mainstream culture to replicate, through narrative and imagery, racial inequalities and biases which exist throughout society. I derive the term "dominant gaze" from Laura Mulvey's feminist critique of Hollywood movies, "Visual Pleasure and Narrative Cinema,"[1] in which she contends that popular film essentially serves the political function of subjugating female bodies and experiences to the interpretation and control of a heterosexual "male gaze." According to Mulvey, any observer's potential to experience visual and visceral pleasure from watching Hollywood movies is completely predicated upon acceptance of a patriarchal world view in which men look and women are looked at, men act and women are acted upon. She further contends that this distinctly male-oriented perspective insidiously perpetuates sexual inequality by forcing the viewer (whether male or female) to identify with and adopt a perspective which objectifies and dehumanizes women. Finally, she asserts that only through concerted deconstruction and disruption of the male gaze can women achieve true equality in societal relations and in the cultural representations which reinforce them.

Extending Mulvey's metaphor, I use the term "dominant gaze" to describe the tendency of American popular cinema to objectify and trivialize the racial identity and experiences of people of color, even when it purports to represent them. Like Mulvey's male gaze, the dominant gaze subtly invites the viewer to empathize and identify with its viewpoint as natural, universal, and beyond challenge; it marginalizes other perspectives to bolster its own legitimacy in defining narratives and images. As D. W. Griffith illustrated so effectively in *Birth of a Nation*, the dominant gaze's power lies in projecting stereotypes and biases as essential "truths." Mas'ud Zavarzadeh notes in *Seeing Films Politically*[2] that both momentous and trivial films fulfill this hegemonic function. In fact, he argues, the distortive messages conveyed in so-called "minor" or "trivial" films have a far greater effect on popular culture precisely because of their insignificant nature; they create "the space in which the daily is negotiated; it is the space that is represented in the common sense as 'real.' "[3]

As one intrigued by the relationship between law and popular culture in forging societal norms about race, I think it important to detect and dissect the dominant gaze that pervades the representation of Blacks in American cinema. Much as analyzing jurisprudential artifacts such as *Dred Scott v. Sandford* and *Plessy v. Ferguson* remains essential to a full understanding of the persistent effects of racism in our legal system, film classics such as *Birth of a Nation* provide a useful starting point for analysis of the narratives and images that perpetuate legacies of bigotry in our popular culture and in our laws.

Doing the Hollywood Shuffle: Racial Stereotypes in American Popular Films

In 1941, in commenting on a demeaning and unintelligible line of dialogue written for her role as a mammy-ish maid in *Affectionately Yours*, Black Hollywood actress Butterfly McQueen confessed: "I never thought I would have to say a line like that. I had imagined that since I was an intelligent woman, I could play any kind of role."[4] McQueen's dismay stemmed from the realization that Hollywood had no roles for an intelligent Black woman—only ones for "toms, coons, mulattoes, mammies, and bucks." Nearly fifty years later, Black filmmaker Robert Townsend expressed a similar point in the 1987 comedy *Hollywood Shuffle*. Townsend lambastes the Hollywood film and television community as manipulative buffoons who use Black actors only for roles as pimps, drug addicts, and prostitutes; accordingly, the film's Black characters realize that their livelihood depends upon conforming to these debilitating images—that is, doing the "Hollywood Shuffle."

According to Donald Bogle, racial stereotypes in American movies are as old as movies themselves: the Tom (Edwin S. Porter's *Uncle Tom's Cabin*, 1903); the Coon (Thomas Alva Edison's *Ten Little Pickaninnies*, 1904); the Tragic Mulatto (*The Octoroon*, 1913); the Mammy (*Coontown Suffragettes*, 1914—a blackface version of Aristophanes' *Lysistrata*); and the Buck (*Birth of a Nation*, 1915. All these movies inscribed on the nation's consciousness cinematic images which persist to this day. One need only look at contemporary analogues of these stereotypes (from Aunt Jemima pancake mix and "Buckwheat" T-shirts to "mammy" figures in television situation comedies) to recognize their continuing resonance in our popular discourse.

How has the dominant gaze operated to perpetuate the subordination of Blacks in mainstream Hollywood films? Consider three distinct ways in which the dominant gaze functions: (1) in the proliferation of degrading stereotypes which serve to dehumanize Blacks' history, lives, and experiences; (2) in the marginalization or complete absence of indigenous perspectives on Blacks' history, lives, and experiences; and (3) in the co-optation—or "Hollywood-ization"—of ostensibly "racial" themes to capitalize on the perceived trendiness or fashionableness of such perspectives. In marginalizing Blacks and other minorities from popular discourse, the three trends frequently overlap in particular films. *Birth of a Nation*, for example, both disseminates negative stereotypes and obscures indigenous perspectives; a more recent film such as *Driving Miss Daisy* might be seen as a benignly intended example of the second and third trends; and slick Eddie Murphy vehicles such as *Beverly Hills Cop* illustrate all three.

It is important to understand the history of exploitation of Blacks in American films, for it is from this ideological cinema-scape that contemporary movies emerge. Over time, such distortion and erasure create damage both subtle and severe; as Carol Sanger has noted regarding the debilitating effects of both pornography and so-called "harmless" (but nevertheless misogynistic) pop novels, both cultural forms condition their female objects to become "seasoned to the use" of demeaning images.[5] Similarly, the unchallenged transmission of racial stereotypes in films not only weakens resistance to their falsity but also strengthens the legitimacy of their narrative source.

With these concerns in mind, I must concede that I approach movies not only with an avid fan's enthusiasm and curiosity, but with a skeptic's critical eye as well. It was in this frame of mind that I first saw *Soul Man* — a fairytale romance of a white student who pretends to be Black so that he can go to Harvard Law School.

Soul Man: *Variations on the Gaze*

This is the Eighties! It's the Cosby decade—
America LOVES Black people!

With these cheery words, the white protagonist of *Soul Man* attempts to reassure a doubting friend of the wisdom of his decision to "turn Black" in order to win a minority scholarship to Harvard Law School. As the flippancy of this dialogue might suggest, *Soul Man* aims both stylistically and substantively to be very much an "Eighties" flick. Advertised as "A Comedy With Heart . . . and Soul," it sparkles with several (by now de rigueur) attributes bound to please the youthful, upwardly mobile moviegoer: a hip title; a musical soundtrack studded with soul, rock, and blues standards; and a plot featuring attractive, well-educated, and basically conventional young people. Its obvious theme (and target audience) of "twentysomething" self-interest is carefully tempered by the presence of a few prominent older stars (James Earl Jones and Leslie Nielsen) to draw a wider audience. The slickly packaged story provides carefully measured doses of comedy, romance, sex, conflict, and moralizing before reaching a happy and uncomplicated denouement.

Not coincidentally, *Soul Man*'s narrative premise is also characteristic of its era; it is a post-*Bakke*[6] fantasy about the dangerous possibilities of affirmative action, minority scholarships, and other race-conscious remedies. Mark Watson, an upper-middle-class, white male college graduate, fears that he will be prevented from attending the law school of his dreams. To obtain his "rightful" place at Harvard, he decides to fake being Black so that he can win a minority scholarship. With the help of a friend, Mark obtains chemicals to darken his skin, interviews successfully for the scholarship, and—voila!—embarks on his new life as a Black man at Harvard.

Mark continues this ruse without hesitation until he falls in love with Sarah Walker (Rae Dawn Chong), a brilliant and beautiful Black law student, and learns that *she* would have received the scholarship if *he* had not happened along. Torn with guilt and driven by his desire to please the unknowing Sarah, Mark confesses his deception to a Black law professor (Jones) and submits to prosecution by the Harvard disciplinary council. After a climactic trial scene before the council and his fellow students, he is exonerated—at least, permitted to remain at Harvard Law School. As the film ends, a wiser and more sensitive Mark returns to his life as a white student, now accompanied by Sarah, who has forgiven his transgressions and realized her true, color-blind love for him.

As one might surmise from this synopsis, in many ways *Soul Man* is—beneath its hip, race-conscious veneer—simply another romantic comedy in the old-style Hollywood tradition: Boy Meets Girl, Boy Gets Girl, Boy Loses Girl, Boy Gets Girl Back. Other familiar cinematic motifs underscore this basic conventionality of structure: the fraternal camaraderie between Mark and his buddy; the ambivalent mixture of flippancy and respect with which Mark views his intimidating, "father-figure" professor; the presence of a desperate "other woman" whose attention is unwanted by Mark; the rivalry with another male who covets Mark's spot at Harvard Law School; and most critically, the kind of dewy-eyed ending crafted to warm the viewer's heart and provide reassurance that all is right with the world.

However, what renders this movie an especially revealing artifact of its era is its willingness (indeed eagerness) to use race explicitly as a gimmick to advance its old-fashioned story line. *Soul Man*'s comic effectiveness depends upon the viewer's willingness to accept racial stereotypes as comedy and racial identity as a gag. Significantly, the movie transmits its putative wisdom about Black experience not through the eyes of its Black characters, but through the gaze of a white person aiming to carry out a self-serving schoolboy scheme. In using such a dominant gaze, the film undermines its own "enlightened" pretensions in commenting on law, race, and the reality of racial discrimination. To understand how this diminution is accomplished, it is helpful to clarify the perspective of race that permeates the film.

Watson's Plot: A View of the Bottom from the Top

Three early scenes in *Soul Man* set the stage for Mark's racial transformation. As the movie begins, the camera's eye introduces us to Mark Watson's world of collegiate ease and privilege: a student's messy bedroom, replete with carelessly strewn clothes, tennis balls, frisbees, and other sports paraphernalia. A radio blares blues music; a large kitschy figurine of a bikini-clad white woman decorates a corner. Mark has just awakened from the previous night's revelry, to find a blonde woman (whom he obviously does not recognize) asleep beside him. Suddenly, his roommate bursts loudly into the room, waving two envelopes that have just arrived in the mail—letters from Harvard Law School! Before they can open the momentous letters to discover acceptance or rejection, Mark offers his roommate Gordon a mock-solemn, man-to-man vow: "You're my best friend and

I love you; but if you get into Harvard and I don't, I hope you rot in hell." They rip open the letters; both of them have been accepted! Joyous, fraternistic whooping follows, as Mark's anonymous bedmate fades into the background. The "buddy" strand of the plot has been established.

The next scene brings us to Mark's parents' lavish Southern California home, where we are invited to share Mark's shock as his self-centered, nouveau–New Age father explains why he will not pay Mark's way through Harvard: Dad has already spoiled Son by giving him everything he desired, and now it is fiftyish Dad's turn to indulge a mid-life crisis by buying a condo in Bermuda. Mark's subsequent conversation with friend Gordon invites us to commiserate with Mark; how will he ever obtain the $50,000 he needs to get through Harvard Law School? Thus, the moral urgency of Mark's dilemma has been established.

In the third major episode, Mark and Gordon desperately plow through the Harvard catalogue, trying to find scholarships that might solve Mark's problem. After dismissing several options, they find one that intrigues Mark—the Henry Bouchard Scholarship for the most qualified Black student from the Los Angeles area. In a stroke of ingenuity, Mark makes himself "qualified" by making himself Black. Dismissing his friend's ethical objections, Mark explains that the scholarship would have gone to waste because the only qualified Black "got a better deal from Stanford." But Gordon asks, is Mark really ready to *be* a Black person? Of course, Mark responds—"America loves Black People!" Thus, the ethical rationale for Mark's behavior is established, and the viewer is invited to root for his "harmless" deception.

Once these introductory scenes have established the film's narrative framework, the rest of *Soul Man* focuses on Mark's blackface experience at Harvard Law. It is worth noting that *Soul Man*'s central plot gimmick—a white protagonist in blackface—is hardly a new phenomenon; films such as *Birth of a Nation* and *Uncle Tom's Cabin* featured white actors playing Black roles, and vaudevillian blackface was a major entertainment form in the early part of the century. The effect of blackface in *Soul Man*—as in these earlier representations—is to create a disquieting narrative undercurrent, a dysfunction between surface and substance. The viewer is expected not to question this dissonance, but to accept it as a gag for the purposes of being entertained.

In this respect, *Soul Man*'s use of blackface more closely resembles these earlier regressive films than it does two more recent movies using blackface themes to advance serious points. *Watermelon Man* (1970) focuses on the tragicomic dilemma of a white character who wakes up one day and discovers that he has turned Black overnight; however, a critical distinction between this film and *Soul Man* rests upon the viewer's knowledge that the white character is in fact played by a Black actor, Godfrey Cambridge. *Black Like Me* (1965), based on the well-known autobiography of John Howard Griffin, dramatizes the prejudice and hatred confronted by a white journalist who deliberately darkens his skin to learn first-hand the treatment of Blacks in the South in the early 1960s. Unlike *Soul Man*, *Black Like Me* is a serious tale of degradation and cruelty; the protagonist cannot find lodging, work, transportation, or even a place to go to the bathroom. He suffers the indignities of racial slurs, ignorant comments, and outright threats of violence; his experience of life in the South is almost unremittingly somber and bleak.

Unlike *Watermelon Man* or *Black Like Me, Soul Man* uses blackface to portray the issue of crossing of color line as a farcical, frat-boy romp. Mark Watson's indignities seem to be limited to suffering the occasional bigoted apartment manager or tasteless racist joke from fellow students—hardly an inconvenience when compared to the "benefits" that he derives from being Black. Moreover, *Soul Man* presents these incidents as comic fodder, intended to amuse rather than to provoke or disturb. As a result, the depiction of racist incidents in this film is stripped of affective power and validity and subsumed within Mark's dominant gaze.

In scene after scene, the plot trots out hoary old stereotypes and invites the viewer to find them amusing. In a pivotal scene, we watch Mark's tense visit to the home of the white Radcliffe student's wealthy and bigoted family, and are asked to observe the event through Mark's eyes. Through his gaze, we see racist stereotypes which Mark imagines are being projected upon him by the family: that he is a vicious drug addict and pimp who will abuse their pure daughter; or a lascivious island native who wants to seduce the mother; or a Prince-style, pelvis-thrusting rocker who will corrupt the young son. I experience this scene not as a satiric comment on racist perspectives, but rather as an invitation to identify with the prejudices that have fostered the absurd stereotypes imagined by Mark. By filtering its parody of ignorance and bias through the eyes of Mark—hardly a true "victim" of prejudice—the scene lacks both the irony and the empathic power necessary to convey its ostensibly well-intended message. Unlike, say, the famous (and hilariously effective) scene in Woody Allen's *Annie Hall* (1978) in which Allen invites us to imagine through Jewish eyes the way in which his gentile girlfriend's family must be scrutinizing and objectifying him, *Soul Man*'s recycled version gives the viewer no opportunity for genuine empathy with the oppressed person's point of view. Instead, since Mark is clearly not Black and not in a subordinate role to anyone, this viewer was left with the sense that Mark's dilettantish exposure to racism in this scene was somehow being equated with Blacks' everyday experiences with racism, and that the hyperbolically bigoted whites were being equated with Blacks' everyday experiences with racists. Such a message distressingly discourages viewers from recognizing that often bigotry wears a mask not burlesque-style and latent, but subtle and insidious.

Conclusion: Social Change and the Dominant Gaze

In defending his film *Do the Right Thing* (1989) against the criticism that it might make mainstream white audiences feel uncomfortable, Spike Lee asserted, "[T]hat's the way it is all the time for Black people." Lee's point was that the dominant gaze still prevails; "uncomfortable" perspectives are marginalized, criticized, or, worst of all, simply ignored. A film such as *Soul Man,* which capitalizes on an ostensibly alternative perspective to tell a tale about contemporary race relations, is ultimately fatally flawed by the dominance of its vision. By exploiting the effect of racial stereotypes without reminding the viewers of their continuing destructive force, *Soul Man* misses the opportunity to make—either seriously or comically—a truly instructive comment about the nature of racism in our society.

bell hooks argues that we must create "counterhegemonic art" to liberate our culture from the stigma of racist, sexist, homophobic, and other degrading stereotypes. In her view, only through transformative counter-images can the dominant gaze be subverted; toward this end, popular culture has enormous potential not only for entertainment but also for political and social change as well. Given the power of mainstream films both to reflect and to shape dominant visions of race, law, and equality, I find hooks' assertion persuasive, if somewhat unrealistic. But perhaps anticipating the growth of a truly "counterhegemonic" popular culture is similar to advocating radical legal reform; both goals may be hopelessly Panglossian, but they can be buttressed by concrete, interim steps along the way. To this ardent but skeptical admirer of popular film, that means continuing to watch, to critique, and to subvert the dominant gaze.

NOTES

1. Laura Mulvey, *Visual Pleasure and Narrative Cinema,* 16 SCREEN 6–18 (1975). *See also* THE FEMALE GAZE: WOMEN AS VIEWERS OF POPULAR CULTURE (Lorraine Gamman & Margaret Marshman eds., 1989).

2. MAS'UD ZAVARZADEH, SEEING FILMS POLITICALLY 1–4 (1991).

3. *Id.* at vi.

4. DONALD BOGLE, TOMS, COONS, MULATTOES, MAMMIES, AND BUCKS: AN INTERPRETIVE HISTORY OF BLACKS IN AMERICAN FILMS 93 (1973).

5. Carol Sanger, *Seasoned to the Use,* 87 MICH. L. REV. 1334, 1363 (1989).

6. Regents of the University of California v. Bakke, 438 U.S. 265 (1978).

SECTION TWO
THEORIZING ABOUT COUNTERSTORIES

7　Legal Storytelling: Storytelling for Oppositionists and Others: A Plea for Narrative

RICHARD DELGADO

Storytelling

Everyone has been writing stories these days. And I don't just mean writing *about* stories or narrative theory, important as those are. I mean actual stories, as in "once-upon-a-time" type stories. Many, but by no means all, who have been telling legal stories are members of what could be loosely described as outgroups, groups whose marginality defines the boundaries of the mainstream, whose voice and perspective—whose consciousness—has been suppressed, devalued, and abnormalized. The attraction of stories for these groups should come as no surprise. For stories create their own bonds, represent cohesion, shared understandings, and meanings. The cohesiveness that stories bring is part of the strength of the outgroup. An outgroup creates its own stories, which circulate within the group as a kind of counter-reality.

The dominant group creates its own stories, as well. The stories or narratives told by the ingroup remind it of its identity in relation to outgroups, and provide it with a form of shared reality in which its own superior position is seen as natural.

The stories of outgroups aim to subvert that reality. In civil rights, for example, many in the majority hold that any inequality between blacks and whites is due either to cultural lag or inadequate enforcement of currently existing beneficial laws—both of which are easily correctable. For many minority persons, the principal instrument of their subordination is neither of these. Rather, it is the prevailing *mindset* by means of which members of the dominant group justify the world as it is, that is, with whites on top and browns and blacks at the bottom.

87 MICH. L. REV. 2411 (1989). Originally published in the Michigan Law Review. Reprinted by permission.

Stories, parables, chronicles, and narratives are powerful means for destroying mindset—the bundle of presuppositions, received wisdoms, and shared understandings against a background of which legal and political discourse takes place. These matters are rarely focused on. They are like eyeglasses we have worn a long time. They are nearly invisible; we use them to scan and interpret the world and only rarely examine them for themselves. Ideology—the received wisdom—makes current social arrangements seem fair and natural. Those in power sleep well at night—their conduct does not seem to them like oppression.

The cure is storytelling (or, as I shall sometimes call it, counterstorytelling). As Derrick Bell, Bruno Bettelheim, and others show, stories can shatter complacency and challenge the status quo. Stories told by underdogs are frequently ironic or satiric; a root word for "humor" is *humus*—bringing low, down to earth.[1] Along with the tradition of storytelling in black culture[2] there exists the Spanish tradition of the picaresque novel or story, which tells of humble folk piquing the pompous or powerful and bringing them down to more human levels.[3]

Most who write about storytelling focus on its community-building functions: stories build consensus, a common culture of shared understandings, and a deeper, more vital ethics. But stories and counterstories can serve an equally important destructive function. They can show that what we believe is ridiculous, self-serving, or cruel. They can show us the way out of the trap of unjustified exclusion. They can help us understand when it is time to reallocate power. They are the other half—the destructive half—of the creative dialectic.

Storytelling and Counterstorytelling

The same object, as everyone knows, can be described in many ways. A rectangular red object on my living room floor may be a nuisance if I stub my toe on it in the dark, a doorstop if I use it for that purpose, further evidence of my lackadaisical housekeeping to my visiting mother, a toy to my young daughter, or simply a brick left over from my patio restoration project. There is no single true, or all-encompassing, description. The same holds true of events. Watching an individual perform strenuous repetitive movements, we might say that he or she is exercising, discharging nervous energy, seeing to his or her health under doctor's orders, or suffering a seizure or convulsion. Often, we will not be able to ascertain the single best description or interpretation of what we have seen. We participate in creating what we see in the very act of describing it.[4]

Social and moral realities, the subject of this chapter, are just as indeterminate and subject to interpretation as single objects or events, if not more so. For example, what is the "correct" answer to the question, The American Indians are—(A) a colonized people; (B) tragic victims of technological progress; (C) subjects of a suffocating, misdirected federal beneficence; (D) a minority stubbornly resistant to assimilation; or (E)———; or (F)———?

My premise is that much of social reality is constructed. We decide what is, and, almost simultaneously, what ought to be. Narrative habits, patterns of seeing, shape what we see and that to which we aspire.[5] These patterns of perception become habitual, tempting us to believe that the way things are is inevitable, or the best that can be in an imperfect world. Alternative visions of reality are not explored, or, if they are, rejected as extreme or implausible.

How can there be such divergent stories? Why do they not combine? Is it simply that members of the dominant group see the same glass as half full, blacks as half empty? I believe there is more than this at work; there is a war between stories. They contend for, tug at, our minds. To see how the dialectic of competition and rejection works—to see the reality-creating potential of stories and the normative implications of adopting one story rather than another—consider the following series of accounts, each describing the same event.

A STANDARD EVENT AND A STOCK STORY THAT EXPLAINS IT

The following series of stories revolves around the same event: A black lawyer interviews for a teaching position at a major law school (school X), and is rejected. Any other race-tinged event could have served equally well for purposes of illustration. This particular event was chosen because it occurs on familiar ground—many readers of this book are past or present members of a university community who have heard about or participated in events like the one described.

SETTING.   A professor and student are talking in the professor's office. Both are white. The professor, Blas Vernier, is tenured, in mid-career, and well regarded by his colleagues and students. The student, Judith Rogers, is a member of the student advisory appointments committee.

Rogers: Professor Vernier, what happened with the black candidate, John Henry? I heard he was voted down at the faculty meeting yesterday. The students on my committee liked him a lot.

Vernier: It was a difficult decision, Judith. We discussed him for over two hours. I can't tell you the final vote, of course, but it wasn't particularly close. Even some of my colleagues who were initially for his appointment voted against him when the full record came out.

Rogers: But we have no minority professors at all, except for Professor Chen, who is untenured, and Professor Tompkins, who teaches Trial Practice on loan from the district attorney's office once a year.

Vernier: Don't forget Mary Foster, the Assistant Dean.

Rogers: But she doesn't teach, just handles admissions and the placement office.

Vernier: And does those things very well. But back to John Henry. I understand your disappointment. Henry was a strong candidate, one of the stronger blacks we've interviewed recently. But ultimately he didn't measure up. We didn't think he wanted to teach for the right reasons. He was vague and diffuse about his research interests. All he could say was that he wanted to write about equality and civil rights, but so far as we could tell he had nothing new to say about those areas. What's more, we had some problems with his teaching interests. He wanted to teach peripheral courses, in areas where we already have enough people. And we had the sense that he wouldn't be really rigorous in those areas, either.

Rogers: But we need courses in employment discrimination and civil rights. And he's had a long career with the NAACP Legal Defense Fund and really seemed to know his stuff.

Vernier: It's true we could stand to add a course or two of that nature, although as you know our main needs are in Commercial Law and Corporations, and Henry doesn't teach either. But I think our need is not as acute as you say. Many of the topics you're interested in are covered in the second half of the Constitutional Law course taught by Professor White, who has a national reputation for his work in civil liberties and freedom of speech.

Rogers: But Henry could have taught those topics from a black perspective. And he would have been a wonderful role model for our minority students.

Vernier: Those things are true, and we gave them considerable weight. But when it came right down to it, we felt we couldn't take that great a risk. Henry wasn't on the law review at school, as you are, Judith, and has never written a line in a legal journal. Some of us doubted he ever would. And then, what would happen five years from now when he came up for tenure? It wouldn't be fair to place him in an environment like this. He'd just have to pick up his career and start over if he didn't produce.

Rogers: With all due respect, Professor, that's paternalistic. I think Henry should have been given the chance. He might have surprised us.

Vernier: So I thought, too, until I heard my colleagues' discussion, which I'm afraid, given the demands of confidentiality, I can't share with you. Just let me say that we examined his case long and hard and I am convinced, fairly. The decision, while painful, was correct.

Rogers: So another year is going to go by without a minority candidate or professor?

Vernier: These things take time. I was on the appointments committee last year, chaired it in fact. And I can tell you we would love nothing better than to find a qualified black. Every year, we call the Supreme Court to check on current clerks, telephone our colleagues at other leading law schools, and place ads in black newspapers and journals. But the pool is so small. And the few good ones have many opportunities. We can't pay nearly as much as private practice, you know.

[Rogers, who would like to be a legal services attorney, but is attracted to the higher salaries of corporate practice, nods glumly.]

Vernier: It may be that we'll have to wait another few years, until the current crop of black and minority law students graduates and gets some experience. We have some excellent prospects, including some members of your very class.

Rogers: [Thinks: I've heard that one before, but says] Well, thanks, Professor. I know the students will be disappointed. But maybe when the committee considers visiting professors later in the season it will be able to find a professor of color who meets its standards and fits our needs.

Vernier: We'll try our best. Although you should know that some of us believe that merely shuffling the few minorities in teaching from one school to another does nothing to expand the pool. And once they get here, it's hard to say no if they express a desire to stay on.

Rogers: [*Thinks: That's a lot like tenure. How ironic; there are certain of your colleagues we would love to get rid of, too. But says*] Well, thanks, Professor. I've got to get to class. I still wish the vote had come out otherwise. Our student committee is preparing a list of minority candidates that we would like to see considered. Maybe you'll find one or more of them worthy of teaching here.

Vernier: Judith, believe me, there is nothing that would please me more.

In the above dialogue, Professor Vernier's account represents the stock story—the one the institution collectively forms and tells about itself. This story picks and chooses from among the available facts to present a picture of what happened: an account that justifies the world as it is. It emphasizes the school's benevolent motivation ("look how hard we're trying") and good faith. It stresses stability and the avoidance of risks. It measures the black candidate through the prism of preexisting, well-agreed-upon criteria of conventional scholarship and teaching. Given those standards, it purports to be scrupulously meritocratic and fair; Henry would have been hired had he measured up. No one raises the possibility that the merit criteria employed in judging Henry are themselves debatable, *chosen*—not inevitable. No one, least of all Vernier, calls attention to the way in which merit functions to conceal the contingent connection between institutional power and the things rated.

There is also little consideration of the possibility that Henry's presence on the faculty might have altered the institution's character, helped introduce a different prism and different criteria for selecting future candidates. The account is highly procedural—it emphasizes that Henry got a full, careful hearing—rather than substantive: a black was rejected. It emphasizes certain "facts" without examining their truth—namely, that the pool is very small, that good minority candidates have many choices, and that the appropriate view is the long view; haste makes waste.

The dominant fact about this first story, however, is its seeming neutrality. It scrupulously avoids issues of blame or responsibility. Race played no part in the candidate's rejection; indeed, the school leaned over backwards to accommodate him. A white candidate with similar credentials would not have made it as far as Henry did. The story comforts and soothes. And Vernier's sincerity makes him an effective apologist for his system.

Vernier's story is also deeply coercive, although the coercion is disguised. Judith was aware of it but chose not to confront it directly; Vernier holds all the cards. He pressures her to go along with the institution's story by threatening her prospects at the same time that he flatters her achievements. A victim herself, she is invited to take on and share the consciousness of her oppressor. She does not accept Vernier's story, but he does slip a few doubts through cracks in her armor. The professor's story shows how forceful and repeated storytelling can perpetuate a particular view of reality. Naturally, the stock story is not the only one that can be told. By emphasizing other events and giving them slightly different interpretations, a quite different picture can be made to emerge.

AL-HAMMAR X'S COUNTERSTORY

A few days after word of Henry's rejection reached the student body, Noel Al-Hammar X, leader of the radical Third World Coalition, delivered a speech at noon on the steps of the law school patio. The audience consisted of most of the black and brown students at the law school, several dozen white students, and a few faculty members. Chen was absent, having a class to prepare for. The Assistant Dean was present, uneasily taking mental notes in case the Dean asked her later what she heard.

Al-Hammar's speech was scathing, denunciatory, and at times downright rude. He spoke several words that the campus newspaper reporter wondered if his paper would print. He impugned the good faith of the faculty, accused them of institutional if not garden-variety racism, and pointed out in great detail the long history of the faculty as an all-white club. He said that the law school was bent on hiring only white males, "ladies" only if they were well-behaved clones of white males, and would never hire a black unless forced to do so by student pressure or the courts. He exhorted his fellow students not to rest until the law faculty took steps to address its own ethnocentricity and racism. He urged boycotting or disrupting classes, writing letters to the state legislature, withholding alumni contributions, setting up a "shadow" appointments committee, and several other measures that made the Assistant Dean wince.

Al-Hammar's talk received a great deal of attention, particularly from the faculty who were not there to hear it. Several versions of his story circulated among the faculty offices and corridors ("Did you hear what he said?"). Many of the stories-about-the-story were wildly exaggerated. Nevertheless, Al-Hammar's story is an authentic counterstory. It directly challenges—both in its words and tone—the corporate story the law school carefully worked out to explain Henry's non-appointment. It rejects many of the institution's premises, including we-try-so-hard, the-pool-is-so-small, and even mocks the school's meritocratic self-concept. "They say Henry is mediocre, has a pedestrian mind. Well, they ain't sat in none of my classes and listened to themselves. Mediocrity they got. They're experts on mediocrity." Al-Hammar denounced the faculty's excuse making, saying there were dozens of qualified black candidates, if not hundreds. "There isn't that big a pool of Chancellors, or quarterbacks," he said. "But when they need one, they find one, don't they?"

Al-Hammar also deviates stylistically, as a storyteller, from John Henry. He rebels against the "reasonable discourse" of law. He is angry, and anger is out of bounds in legal discourse, even as a response to discrimination. John Henry was unsuccessful in getting others to listen. So was Al-Hammar, but for a different reason. His counterstory overwhelmed the audience. More than just a narrative, it was a call to action, a call to join him in destroying the current story. But his audience was not ready to act. Too many of his listeners felt challenged or coerced; their defenses went up. The campus newspaper the next day published a garbled version, saying that he had urged the law faculty to relax its standards in order to provide minority students with role models. This prompted three letters to the editor asking how an unqualified black professor could be a good role model for anyone, black or white.

Moreover, the audience Al-Hammar intended to affect, namely the faculty, was even more unmoved by his counterstory. It attacked them too frontally. They were quick to dismiss him as an extremist, a demagogue, a hothead—someone to be taken seriously only for the damage he might do should he attract a body of followers. Consequently, for the next week the faculty spent much time in one-on-one conversations with "responsible" student leaders, including Judith Rogers.

By the end of the week, a consensus story had formed about Al-Hammar's story. That story-about-a-story held that Al-Hammar had gone too far, that there was more to the situation than Al-Hammar knew or was prepared to admit. Moreover, Al-Hammar was portrayed *not* as someone who had reached out, in pain, for sympathy and friendship. Rather, he was depicted as a "bad actor," someone with a "chip on his shoulder," someone no responsible member of the law school community should trade stories with. Nonetheless, a few progressive students and faculty members believed Al-Hammar had done the institution a favor by raising the issues and demanding that they be addressed. They were a distinct minority.

THE ANONYMOUS LEAFLET COUNTERSTORY

About a month after Al-Hammar spoke, the law faculty formed a special committee for minority hiring. The committee contained practically every young liberal on the faculty, two of its three female professors, and the Assistant Dean. The Dean announced the committee's formation in a memorandum sent to the law school's ethnic student associations, the student government, and the alumni newsletter, which gave it front-page coverage. It was also posted on bulletin boards around the law school.

The memo spoke about the committee and its mission in serious, measured phrases—"social need," "national search," "renewed effort," "balancing the various considerations," "identifying members of a future pool from which we might draw." Shortly after the memo was distributed, an anonymous four-page leaflet appeared in the student lounge, on the same bulletin boards on which the Dean's memo had been posted, and in various mailboxes of faculty members and law school organizations. Its author, whether student or faculty member, was never identified.[6]

The leaflet was entitled, "Another Committee, Aren't We Wonderful?" It began with a caricature of the Dean's memo, mocking its measured language and high-flown tone. Then, beginning in the middle of the page the memo told, in conversational terms, the following story:

And so, friends and neighbors [the leaflet continued], how is it that the good law schools go about looking for new faculty members? Here is how it works. The appointments committee starts out the year with a model new faculty member in mind. This mythic creature went to a leading law school, graduated first or second in his or her class, clerked for the Supreme Court, and wrote the leading note in the law review on some topic dealing with the federal courts. This individual is brilliant, personable, humane, and has just the right amount of practice experience with the right firm.

Schools begin with this paragon in mind and energetically beat the bushes, beginning in September, in search of him or her. At this stage, they believe themselves genuinely and sincerely colorblind. If they find such a mythic figure who is black or Hispanic or gay or lesbian, they will hire this person in a flash. They will of course do the same if the person is white.

By February, however, the school has not hired many mythic figures. Some that they interviewed turned them down. Now, it's late in the year and they have to get someone to teach Trusts and Estates. Although there are none left on their list who are Supreme Court clerks, etc., they can easily find several who are a notch or two below that—who went to good schools, but not Harvard, or who went to Harvard, yet were not first or second in their classes. Still, they know, to a degree verging on certainty, that this person is smart and can do the job. They know this from personal acquaintance with this individual, or they hear it from someone they know and trust. Joe says Bill is really smart, a good lawyer, and will be terrific in the classroom.

So they hire this person because, although he or she is not a mythic figure, functionally equivalent guarantees—namely, first- or second-hand experience—assure them that this person will be a good teacher and scholar. And so it generally turns out—the new professor does just fine.

Persons hired in this fashion are almost always white, male, and straight. The reason: We rarely know blacks, Hispanics, women, and gays. Moreover, when we hire the white male, the known but less-than-mythic quantity, late in February, *it does not seem to us like we are making an exception.* Yet we are. We are employing a form of affirmative action—bending the stated rules so as to hire the person we want.

The upshot is that whites have two chances of being hired—by meeting the formal criteria we start out with in September (that is, by being mythic figures) and also by meeting the second, informal, modified criteria we apply later to friends and acquaintances when we are in a pinch. Minorities have just one chance of being hired—the first.

To be sure, once every decade or so a law school, imbued with crusading zeal, will bend the rules and hire a minority with credentials just short of Superman or Superwoman. And, when it does so, *it will feel like an exception.* The school will congratulate itself—it has lifted up one of the downtrodden. And, it will remind the new professor repeatedly how lucky he or she is to be here in this wonderful place. It will also make sure, through subtle or not-so-subtle means, that the students know so, too.

But (the leaflet continued), there is a coda.

If, later, the minority professor hired this way unexpectedly succeeds, this will produce consternation among his or her colleagues. For, things were not intended to go that way. When he or she came aboard, the minority professor lacked those standard indicia of merit—Supreme Court clerkship, high LSAT score, prep school background—that the majority-race professors had and believe essential to scholarly success.

Yet the minority professor is succeeding all the same—publishing in good law reviews, receiving invitations to serve on important commissions, winning popularity with students. This is infuriating. Many majority-race professors are persons of relatively slender achievements—you can look up their publishing record any time you have five minutes. Their principal achievements lie in the distant past, when, aided by their parents' upper-class background, they did well in high school and college, and got the requisite test scores on standardized tests which test exactly the accumulated cultural capital they acquired so easily and naturally at home. Shortly after that, their careers started to stagnate. They publish an article every five years or so, often in a minor law review, after gallingly having it turned down by the very review they served on as editor twenty years ago.

So, their claim to fame lies in their early exploits, the badges they acquired up to about the age of twenty-five, at which point the edge they acquired from Mummy and Daddy began to lose effect. Now, along comes the hungry minority professor, imbued with a fierce desire to get ahead, a good intellect, and a willingness to work 70 hours a week if necessary to make up for lost time. The minority person lacks the merit badges awarded early in life, the white professor's main source of security. So, the minority's colleagues don't like it and use perfectly predictable ways to transfer the costs of their discomfort to the misbehaving minority.

So that, my friends, is why minority professors
(i)   have a hard time getting hired; and,
(ii) have a hard time if they are hired.

When you and I are running the world, we won't replicate this unfair system, will we? Of course not—unless, of course, it changes us in the process.

This second counterstory attacks the faculty less frontally in some respects— for example it does not focus on the fate of any particular black candidate, such as Henry, but attacks a general mindset. It employs several devices, including narrative and careful observation—the latter to build credibility (the reader says, "That's right"), the former to beguile the reader and get him or her to suspend judgment. (Everyone loves a story.) The last part of the story is painful; it strikes close to home. Yet the way for its acceptance has been paved by the earlier parts, which paint a plausible picture of events, so that the final part demands consideration. It generalizes and exaggerates—many majority-race professors are *not* persons of slender achievement. But such broad strokes are part of the narrator's art. The realistically drawn first part of the story, despite shading off into caricature at the end, forces readers to focus on the flaws in the good face the dean attempted to put on events. And, despite its somewhat accusatory thrust, the story, as was mentioned, debunks only a mindset, not a person. Unlike Al-Hammar X's story, it does not call the chair of the appointments committee, a much-loved senior professor, a racist. (But did Al-Hammar's story, confrontational as it was, pave the way for the generally positive reception accorded the anonymous account?)

The story invites the reader to alienate herself or himself from the events described, to enter into the mental set of the teller, whose view is different from the reader's own. The oppositional nature of the story, the manner in which it challenges and rebuffs the stock story, thus causes him or her to oscillate between poles. It is insinuative: At times, the reader is seduced by the story and its logical coherence—it is a plausible counter-view of what happened; it has a degree of explanatory power.

Yet the story places the majority-race reader on the defensive. He or she alternately leaves the storyteller's perspective to return to his or her own, saying, "That's outrageous, I'm being accused of. . . ." The reader thus moves back and forth between two worlds, the storyteller's, which the reader occupies vicariously to the extent the story is well told and rings true, and his or her own, which he or she returns to and reevaluates in light of the story's message. Can my world still stand? What parts of it remain valid? What parts of the story seem true? How can I reconcile the two worlds, and will the resulting world be a better one than the one with which I began?

NOTES

1. J. SHIPLEY, THE ORIGINS OF ENGLISH WORDS 441 (1984) (*humor* derives from *ugu,* a word for wetness; related to *humus*—earth or earthly sources of wetness); *see also* THE OXFORD DICTIONARY OF ENGLISH ETYMOLOGY 452 (C. Onions ed., 1966).

2. *See* THE BOOK OF NEGRO FOLKLORE (L. Hughes & A. Bontemps eds., 1958); THE NEGRO AND HIS FOLKLORE IN NINETEENTH CENTURY PERIODICALS (B. Jackson ed., 1967); Greene, *A Short Commentary on the Chronicles,* 3 HARV. BLACKLETTER J. 60, 62 (1986); *see also* L. PARRISH, SLAVE SONGS OF THE GEORGIA SEA ISLANDS (1942).

3. *See, e.g.,* M. CERVANTES, DON QUIXOTE OF LA MANCHA (W. Starkie trans./ed., 1954) (1605). For ironic perspectives on modern Chicano culture, see R. RODRIGUEZ, HUNGER OF MEMORY (1980); Gerald Lopez, *The Idea of a Constitution in the Chicano Tradition,* 37 J. LEGAL EDUC. 162 (1987); Richard Rodriguez, *The Fear of Losing a Culture,* TIME, July 11, 1988, at 84. *Cf.* Richard Delgado, *The Imperial Scholar,* 132 U. Pa. L. Rev. 561 (1984) (ironic examination of the dearth of minority scholarship in the civil rights field).

4. *See, e.g.,* R. AKUTAGAWA, *In a Grove, in* RASHOMON AND OTHER STORIES 19 (T. Kojima trans., 1970); R. LEONCAVALLO, I PAGLIACCI (1892) (in the Prologue, hunchbacked clown Tonio explains that stories are real, perhaps the most real thing of all, turning commedia dell'arte—"it's only a play, we're just acting"—on its head).

5. *See* J. B. WHITE, HERACLES' BOW 175 (1985); John Cole, *Thoughts from the Land of And,* 39 MERCER L. REV. 907, 921–25 (1988) (discussing theories that language determines the physical world, rather than the opposite); J. White,

Thinking About Our Language, 96 YALE L.J. 1960, 1971 (1987) (describing the dangers of reification). *See generally* N. GOODMAN, WAYS OF WORLDMAKING (1978); E. CASSIRER, LANGUAGE AND MYTH (1946).

I say "shape," not "create" or "determine," because I believe there is a degree of intersubjectivity in the stories we tell. *See infra,* recounting an event in the form of different stories. Every well-told story is virtually an archetype—it rings true in light of the hearer's stock of preexisting stories. But stories may expand that empathic range if artfully crafted and told; that is their main virtue.

6. Like all the stories, the leaflet is purely fictional; perhaps it was born as an "internal memo," stimulated by Al-Hammar's speech, in the minds of many progressive listeners at the same time.

8   Property Rights in Whiteness— Their Legal Legacy, Their Economic Costs

DERRICK BELL

A F E W years ago, I was presenting a lecture in which I enumerated the myriad ways in which black people have been used to enrich this society and made to serve as its proverbial scapegoat. I was particularly bitter about the country's practice of accepting black contributions and ignoring the contributors. Indeed, I suggested, had black people not existed, America would have invented them.

From the audience, a listener reflecting more insight on my subject than I had shown shouted out, "Hell man, they did invent us." The audience immediately understood and responded to the comment with a round of applause in which I joined. Whether we are called "colored," "Negroes," "Afro-Americans," or "blacks," we are marked with the caste of color in a society still determinedly white. As a consequence, we are shaped, molded, changed, from what we might have been . . . into what we are. Much of what we are—considering the motivations for our "invention—" is miraculous. And much of that invention—as you might expect—is far from praiseworthy . . . scarred as it is by all the marks of oppression.

Not the least of my listener's accomplishments was the seeming answer to the question that is implicit in the title of this essay. And indeed, racial discrimination has wrought and continues to place a heavy burden on all black people in this country. A major function of racial discrimination is to facilitate the exploitation of black labor, to deny us access to benefits and opportunities that would otherwise be available, and to blame all the manifestations of exclusion-bred despair on the asserted inferiority of the victims.

But the costs and benefits of racial discrimination are not so neatly summarized. There are two other inter-connected political phenomena that emanate from the widely shared belief that whites are superior to blacks that have served critically important stabilizing functions in the society. First, whites of widely varying socio-economic status employ white supremacy as a catalyst to negotiate policy differences, often through compromises that sacrifice the rights of blacks.

Second, even those whites who lack wealth and power are sustained in their

33 Vill. L. Rev. 767 (1988). Originally published in the Villanova Law Review. Reprinted by permission.

sense of racial superiority, and thus rendered more willing to accept their lesser share, by an unspoken but no less certain property right in their "whiteness." This right is recognized and upheld by courts and the society like all property rights under a government created and sustained primarily for that purpose.

Let us look first at the compromise-catalyst role of racism in American policy-making. When the Constitution's Framers gathered in Philadelphia, it is clear that their compromises on slavery were the key that enabled Southerners and Northerners to work out their economic and political differences.

The slavery compromises set a precedent under which black rights have been sacrificed throughout the nation's history to further white interests. Those compromises are far more than an embarrassing blot on our national history. Rather, they are the original and still definitive examples of the on-going struggle between individual rights reform and the maintenance of the socio-economic status quo.

Why did the Framers do it? Surely, there is little substance in the traditional rationalizations that the slavery provisions in the Constitution were merely unfortunate concessions pressured by the crisis of events and influenced by then prevailing beliefs that: (1) slavery was on the decline and would soon die of its own weight; or that (2) Africans were thought a different and inferior breed of beings and their enslavement carried no moral onus.

The insistence of southern delegates on protection of their slave property was far too vigorous to suggest that the institution would soon be abandoned.[1] And the anti-slavery statements by slaves and white abolitionists alike were too forceful to suggest that the slavery compromises were the product of men who did not know the moral ramifications of what they did.[2]

The question of what motivated the Framers remains. My recent book, *And We Are Not Saved*,[3] contains several allegorical stories intended to explore various aspects of American racism using the tools of fiction. In one, Geneva Crenshaw, a black civil rights lawyer gifted with extraordinary powers, is transported back to the Constitutional Convention of 1787.

There is, I know, no mention of this visit in Max Farrand's records of the Convention proceedings. James Madison's compulsive notes are silent on the event. But the omission of the debate that followed her sudden appearance in the locked meeting room, and the protection she is provided when the delegates try to eject her, is easier to explain than the still embarrassing fact that these men—some of the outstanding figures of their time—could incorporate slavery into a document committed to life, liberty, and the pursuit of happiness for all.

Would they have acted differently had they known the great grief their compromises on slavery would cause? Geneva's mission is to use her knowledge of the next two centuries to convince the Framers that they should not incorporate recognition and protection of slavery in the document they are writing. To put it mildly, her sudden arrival at the podium was sufficiently startling to intimidate even these men. But outrage quickly overcame their shock. Ignoring Geneva's warm greeting and her announcement that she had come from 200 years in the future, some of the more vigorous delegates, outraged at the sudden appearance in their midst of a woman, and a black woman at that, charged towards her. As Geneva described the scene:

> Suddenly, the hall was filled with the sound of martial music, blasting trumpets, and a deafening roll of snare drums. At the same time—and as the delegates were almost upon me—a cylinder composed of thin vertical bars of red, white, and blue light descended swiftly and silently from the high ceiling, nicely encapsulating the podium and me.
>
> To their credit, the self-appointed eviction party neither slowed nor swerved. As each man reached and tried to pass through the transparent light shield, there was a loud hiss, quite like the sound electrified bug zappers make on a warm, summer evening. While not lethal, the shock the shield dealt each attacker was sufficiently strong to literally knock him to the floor, stunned and shaking.

This phenomenon evokes chaos rather than attention in the room, but finally during a lull in the bedlam Geneva tries for the third time to be heard. "Gentlemen," she begins again, "Delegates,"—then paused and, with a slight smile, added, "fellow citizens. I have come to urge that, in your great work here, you not restrict to white men of property the sweep of Thomas Jefferson's self-evident truths. For all men (and women too) are equal and endowed by the Creator with inalienable rights, including 'Life, Liberty and the pursuit of Happiness.' "

The debate that ensues between Geneva and the Framers is vigorous, but, despite the extraordinary powers at her disposal, Geneva is unable to alter the already reached compromises on slavery. She tries to embarrass the Framers by pointing out the contradiction in their commitment to freedom and liberty and their embrace of slavery. They will not buy it:

> "There is no contradiction," replied a delegate. "Gouverneur Morris of Pennsylvania . . . has admitted that 'Life and liberty were generally said to be of more value, than property . . . [but] an accurate view of the matter would nevertheless prove that property is the main object of Society.' "[4]
>
> "A contradiction," another added, "would occur were we to follow the course you urge. We are not unaware of the moral issues raised by slavery, but we have no response to the [Southern delegate] who has admonished us that 'property in slaves should not be exposed to danger under a Government instituted for the protection of property.' "[5]
>
> "Government, was instituted principally for the protection of property and was itself . . . supported by property. Property is the great object of government; the great cause of war; the great means of carrying it on."[6] The security the Southerners seek is that their Negroes may not be taken from them. After all, Negroes are their wealth, their only resource.

Where, Geneva wondered, were those delegates from northern states, many of whom abhorred slavery and had already spoken out against it in the Convention? She found her answer in the castigation she received from one of the Framers, who told her:

Woman, we would have you gone from this place. But if a record be made, that record should show that the economic benefits of slavery do not accrue only to the South. Plantation states provide a market for Northern factories, and the New England shipping industry and merchants participate in the slave trade. Northern states, moreover, utilize slaves in the fields, as domestics, and even as soldiers to defend against Indian raids.

Slavery has provided the wealth that made independence possible, another delegate told her. The profits from slavery funded the Revolution. It cannot be denied. At the time of the Revolution, the goods for which the United States demanded freedom were produced in very large measure by slave labor. Desperately needing assistance from other countries, we purchased this aid from France with tobacco produced mainly by slave labor. The nation's economic well-being depended on the institution, and its preservation is essential if the Constitution we are drafting is to be more than a useless document. At least, that is how we view the crisis we face.

At the most dramatic moment of the debate, a somber delegate got to his feet, and walked fearlessly right up to the shimmering light shield. Then he spoke seriously and with obvious anxiety:

This contradiction is not lost on us. Surely we know, even though we are at pains not to mention it, that we have sacrificed the freedom of your people in the belief that this involuntary forfeiture is necessary to secure the property interests of whites in a society espousing, as its basic principle, the liberty of all. Perhaps we, with the responsibility of forming a radically new government in perilous times, see more clearly than is possible for you in hindsight that the unavoidable cost of our labors will be the need to accept and live with what you call a contradiction.

Realizing that she was losing the debate, Geneva intensified her efforts. But the imprisoned delegates' signals for help had been seen and the local militia summoned. Hearing some commotion beyond the window, she turned to see a small cannon being rolled up, and aimed at her. Then, in quick succession, a militiaman lighted the fuse; the delegates dived under their desks; the cannon fired; and, with an ear-splitting roar, the cannonball broke against the light shield and splintered, leaving the shield intact, but terminating both the visit and all memory of it.

The Framers felt—and likely they were right—that a government committed to the protection of property could not have come into being without the race-based, slavery compromises placed in the Constitution. It is surely so that the economic benefits of slavery and the political compromises of black rights played a very major role in the nation's growth and development. In short, without slavery, there would be no Constitution to celebrate. This is true not only because slavery provided the wealth that made independence possible but also because it afforded an ideological basis to resolve conflict between propertied and unpropertied whites.

According to historians, including Edmund Morgan[7] and David Brion Davis,[8] working-class whites did not oppose slavery when it took root in the mid-1660s.

They identified on the basis of race with wealthy planters even though they were and would remain economically subordinate to those able to afford slaves. But the creation of a black subclass enabled poor whites to identify with and support the policies of the upper class. And large landowners, with the safe economic advantage provided by their slaves, were willing to grant poor whites a larger role in the political process.[9] Thus, paradoxically, slavery for blacks led to greater freedom for poor whites, at least when compared with the denial of freedom to African slaves. Slavery also provided mainly propertyless whites with a property in their whiteness.

My point is that the slavery compromises continued, rather than set a precedent under which black rights have been sacrificed throughout the nation's history to further white interests. Consider only a few examples:

The long fight for universal male suffrage was successful in several states when opponents and advocates alike reached compromises based on their generally held view that blacks should not vote. Historian Leon Litwack reports that "utilizing various political, social, economic, and pseudo-anthropological arguments, white suffragists moved to deny the vote to the Negro. From the admission of Maine in 1819 until the end of the Civil War, every new state restricted the suffrage to whites in its constitution."[10]

By 1857, the nation's economic development had stretched the initial slavery compromises to the breaking point. The differences between planters and business interests that had been papered over 70 years earlier by greater mutual dangers could not be settled by a further sacrifice of black rights in the *Dred Scott* case.[11]

Chief Justice Taney's conclusion in *Dred Scott* that blacks had no rights whites were bound to respect represented a renewed effort to compromise political differences between whites by sacrificing the rights of blacks. The effort failed, less because Taney was willing to place all blacks—free as well as slave—outside the ambit of constitutional protection, than because he rashly committed the Supreme Court to one side of the fiercely contested issues of economic and political power that were propelling the nation toward the Civil War.

When the Civil War ended, the North pushed through constitutional amendments, nominally to grant citizenship rights to former slaves, but actually to protect its victory. But within a decade, when another political crisis threatened a new civil war, black rights were again sacrificed in the Hayes-Tilden Compromise of 1877. Constitutional jurisprudence fell in line with Taney's conclusion regarding the rights of blacks vis-à-vis whites even as his opinion was condemned. The country moved ahead, but blacks were cast into a status that only looked positive when compared with slavery itself.

The reader, I am sure, could add several more examples, but I hope these suffice to illustrate the degree to which whites have used white supremacy to bridge broad gaps in wealth and status to negotiate policy compromises that sacrifice blacks and the rights of blacks.

In the post-Reconstruction era, the constitutional amendments initially promoted to provide rights for the newly emancipated blacks were transformed into the major legal bulwarks for corporate growth. The legal philosophy of that era espoused liberty of action untrammelled by state authority, but the only logic of the ideology—and its goal—was the exploitation of the working class, whites as well as blacks.

As to whites, consider *Lochner v. New York*,[12] where the Court refused to find that the state's police powers extended to protecting bakery employees against employers who required them to work in physically unhealthy conditions for more than 10 hours per day and 60 hours per week. Such maximum hour legislation, the Court held, would interfere with the bakers' inherent freedom to make their own contracts with the employers on the best terms they could negotiate. In effect, the Court simply assumed in that pre-union era that employees and employers bargained from positions of equal strength. Liberty of that sort simply legitimated the sweat shops in which men, women, and children were quite literally worked to death.

For blacks, of course, we can compare *Lochner* with the decision in *Plessy v. Ferguson*,[13] decided only eight years earlier. In *Plessy*, the Court upheld the state's police power to segregate blacks in public facilities even though such segregation must, of necessity, interfere with the liberties of facilities' owners to use their property as they saw fit.

Both opinions are quite similar in the Court's use of fourteenth amendment fictions: the assumed economic "liberty" of bakers in *Lochner*, and the assumed political "equality" of blacks in *Plessy*. Those assumptions, of course, required the most blatant form of hypocrisy. Both decisions protected existing property and political arrangements, while ignoring the disadvantages to the powerless caught in those relationships: the exploited whites (in *Lochner*) and the segregated blacks (in *Plessy*).

The effort to form workers' unions to combat the ever-more powerful corporate structure was undermined because of the active antipathy against blacks practiced by all but a few unions. Excluded from jobs and the unions because of their color, blacks were hired as scab labor during strikes, increasing the hostility of white workers that should have been directed toward their corporate oppressors.

The Populist Movement in the latter part of the nineteenth century attempted to build a working-class party in the South strong enough to overcome the economic exploitation by the ruling classes. But when neither Populists nor the conservative Democrats were able to control the black vote, they agreed to exclude blacks entirely through state constitutional amendments, thereby leaving whites to fight out elections themselves. With blacks no longer a force at the ballot box, conservatives dropped even the semblance of opposition to Jim Crow provisions pushed by lower-class whites as their guarantee that the nation recognized their priority citizenship claim, based on their whiteness.

Southern whites rebelled against the Supreme Court's 1954 decision declaring school segregation unconstitutional precisely because they felt the long-standing priority of their superior status to blacks had been unjustly repealed. This year, we celebrate the thirty-fourth anniversary of the Court's rejection of the "separate but equal" doctrine of *Plessy v. Ferguson*,[14] but in the late twentieth century, the passwords for gaining judicial recognition of the still viable property right in being white include "higher entrance scores," "seniority," and "neighborhood schools." There is as well the use of impossible to hurdle intent barriers to deny blacks remedies for racial injustices, where the relief sought would either undermine white expectations and advantages gained during years of overt discrimination, or where such relief would expose the deeply imbedded racism in a major institution, such as the criminal justice system.[15]

The continuing resistance to affirmative action plans, set-asides, and other meaningful relief for discrimination-caused harm is based in substantial part on the perception that black gains threaten the main component of status for many whites: the sense that, as whites, they are entitled to priority and preference over blacks. The law has mostly encouraged and upheld what Mr. Plessy argued in *Plessy v. Ferguson* was a property right in whiteness, and those at the top of the society have been benefitted because the masses of whites are too occupied in keeping blacks down to note the large gap between their shaky status and that of whites on top.

Blacks continue to serve the role of buffers between those most advantaged in the society and those whites seemingly content to live the lives of the rich and famous through the pages of the tabloids and television dramas like *Dallas, Falcon Crest,* and *Dynasty.* Caught in the vortex of this national conspiracy that is perhaps more effective because it apparently functions without master plans or even conscious thought, the wonder is not that so many blacks manifest self-destructive or non-functional behavior patterns, but that there are so many who continue to strive and sometimes succeed.

The cost to black people of racial discrimination is high, but beyond the bitterness that blacks understandably feel there is the reality that most whites too, are, as Jesse Jackson puts it, victims of economic injustice. Indeed, allocating the costs is not a worth-while use of energy when the need now is so clearly a cure.

There are today—even in the midst of outbreaks of anti-black hostility on our campuses and elsewhere—some indications that an increasing number of working-class whites are learning what blacks have long known: that the rhetoric of freedom so freely voiced in this country is no substitute for the economic justice that has been so long denied.

True, it may be that the structure of capitalism, supported as was the Framers' intention by the Constitution, will never give sufficiently to provide real economic justice for all. But in the beginning, that Constitution deemed those who were black as the fit subject of property. The miracle of that document—too little noted during its bicentennial—is that those same blacks and their allies have in their quest for racial justice brought to the Constitution much of its current protection of individual rights.

The challenge is to move the document's protection into the sacrosanct area of economic rights this time to insure that opportunity in this sphere is available to all. Progress in this critical area will require continued civil rights efforts, but may depend to a large extent on whites coming to recognize that their property right in being white has been purchased for too much and has netted them only the opportunity, as one noted historian put it, to harbor sufficient racism to feel superior to blacks while nevertheless working at a black's wages.[16]

The cost of racial discrimination is levied against us all. Blacks feel the burden and strive to remove it. Too many whites have felt that it was in their interest to resist those freedom efforts. But the efforts to achieve racial justice have already performed a miracle of transforming the Constitution—a document primarily intended to protect property rights—into a vehicle that provides a measure of protection for those whose rights are not bolstered by wealth, power, and property.

NOTES

1. Even on the unpopular subject of importing slaves, Southern delegates were adamant. John Rutledge from South Carolina warned: "If the Convention thinks that N.C.; S.C. & Georgia will ever agree to the plan, unless their fight to import slaves be untouched, the expectation is vain. The people of those States will never be such fools as to give up so important an interest." II THE RECORDS OF THE FEDERAL CONVENTION OF 1787, at 373 (M. Farrand ed., 1911).

2. The debate over the morality of slavery had raged for years with influential Americans denouncing slavery as a corrupt and morally unjustifiable practice. *See, e.g.,* W. WIECEK, THE SOURCES OF ANTISLAVERY CONSTITUTIONALISM IN AMERICA: 1760–1848, at 42–43 (1977). And slaves themselves petitioned governmental officials and legislatures to abolish slavery. *See* I A DOCUMENTARY HISTORY OF THE NEGRO PEOPLE IN THE UNITED STATES 5–12 (H. Aptheker ed., 1968).

3. D. BELL, AND WE ARE NOT SAVED: THE ELUSIVE QUEST FOR RACIAL JUSTICE (1987).

4. *See generally* I THE RECORDS OF THE FEDERAL CONVENTION OF 1787, at 533 (M.Farrand ed., 1911).

5. *Id.* at 593–94.

6. *Id.* at 542.

7. E. MORGAN, AMERICAN SLAVERY, AMERICAN FREEDOM: THE ORDEAL OF COLONIAL VIRGINIA (1975).

8. D. DAVIS, THE PROBLEM OF SLAVERY IN THE AGE OF REVOLUTION: 1770–1820 (1975).

9. E. MORGAN, *supra* note 7, at 380–81.

10. L. LITWACK, NORTH OF SLAVERY: THE NEGRO IN THE FREE STATES 1790–1860, at 79 (1967).

11. Dred Scott v. Sandford, 60 U.S. (19 How.) 393 (1857).

12. 198 U.S. 45 (1905) (overruled by Ferguson v. Skrupa, 372 U.S 726, 730 (1963) ("[D]octrine that . . . due process authorizes courts to hold laws unconstitutional when they believe the legislature has acted unwisely [is] . . . discarded.")).

13. 163 U.S. 537 (1896).

14. Brown v. Board of Educ., 347 U.S. 483 (1954).

15. McCleskey v. Kemp, 107 S. Ct. 1756 (1987).

16. C. VANN WOODWARD, THE STRANGE CAREER OF JIM CROW (3d ed. 1974) (on the function of racism in society).

9 Alchemical Notes: Reconstructing Ideals from Deconstructed Rights

PATRICIA J. WILLIAMS

O N C E upon a time, there was a society of priests who built a Celestial City whose gates were secured by Word-Combination locks. The priests were masters of the Word, and, within the City, ascending levels of power and treasure became accessible to those who could learn ascendingly intricate levels of Word Magic. At the very top level, the priests became gods; and because they then had nothing left to seek, they engaged in games with which to pass the long hours of eternity. In particular, they liked to ride their strong, sure-footed steeds, around and around the perimeter of heaven: now jumping word-hurdles, now playing polo with the concepts of the moon and of the stars, now reaching up to touch that pinnacle, that fragment, that splinter of Refined Understanding which was called Superstanding, the brass ring of their merry-go-round.

In time, some of the priests-turned-gods tired of this sport, denounced it as meaningless. They donned the garb of pilgrims, seekers once more, and passed beyond the gates of the Celestial City. In this recursive passage, they acquired the knowledge of Undoing Words.

Beyond the walls of the City lay a Deep Blue Sea. The priests built themselves small boats and set sail, determined to explore the uncharted courses, the open vistas of this new and undefined domain. They wandered for many years in this manner, until at last they reached a place that was half-a-circumference away from the Celestial City. From this point, the City appeared as a mere shimmering illusion; and the priests knew that at last they had reached a place which was Beyond the Power of Words. They let down their anchors, the plumb lines of their reality, and experienced godhood once more.

THE STORY

Under the Celestial City, dying mortals called out their rage and suffering, battered by a steady rain of sharp hooves whose thundering, sound-drowning path described the wheel of their misfortune.

At the bottom of the Deep Blue Sea, drowning mortals reached silently and desperately for drifting anchors dangling from short chains far, far overhead, which they thought were life-lines meant for them.

I W R O T E the above parable in response to a friend who asked me what Critical Legal Studies was *really* all about; the Meta-Story was my impressionistic attempt to explain. Then my friend asked me if there weren't lots of blacks and minorities, organizers and grass-roots types in an organization so diametrically removed from tradition. Her question immediately called to mind my first days on my first job out of law school: armed with fresh degrees and shiny new theories, I walked through the halls of the Los Angeles Criminal and Civil Courthouses, from assigned courtroom to assigned courtroom. The walls of every hall were lined with waiting defendants and families of defendants,[1] almost all poor, Hispanic and/or black. As I passed, they stretched out their arms and asked me for my card; they asked me if I were a lawyer, they called me 'sister' and 'counselor.' The power of that memory is fused with my concern about the disproportionately low grass-roots membership in or input to CLS. CLS wields significant power in shaping legal strategies which affect—literally from on high—the poor and oppressed. The irony of that reproduced power imbalance prompted me to complete 'The Brass Ring and the Deep Blue Sea' with the Story.

In my experience, most non-corporate clients looked to lawyers almost as gods. They were frightened, pleading, dependent (and resentful of their dependence), trusting only for the specific purpose of getting help (because they had no choice), and distrustful in a global sense (again, because they most often had no choice). Subservience is one way I have heard the phenomenon described (particularly by harried, well-meaning practitioners who would like to see their clients be more assertive, more responsible, and more forthcoming), but actually I think its something much worse, and more complexly worse.

I think what I saw in the eyes of those who reached out to me in the hallways of the courthouse was a profoundly accurate sense of helplessness—a knowledge that without a sympathetically effective lawyer (whether judge, prosecutor, or defense attorney) they would be lining those halls and those of the lockup for a long time to come. I probably got more than my fair share of outstretched arms because I was one of the few people of color in the system at that time; but just about every lawyer who has frequented the courthouse enough has had the experience of being cast as a saviour. I have always tried to take that casting as a real request—not as a literal message that I am a god, but as a rational demand that I work the very best of whatever theory-magic I learned in law school on their behalves. CLS has a good deal of powerful theory-magic of its own to offer; but I think it has failed to make its words and un-words tangible, *reach*-able and applicable to those in this society who need its powerful assistance most.

In my Story, the client-mortals reached for help because they needed help; in CLS, I have sometimes been left with the sense that lawyers and clients engaged in the pursuit of 'rights' are viewed as foolish, 'falsely conscious,' benighted, or misled. Such an attitude indeed gives the courthouse scenario a cast not just of subservience but of futility. More important, it may keep CLS from reaching back; or, more ironically still, keep CLS reaching in the wrong direction, locked in refutation of formalist legal scholarship.

This chapter is an attempt to detail my discomfort with that part of CLS which rejects rights-based theory, particularly that part of the debate and critique which applies to the black struggle for civil rights.

I by no means want to idealize the importance of rights in a legal system in which rights are so often selectively invoked to draw boundaries, to isolate, and to limit. At the same time, it is very hard to watch the idealistic or symbolic importance of rights being diminished with reference to the disenfranchised, who experience and express their disempowerment as nothing more or less than the denial of rights. It is my belief that blacks and whites do differ in the degree to which rights-assertion is experienced as empowering or disempowering. The expression of these differing experiences creates a discourse boundary, reflecting complex and often contradictory societal understandings. It is my hope that in redescribing the historical alchemy of rights in black lives, the reader will experience some reconnection with that part of the self and of society whose story unfolds beyond the neatly staked bounds of theoretical legal understanding.

A Tale with Two Stories

Mini-Story (In Which Peter Gabel and I Set Out to Teach Contracts in the Same Boat While Rowing in Phenomenological Opposition)

Some time ago, Peter Gabel[2] and I taught a contracts class together. Both recent transplants from California to New York, each of us hunted for apartments in between preparing for class and ultimately found places within one week of each other. Inevitably, I suppose, we got into a discussion of trust and distrust as factors in bargain relations. It turned out that Peter had handed over a $900 deposit, in cash, with no lease, no exchange of keys, and no receipt, to strangers with whom he had no ties other than a few moments of pleasant conversation. Peter said that he didn't need to sign a lease because it imposed too much formality. The handshake and the good vibes were for him indicators of trust more binding than a distancing form contract. At the time, I told Peter I thought he was stark raving mad, but his faith paid off. His sublessors showed up at the appointed time, keys in hand, to welcome him in. Needless to say, there was absolutely nothing in my experience to prepare me for such a happy ending.

I, meanwhile, had friends who found me an apartment in a building they owned. In *my* rush to show good faith and trustworthiness, I signed a detailed, lengthily negotiated, finely printed lease firmly establishing me as the ideal arm's length transactor.

As Peter and I discussed our experiences, I was struck by the similarity of what each of us was seeking, yet in such different terms, and with such polar approaches. We both wanted to establish enduring relationships with the people in whose houses we would be living; we both wanted to enhance trust of ourselves and to allow whatever closeness, whatever friendship, was possible. This similarity of desire, however, could not reconcile our very different relations to the word of law. Peter, for example, appeared to be extremely self-conscious of his power potential (either real or imagistic) as a white or male or lawyer authority figure. He therefore seemed to go to some lengths to overcome the wall which that image might impose. The logical ways of establishing some measure of trust between strangers were for him an avoidance of conventional expressions of power and a preference for informal processes generally.[3]

I, on the other hand, was raised to be acutely conscious of the likelihood that, no matter what degree of professional or professor I became, people would greet and dismiss my black femaleness as unreliable, untrustworthy, hostile, angry, powerless, irrational, and probably destitute. Futility and despair are very real parts of my response. Therefore it is helpful for me, even essential for me, to clarify boundary; to show that I can speak the language of lease is my way of enhancing trust of me in my business affairs. As a black, I have been given by this society a strong sense of myself as already too familiar, too personal, too subordinate to white people. I have only recently evolved from being treated as three-fifths of a human,[4] a subpart of the white estate. I grew up in a neighborhood where landlords would not sign leases with their poor, black tenants, and *demanded* that rent be paid in cash; although superficially resembling Peter's transaction, such 'informality' in most white-on-black situations signals distrust, not trust. Unlike Peter, I am still engaged in a struggle to set up transactions at arms' length, as legitimately commercial, and to portray myself as a bargainer of separate worth, distinct power, sufficient *rights* to manipulate commerce, rather than to be manipulated as the object of commerce.

Peter, I speculate, would say that a lease or any other formal mechanism would introduce distrust into his relationships and that he would suffer alienation, leading to the commodification of his being and the degradation of his person to property. In contrast, the lack of a formal relation to the other would leave me estranged. It would risk a figurative isolation from that creative commerce by which I may be recognized as whole, with which I may feed and clothe and shelter myself, by which I may be seen as equal—even if I am stranger. For me, stranger-stranger relations are better than stranger-chattel.

The unifying theme of Peter's and my experiences (assuming that my hypothesizing about Peter's end of things has any validity at all) is that one's sense of empowerment defines one's relation to the law, in terms of trust-distrust, formality-informality, or rights–no rights (or 'needs'). In saying this I am acknowl-edging and affirming points central to CLS literature: that rights may be unsta-ble[5] and indeterminate.[6] Despite this recognition, however, and despite a mutual struggle to reconcile freedom with alienation, and solidarity with oppression, Pe-ter and I found the expression of our social disillusionment lodged on opposite sides of the rights/needs dichotomy.

On a semantic level, Peter's language of circumstantially defined need—of in-formality, of solidarity, of overcoming distance—sounded dangerously like the language of oppression to someone like me who was looking for freedom through the establishment of identity, the *form*-ation of an autonomous social self. To Pe-ter, I am sure, my insistence on the protective distance which rights provide seemed abstract and alienated.

Similarly, while the goals of CLS and of the direct victims of racism may be very much the same, what is too often missing from CLS works is the acknowl-edgment that our experiences of the same circumstances may be very, very dif-ferent; the same symbol may mean different things to each of us. At this level, for example, the insistence of Mark Tushnet, Alan Freeman, and others[7] that the 'needs' of the oppressed should be emphasized rather than their 'rights' amounts to no more than a word game. It merely says that the choice has been made to put 'needs' in the mouth of a rights discourse— thus transforming 'need' into a new form of right. 'Need' then joins 'right' in the pantheon of reified representations of what it is that you, I, and we want from ourselves and from society.

While rights may not be ends in themselves, it remains that rights rhetoric has been and continues to be an effective form of discourse for blacks. The vo-cabulary of rights speaks to an establishment that values the guise of stability, and from whom social change for the better must come (whether it is given, taken, or smuggled). Change argued for in the sheep's clothing of stability (i.e., 'rights') can be effective, even as it destabilizes certain other establishment val-ues (i.e., segregation). The subtlety of rights' real instability thus does not render unusable their persona of stability.

What is needed, therefore, is not the abandonment of rights language for all purposes, but an attempt to become multilingual in the semantics of each other's rights-valuation. One summer when I was about six, my family drove to Maine. The highway was very straight and hot and shimmered darkly in the sun. My sister and I sat in the back seat of the Studebaker and argued about what color the road was. I said black. My sister said purple. After I had successfully harangued her into admitting that it was indeed black, my father gently pointed out that my sister still saw it as purple. I was unimpressed with the relevance of that at the time, but with the passage of years, and much more observation, I have come to see endless overheated highways as slightly more purpley than black. My sister and I will probably argue about the hue of life's roads forever. But, the lesson I learned from listening to her wild perceptions is that it really is possible to see things—even the most concrete things—simultaneously yet differently; and that seeing simultaneously yet differently is more easily done by two people than one; but that one person can get the hang of it with lots of time and effort.

In addition to our differing word usage, Peter and I had qualitatively different *experiences* of rights. For example, for me to understand fully the color my sister saw when she looked at a road involved more than my simply knowing that her 'purple' meant my 'black.' It required as well a certain 'slippage of perception' that came from my finally experiencing how much her purple *felt* like my black.

In Peter's and my case, such a complete transliteration of each other's experiences is considerably harder to achieve. If it took years for me to understand fully my own sister, probably the best that Peter and I can do—as friends and colleagues, but very different people—is to listen intently to each other so that maybe our respective children can bridge the experiential distance. Bridging such gaps requires listening at a very deep level to the uncensored voices of others. To me, therefore, one of the most troubling positions advanced by some in CLS is that of rights' actual disutility in political advancement. That position seems to discount entirely the voice and the experiences of blacks in this country, for whom politically effective action has occurred mainly in connection with asserting or extending rights.

For blacks, therefore, the battle is not deconstructing rights, in a world of no rights; nor of constructing statements of need, in a world of abundantly apparent need. Rather, the goal is to find a political mechanism that can confront the *denial* of need. The argument that rights are disutile, even harmful, trivializes this aspect of black experience specifically, as well as that of any person or group whose genuine vulnerability has been protected by that measure of actual entitlement which rights provide.

For many white CLSers, the word 'rights' seems to be overlaid with capitalist connotations of oppression, universalized alienation of the self, and excessive power of an external and distancing sort. The image of the angry bigot locked behind the gun-turreted, barbed wire walls of his white-only enclave, shouting 'I have my rights!!' is indeed the rhetorical equivalent of apartheid. In the face of such a vision, 'token bourgeoisification'[8] of blacks is probably the best—and the worst—that can ever be imagined. From such a vantage point, the structure of rights is akin to that of racism in its power to constrict thought, to channel broad human experience into narrowly referenced and reified stereotypes. Breaking through such stereotypes would naturally entail some 'unnaming' process.

For most blacks, on the other hand, running the risk—as well as having the power—of 'stereo-typing' (a misuse of the naming process; a reduction of considered dimension rather than an expansion) is a lesser historical evil than having been unnamed altogether. The black experience of anonymity, the estrangement of being without a name, has been one of living in the oblivion of society's inverse, beyond the dimension of any consideration at all. Thus, the experience of rights-assertion has been one of both solidarity and freedom, of empowerment of an internal and very personal sort; it has been a process of finding the self.

The individual and unifying cultural memory of black people is the helplessness, the uncontrollability of living under slavery. I grew up living in the past: the future, some versions of which had only the sheerest possibility of happening, was treated with the respect of the already-happened, seen through the expansively prismatic lenses of what had already happened. Thus, when I decided to go to law school, my mother told me that 'the Millers were lawyers so you have it in your blood.' Now the Millers were the slaveholders of my maternal grandmother's clan. The Millers were also my great-great-grandparents and great-aunts and who knows what else. My great-great-grandfather Austin Miller, a thirty-five-year-old lawyer, bought my eleven-year-old great-great-grandmother, Sophie, and her parents (being 'family Negroes,' the previous owner sold them as a matched set). By the time she was twelve, Austin Miller had made Sophie the mother of a child, my great-grandmother Mary. He did so, according to family lore, out of his desire to have a family. Not, of course, a family with my great-great-grandmother, but with a wealthy white widow whom he in fact married shortly thereafter. He wanted to *practice* his sexual talents on my great-great-grandmother. In the bargain, Sophie bore Mary, who was taken away from her and raised in the Big House as a house servant, an attendant to his wife, Mary (after whom Sophie's Mary, my great-grandmother, had been named), and to his legitimated white children.

In ironic, perverse obeisance to the rationalizations of this bitter ancestral mix, the image of this self-centered child molester became the fuel for my survival during the dispossessed limbo of my years at Harvard; the *Bakke* years, the years when everyone was running around telling black people that they were very happy to have us there, but after all they did have to lower the standards and readjust the grading system, but Harvard could *afford* to do that because Harvard was Harvard. And it worked. I got through law school, quietly driven by the false idol of the white-man-within-me, and I absorbed a whole lot of the knowledge and the values which had enslaved me and my foremothers.

I learned about images of power in the strong, sure-footed arms' length transactor. I learned about unique power-enhancing lands called Whiteacre and Blackacre, and the mystical fairy rings which encircled them, called restrictive covenants. I learned that excessive power overlaps generously with what is seen as successful, good, efficient, and desirable in our society.

I learned to undo images of power with images of powerlessness; to clothe the victims of excessive power in utter, bereft naiveté; to cast them as defenseless supplicants raising—*pleading*—defenses of duress, undue influence, and fraud. I learned that the best way to give voice to those whose voice had been suppressed was to argue that they had no voice.

Some time ago, a student gave me a copy of *Pierson v. Post*[9] as reinterpreted by her six-year-old, written from the perspective of the wild fox. In some ways it resembled Peter Rabbit with an unhappy ending; most importantly it was a tale retold from the doomed prey's point of view, the hunted reviewing the hunter. I had been given this story the same week that my sister had gone to the National Archives and found something which may have been the contract of my great-great-grandmother Sophie's sale (whether hers or not, it was someone's) as well as the census accounting which listed her, along with other, inanimate evidence of wealth, as the 'personal property' of Austin Miller.

In reviewing those powerfully impersonal documents, I realized that both she and the fox shared a common lot, were either owned or unowned, never the owner. And whether owned or unowned, rights over them never filtered down *to* them; rights to their persons never vested in them. When owned, issues of physical, mental, and emotional abuse or cruelty were assigned by the law to the private tolerance, whimsy, or insanity of an external master. And when unowned— i.e., free, freed, or escaped—again their situation was uncontrollably precarious, for as objects *to be* owned, they and the game of their conquest were seen only as potential enhancements to some other self. They were fair game from the perspective of those who had rights; but from their own point of view, they were objects of a murderous hunt.

This finding of something which could have been the contract of sale of my great-great-grandmother irretrievably personalized my analysis of the law of her exchange. Repeatedly since then, I have tried to analyze, rationalize, and rescue her fate, employing the tools I learned in law school: adequacy of valuable consideration, defenses to formation, grounds for discharge and remedies (for whom?). That this was to be a dead-end undertaking was all too obvious, but it was interesting to see how the other part of my heritage, Austin Miller, the lawyer, and his confreres had constructed their world so as to nip quests like mine in the bud.

The very best I could do for my great-great-grandmother was to throw myself, in whimpering supplication, upon the mercy of an imaginary, patriarchal court and appeal for an exercise of its extraordinary powers of conscionability and 'humanitarianism.'[10] I found that it helped to appeal to that court's humanity, and not to stress the fullness of her own. I found that the best way to get anything for her, whose needs for rights were so compellingly, overwhelmingly manifest, was to argue that she, poor thing, had no rights.[11] It is this experience of having, for survival, to argue our own invisibility in the passive, unthreatening rhetoric of 'no-rights' which, juxtaposed with the CLS abandonment of rights theory, is both paradoxical and difficult for minorities to accept.

To say that blacks never fully believed in rights is true; yet it is also true that blacks believed in them so much and so hard that we gave them life where there was none before. We held onto them, put the hope of them into our wombs, and mothered them—not just the notion of them. We nurtured rights and gave rights life. And this was not the dry process of reification, from which life is drained and reality fades as the cement of conceptual determinism hardens round—but its opposite. This was the resurrection of life from 400-year-old ashes; the parthenogenesis of unfertilized hope.

The making of something out of nothing took immense alchemical fire: the fusion of a whole nation and the kindling of several generations. The illusion became real for only a very few of us; it is still elusive and illusory for most. But if it took this long to breathe life into a form whose shape had already been forged by society and which is therefore idealistically if not ideologically accessible, imagine how long would be the struggle without even that sense of definition, without the power of that familiar vision. What hope would there be if the assignment were to pour hope into a timeless, formless futurism? The desperate psychological and physical oppression suffered by black people in this society makes such a prospect either unrealistic (i.e., experienced as unattainable) or other-worldly (as in the false hopes held out by many religions of the oppressed).

It is true that the constitutional foreground of 'rights' was shaped by whites, parcelled out to blacks in pieces, ordained in small favors, as random insulting gratuities. Perhaps the predominance of that imbalance obscures the fact that the recursive insistence of those rights is also defined by black desire for them, desire not fueled by the sop of minor enforcement of major statutory schemes like the Civil Rights Act, but by knowledge of, and generations of existing in, a world without any meaningful boundaries. And 'without boundary' for blacks has meant not untrammelled vistas of possibility, but the crushing weight of totalistic—bodily and spiritual—*intrusion*. 'Rights' feels so new in the mouths of most black people. It is still so deliciously empowering to say. It is a sign for and a gift of selfhood that is very hard to contemplate reconstructing (deconstruction is too awful to think about!) at this point in history. It is the magic wand of visibility and invisibility, of inclusion and exclusion, of power and no-power. The concept of rights, both positive and negative, is the marker of our citizenship, our participatoriness, our relation to others.

In many mythologies, the mask of the sorcerer is also the source of power. To unmask the sorcerer is to depower.[12] So CLS' unmasking rights mythology in liberal America is to reveal the source of much powerlessness masquerading as strength. It reveals a universalism of need and oppression among whites as well as blacks.

In those ancient mythologies, however, unmasking the sorcerer was only part of the job. It was impossible to destroy the mask without destroying the balance of things, without destroying empowerment itself. Therefore, the mask had to be donned by the acquiring shaman, and put to good ends. As rulers range from despotic to benign, as anarchy can become syndicalism, so the power mask in the right hands can transform itself from burden into blessing.

The task for CLS, therefore, is not to discard rights, but to see through or past them so that they reflect a larger definition of privacy, and of property: so that privacy is turned from exclusion based on *self*-regard into regard for another's fragile, mysterious autonomy; and so that property regains its ancient connotation of being a reflection of that part of the self which by virtue of its very externalization is universal. The task is to expand private property rights into a conception of civil rights, into the right to expect civility from others.[13]

In discarding rights altogether, one discards a symbol too deeply enmeshed in the psyche of the oppressed to lose without trauma and much resistance. Instead, society must give them away. Unlock them from reification by giving them to slaves. Give them to trees. Give them to cows. Give them to history. Give them to rivers and rocks. Give to all of society's objects and untouchables the rights of privacy, integrity, and self-assertion; give them distance and respect. Flood them with the animating spirit which rights-mythology fires in this country's most oppressed psyches, and wash away the shrouds of inanimate object status, so that we may say not that we own gold, but that a luminous golden spirit owns us.

NOTES

1. Few plaintiffs ever seemed to wait around as much as defendants did. In part, this was due to the fact that, in the courts in which I practiced, unlike, for example, a family court, the plaintiffs were largely invisible entities—like the state or a bank or a corporate creditor—whose corporeal manifestations were their lawyers.

2. Peter Gabel was one of the first to bring critical theory to legal analysis; as such he is considered one of the 'founders' of Critical Legal Studies.

3. *See generally* R. Delgado et al., *Fairness and Formality: Minimizing the Risk of Prejudice in Alternative Dispute Resolution*, 1985 WIS. L. REV. 1359 [hereinafter *Fairness and Formality*].

4. *See* U.S. Const. art. I, § 2.

5. 'Can anyone seriously think that it helps either in changing society or in understanding how society changes to discuss whether [someone is] exercising rights protected by the First Amendment? It matters only whether they engaged in politically effective action.' M. Tushnet, *An Essay on Rights*, 62 TEX. L. REV. 1363, 1370–71 (1984); *see also* THE POLITICS OF LAW: A PROGRESSIVE CRITIQUE (D. Kairys ed., 1982); G. Frug, *The Ideology of Bureaucracy in American Law*, 97 HARV. L. REV. 1276 (1984); P. Gabel, *Reification in Legal Reasoning*, 3 RES. IN L. & SOC. 25 (1980); P. Gabel & P. Harris, *Building Power and Breaking Images: Critical Legal Theory and the Practice of Law*, 11 N.Y.U. REV. L. & SOC. CHANGE 369 (1982–83); D. Kennedy, *The Structure of Blackstone's Commentaries*, 28 BUFF. L. REV. 205 (1979); D. Kennedy, *Form and Substance in Private Law Adjudication*, 89 HARV. L. REV. 1685 (1976).

6. *See* Tushnet, *supra* note 5, at 1375; *see also* R. Gordon, *Historicism in Legal Scholarship*, 90 YALE L.J. 1017 (1981); R. Unger, *The Critical Legal Studies Movement*, 96 HARV. L. REV. 561 (1983).

7. *See* Tushnet, *supra* note 5; A. Freeman, *Legitimizing Racial Discrimination Through Anti-Discrimination Law: A Critical Review of Supreme Court Doctrine*, 62 MINN. L. REV. 1049 (1978); *see also* D. HAY, ET AL., ALBION'S FATAL TREE (1975).

8. A. Freeman, *Antidiscrimination Law: A Critical Review, in* THE POLITICS OF LAW: A PROGRESSIVE CRITIQUE 96, 114 (D. Kairys ed., 1982).

9.

Post, being in possession of certain dogs and hounds under his command, did, 'upon a certain wild and uninhabited, unpossessed and waste land, called the beach, find and start one of those noxious beasts called a fox,' and whilst there hunting, chasing and pursuing the same with his dogs and hounds, and when in view thereof, Pierson, well knowing the fox was so hunted and pursued, did, in the sight of Post, to prevent his catching the same, kill and carry it off.

3 Cai. R. 175, 175 (N.Y. Sup. Ct. 1805).

10. *See* S. ELKINS, SLAVERY: A PROBLEM IN AMERICAN INSTITUTIONAL AND INTELLECTUAL LIFE 237 (2d ed. 1963), in which the 'conduct and character' of slave traders is described as follows: 'Between these two extremes [from 'unscrupulous' to 'guilt-ridden'] must be postulated a wide variety of acceptable, genteel, semi-personalized, and doubtless relatively *humane* commercial transactions whereby slaves in large numbers could be transferred in exchange for money' (emphasis added).

11. *See* D. Bell, *Social Limits on Basic Protections for Blacks, in* RACE, RACISM AND AMERICAN LAW 280 (1980).

12. The 'unmasking' can occur in a number of less-than-literal ways: killing the totemic animal from whom the sorcerer derives power; devaluing the magician as merely the village psychotic; and, perhaps most familiarly in our culture, incanting sacred spells backwards. C. LÉVI-STRAUSS, THE RAW AND THE COOKED 28 (1979); M. ADLER, DRAWING DOWN THE MOON 321 (1979); W. LA BARRE, THE GHOST DANCE 315–19 (1970). Almost every culture in the world has its share of such tales: Plains Indian, Eskimo, Celtic, Siberian, Turkish, Nigerian, Cameroonian, Brazilian, Australian and Malaysian stories—to name a few—describe the phenomenon of the power mask or power object. *See generally* L. ANDREWS, JAGUAR WOMAN AND THE WISDOM OF THE BUTTERFLY TREE, 151–76 (1985); J. HALIFAX, SHAMANIC VOICES (1979); A. Kamenskii, *Beliefs About Spirits and Souls of the Dead, in* RAVENS BONES 67 (A. Hope III, ed. 1982); J. FRAZER, THE GOLDEN BOUGH 810 (1963).

13.

He had to choose. But it was not a choice
Between excluding things. It was not a choice
Between, but of. He chose to include the things
That in each other are included, the whole,
The complicate, the amassing harmony.

W. STEVENS, *Notes Toward a Supreme Fiction, in* THE COLLECTED POEMS OF WALLACE STEVENS 403 (1981).

From the Editor:
Issues and Comments

D O E S law—court opinions, statutes, briefs, and the like—have a story or stories? Or is it a collection of facts, prescriptions, and guidelines? If law does contain implicit stories, what are they, and how should we analyze them? Is whiteness itself such a story? When outsiders tell stories like Professor Patricia Williams's, do they, too, become part of "law"? Are there any dangers implicit in legal story-telling, or seeing law as a mass of stories and narratives? Can a story be false, or dishonest, or manipulative? Is law, as Torres and Milun imply, a kind of official story-cide, a system that kills, prevents the telling of, certain stories such as those of the Mashpee Indians? Does any majoritarian cultural artifact, such as the movie *Soul Man*, do that as well? If so, (a) is that a problem? and (b) what is the cure?

For further work on telling and retelling, see Parts III (on revisionist history) and XI (Critical Race Feminism, in which several writers examine and revise dominant stories about women). On judges as story-tellers and story-hearers, see the article by Delgado and Stefancic listed in the Suggested Readings; for a subtle exploration of the stories of lawyers and "lay lawyers," see the article by Gerald López.

Suggested Readings

Austin, Regina, *Sapphire Bound!*, 1989 WIS. L. REV. 539.

Ball, Milner S., *Stories of Origin and Constitutional Possibilities*, 87 MICH. L. REV. 2280 (1989).

Barnes, Robin D., *An Extra-Terrestrial Trade Proposition Brings an End to the World as We Know It*, 34 ST. LOUIS L.J. 413 (1990).

Bell, Derrick A., Jr., *The Final Report: Harvard's Affirmative Action Allegory*, 87 MICH. L. REV. 2382 (1989).

Brown, Kevin, *The Social Construction of a Rape Victim: Stories of African-American Males About the Rape of Desiree Washington*, 1992 U. ILL. L. REV. 997.

Davis, Peggy C., *Contextual Legal Criticism: A Demonstration Exploring Hierarchy and "Feminine" Style*, 66 N.Y.U. L. REV. 1635 (1991).

Delgado, Richard & Jean Stefancic, *Norms and Narratives: Can Judges Avoid Serious Moral Error?*, 69 TEX. L. REV. 1929 (1991).

Green, Dwight L., *Drug Decriminalization: A Chorus in Need of Masterrap's Voice*, 18 HOFSTRA L. REV. 457 (1990).

Hernadez Truyol, Berta Esperanza, *Building Bridges—Latinas and Latinos at the Crossroads: Realities, Rhetoric, and Replacement*, 25 COLUM. HUMAN RIGHTS L. REV. 369 (1994).

López, Gerald P., *Lay Lawyering*, 32 UCLA L. REV. 1 (1984).

Matsuda, Mari J., *Public Response to Racist Speech: Considering the Victim's Story*, 87 MICH. L. REV. 2320 (1989).

Robinson, Reginald Leamon, *"The Other Against Itself": Deconstructing the* Violent Discourse *Between Korean and African Americans*, 67 S. CAL. L. REV. 15 (1993).

Ross, Thomas, *Innocence and Affirmative Action*, 43 VAND. L. REV. 297 (1990).

Williams, Patricia J., *The Obliging Shell: An Informal Essay on Formal Equal Opportunity*, 87 MICH. L. REV. 2128 (1989).

Williams, Robert A., Jr., *Taking Rights Aggressively: The Perils and Promise of Critical Legal Theory for Peoples of Color*, 5 LAW & INEQ. J. 103 (1987).

PART III

REVISIONIST INTERPRETATIONS OF HISTORY AND CIVIL RIGHTS PROGRESS

S O M E of the best Critical writing has concerned itself with the history, development, and interpretation of U.S. race relations law. Many Criticalists write about the idea of progress (is the arrow of development forward or backward?) or why change is so often cyclical—consisting of alternating periods of advance and retrenchment. Authors try to understand the role of conquest, colonialism, economic exploitation, or white self-interest in driving legal relations between the majority group and minority communities of color.

Part III opens with a selection by Robert Williams, an eminent young Indian legal scholar, who shows how the crude discourses of earlier times, which were used to justify ruthless treatment of Native Americans, retain their malevolent efficacy today. Mary Dudziak then puts forward the surprising thesis that progressive sentiment and altruism played relatively little role in *Brown v. Board of Education*; as she sees it, white self-interest and the needs of elite groups engaged in opposing Communism worldwide called the tune. Next, James Gordon puts forward the astonishing thesis that Robert Harlan, a light-skinned, blue-eyed man who grew up in the household of James Harlan, father of the future Supreme Court Justice John Marshall Harlan, author of the famous dissent in *Plessy v. Ferguson*, was black. The young Justice-to-be thus had a black brother, and his special relation to Robert may have shaped his dream of an America free of the scourge of race and racism.

In a final selection, Robert Cottrol and Raymond Diamond's brief against gun control for the black community, the authors argue that the Second Amendment (which guarantees the right to bear arms) is especially important to the black community in light of the violence and neglect it has suffered at the hands of whites.

10 Documents of Barbarism: The Contemporary Legacy of European Racism and Colonialism in the Narrative Traditions of Federal Indian Law

ROBERT A. WILLIAMS, JR.

A S A N eastern Indian who moved West, I have become more appreciative of the importance of a central theme of all American Indian thought and discourse, the circle. To come West, and listen to so many Indian people speak and apply a vital and meaningful discourse of tribal sovereignty, has been a redemptive experience. It has enabled me to envision what must have been for all Indian peoples before Europeans established their hegemony in America.

As an eastern Indian moved West, I continually reflect on the cycles of confrontation between white society and American Indian tribalism. I am most alarmed by the structural similarities which can be constructed between the early nineteenth century Removal era and the modern West today. In the early nineteenth century, white society confronted the unassimilability of an intransigent tribalism in the East, and responded with an uncompromising and racist legal discourse of opposition to tribal sovereignty. The full-scale deployment of this discourse resulted in tribalism's virtual elimination from the eastern United States. In the modern West today, white society again finds itself confronting a resurgent discourse of tribal sovereignty as its intercourse with once remote Indian Nations increases. The revival of an uncompromising and racist legal discourse of opposition to tribal sovereignty, articulated by many segments of white society today, just as certainly seeks tribalism's virtual elimination from the western United States. While there are many differences between the Removal era confrontations with tribalism and the confrontations occurring today in Indian Country over the place and meaning of tribal sovereignty in contemporary United States society, the importance of the circle in American Indian thought and discourse particularly alerts me to many alarming similarities.

31 ARIZ. L. REV. 237 (1989). Copyright © 1989 by the Arizona Board of Regents. Reprinted by permission.

The Removal of Tribalism in the East

DOCUMENTS OF CIVILIZATION: THE CHEROKEES' DISCOURSE OF TRIBAL SOVEREIGNTY

In his illuminating *Theses on the Philosophy of History* written in 1940, a few months prior to his death in the face of Hitler's final solution, the German-Jewish writer Walter Benjamin observed that there is no document of civilization which is not at the same time a document of barbarism.[1] By all documented accounts, the United States' forced removal of the Five "Civilized" tribes of the Indians—the Cherokees, Creeks, Chickasaws, Choctaws and Seminoles—from their ancestral homelands in the south across the Great Father of Waters was an act of barbarism. In his classic and ironically titled text, *Democracy in America*,[2] Alexis de Tocqueville, who was *there* when the Choctaws crossed the Mississippi at Memphis in 1831, described the horrible scene as follows:

> It was then in the depths of winter, and that year the cold was exceptionally severe; the snow was hard on the ground, and huge masses of ice drifted on the river. The Indians brought their families with them; there were among them the wounded, the sick, newborn babies, and old men on the point of death. They had neither tents nor wagons, but only some provisions and weapons. I saw them embark to cross the great river, and the sign will never fade from my memory. Neither sob nor complaint rose from that silent assembly. Their afflictions were of long standing, and they felt them to be irremediable.[3]

While Tocqueville was a witness to Removal, his most famous insight into the American character was his notation of a national obsession with the legal process. Thus, Tocqueville's digressions in *Democracy in America* on United States Indian policy in general contain a special poignancy in light of his reflections on the Choctaw removal. Commenting on the history of the nation's treatment of Indian tribal peoples, Tocqueville noted the United States' "singular attachment to the formalities of law" in carrying out a policy of Indian extermination.[4] Contrasting the Spaniards' Black Legend of Indian atrocities, Tocqueville's *Democracy in America* complimented the United States for its clean efficiency in "legally" dealing with its Indian problem. It would be "impossible," the Frenchman declared in mock admiration of the Americans' Indian policy, "to destroy men with more respect for the laws of humanity."[5]

The cases, treatises and other scholarly commentary comprising the textual corpus of modern federal Indian law discourse revere the documents of an ineffectual United States Supreme Court declaring the Cherokee Nations' impotent rights to resist the forces intent on their destruction. In particular, the celebratory narrative traditions of federal Indian law scholarship regard the Marshall Court's 1832 decision in *Worcester v. Georgia*,[6] recognizing the inherent sovereignty of Indian Tribes, as perhaps the Removal era's most important legacy for American tribalism. But there was a competing legal discourse in the early nineteenth century on tribalism's rights and status east of the Mississippi that denied, and in fact overcame, the assertions of tribal sovereignty contained in the Marshall Court's much-celebrated *Worcester* opinion.

The dominant forces of political and legal power in United States society effectively ignored Marshall's declaration in *Worcester* that the Cherokee Nation "is a distinct community occupying its own territory, with boundaries accurately described, in which the laws of Georgia can have no force, and which the citizens of Georgia have no right to enter."[7] The Cherokees, along with the other southern tribes, were coerced into abandoning their territory and were resettled in the West. The laws of Georgia are now in force in the Cherokees' ancestral homelands; in fact, the traces of many once vital forms of tribalism east of the Mississippi can be found only in the pages of the historian and place names on road maps. And, as noted by the witness Tocqueville, it was all accomplished with a "singular attachment to the formalities of law"; a law violently opposed to that laid down by Chief Justice Marshall in his *Worcester* opinion.

The period's best preserved discourse of tribal sovereignty is that articulated by the Cherokee Nation. Having survived their military subjugation by the United States in the post-Revolutionary period, the Cherokees' war against white repression was continued through other means, by law and politics. Thus, there exists a large corpus of official documents declaring Cherokee resistance preserved in enabling acts of Cherokee self-government, memorials to Congress, and arguments made before United States tribunals of justice. The basic themes of this discourse asserted the Cherokees' fundamental human right to live on the land of their elders, their right to the sovereignty and jurisdiction over that land, and the United States' acknowledgment and guarantee of those rights in treaties negotiated with the tribe.

The tribe's 1830 memorial to Congress contains perhaps the most concise summary of the principal themes of the Cherokees' discourse of sovereignty. The Cherokees presented their petition to the national government shortly after the passage of the Removal Act. The Cherokee memorial declared the tribe's firm opposition to abandoning its eastern homeland in the following terms:

> We wish to remain on the lands of our fathers. We have a perfect and original right to remain without interruption or molestation. The treaties with us, and the laws of the United States made in pursuance of treaties, guaranty our residence and privileges, and secures us against intruders. Our only request is, that these treaties may be fulfilled, and these laws executed.[8]

The Cherokees' discourse of resistance, with its organizing theme of an Indian tribe's fundamental human right to retain and rule over its ancestral homeland, asserted itself most threateningly in an adamant refusal to remove voluntarily from Georgia westward to an Indian Territory beyond the Mississippi River. It was the Cherokees' refusal to abandon their homeland that rendered their discourse so "presumptuous" and intolerable to those segments of United States society determined to see tribalism eliminated from within the borders of white civilization.

In response to the Cherokees' legal discourse of sovereignty over their ancestral lands, Georgia enacted a series of laws that partitioned the Cherokee country
to several of the state's counties, extended its jurisdiction over the territory, and
declared all Indian customs null and void. Under these laws, Indians were also
deemed incompetent to testify in Georgia's courts in cases involving whites.

These positive expressions of Georgia's intent to exercise political jurisdiction over the Cherokee country were accompanied by a legal discourse stridently
opposed to the Cherokees' own discourse of tribal sovereignty. This legal discourse of opposition to tribal sovereignty was not, however, directed only at the
Cherokees, and was not the exclusive possession of the Georgians. The themes
of this discourse focused beyond the Cherokee controversy, and were embraced
by many members of the dominant white society who denied all Indian tribes the
right to retain sovereignty over their ancestral lands. According to this discourse,
tribal Indians, by virtue of their radical divergence from the norms and values of
white society regarding use of and entitlement to lands, could make no claims to
possession or sovereignty over territories which they had not cultivated and
which whites coveted. Treaties of the federal government allegedly recognizing
tribal rights to ancestral homelands had been negotiated primarily to protect the
tribes from certain destruction. Destruction of the tribes now appeared inevitable, however, as the territories reserved to the tribes east of the Mississippi
were being surrounded by land hungry whites.[9] Because conditions had changed
so dramatically from the time of the treaties' negotiation, the treaties could no
longer be regarded as binding. Only removal could save the tribes from inevitable
destruction.

In 1830, Georgia Governor George C. Gilmer summed up the basic thesis of
the legal discourse legitimating the breach of treaties required by the Removal
policy as follows: "[T]reaties were expedients by which ignorant, intractable and
savage people were induced without bloodshed to yield up what civilized peoples
had a right to possess by virtue of that command of the Creator delivered to man
upon his formation—be fruitful, multiply and replenish the earth, and subdue it."

Georgia Congressman, later governor, Wilson Lumpkin made virtually the
same claim in his speech before the House of Representatives in support of the
1830 Removal Act, which would facilitate the expulsion of all remaining tribal
Indians to the western Indian territory.

> The practice of buying Indian lands is nothing more than the substitute of hu-
> manity and benevolence, and has been resorted to in preference to the sword, as
> the best means for agricultural and civilized communities entering into the en-
> joyment of their natural and just right to the benefits of the earth, evidently de-
> signed by *Him* who formed it for purposes more useful than Indian hunting
> grounds.[10]

The Georgians consistently stressed that tribalism's claims to sovereignty
and ownership over lands coveted by a civilized community of cultivators were
inconsistent with natural law. Tribalism's asserted incompatibility with United

States society east of the Mississippi was in fact the most frequently articulated theme in the argument of all the advocates of the Removal policy. President John Quincy Adams, in a message to Congress in 1828, recognized the need for a "remedy" to the anomaly of independence-claiming tribal communities in the midst of white civilization. This "remedy," of course, was removal of the Indians to the west, an idea which has been debated as the final solution to the "Indian problem" since Jefferson's 1803 Louisiana Purchase.[11] Noting that the nation had been far more successful in acquiring the eastern tribes' territory "than in imparting to them the principles of inspiring in them the spirit of civilization,"[12] Adams observed that:

> [I]n appropriating to ourselves their hunting grounds we have brought upon ourselves the obligation of providing them with subsistence; and when we have had the same good fortune of teaching them the arts of civilization and the doctrines of Christianity we have unexpectedly found them forming in the midst of ourselves communities claiming to be independent of ours and rivals of sovereignty within the territories of the members of our Union. This state of things requires that a remedy should be provided—a remedy which, while it shall do justice to those unfortunate children of nature, may secure to the members of our confederates their right of sovereignty and soil.[13]

Even so-called "friends of the Indian" argued that tribalism's incompatibility with the values and norms of white civilization left removal as the only means to save the Indian from destruction. In 1829, Thomas L. McKenney, head of the national government's Office of Indian Affairs, organized New York's Board for the Emigration, Preservation, and Improvement of the Aborigines. McKenney formed the Board to gain support from missionaries and clergymen for the government's removal plan. He asked former Michigan territorial governor Lewis Cass, a well-regarded expert on the Indian in early nineteenth century white society, to publish the argument in favor of the Removal policy in the widely circulated *North American Review*.[14] As Cass explained in one article:

> A barbarous people, depending for subsistence upon the scanty and precarious supplies furnished by the chase, cannot live in contact with a civilized community. As the cultivated border approaches the haunts of the animals, which are valuable for food or furs, they recede and seek shelter in less accessible situations. ... [W]hen the people, whom they supply with the means of subsistence, have become sufficiently numerous to consume the excess annually added to the stock, it is evident, that the population must become stationary, or, resorting to the principle instead of the interest, must, like other prodigals, satisfy the wants of to-day at the expense of to-morrow.[15]

Cass further argued that any attempt by the tribes to establish independent sovereign governments in the midst of white civilization "would lead to their inevitable ruin."[16] The Indians had to be removed from the path of white civilization for their own good.

JOHN LOCKE'S CONTRIBUTIONS TO THE NARRATIVE TRADITION OF TRIBALISM'S INFERIOR LAND RIGHTS

On both sides of the Atlantic and throughout the seventeenth and eighteenth centuries, the narrative tradition of tribalism's incompatibility with white civilization generated a rich corpus of texts and legal arguments for dispossessing the Indian. These texts and arguments, while enriching and extending the tradition itself, enabled English-Americans to better understand and relate the true nature of the Indian problem confronting their transplanted New World society. John Locke's chapter on *Property*, contained in his widely read *Second Treatise of Government*,[17] was but one famous and influential text that can be located within this tradition. Written towards the end of the seventeenth century, Locke's text illustrates the widely diffused nature of the impact of more than seventy years of English colonial activity in the New World on so many aspects of English life and society.

Locke himself was a one-time functionary in the slave plantation enterprise of the colonial proprietors of South Carolina.[18] His late seventeenth century philosophical discussion on the natural law rights of an individual to acquire "waste" and common lands by labor assumed the status of a canonical text in a number of still vital narrative traditions emerging out of early United States political and legal culture.[19] With respect to the narrative tradition of tribalism's incompatibility with white norms and values, Locke's famous text represents the principal philosophical delineation of the normative arguments supporting white civilization's conquest of America.

The *Second Treatise*'s legitimating discourse of a civilized society of cultivators' superior claim to the "waste" and underutilized lands roamed over by savage tribes provided a more rigidly systematized defense of the natural law–grounded set of assumptions by which white society had traditionally justified dispossessing Indian society of the New World. The primary philosophical problem set out in Locke's famous chapter on *Property* in his *Second Treatise* was a demonstration of "how men might come to have a property in several parts of that which God gave to mankind in common, and that without any express compact of all the commoners."[20] Thus, Locke's text constructed its methodically organized argument for dispossessing the Indian of the presumed great "common" that was America in indirect fashion, through abstraction. Locke sought to demonstrate, through a series of carefully calculated contrasts between English and American Indian land use practices, how individual labor upon the commons removes "it out of the state of nature" and "begins the [private] property."[21] For Locke, the narrative tradition of tribalism's normative deficiency provided the needed illustrations for his principal argument that " 'Tis labour indeed that puts the difference of value on everything."[22] In turn, this "difference" was the source of a cultivator society's privileges to deny the wasteful claims of tribalism to the underutilized "commons" of America. Locke wrote:

> There cannot be a clearer demonstration of any thing, than several Nations of the Americans are of this [the value added to land by labor] who are rich in Land, and

poor in all Comforts of Life; whom nature having furnished as liberally as any other people, with the materials of Plenty, i.e., a fruitful soil, apt to produce in abundance, what might serve for food, rayment, and delight; yet for want of improving it by labour, have not one hundredth part of the Conveniences we enjoy; and the king of a large fruitful territory there feeds, lodges, and is clad worse than a day labourer in the *England*.[23]

Locke's argument was firmly grounded in a narrative tradition familiar to any late seventeenth century Englishman who had heard the countless sermons or read the voluminous promotional literature designed to encourage English colonization of the unenclosed, uncultivated expanses of territory in America claimed by Indian tribes. Locke's gross anthropological overgeneralizations of the living conditions of the kings "of several Nations of the Americans"[24] serve to illustrate his basic theme that land without labor-added value, such as Indian-occupied land, remains in the state of nature free for individual English appropriation as property. This use of the Indian's "difference" as a shorthand device to demonstrate the value added to uncultivated land by labor illuminates the economizing and legitimating functions of a narrative tradition when skillfully deployed in expository and rhetorical discourses.

Locke's famous argument in his *Second Treatise* that land lying waste and uncultivated has no owner and can therefore be appropriated by labor actually contained an express normative judgment on the Indian's claims under natural law to the "in-land parts of America."[25] Drawing on the narrative tradition's dominant theme of tribalism's deficiency and unassimilability respecting land use, Locke declared toward the end of his text:

Yet there are still *great tracts of ground* to be found, which (the inhabitants thereof not having joined with the rest of mankind, in the consent of the use of their common money) lie waste, and are more than the people, who dwell on it, do, or can make use of, and so still be in common. Tho' this can scarce happen amongst that part of mankind, that have consented to the use of money.[26]

Locke's refrain in the closing sentences of his discussion in *Property* that "thus, in the beginning, all the world was America,"[27] was therefore far more than a metaphorical illustration of the conditions of the state of nature from which private property emerged. The oft-quoted allusion was also a tactical deployment of a principal theme of a narrative tradition that had legitimated and energized the call to colonization of the vast "commons" that was supposedly the Indian's America since the beginnings of the English invasion of the New World.

Locke's natural law thematic of the Indian's failure to adopt the supposedly universal "rational" norms by which Englishmen assessed claims to natural rights drew heavily on the narrative tradition of tribalism's normatively deficient land use practices. In supporting the claims of a society of cultivators to the Indian's America, Locke in turn strongly reinforced and extended that same tradition. But while extremely influential, Locke's philosophical text simply supplemented the cumulative burden already placed upon Indian land rights in a narrative tradition focused on tribalism's difference from white culture. Nevertheless, Locke more systematically rationalized the privileges flowing to white society by virtue of that difference, and, for a society that valued systemic rationalization as a confirmation of divinely inspired natural law,[28] this was indeed an enlightening achievement.

The Discourse of Opposition to Tribal Sovereignty in Contemporary United States Society

THE TASK OF HEARING WHAT HAS ALREADY BEEN SAID

The pre–nineteenth century narrative tradition on tribalism's deficiency and unassimilability with white civilization provided the Removal era's legal discourse of opposition to tribal sovereignty with a number of valuable and venerable themes and thematic devices. Its central vision of tribalism's normative deficiency respecting land use grounded the claims of Georgia and the other southern states to superior rights of ownership and sovereignty over Indian Country. Its intimately connected themes of tribalism's unassimilability and doomed fate in the face of white civilization's superior difference and privileges arising from that difference perfectly complemented the advocates of Removal's claims that the only way to save the tribes was to banish them from the midst of white civilization.

As has been illustrated, the idea that tribalism east of the Mississippi was incompatible with the territorial ambitions and superior claims of United States society had been an integral component of United States public discourses on Indian policy long prior to the emergence of the Removal era's dominant legal discourse of opposition to tribal sovereignty. The widely asserted position of the early nineteenth century advocates of Removal that tribalism was doomed to extinction in its confrontation with United States civilization east of the Mississippi was appropriated from a narrative tradition refined by Europeans in the New World in the course of two centuries of colonial contact with American Indians.

Just as it is possible to reconstruct the emergence of the early nineteenth century Removal era's dominant legal discourse of opposition to tribal sovereignty out of a broader legitimating narrative tradition on tribalism's normative deficiency and unassimilability with white civilization, so too can this tradition itself be explained as a localized extension of a more global discursive legacy. That legacy, of course, would be the colonizing discourses and discursive strategies of the West's one-thousand-year-old tradition of repression of peoples of color.[29] For so many of the world's peoples of color, their history has been dominated by the seemingly eternal recurrence of the West's articulation and rearticulation of the privileges of its superior difference in their homelands.[30]

To say that it has all been heard before does not trivialize the significance of the circle in the thought of so many of the world's peoples of color, particularly the tribal peoples of America. Rather, it resignifies the importance of the circle's organizing vision that, borrowing from an apostate's discourse of opposition to the West's mythos of historical linearity,[31] "a meaning has taken shape that hangs over us, leading us forward in our blindness, but awaiting in the darkness for us to attain awareness before emerging into the light of day and speaking."[32]

While the strategy of stressing the Indian's difference has been frequently deployed throughout the history of public discourses on United States Indian policy, the modern United States Supreme Court also frequently cites tribalism's continuing difference from the norms of the dominant society in its opinions articulating the inherent limitations on tribal sovereignty.[33] The strategy of stressing difference in order to intensify the exclusion by which tribalism was placed outside white civilization clearly animates the discussion of then–Associate Justice William Rehnquist's 1978 majority opinion in *Oliphant v. Suquamish Indian Tribe*.[34] *Oliphant* is the modern Supreme Court's most important discussion on the inherent limitations on tribal sovereignty. The Court held in *Oliphant* that Indian tribes lacked the inherent sovereign power to try and punish non-Indians for minor crimes committed in Indian Country.[35] The decision constrained the exercise of tribal sovereign power so as not to interfere with the interests of United States citizens to be protected from "unwarranted intrusions" on their personal liberty.[36] The decision also obviously constrains the ability of tribal government to maintain law and order in Indian Country according to a possibly divergent tribal vision.[37]

Rehnquist's *Oliphant* text legitimated these Supreme Court–created constraints on modern tribalism by first noting the following historical distinctions marking the administration of tribal criminal jurisdiction:

> Until the middle of this century, few Indian tribes maintained any semblance of a formal court system. Offenses by one Indian against another were usually handled by social and religious pressure and not by formal judicial processes; emphasis was on restitution rather than on punishment. In 1834 the Commissioner of Indian Affairs described the then status of Indian criminal systems: 'With the exception of two or three tribes . . . the Indian tribes are without laws, and the chiefs without much authority to exercise any restraint.'[38]

Having identified this historical difference by which the exercise of tribal criminal jurisdiction was placed outside white civilization, Rehnquist's opinion in *Oliphant* declared that this difference had been essentially continued in the contemporary divergence of modern tribal court systems from the norms governing the exercise of criminal jurisdiction in the dominant society's courts.[39] Citing to the Indian Civil Rights Act of 1968, a congressional act extending to tribal court criminal defendants "many of the due process protections accorded to defendants in federal or state criminal proceedings,"[40] Rehnquist observed that the protections afforded defendants in tribal court "are not identical" to those accorded defendants in non-Indian courts.[41] "Non-Indians, for example, are excluded from . . . tribal court juries" in a tribal criminal prosecution, Rehnquist noted, even if the defendant is a non-Indian.[42] It was this and other substantive differences stated and implied throughout the opinion between tribal and federal and state court proceedings[43] that determined, in Rehnquist's opinion, that Indian tribes do not possess the "power to try non-Indian citizens of the United States except in a manner acceptable to Congress."[44] Quoting from an 1834 House of Representatives report,[45] Rehnquist declared that the "principle" that tribes, by virtue of their difference, lacked criminal jurisdiction over non-Indians

> would have been obvious a century ago when most Indian tribes were characterized by a "want of fixed laws [and] of competent tribunals of justice." It should be no less obvious today, even though present-day Indian tribal courts embody dramatic advances over their historical antecedents.[46]

Rehnquist's implication in *Oliphant* was clear; despite their "dramatic advances," tribal courts operate according to norms that are too radically different from those governing United States courts. Tribes cannot be permitted to exercise their deficient forms of criminal jurisdiction over white society.[47]

Conclusion

The legacy of a thousand years of European colonialism and racism can be located in the underlying shared assumptions of Indian cultural inferiority reflected in the narrative tradition of tribalism's normative deficiency, the Removal era's dominant discourse of opposition to tribal sovereignty, and in those contemporary Indian policy discourses seeking to constrain tribalism. Since its invasion of America, white society has sought to *justify*, through law and legal discourse, its privileges of aggression against Indian people by stressing tribalism's incompatibility with the superior values and norms of white civilization. For half a millennium, the white man's Rule of Law has most often served as the fundamental mechanism by which white society has absolved itself for any injustices arising from its assumed right of domination over Indian people.

European-derived racist-imperial discourse illuminates the continuing determinative role of racism and cultural imperialism in United States public discourses on the legal rights and status of Indian tribes. The racist attitude, focusing on the tribal Indian's cultural inferiority as the source of white society's privilege of acting as rightful judge over the Indian, can be located in the discourses of seventeenth century Puritan divines, nineteenth century Georgia legislators, and twentieth century members of Congress, the federal judiciary, and federal executive branch.

The relationship between the thousand-year-old legacy of European racism and colonialism and United States public discourses of law and politics regarding Indian rights and status can be more precisely defined by focusing on the racist attitude itself. This racist attitude can be found recurring throughout the history of white society's contact with Indian tribalism. *The legacy of European colonialism and racism in federal Indian law and policy discourses can be located most definitively, therefore, in those Indian policy discourses that seek to jus-*

tify white society's privileges or aggression in the Indian's Country on the basis of tribalism's asserted deficiency and unassimilability. That so many contemporary Indian policy discourses unhesitatingly cite tribalism's deficient difference as the legitimating source of white society's role as rightful judge over Indian people understandably causes great alarm to those who appreciate the significance of the circle in American Indian thought. The genocidal legacy of European racism and colonialism in the narrative traditions of federal Indian law continues to threaten tribalism with elimination from what once was the Indian's America.

NOTES

1. In W. BENJAMIN, ILLUMINATIONS 256–57 (H. Arendt ed., 1969).
2. A. DE TOCQUEVILE, DEMOCRACY IN AMERICA 298–99 (J. Mayer & M. Lerner eds. & G. Lawrence trans., 1966).
3. *Quoted in* F. PRUCHA, I THE GREAT FATHER: THE UNITED STATES GOVERNMENT AND THE AMERICAN INDIANS 218 (1984).
4. A. DE TOCQUEVILLE, 1 DEMOCRACY IN AMERICA 336–55 (H. Reeve trans., 1945), *quoted in* R. Strickland, *Genocide-at-Law: An Historic and Contemporary View of the Native American Experience,* 34 U. KAN L. REV. 713, 718 (1986).
5. *Quoted in* R. STRICKLAND, FIRE AND THE SPIRITS 718 (1975).
6. 31 U.S. (6 Pet.) 515 (1832).
7. 31 U.S. at 561.
8. A. GUTTMAN, STATES' RIGHTS AND INDIAN REMOVAL 58 (1965).
9. *See, e.g., Andrew Jackson's First Annual Message to Congress* (Dec. 8, 1829), in II A COMPILATION OF MESSAGES AND PAPERS OF THE PRESIDENTS 456–59 (J. Richardson ed., 1907).
10. W. LUMPKIN, THE REMOVAL OF THE CHEROKEE INDIANS FROM GEORGIA 83, 196 (1969).
11. *See* F. PRUCHA, *supra* at 3, at 183–84.
12. John Quincy Adams' Message to Congress (Dec. 2, 1828), in II A COMPILATION OF MESSAGES AND PAPERS OF THE PRESIDENTS 415 (J. Richardson ed., 1907).
13. *Id.* at 416.
14. *Governor Cass on the Need for Removal,* 30 N. AM. REV. 62–121 (1830), *reprinted in* A. GUTTMAN, *supra* note 8, at 30–36.
15. *Id.* at 31.
16. *Id.* at 35.
17. J. LOCKE, TWO TREATISES OF GOVERNMENT (P. Laslett rev. ed., 1963).
18. *See* K. STAMP, THE PECULIAR INSTITUTION: SLAVERY IN THE ANTEBELLUM SOUTH 18 (1956). It was Secretary Locke who drafted the Carolina Lord Proprietors' 1669 "Fundamental Constitutions," which granted every English colonial freeman "absolute power and authority over his negro slaves." *See id.*
19. *See, e.g.,* R. EPSTEIN, TAKINGS (1987). For varying assessments of Locke's contributions to the narrative traditions of Anglo-American political and legal culture, *see, e.g.,* C. MACPHERSON, THE POLITICAL THEORY OF POSSESSIVE INDI-

VIDUALISM (1962); J. TULLY, A DISCOURSE ON PROPERTY: JOHN LOCKE AND HIS AD-VERSARIES (1980); L. HARTZ, THE LIBERAL TRADITION IN AMERICA (1955).

20. J. Locke, *supra* note 17, at 327.

21. *Id.* at 330.

22. *Id.* at 338.

23. *Id.* at 338–39.

24. There were "several" hundred American tribal nations, with widely disparate land use practices, traditions of wealth accumulation, and political organization at the time Locke wrote. *See generally* H. DRIVER, INDIANS OF NORTH AMERICA (2d ed. 1975).

25. *Id.*

26. *Id.* at 341.

27. *Id.* at 343.

28. *See generally* R. Williams, *Jefferson, the Norman Yoke , and American Indian Lands,* 29 ARIZ. L. REV. 165 (1987).

29. R. Williams, *The Algebra of Federal Indian Law: The Hard Trail of Decolonizing and Americanizing the White Man's Indian Jurisprudence,* 1986 WIS. L. REV. 219 [hereinafter Williams, *The Algebra*].

30. We are, after all, borrowing Foucault's haunting words, "doomed historically to history, to the patient construction of discourses about discourses, and to the task of hearing what has already been said." M. FOUCAULT, THE BIRTH OF THE CLINIC: AN ARCHAEOLOGY OF MEDICAL PERCEPTION XV–XVI (1975).

31. See M. Foucault, *Nietzsche, Genealogy, History, in* LANGUAGE, COUNTER-MEMORY, PRACTICE 139–64 (1977), which contains the best short account of Foucault's problematization of the idea of historical linear development in Western thought.

32. M. Foucault, *supra* note 30, at xv–xvi.

33. *See* Williams, *The Algebra, supra* note 29, at 267–89.

34. 435 U.S. 191 (1978).

35. *Oliphant,* 435 U.S. at 210.

36. *Id.*

37. *See* Williams, *The Algebra, supra* note 29, at 272–74.

38. *Oliphant,* 435 U.S. at 197.

39. *Id.* at 194–94.

40. *Id.* at 194.

41. *Id.*

42. *Id.*

43. *See* Williams, *The Algebra, supra* note 29, at 267–74.

44. *Oliphant,* 435 U.S. at 210.

45. *Id.* (quoting H.R. REP. NO. 474, 23d Cong., 1st Sess. 18 (1834)).

46. *Id.*

47. *See* Williams, *The Algebra, supra* note 29, at 272–74.

11 Desegregation as a Cold War Imperative

MARY L. DUDZIAK

AT THE height of the McCarthy era, when Congressional committees were exposing "communist infiltration" in many areas of American life, the Supreme Court was upholding loyalty oath requirements, and the executive branch was ferreting out alleged communists in government, the U.S. Attorney General filed a pro–civil rights brief in what would become one of the most celebrated civil rights cases in American history: *Brown v. Board of Education.* Although seemingly at odds with the restrictive approach to individual rights in other contexts, the U.S. government's participation in the desegregation cases during the McCarthy era was no anomaly.

In the years following World War II, racial discrimination in the United States received increasing attention from other countries. Newspapers throughout the world carried stories about discrimination against non-white visiting foreign dignitaries, as well as against American blacks. At a time when the U.S. hoped to reshape the postwar world in its own image, the international attention given to racial segregation was troublesome and embarrassing. The focus of American foreign policy at this point was to promote democracy and to "contain" communism. However, the international focus on U.S. racial problems meant that the image of American democracy was tarnished. The apparent contradictions between American political ideology and practice led to particular foreign policy difficulties with countries in Asia, Africa, and Latin America. U.S. government officials realized that their ability to sell democracy to the Third World was seriously hampered by continuing racial injustice at home. Accordingly, efforts to promote civil rights within the United States were consistent with, and important to, the more central U.S. mission of fighting world communism.

The literature on desegregation during the 1940s and 1950s has failed to consider the subject within the context of other important aspects of American cultural history during the postwar era. Most scholars seem to assume that little outside the subject of race relations is relevant to the topic.[1] As a result, historians of *Brown* seem to write about a different world than do those who consider other aspects of postwar American culture. The failure to contextualize *Brown* reinforces the sense that the movement against segregation somehow happened in spite of everything else that was going on. During a period when civil liberties and social change were repressed in other contexts, somehow, some way, *Brown* managed to happen.

This chapter represents an effort to begin to examine the desegregation cases within the context of the cultural and political period in which they occurred. The wealth of primary historical documents on civil rights during the Cold War that explicitly draw connections between civil rights and anticommunism suggests that an effort to examine desegregation within the context of Cold War American culture may be more than an interesting addition to a basically well told tale. It may ultimately cause us to recast our interpretations of the factors motivating the critical legal and cultural transformation that *Brown* has come to represent.

In one important deviation from the dominant trend in scholarship on desegregation, Derrick Bell has suggested that the consensus against school segregation in the 1950s was the result of a convergence of interests on the part of whites and blacks, and that white interests in abandoning segregation were in part a response to foreign policy concerns and an effort to suppress the potential of black radicalism at home. According to Bell, without a convergence of white and black interests in this manner, *Brown* would never have occurred.[2] While Bell's work is important and suggestive, neither Bell nor other scholars have developed this approach historically.

One need not look far to find vintage '50s Cold War ideology in primary historical documents relating to *Brown*. For example, the amicus brief filed in *Brown* by the U.S. Justice Department argued that desegregation was in the national interest in part due to foreign policy concerns. According to the Department, the case was important because "[t]he United States is trying to prove to the people of the world, of every nationality, race and color, that a free democracy is the most civilized and most secure form of government yet devised by man."[3] Following the decision, newspapers in the United States and throughout the world celebrated *Brown* as a "blow to communism" and as a vindication of American democratic principles. As was true in so many other contexts during the Cold War era, anticommunist ideology was so pervasive that it set the terms of the debate on all sides of the civil rights issue.

In addition to its important consequences for U.S. race relations, *Brown* served U.S. foreign policy interests. The value of a clear Supreme Court statement that segregation was unconstitutional was recognized by the State Department. Federal government policy on civil rights issues during the Truman Administration was framed with the international implications of U.S. racial problems in mind. And through a series of amicus briefs detailing the effect of racial segregation on U.S. foreign policy interests, the Administration impressed upon the Supreme Court the necessity for world peace and national security of upholding black civil rights at home.

As has been thoroughly documented by other historians, the federal government's efforts in the late 1940s and early 1950s to achieve some level of racial equality had much to do with the personal commitment on the part of some in government to racial justice, and with the consequences of civil rights policies for domestic electoral politics. In addition to these motivating factors, the effect of U.S. race discrimination on international relations during the postwar years was a critical motivating factor in the development of federal government policy. Without attention to the degree to which desegregation served important foreign policy interests, the federal government's posture on civil rights issues in the postwar years cannot be fully understood.

American Racism in the Eyes of the World

Apart from pressure from civil rights activists and electoral politics at home, the Truman Administration had another reason to address domestic racism: other countries were paying attention to it. Newspapers in many corners of the world covered stories of racial discrimination against visiting non-white foreign dignitaries and Americans. And as tension between the United States and the Soviet Union increased in the years after the war, the Soviets made effective use of U.S. failings in this area in anti-American propaganda. Concern about the effect of U.S. race discrimination on Cold War American foreign policy led the Truman Administration to consider a pro–civil rights posture as part of its international agenda to promote democracy and contain communism.

In one example of foreign press coverage, in December 1946 the *Fiji Times & Herald* published an article entitled "Persecution of Negroes Still Strong in America." According to the Fiji paper, "the United States has within its own borders, one of the most oppressed and persecuted minorities in the world today." In the Southern states, "hundreds of thousands of negroes exist today in an economic condition worse than the out-and-out slavery of a century ago." Treatment of blacks was not merely a question of race discrimination; "it is frequently a question of the most terrible forms of racial persecution."

The article described the 1946 lynching of four blacks in Georgia. "This outrage," the article continued, followed Supreme Court action invalidating Georgia voting restrictions. "The decision gave the negro the legal right to vote but [Georgia Governor] Talmadge challenged him to exercise it. He also flung a defiance to the Court itself and asked the voters of his State to back him up, which they did." According to the paper, "[v]ery few negroes dared to vote, even though the country's highest tribunal had found them entitled to. Most of those who did, or tried to, were badly mauled by white ruffians." The article noted that federal anti-lynching legislation had been proposed in the past, and "further attempts are certain in the next Congress."

The *Fiji Times & Herald* was not entirely critical. Reporting that a recent dinner honoring black journalists had brought together blacks and white Southerners, the paper concluded that "[t]he point is that the best culture of the south, in America, is opposed to the Bilbo-Talmadge anti-negro oppression and seems today more than ever inclined to join with the north in fighting it." Efforts against racial intolerance had particular consequences in the U.S., for "there cannot be, on the basic tenants [sic] of Americanism, such a thing as second class citizenship." The issue also had broader implications, however. "The recognition and acceptance of the concept of a common humanity should, and must, shatter the longstanding bulwarks of intolerance, racial or otherwise, before anything entitled to call itself true civilisation can be established in America or any other country."

The American Consul in Fiji was unhappy with the *Times & Herald* article, which it saw as "an indication of certain of the anti-American and/or misinformation or propaganda now carried" in the paper. A response to the article seemed appropriate and necessary. "If and when a favorable opportunity occurs, the matter of the reasonableness or justification in the publication of such biased and unfounded material, obviously prejudicial to American prestige throughout this area, will be tactfully broached to the Editor and appropriate government officials."

In Ceylon, American Embassy officials were concerned about what they considered to be "Asian preoccupation with racial discrimination in the United States." Ceylon newspapers ran stories on U.S. racial problems picked up from Reuters wire service. In addition, a Ceylon *Observer* columnist focused on the issue, particularly the seeming contradiction of segregation in the capital of American democracy. In his article, Lakshman Seneviratne quoted *Time* magazine as saying, "[i]n Washington, the seated figure of Abraham Lincoln broods over the capital of the U.S. where Jim Crow is the rule." According to Seneviratne, in Washington "the colour bar is the greatest propaganda gift any country could give the Kremlin in its persistent bid for the affections of the coloured races of the world, who, if industrialized, and technically mobilized, can well dominate, if domination is the obsession, the human race."

The effect of U.S. race discrimination on the country's leadership in postwar world politics was discussed in the Chinese press. The Shanghai *Ta Kung Pao* covered the May 2, 1948, arrest of U.S. Senator Glen Taylor for violating Alabama segregation laws. Criticizing Taylor's arrest, the paper noted that "[t]he Negro problem is a problem of U.S. internal politics, and naturally, it is unnecessary for anybody else to meddle with it." However, the issue had international ramifications.

> [W]e cannot help having some impressions of the United States which actually already leads half of the world and which would like to continue to lead it. If the United States merely wants to "dominate" the world, the atomic bomb and the U.S. dollar will be sufficient to achieve this purpose. However, the world cannot be "dominated" for a long period of time. If the United States wants to "lead" the world, it must have a kind of moral superiority in addition to military superiority.

According to the paper, "the United States prides itself on its 'liberal traditions,' and it is in the United States itself that these traditions can best be demonstrated."

The American Consul General in Shanghai believed that the *Ta Kung Pao* editorial "discusses the Negro problem in the U.S. in a manner quite close to the Communist Party line." The Consul General preferred an editorial in the *China Daily Tribune* which cast American race discrimination as a problem generated by a small minority who were acting against the grain. According to that paper, "Prejudice against people of color seems to die hard in some parts of the United States despite all that President Truman and the more enlightened leaders of the nation are doing to ensure that race equality shall become an established fact."

Indian newspapers were particularly attuned to the issue of race discrimination in the U.S. According to the American Consul General in Bombay, "[t]he color question is of intense interest in India." Numerous articles with titles like "Negro Baiting in America," "Treatment of Negroes a Blot on U.S.," and "Untouchability Banished in India: Worshipped in America" appeared in the Indian press. Regarding the latter article, the American Consul General commented that it was "somewhat typical of the irresponsible and malicious type of story on the American Negro which appears not too infrequently in segments of the Indian press. . . ." The article was written by Canadian George T. Prud'homme, who the Consul General described as a "communist writer." It concerned a trip through the South, and included a photograph of a chain gang. According to Prud'homme, "[t]he farther South one travels, the less human the Negro status becomes, until in Georgia and Florida it degenerates to the level of the beast in the field."

Prud'homme described an incident following his attempt to speak to blacks seated behind him on a segregated bus. He was later warned "not to talk to 'those damned niggers.' "

> "We don't even talk to niggers down here," said [a] blond young man.
> "You better not either . . . unless you want to get beaten up."
> I replied I didn't think the Negroes would attempt to beat me up with the bus half-filled with whites.
> *"It isn't the niggers that will beat you up, it's the whites you have to look out for,"* confided the driver. *"This ain't the North. Everything is different down here."*

The article discussed segregation, the history of the Ku Klux Klan, and the denial of voting rights through poll taxes and discriminatory voter registration tests. The writer believed that American treatment of blacks "strangely resembles the story of India under British domination." The "only bright spot in this picture" was provided by individuals such as a white Baptist pastor who was committed to racial equality. But the minister told Prud'homme, "If one of us fights for true democracy and progress, he is labelled a Communist. . . . That is an effective way of shutting him up."

Of particular concern to the State Department was coverage of U.S. racism by the Soviet media. The U.S. Embassy in Moscow believed that a number of articles in 1946 "may portend stronger emphasis on this theme as [a] Soviet propaganda weapon." In August 1946, the U.S. Embassy in Moscow sent the State Department a translation of an editorial from the periodical *Trud* which was "representative of the frequent Soviet press comment on the question of Negro discrimination in the United States." The *Trud* article was based on information the Soviets had gathered from the "progressive American press," and it concerned lynching and black labor in the South.

According to *Trud*, American periodicals had reported "the increasing frequency of terroristic acts against negroes," including "the bestial mobbing of four negroes by a band of 20 to 25 whites" in July 1946 in Monroe, Georgia. In another incident near Linden, Louisiana, "a crowd of white men tortured a negro war veteran, John Jones, tore his arms out and set fire to his body. The papers stress the fact that the murderers, even though they are identified, remain unpunished." U.S. census figures indicated that three quarters of American blacks lived in the South. In the Southern "Black Belt," "the negroes are overwhelmingly engaged in agriculture, as small tenant-farmers, share-croppers and hired hands. Semi-slave forms of oppression and exploitation are the rule. . . ." Blacks were denied economic rights due to the way the legal system protected the interests of the landowners upon whose property share-croppers and tenant farmers labored. In addition, "[t]he absence of economic rights is accompanied by the absence of social rights. The poll tax, in effect in the Southern States, deprives the overwhelming majority of negroes of the right to vote." *Trud* observed that "[t]he movement for full economic, political and social equality is spreading among the negro population," but that "[t]his movement has evoked exceptional fury and resistance." According to the paper, "[t]he progressive public opinion of the USA is indignant at the baiting of negroes, and rightly sees in this one of the means by which reaction is taking the offensive against the working people."

By 1949, according to the U.S. Embassy in Moscow, "the 'Negro question' [was] [o]ne of the principal Soviet propaganda themes regarding the United States." "[T]he Soviet press hammers away unceasingly on such things as 'lynch law,' segregation, racial discrimination, deprivation of political rights, etc., seeking to build up a picture of an America in which the Negroes are brutally downtrodden with no hope of improving their status under the existing form of government." An Embassy official believed that "this attention to the Negro problem serves political ends desired by the Soviet Union and has nothing whatsoever to do with any desire to better the Negro's position. . . ." The "Soviet press seizes upon anything showing the position of the US Negro in a derogatory light while ignoring entirely the genuine progress being made in America in improving the situation."

A powerful critique of U.S. racism, presented before the United Nations, came from American blacks. On October 23, 1947, the NAACP filed a petition in the United Nations protesting the treatment of blacks in the U.S. called *An Appeal to the World*. The petition denounced U.S. race discrimination as "not only indefensible but barbaric." It claimed that racism harmed the nation as a whole. "It is not Russia that threatens the United States so much as Mississippi; not Stalin and Molotov but Bilbo and Rankin; internal injustice done to one's brothers is far more dangerous than the aggression of strangers from abroad." The consequences of American failings were potentially global. "[T]he disfranchisement of the American Negro makes the functioning of all democracy in the nation difficult; and as democracy fails to function in the leading democracy in the world, it fails the world." According to W.E.B. Du Bois, the principal author of the petition, the purpose behind the appeal was to enable the UN "to prepare this nation to be just to its own people."

The NAACP petition "created an international sensation." It received extensive coverage in the American and foreign media. Meanwhile, U.S. Attorney General Tom Clark remarked, "I was humiliated . . . to realize that in our America there could be the slightest foundation for such a petition." Although she was a member of the Board of Directors of the NAACP, Eleanor Roosevelt, who was also a member of the American UN delegation, refused to introduce the NAACP petition in the United Nations out of concern that it would harm the international reputation of the United States. The Soviet Union, however, proposed that the NAACP's charges be investigated. On December 4, 1947, the UN Commission on Human Rights rejected that proposal, and the UN took no action on the petition. Nevertheless, the *Des Moines Register* remarked that the petition had "accomplished its purpose of arousing interest in discrimination." Although the domestic press reaction was generally favorable, the West Virginia *Morgantown Post* criticized the NAACP for "furnishing Soviet Russia with new ammunition to use against us."

The Truman Justice Department first participated as amicus curiae in civil rights cases involving restrictive covenants.[4] In previous civil rights cases, the Solicitor General participated when the litigation involved a federal agency,[5] and when the question in the case concerned the supremacy of federal law.[6] A different sort of federal interest was involved in the restrictive covenant cases. According to Solicitor General Phillip Perlman, racially restrictive covenants hampered the federal government "in doing its duty in the fields of public health, housing, home finance, and in the conduct of foreign affairs."[7] The Brief for the United States in *Shelley v. Kraemer*[8] relied on the State Department's view that "the United States has been embarrassed in the conduct of foreign relations by acts of discrimination taking place in this country."[9] To support this argument, the brief quoted at length from the letter Acting Secretary of State Acheson had written to the FEPC in 1946.

Although not addressing the international implications of the case, the Supreme Court agreed with the result sought by the Justice Department. The Court ruled that enforcement of racially restrictive covenants in state courts constituted state action which violated the rights of blacks to equal protection of the laws.[10]

The Solicitor General's office continued its efforts in civil rights cases in 1949. In *Henderson v. United States*,[11] the Department of Justice took a position contrary to the Interstate Commerce Commission on the question of the validity of railroad dining car segregation under the Interstate Commerce Act.[12] As in

Shelley, an important motivation behind the government's anti-segregation position was the international implications of segregation.[13] The *Henderson* brief
elaborated more fully on the problem. One area in which international criticism
of the U.S. manifested itself was the United Nations. The brief quoted from recent statements made by representatives of other governments in a UN subcom-
mittee meeting which "typify the manner in which racial discrimination in this
country is turned against us in the international field."[14] For example, a representative of the Soviet Union had commented: "Guided by the principles of the
United Nations Charter, the General Assembly must condemn the policy and
practice of racial discrimination in the United States and any other countries of
the American continent where such a policy was being exercised."[15] Similarly,
the representative from Poland "did not . . . believe that the United States Government had the least intention to conform to the recommendations which
would be made by the United Nations with regard to the improvement of living
conditions of the coloured population of that country."[16]

As it had in *Shelley*, the Justice Department made reference to foreign press
coverage of U.S. race discrimination, noting that "[t]he references to this subject
in the unfriendly foreign press are frequent and caustic."[17] This time the brief bolstered this claim with examples from Soviet publications. *The Bolshevik*, for example, carried an article which claimed that

> [t]he theory and practice of racial discrimination against the negroes in America
> is known to the whole world. The poison of racial hatred has become so strong in
> post-war America that matters go to unbelievable lengths; for example a Negress
> injured in a road accident could not be taken to a neighbouring hospital since this
> hospital was only for "whites."[18]

Through its reliance on UN statements and the Soviet press, the *Henderson* brief
powerfully made the point that racial segregation hampered the U.S. government's fight against world communism.

The Impact of *Brown* on American
Foreign Policy Interests

When *Brown v. Board of Education* was decided, the opinion gave
the State Department the counter to Soviet propaganda it had been looking for,
and the State Department wasted no time in making use of it. Within an hour after the decision was handed down, the Voice of America broadcast the news to
Eastern Europe.[19] An analysis accompanying the "straight news broadcasts" emphasized that "the issue was settled by law under democratic processes rather
than by mob rule or dictatorial fiat."[20] The *Brown* broadcast received "top priority on the Voice's programs," and was to be "beamed possibly for several days,
particularly to Russian satellites and Communist China." The *New York Times*
quoted a Voice of America official as commenting that "[i]n these countries . . .
the people would know nothing about the decision except what would be told

them by the Communist press and radio, which you may be sure would be twisted and perverted. They have been told that the Negro in the United States is still practically a slave and a declassed citizen."[21]

The *Brown* decision had the kind of effect on international opinion that the U.S. government had hoped for. Favorable reaction to the opinion spanned the globe. On May 21, 1954, for example, the President of the Municipal Council of Santos, São Paulo, Brazil, sent a letter to the U.S. Embassy in Rio de Janeiro celebrating the *Brown* decision. The Municipal Council had passed a motion recording "a vote of satisfaction" with the ruling. They viewed *Brown* as "establishing the just equality of the races, essential to universal harmony and peace." The Council desired that "the Consul of that great and friendly nation be officially notified of our desire to partake in the rejoicing with which the said decision was received in all corners of the civilized world."

Newspapers in Africa gave extensive coverage to the decision. According to a dispatch from the American Consul in Dakar, *Brown* was "greeted with enthusiasm in French West Africa although the press has expressed some slight skepticism over its implementation." *Afrique Nouvelle*, a weekly paper that was a "highly vocal opponent of all racial discrimination," carried an article under the headline "At last! Whites and Blacks in the United States on the same school benches." The dispatch noted that the writer was concerned that there would be

> "desperate struggles" in some states against the decision but expresses the hope that the representatives of the negroes and the "spiritual forces" of the United States will apply themselves to giving it force and life. The article concludes by saying that "all the peoples of the world can salute with joy this measure of progress."

The American Consul concluded the dispatch by observing that

> [w]hile it is, of course, too soon to speculate on the long range effects of the decision in this area, it is well to remember that school segregation more than any other single factor has lowered the prestige of the United States among Africans here and the over-all results, therefore, can hardly fail to be beneficial.

Although the initial decision to participate in *Brown* had been made by the Truman Administration, the Republican National Committee (RNC) was happy to take credit for it. On May 21, 1954, the RNC issued a statement which claimed that the decision "falls appropriately within the Eisenhower Administration's many-frontal attack on global Communism. Human equality at home is a weapon of freedom. . . . [I]t helps guarantee the Free World's cause."[22]

Conclusion

The desegregation cases came before the Court at a time when the sanctity of American democracy had tremendous implications for U.S. foreign policy interests. The U.S. hoped to save the world for democracy, and promoted its ideology and form of government as providing for greater personal freedom. In the U.S., the Voice of America proclaimed, the Bill of Rights and the Constitution protected American citizens from state tyranny. Yet as news story after news story of voting rights abuses, state-enforced segregation, and lynchings appeared in the world media, many questioned whether American constitutional rights and democratic principles had any meaning. In many African and Asian countries, where issues of race, nationalism, and anti-colonialism were of much greater import than Cold War tensions between the superpowers, the reality of U.S. racism was particularly problematic. America could not save the Third World for democracy if democracy meant white supremacy. The Soviet Union's efforts to take advantage of this American dilemma reinforced its Cold War implications.

In responding to foreign critics, State Department officials attempted to characterize American racism as a regional, rather than a national, problem, and as something that was on its way out. They argued that democracy was working, and that it would eventually overcome the anachronistic practices of a marginal few. The desegregation cases posed a threat to this characterization. If the Supreme Court had ruled in favor of the defendants in *Shelley, Henderson, Sweatt, McLaurin,* and *Brown,* the Court would have reaffirmed the idea that the American Constitution accommodated the racist practices challenged in those cases. American Embassy officials in Nigeria would have found it difficult to counter arguments that the Communist Party was more committed to the interests of people of color, if the Court had interpreted the document embodying the principles of democracy and individual rights to be consistent with racial segregation.

NOTES

1. As Gerald Horne has noted, "the fact that the *Brown* ruling came in the midst of a concerted governmental campaign against international and domestic communism is one of the most overlooked aspects of the decision." G. HORNE, BLACK AND RED: W.E.B. DU BOIS AND THE AFRO-AMERICAN RESPONSE TO THE COLD WAR, 1944–1963, at 227 (1986).

2. D. Bell, *Brown v. Board of Education and the Interest-Convergence Dilemma,* 93 HARV. L. REV. 518 (1980), reprinted in D. BELL, SHADES OF BROWN: NEW PERSPECTIVES ON SCHOOL DESEGREGATION (1980) [hereinafter Bell, *Convergence Dilemma*]; *see also* D. Bell, *Racial Remediation: An Historical Perspective on Current Conditions,* 52 NOTRE DAME L. REV. 5, 12 (1976).

3. Brief for the United States as Amicus Curiae at 6, Brown v. Board of Education, 347 U.S. 483 (1954).

4. *See* Shelley v. Kraemer, 334 U.S. 1 (1948); Hurd v. Hodge, 334 U.S. 24 (1948). According to Solicitor General Perlman, the brief filed in the restrictive covenant cases was "the first instance in which the Government had intervened in a case to which it was not a party and in which its sole purpose was the vindication of rights guaranteed by the Fifth and Fourteenth Amendments." J. ELLIFF,

THE UNITED STATES DEPARTMENT OF JUSTICE AND INDIVIDUAL RIGHTS 1937–1962, 258 (1987) (quoting Address by Perlman to the National Civil Liberties Clearing House (Feb. 23, 1950)).

Because my purpose is to examine the Truman Administration's participation in these cases, this article does not dwell on the crucial role in the cases played by the NAACP. For excellent treatments of the NAACP's litigation efforts, see M. TUSHNET, THE NAACP'S LEGAL STRATEGY AGAINST SEGREGATED EDUCATION, 1925–1950 (1987); R. KLUGER, SIMPLE JUSTICE (1975).

5. *See* Mitchell v. United States, 313 U.S. 80 (1941).

6.. *See* Taylor v. Georgia, 315 U.S. 25 (1942).

7. Oral argument of Solicitor General Perlman, 16 U.S.L.W. 3219 (Jan. 20, 1948) (paraphrased account of argument); see also C. VOSE, CAUCASIANS ONLY: THE SUPREME COURT, THE NAACP, AND THE RESTRICTIVE COVENANT CASES 200 (1959).

8. 334 U.S. 1 (1948). In *Shelley*, whites sold residential property to blacks in violation of a covenant among landowners prohibiting sales to nonwhites. State Supreme Courts in Missouri and Michigan had ruled that the covenants were enforceable. *Id.* at 6–7. The question in *Shelley* was whether judicial enforcement of the covenants constituted state action violating the fourteenth amendment rights of the blacks who purchased the property. The Supreme Court ruled that it did. *Id.* at 20.

9. Brief for the United States as Amicus Curiae at 19, Shelley v. Kraemer, 334 U.S. 1 (1948) (quoting letter from Ernest A. Gross, Legal Adviser to the Secretary of State, to the Attorney General (Nov. 4, 1947)).

10. 334 U.S. at 20.

11. 339 U.S. 816 (1950).

12. The Interstate Commerce Act provided that "[i]t shall be unlawful for any common carrier . . . to make, give, or cause any undue or unreasonable preference or advantage to any particular person . . . in any respect whatsoever; or to subject any particular person . . . to any undue or unreasonable prejudice or disadvantage in any respect whatsoever. . . ." Interstate Commerce Act, ch. 722, § 5(a), 54 Stat. 898, 902, 49 U.S.C. § 3(1) (1946) (codified as amended at 49 U.S.C. § 1074(b) (1982)). The Interstate Commerce Commission ruled that the Southern Railway Company's practice of providing separate seating behind a curtain in dining cars for black passengers did not violate the Act. *See* Henderson v. United States, 339 U.S. 816, 820–22 (1950). On appeal, the ICC defended its interpretation of the Act, and the Justice Department filed a brief on behalf of the United States arguing that (1) dining car segregation violated the Act, and (2) segregation violated the equal protection clause. *See* Brief for the United States at 9–11, Henderson v. United States, 339 U.S. 816 (1950).

13. The brief quoted from the same letter from Dean Acheson that the Department had relied on in *Shelley*. *See* Brief for the United States at 60–61, Henderson v. United States, 339 U.S. 816 (1950).

14. *Id.* at 61.

15. *Id.* (quoting United Nations, General Assembly, *Ad Hoc* Political Committee, Third Session, Part II, Summary Record of the Fifty-Third Meeting (May 11, 1949), at 12).

16. *Id.* (quoting United Nations, General Assembly, *Ad Hoc* Political Committee, Third Session, Part II, Summary Record of Fifty-Fourth Meeting (May 13, 1949), at 6).

17. *Id.*

18. *Id.* at 61 n.73 (quoting Frantsov, *Nationalism—The Tool of Imperialist Reaction*, THE BOLSHEVIK (U.S.S.R.), No. 15 (1948)).

In another example, a story in the Soviet *Literary Gazette* titled "The Tragedy of Coloured America" stated:

> It is a country within a country. Coloured America is not allowed to mix with the other white America, it exists within it like the yolk in the white of an egg. Or, to be more exact, like a gigantic ghetto. The walls of this ghetto are invisible but they are nonetheless indestructible. They are placed within cities where the Negroes live in special quarters, in buses where the Negroes are assigned only the back seats, in hairdressers where they have special chairs.

Id. (quoting Berezko, *The Tragedy of Coloured America*, THE LITERARY GAZETTE (U.S.S.R.), No. 51 (1948)).

19. N.Y. TIMES, May 18, 1954, at 1, col. 7. The Voice of America's ability to effectively use the decision was enhanced by the fact that the opinion was short and easily understandable by lay persons. Chief Justice Earl Warren intended to write "a short opinion so that any layman interested in the problem could read the entire opinion [instead of getting just] a little piece here and a little piece there. . . . I think most of the newspapers printed the entire decision." *See* J. WILKINSON, FROM BROWN TO BAKKE: THE SUPREME COURT AND SCHOOL INTEGRATION, 1954–1978 30 (1979) (quoting H. ABRAHAM, FREEDOM AND THE COURT 372 n. 90 (3d ed. 1977)).

20. N.Y. TIMES, May 18, 1954, at 1, col. 7.

21. *Id.*

22. Republican National Committee, News Release, May 21, 1954, at 3, White House Files—Civil Rights—Republican National Committee 1954, Box 37, Philleo Nash Papers, Harry S. Truman Library.

President Eisenhower himself was less enthusiastic. He repeatedly refused to publicly endorse *Brown. See* R. BURK, THE EISENHOWER ADMINISTRATION AND BLACK CIVIL RIGHTS 144, 162, 165–66 (1984). *See generally* Mayer, *With Much Deliberation and Some Speed: Eisenhower and the Brown Decision*, 52 J. SOUTHERN HIST. 43 (1986). Eisenhower criticized "foolish extremists on both sides" of the school desegregation controversy, R. BURK, *supra* at 163, and, in an effort to distance his administration from the Supreme Court's ruling, he "rebuked Vice President Nixon for referring to Earl Warren as the 'Republican Chief Justice'. . . ." *Id.* at 162. Chief Justice Warren was angered by Eisenhower's stance. He believed that if Eisenhower had fully supported *Brown,* "we would have been relieved . . . of many of the racial problems that have continued to plague us." E. WARREN, THE MEMOIRS OF EARL WARREN 291 (1977); *see* J. WILKINSON, *supra* note 19, at 24.

12 Did the First Justice Harlan Have a Black Brother?

JAMES W. GORDON

Introduction

On September 18, 1848, James Harlan, father of future Supreme Court Justice John Marshall Harlan, appeared in the Franklin County Court for the purpose of freeing his mulatto slave, Robert Harlan.[1] This appearance formalized Robert's free status and exposed a remarkable link between this talented mulatto and his prominent lawyer politician sponsor.

This event would have little historical significance but for the fact that Robert Harlan was no ordinary slave. Born in 1816, and raised in James Harlan's household, blue-eyed, light-skinned Robert Harlan had been treated by James Harlan more like a member of the family than like a slave. Robert was given an informal education and unusual opportunities to make money and to travel. While still a slave in the 1840s, he was permitted sufficient freedom to have his own businesses, first in Harrodsburg, Kentucky, and then later in Lexington, Kentucky. More remarkably still, he was permitted to hold himself out to the community as a free man of color at least as early as 1840, not only with James Harlan's knowledge, but apparently with his consent.[2] After making a fortune in California during the Gold Rush, Robert moved to Cincinnati in 1850 and invested his money in real estate and a photography business.[3] In the years that followed, he became a member of the Northern black elite, and, in the period after 1870, established himself as one of the most important black Republican leaders in Ohio.[4]

Although a humane master, James Harlan's treatment of Robert was paradoxical. James' tax records show that he bought and sold slaves throughout his life. The slave census of 1850 lists fourteen slaves in James Harlan's household, ranging in age from three months to seventy years. The census for 1860 lists twelve slaves ranging in age from one to fifty-three years. James neither routinely educated nor often emancipated his slaves, although his ambivalence about the "peculiar institution" was well enough known to become a political liability in Kentucky, a state which was firmly committed to the preservation of slavery.

What about Robert Harlan was so special as to lead to such exceptional treatment by James? In the view of two scholars, the peculiarity of James Harlan's re-

15 W. NEW ENG. L. REV. 159 (1993). Copyright © 1993 by Western New England Law Review Association, Inc. All rights reserved. Reprinted by permission.

lationship with Robert Harlan is easily explained. Robert Harlan, they assert, was James Harlan's son.[5] If true, this means that another of James' sons, the first Justice John Marshall Harlan, had a black half-brother.

When James emancipated Robert, John Harlan was fifteen years old. Thereafter, James and Robert continued to have contacts. After James' death in 1863, John and Robert remained in touch. Robert was an anomalous feature of John's childhood in slaveholding Kentucky and remained a part of his perception of blacks as an adult.

John deeply loved and respected his father, James. He lived in his father's house until after his own marriage. James taught John law and politics. In both arenas, father and son were partners and seem to have confided freely in one another. James remained the most important influence in John's life until the older man died in 1863, when John was thirty years old.

James Harlan's ambivalent, but generally negative, feelings about slavery surely influenced John's views on the subject. But even more importantly, James' peculiar relationship with Robert during John's youth, and the ongoing contacts between James, John, and Robert after Robert's emancipation, must have affected John's attitudes toward blacks. Robert was smart and ambitious, but lived his life in the twilight between two worlds, one black, the other white. He was never completely at home in either. Robert's lifelong experience of the significance of the color line became, vicariously, a part of John's experience. Robert was also a continuing example of something John Harlan could not later, as a Supreme Court Justice, bring himself to deny—the humanity of blacks, and the profound unfairness of their treatment by a racist America.

Given his connection to Robert, Justice John Harlan's progressive views on race, views which he repeatedly articulated in his famous dissents as an Associate Justice of the United States Supreme Court, become more comprehensible.[6] Indeed, it is reasonable to assume that we will never understand fully the sources of Justice Harlan's advanced views on race until we better understand his relationship with the black man who might have been his half-brother. Justice Harlan argued repeatedly that the Civil War Amendments had given black Americans the same civil rights as whites:

> [T]here cannot be, in this republic, any class of human beings in practical subjection to another class, with power in the latter to dole out to the former just such privileges as they may choose to grant. The supreme law of the land has decreed that no authority shall be exercised in this country upon the basis of discrimination, in respect of civil rights, against [free men] and citizens because of their race, color, or previous condition of servitude.[7]

Harlan further denied that blacks constituted

> a class which may still be discriminated against, even in respect of rights of a character so necessary and supreme, that, deprived of their enjoyment in common with others, a [free man] is not only branded as one inferior and infected, but, in the competitions of life, is robbed of some of the most essential means of existence.[8]

In *Plessy v. Ferguson*, Harlan, standing alone against the rest of the Court, again dissented:

> In respect of civil rights, common to all citizens, the Constitution of the United States does not . . . permit any public authority to know the race of those entitled to be protected in the enjoyment of such rights. . . . I deny that any legislative body or judicial tribunal may have regard to the race of citizens when the civil rights of those citizens are involved.[9]

Elsewhere in the same opinion, in words that have since become famous, Harlan wrote,

> in view of the Constitution, in the eye of the law, there is in this country no superior, dominant, ruling class of citizens. There is no caste here. Our Constitution is color-blind, and neither knows nor tolerates classes among citizens. In respect of civil rights, all citizens are equal before the law.[10]

If Robert and John were brothers, a provocative dimension for contemplation is opened. The careers of these two talented, ambitious men offer us parallel examples of life on different sides of the color line in nineteenth century America. They grew up in the same household, and, if brothers, carried many of the same genes. Each was given every opportunity that his status and skin color permitted. Each succeeded to a remarkable extent, again, within the limits imposed upon him by the society in which they both lived. Each man was shaped by his own perceptions of these limits and by their reality. In the end, John Harlan climbed as high as his society permitted *any man*. Robert Harlan climbed as high as his society permitted *any black man*. Although in the end Robert did not rise as high as did John, his achievements were, upon reflection, equally impressive and worthy of exploration.

JOHN MARSHALL HARLAN (1833–1911)

John Harlan was born on June 1, 1833, near Danville on the family farm, Harlan Station.[11] His father, James, was by then an established lawyer and a rising politician, having already served as Commonwealth's Attorney in the circuit court. John received local primary schooling and then attended Presbyterian Centre College. After he graduated from Centre in 1850, he attended Transylvania Law School, in Lexington, and then completed his legal training in his father's law office in Frankfort. John practiced with his father until 1860, when he moved to Louisville in order to expand his professional opportunities. John received his political baptism in the mid-1850s as a successful stump speaker, and quickly became a rising political star. Following the Civil War, he reluctantly joined the Republican Party, and, in partnership with men like his law partner Benjamin Bristow, became one of the "Great Men" of the party in Kentucky.

By switching the Kentucky delegation from Bristow to Rutherford B. Hayes in the 1876 Republican National Convention after it became clear that Bristow could not be nominated, Harlan earned Hayes' gratitude. This gratitude eventually led Hayes to nominate John Harlan to be an Associate Justice of the United States Supreme Court in 1877, and to give Harlan the platform from which to proclaim that blacks deserved the full rights of American citizens under our "color-blind" Constitution.

ROBERT HARLAN (1816–1897)

Much less is known for certain about Robert Harlan than about John. Black men and women, as individuals, were nearly invisible in Kentucky during the slavery period. Surviving accounts almost invariably treat blacks in the aggregate, noting few personal characteristics. Individual slaves had less personal history than fast horses or pedigreed dogs. Writers took little notice of them as individuals, and they rarely appeared in public records other than the minute books of the county courts, where individuals occasionally brushed against local authorities. Robert Harlan lived the first thirty-four years of his life as a member of this faceless human scenery. For this reason, his years in Kentucky are obscure. Most of the reliable information about him comes from his years in Cincinnati—after he acquired wealth and became active in Republican politics.

The most important narrative source of information about Robert Harlan's life is a brief sketch written by William J. Simmons, a black educator, and published in 1887 in Simmons' collection of biographies of notable black Americans, *Men of Mark: Eminent, Progressive and Rising*.[12] At the time this book was first published, Robert Harlan was in the Ohio legislature serving as one of the first elected black members of the state House of Representatives. Simmons reports that Robert Harlan was born in Mecklenburg County, Virginia, December 12, 1816, the son of a white father and a slave mother who was "three-parts" white. Simmons further states that Robert was brought to Kentucky at the age of eight and raised by James Harlan, the "father of the Hon. John M. Harlan, at present associate justice of the Supreme Court of the United States."

This is all the information about Robert's origin provided by Simmons or any other source published during Robert Harlan's lifetime. It is possible that Robert knew no more than this about his origin, however, this seems unlikely unless he was separated from his mother at a very early age.[13] If he knew or suspected who his father was, his public silence on this question is strange, unless he maintained his silence for his father's sake or that of his father's family.

Whatever may be the truth about the place of his birth, there is no doubt about his exceptional treatment at the hands of James Harlan. Robert was intelligent and ambitious, and was given some education in the Harlan household. Although Kentucky, unlike her sister states further South, never made it a crime to teach slaves to read and write, such behavior was not encouraged. Most slaveholders believed that a slave who could read would prove less manageable than one who could not. Slaves who could write were a direct threat to the slave system because that system relied upon written passes to restrict a slave's mobility.[14] A slave who could write could forge passes facilitating his own flight to freedom or assisting others in theirs.

Simmons wrote that James Harlan attempted to send Robert to school with James' own sons, but that Robert was "discovered" to be black and sent home. Simmons says that Robert was thereafter educated at home by James' older sons.[15] Surviving examples of Robert's speeches and letters show that he learned a great deal from these informal educational opportunities, although his polished work displays much more refinement than do his private letters. Because of his light skin and his education, Robert was almost certainly a house slave who spent much time with the Harlan family. Simmons wrote that Robert was trained as a barber, subsequently opened a barber shop in Harrodsburg, and later a grocery in Lexington.

Robert also seems to have been permitted to travel while still formally a slave. Simmons asserted that Robert had visited "almost every state in the Union [and Canada]," "with the consent of his owner" and "without restriction." This would represent remarkable freedom of movement for a man who was still nominally a slave. It is certain that he traveled widely after formal emancipation, and the restlessness he displayed later—a restlessness which took him to California in 1849 and produced later trips to Europe—coupled with his early interest in horse racing, offer some support for Simmons' report in this regard. Permitting such travel would have been consistent with James' other extraordinary treatment of Robert, although it entailed some risk of Robert being swept up by white patrollers.[16]

In 1848, James formally emancipated Robert. John Harlan was fifteen at the time. Frankfort was then a small community. It seems likely that John knew what his father intended to, and did do, that September morning before the county court. The county court records show that emancipations were unusual events, and it is likely that this one, especially since it involved a slave who was already believed to be a free man, elicited comment from James' neighbors. Surely John would have discussed Robert's unique status with his father at this time.

In late 1848, or early 1849, after reconnecting publicly with James Harlan long enough to be formally emancipated, Robert left his family and went to California in search of wealth.[17]

Robert went no further than San Francisco, where he amassed a fortune of $45,000 in less than two years.[18] Simmons does not state how Harlan made his money in California. One account printed after Harlan's death says he opened a store in San Francisco and made his fortune through trade.[19] If this were true, Simmons would probably have reported it. It also seems unlikely that Harlan could have accumulated so much money so quickly in this fashion. He may have obtained this money by gambling, by running either a faro or monte table in a San Francisco saloon. This seems confirmed by an admission later elicited from Robert by one of his political enemies, that gambling was the foundation of his wealth.[20]

When Harlan returned East in 1850, to settle in Cincinnati, Ohio, he was a very rich man. Robert's Kentucky wife had died during his absence, but as soon as he was established in Cincinnati he sent for his three surviving daughters and their grandmother. Legally free, and with money to invest, he bought real estate and a photography business. As a man of leisure, he began to concentrate on what was apparently the first love of his life, horse racing.[21] It stretches belief to imagine that Robert could have restrained himself from communicating his financial good fortune to his former master. If Robert informed James Harlan of his dramatic change of circumstances, such startling news would have been made known to John as well. John was living in his father's house during many of these years (he did not marry Malvina French Shanklin until 1856) and practicing law and politics at his father's side.

By 1852, Robert had remarried. Robert's first son was born in 1853 and was named Robert James Harlan.[22] That his son should be named after both Robert and Robert's benefactor is not surprising. It suggests that Robert felt good will toward James. It may also hint that Robert privately made a claim to a closer relationship to James than any he put forward in public. It would be remarkable if Robert had not announced to James Harlan the birth of a child named for him. This also suggests that contact between the Frankfort Harlans and the Cincinnati Harlans was maintained. Within a few months of the birth of his son, Robert Jr., Robert's second wife, Josephine M. Harlan, died.

Robert spent the 1850s speculating in real estate and racing horses. Having visited England in 1851, he decided in 1858 to emigrate with his family, reportedly taking his race horses, a trainer, and a jockey with him.

Perhaps it was the emotional impact of the United States Supreme Court's infamous *Dred Scott* decision, issued in 1857, that prompted Harlan to give up on the United States. This decision validated federal protection for the South's "peculiar institution" and sketched, in unmistakably bleak terms, the withered prospects for American blacks, North or South, slave or free.[23] It might have been, instead, the raising and then dashing of hope nearer home which finally convinced Robert Harlan that he had no future in his own country. In 1857, in apparent reaction to the *Dred Scott* decision, the Ohio legislature—under Republican leadership—enacted three new statutes granting blacks important rights. This must have taken some of the sting out of the Supreme Court opinion and the federal commitment to the apprehension of fugitive slaves. However, the next year, the Republican Party lost control of both houses of the Ohio legislature. The new Democratic majority quickly repealed all three of the 1857 acts, and passed a "visible admixture" law which made it a criminal offense for election officials to allow people with a "visible admixture of Negro blood" to vote. For Harlan, who was seven-eighths white, this must have seemed a burning, personal affront since it disenfranchised him.

Robert Harlan lived abroad for ten years, from late 1858 or early 1859, until 1869. He missed most of the turbulent decade of the 1860s, returning to Cincinnati in 1869, having lost most of his financial resources due to the dislocation of his investments during the Civil War. His financial decline was almost certainly exacerbated by gambling losses and the failure of his horse racing ventures in

Great Britain. It is possible that the passage of a bill granting suffrage to Ohio blacks in 1869 played a part in inducing Robert to return to Cincinnati.[24]

Whatever prompted his return to the United States in 1869, Cincinnati, at that time, offered to talented, ambitious black men opportunities that had never before been available. The triumph of the North in the Civil War, the ratification of the Fifteenth Amendment, guaranteeing northern blacks the vote, and the partisan interests of the Republican Party combined to open apparently breath-taking opportunities for prominent blacks. All they need do was to attach the new black voters to the Republican electoral machine—*attach* them to the party, *not integrate* them into it. Robert Harlan recognized these possibilities and, in early 1870, threw himself into politics as a vocation. He set about making himself useful to the white Republican leadership of the city and the state, and quickly became a thoroughgoing party man.

By 1871, Robert was deeply engaged in Republican politics in Ohio. He was given serious consideration as a candidate for the state legislature from Cincinnati in 1871, and acquired substantial support before being defeated in the county convention. He met President Grant in the summer of 1871, and became one of Grant's most important adherents in the Ohio black community.[25] In 1872, Harlan became one of two representatives from Cincinnati elected to the Republican State Central Committee, the second black man ever to serve in this capacity. Also in 1872, he attended the national Republican convention held in Philadelphia as one of six Ohio alternates at-large. In this delegation, as a delegate-at-large, was future President Rutherford B. Hayes. In the presidential election of that year, Robert worked hard for Grant's re-election.

For his efforts on behalf of the party, Harlan received the first significant federal patronage position given to an Ohio black man. He was appointed in 1873 as Special Inspector of the United States Post Office at Cincinnati. The 1873 register of federal employees lists Harlan as a Special Agent for "mail depredations."[26] The postal laws and regulations that were in effect in 1873 fixed a special agent's salary at $1600 per year, and a Post Office *Register* entry for 1873 lists Harlan's compensation in this amount. The regulations also provided for the payment of five dollars per day "for traveling and incidental expenses, while actually employed in the service." Robert had found in politics the additional income he needed to again enjoy "the good life." But his good fortune was short-lived. It appears that he was removed from office in January or February 1875.

Part of Robert Harlan's importance was fortuitous. Ohio was a critically important state in any national campaign in the 1870s and 1880s. This was reflected in the Republican presidential candidacies of Hayes and James A. Garfield in 1876 and 1880 respectively. Because Ohio was so important, and because it was evenly balanced between the Republican and Democratic parties during this period, the importance of the state's black vote was magnified. Robert Harlan was the right man in the right place at the right time. He was lucky, but he was astute in his seizure of the opportunity presented by this state of affairs.

In these years Robert also saw to the education and support of his son, Robert

Jr. He sent him to Woodward High School—a white school—where William Howard Taft was a classmate. Robert Jr. attended the Cincinnati Law College, and worked as a clerk from 1872 until 1878, when the younger man was appointed a deputy United States internal revenue collector. In 1887, Robert Jr.'s occupation was listed for the first time as "attorney" in the Cincinnati directory, and he was listed in the same way in the directories for 1890 and 1891.

Meanwhile, Robert attended Ohio state Republican conventions throughout the 1870s and 1880s.[27] He also attended the national Republican conventions held in 1884 and 1888 in Chicago, serving in the Ohio delegations with future President William McKinley, Jr., in 1884, and with Governor, later United States Senator, Joseph B. Foraker in 1888. In the late 1870s, Robert Harlan aligned himself with the Garfield forces in Ohio and nationally.[28] In the 1880s, after President Garfield's assassination, he supported Joseph Foraker, defending him against charges that Foraker was cool in his support of black rights.[29]

After nearly winning a seat in the state legislature from Cincinnati in 1880, Robert succeeded in obtaining a second federal patronage job in 1882, when he was appointed Special United States Customs Inspector at Cincinnati by President Chester A. Arthur. Harlan's application and recommendation file[30] has survived and opens a small window into his political life. Applying originally for reappointment to the position as special postal agent that he had held under Grant, Harlan solicited and received letters of support from many important Republican politicians.

Robert was able to obtain letters of recommendation from former President Grant as well as from prominent local and state Ohio Republicans. Grant's letter, dated December 6, 1881, states, "I know the Colonel very well. . . . I think him in every way well qualified for the place."[31] In addition to that of Grant, Harlan's application file contains letters from William Lawrence, who calls Harlan "my friend" and writes,

> [h]is long service as a Republican, his capacity for usefulness and the fact that he
> is a representative man of his race give him strong claims which I hope you can
> find it practical to recognize—His many friends, of whom I am one would be grat-
> ified if this can be done.[32]

Both Cincinnati Republican Congressmen, Thomas L. Young and Benjamin Butterworth, supported Harlan's appointment, as did Ohio United States Senator George H. Pendleton, of Cincinnati, and eleven other Ohio congressmen. Butterworth pressed repeatedly and hard for Harlan's appointment. All of these men commented upon Harlan's service and usefulness to the Republican party. A number noted the importance of appointing a black man to office. Halstead, the long-time editor and publisher of the *Cincinnati Commercial*, the leading Republican newspaper in southern Ohio, wrote in support of Harlan's appointment, as did Alphonso Taft, the father of future President and Chief Justice William Howard Taft.[33]

The list of references is remarkable, demonstrating both Harlan's sophistication about who controlled federal patronage in Ohio and his ability to obtain support from southern Ohio's most important Republican officials. There is no reference from John Marshall Harlan in the file, but given Robert's clout in Ohio Republican circles by this time, this fact is less surprising than it would have been in 1873. By now, Robert Harlan had a long political reach of his own. In 1877, when John Harlan's name was being suggested for appointment to the Supreme Court, John apparently asked Robert to support his nomination among Robert's Ohio contacts. Robert made overtures to his friends (who were friends of President Hayes) and wrote to John to reassure him that his name would be submitted.[34] Robert had less reason to appeal to John for help now than he had in 1873, and John may well have been less well placed to provide written assistance of this kind once he took his place on the United States Supreme Court in 1877. Certainly, he did not have the same private connection to the Arthur administration that Bristow at first had provided him to Grant.

In 1886, after fifteen years of effort, Robert Harlan won a seat in the Ohio legislature. He was the second black man elected to one of the Cincinnati seats—the first being attorney George Washington Williams in 1880—and the fourth black man ever elected to the state House of Representatives. Harlan listed his occupation as "Horseman."[35]

Throughout this period, Robert retained his position as a special inspector in the United States customs service, serving until 1892. In these years, he was also able to obtain patronage appointments for his son. Robert Jr., who had been trained as a lawyer, served as a surveyor in the Cincinnati City Water Works in 1889. He was appointed a license deputy in the City Auditor's office in 1892, and a deputy in the County Treasurer's office in 1893, a position which he seems to have held at least until the late 1890s. This suggests that Robert was also well connected to the Republican city administration of George B. Cox—"Boss" Cox of Cincinnati.

In his final years, Robert was less visible politically, and it is not certain that he maintained his importance in the Republican Party. What seems clear is that he continued to struggle to promote the interests of his son, Robert Jr., as long as he was able, attempting to pass to him whatever resources he commanded. Most of these were political rather than financial. After being ejected from his third wife's home on Harrison Street in 1895, and after living alone for a year, Robert Harlan moved into his son's house on Baymiller Street. He died there, two months short of his eighty-first birthday, on the morning of September 19, 1897. No will was probated and no dying statements concerning his paternity were reported. Most of Cincinnati's prominent black citizens attended his funeral.

Robert Harlan had struggled his entire life to obtain a shadow of the opportunities presented to John Harlan at birth. Robert had been forced to swim against the current of racism in both Kentucky and Cincinnati. He learned what was necessary in order to maximize the limited autonomy Kentucky society permitted blacks, and he succeeded in finding a niche in the power structure of Cincinnati.

He seized opportunities whenever they presented themselves both for himself and for his son, Robert Jr. Robert was strong enough to make a reasonably good life for himself and his family, but he also suffered from the personal flaws that were produced in him by lifelong oppression. As an illegitimate son he craved recognition, and he sought the respect of people who would never give it to a black man. He suffered racist abuse even from his Republican allies in Cincinnati, receiving the message over and over again that he was important not as an individual, but as an instrument. Even in post-war Ohio, he was not a person, but a thing.

He lived by his wits, and when necessary did so at the expense of others. His success was a reflection of his intelligence and his willingness to seize the main chance. His restlessness is apparent from the range of his wanderings. He seems to have been a man who never quite got what he wanted, though he often came close. His influence depended on his ability to be useful. He surely must have experienced the insecurity that awareness of this would bring.

He was as courageous, in his own way, as James or John Harlan. Despite being white enough to "pass," he seems never to have made the attempt. His position throughout his life enabled him to see far across the color line. He knew the possibilities of life on the white side of that line, and yet throughout his life he chose to remain "black" and struggle against the prejudices and handicaps he could have left behind. In all of his contacts with white politicians, he seems to have emphasized his black status, and to have appealed to them as a representative of the black community. For a relatively brief period, in the 1870s, his skin color became an asset instead of an unmitigated liability. Thereafter, he was trapped in the role when the circumstances of the country changed in the last two decades of the nineteenth century. The national Republican Party shifted its focus from race to economics, and the country reverted to its antebellum racist consensus. As a result, Robert's influence waned. He was unable to transfer that influence intact to his son, who found that the strategies that had worked for his father in the 1870s worked no longer.

Who Was Robert Harlan's Father?

MISCEGENATION IN THE ANTEBELLUM UPPER SOUTH: A PATTERN OF CONDUCT

Robert Harlan was born into a biracial Southern world in which whites owned human beings and blacks were forced to submit to nearly absolute white authority or die. It was a society in which the races were separated by a strict caste line that was supported by profound social, economic, and ideological differences between the races. But it was also a society in which blacks and whites were constantly brought into intimate contact with each other by the slave system.

The racial intimacy required by the slave system in the South and the profound vulnerability of blacks when presented with demands from white masters and satellite whites produced common, if disapproved, interracial sexual encounters. These encounters in turn produced large numbers of mulatto offspring. Robert Harlan was one of these children. If Robert Harlan's mother was one-quarter black, a "quadroon," and his father was a white man, Robert was one-eighth black, an "octoroon"[36]—he had one black great-grandparent, like Plessy in the famous "separate but equal" case, *Plessy v. Ferguson*.[37] Perhaps it was more than coincidence that led John Marshall Harlan to write one of his most famous and impassioned dissents in defense of the civil rights of black Americans on Plessy's behalf. Because of the character of Robert's birth and the scarcity of historical records on slave births, we will never know the names of his parents with certainty.[38]

Is it possible that Robert knew or suspected that he had a Harlan father and chose to conceal this fact from the public during his lifetime? If he had claimed his patrimony publicly, at any time, the claim would have been doubted in the absence of acknowledgment by James or some other member of the white Harlan family. It seems likely that Robert was genuinely grateful to James for his humane treatment, and that there were bonds of affection between these men that prevented the younger man from publicly proclaiming their blood tie. Affection and gratitude for James is suggested by Robert's naming his only son after his former master. Affection also comes through occasionally in Robert's letters to John. When John agreed to serve on the Louisiana election commission in April 1877, Robert wrote him:

> I beg to repeat to you the words of an old colored man that formerly belong [sic] to your father—they were do-do-take care.
> I do not care which way you may decide the Louisiana question your [sic] bound to make enemies especially if you take a leading part in the matter.[39]

Disclosure would certainly have embarrassed James and John, and deeply hurt their family. It also would have damaged James' own political prospects and those of his legitimate son, John. It is possible that there were conditions attached to James' generosity toward, and sponsorship of, Robert—one condition being that Robert never publicly claim the blood relationship. It is possible that any secret assistance Robert may have received from John Harlan later was given upon the same terms. All of these possibilities rest on speculation, but the point is that there may have been reasons for Robert to maintain consistently a lie about the circumstances of his birth. There is a reference in one of Robert's letters to John that suggests that some of Robert's political associates in Cincinnati were aware of some connection between Robert and John. In a letter dated October 4, 1873, Robert invited John to make a campaign speech in Cincinnati in support of Republican candidates. In the letter Robert explained, "The campaign committee requested me to write you thinking I might have more influence with you than they had."[40] This reference does not necessarily relate to a claim of blood ties, but it does suggest that there was an awareness, at least in some Republican circles in Cincinnati, that Robert had a special relationship with John.

WAS JAMES HARLAN ROBERT HARLAN'S FATHER?
PHYSICAL CHARACTERISTICS

Although by no means conclusive, Robert's size and physical resemblance to the "Big Red" branch of the Harlan family argues strongly against the paternity of a stranger to that clan. Robert Harlan was a big man. He stood over six feet tall and weighed more than 200 pounds.[41] He had blue-grey eyes, light skin, and black, straight hair. He was physically vigorous and healthy his whole life and traveled extensively. When Robert died in 1897, at age eighty, the average life expectancy for a black man was thirty-two years. That of white males was only forty-eight. Robert Harlan's son, Robert Jr., also lived at least into his late seventies. Both men were long-lived, and modern mortality studies indicate that heredity is an important factor in family longevity.

There are a number of portraits of Robert Harlan that were published during his lifetime. The best of these appeared in 1886 in an Ohio newspaper.[42] In this detailed etching, which is captioned "Col. Robert Harlan, Member of the Ohio Legislature," Harlan's fine features stare out in a right full-face profile. His most prominent features are a rounded pate with a high, full forehead crowned by a receding hairline of short, straight hair which has reached the peak of his head. He has large ears with full earlobes and a firm, well-defined jawline. A large, full mustache sitting below a straight, slightly bulbous nose dominates the face and covers the mouth, preventing any view of the lips. The smooth skin of the face—it is remarkably wrinkle free given his age—ends in a pointed chin. Heavy brows cover narrow eyes which turn down at the outside, imparting almost a squinting expression. The entire face is lean and shows strength.

When I first saw this picture, I was struck by the similarity it bore to a famous picture of Justice John Marshall Harlan taken while he was a member of the Supreme Court. In that picture, John Harlan's rounded dome of a head with its crowning fringe of hair displays, it seems to me, a number of the same features. The shape of the head is similar. The large forehead is similar. The receding hairline, the short, straight hair (which had been red in his youth), and the large ears are there, as is the large earlobe and the strong jaw. The nose is the same, though fuller and more bulbous. The smooth skin, the heavy brows, the squinting eyes—they too were blue—and the pointed chin are all there. The wide mouth, with its narrow lips and distinctive scowl, made me long for the look behind Robert Harlan's mustache that I will never have. Although John Harlan's face is fuller—John was overweight in his later years—I thought they could be brothers. Of course, my "perception" may have been affected by my knowledge that Robert had grown up in James Harlan's household.

The only portrait of James Harlan, John's father, with which I am familiar is an oil painting by an unknown artist in the collection of the Kentucky State Historical Society's museum at the Old Statehouse in Frankfort, Kentucky. That portrait shows a middle-aged man with a high forehead and thinning straight red hair, with the familiar Harlan nose and strong jawline. His eyes appear to be grey or hazel, although it is difficult to tell what color was intended by the artist. They look out from behind wire-rimmed antique glasses and heavy brows. The earlobe of the left ear, which is just visible below the long hair on the side of James' head, is large. The mouth is firmly set and surrounded by thin lips. The face is ruddy, and thinner than John Harlan's—in this respect more resembling Robert's than John's—but the resemblance between father and son, between James and John, is pronounced.

Both James Harlan and John Marshall Harlan, like Robert Harlan, were big men. James was over six feet tall.[43] John was six feet two. James probably had grey or hazel eyes. John's eyes were blue. Both men had ruddy complexions, and sandy red hair.

The factors discussed here do not prove the existence of a blood relationship between James Harlan and Robert Harlan. Physical resemblance is a matter of opinion and the presence of blue eyes, straight hair, and large size do not establish blood relationship. Their cumulative effect, as with so much else about this tale, is suggestive. When considered along with other factors, they become more so.

JAMES HARLAN'S TREATMENT OF ROBERT HARLAN

In his powerful treatment of slavery, *Roll, Jordan, Roll*, Eugene Genovese concluded that "[t]hose mulattoes who received special treatment usually were kin to their white folks."[44] While by no means conclusive, evidence of Robert's special treatment by James is important to any consideration of the relationship between these two men.

Sometimes little things escape notice. Robert Harlan lived under that name throughout his life (as far as public records can establish this fact), and as Paul McStallworth[45] indicated, it was no small thing for Robert to have been permitted to take the Harlan family name, and use it while still a slave.

Although it was common for freed slaves to take the family name of their former masters after the Civil War, this practice was rarer in the antebellum South. Perhaps this was simply because the planter families frowned upon it. Perhaps they did so for no more obscure reason than that use of the family name bestowed more humanity upon slaves than most owners found comfortable. One could call many other chattels by name, a horse or a dog, for example, but few of these "things" had two names, one of which associated it directly with the master's family. Perhaps it was this public association that was unacceptable, because it invited speculation and rumors that a family with self-respect and social position preferred to prevent. It was a rare thing indeed for a slave to be permitted to use the family name while still in bondage. Such permission came very close to an informal acknowledgment of familial connection. But allowing Robert Harlan to use the Harlan family name was not the only unusual privilege which James Harlan extended to his slave, Robert.

At least as early as 1840—eight years before his formal emancipation—Robert Harlan appears in the public records of Lexington, Kentucky, with the designation "free man of color" next to his name.[46] Accounts of Robert's life state that James Harlan permitted Robert to set up in Harrodsburg as a barber in the 1830s, and as a grocer in Lexington in the 1840s. While in Harrodsburg, Robert might still have been living in James' household. However, James moved to Frankfort in 1840 to become Secretary of State, and Robert established himself in Lexington that same year. Robert must have been living on his own in Lexington. The city tax records for Lexington support this hypothesis. The records listed heads of household and independent individuals only. Robert's "household" appears in the records in the years 1841–1848.[47] Robert lived with a free woman "of color" throughout the 1840s, and she bore him five daughters between 1842 and 1848, when Robert disappeared from the Lexington records.[48]

Robert's status as a "non-slave" is especially surprising since it was illegal under the laws of Kentucky for Robert to live as a free man, working for his own account in Harrodsburg and Lexington. It was a criminal offense for James Harlan to permit him to do so and James could not have been ignorant of this fact.

The risks for James grew more immediate in 1847. Robert was living in Lexington and James in Frankfort, twenty miles away. James could no longer provide Robert with the informal protection that was probably possible when they both lived in Harrodsburg in the 1830s. Now, too, James' visibility as a Whig leader in the state made both men more vulnerable to James' political enemies. This point must have been driven home to James when the court of appeals handed down its decision in *Parker v. Commonwealth*,[49] in December 1847.

In *Parker*, the court sustained a verdict against a slaveholder under an indictment that was challenged as insufficient. The slaveholder was indicted for permitting her slave, Clarissa, "to go at large and hire herself by permission of the plaintiff in error, who was her owner."[50]

It is possible that the *Parker* decision influenced James to convert Robert's de facto emancipation into formal, de jure manumission in September 1848. However, it must have been Robert's decision to leave the state—and James' protection—for the California gold fields, which made legal emancipation absolutely necessary.

Robert remained in contact with John's brother James. James had practiced law with John in Louisville in the 1870s and served later as a judge in Louisville. However, James appears to have been an alcoholic and to have suffered a tragic decline. His correspondence with John about his circumstances and his need for money is agitated and moving. John apparently tried to assist James in ways which would not result in supplying his brother with liquor.

> In some of James' letters he refers to Robert Harlan. In May 1888, James wrote John: It is well settled beyond change that I cant [sic] stay here. I am afraid to do so. Bob Harlan has often [the word "promised" is struck through] offered to asst [sic] me but I do not wish to be driven to the necessity of appealing to him—My position is as despicable and contemptible as it can be and few have been so utterly abandoned by fate as I have.[51]

In another letter, James seems almost to threaten John with an appeal to Robert: "If you cant [sic] help me I can try others—Bob Harlan will let me have the money if he has it . . . ."[52] In July of the same year, James' fortunes took a turn for the better, and he wrote John a newsy letter from James' new home in the Indian (soon to be Oklahoma) Territory. In it he told John that "Bob Harlan has for two years been unusually kind to me, not however putting me under obligation."[53]

Surely James would not have turned to Robert for money unless he believed the older man had financial means. It is possible, of course, that James turned to Robert not as a family member, but as a former family slave who owed the Harlan family a great debt of gratitude. However, from the content of James' surviving letters to John it appears that his appeals for financial help were directed primarily at family or very close friends of the family, like John's former law partner, Augustus Willson. The fact that James maintained contact with Robert and looked to him for financial assistance is suggestive. The anguish James felt when driven to ask for Robert's assistance, and his assumption that such an appeal would discomfit John enough to wring money from the Justice, offers support for the family connection hypothesis when added to the rest of the evidence.

Did Robert Harlan Help Shape John Marshall Harlan's Views on Race?

Most of the scholarly writings about the first Justice Harlan offer, at best, tentative explanations for his behavior on the Supreme Court. We need more studies of the details of his life and personal relationships if we are to understand better this complex and important Justice. One of the most important enigmas about John Harlan that remains is the source of his progressive attitude concerning the legal rights of America's black citizens.

My own research has convinced me that one of the keys to understanding the sources of John Harlan's personal and judicial values is his relationship with his father, James. John Harlan loved and respected his father. Through James' relationship with Robert Harlan, and through John's own contacts with Robert, Robert was well situated to influence John's understanding of race. John's own contacts with Robert began in childhood and continued at least until the time of John's appointment to the Supreme Court. John's experiences with Robert were different in quality from those he had with other blacks because of Robert's special relationship with James Harlan. If the blood tie I have suggested existed, and if John knew it, then Robert's effect on John would have been profound. Even if my hypothesis of a blood relationship is rejected, the duration and intensity of contacts between John, James, and Robert are certain to have had some impact on the future Justice and should be explored as fully as the surviving sources permit.

At the very least, John's connection to Robert would have made empty abstractions about race impossible for John. Robert humanized, for John, all cases involving the rights of black Americans. John knew through personal experience what the legal disabilities imposed upon blacks—the disabilities against which John Harlan raged in his Supreme Court opinions—meant in people's lives. At the very least, Robert put a face on the millions of human beings who were forced to live their lives in the shadow of the Supreme Court's racist opinions. Robert made John see the human beings behind the briefs. This must certainly have been true in a case like *Plessy v. Ferguson*,[54] where the plaintiff was seven-eighths white—like Robert. John's devotion to his religion offers another key to understanding his behavior—a topic I hope to explore in the future. Once John Harlan could see blacks as individual human beings, his religious convictions compelled him to extend to them the rights all human beings deserved. This alone might have set John Harlan apart from his fellow Justices, for whom race was largely an abstract matter.

Through Robert, John would also have experienced, vicariously, the consequences of the color line. Robert was raised in the household of a humane slaveholder. He had money and great opportunity for a man of color in his time. Despite these "advantages," Robert was denied all of the opportunities that were John's from birth. Through Robert, John could experience the pain of butting doors which would never open no matter how meritorious he might be as an individual. In reviewing the story of Robert's life, John must have been acutely aware of the significance of the color line. Robert's slightly brown skin had rendered his considerable talents largely irrelevant to a color-conscious, racist society. Indeed, this circumstance alone had robbed Robert of the Harlan birthright which helped John to prosper throughout his life.

If Robert Harlan helped to shape John Harlan's views about race in any of these ways, he made a lasting contribution to John's fame. Through John's words, Robert also left a mark on his country. He helped to start America's eventual, painful re-examination of the assumptions underlying its racist consensus. In this way, Robert left his descendants and his country a wonderful legacy.

Separate, but Never Equal

A concealing fog curls about Robert Harlan's connection to the Harlans of Kentucky. It may be the kind of fog one occasionally finds hiding the violation of a taboo. It is also possible that this fog is of the ordinary variety, the kind that rises without assistance from the passage of time and the loss or deterioration of historical sources. The critical difficulty in the case of the Harlans is to distinguish this kind of "normal" obscurity from the other.

In the case of the Harlans, religious standing, guilt over a breach of private morality, and concern over the potential destructive political power of damaging information would have encouraged both James and John to conceal Robert's blood tie if it existed. But genuine religious conviction and mature moral character would also have encouraged both to take responsibility for ameliorating Robert's life to the extent that it was in their power to do so. Robert might have concealed his paternity out of love or gratitude, or he may not have known whether his father was a Harlan or not. Given the character of the problem addressed and the paucity of the surviving sources, we probably can never be certain whether or not Robert Harlan was James Harlan's son. In my own mind, however, I am convinced that he was.

James Harlan gave all four of his acknowledged sons good educations, ultimately training them all for the bar. John attended the best local grammar school, the best local college (Centre), and the best law school in the West (Transylvania). James could offer no such opportunities to Robert. James could entertain no such plans for him.

No vocation in law or politics was possible. Just as James could not provide Robert with formal education, neither could he treat him like a son in other respects given the time and place in which they lived.

John received the benefits of being the son of a famous father, and a member of a powerful family. He received counsel from that father and James' help in launching his political career. Robert fought through most of his life alone, illegitimate, black, and unacknowledged. Still he managed to succeed. James Harlan was a good master to his slaves and to Robert in particular. But, at best, Robert received a modest start from James. The great irony of his story is that the treatment he received was so much better than that received by so many others with "tainted" blood like Plessy's and his own.

Even in the ranks of the party that had destroyed slavery and nationalized freedom, the disparity of treatment continued. The Republican Party could serve John Marshall Harlan's ambitions; Robert Harlan could only serve the party. John Harlan could aspire to the governorship of his state and win the prize of a seat on the United States Supreme Court. Robert Harlan labored long and hard among black Ohioans on behalf of that same party, receiving in return two federal patronage jobs and, eventually, a contested one-term seat in the Ohio House of Representatives.

John could lead the party; Robert could only follow it. John could reshape the party; Robert was forced to shape himself to it. John was admired and lionized, while Robert was forced to suffer chronic contempt from his white allies, and the jibes of some of his own people that he was too white. John could educate his sons at the finest schools and offer them access into the best social, economic, and political circles in white America. Robert struggled his entire life to capture and hold onto minor but respectable patronage jobs for his only son, Robert Jr., in order to prevent that son's descent into poverty and disgrace. In short, John Harlan could aspire to and achieve his heart's desire. Robert Harlan was forced to dream smaller dreams, swallow more bile, and content himself with a scrambling and precarious political existence.

John Harlan was a remarkable, talented, and ambitious man. He had the great good fortune to be born the son of a father who was a political leader in his native state, and to find himself on the top side of the color line. Robert was also remarkable, talented, and ambitious. It is possible that he was born the son of the same father, although at a time when James was still really a child himself and dependent upon his own parents. It was Robert's misfortune to find himself on the bottom side of the color line. His disability was to be the illegitimate son of racially mixed parents in a society that empowered white slaveholders and their sons to sire mulatto children, and then cursed these children because they were constant reminders of the moral implications, for masters and slaves, of absolute human bondage. It was Robert Harlan's misfortune to have been born a slave of mixed blood and thus consigned by white society to a limbo between masters and slaves. It was his good fortune, as it was John's, to have been raised in the household of a man who, as an adult, was strong enough and moral enough to feel obligations to *all* of his sons.

James Harlan gave Robert all that Kentucky slave society would permit. In many ways, he even went secretly beyond what his neighbors could accept. He tried to give Robert some education, his de facto freedom, and a start in life. From these assets Robert built a relatively good life. In the process, he gave James' famous son a gift. He gave the first Justice Harlan insight. Through his contact with Robert, John Harlan developed a special way of seeing the problems involving race which came before him as a judge. It was this insight that made him unique in his understanding of the real costs, to both blacks and whites, of the color line.

One year before Robert Harlan's death, John Harlan wrote in dissent in *Plessy v. Ferguson*, "The destinies of the two races, in this country, are indissolubly linked together, and the interests of both require that the common government of all shall not permit the seeds of race hate to be planted under the sanction of law."[55] I wonder whether, when John Harlan penned these words, he reflected on their truth in his own life. His life, his father's life, and Robert's life had indeed been "indissolubly linked together." That link, like the country's, was forged in slavery and continued into an ambiguous twilight of freedom. Drawing upon his own experience for inspiration, John Harlan wrote of a color-blind future, and by writing about it began the process of creating it. In a way, the writing of these words was John Marshall Harlan's greatest achievement.

Given his opportunities and the culture into which he was born and against which he had to fight every day of his life, Robert Harlan's successes were quite as remarkable as those of his half-brother John. John Harlan proved a worthy son of a worthy father. When all is considered, so did Robert.

NOTES

1. The entry on the *Order Book* of the Franklin County Court reads as follows: "A Deed of emancipation from James Harlan to his Slave Robert Harlan was this day produced in Court, and acknowledged by said James Harlan to be his act and deed, Whereupon it is ordered that the Clerk of this Court Issue to Said Robert Harlan who is ascertained to be of the following description vis aged thirty two years 12th decr next six feet high yellow big straight black hair Blue Gray eyes a Scar on his right wrist about the Size of a dime and Also a small [illegible] Scar on the upper lip. A certificate of his freedom accordingly, upon his giving bond with Security in the penalty of five hundred dollars Conditioned that the said Robert

Harlan shall not become a charge upon any County in this Commonwealth and thereupon the said James Harlan with George W Craddock his Security entered into and acknowledged bound to the Commonwealth accordingly which is approved by the Court."

FRANKLIN COUNTY COURT ORDER BOOK, Sept. 18, 1848, at 3.

2. FAYETTE COUNTY [KENTUCKY] MARRIAGE BONDS "COLORED," 1823–1874; LEXINGTON, KENTUCKY, CITY TAX RECORDS, 1841–1848.

3. WILLIAM J. SIMMONS, MEN OF MARK: EMINENT, PROGRESSIVE AND RISING 421 (Ebony Classics 1970) (1887).

4. *Id. See also* WILLARD B. GATEWOOD, ARISTOCRATS OF COLOR: THE BLACK ELITE, 1880–1920, at 19, 115–17 (1990); DAVID A. GERBER, BLACK OHIO AND THE COLOR LINE, 1860–1915, at 117–36, 209–44 (1976). Gatewood describes Robert Harlan as James Harlan's son. GATEWOOD, *supra* at 116. This assertion appears to rest on Paul McStallworth's statement to that effect in the *Dictionary of American Negro Biography* rather than on supplemental evidence. DICTIONARY OF AMERICAN NEGRO BIOGRAPHY 287–88 (Rayford W. Logan & Michael R. Winston eds., 1983); *see infra*.

5. This connection was made by Dr. Paul McStallworth in his brief biographical entry on "Robert James Harlan" in the *Dictionary of American Negro Biography*. DICTIONARY OF AMERICAN NEGRO BIOGRAPHY, *supra* note 4, at 287–88. Dr. McStallworth's conclusion appears to rest primarily upon a biographical article about Robert Harlan that was published in a Cincinnati newspaper 37 years after Robert's death. *See Brief Biography of Colonel Robert Harlan*, CINCINNATI UNION, Dec. 13, 1934.

A newly published biography of John Marshall Harlan refers to the blood relationship between John Harlan and Robert Harlan as an established fact, and puts Robert into the Harlan family tree on the inside cover of the book—as either the son of John's father, James, or as the son of John's grandfather, James the elder. The textual discussion of Robert is brief, covering less than two pages. LOREN P. BETH, JOHN MARSHALL HARLAN: THE LAST WHIG JUSTICE 12–13 (1992).

6. *See, e.g.*, Plessy v. Ferguson, 163 U.S. 537, 552–64 (1896) (Harlan, J., dissenting); Civil Rights Cases, 109 U.S. 3, 26–62 (1883) (Harlan, J., dissenting); *see also* BETH, *supra* note 5, at 223–39.

7. *Civil Rights Cases*, 109 U.S. at 62 (Harlan, J., dissenting).

8. *Id.* at 39–40.

9. *Plessy*, 163 U.S. at 554–55 (Harlan, J., dissenting).

10. *Id.* at 559.

11. John Harlan has been the subject of several articles, although fewer than he deserves. For a more detailed treatment of John's career and legal philosophy, as well as the biographical details outlined in this chapter, the reader is encouraged to refer to the following sources. *See generally* BETH, *supra* note 5 (the first book-length biography of Harlan); FLOYD B. CLARK, THE CONSTITUTIONAL DOCTRINES OF JUSTICE HARLAN (Da Capo Press 1969) (1915); Henry J. Abraham, *John Marshall Harlan: A Justice Neglected*, 41 Va. L. Rev. 871 (1955); Henry J. Abraham, *John Marshall Harlan: The Justice and the Man*, 46 Ky. L.J. 449 (1958); Florian Bartosic, *The Constitution, Civil Liberties and John Marshall Harlan*, 46 Ky. L.J. 407 (1958); Loren P. Beth, *President Hayes Appoints a Justice*, Y.B. Sup. Ct. Hist. Soc'y 68 (1989); David G. Farrelly, *A Sketch of John Marshall Harlan's Pre-*

Court Career, 10 VAND. L. REV. 209 (1957); David G. Farrelly, *Harlan's Formative Period: The Years Before the War*, 46 KY. L.J. 367 (1958) in LOUIS HARTZ, JOHN M. HARLAN IN KENTUCKY, 1855–1877: The Story of His Pre-Court Political Career, 14 Filson Club Hist. Q. 17 (1940). (the best published study of Harlan's political career before his appointment to the Court); Ellwood W. Lewis, *The Appointment of Mr. Justice Harlan*, 29 IND. L.J. 46 (1953); Lewis I. Maddocks, *The Two Justices Harlan on Civil Rights and Liberties: A Study in Judicial Contrasts*, 68 KY. L.J. 301 (1979–80); Robert T. McCracken, *Justice Harlan*, 60 U. PA. L. REV. 297 (1912); Edward F. Waite, *How "Eccentric" Was Mr. Justice Harlan?*, 37 MINN. L. REV. 173 (1953); Alan F. Westin, *The First Justice Harlan: A Self-Portrait from His Private Papers*, 46 KY. L.J. 321 (1958); Lewis I. Maddocks, Justice John Marshall Harlan: Defender of Individual Rights (1959) (unpublished Ph.D. dissertation, Ohio State University).

12. Simmons, *supra* note 3, at 421–22.

13. Separating small children from their slave mothers was a taboo that slaveholders seldom violated. *See generally* EUGENE D. GENOVESE, ROLL, JORDAN, ROLL 453–54 (Vintage Books 1976) (1972). Therefore, it seems likely that there would have been some time for Robert's mother to tell him something of his paternity.

14. *See* Jarrett v. Higbee, 21 Ky. (1 T.B. Mon.) 546 (1827).

15. Simmons, *supra* note 3. This seems unlikely since James did not marry until 1822, and had his first sons, Richard D. Harlan and William L. Harlan, in 1823 and 1825. By the time either of James' "older" sons could have taught Robert to read and write, he would have been a young adult. If he was educated in the Harlan household, it seems likely that James and his wife, Eliza Davenport Harlan, were his teachers. The editor of the *Cincinnati Enquirer* reported in Harlan's obituary:

> When this colored boy became old enough to go to school Judge Harlan sent him to the village school at Harrodsburg, along with his own boys. Although his appearance would hardly reveal the fact of his being a colored child, some one [sic] informed the school authorities of the fact the same day that the boy was admitted to the school and he was summarily discharged. Out of this circumstance Colonel Harlan often remarked that he had only "a half a day's schooling."

Life of Robert Harlan, CINCINNATI ENQUIRER, Sept. 22, 1897, at 6.

16. In describing such patrolling in Kentucky, J. Winston Coleman wrote, "It was the duty of the 'patterollers' to seize and whip every slave found away from home, unless on business or with the permission of his master or overseer, which had to be stated in writing." J. Winston Coleman, Jr., Slavery in Kentucky 99 (1940). For an example of a slave who seems to have been in the same position as Robert and who was arrested, see Jarrett v. Higbee, 21 Ky. (1 T.B. Mon.) 546 (1827).

17. SIMMONS, *supra* note 3, at 421.

18. *Id.* at 421.

19. *Life of Robert Harlan*, CINCINNATI ENQUIRER, Sept. 22, 1897, at 6.

20. *Colonel Harlan Visits the West End and Attends a Meeting—A Bit of His Political History By One Who Knows and Other Matters of Interest*, CINCINNATI COMMERCIAL, Sept. 4, 1871, at 8.

21. Robert Harlan's fascination with race horses seems to go back to his early youth. Although considered not quite respectable by middle class blacks in the late nineteenth century North, an interest in horse racing was a sign of breeding and social position in much of the South. Simmons wrote in 1887 that Harlan "enjoys sport as much as any one: indeed he is specially fond of horse-flesh, and can relish a fine animal as only a native Kentuckian knows how." Simmons, *supra* note 3, at 422.

22. DICTIONARY OF AMERICAN NEGRO BIOGRAPHY, *supra* note 4, at 288.

23. Dred Scott v. Sandford, 60 U.S. (19 How.) 393 (1856).

24. BLACKS IN OHIO HISTORY: A CONFERENCE TO COMMEMORATE THE BICENTENNIAL OF THE AMERICAN REVOLUTION 18 (Ruben F. Weston ed., n.d.). (In the collection of the National Afro-American Museum and Cultural Center of Wilberforce, Ohio.)

25. Robert Harlan loyally clung to the Republican Party, even when other influential blacks expressed dismay at the party's refusal to share patronage with its black adherents and to nominate black candidates for office. *See* GERBER, *supra* note 4, at 209–44. Gerber calls Harlan "the Grant administration's leading black officeholder in Ohio." *Id.* at 221. Gerber's book offers a lucid and complete treatment of black life in Ohio. His discussion of politics is especially enlightening. From Gerber's treatment, it is clear that Robert Harlan was an extremely important black politician in the 1870s and 1880s.

26. REGISTER OF THE OFFICERS AND AGENTS, CIVIL, MILITARY, AND NAVAL, IN THE SERVICE OF THE UNITED STATES, ON THE THIRTIETH OF SEPTEMBER, 1873, at 438.

27. *See* Letter from Robert Harlan to John Marshall Harlan (Mar. 28, 1876).

28. *See* Letter from Robert Harlan to James Garfield (Sept. 3, 1880) (available in James A. Garfield Papers, Library of Congress); Telegram from Robert Harlan to James Garfield (Nov. 3, 1880) (available in James A. Garfield Papers, Library of Congress).

29. *Letter to the Editor by Robert Harlan,* CLEVELAND GAZETTE (Feb. 7, 1885).

30. Record Group 56, Special Agents Applications and Recommendations File for Robert J. Harlan (available in General Records of the Treasury Department, National Archives).

31. Letter from Ulysses S. Grant to Charles J. Folger, Secretary of the Treasury (Dec. 6, 1881) (in Record Group 56, Special Agents Applications and Recommendations File for Robert J. Harlan (available in General Records of the Treasury Department, National Archives)).

32. Letter from William Lawrence to Chester A. Arthur (Dec. 3, 1881) (in Record Group 56, Special Agents Applications and Recommendations File for Robert J. Harlan (available in General Records of the Treasury Department, National Archives)).

33. *See* Record Group 56, *supra* note 30.

34. "[A]s regards your matter I spoke to John W. Heron about it. He informed me that he and others had spoke [sic] to the President while here in your favor, and that he had no doubt that you would be appointed." Letter from Robert Harlan to John Marshall Harlan (Oct. 10, 1877) (available in John Marshall Har-

lan Papers, Library of Congress). Robert may have been one of the first people to write to John about the younger man's appointment to the high court. In a letter written in early March 1877, Robert reported,

> Mr. Halstead [the editor/publisher of the Republican *Cincinnati Commercial*] said to me this afternoon that Hayes told him that you were on his Slate for anything you wanted—he further said that he could not understand it in way [sic] others worry that Hayes intended to offer you Judge Davis's [sic] place on the bench.

Letter from Robert Harlan to John Marshall Harlan (Mar. 7, 1877) (available in John Marshall Harlan Papers, Library of Congress).

35. BLACKS IN OHIO HISTORY, *supra* note 24, at 19.

36. The word "mulatto" was generally used to describe anyone with a visible mixture of white and black blood. *See* JOEL WILLIAMSON, NEW PEOPLE: MISCEGENATION AND MULATTOES IN THE UNITED STATES xii (1980). A "quadroon" was a person with one black grandparent.

References to Robert Harlan frequently described him as blue-eyed and very lightskinned. Various accounts commented on Robert's "whiteness" and observed that it was hard to distinguish him from a white man. Some people questioned his right to represent blacks because he was so white in appearance. *See,. e.g.,* CINCINNATI COMMERCIAL, Sept. 7, 1871, at 4. One of these compared Robert Harlan to a white political rival and commented that there was no detectable difference in their skin color. Ulysses S. Grant made a similar observation about Robert's white appearance in 1881 when he wrote, "I know the Colonel very well. He is an intelligent colored man (although you would probably not discover that unless your attention was called to the fact) . . . ." Letter from Ulysses S. Grant to Charles J. Folger (Dec. 6, 1881), Record Group 56, *supra* note 31.

37. 163 U.S. 537 (1896).

38. The breadth of this problem is well illustrated by the examples of the two most prominent mulattoes in nineteenth century America. Neither Frederick Douglass, the great black abolitionist orator, nor Booker T. Washington, the founder of Tuskegee Institute and Douglass' successor as spokesman for black America, ever identified their white fathers. In both of these cases, neither man seems to have known who his father was, and there is no existing evidence which would permit biographers to fill in this important blank. The problem becomes obviously even more pronounced when one seeks information about less prominent mulattoes.

39. Letter from Robert Harlan to John Marshall Harlan (Apr. 14, 1877) (available in John Marshall Harlan Papers, Library of Congress).

40. Letter from Robert Harlan to John Marshall Harlan (Oct. 4, 1873) (available in John Marshall Harlan Papers, Library of Congress).

41. *"Colonel" Robert Harlan,* CLEVELAND GAZETTE, Oct. 2, 1897, at 1. See also the physical description of Robert contained in his emancipation record. FRANKLIN COUNTY COURT ORDER BOOK, *supra* note 1.

42. *Honorable Robert Harlan,* CINCINNATI GAZETTE, May 1, 1886.

43. *Lawyers and Lawmakers of Kentucky,* the late-nineteenth-century collective biography of the Kentucky bar, described James Harlan as "the huge,

brawny, fair-haired, near-sighted, generous attorney general, . . . gigantic in body and mind." LAWYERS AND LAWMAKERS OF KENTUCKY 108 (Southern Historical Press 1982) (H. Levin ed., 1897).

44. GENOVESE, *supra* note 13, at 429.

45. DICTIONARY OF AMERICAN NEGRO BIOGRAPHY, *supra* note 4, at 287.

46. *See* FAYETTE COUNTY MARRIAGE BONDS (Nov. 19, 1840), *supra* note 2; LEXINGTON CITY TAX RECORDS (1840), *supra* note 2.

47. *See* LEXINGTON CITY TAX RECORDS (1841–48), *supra* note 2.

48. *Id.* One of these daughters died in 1845. LEXINGTON CITY TAX RECORDS (1845), *supra.*

49. Parker v. Commonwealth, 47 Ky. (8 B. Mon.) 30 (1847).

50. *Id.* at 30.

51. Letter from James Harlan to John Marshall Harlan (May 10, 1888) (available in John Marshall Harlan Papers, University of Louisville Law School).

52. Letter from James Harlan to John Marshall Harlan (May 14, 1888) (available in John Marshall Harlan Papers, University of Louisville Law School).

53. Letter from James Harlan to John Marshall Harlan (July 27, 1888) (available in John Marshall Harlan Papers, University of Louisville Law School).

54. 163 U.S. 537 (1896).

55. Plessy v. Ferguson, 163 U.S. 537, 560 (1896) (Harlan, J., dissenting).

13 The Second Amendment: Toward an Afro-Americanist Reconsideration

ROBERT J. COTTROL and RAYMOND T. DIAMOND

T H E threat that free blacks posed to southern slavery was twofold. First, free blacks were a bad example to slaves. For a slave to see free blacks enjoy the trappings of white persons—freedom of movement, expression, and association, relative freedom from fear for one's person and one's family, and freedom to own the fruits of one's labor—was to offer hope and raise desire for that which the system could not produce. A slave with horizons limited only to a continued existence in slavery was a slave who did not threaten the system, whereas a slave with visions of freedom threatened rebellion.

This threat of rebellion is intimately related to the second threat that free blacks posed to the system of Negro slavery, the threat that free blacks might instigate or participate in a rebellion by their slave brethren. To forestall this threat of rebellion, southern legislatures undertook to limit the freedom of movement and decision of free blacks.[1] States limited the number of free blacks who might congregate at one time;[2] they curtailed the ability of free blacks to choose their own employment,[3] and to trade and socialize with slaves.[4] Free blacks were subject to question, to search, and to summary punishment by patrols established to keep the black population, slave and free, in order.[5] To forestall the possibility that free blacks would rebel either on their own or with slaves, the southern states limited not only the right of slaves, but also that of free blacks, to bear arms.

The idea was to restrict the availability of arms to blacks, both slave and free, to the extent consistent with local conceptions of safety. At one extreme was Texas, which, between 1840 and 1850, prohibited slaves from using firearms altogether.[6] Also at this extreme was Mississippi, which forbade firearms to both free blacks and slaves after 1852.[7] At the other extreme was Kentucky, which merely provided that, should slaves or free blacks "wilfully and maliciously" shoot at a white person, or otherwise wound a free white person while attempting to kill another person, the slave or free black would suffer the death penalty.[8]

More often than not, slave state statutes restricting black access to firearms were aimed primarily at free blacks, as opposed to slaves, perhaps because the vigilant master was presumed capable of denying arms to all but the most trustwor-

80 GEO. L.J. 309 (1991). Copyright © 1991 Georgetown Law Journal & Georgetown University. Reprinted by permission.

thy slaves, and would give proper supervision to the latter. Thus, Louisiana provided that a slave was denied the use of firearms and all other offensive weapons,[9] unless the slave carried written permission to hunt within the boundaries of the owner's plantation.[10] South Carolina prohibited slaves outside the company of whites or without written permission from their master from using or carrying firearms unless they were hunting or guarding the master's plantation.[11] Georgia, Maryland, and Virginia did not statutorily address the question of slaves' access to firearms, perhaps because controls inherent to the system made such laws unnecessary in these states' eyes.

By contrast, free blacks, not under the close scrutiny of whites, were generally subject to tight regulation with respect to firearms. The State of Florida, which had in 1824 provided for a weekly renewable license for slaves to use firearms to hunt and for "any other necessary and lawful purpose,"[12] turned its attention to the question of free blacks in 1825. Section 8 of "An Act to Govern Patrols"[13] provided that white citizen patrols "shall enter into all negro houses and suspected places, and search for arms and other offensive or improper weapons, and may lawfully seize and take away all such arms, weapons, and ammunition . . . ." By contrast, the following section of that same statute expanded the conditions under which a slave might carry a firearm; a slave might do so under this statute either by means of the weekly renewable license or if "in the presence of some white person."[14]

Immediately after the Civil War and the emancipation it brought, white Southerners adopted measures to keep the black population in its place. Southerners saw how Northerners had used segregation as a means to avoid the black presence in their lives, and they already had experience with segregation in southern cities before the war. Southerners extended this experience of segregation to the whole of southern life through the mechanism of "Jim Crow."[15] Jim Crow was established both by the operation of law, including the black codes and other legislation, and by an elaborate etiquette of racially restrictive social practices. The *Civil Rights Cases*[16] and *Plessy v. Ferguson*[17] gave the South freedom to pursue the task of separating black from white. The *Civil Rights Cases* went beyond *Cruikshank*, even more severely restricting congressional power to provide for the equality of blacks under Section 5 of the Fourteenth Amendment, and *Plessy v. Ferguson* declared separate facilities for blacks and whites to be consonant with the Fourteenth Amendment's mandate of "equal protection of the laws."[18] In effect, states and individuals were given full freedom to effect their "social prejudices"[19] and "racial instincts"[20] to the detriment of blacks throughout the South and elsewhere.

These laws and customs were given support and gruesome effect by violence. In northern cities, violence continued to threaten blacks after Reconstruction and after the turn of the century. For instance, in New York, hostility between blacks and immigrant whites ran high. Negro strikebreakers were often used to break strikes of union workers. Regular clashes occurred between blacks and the Irish throughout the nineteenth century, until finally a major race riot broke out in 1900 that lasted four days.[21] And in 1919, after a Chicago race riot, 38 deaths and 537 injuries were reported as a result of attacks on the black population.[22]

In the South, racism found expression not only through the power of unorganized mobs but also under the auspices of organized groups like the Ku Klux Klan. The Klan started in 1866 as a social organization of white Civil War veterans in Pulaski, Tennessee, complete with pageantry, ritual, and opportunity for plain and innocent amusement. But the group soon expanded and turned its attention to more sinister activities. The Klan's activities, primarily in the South, expanded to playing tricks on blacks and then to terroristic nightriding against them. The Ku Klux Klan in this first incarnation was disbanded, possibly as early as January 1868, and no later than May 1870. By that time, the Klan's activities had come to include assaults, murder, lynchings, and political repression against blacks, and Klan-like activities would continue and contribute to the outcome of the federal election of 1876 that ended Reconstruction.[23] As one author has put it, "The Invisible Empire faded away, not because it had been defeated, but because it had won."[24]

The Ku Klux Klan would be revived in 1915 after the release of D. W. Griffith's film *Birth of a Nation*, but both in its early and later guises, Klan tactics would play a familiar role in the lives of black people in the South; for up to the time of the modern civil rights movement, lynching would be virtually an everyday occurrence. Between 1882 and 1968, 4,743 persons were lynched, the overwhelming number of these in the South; 3,446 of these persons were black, killed for the most part for being accused in one respect or another of not knowing their place. These accusations were as widely disparate as arson, theft, sexual contact or even being too familiar with a white woman, murdering or assaulting a white person, hindering a lynch mob, protecting one's legal rights, not showing proper respect, or simply being in the wrong place at the wrong time.

This is not to say that blacks went quietly or tearfully to their deaths. Oftentimes they were able to use firearms to defend themselves, though usually not with success: Jim McIlherron was lynched in Estell Springs, Tennessee, after having exchanged over one thousand rounds with his pursuers.[25] The attitude of individuals such as McIlherron is summed up by Ida B. Wells-Barnett, a black anti-lynching activist who wrote of her decision to carry a pistol:

> I had been warned repeatedly by my own people that something would happen if I did not cease harping on the lynching of three months before. . . . I had bought a pistol the first thing after [the lynching], because I expected some cowardly retaliation from the lynchers. I felt that one had better die fighting against injustice than to die like a dog or a rat in a trap. I had already determined to sell my life as dearly as possible if attacked. I felt if I could take one lyncher with me, this would even up the score a little bit.[26]

When blacks used firearms to protect their rights, they were often partially successful but were ultimately doomed. In 1920, two black men in Texas fired on and killed two whites in self-defense. The black men were arrested and soon lynched.[27] When the sheriff of Aiken, South Carolina, came with three deputies to a black household to attempt a warrantless search and struck one female family member, three other family members used a hatchet and firearms in self-defense, killing the sheriff. The three wounded survivors were taken into custody, and after one was acquitted of murdering the sheriff, with indications of a similar verdict for the other two, all three were lynched.[28]

Although individual efforts of blacks to halt violence to their persons or property were largely unsuccessful, group activity sometimes worked. In her autobiography, Ida Wells-Barnett reported an incident in Memphis in 1891 in which a black militia unit for two or three nights guarded approximately 100 jailed blacks who were deemed at risk of mob violence. When it seemed the crisis had passed, the militia unit ceased its work. It was only after the militia unit left that a white mob stormed the jail and lynched three black inmates.[29]

A. Philip Randolph, the longtime head of the Brotherhood of Sleeping Car Porters, and Walter White, onetime executive secretary of the National Association for the Advancement of Colored People, vividly recalled incidents in which their fathers had participated in collective efforts to use firearms to successfully forestall lynchings and other mob violence. As a thirteen-year-old, White participated in his father's experiences, which, he reported, left him "gripped by the knowledge of my own identity, and in the depths of my soul, I was vaguely aware that I was glad of it."[30] After his father stood armed at a jail all night to ward off lynchers, Randolph was left with a vision, not "of powerlessness, but of the 'possibilities of salvation,' which resided in unity and organization."[31]

The willingness of blacks to use firearms to protect their rights, their lives, and their property, alongside their ability to do so successfully when acting collectively, renders many gun control statutes, particularly of Southern origin, all the more worthy of condemnation. This is especially so in view of the purpose of these statutes, which, like that of the gun control statutes of the black codes, was to disarm blacks.

This purpose has been recognized by some state judges. The Florida Supreme Court in 1941 refused to extend a statute forbidding the carrying of a pistol on one's person to a situation in which the pistol was found in an automobile glove compartment. In a concurrence, one judge spoke of the purpose of the statute:

> I know something of the history of this legislation. The original Act of 1893 was passed when there was a great influx of negro laborers in this State drawn here for the purpose of working in the turpentine and lumber camps. The same condition existed when the Act was amended in 1901 and the Act was passed for the purpose of disarming the negro laborers and to thereby reduce the unlawful homicides that were prevalent in turpentine and saw-mill camps and to give the white citizens in sparsely settled areas a better feeling of security. The statute was never intended to be applied to the white population and in practice has never been so applied.[32]

The Ohio Supreme Court in 1920 construed the state's constitutional right of the people "to bear arms for their defense and security" not to forbid a statute outlawing the carrying of a concealed weapon.[33] In so doing, the court followed the lead of sister courts in Alabama,[34] Arkansas,[35] Georgia,[36] and Kentucky,[37] over the objections of a dissenting judge who recognized that "the race issue [in Southern states] has intensified a decisive purpose to entirely disarm the negro, and this policy is evident upon reading the opinions."[38]

That the Southern states did not prohibit firearms ownership outright is fortuitous. During the 1960s, while many blacks and white civil rights workers were threatened and even murdered by whites with guns, firearms in the hands of blacks served a useful purpose, to protect civil rights workers and blacks from white mob and terrorist activity.[39]

While the rate of lynchings in the South had slowed somewhat, it was still clear by 1960 that Southerners were capable of murderous violence in pursuit of the Southern way of life. The 1955 murder of Emmett Till, a fourteen-year-old boy killed in Money, Mississippi, for wolf-whistling at a white woman, sent shock waves throughout the nation.[40] Two years later, the nation again would be shocked, this time by a riotous crowd outside Little Rock's Central High School bent on preventing nine black children from integrating the school under federal court order; President Eisenhower ordered federal troops to effectuate the court order.[41] News of yet another prominent lynching in Mississippi reached the public in 1959.

In the early 1960s, Freedom Riders and protesters at sit-ins were attacked, and some suffered permanent damage at the hands of white supremacists.[42] In 1963, Medgar Evers, Mississippi secretary of the NAACP, was killed.[43] Three college students were killed in Mississippi during the 1964 "Freedom Summer"; this killing would render their names—Andrew Goodman, James Chaney, and Michael Schwerner—and their sacrifice part of the public domain.[44] A church bombing in Birmingham that killed four small black children,[45] the killing of a young white housewife helping with the march from Montgomery to Selma,[46] and the destructive riot in Oxford, Mississippi,[47] that left two dead when James Meredith entered the University of Mississippi helped make clear to the nation what blacks in the South had long known: white Southerners were willing to use weapons of violence, modern equivalents of rope and faggot, to keep blacks in their place.

It struck many, then, as the height of blindness, confidence, courage, or moral certainty for the civil rights movement to adopt nonviolence as its credo, and to thus leave its adherents open to attack by terrorist elements within the white South. Yet, while nonviolence had its adherents among the mainstream civil rights organizations, many ordinary black people in the South believed in resistance and in the necessity of maintaining firearms for personal protection, and these people lent their assistance and their protection to the civil rights movement.

Daisy Bates, the leader of the Little Rock NAACP during the desegregation crisis, wrote in her memoirs that armed volunteers stood guard over her home.[48] Moreover, there are oral histories of such assistance. David Dennis, the black Congress of Racial Equality (CORE) worker who had been targeted for the fate that actually befell Goodman, Schwerner, and Chaney during the Freedom Summer,[49] has told of black Mississippi citizens with firearms who followed civil rights workers in order to keep them safe.[50]

Ad hoc efforts were not the sole means by which black Southern adherents of firearms protected workers in the civil rights movement. The Deacons for Defense and Justice were organized first in 1964 in Jonesboro, Louisiana, but received prominence in Bogalousa, Louisiana.[51] The Deacons organized in Jonesboro after their founder saw the Ku Klux Klan marching in the street and realized that the "fight against racial injustice include[d] not one but two foes: White reactionaries and police." Jonesboro's Deacons obtained a charter and weapons, and vowed to shoot back if fired upon. The word spread throughout the South, but most significantly to Bogalousa, where the Klan was rumored to have its largest per capita membership. There, a local chapter of the Deacons would grow to include "about a tenth of the Negro adult male population," or about 900 members, although the organization was deliberately secretive about exact numbers.[52] What is known, however, is that in 1965 there were fifty to sixty chapters across Louisiana, Mississippi, and Alabama. In Bogalousa, as elsewhere, the Deacons' job was to protect black people from violence, and they did so by extending violence to anyone who attacked. This capability and willingness to use force to protect blacks provided a deterrent to white terroristic activity.

A prime example of how the Deacons accomplished their task lies in the experience of James Farmer, then head of CORE, a frontline, mainstream civil rights group. Before Farmer left on a trip for Bogalousa, the Federal Bureau of Investigation informed him that he had received a death threat from the Klan. The FBI apparently also informed the state police, who met Farmer at the airport. But at the airport also were representatives of the Bogalousa chapter of the Deacons, who escorted Farmer to the town. Farmer stayed with the local head of the Deacons, who provided close security throughout the rest of this stay and Farmer's next. Farmer later wrote in his autobiography that he was secure with the Deacons, "in the knowledge that unless a bomb were tossed . . . the Klan could only reach me if they were prepared to swap their lives for mine."[53]

Blacks in the South found the Deacons helpful because they were unable to rely upon police or other legal entities for racial justice. This provided a practical reason for a right to bear arms: In a world in which the legal system was not to be trusted, perhaps the ability of the system's victims to resist might convince the system to restrain itself.

Conclusion: Self-Defense and the Gun Control Question Today

While discussion of the Second Amendment has been relegated to the margin of academic and judicial discourse, the realization that there is a racial dimension to the question, and that the right may have had greater and different significance for blacks and others less able to rely on the government's protection, has been even further on the periphery. The history of blacks and the right to bear arms, and the failure of most constitutional scholars and policymakers to seriously examine that history, is in part another instance of the difficulty of integrating the study of the black experience into larger questions of legal and social policy.

Throughout American history, black and white Americans have had radically different experiences with respect to violence and state protection. Perhaps another reason the Second Amendment has not been taken very seriously by the courts and the academy is that for many of those who shape or critique constitutional policy the state's power and inclination to protect them is a given. But for all too many black Americans, that protection historically has not been available. Nor, for many, is it readily available today. If in the past the state refused to protect black people from the horrors of white lynch mobs, today the state seems powerless in the face of the tragic black-on-black violence that plagues the mean streets of our inner cities, and at times seems blind to instances of police brutality visited upon minority populations.[54]

NOTES

1. Eugene D. Genovese, *The Slave States of North America, in* NEITHER SLAVE NOR FREE: THE FREEDMEN OF AFRICAN DESCENT IN THE SLAVE SOCIETIES OF THE NEW WORLD 258, 261–62 (David W. Cohen & Jack P. Greene eds., 1972).

2. JOHN H. FRANKLIN, FROM SLAVERY TO FREEDOM: A HISTORY OF NEGRO AMERICANS 139–40 (6th ed. 1988).

3. *Id.* at 140.

4. *Id.* at 140–41.

5. KENNETH STAMPP, THE PECULIAR INSTITUTION 214–16 (1956).

6. An Act Concerning Slaves, § 6, 1840 Laws of Tex. 171, 172. Chapter 58 of the Texas Acts of 1850 provided penalties for violators of the 1840 statute. Act of Dec. 3, 1850, ch. 58, § 1, 1850 Laws of Tex. 42–44 (amending § 6 of An Act Concerning Slaves). Masters, overseers, or employers were to be fined between $25 and $100, and the slave was to receive not less than 39 nor more than 50 lashes. But also under the 1850 Act, slaves were allowed to carry firearms on the premises of the master, overseer, or employer, where they presumably would receive proper supervision.

7. Act of Mar. 15, 1852, ch. 206, 1852 Laws of Miss. 328 (prohibiting magistrates from issuing licenses for blacks to carry and use firearms). This act repealed Chapter 73, sections 10 and 12 of the Mississippi Acts of 1822, allowing slaves and free blacks respectively to obtain a license to carry firearms. See Act of June 18, 1822, ch. 73, §§ 10, 12, 1822 Laws of Miss. 179, 181–82.

8. Chapter 448, § 1, of the Kentucky Acts of 1818 was limited solely to slave offenders. Act of Feb. 10, 1819, ch. 448, § 1, 1819 Acts of Ky. 787. The Kentucky Acts of 1850 extended these provisions to free blacks as well. Act of Mar. 24, 1851, ch. 617, art. VII, § 7, 1850 Acts of Ky. 291, 300–01.

9. Black Code, ch. 33, 19, Laws of La. 150, 160 (1806).

10. *Id.* § 20. Moreover, in 1811, Louisiana forbade peddlers from selling arms to slaves, upon a fine of $500 or one year in prison. Act of Apr. 8, 1811, ch.

14, 1811 Laws of La. 50, 53–54 (supplementing act relative to peddlers and hawkers).

11. Act of Dec. 18, 1819, 1819 Acts of S.C. 28, 31 (providing more effective performance of patrol duty).

12. An Act Concerning Slaves, § 11, Acts of Fla. 289, 291 (1824). In 1825, Florida had provided a penalty for slaves using firelight to hunt at night, but this seems to have been a police measure intended to preserve wooded land, for whites were also penalized for this offense, albeit a lesser penalty. Act of Dec. 10, 1825, § 5, 1825 Laws of Fla. 78–80. Penalties for "firehunting" were reenacted in 1827, Act of Jan. 1, 1828, 1828 Laws of Fla. 24–25, and the penalties for a slave firehunting were reenacted in 1828, Act of Nov. 21, 1828, § 46, 1828 Laws of Fla. 174, 185.

13. 1825 Acts of Fla. 52, 55.

14. *Id.* § 9.

15. *See generally* C. VANN WOODWARD, THE STRANGE CAREER OF JIM CROW (3d ed. 1974).

> Jim Crow has been said to have established an etiquette of discrimination. It was not enough for blacks to be second class citizens, denied the franchise and consigned to inferior schools. Black subordination was reinforced by a racist punctilio dictating separate seating on public accommodations, separate water fountains and restrooms, separate seats in courthouses, and separate Bibles to swear in black witnesses about to give testimony before the law. The list of separations was ingenious and endless. Blacks became like a group of American untouchables, ritually separated from the rest of the population.

Raymond T. Diamond & Robert J. Cottrol, Codifying Caste: Louisiana's Racial Classification Scheme and the Fourteenth Amendment, 29 Loy. L. Rev. 255, 264–65 (1983).

16. 109 U.S. 3 (1883).

17. 163 U.S. 537 (1896).

18. 163 U.S. at 548.

19. *Id.* at 551.

20. *Id.*

21. GILBERT OSOFSKY, HARLEM: THE MAKING OF A GHETTO: NEGRO NEW YORK 1890–1930, at 42–52 (1963).

22. CHICAGO COMMISSION ON RACE RELATIONS, THE NEGRO IN CHICAGO: A STUDY OF RACE RELATIONS AND A RACE RIOT (1922) 595–98, 602, 640–49, *reprinted in* THE NEGRO AND THE CITY 126–33 (Richard B. Sherman ed., 1970). An outbreak of racial violence against blacks was recorded from 1917 to 1921. Riots occurred in Chicago, Omaha, Washington, D.C., and East St. Louis, Illinois. *Id.* at 126.

23. WYN CRAIG WADE, THE FIERY CROSS: THE KU KLUX KLAN IN AMERICA 33 (1987).

24. *See generally* WILLIAM L. KATZ, THE INVISIBLE EMPIRE: THE KU KLUX KLAN IMPACT ON HISTORY 58 (1986).

25. *Blood-Curdling Lynching Witnessed by 2,000 Persons*, CHATTANOOGA TIMES, Feb. 13, 1918, reprinted in RALPH GINZBURG, 100 YEARS OF LYNCHINGS 114–16 (1988).

26. IDA B. WELLS-BARNETT, CRUSADE FOR JUSTICE: THE AUTOBIOGRAPHY OF IDA B. WELLS 62 (Alfreda M. Duster ed., 1970). Wells-Barnett's fears for her safety, fortunately, were never realized. Born a slave in 1862, she died of natural causes in 1931. *Id.* at xxx–xxxi, 7. Eli Cooper of Caldwell, Georgia, was not so lucky, however. Cooper was alleged to have said that the "Negro has been run over for fifty years, but it must stop now, and pistols and shotguns are the only weapons to stop a mob." Cooper was dragged from his home by a mob of 20 men and killed as his wife looked on. *Church Burnings Follow Negro Agitator's Lynching*, CHI. DEFENDER, Sept. 6, 1919, *reprinted in* GINZBURG, *supra* note 25, at 124.

27. *Letter from Texas Reveals Lynching's Ironic Facts*, N.Y. NEGRO WORLD, Aug. 22, 1920, *reprinted in* GINZBURG, *supra* note 25, at 139–40.

28. *Lone Survivor of Atrocity Recounts Events of Lynching*, N.Y. AMSTERDAM NEWS, June 1, 1927, *reprinted in* GINZBURG, *supra* note 25, at 175–78.

29. WELLS-BARNETT, *supra* note 26, at 50. To forestall the occurrence of future incidents of the same nature, a Tennessee court ordered the local sheriff to take charge of the arms of the black militia unit. *Id.*

30. Walter White, *A Man Called White*, *reprinted in* THE NEGRO AND THE CITY, *supra* note 22, at 121–26.

31. JERVIS ANDERSON, A. PHILIP RANDOLPH: A BIOGRAPHICAL PORTRAIT 41–42 (1973).

32. Watson v. Stone, 4 So. 2d 700, 703 (Fla. 1941).

33. State v. Nieto, 130 N.E. 663 (Ohio 1920).

34. Dunston v. State, 27 So. 333 (Ala. 1900).

35. Carroll v. State, 28 Ark. 99 (1872).

36. Brown v. State, 39 S.E. 873 (Ga. 1901).

37. Commonwealth v. Walker, 7 Ky. L. Rptr. 219 (1885) (abstract).

38. *Nieto*, 130 N.E. at 669 (Wanamaker, J., dissenting).

39. *See, e.g.,* John R. Salter, Jr., & Donald B. Kates, Jr., *The Necessity of Access to Firearms by Dissenters and Minorities Whom Government Is Unwilling or Unable to Protect, in* RESTRICTING HANDGUNS: THE LIBERAL SKEPTICS SPEAK OUT 185, 189–93 (Donald B. Kates, Jr., ed., 1979).

40. *See* STEPHEN J. WHITFIELD, A DEATH IN THE DELTA: THE STORY OF EMMETT TILL 23–108 (1988); *see also Eyes on the Prize: America's Civil Rights Years, 1954–1965: Awakenings (1954–56)* (PBS Television Broadcast, Jan. 21, 1986).

41. *See* Cooper v. Aaron, 358 U.S. 1 (1958); *see also* TONY A. FREYER, THE LITTLE ROCK CRISIS: A CONSTITUTIONAL INTERPRETATION (1984); Raymond T. Diamond, *Confrontation as Rejoinder to Compromise: Reflections on the Little Rock Desegregation Crisis*, 11 NAT'L BLACK L.J. 151, 152–64 (1989); *Eyes on the Prize: America's Civil Rights Years, 1954–1965: Fighting Back (1957–62)* (PBS Television Broadcast, Jan. 28, 1986).

42. RHONDA BLUMBERG, CIVIL RIGHTS: THE 1960s FREEDOM STRUGGLE 65–81 (1984).

43. CIVIL RIGHTS: 1960–66, at 190–91 (Lester A. Sobel ed., 1967).

44. *Id.* at 244–46.

45. *Id.* at 187–88.

46. *Id.* at 303–05.

47. *Id.* at 110–18.

48. DAISY BATES, THE LONG SHADOW OF LITTLE ROCK, A MEMOIR 94 (1982).

49. HOWELL RAINES, MY SOUL IS RESTED: MOVEMENT DAYS IN THE DEEP SOUTH REMEMBERED 275–76 (1977).

50. Telephone interview with David Dennis (Oct. 30, 1991).

51. Hamilton Bims, *Deacons for Defense*, EBONY, Sept. 1965, at 25, 26; *see also* Roy Reed, *The Deacons, Too, Ride by Night*, N.Y. TIMES, Aug. 15, 1965 (Magazine), at 10.

52. *See* Bims, *supra* note 51, at 26.

53. JAMES FARMER, LAY BARE THE HEART 288 (1983).

54. The beating of Rodney King on March 3, 1991, by members of the Los Angeles Police Department, serendipitously captured on tape by an amateur photographer, has focused attention recently on the problem of police brutality, though the problem predates and presumably continues beyond the incident. *See* Tracey Wood & Faye Fiore, *Beating Victim Says He Obeyed Police*, L.A. Times, Mar. 7, 1991, at A1.

From the Editor:
Issues and Comments

ON SOME level, all five authors seem to agree that history—what happened—is a contested construct, subject to multiple interpretations and assignments of meaning. There is no standard account, no unquestionable view of what happened, why it did, or who did what to whom. Do colonial conquerors, as Williams suggests, always devise and circulate devastating stories to demonize the subjugated population and thus rationalize their own plundering of their riches and lands—and do we continue to do this to Native Americans even today? Dudziak argues that in *Brown* whites did not so much do a favor for blacks as for each other. Is this a tenable hypothesis? If the first Justice Harlan indeed had a black brother, does this help explain his courageous attitudes and positions on race? If so, what does this say about the possibility of racial harmony in *our* time? Does the frightening history of violence suffered at the hands of whites mean, as Cottrol and Diamond argue, that blacks should own guns and resist gun control—or the opposite?

For further reading, consult the essays of Gotanda (on Japanese internment), Aleinikoff (on today's racism), and Lâm (on the Hawaiian land question), all listed in Suggested Readings, following.

Suggested Readings

Aleinikoff, T. Alexander, *The Constitution in Context: The Continuing Significance of Racism*, 63 U. COLO. L. REV. 325 (1992).

Bell, Derrick A., Jr., Bakke, *Minority Admissions, and the Usual Price of Racial Remedies*, 67 CAL. L. REV. 3 (1979).

Bell, Derrick A., Jr., *Civil Rights Lawyers on the Bench*, 91 YALE L.J. 814 (1982).

Brown, Kevin, *Has the Supreme Court Allowed the Cure for De Jure Segregation to Replicate the Disease?*, 78 CORNELL L. REV. 1 (1992).

Davis, Peggy C., *Neglected Stories and the Lawfulness of* Roe v. Wade, 28 HARV. C.R.-C.L. L. REV. 299 (1993).

Dudziak, Mary L., *The Limits of Good Faith: Desegregation in Topeka, Kansas, 1950–1956*, 5 LAW & HIST. REV. 351 (1987).

Gotanda, Neil, *"Other Non-Whites" in American Legal History: A Review of* Justice at War, 85 COLUM. L. REV. 1186 (1985) (reviewing Peter Irons, *Justice at War* (1983)).

Harris, Cheryl I., *Whiteness as Property*, 106 HARV. L. REV. 1707 (1993).

Horwitz, Morton J., *Rights*, 23 Harv. C.R.-C.L. L. REV. 393 (1988).

Lâm, Maivân Clech, *The Kuleana Act Revisited: The Survival of Traditional Hawaiian Commoner Rights in Land*, 64 WASH. L. REV. 233 (1989).

Martinez, George A., *Legal Indeterminacy, Judicial Discretion and the Mexican-American Litigation Experience: 1930–1980*, 27 U.C. DAVIS L. REV. 555 (1994).

Perea, Juan F., *Demography and Distrust: An Essay on American Language, Cultural Pluralism, and Official English*, 77 MINN. L. REV. 269 (1992).

WEST, CORNEL, RACE MATTERS (1993).

Williams, Robert A., Jr., *The Algebra of Federal Indian Law: The Hard Trail of Decolonizing and Americanizing the White Man's Indian Jurisprudence*, 1986 WIS. L. REV. 219.

WILLIAMS, ROBERT A., JR., THE AMERICAN INDIAN IN WESTERN LEGAL THOUGHT: THE DISCOURSES OF CONQUEST (1990).

PART IV

CRITICAL UNDERSTANDING OF THE SOCIAL SCIENCE UNDERPINNINGS OF RACE AND RACISM

A NUMBER of Critical Race Theory writers have been applying the insights of social science to understand how race and racism work in our society, and in the legal system. For example, Derrick Bell and others have explored the reasons why interracial sex and marriages remain surrounded by strong taboos. Other writers have tried to understand the constraints that affect the judiciary, and why even seemingly fair-minded judges continue to hand down decisions tinged by unfairness to black litigants. Others have addressed the question of whether the movement toward alternative dispute resolution—mediation, arbitration, and a host of streamlined, nonformal alternatives to litigation—will help or hurt disempowered disputants.

The selections that follow show Critical theorists grappling with some of the thorniest problems of race and law. The first, Richard Delgado's classic "Words That Wound," addresses the question of what the law can do about racial insults and name-calling, marshaling social science evidence that shows the harm of racist epithets. In the second, judge and law professor Peggy C. Davis employs cognitive psychology and the notion of "microaggressions" to explain why persons of color continue to believe the legal system biased. Next, Cornell professor Sheri Lynn Johnson sets forth social science research showing a strong tendency on the part of whites to convict black defendants in situations where whites would have been acquitted. She argues that existing legal protections (such as voir dire—questioning of prospective jurors) are not adequate to guard against deep-seated prejudice, and she urges new procedures to exclude bias and racism from jury trials. And in the final selection Ian Haney López puts forward the view that race and races do not exist—that they have little or no biological reality and are constructs that society invents for its own (usually questionable) purposes. Moreover, we all have a *choice* whether to acquiesce in the construction others assign to us; if we agree to "be black" or Latino, for example, we do so as a matter of our own agency.

Readers interested in pursuing further the lively discussion of hate speech are invited to consult Richard Delgado's *Words That Wound* (Westview, 1993), as well as the writings in the law review literature of Mari Matsuda, Charles Lawrence, Richard Delgado, and Catharine MacKinnon, most of which are cited in the various Suggested Readings sections of this volume.

14 Words That Wound: A Tort Action for Racial Insults, Epithets, and Name-Calling

RICHARD DELGADO

Psychological, Sociological, and Political Effects of Racial Insults

American society remains deeply afflicted by racism. Long before slavery became the mainstay of the plantation society of the antebellum South, Anglo-Saxon attitudes of racial superiority left their stamp on the developing culture of colonial America.[1] Today, over a century after the abolition of slavery, many citizens suffer from discriminatory attitudes and practices, infecting our economic system, our cultural and political institutions, and the daily interactions of individuals. The idea that color is a badge of inferiority and a justification for the denial of opportunity and equal treatment is deeply ingrained.

The racial insult remains one of the most pervasive channels through which discriminatory attitudes are imparted. Such language injures the dignity and self-regard of the person to whom it is addressed, communicating the message that distinctions of race are distinctions of merit, dignity, status, and personhood. Not only does the listener learn and internalize the messages contained in racial insults, these messages color our society's institutions and are transmitted to succeeding generations.

The Harms of Racism

The psychological harms caused by racial stigmatization are often much more severe than those created by other stereotyping actions. Unlike many characteristics upon which stigmatization may be based, membership in a racial minority can be considered neither self-induced, like alcoholism or prostitution, nor alterable. Race-based stigmatization is, therefore, "one of the most fruitful causes of human misery. Poverty can be eliminated—but skin color cannot."[2] The plight of members of racial minorities may be compared with that of persons with physical disfigurements; the point has been made that

[a] rebuff due to one's color puts [the victim] in very much the situation of the very ugly person or one suffering from a loathsome disease. The suffering . . . may be aggravated by a consciousness of incurability and even blameworthiness, a self-reproaching which tends to leave the individual still more aware of his loneliness and unwantedness.[3]

The psychological impact of this type of verbal abuse has been described in various ways. Kenneth Clark has observed, "Human beings . . . whose daily experience tells them that almost nowhere in society are they respected and granted the ordinary dignity and courtesy accorded to others will, as a matter of course, begin to doubt their own worth."[4] Minorities may come to believe the frequent accusations that they are lazy, ignorant, dirty, and superstitious.[5] "The accumulation of negative images . . . present[s] them with one massive and destructive choice: either to hate one's self, as culture so systematically demand[s], or to have no self at all, to be nothing."[6]

The psychological responses to such stigmatization consist of feelings of humiliation, isolation, and self-hatred. Consequently, it is neither unusual nor abnormal for stigmatized individuals to feel ambivalent about their self-worth and identity.[7] This ambivalence arises from the stigmatized individual's awareness that others perceive him or her as falling short of societal standards, standards which the individual has adopted. Stigmatized individuals thus often are hypersensitive and anticipate pain at the prospect of contact with "normals."[8]

It is no surprise, then, that racial stigmatization injures its victims' relationships with others. Racial tags deny minority individuals the possibility of neutral behavior in cross-racial contacts,[9] thereby impairing the victims' capacity to form close interracial relationships. Moreover, the psychological responses of self-hatred and self-doubt unquestionably affect even the victims' relationships with members of their own group.[10]

The psychological effects of racism may also result in mental illness and psychosomatic disease.[11] The affected person may react by seeking escape through alcohol, drugs, or other kinds of anti-social behavior. The rates of narcotic use and admission to public psychiatric hospitals are much higher in minority communities than in society as a whole.[12]

The achievement of high socioeconomic status does not diminish the psychological harms caused by prejudice. The effort to achieve success in business and managerial careers exacts a psychological toll even among exceptionally ambitious and upwardly mobile members of minority groups. Furthermore, those who succeed "do not enjoy the full benefits of their professional status within their organizations, because of inconsistent treatment by others resulting in continual psychological stress, strain, and frustration."[13] As a result, the incidence of severe psychological impairment caused by the environmental stress of prejudice and discrimination is not lower among minority group members of high socioeconomic status.[14]

One of the most troubling effects of racial stigmatization is that it may affect parenting practices among minority group members, thereby perpetuating a tradition of failure. A recent study[15] of minority mothers found that many denied the real significance of color in their lives, yet were morbidly sensitive to matters of race. Some, as a defense against aggression, identified excessively with whites, accepting whiteness as superior. Most had negative expectations concerning life's chances. Such self-conscious, hypersensitive parents, preoccupied with the ambiguity of their own social position, are unlikely to raise confident, achievement-oriented, and emotionally stable children.

In addition to these long-term psychological harms of racial labeling, the stresses of racial abuse may have physical consequences. There is evidence that high blood pressure is associated with inhibited, constrained, or restricted anger, and not with genetic factors,[16] and that insults produce elevation in blood pressure.[17] American blacks have higher blood pressure levels and higher morbidity and mortality rates from hypertension, hypertensive disease, and stroke than do white counterparts.[18] Further, there exists a strong correlation between degree of darkness of skin for blacks and level of stress felt, a correlation that may be caused by the greater discrimination experienced by dark-skinned blacks.[19]

In addition to such emotional and physical consequences, racial stigmatization may damage a victim's pecuniary interests. The psychological injuries severely handicap the victim's pursuit of a career. The person who is timid, withdrawn, bitter, hypertense, or psychotic will almost certainly fare poorly in employment settings. An experiment in which blacks and whites of similar aptitudes and capacities were put into a competitive situation found that the blacks exhibited defeatism, half-hearted competitiveness, and "high expectancies of failure."[20] For many minority group members, the equalization of such quantifiable variables as salary and entry level would be an insufficient antidote to defeatist attitudes because the psychological price of attempting to compete is unaffordable; they are "programmed for failure."[21] Additionally, career options for the victims of racism are closed off by institutional racism—the subtle and unconscious racism in schools, hiring decisions, and the other practices which determine the distribution of social benefits and responsibilities.

Unlike most of the actions for which tort law provides redress to the victim, racial labeling and racial insults directly harm the perpetrator. Bigotry harms the individuals who harbor it by reinforcing rigid thinking, thereby dulling their moral and social senses[22] and possibly leading to a "mildly . . . paranoid" mentality.[23] There is little evidence that racial slurs serve as a "safety valve" for anxiety which would otherwise be expressed in violence.[24]

Racism and racial stigmatization harm not only the victim and the perpetrator of individual racist acts but also society as a whole. Racism is a breach of the ideal of egalitarianism, that "all men are created equal" and each person is an equal moral agent, an ideal that is a cornerstone of the American moral and legal system. A society in which some members regularly are subjected to degradation because of their race hardly exemplifies this ideal. The failure of the legal system to redress the harms of racism, and of racial insults, conveys to all the lesson that egalitarianism is not a fundamental principle; the law, through inaction, implicitly teaches that respect for individuals is of little importance. Moreover, unre-dressed breaches of the egalitarian ideal may demoralize all those who prefer to live in a truly equal society, making them unwilling participants in the perpetu-ation of racism and racial inequality.

To the extent that racism contributes to a class system, society has a para-mount interest in controlling or suppressing it. Racism injures the career prospects, social mobility, and interracial contacts of minority group members. This, in turn, impedes assimilation into the economic, social, and political main-stream of society and ensures that the victims of racism are seen and see them-selves as outsiders. Indeed, racism can be seen as a force used by the majority to preserve an economically advantageous position for themselves. But when indi-viduals cannot or choose not to contribute their talents to a social system because they are demoralized or angry, or when they are actively prevented by racist in-stitutions from fully contributing their talents, society as a whole loses.

Finally, and perhaps most disturbingly, racism and racial labeling have an even greater impact on children than on adults. The effects of racial labeling are discernible early in life; at a young age, minority children exhibit self-hatred be-cause of their color, and majority children learn to associate dark skin with un-desirability and ugliness.[25] A few examples readily reveal the psychological dam-age of racial stigmatization on children. When presented with otherwise identical dolls, a black child preferred the light-skinned one as a friend; she said that the dark-skinned one looked dirty or "not nice."[26] Another child hated her skin color so intensely that she "vigorously lathered her arms and face with soap in an ef-fort to wash away the dirt."[27] She told the experimenter, "This morning I scrubbed and scrubbed and it came almost white."[28] When asked about making a little girl out of clay, a black child said that the group should use the white clay rather than the brown "because it will make a better girl."[29] When asked to de-scribe dolls which had the physical characteristics of black people, young chil-dren chose adjectives such as "rough, funny, stupid, silly, smelly, stinky, dirty."[30] Three-fourths of a group of four-year-old black children favored white play com-panions;[31] over half felt themselves inferior to whites.[32] Some engaged in denial or falsification.[33]

The Harms of Racial Insults

Immediate mental or emotional distress is the most obvious direct harm caused by a racial insult. Without question, mere words, whether racial or otherwise, can cause mental, emotional, or even physical[34] harm to their target, especially if delivered in front of others[35] or by a person in a position of author-ity.[36] Racial insults, relying as they do on the unalterable fact of the victim's race and on the history of slavery and race discrimination in this country, have an even greater potential for harm than other insults.

Although the emotional damage caused is variable and depends on many fac-tors, only one of which is the outrageousness of the insult, a racial insult is always a dignitary affront, a direct violation of the victim's right to be treated respectfully. Our moral and legal systems recognize the principle that individuals are entitled to treatment that does not denigrate their humanity through disrespect for their privacy or moral worth. This ideal has a high place in our traditions, finding expression in such principles as universal suffrage, the prohibition against cruel and unusual punishment, the protection of the fourth amendment against unreasonable searches, and the abolition of slavery. A racial insult is a serious transgression of this principle because it derogates by race, a characteristic central to one's self-image.

The wrong of this dignitary affront consists of the expression of a judgment that the victim of the racial slur is entitled to less than that to which all other citizens are entitled. Verbal tags provide a convenient means of categorization so that individuals may be treated as members of a class and assumed to share all the negative attitudes imputed to the class.[37] Racial insults also serve to keep the victim compliant. Such dignitary affronts are certainly no less harmful than others recognized by the law. Clearly, a society whose public law recognizes harm in the stigma of separate but equal schooling[38] and the potential offensiveness of the required display of a state motto on automobile license plates,[39] and whose private law sees actionable conduct in an unwanted kiss[40] or the forcible removal of a person's hat,[41] should also recognize the dignitary harm inflicted by a racial insult.

The need for legal redress for victims also is underscored by the fact that racial insults are intentional acts. The intentionality of racial insults is obvious: what other purpose could the insult serve? There can be little doubt that the dignitary affront of racial insults, except perhaps those that are overheard, is intentional and therefore most reprehensible. Most people today know that certain words are offensive and only calculated to wound.[42] No other use remains for such words as "nigger," "wop," "spick," or "kike."

In addition to the harms of immediate emotional distress and infringement of dignity, racial insults inflict psychological harm upon the victim. Racial slurs may cause long-term emotional pain because they draw upon and intensify the effects of the stigmatization, labeling, and disrespectful treatment that the victim has previously undergone. Social scientists who have studied the effects of racism have found that speech that communicates low regard for an individual because of race "tends to create in the victim those very traits of 'inferiority' that it ascribes to him."[43] Moreover, "even in the absence of more objective forms of discrimination—poor schools, menial jobs, and substandard housing—traditional stereotypes about the low ability and apathy of Negroes and other minorities can operate as 'self- fulfilling prophecies.' "[44] These stereotypes, portraying members of a minority group as stupid, lazy, dirty, or untrustworthy, are often communicated either explicitly or implicitly through racial insults.

Because they constantly hear racist messages, minority children, not surprisingly, come to question their competence, intelligence, and worth. Much of the blame for the formation of these attitudes lies squarely on value-laden words, epithets, and racial names.[45] These are the materials out of which each child "grows his own set of thoughts and feelings about race."[46] If the majority "defines them and their parents as no good, inadequate, dirty, incompetent, and stupid," the child will find it difficult not to accept those judgments.[47]

Victims of racial invective have few means of coping with the harms caused by the insults. Physical attacks are of course forbidden. "More speech" frequently is useless because it may provoke only further abuse or because the insulter is in a position of authority over the victim. Complaints to civil rights organizations also are meaningless unless they are followed by action to punish the offender. Adoption of a "they're well meaning but ignorant" attitude is another impotent response in light of the insidious psychological harms of racial slurs. When victimized by racist language, victims must be able to threaten and institute legal action, thereby relieving the sense of helplessness that leads to psychological harm and communicating to the perpetrator and to society that such abuse will not be tolerated, either by its victims or by the courts.

Minority children possess even fewer means for coping with racial insults than do adults. "A child who finds himself rejected and attacked . . . is not likely to develop dignity and poise. . . . On the contrary he develops defenses. Like a dwarf in a world of menacing giants, he cannot fight on equal terms."[48] The child who is the victim of belittlement can react with only two unsuccessful strategies, hostility or passivity. Aggressive reactions can lead to consequences that reinforce the harm caused by the insults; children who behave aggressively in school are marked by their teachers as troublemakers, adding to the children's alienation and sense of rejection.[49] Seemingly passive reactions have no better results; children who are passive toward their insulters turn the aggressive response on themselves;[50] robbed of confidence and motivation, these children withdraw into moroseness, fantasy, and fear.[51]

It is, of course, impossible to predict the degree of deterrence a cause of action in tort would create. However, as Professor van den Berghe has written, "for most people living in racist societies racial prejudice is merely a special kind of convenient rationalization for rewarding behavior."[52] In other words, in racist societies "most members of the dominant group will exhibit both prejudice and discrimination,"[53] but only in conforming to social norms. Thus, "[W]hen social pressures and rewards for racism are absent, racial bigotry is more likely to be restricted to people for whom prejudice fulfills a psychological 'need.' In such a tolerant milieu prejudiced persons may even refrain from discriminating behavior to escape social disapproval."[54] Increasing the cost of racial insults thus would certainly decrease their frequency. Laws will never prevent violations altogether, but they will deter "whoever is deterrable."[55]

Because most citizens comply with legal rules, and this compliance in turn "reinforce[s] their own sentiments toward conformity,"[56] a tort action for racial insults would discourage such harmful activity through the teaching function of the law.[57] The establishment of a legal norm "creates a public conscience and a standard for expected behavior that check overt signs of prejudice."[58] Legislation aims first at controlling only the acts that express undesired attitudes. But "when expression changes, thoughts too in the long run are likely to fall into line."[59] "Laws . . . restrain the middle range of mortals who need them as a mentor in molding their habits."[60] Thus, "If we create institutional arrangements in which exploitative behaviors are no longer reinforced, we will then succeed in changing attitudes [that underlie these behaviors]."[61] Because racial attitudes of white Americans "typically follow rather than precede actual institutional [or legal] alteration,"[62] a tort for racial slurs is a promising vehicle for the eradication of racism.

[*Ed.* In the remainder of the article Professor Delgado outlines his proposed tort remedy, discusses case law that is moving in this direction, and defends his approach in the face of objections, including that it would violate the First Amendment.]

NOTES

1. *See generally* A. HIGGINBOTHAM, IN THE MATTER OF COLOR (1978).
2. P. MASON, RACE RELATIONS 2 (1970).
3. O. COX, CASTE, CLASS AND RACE 383 (1948).
4. K. CLARK, DARK GHETTO 63–64 (1965).
5. *See* G. ALLPORT, THE NATURE OF PREJUDICE 152 (1954).
6. J. KOVEL, WHITE RACISM: A PSYCHOHISTORY 195 (1970).
7. *See* E. GOFFMAN, STIGMA 7 (1963). *See also* J. GRIFFIN, BLACK LIKE ME (1960) (white journalist dyed skin, assumed black identity, traveled through South, was treated as a black; began to assume physical demeanor and psychological set of black itinerant).
8. *See* GOFFMAN, *supra* note 7, at 17, 131.
9. *See* S. HAYAKAWA, SYMBOL, STATUS, AND PERSONALITY 76–78 (1966).
10. *See, e.g.,* ALLPORT, *supra* note 5, at 9, 148–49; M. GOODMAN, RACE AWARENESS IN YOUNG CHILDREN 46–47, 55–58, 60 (rev. ed. 1964). *See also* Cota Robles de Suarez, *Skin Color as a Factor of Racial Identification and Preference of Young Chicano Children,* CHI. J. SOC. SCI. & ARTS, Spring 1971, at 107; Stevenson & Stewart, *A Developmental Study of Racial Awareness in Young Children,* 29 CHILD DEV. 399 (1958).
11. *See, e.g.,* Harburg et al., *Socio-Ecological Stress, Suppressed Hostility, Skin Color, and Black-White Male Blood Pressure: Detroit,* 35 PSYCHOSOMATIC MED. 276 (1973) [hereinafter Harburg] (suppressed hostility and darker skin "interact for high stress males and relate to high blood pressure"); Kiev, *Psychiatric Disorders in Minority Groups, in* PSYCHOLOGY AND RACE 416, 420–24 (P. Watson ed., 1973).
12. *See* CLARK, *supra* note 4, at 82–84, 90. *See generally* W. GRIER & P. COBBS, BLACK RAGE 161 (1968) (paranoid symptoms are significantly more frequent among mentally ill blacks than among mentally ill whites); SPECIAL POPULATIONS SUB-TASK PANEL ON MENTAL HEALTH OF HISPANIC AMERICANS, REPORT TO THE PRESIDENT'S COMMISSION ON MENTAL HEALTH 2, 10–11, 40 (1978).
13. J. MARTIN & C. FRANKLIN, MINORITY GROUP RELATIONS 3 (1979).

14. *See* JOINT COMMISSION ON MENTAL HEALTH OF CHILDREN, SOCIAL CHANGE AND THE MENTAL HEALTH OF CHILDREN 99–100 (1973).

15. Kiev, *supra* note 11, at 416, 420–21.

16. *See* Harburg, *supra* note 11, at 292.

17. *See* Gentry, *Effects of Frustration, Attack, and Prior Aggressive Training on Overt Aggression and Vascular Processes*, 16 J. PERSONALITY & SOC. PSYCHOLOGY 718 (1970).

18. *See* Harburg, *supra* note 11, at 294. *See generally* L.A. TIMES, Jan. 14, 1981, § I-A, at 4, col. 1 (discussing report of Children's Defense Fund) (black children more likely to be sick and without regular source of health care than white children; black children three times as likely as white children to be labeled mentally retarded, and twice as likely to drop out of school before the twelfth grade).

19. *See* Harburg, *supra* note 11, at 285–90.

20. MARTIN & FRANKLIN, *supra* note 13, at 43. *See* ALLPORT, *supra* note 5, at 159.

21. MARTIN & FRANKLIN, *supra* note 13, at 4.

22. *See* ALLPORT, *supra* note 5, at 170–86, 371–84, 407–08.

23. G. Allport, *The Bigot in Our Midst*, 40 COMMONWEAL 582 (1944), *reprinted in* ANATOMY OF RACIAL INTOLERANCE 161, 164 (G. deHuszar ed., 1946).

24. *See* ALLPORT, *supra* note 5, at 62, 252, 460–61, 467–72 (rejecting view of racist conduct as catharsis and arguing that racist attitudes themselves can be curtailed by law). *But see* R. WILLIAMS, THE REDUCTION OF INTERGROUP TENSIONS 41 (1947); L. Berkovitz, *The Case for Bottling Up Rage*, PSYCHOLOGY TODAY, July 1973, at 24; L. Magruder, *Mental and Emotional Disturbance in the Law of Torts*, 49 HARV. L. REV. 1033, 1053 (1936) ("[I]t would be unfortunate if the law closed all safety valves through which irascible tempers might legally blow off steam.").

25. *See* GOODMAN, *supra* note 10, at 36–60. *See also* ALLPORT, *supra* note 5, at 289–301.

26. GOODMAN, *supra* note 10, at 55.

27. *Id.* at 56.

28. *Id.* at 58.

29. *Id.*

30. *Id.*

31. *See id.* at 83.

32. *See id.* at 86.

33. *See id.* at 60–73.

34. *E.g.*, Wilkinson v. Downton, [1897] 2 Q.B. 57 (defendant falsely told plaintiff her husband had had both legs broken in an accident; plaintiff suffered permanent physical harm).

35. *E.g.*, Fisher v. Carrousel Motor Hotel, Inc., 424 S.W.2d 627 (Tex. 1967).

36. *E.g.*, Alcorn v. Anbro Eng'g, Inc., 2 Cal. 3d 493, 468 P.2d 216, 86 Cal. Rptr. 88 (1970); Contreras v. Crown Zellerbach, Inc., 88 Wash. 2d 735, 565 P.2d 1173 (1977) (en banc).

37. *See* F. WERTHAM, A SIGN FOR CAIN 89 (1966) (racial prejudice depersonalizes the victim, thereby rationalizing violence and inhumane treatment).

38. *See generally* Brown v. Board of Educ., 347 U.S. 483 (1954). *Brown*

turned, clearly, on the stigmatizing effect—the indignity or affront of separate schools—because by hypothesis the schools were "equal." *See id.* at 492.

39. Wooley v. Maynard, 430 U.S. 705 (1977) (considerations of privacy and autonomy held to prevent New Hampshire from punishing citizens for putting tape over state motto "Live Free or Die" on license plates).

40. *See* W. PROSSER, HANDBOOK OF THE LAW OF TORTS, § 10, at 36 & n.85 (4th ed. 1971).

41. *See id.* § 10, at 36 & n.78.

42. *See* Allport, *supra* note 5, at 177 (When a speaker uses terms like "nigger," "spick," or "wop," "we can be almost certain that the speaker *intends* not only to characterize the person's membership, but also to disparage and reject him.") (emphasis in original). *See generally* HAYAKAWA, *supra* note 9, at 25 (racial and religious classifications serve no nondiscriminatory, predictive ends).

43. M. DEUTSCH, ET AL., SOCIAL CLASS, RACE AND PSYCHOLOGICAL DEVELOPMENT 175 (1968).

44. *Id.*

45. *See* ALLPORT, *supra* note 5, at vi; GOODMAN, *supra* note 10, at 73, 127–31, 135–36, 159–60, 163–64, 211, 232, 238–39; G. deHuszar, *Preface* to ANATOMY OF RACIAL INTOLERANCE, *supra* note 23, at 3.

46. GOODMAN, *supra* note 10, at 246.

47. K. KENISTON, ALL OUR CHILDREN 33 (1977).

48. Allport, *supra* note 5, at 139.

49. *See generally* H. JAMES, CHILDREN IN TROUBLE 278 (1970); J. KOZOL, DEATH AT AN EARLY AGE (1967); Vredeval, *Embarrassment and Ridicule*, NAT'L EDUC. A. J., Sept. 1963, at 17. Black teenagers have a one in ten chance of getting into trouble with the law and are five times more likely to be murdered than white teenagers. *See* L.A. TIMES, *supra* note 18. Black children are suspended from schools at twice the rate of white children. *See id.*

50. *See* M. MCDONALD, NOT BY THE COLOR OF THEIR SKIN 131 (1970).

51. *See generally* CLARK, *supra* note 4, at 65 (sense of inferiority is the most serious race-related injury to black child); M. DEUTSCH, THE DISADVANTAGED CHILD 106 (1968) ("[B]lack children tend to be more passive, more fearful and more diseuphoric than white.").

Deutsch has produced evidence to show that personality traits of defeatism and self-rejection in minority children are to a significant extent independent of income level. In a study comparing aptitude scores and self-image ratings among groups of low-income white children and similar black children, it was found that the latter had lower scores on aptitude tests and more negative self-images. *See* DEUTSCH, *supra* at 106. Another study found that although I.Q. levels increased with education and prestige ratings of occupations of the parents of both white and black children, the gains were considerably less for black children. *See id.* at 295. These studies seem to show that although poverty has a negative effect on a child's self-image and academic performance, the racial factor is even more significant. *See also* Kacser, *Background Paper, in* SUBCOMM. ON EXECUTIVE REORGANIZATION AND GOVERNMENT RESEARCH OF THE SENATE COMM. ON GOVERNMENT OPERATIONS, GOVERNMENT RESEARCH ON THE PROBLEMS OF CHILDREN AND YOUTH: BACKGROUND PAPERS PREPARED FOR THE 1970–71 WHITE HOUSE CON-

FERENCE ON CHILDREN AND YOUTH, 92d Cong., 1st Sess. 1, 15 (1971) (children who suffer from discrimination become convinced they are inferior and unworthy of help or affection, and respond by aggression, neurotic repression, withdrawal, and fantasy).

52. P. VAN DEN BERGHE, RACE AND RACISM 21 (2d ed. 1978).

53. *Id.* at 20.

54. *Id.*

55. ALLPORT, *supra* note 5, at 472.

56. WILLIAMS, *supra* note 24, at 73.

57. *See* Olmstead v. United States, 277 U.S. 438, 485 (1928) (Brandeis, J., dissenting) (teaching role of the law).

58. ALLPORT, *supra* note 5, at 470.

59. *Id.*

60. *Id.* at 439. *See also* G. Allport, *Prejudice: A Problem in Psychological and Social Causation* 4, Supp. Ser. No. 4, J. SOC. ISSUES (1950) (examination of prejudice as a mode of mental functioning).

61. H. Triandis, *The Impact of Social Change on Attitudes, in Attitudes, Conflict and Social Changes* 132 (1972) (quoted in P. Katz, *Preface* to TOWARD THE ELIMINATION OF RACISM 8 (P. Katz ed., 1976)).

62. GUNNAR MYRDAL, AN AMERICAN DILEMMA 20 (1962) (fallacy of theory that law cannot change custom).

15 Law as Microaggression

PEGGY C. DAVIS

I N   J A N U A R Y of 1988, the Chief Judge of the highest court of New York commissioned sixteen citizens to consider whether minorities in that state believe the court system to be biased. The answer was immediately apparent. With striking regularity minority people, in New York and elsewhere in the United States, report conviction that the law will work to their disadvantage. Every relevant opinion poll of which the Commission is aware finds that minorities are more likely than other Americans to doubt the fairness of the court system.

Having quickly discovered evidence of a widespread minority perception of bias within the courts, the Commission was left to consider its causes. The causes are not easily established. Those who perceive the courts as biased admit that incidents of alleged bias are usually ambiguous; that systematic evidence of bias is difficult to compile; and that evidence of bias in some aspects of the justice system is balanced by evidence that the system acts to correct or to punish bias in other sectors of the society.

The Lens Through Which Blacks Are Perceived

The work of Professor Charles Lawrence has sensitized legal scholars to basic psychological facts about race and perception. In urging that anti-discrimination laws be liberated from existing standards of intentionality, Lawrence argues that, as a matter of history, culture, and psychology, American racism is pervasive and largely unconscious:

> Americans share a common historical and cultural heritage in which racism has played and still plays a dominant role. Because of this shared experience, we also inevitably share many ideas, attitudes, and beliefs that attach significance to an individual's race and induce negative feelings and opinions about nonwhites. To the extent that this cultural belief system has influenced all of us, we are all racists. At the same time, most of us are unaware of our racism.[1]

The claim of pervasive, unconscious racism is easily devalued. The charge has come to be seen as egregious defamation and to carry an aura of irresponsibility.

98 YALE L.J. 1559 (1989). Originally published in The Yale Law Journal. Reprinted by permission of The Yale Law Journal Company and Fred B. Rothman & Company.

Nonetheless, the claim is well founded. It must be examined and understood, rather than resisted. It is examined here in the context of a small incident. The incident, reported below, will be analyzed first from the point of view of a white participant and as an instance of stereotyping. Then, it will be analyzed from the point of view of a black participant and as an instance of the "incessant, often gratuitous and subtle offenses" defined by black mental health professionals as "microaggressions."[2]

The scene is a courthouse in Bronx, New York. A white assistant city attorney takes the court elevator up to the ninth floor. At the fifth floor, the doors open. A black woman asks: "Going down?" "Up," says [the city attorney]. And then, as the doors close: "You see? They can't even tell up from down. I'm sorry, but it's true."

The black woman's words are subject to a variety of interpretations. She may have thought it efficient, appropriate, or congenial to ask the direction of the elevator rather than to search for the indicator. The indicator may have been broken. Or, the woman may have been incapable of competent elevator travel. The city attorney is led, by cognitive habit and by personal and cultural history, to seize upon the pejorative interpretation.

The city attorney lives in a society in which blacks are commonly regarded as incompetent. The traditional stereotype of blacks includes inferior mentality, primitive morality, emotional instability, laziness, boisterousness, closeness to anthropoid ancestors, occupational instability, superstition, care-free attitude, and ignorance.[3] Common culture reinforces the belief in black incompetence in that the black is "less often depicted as a thinking being."[4] If, for example, the city attorney watches television, she has observed that whites, but not blacks, are likely to exert authority or display superior knowledge; that whites, but not blacks, dispense goods and favors; and that blacks are disproportionately likely to be dependent and subservient.[5]

Cognitive psychologists tell us that the city attorney shares with all human beings a need to "categorize in order to make sense of experience. Too many events occur daily for us to deal successfully with each one on an individual basis; we must categorize in order to cope."[6] In a world in which sidewalk grates routinely collapsed under the weight of an average person, we would walk around sidewalk grates. We would not stop to inspect them and distinguish secure ones from loose ones. It is more efficient to act on the basis of a stereotyping heuristic. In a world in which blacks are commonly thought to be incompetent (or dangerous, or musical, or highly sexed), it is more efficient for the city attorney to rely on the generalization than to make individuating judgments.

It is likely that the city attorney assimilated negative stereotypes about blacks before she reached the age of judgment. She will, therefore, have accepted them as truth rather than opinion. Having assimilated the stereotypes, the city attorney will have developed a pattern of interpreting and remembering ambiguous events in ways that confirm, rather than unsettle, her stereotyped beliefs. If she sees or hears of two people on a subway, one white, one black, and one holding a knife, she is predisposed to form an impression that the black person held the knife, regardless of the truth of the matter. She will remember examples of black incompetence and may fail to remember examples of the opposite.[7]

Psychoanalysts tell us that the stereotype serves the city attorney as a mental repository for traits and impulses that she senses within herself and dislikes or fears. According to this view, people manage normal developmental conflicts involving impulse control by projecting forbidden impulses onto an outgroup. This defense mechanism allows the city attorney to distance herself psychologically from threatening traits and thoughts. In this respect, the pejorative outgroup stereotype serves to reduce her level of stress and anxiety.

Historians tell us of the rootedness of the city attorney's views. During the early seventeenth century, the circumstances of blacks living in what was to become the United States were consistent with principles of open, although not equal, opportunity. African-Americans lived both as indentured servants and as free people.[8] This early potential for egalitarianism was destroyed by the creation of a color-caste system. Colonial legislatures enacted slavery laws that transformed black servitude from a temporary status, under which both blacks and whites labored, to a lifelong status that was hereditary and racially defined. Slavery required a system of beliefs that would rationalize white domination and laws and customs that would assure control of the slave population.

The beliefs that served to rationalize white domination are documented in an 1858 treatise. In many respects, they echo the beliefs identified one hundred years later as constitutive of the twentieth century black stereotype:

[T]he negro, . . . whether in a state of bondage or in his native wilds, exhibits such a weakness of intellect that . . . "when he has the fortune to live in subjection to a wise director, he is, without doubt, fixed in such a state of life as is most agreeable to his genius and capacity."

. . . .

. . . So debased is their [moral] condition generally, that their humanity has been even doubted. . . . [T]he negro race is habitually indolent and indisposed to exertion. . . .

In connection with this indolent disposition, may be mentioned the want of thrift and foresight of the negro race.

The negro is not malicious. His disposition is to forgive injuries, and to forget the past. His gratitude is sometimes enduring, and his fidelity often remarkable. His passions and affections are seldom very strong, and are never very lasting. The dance will allay his most poignant grief, and a few days blot out the memory of his most bitter bereavement.

The negro is naturally mendacious, and as a concomitant, thievish. . . .

. . . Lust is his strongest passion; and hence, rape is an offence of too frequent occurrence.[9]

The laws and customs that assured control of the slave population reinforced the image of blacks as incompetent and in need of white governance. The master was afforded ownership, the right to command labor, and the virtually absolute right of discipline. Social controls extending beyond the master-slave relationship served to exclude the slave—and in some respects to exclude free blacks—from independent, self-defining activity. The slave could not obtain education, marry, maintain custody of offspring against the wishes of the master, or engage in commerce. Rights of assembly and movement were closely controlled. Social relationships between whites and blacks were regulated on the basis of caste hierarchy: Breaches of the social order, such as "insolence" of a slave towards a white person, were criminally punishable.

This history is part of the cultural heritage of the city attorney. The system of legal segregation, which maintained caste distinctions after abolition, is part of her life experience. This "new system continued to place all Negroes in inferior positions and all whites in superior positions."[10] The city attorney is among the

> two-thirds of the current population [that] lived during a time when it was legal and customary in some parts of this country to require that blacks sit in the back of a bus, give up their seats to whites, use different rest rooms and drinking fountains, and eat at different restaurants.[11]

The civil rights movement and post-1954 desegregation efforts are also part of the city attorney's cultural heritage. As an educated woman in the 1980s, she understands racial prejudice to be socially and morally unacceptable. Psychological research that targets her contemporaries reveals an expressed commitment to egalitarian ideals along with lingering negative beliefs and aversive feelings about blacks. "Prejudiced thinking and discrimination still exist, but the contemporary forms are more subtle, more indirect, and less overtly negative than are more traditional forms."[12]

Recent research also suggests that the city attorney can be expected to conceal her anti-black feelings except in private, homoracial settings. Many of her white contemporaries will suppress such feelings from their conscious thoughts. White Americans of the city attorney's generation do not wish to appear prejudiced. "[T]he contemporary form[] of prejudice is expressed [at least in testing situations] in ways that protect and perpetuate a nonprejudiced, nondiscriminating self-image."[13] Americans of the city attorney's generation live under the combined influence of egalitarian ideology and "cultural forces and cognitive processes that . . . promote prejudice and racism."[14] Anti-black attitudes persist in a climate of denial.

The denial and the persistence are related. It is difficult to change an attitude that is unacknowledged. Thus, "like a virus that mutates into new forms, old-fashioned prejudice seems to have evolved into a new type that is, at least temporarily, resistant to traditional . . . remedies."[15]

The View from the Other Side
of the Lens: Microaggression

Return to the fifth floor and to the moment at which the elevator door opened. The black woman sees two white passengers. She inquires and perceives the response to her inquiry. She sees and hears, or thinks she sees and hears, condescension. It is in the tone and body language that surround the word "Up." Perhaps the tone is flat, the head turns slowly in the direction of the second passenger, and the eyes roll upward in apparent exasperation. Perhaps the head remains lowered, and the word is uttered as the eyes are raised to a stare that suggests mock disbelief. The woman does not hear the words spoken behind the closed elevator doors. Yet she feels that she has been branded incompetent, even for elevator travel. This feeling produces anger, frustration, and a need to be hypervigilant against subsequent, similar brandings.

The elevator encounter is a microaggression. "These are subtle, stunning, often automatic, and non-verbal exchanges which are 'put downs' of blacks by offenders."[16] Psychiatrists who have studied black populations view them as "incessant and cumulative" assaults on black self-esteem.[17]

> Microaggressions simultaneously sustain[] defensive-deferential thinking and erode[] self confidence in Blacks. . . . [B]y monopolizing . . . perception and action through regularly irregular disruptions, they contribute[] to relative paralysis of action, planning and self-esteem. They seem to be the principal foundation for the verification of Black inferiority for both whites and Blacks.[18]

The management of these assaults is a preoccupying activity, simultaneously necessary to and disruptive of black adaptation.

> [The black person's] self-esteem suffers . . . because he is constantly receiving an unpleasant image of himself from the behavior of others to him. This is the subjective impact of social discrimination. . . . It seems to be an ever-present and unrelieved irritant. Its influence is not alone due to the fact that it is painful in its intensity, but also because the individual, in order to maintain internal balance and to protect himself from being overwhelmed by it, must initiate restitutive maneuvers . . .—all quite automatic and unconscious. In addition to maintaining an internal balance, the individual must continue to maintain a social facade and some kind of adaptation to the offending stimuli so that he can preserve some social effectiveness. All of this requires a constant preoccupation, notwithstanding . . . that these adaptational processes . . . take place on a low order of awareness.[19]

Vigilance and psychic energy are required not only to marshal adaptational techniques but also to distinguish microaggressions from differently motivated actions and to determine "which of many daily microaggressions one must undercut."[20]

The Legal System Perceived by Victims of Microaggression

We do not know what business the black elevator traveler has in the courthouse. Whether she is a judge, a litigant, a court officer, or a vagrant, it is likely that her view of the legal system is affected by her status as a regular target of microaggression. If she has a role in the system, she will be concerned about the ways in which she is heard and regarded. When a court decides matters of fact, she will wonder whether the judgment has been particularized or based upon generalizations from immutable irrelevancies. When a court decides matters of law, she will wonder whether it considers and speaks to a community in which she is included. She will know that not every legal outcome is the product of bias. Sometimes the person on the sidewalk who will not yield turns out to be blind, or stopping to speak, or also black. Sometimes contrary evidence is so powerful that stereotypes are overwhelmed; a black person may perform in such an obviously competent manner that s/he is *perceived* as competent. Sometimes contrary evidence is so weak that the influence of stereotypes is harmless; a black person who asks a seemingly stupid question may *be* stupid. At other times, the concerns of the black elevator traveler seem justified. The two situations described below are the sort that seem to justify her concerns. The first involves matters of fact and the experiences of three black jurors. The second involves matters of law and the perspectives from which blacks regard legal pronouncements.

JURORS UNDER THE INFLUENCE OF MICROAGGRESSION

Robert Nickey has three times assumed the role of juror in the legal system. On the last occasion, he sat in judgment of a young man of privilege accused of murdering a female companion. Mr. Nickey was one of three black jurors hearing the case of *New York v. Chambers*. Mr. Nickey has worked all of his adult life as a mortician; he considered himself well qualified to evaluate the evidence in a trial dominated by forensic testimony. When the deliberations began, he felt that his views were unheeded by white jurors. At hearings convened by New York's Judicial Commission on Minorities, Mr. Nickey testified that a particular moment in the deliberations confirmed in his mind a growing sense that racial difference lay at the heart of juror disagreement:

> *Mr. Nickey:* [The second black juror] asked the remaining jurors, he said, if this man was black, would any of you all have any difficult[y] convicting him of murder with intent.
> *Mr. Chairman:* He asked that in the jury room?
> *Mr. Nickey:* He asked that in the jury room, and I'm here to tell you there was a hush[ed] sound in that jury room. Nobody spoke for five minutes.
> And right then we were convinced there was some prejudice because the young man was white, young, a lot of money was behind him.

Mr. Nickey interpreted this moment in the jury room in light of a life history of microaggression. He had encountered whites who started or stiffened as he approached on a dark street or subway car but remained relaxed upon the approach of whites whose appearance and demeanor were no more threatening. He had encountered whites who did not give way if he approached on a busy street but yielded to a similarly situated white. He had often sensed that whites heard his ambiguous or perfectly sensible words and formed the thought that he "didn't know up from down." Robert Chambers did not fit the white jurors' stereotype of an intentional killer. From Mr. Nickey's perspective, their inability to conceive of Chambers as an intentional killer combined with an inability to credit the views of black jurors to produce intransigence and deadlock. He concluded that "beyond reasonable doubt" meant one thing for white defendants and another for blacks:

> [*Mr. Nickey:*] So I'm saying there is two kinds of justice[] here in the State of New York. One is for the rich and in my opinion, the rich, he gets off. He gets like what they call a hand slap. You know, a little time or no time at all.
>
> But if you are a minority and you don't have any money, you go to jail, it's as simple as that. You go to jail and you do your time.
>
> And I always felt and was taught that justice was blind to race, color, or creed. But that is not so here in New York.

A second black juror referred to the same moment in the jury room as the basis of a "strong belief of racial prejudice" that led him to seek to be relieved from further service. The third black juror, a woman, concluded that "racial prejudice, sexual harassment, sexism, chauvinistic and elitist attitudes . . . permeated the jury's deliberation process."

These jurors experienced microaggression on two levels. In the context of the deliberations, a message of inferiority and subordination was delivered as their views were disregarded. The stereotyped thinking of white jurors caused both a different evaluation of the evidence and an inability to credit the competing views and perspectives of the black jurors. As a result, the black jurors were rendered ineffective in the deliberative process. The theory of microaggression instructs that the black jurors' perception of being disregarded and marginalized in the deliberative process produced stress in direct proportion to the restriction that marginalization imposed upon their ability to function as factfinders.[21]

At a more general level, a social message of inferiority and subordination was delivered. The black jurors were struck not only by their own isolation and ineffectiveness in the factfinding process but also by the racialist character of the process. They took from the deliberations a belief that legal claims are consigned to a system unable in important respects to particularize factual judgments, and prone to deliver judgment in accordance with racial stereotypes. The belief that particular jurors were, as a general matter, inappropriately empathetic or indifferent to the plight of the defendant may have been disquieting, but the belief that they were empathetic or indifferent *in racially determined ways* was an affront.

It said to the black jurors that they, as black people, could not expect impartial consideration were they before the court as defendants or complainants. It increased their subjective need to be hypervigilant against manifestations of arbitrary prejudice and contributed to "the ongoing, cumulative racial stress[,] . . . anger, energy depletion, and uneasiness that result from the time spent preoccupied by color-related aspects of one's [life and work]."[22]

LAW AS MICROAGGRESSION

Mr. Nickey lacks scientific evidence of bias in the court system. He has as a basis for his assertions only his sense of the cognitive dissonance between black and white jurors in a particular case, educated by experiences of American racism and awareness of American history and culture. His beliefs about decisionmaking in the legal system are, however, consistent with the results of a research effort that has been described as "far and away the most complete and thorough analysis of sentencing that [has] ever been done." The study addressed the combined effects of the race of the victim and the race of the defendant upon a sentencer's decision of whether to impose the penalty of death.

This research, conducted by Professor David Baldus, established that when a black person has been accused of murdering a white person the likelihood that the killer will be sentenced to death is far greater than when homicide victims and perpetrators fall into any other racial pattern. The assertions offered earlier will, if credited, render this fact unsurprising: "If caste values and attitudes mean anything at all, they mean that offenses by or against Negroes will be defined not so much in terms of their intrinsic seriousness as in terms of their importance in the eyes of the dominant group."[23] It is a fact that certainly would not surprise Mr. Nickey.

Two years ago, the Supreme Court considered whether the Baldus research, which contained statistical evidence of an extreme manifestation of this racial pattern of capital sentencing in the State of Georgia, supported a claim that Georgia death sentencing procedures violate equal protection guarantees or prohibitions against cruel and unusual punishment.[24] The Court found the evidence inadequate to demonstrate "a constitutionally significant risk of racial bias affecting the Georgia capital sentencing process."[25] With arguments that wither (if they do not die) in the light of Professor Lawrence's explication of automatic and unconscious racism,[26] the Court found McCleskey's equal protection claim wanting by reason of his failure to prove the decisionmakers in his case guilty of intentional discrimination or the State of Georgia guilty of creating its system of capital punishment with a consciously discriminatory purpose.[27] With respect to the claim of cruel and unusual punishment, the Court also found that too little had been proven to warrant correction of the Georgia death sentencing scheme.[28]

When the Court announces law, as it did in *McCleskey*, it "constructs a response to the question 'What kind of community should we . . . establish with each other . . . ?'"[29] The law is perceived as just to the extent that it hears and respects the claims of each affected class. James Boyd White explains the point by example:

> In evaluating the law that regulates the relations between police officials and citizens . . . the important question to be asked is not whether it is "pro-police" or "pro-suspect" in result, nor even how it will work as a system of incentives and deterrents, but what room it makes for the officer and the citizen each to say what reasonably can be said, from his or her point of view, about the transaction—the street frisk, the airport search, the barroom arrest—that they share. . . . [T]he central concern is with voices: whether the voice of the judge leaves room for the voices of the parties.[30]

The relevant voices are not just those of the immediate parties, but those of all persons whose lives, status, and rights are affected by the announced law. The rules governing street frisks will be better rules to the extent that the rulemaker looks beyond the situations of the prosecutor and the frisked person to consider the positions of, inter alia, the police officer, the citizen who might be frisked, the citizen who might be victimized, and the community that shares the ambiguous or neutral characteristics that aroused suspicion and provoked the frisk.

Having in mind these questions of "voice," consider the reaction of James Nickey upon announcement of the *McCleskey* decision. Mr. Nickey will bring a question to the text: When this matter of constitutional law was debated, was there room in the argument for my voice? The accumulated effects of microaggressions give cause for skepticism. If there is a cultural pattern of reacting instinctively to blacks as inferior and subject to control, it is unlikely that blacks will have figured in legal discourse as part of the "we" that comes to mind as courts consider how "we" will govern ourselves and relate to one another. Just as the apparently incompetent elevator traveler will not be a credible witness, the being for whom one does not think of yielding on the sidewalk will not be thought of as an equal partner when the requirements of justice are calculated.

The *McCleskey* decision strikes the black reader of law as microaggression—stunning, automatic acts of disregard that stem from unconscious attitudes of white superiority and constitute a verification of black inferiority. The Court was capable of this microaggression because cognitive habit, history, and culture left it unable to hear the range of relevant voices and grapple with what reasonably might be said in the voice of discrimination's victims.

NOTES

1. Lawrence, *The Id, the Ego, and Equal Protection: Reckoning with Unconscious Racism*, 39 STAN. L. REV. 317, 322 (1987).

2. C. Pierce & W. Profit, Homoracial Behavior in the U.S.A. 2–3 (1986) (unpublished manuscript).

3. G. ALLPORT, THE NATURE OF PREJUDICE 196–98 (1954). The stereotype also includes overassertiveness, religious fanaticism, fondness for gambling,

gaudy and flashy dress, violence, a high birth rate, and susceptibility to bribery. *Id.*

More recent opinion studies indicate a reduction in self-reported negative associations with blacks. J. DOVIDIO & S. GAERTNER, PREJUDICE, DISCRIMINATION, AND RACISM 3–6 (1986). The relationship between self-reported beliefs and actual beliefs is, however, problematic in this context.

4. Pierce, *Psychiatric Problems of the Black Minority, in* AMERICAN HANDBOOK OF PSYCHIATRY 512, 514 (S. Arieti ed., 1974).

> For instance, although he is the district attorney in a [television] program, the black solves a case with his fists; an underling, who is a white police lieutenant, uses his brains to solve the same problem. That is, while the district attorney is being beat up, the lieutenant is deploying squad cars, securing laboratory assistance, and reasoning out his next move. Gratuitously . . . the show depicts the lieutenant speaking with a force and an arrogance that would not be tolerated in a real life situation between a district attorney and his subordinate.

Id. See also Pierce et al., *An Experiment in Racism: TV Commercials, in* TELEVISION AND EDUCATION 62 (C. Pierce ed., 1978).

5. C. Pierce et al., *supra* note 4, at 82; *see also* DOVIDIO & GAERTNER, *SUPRA* note 3, at 8–9, 64–65.

6. Lawrence, *supra* note 1, at 337.

7. *See* G. ALLPORT & L. POSTMAN, THE PSYCHOLOGY OF RUMOR 12–13, 99–115 (1947); *see also* S. Fiske & S. Neuberg, Alternatives to Stereotyping: Informational and Motivational Conditions for Individuating Processes 11, 12–13 (1986) (unpublished manuscript) ("Once perceiver has accessed a social category, it is difficult for the perceiver to respond accurately to the targets individuating characteristics.").

8. *See* Burns, *Black People and the Tyranny of American Law*, 407 ANNALS 156, 157–58 (1973) and authorities cited therein.

9. T. COBB, AN INQUIRY INTO THE LAW OF NEGRO SLAVERY 34–40 (1858) (footnotes omitted).

10. A. DAVIS ET AL., DEEP SOUTH 4 (1941).

11. DOVIDIO & GAERTNER, *supra* note 3, at 1.

12. *Id.* at 84.

13. *Id.* The authors show, for example, that anti-black feelings may be masked to the extent that they are displayed only when there is a nonracial factor that can be used to rationalize them. White research subjects led to believe that a person was in distress responded in nearly similar ways to black and to white victims (with a somewhat greater response in the case of black victims) if there was no apparent justification for a failure to respond. If the subjects knew of the availability of another who might respond, they "helped black victims much less frequently than they helped white victims (38 percent vs. 75 percent) . . . [and] showed lower levels of arousal with black than with white victims (Means +2.40 vs. 10.84 [heart]beats per minute). These subjects thus showed much less evidence of personal concern, in terms of both physiological response and helping behavior, for black victims than for white victims." *Id.* at 77–78.

14. *Id.* at 85.

15. *Id.* at 85–86.

16. Pierce et al., *supra* note 4, at 66.

17. Pierce, *supra* note 4, at 515.

18. C. Pierce, Unity in Diversity: Thirty-Three Years of Stress 17 (unpublished manuscript 1986).

19. A. KARDINER & L. OVESEY, THE MARK OF OPPRESSION 302–03 (1951).

20. Pierce, *supra* note 18, at 18; *see also* Dudley, *Blacks in Policy-Making Positions, in* BLACK FAMILIES IN CRISIS, (A. Coner-Edwards & J. Spurlock eds. 1988) 22 (describing psychic work associated with distinguishing racially influenced from other behaviors and fashioning response).

21. *See* C. Pierce, *Stress in the Workplace, in* BLACK FAMILIES IN CRISIS, *supra* note 20, at 31 ("a Black worker is stressed in direct proportion to the inhibition to control space, time, energy, and movement secondary to overt or covert racial barriers").

22. *Id.* at 31.

23. Johnson, *The Negro and Crime,* 217 ANNALS 93, 98 (Sept. 1941).

24. McCleskey v. Kemp, 481 U.S. 279 (1987).

25. *Id.* at 313.

26. *See* S. Johnson, *Unconscious Racism and the Criminal Law,* 73 CORNELL L. REV. 1016 (1988).

27. *McCleskey,* 481 U.S. at 279–82.

28. *Id.* at 312–13 ("[A]t most, the Baldus study indicates a discrepancy that appears to correlate with race. Apparent disparities in sentencing are an inevitable part of our criminal justice system. . . . '[T]here can be "no perfect procedure for deciding in which cases governmental authority should be used to impose death. . . ."' Where the discretion that is fundamental to our criminal process is involved, we decline to assume that what is unexplained is invidious.") (citation omitted). This disinclination to find a relationship between racial disparity and attitudes about race will remain a feature of the Court's jurisprudence so long as the mechanisms of contemporary racialism remain unacknowledged. For a recent example of this phenomenon, *see* City of Richmond v. J.A. Croson Co., 109 S. Ct. 706, 723–27 (1989) (discounting evidence of racial disparity among recipients of city contracts and members of contractors' associations as justifications for time-limited minority set aside program).

29. J. WHITE, HERACLES' BOW: ESSAY ON THE RHETORIC AND POETICS OF THE LAW 34 (1985).

30. *Id.* at 47–48.

16 Black Innocence and the White Jury

SHERI LYNN JOHNSON

H O W does racial bias influence the determination of guilt? If juries were approximately half black and half white, we probably would not need to ask this question because any individual juror's biases would be unlikely to alter the verdict. But many American juries are all white or almost all white, in part because of the racial proportions of our population and in part because of the system of juror selection. This state of affairs leads to a more specific question: Are innocent black defendants tried by white juries disproportionately subject to conviction?

To answer the question of whether black defendants are more likely to be convicted merely because they are black means, in social science terms, testing the null hypothesis that race is not a factor in the determination of guilt. The data relevant to the testing of this hypothesis may be divided into three categories: observations and statistics from real criminal trials, results of mock jury experiments, and conclusions from general research on racial prejudice. Although each of these data sources considered in isolation is incomplete, taken together they provide sufficient evidence to warrant rejecting the null hypothesis.

Trial Data

Data from the field, or "real life," are intuitively attractive; if large numbers of events could be studied in great detail, the results of those studies would be extremely persuasive. Unfortunately, it is extremely expensive and time-consuming to study people's behavior in natural settings. Refusals to cooperate often make such studies completely impossible. Therefore, observers usually must choose between studying a small number of occurrences quite thoroughly and collecting rather limited information about a large number of occurrences.

One of the earliest case studies was conducted by the University of Chicago Jury Project.[1] All jury trials arising in a single northern United States district between January 1954 and June 1955 were observed and, following each trial, all lawyers and jurors were extensively interviewed. Of the twenty-three trials stud-

83 MICH. L. REV. 1611 (1985). Originally published in the Michigan Law Review. Reprinted by permission.

ied, four were criminal trials of black defendants. The interviewer reported that racial prejudice influenced the jury deliberations in all four cases, including the one case in which the defendant was acquitted.[2] Several jurors explicitly argued during deliberations that the defendant should be convicted simply because he was black.[3] Many other jurors expressed unsolicited derogatory views of blacks to the interviewer.[4]

In the early 1960s Kalven and Zeisel investigated the functioning of the jury through a different technique: they interviewed trial judges concerning their views of jury verdicts in 1191 cases.[5] In 293 of these cases, the presiding judge disagreed with the jury's determination and was asked to explain the jury's behavior. If the judges' observations and impressions are to be trusted, the race of the defendant affected jury deliberations in three ways. First, in only twenty-two cases did the jury vote to convict when the judge would have acquitted; in four of these cases, the judge saw substantial evidentiary problems and explained the jury's verdict as prompted by the jurors' antagonism toward the defendant's involvement in interracial sex.[6] Second, the juries tended toward undue leniency in black defendant/black victim assault cases.[7] Third, although judges thought that jurors often acquitted guilty defendants out of sympathy for the particular defendant (this explanation was offered for 22 percent of all judge/jury disagreements, or 4 percent of *all* verdicts rendered),[8] black defendants were much less likely than white defendants to be the recipients of such leniency because they were viewed as extremely unsympathetic.[9]

Conviction Rates

Three studies find significant differences in the conviction rates of black and white defendants. Gerard and Terry report their analysis of data gathered in several Missouri counties in 1962.[10] The data were comprised of a randomly selected sample of all cases in which an information or indictment charging the commission of a felony had been filed; nineteen of these cases were tried by a jury.[11] Juries convicted ten of thirteen black defendants but only two of six whites.[12] Uhlman's sample of all felony cases docketed and disposed of between July 1968 and June 1974 in a large northeastern metropolitan area also found a statistically significant greater overall conviction rate for black defendants; 72 percent of all white defendants were found guilty and 75.9 percent of black defendants were found guilty.[13] Uhlman did not isolate jury trial verdicts, but he did investigate 24,100 bench trials presided over by twenty judges. Both black and white judges convicted black defendants more often than white defendants, but the interracial disparity was greater for white than for black judges.[14] Aggregating these rates across judges concealed enormous individual variation: for two white judges, the conviction rates of black and white defendants differed by *more than 70 percent,* and for another two the conviction rates differed by *more than 40 percent.*[15] While it is possible that factors not controlled for by the researchers accounted for the overall difference in conviction rates of black and white defendants, it seems unlikely that the extraordinary differences reported for these four judges did not reflect racial bias. Finally, a study of all persons indicted for first degree murder in twenty-one Florida counties between 1972 and 1978 revealed that black defendants were significantly more likely to be found guilty than were white defendants.[16]

Other Sentencing Data

Because judges rather than juries determine noncapital sentences, other sentencing data are even less directly probative of the bias in guilt adjudications than are death penalty statistics. Nevertheless, evidence of bias in sentencing would be especially disturbing because one would expect judges to be less racially biased—or to control their biases better—than jurors.[17]

Early studies of sentencing all showed substantial race effects, but many such studies did not attempt to control for other factors, such as type of offense or prior criminal record.[18] Numerous recent studies, some with adequate controls, have produced conflicting results.[19] One commentator has attempted to reconcile these studies by pointing out that even those finding statistically significant discrepancies show these to be of a small magnitude.[20] However, other commentators have argued that the apparent disparities may be only the tip of the iceberg: several forms of racial bias may operate in the sentencing of individual defendants but statistically cancel each other out.[21] There is some empirical support for this position. For example, harsher sentencing of black defendants convicted of interracial crimes may be offset by more lenient sentencing of black defendants convicted of intraracial crimes, as appears to be true in capital cases.[22] And, as another study has suggested, whites may be favored in the decision to incarcerate due to racial stereotypes about recidivism, but this may be offset by longer sentences for whites who are incarcerated, because their criminal success may be of a greater magnitude, particularly for larcenous crimes.[23] Finally, the harshness of some judges toward black defendants may sometimes be "balanced" by the lenience of other judges toward black defendants. Thus, Gibson has found that aggregate statistics showing no racial discrimination masked a mixture of pro-black and anti-black judges.[24]

Mock Jury Studies

Mock jury studies provide the strongest evidence that racial bias frequently affects the determination of guilt. These studies, like other laboratory experiments, do not suffer from lack of control, for the good experimenter assures that the *only* variable altered is the one being investigated. The problem of external validity, however, now arises; there is always the risk that causal relationships found in the laboratory are not present in the real world. This may occur because the laboratory setting interacted with the measured variables; for example, the condition of being observed might cause the subjects to try to conceal their racial bias. A second reason laboratory findings may not reflect real world phenomena is that the measured variables may not affect the subjects in the same way that their real world counterparts do; for example, the stimulus of reading that the defendant is black may not be functionally equivalent to the stimulus of seeing a black defendant through the course of a trial. Because of the strength and direction of the mock jury study findings, the question of external validity assumes particular importance.

Laboratory Findings

Laboratory findings concerning the influence of race on white subjects' perception of criminal defendants are quite consistent. More than a dozen mock jury studies provide support for the hypothesis that racial bias affects the determination of guilt. Of the handful of studies whose findings initially appear to support the null hypothesis, all, upon close examination, are ambiguous in their import. The mock jury studies may be divided into three categories: experiments investigating race and guilt attribution, experiments investigating race and sentencing, and experiments investigating the interaction among race, attractiveness, and blameworthiness.

RACE AND GUILT ATTRIBUTION.   Studies investigating the relationship between race and determination of guilt provide subjects with a transcript or a videotape of a trial in which the race of one of the participants—the defendant, the victim, or the attorney, depending on the study—is randomly varied while all other aspects of the case are held constant. The subject is asked to determine whether the defendant is guilty, and correlations between the race of the trial participant and the judgment of guilt are tested for statistical significance. Because the only factor that has been varied is a participant's race, statistically significant differences can be interpreted as reflecting a causal relationship between race and guilt attribution.

RACE OF THE DEFENDANT.   Nine very recent experiments find that the race of the defendant significantly and directly affects the determination of guilt. White subjects in all of these studies were more likely to find a minority-race defendant guilty than they were to find an identically situated white defendant guilty. Four studies find a significant interaction between the race of the defendant, guilt attribution, and some third variable. The one study that did not find any differences based on the race of the defendant may be reconciled with these findings based upon a careful analysis of its methodology.

The least complicated of these studies was published by McGlynn, Megas, and Benson in 1976.[25] The subjects were 208 white college students at a Texas university. Subjects read a summary of a violent murder case in which an insanity defense was presented and were asked to vote guilty or insane and to recommend a sentence for the defendant. Black males were found guilty in 69 percent of the cases, black females in 56 percent of the cases; both white males and females were found guilty in 54 percent of the cases.[26]

Two experiments published by Ugwuegbu systematically varied the victim's race, the defendant's race, and the amount of evidence pointing toward guilt (near zero, marginal, or strong).[27] The subjects in the first experiment were 256 white undergraduates at a midwestern university; the subjects in the second were 196 black undergraduates at the African American Affairs Institute.[28] After reading case transcripts, subjects in both experiments were asked four questions assessing the defendant's culpability;[29] answers to those questions were then correlated with each of the independent variables. For white subjects, the correlation between the defendant's race and culpability was significant: those subjects rated a black defendant more culpable than a white one.[30] Additional statistical tests revealed that the significance of the defendant's race varied with the strength of the evidence: when the evidence of guilt was strong or near zero the white subjects rated black and white defendants equally culpable, but when the evidence was marginal they rated black defendants more culpable. As the author explained, "[W]hen the evidence is not strong enough for conviction a white juror gives the benefit of the doubt to a white defendant but not to a black defendant."[31]

Ugwuegbu's second experiment, investigating the responses of black subjects, revealed a similar pattern of own-race bias. Black subjects rated the black defendant as significantly less culpable than the white defendant, and again the significance of the defendant's race depended upon the strength of the evidence.[32] Like white subjects, black subjects held a racially dissimilar defendant more culpable than a racially similar defendant when the evidence was marginal and were unaffected by the defendant's race when the evidence was weak.[33] Unlike white subjects, however, black subjects also judged a dissimilar defendant more harshly than a similar defendant in the strong evidence condition; "black subjects tended to grant the black defendant the benefit of the doubt not only when the evidence is doubtful but even when there was strong evidence against him."[34]

In a sophisticated study published in 1979, Bernard examined the effect of the defendant's race on the verdicts of juries with various racial compositions.[35] To increase verisimilitude, the experiment presented a videotaped "trial" (rather than a transcript) to a panel of jurors who were first asked for an individual verdict and then asked to deliberate and arrive at a unanimous verdict. The charge was assault and battery on a police officer, to which a defense of provocation and police brutality was offered. Deliberately ambiguous evidence was offered on the officer's propensity for violence and the defendant's intoxication. At the close of the testimony, the judge instructed the subjects on the applicable law. Five juries saw the videotape with a black defendant and five saw the videotape with a white defendant; in each set, one jury was 100 percent black, one 75 percent black and 25 percent white, one 50 percent black and 50 percent white, one 25 percent black and 75 percent white, and one 100 percent white.

On the individual ballot, white jurors tended to find the black defendant guilty more often than the white defendant, black jurors showing a reciprocal tendency to find white defendants guilty more often than black defendants, although neither trend was statistically significant due to the small sample size.[36] There was a pronounced tendency for jurors to shift their votes toward acquittal as a result of group discussion, with one notable exception: white jurors who found the black defendant guilty on their first ballot tended to hold to this decision and not be influenced by group discussion. By the final individual ballot, the number voting guilty had decreased to 15 percent and *all* of these guilty votes came from white subjects viewing the black defendant.[37]

An examination of the group verdicts is also anecdotally instructive. The only jury unable to reach a verdict was racially balanced (50 percent black and 50 percent white) and assigned to view the black defendant. By the second ballot, all white jurors in this jury voted guilty and all black jurors voted not guilty; this polarization persisted through two more ballots, when the jury reported itself incapable of reaching a decision. A second jury with the same jury-defendant combination was run and this jury also reported itself unable to render a verdict. Furthermore, only one jury ultimately reached a unanimous verdict of guilty: this was an all-white jury viewing the black defendant.[38]

RACE OF THE VICTIM.   Three studies consider whether the race of the victim influences guilt attribution, all finding a statistically significant effect. These findings are important in two ways. First, by revealing one way in which racial bias affects determinations of guilt, they increase the plausibility of the hypothesis that racial bias infects criminal trials in other ways, thus indirectly supporting the findings that the race of the defendant affects guilt attribution. Second, they pose the possibility of a cumulative effect of the race of the defendant and the race of the victim, such that the black defendant on trial for a crime against a white victim is doubly disadvantaged.

Miller and Hewitt's subjects were 133 students at a Missouri university, approximately half of whom were black and half white.[39] Subjects saw a videotape of the beginning of an actual court case involving rape, showing a judge and a defense attorney conversing in the courtroom with the accused, a thirty-year-old black male. Subjects were then given written summaries of the prosecution and defense arguments actually used in the trial. All subjects were told that the victim was a thirteen-year-old female, but half were told that the victim was black and half were told that she was white. Subjects were then asked how they would have voted had they been on the jury. When the mock jurors were white, 65 percent voted for conviction in the white victim condition but only 32 percent voted for conviction in the black victim condition; when the mock jurors were black, 80 percent voted for conviction when the victim was black but only 48 percent voted for conviction when the victim was white.[40]

Ugwuegbu's study, described earlier for its findings on culpability and the race of the defendant, also investigated the effect of the victim's race on culpability.[41] For both black and white subjects, the defendant was rated significantly less culpable when his victim was racially different from the subject.[42]

Klein and Creech's study investigated only white subjects.[43] Their first experiment revealed that for three out of four hypothetical crimes, regardless of the race of the defendant, subjects estimated the defendant's guilt to be greater if the victim were white than if the victim were black.[44] In their second experiment, they found that the black victim of a black assailant was judged significantly less truthful than other victims.[45]

[*Ed.* Professor Johnson goes on to discuss additional studies relating to the race of the defendant and victim.]

RACE, ATTRACTIVENESS, AND BLAMEWORTHINESS. Studies relating attractiveness, race, and blameworthiness provide additional support—and perhaps a partial explanation—for the findings on race and guilt attribution discussed above.

ATTRACTIVENESS AND BLAMEWORTHINESS. Investigation of the relationship between attractiveness and perceived blameworthiness has yielded consistent results. In their judgments of blameworthiness, subjects respond to the defendant's physical beauty, his social status, and the similarity of his attitudes to their own. One study found crime-specific facial stereotypes and correlations of those stereotypes with judgments of guilt,[46] while two more found that physically attractive defendants are less likely to be judged guilty.[47] Three mock jury studies found greater leniency in the sentencing of physically attractive defendants.[48] Furthermore, as with findings on race and blameworthiness, the effects of physical attractiveness operate on subjects through the victim's beauty as well as the defendant's: subjects tend to punish offenders whose victims were physically attractive more harshly than those whose victims were physically unattractive.[49] Socially desirable attributes, as well as physical beauty, appear to influence judgments of blameworthiness. One mock jury study found that defendants described as middle class were judged less guilty and assigned fewer years in prison than were defendants of a lower-class background. Three studies found that defendants described as working class and divorced were sentenced more harshly than were defendants described as middle-class family men. Finally, jurors' judgments of blameworthiness are altered by the extent to which the defendant's attitudes resemble their own: two studies found that subjects were more likely to find defendants with dissimilar attitudes guilty than defendants with similar attitudes.[50]

RACE AND ATTRACTIVENESS. The findings on attractiveness and blameworthiness assume significance when considered with findings relating race to attractiveness. White subjects have more trouble distinguishing black faces than white faces[51] and are likely to perceive black faces as less beautiful than white ones;[52] white mock jurors tend to perceive black defendants as coming from a lower socioeconomic class than white defendants despite otherwise identical descriptions of the defendants; and white subjects without information on the attitude of other persons assume greater attitude dissimilarity from black persons.[53] It would appear that white subjects tend to assume less favorable characteristics about black defendants than white defendants and that such assumptions contribute to these subjects' greater tendency to find black defendants guilty.

NOTES

1. Dale W. Broeder, *The Negro in Court*, 1965 DUKE L.J. 19, 20 n.3.
2. *Id.* at 21–22.
3. *Id.* at 23.
4. *Id.* at 24.
5. H. KALVEN & H. ZEISEL, THE AMERICAN JURY (1966).
6. *Id.* at 409. At least three of these cases involved a black defendant. *Id.* at 398.
7. Kalven and Zeisel reported four such cases. *Id.* at 340–41.
8. *Id.* at 217.
9. *Id.* at 343–44.
10. Gerard & Terry, *Discrimination Against Negroes in the Administration of Criminal Law in Missouri*, 1970 WASH. U. L.Q. 415.
11. *Id.* at 430.
12. *Id.*
13. T. UHLMAN, RACIAL JUSTICE 37, 78 (1979). A difference of 4 percent is statistically significant, extremely unlikely to have been caused by chance—because of the large number of cases involved. Whether it is of practical importance depends upon the interpretation of the correlation. Is it spurious, resulting from correlations with other variables, or does it represent the effect of racial prejudice in marginal evidence cases, as suggested by the mock jury studies described *infra?* If the former interpretation is correct, there is no practical importance in these findings; if the latter is correct, 4 percent of the black defendants who went to trial in that city were wrongfully convicted.
14. *Id.* at 66.
15. *Id.* at 68.
16. L. Foley, The Effect of Race on the Imposition of the Death Penalty (1979) (paper presented at the meeting of the American Psychological Association in New York, Sept. 1979).
17. *Cf.* S. NAGEL, THE LEGAL PROCESS FROM A BEHAVIORAL PERSPECTIVE 94–95, 109 (1969) (probation officers more often discriminated on the basis of race and economic class than did judges).
18. *See, e.g.,* Henry Bullock, *Significance of the Racial Factor in the Length of Prison Sentences*, 52 J. CRIM. L., CRIMINOLOGY & POLICE SCI. 411 (1946) (classic study finding racial disparities in sentence length); Garfinkel, *Research Note on Inter- and Intra-Racial Homicides*, 27 SOCIAL FORCES 369 (1949) (black offenders treated more severely than white offenders); Guy B. Johnson, *The Negro and Crime*, 217 ANNALS 93 (1941) (differential sentencing for black offenders, particularly those with white victims).

19. For a review of recent studies, *see* R. MCNEELY & C. POPE, RACE, CRIME, AND CRIMINAL JUSTICE 17–21 (1981); Hagan, *Extra-Legal Attributes and Criminal Sentencing: An Assessment of a Sociological Viewpoint*, 8 LAW & SOC'Y REV. 357 (1974).

20. Hagan, *supra* note 19, at 362–69.

21. Nagel & Neef, *Racial Disparities That Supposedly Do Not Exist: Some Pitfalls in Analysis of Court Records*, 52 NOTRE DAME LAW. 87 (1976).

22. *See supra* and accompanying text.

23. Nagel & Neef, *supra* note 21, at 90.

24. James L. Gibson, *Race as a Determinant of Criminal Sentences: A Methodological Critique and a Case Study*, 12 LAW & SOC'Y REV. 455 (1978). *See also* T. UHLMAN, *supra* note 13, at 37, 68, 78 (Although overall conviction rates varied only 4 percent, for two white judges the difference in conviction rates between black and white defendants was more than 70 percent, and for another two judges the conviction rates differed by more than 40 percent.).

25. Richard P. McGlynn et al., *Sex and Race as Factors Affecting the Attribution of Insanity in a Murder Trial*, 93 J. PSYCHOLOGY 93 (1976).

26. *Id.* at 96.

27. Denis Chimaeze E. Ugwuegbu, *Racial and Evidential Factors in Juror Attribution of Legal Responsibility*, 15 J. EXPERIMENTAL SOC. PSYCHOLOGY 133 (1979).

28. The responses of twelve white and ten black undergraduates were deleted from the data analysis for various reasons.

29. The dependent variables include the following questionnaire items:

1. I feel that the defendant's *intention* was to cause the plaintiff, Miss Brown: (No harm at all, Some harm, Extreme harm).
2. To what extent was Mr. Williams, the defendant, *responsible* for the rape?: (Not at all responsible, Moderately responsible, Very much responsible.)
3. With respect to my *verdict*, I feel the defendant is guilty as charged: (Not guilty of any crime, Moderately guilty as charged, Exactly guilty as charged.) [sic]
4. Based on the evidence, I feel I would recommend for the defendant as punishment: (No punishment at all; Suspended sentence; 1–5 years in the State Prison; 5–9 years; 10–14 years; 15–20 years; Over 20 years but not life; Life imprisonment; Death penalty.)

All of the items incorporated 9-point rating scales and were scored 1–9. The extremes and midpoints of items 1, 2, and 3 were verbally anchored with 1 indicating no culpability, 5 average, and 9 strong culpability, respectively. Item 4 was rated on a scale of nine alternatives. In each case, the higher the number the more punitive the judgment.

Ugwuegbu, *supra* note 27, at 137–38 (emphasis in original). The four items were then summed for each subject to derive a total score. *Id.* at 138.

30. *Id.* at 138–39.

31. *Id.* at 139–40.

32. *Id.* at 141.

33. *Id.* at 141–42.

34. *Id.* at 142.

35. J. L. Bernard, *Interaction Between the Race of the Defendant and That of Jurors in Determining Verdicts*, 5 LAW & PSYCHOLOGY REV. 103 (1979).

36. *Id.* at 109.

37. *Id.*

38. *Id.* at 110.

39. Marina Miller & Jay Hewitt, *Conviction of a Defendant as a Function of Juror-Victim Racial Similarity*, 105 J. SOC. PSYCHOLOGY 159 (1978).

40. For both black and white subjects, the greater tendency to vote for the conviction when the victim was racially similar to themselves was significant at the .01 level. *Id.* at 160.

41. Ugwuegbu, *supra* note 27.

42. *Id.* at 139, 141.

43. Kitty Klein & Blanche Creech, *Race, Rape and Bias: Distortion of Prior Odds and Meaning Changes*, 3 BASIC & APPLIED SOC. PSYCHOLOGY 21 (1982).

44. Klein and Creech reported positive results of statistical significance tests for the crime of rape. They did not calculate the statistical significance for the other three crimes, although for two of them (burglary and murder) the estimates of guilt were far higher in the white victim situation than in the black victim situation. It was only for the drug sale, where there were no true victims, that the race-of-the-victim differences were small and interacted with the race of the defendant: the estimates of guilt were slightly higher for black defendants with black "victims" and for white defendants with white "victims." *Id.* at 24.

45. *Id.* at 29.

46. Shoemaker et al., *Facial Stereotypes of Deviants and Judgments of Guilt or Innocence*, 51 SOC. FORCES 427 (1973).

47. Solender & Solender, *Minimizing the Effect of the Unattractive Client on the Jury: A Study of the Interaction of Physical Appearance with Assertions and Self-Experience References*, 5 HUMAN RIGHTS 201, 206–07 (1976).

48. Michael G. Efran, *The Effect of Physical Appearance on the Judgment of Guilt, Interpersonal Attraction, and Severity of Recommended Punishment in a Simulated Jury Task*, 8 J. RESEARCH IN PERSONALITY 45, 49 (1974); Harold Sigall & Nancy Ostrove, *Beautiful but Dangerous: Effects of Offender Attractiveness and Nature of the Crime on Juridic Judgment*, 31 J. PERSONALITY & SOC. PSYCHOLOGY 410, 413 (1975) (finding greater leniency in the sentencing of physically attractive defendants, except where the crimes involved capitalizing on the defendant's attractiveness); Solomon & Schopler, *The Relationship of Physical Attractiveness and Punitiveness: Is the Linearity Assumption Out of Line?*, 4 PERSONALITY & SOC. PSYCHOLOGY BULL. 483, 485 (1978).

49. Kerr, *Beautiful and Blameless: Effects of Victim Attractiveness and Responsibility on Mock Jurors' Verdicts*, 4 PERSONALITY & SOC. PSYCHOLOGY BULL. 479, 480 (1978).

50. Griffitt & Jackson, *Simulated Jury Decisions: The Influence of Jury-Defendant Attitude Similarity-Dissimilarity*, 1 Soc. Behavior & Personality 1, 5–6 (1973); Mitchell & Byrne, *The Defendant's Dilemma: Effects of Jurors' Attitudes and Authoritarianism on Judicial Decisions*, 25 J. PERSONALITY & SOC. PSY-

CHOLOGY 123, 125–26 (finding that similar attitudes influenced authoritarian subjects but did not influence egalitarian subjects).

51. *See* Paul Barkowitz & John C. Brigham, *Recognition of Faces: Own Race Bias, Incentive, and Time Delay*, 12 J. APPLIED SOC. PSYCHOLOGY 255, 261 (1982); John C. Brigham & Paul Barkowitz, *Do "They all look alike"?: The Effect of Race, Sex, Experience and Attitudes on the Ability to Recognize Faces*, 8 J. APPLIED SOC. PSYCHOLOGY 306, 314 (1978); Chance et al., *Differential Experience and Recognition Memory for Faces*, 97 J. SOC. PSYCHOLOGY 243 (1975) (reporting on two experiments); John F. Cross et al., *Sex, Race, Age and Beauty As Factors in Recognition of Faces*, 10 PERCEPTION & PSYCHOPHYSICS 393, 394 (1971); Galper, *"Functional Race Membership" and Recognition of Faces*, 37 PERCEPTUAL & MOTOR SKILLS 455, 458 (1973); Luce, *The Role of Experience in Inter-Racial Recognition*, 1 PERSONALITY & SOC. PSYCHOLOGY BULL. 39, 40 (1974); Roy S. Malpass, *Racial Bias in Eyewitness Identification?*, 1 PERSONALITY & SOC. PSYCHOLOGY BULL. 42, 43 (1974); Roy S. Malpass & Jerome Kravitz, *Recognition for Faces of Own and Other Race*, 13 J. PERSONALITY & SOC. PSYCHOLOGY 330, 332–33 (1969); Roy S. Malpass et al., *Verbal and Visual Training in Face Recognition*, 14 PERCEPTION & PSYCHOPHYSICS 285, 288 (1973); *see also* Sheri L. Johnson, *Cross-Racial Identification Errors in Criminal Cases*, 69 CORNELL L. REV. 934 (1984).

52. Bernstein et al., *Cross vs. Within-Racial Judgments of Attractiveness*, 32 PERCEPTION & PSYCHOPHYSICS 495, 500–01 (1982); *see also* Newman et al., *Ethnic Awareness in Children: Not a Unitary Concept*, 143 J. GENETIC PSYCHOLOGY 103 (1983) (children prefer pictures of same-race children, with this effect particularly strong in white children).

53. Donn Byrne & Terry J. Wong, *Racial Prejudice, Interpersonal Attraction, and Assumed Dissimilarity of Attitudes*, 65 J. ABNORMAL & SOC. PSYCHOLOGY 246, 247 (1962) (prejudiced white subjects assumed greater attitude dissimilarity from blacks than whites, but unprejudiced subjects did not); Hendrick et al., *Race Versus Belief Similarity as Determinants of Attraction: A Search for a Fair Test*, 17 J. PERSONALITY & SOC. PSYCHOLOGY 250, 257 (1971); *see also* Stein et al., *Race and Belief: An Open and Shut Case*, 1 J. PERSONALITY & SOC. PSYCHOLOGY 281 (1965) (white teenagers responded to stimulus teenagers on the basis of similarity of belief when extensive information on the target's belief was supplied, but when that information was withheld, responded on the basis of racial similarity).

17   The Social Construction of Race

IAN F. HANEY LÓPEZ

U N D E R the jurisprudence of slavery as it stood in 1806, one's status followed the maternal line. A person born to a slave woman was a slave, one born to a free woman was free. In that year, three generations of enslaved women sued for freedom in Virginia on the ground that they descended from a free maternal ancestor. Yet, on the all-important issue of their descent, their faces and bodies provided the only evidence they or the owner who resisted their claims could bring before the court.

> The appellees . . . asserted this right [to be free] as having been descended, in the maternal line, from a free Indian woman; but their genealogy was very imperfectly stated. . . . [T]he youngest . . . [had] the characteristic features, the complexion, the hair and eyes . . . the same with those of whites. . . . Hannah, [the mother] had long black hair, was of the right Indian copper colour, and was generally called an Indian by the neighbours. . . .[1]

Because the Wrights, grandmother, mother, and daughter, could not prove they had a free maternal ancestor, nor could their owner, Hudgins, show their descent from a female slave, the side charged with the burden of proof would lose. Allocating that burden required the court to assign the plaintiffs a race. Under Virginia law, Blacks were presumably slaves and thus bore the burden of proving a free ancestor; Whites and Indians were presumably free and thus the burden of proving their descent fell on those alleging slave status. In order to determine whether the Wrights were Black and presumptively slaves or Indian and presumptively free, the court, in the person of Judge Tucker, devised a racial test:

> Nature has stampt upon the African and his descendants two characteristic marks, besides the difference of complexion, which often remain visible long after the characteristic distinction of colour either disappears or becomes doubtful; a flat nose and woolly head of hair. The latter of these disappears the last of all; and so strong an ingredient in the African constitution is this latter character, that it predominates uniformly where the party is in equal degree descended from parents of different complexions, whether white or Indians. . . . So pointed is this distinction between the natives of Africa and the aborigines of America, that a man might as easily mistake the glossy, jetty clothing of an American bear for the wool of a black sheep, as the hair of an American Indian for that of an African, or the

29 HARV. C.R.-C.L. L. REV. 1 (1994). Copyright © 1994 by the President and Fellows of Harvard College. Reprinted by permission.

descendant of an African. Upon these distinctions as connected with our laws, the burden of proof depends.[2]

The fate of the women rode upon the complexion of their face, the texture of their hair, and the width of their nose. Each of these characteristics served to mark their race, and their race in the end determined whether they were free or enslaved. The court decided for freedom:

> [T]he witnesses concur in assigning to the hair of Hannah . . . the long, straight, black hair of the native aborigines of this country. . . .
>
> . . .
>
> [Verdict] pronouncing the appellees absolutely free . . .[3]

After unknown lives lost in slavery, Judge Tucker freed three generations of women because Hannah's hair was long and straight.

Introduction: The Confounding Problem of Race

I begin this chapter with *Hudgins v. Wright* in part to emphasize the power of race in our society. Human fate still rides upon ancestry and appearance. The characteristics of our hair, complexion, and facial features still influence whether we are figuratively free or enslaved. Race dominates our personal lives. It manifests itself in our speech, dance, neighbors, and friends—"our very ways of talking, walking, eating and dreaming are ineluctably shaped by notions of race."[4] Race determines our economic prospects. The race-conscious market screens and selects us for manual jobs and professional careers, red-lines financing for real estate, green-lines our access to insurance, and even raises the price of that car we need to buy.[5] Race permeates our politics. It alters electoral boundaries, shapes the disbursement of local, state, and federal funds, fuels the creation and collapse of political alliances, and twists the conduct of law enforcement.[6] In short, race mediates every aspect of our lives.

Hudgins v. Wright also enables me to emphasize the role of law in reifying racial identities. By embalming in the form of legal presumptions and evidentiary burdens the prejudices society attached to vestiges of African ancestry, *Hudgins* demonstrates that the law serves not only to reflect but to solidify social prejudice, making law a prime instrument in the construction and reinforcement of racial subordination. Judges and legislators, in their role as arbiters and violent creators of the social order, continue to concentrate and magnify the power of race. Race suffuses all bodies of law, not only obvious ones like civil rights, immigration law, and federal Indian law, but also property law,[7] contracts law,[8] criminal law,[9] federal courts,[10] family law,[11] and even "the purest of corporate law questions within the most unquestionably Anglo scholarly paradigm."[12] I assert that no body of law exists untainted by the powerful astringent of race in our society.

In largest part, however, I begin with *Hudgins v. Wright* because the case provides an empirical definition of race. *Hudgins* tells us one is Black if one has a single African antecedent, or if one has a "flat nose" or a "woolly head of hair." I begin here because in the last two centuries our conception of race has not progressed much beyond the primitive view advanced by Judge Tucker.

Despite the pervasive influence of race in our lives and in U.S. law, a review of opinions and articles by judges and legal academics reveals a startling fact: few seem to know what race is and is not. Today most judges and scholars accept the common wisdom concerning race, without pausing to examine the fallacies and fictions on which ideas of race depend. In U.S. society, "a kind of 'racial etiquette' exists, a set of interpretive codes and racial meanings which operate in the interactions of daily life . . . . Race becomes 'common sense'—a way of comprehending, explaining and acting in the world."[13] This social etiquette of common ignorance is readily apparent in the legal discourse of race. Rehnquist-Court Justices take this approach, speaking disingenuously of the peril posed by racial remediation to "a society where race is irrelevant," while nevertheless failing to offer an account of race that would bear the weight of their cynical assertions.[14] Arguably, critical race theorists, those legal scholars whose work seems most closely bound together by their emphasis on the centrality of race, follow the same approach when they powerfully decry the permanence of racism and persuasively argue for race consciousness, yet do so without explicitly suggesting what race might be.[15] Race may be America's single most confounding problem, but the confounding problem of race is that few people seem to know what race is.

In this essay, I define a "race" as a vast group of people loosely bound together by historically contingent, socially significant elements of their morphology and/or ancestry. I argue that race must be understood as a sui generis social phenomenon in which contested systems of meaning serve as the connections between physical features, faces, and personal characteristics. In other words, social meanings connect our faces to our souls. Race is neither an essence nor an illusion, but rather an ongoing, contradictory, self-reinforcing, plastic process subject to the macro forces of social and political struggle and the micro effects of daily decisions. As used here, the referents of terms like Black and White are social groups, not genetically distinct branches of humankind.

Note that Whites exist as a race under this definition. It is not only people of color who find their identities mediated by race, or who are implicated in the building and maintenance of racial constructs. White identity is just as much a racial fabrication, and Whites are equally, or even more highly, implicated in preserving the racially constructed status quo. I therefore explicitly encourage Whites to critically attend to racial constructs. Whites belong among those most deeply dedicated to fathoming the intricacies of race.

In this context, let me situate the theory I advance in terms of the epistemological significance of my own race and biography. I write as a Latino. The arguments I present no doubt reflect the less pronounced role physical features and ancestry play for my community as opposed to Blacks, the group most often considered in the elaboration of racial theories. Perhaps more importantly, I write from a perspective influenced by a unique biography. My older brother, Garth, and I are the only children of a fourth-generation Irish father, Terrence Eugene Haney, and a Salvadoran immigrant mother, Maria Daisy López de Haney. Sharing a similar morphology, Garth and I both have light but not white skin, dark brown hair, and dark brown eyes. We were raised in Hawaii, far from either my father's roots in Spokane, Washington, or my mother's family in San Salvador, El Salvador. Interestingly, Garth and I conceive of ourselves in different racial terms. For the most part, he considers his race transparent, something of a non-issue in the way Whites do, and he relates most easily with the Anglo side of the family. I, on the other hand, consider myself Latino and am in greatest contact with my maternal family. Perhaps presciently, my parents gave Garth my paternal grandfather's name, Mark, for a middle name, thus christening him Garth Mark Haney. They gave me my maternal father's name, Fidencio. Affiliating with the Latino side of the family, in my first year of graduate school I followed Latino custom by appending my mother's family name to my own, rendering my name Ian Fidencio Haney López. No doubt influencing the theories of race I outline and subscribe to, in my experience race reveals itself as plastic, inconstant, and to some extent volitional. That is the thesis of this chapter.

Biological Race

There are no genetic characteristics possessed by all Blacks but not by non-Blacks; similarly, there is no gene or cluster of genes common to all Whites but not to non-Whites.[16] One's race is not determined by a single gene or gene cluster, as is, for example, sickle-cell anemia. Nor are races marked by important differences in gene frequencies, the rates of appearance of certain gene types. The data compiled by various scientists demonstrate, contrary to popular opinion, that intra-group differences exceed inter-group differences. That is, greater genetic variation exists *within* the populations typically labeled Black and White than *between* these populations.[17] This finding refutes the supposition that racial divisions reflect fundamental genetic differences.

Rather, the notion that humankind can be divided along White, Black, and Yellow lines reveals the social rather than the scientific origin of race. The idea that there exist three races, and that these races are "Caucasoid," "Negroid," and "Mongoloid," is rooted in the European imagination of the Middle Ages, which encompassed only Europe, Africa, and the Near East. This view found its clearest modern expression in Count Arthur de Gobineau's *Essay on the Inequality of Races*, published in France in 1853–55.[18] The peoples of the American continents, the Indian subcontinent, East Asia, Southeast Asia, and Oceania—living outside the imagination of Europe and Count Gobineau—are excluded from the three major races for social and political reasons, not for scientific ones. Nevertheless, the history of science has long been the history of failed efforts to justify these social beliefs.[19] Along the way, various minds tried to fashion practical human typologies along the following physical axes: skin color, hair texture, facial angle, jaw size, cranial capacity, brain mass, frontal lobe mass, brain surface fissures and convolutions, and even body lice. As one scholar notes, "[t]he nineteenth century was a period of exhaustive and—as it turned out—futile search for criteria to define and describe race differences."[20]

To appreciate the difficulties of constructing races solely by reference to physical characteristics, consider the attempt to define race by skin color. On the basis of white skin, for example, one can define a race that includes most of the peoples of Western Europe. However, this grouping is threatened by the subtle gradations of skin color as one moves south or east, and becomes untenable when the fair-skinned peoples of Northern China and Japan are considered. In 1922, in *Ozawa v. United States*,[21] the Supreme Court nicely explained this point. When Japanese-born Takao Ozawa applied for citizenship he asserted, as required by the Naturalization Act, that he was a "white person." Counsel for Ozawa pointedly argued that to reject Ozawa's petition for naturalization would be "to exclude a Japanese who is 'white' in color." This argument did not persuade the Court: "Manifestly, the test [of race] afforded by the mere color of the skin of each individual is impracticable as that differs greatly among persons of the same race, even among Anglo-Saxons, ranging by imperceptible gradations from the fair blond to the swarthy brunette, the latter being darker than many of the lighter hued persons of the brown or yellow races."[22] In rejecting Ozawa's petition for citizenship, the Court recognized that racial boundaries do not in fact follow skin color. If they did, some now secure in their White status would have to be excluded, and others firmly characterized as non-Whites would need to be included. As the *Ozawa* Court correctly tells us, "mere color of the skin" does not provide a means to racially divide people.

The rejection of race in science is now almost complete. In the end, we should embrace historian Barbara Fields's succinct conclusion with respect to the plausibility of biological races: "Anyone who continues to believe in race as a physical attribute of individuals, despite the now commonplace disclaimers of biologists and geneticists, might as well also believe that Santa Claus, the Easter Bunny and the tooth fairy are real, and that the earth stands still while the sun moves."[23]

Racial Illusions

Unfortunately, few in this society seem prepared to relinquish fully their subscription to notions of biological race. This includes Congress and the Supreme Court. Congress' anachronistic understanding of race is exemplified by a 1988 statute that explains that "the term 'racial group' means a set of individuals whose identity as such is distinctive in terms of physical characteristics or biological descent."[24] The Supreme Court, although purporting to sever race from biology, also seems incapable of doing so. In *Saint Francis College v. Al-*

Khazraji,[25] the Court determined that an Arab could recover damages for racial discrimination under 42 U.S.C. § 1981. Writing for the Court, Justice White appeared to abandon biological notions of race in favor of a sociopolitical conception, explaining: "Clear-cut categories do not exist. The particular traits which have generally been chosen to characterize races have been criticized as having little biological significance. It has been found that differences between individuals of the same race are often greater than the differences between the 'average' individuals of different races."[26] Despite this seeming rejection of biological race, Justice White continued: "The Court of Appeals was thus quite right in holding that § 1981, 'at a minimum,' reaches discrimination against an individual 'because he or she is genetically part of an ethnically and physiognomically distinctive subgrouping of *homo sapiens.*' "[27] By adopting the lower court's language of genetics and distinctive subgroupings, Justice White demonstrates the Court's continued reliance on blood as a metonym for race. During oral argument in *Metrobroadcasting v. FCC,* Justice Scalia again revealed the Court's understanding of race as a matter of blood. Scalia attacked the argument that granting minorities broadcasting licenses would enhance diversity by blasting "the policy as a matter of 'blood,' at one point charging that the policy reduced to a question of 'blood . . . blood, not background and environment.' "[28]

Racial Formation

Race must be viewed as a social construction. That is, human interaction rather than natural differentiation must be seen as the source and continued basis for racial categorization. The process by which racial meanings arise has been labeled racial formation.[29] In this formulation, race is not a determinant or a residue of some other social phenomenon, but rather stands on its own as an amalgamation of competing societal forces. Racial formation includes both the rise of racial groups and their constant reification in social thought. I draw upon this theory, but use the term "racial fabrication" in order to highlight four important facets of the social construction of race. First, humans rather than abstract social forces produce races. Second, as human constructs, races constitute an integral part of a whole social fabric that includes gender and class relations. Third, the meaning-systems surrounding race change quickly rather than slowly. Finally, races are constructed relationally, against one another, rather than in isolation. Fabrication implies the workings of human hands, and suggests the possible intention to deceive. More than the industrial term "formation," which carries connotations of neutral constructions and processes indifferent to individual intervention, referring to the fabrication of races emphasizes the human element and evokes the plastic and inconstant character of race. An archaeological exploration of the racial identity of Mexicans will illustrate these four elements of race.

In the early 1800s, people in the United States ascribed to Latin Americans nationalities and, separate from these, races. Thus, a Mexican might also be White, Indian, Black, or Asian. By the 1840s and 1850s, however, U.S. Anglos looked with distaste upon Mexicans in terms that conflated and stigmatized their race and nationality. This animus had its source in the Anglo-Mexican conflicts in the Southwest, particularly in Texas and California. In the newly independent Texas, war propaganda from the 1830s and 1840s purporting to chronicle Mexican "atrocities" relied on racial disparagements. Little time elapsed following the U.S. annexation of Mexican territory in 1848 before laws began to reflect and reify Anglo racial prejudices. Social prejudices quickly became legal ones, highlighting the close ties between race and law. In 1855, for example, the California Legislature targeted Mexicans as a racial group with the so-called "Greaser Act." Ostensibly designed to discourage vagrancy, the law specifically applied to "all persons who are commonly known as 'Greasers' or the issue of Spanish and Indian blood . . . and who go armed and are not peaceable and quiet persons."[30]

> Typifying the arrogant belligerence of the times are the writings of T. J. Farnham: No one acquainted with the indolent, mixed race of California, will ever believe that they will populate, much less, for any length of time, govern the country. The law of Nature which curses the mulatto here with a constitution less robust than that of either race from which he sprang, lays a similar penalty upon the mingling of the Indian and white races in California and Mexico. They must fade away; while the mixing of different branches of the Caucasian family in the States will continue to produce a race of men, who will enlarge from period to period the field of their industry and civil domination, until not only the Northern States of Mexico, but the Californias also, will open their glebe to the pressure of its unconquered arm. The old Saxon blood must stride the continent, must command all its northern shores, must here press the grape and the olive, here eat the orange and the fig, and in their own unaided might, erect the altar of civil and religious freedom on the plains of the Californias.[31]

We can use Farnham's racist hubris to illustrate the four points enumerated earlier regarding racial fabrication.

First, the transformation of "Mexican" from a nationality to a race came about through the dynamic interplay of myriad social forces. As the various strains in this passage indicate, Farnham's racialization of Mexicans does not occur in a vacuum, but in the context of dominant ideology, perceived economic interests, and psychological necessity. In unabashedly proclaiming the virtue of raising industry and harnessing nature, Farnham trumpeted the dominant Lockean ideology of the time, an ideology which served to confirm the superiority of the industrialized Yankees and the inferiority of the pastoral Mexicans and Indians, and to justify the expropriation of their lands.[32] By lauding the commercial and economic interests of colonial expansion, Farnham also appealed to the free-booting capitalist spirit of America, recounting to his East Coast readers the riches which lay for their taking in a California populated only by mixed-breed

Mexicans. Finally, Farnham's assertions regarding the racial character of these Mexicans filled the psychological need to justify conquest: the people already in California, Farnham assured his readers, would "fade away" under Nature's curse, and in any event, were as a race "unfit" to govern their own land. Racial fabrication cannot be explained in terms of a few causal factors, but must be viewed as a complex process subject to manifold social forces.

Second, because races are constructed, ideas about race form part of a wider social fabric into which other relations, not least gender and class, are also woven. Farnham's choice of martial and masculine imagery is not accident but a reflection of the close symbiosis in the construction of racial and gender hierarchies during the nineteenth century.[33] This close symbiosis was reflected, for example, in distinct patterns of gender racialization during the era of frontier expansion—the native men of the Southwest were depicted as indolent, slothful, cruel, and cowardly Mexicans, while the women were described as fair, virtuous, and lonely Spanish maidens. Consider the following leaden verse:

> The Spanish maid, with eye of fire,
> At balmy evening turns her lyre
> And, looking to the Eastern sky,
> Awaits our Yankee chivalry
> Whose purer blood and valiant arms,
> Are fit to clasp her budding charms.
>
> The *man*, her mate, is sunk in sloth—
> To love, his senseless heart is loth:
> The pipe and glass and tinkling lute,
> A sofa, and a dish of fruit;
> A nap, some dozen times by day;
> Somber and sad, and never gay.[34]

This doggerel depicts the Mexican women as Spanish, linking their sexual desirability to European origins, while concurrently comparing the purportedly slothful Mexican man to the ostensibly chivalrous Yankee. Social renditions of masculinity and femininity often carry with them racial overtones, just as racial stereotypes invariably embody some elements of sexual identity. The archaeology of race soon becomes the excavation of gender and sexual identity.

Farnham's appeal to industry also reveals the close interconnection between racial and class structures. The observations of Arizona mine owner Sylvester Mowry reflect this linkage: "The question of [resident Mexican] labor is one which commends itself to the attention of the capitalist: cheap, and under proper management, efficient and permanent. They have been peons for generations. They will remain so, as it is their natural condition."[35] When Farnham wrote in 1840 before U.S. expansion into the Southwest, Yankee industry stood in counterpoint to Mexican indolence. When Mowry wrote in 1863, after fifteen years of U.S. regional control, Anglo capitalism stood in a fruitful managerial relationship to cheap, efficient Mexican labor. The nearly diametric change in the conception of Mexicans held by Anglos, from indolent to industrious, reflects the emergence of an Anglo economic elite in the Southwest and illustrates the close connection between class relations and ideas about race. The syncretic nature of racial, gender, and class constructs suggests that a global approach to oppression is not only desirable, it is *necessary* if the amelioration of these destructive social hierarchies is to be achieved.

Third, as evidenced through a comparison of the stereotypes of Mexicans propounded by Farnham and Mowry, racial systems of meaning can change at a relatively rapid rate. In 1821, when Mexico gained its independence, its residents were not generally considered a race. Twenty years later, as Farnham's writing shows, Mexicans were denigrated in explicitly racial terms as indolent cowards. About another two decades after that, Mowry lauds Mexicans as naturally industrious and faithful. The rapid emergence of Mexicans as a race, and the similarly quick transformations wrought in their perceived racial character, exemplify the plasticity of race. Accretions of racial meaning are not sedimentary products which once deposited remain solid and unchanged, or subject only to a slow process of abrasion, erosion, and buildup. Instead, the processes of racial fabrication continuously melt down, mold, shatter, and recast races: races are not rocks, they are plastics.

Fourth and finally, races are relationally constructed. Despite their conflicting views on the work ethic of Mexicans, the fundamental message delivered by Farnham and Mowry is the same: though war, conquest, and expansion separate their writings, both tie race and class together in the exposition of Mexican inferiority and Anglo superiority. The denigration of Mexicans and the celebration of Anglos are inseverable. The attempt to racially define the conquered, subjugated, or enslaved is at the same time an attempt to racially define the conqueror, the subjugator, or the enslaver.[36] Races are categories of difference which exist only in society: they are produced by myriad conflicting social forces; they overlap and inform other social categories; they are fluid rather than static and fixed; and they make sense only in relationship to other racial categories, having no meaningful independent existence. Race is socially constructed.

Conclusion

I close where I began, with *Hudgins v. Wright*. The women in that case lived in a liminal area between races, being neither and yet both Black and Indian. Biologically, they were neither. Any objective basis for racial divisions fell into disrepute a hundred years ago, when early ethnology proved incapable of delineating strict demarcations across human diversity. Despite Judge Tucker's beliefs and the efforts of innumerable scientists, the history of nineteenth-century anthropology convincingly demonstrates that morphological traits cannot be employed as physical arbiters of race. More recently, genetic testing has made clear the close connection all humans share, as well as the futility of explaining those differences that do exist in terms of racially relevant gene codes. The categories of race previously considered objective, such as Caucasoid, Negroid, and Mongoloid, are now widely regarded as empty relics, persistent shadows of the social belief in races that permeated early scientific thought. Biological race is an illusion.

Social race, however, is not, and it is here that the Wrights' race should be measured. At different times, the Wrights were socially both Black and Indian. As slaves and in the mind of Hudgins, they were Black; as free women and in their argument for liberty, they were Indian. The particular racial options confronting the Wrights reflect the history of racial fabrication in the United States. Races are thus not biological groupings, but social constructions. Even though far from objective, race remains obvious. Walking down the street, we consistently rely on pervasive social mythologies to assign races to the other pedestrians. The absence of any physical basis to race does not entail the conclusion that race is wholly hallucination. Race has its genesis and maintains its vigorous strength in the realm of social beliefs.

For the Wrights, their race was not a phantasm but a contested fact on which their continued enslavement turned. Their struggle makes clear the importance of chance, context, and choice in the social mechanics of race. Aspects of human variation like dark skin or African ancestry are chance, not denotations of distinct branches of humankind. These elements stand in as markers widely interpreted to connote racial difference only in particular social contexts. The local setting in turn provides the field of struggle on which social actors make racially relevant choices. For the Wrights, freedom came because they chose to contest their race. Without their decision to argue that they were Indian and thus free, generations to come might have been reared into slavery.

This is the promise of choice at its brightest: by choosing to resist racial constructions, we may emancipate ourselves and our children. Unfortunately, uncoerced choice in the arena of U.S. race relations is rare, perhaps nonexistent. Two facets of this case demonstrate the darkened potential of choice. First, the women's freedom ultimately turned on Hannah's long straight hair, not on their decision to resist. Without the legal presumptions that favored their features, presumptions that were in a sense the concrete embodiments of the social context, they would have remained slaves. Furthermore, these women challenged their race, not the status ascribed to it. By arguing that they were Indian and not Black, free rather than enslaved, the women lent unfortunate legitimacy to the legal and social presumptions in favor of Black slavery. The context and consequences of the Wrights' actions confirm that choices are made in a harsh racist social setting that may facilitate but more likely will forestall freedom; and that in our decisions to resist, we may shatter but more probably will inadvertently strengthen the racial structures around us. Nevertheless, race is not an inescapable physical fact. Rather, it is a social construction that, however perilously, remains subject to contestation at the hands of individuals and communities alike.

NOTES

1. Hudgins v. Wright, 11 Va. 134 (1 Hen. & M.) (Sup. Ct. App. 1806).

2. *Id.* at 139–40.

3. *Id.* at 140–41.

4. MICHAEL OMI & HOWARD WINANT, RACIAL FORMATION IN THE UNITED STATES: FROM THE 1960S TO THE 1980S 63 (1986).

5. *See* Ian Ayers, *Fair Driving: Gender and Race Discrimination in Retail Car Negotiations*, 104 HARV. L. REV. 817 (1991).

6. *See, e.g., Developments in the Law—Race and the Criminal Process*, 101 HARV. L. REV. 1472 (1988).

7. *See, e.g.,* Frances Lee Ansley, *Race and the Core Curriculum in Legal Education*, 79 CAL. L. REV. 1511, 1521–26 (1991).

8. *See, e.g.,* PATRICIA J. WILLIAMS, THE ALCHEMY OF RACE AND RIGHTS (1991).

9. *See, e.g.,* Randall Kennedy, McCleskey v. Kemp: *Race, Capital Punishment, and the Supreme Court*, 101 HARV. L. REV. 1388 (1988); *Developments in the Law, supra* note 6.

10. *See, e.g.,* Judith Resnick, *Dependent Sovereigns: Indian Tribes, States, and the Federal Courts*, 56 U. CHI. L. REV. 671 (1989).

11. *See, e.g.,* Elizabeth Bartholet, *Where Do Black Children Belong? The Politics of Race Matching in Adoption*, 139 U. PENN. L. REV. 1163 (1991); Twila Perry, *Race and Child Placement: The Best Interests Test and the Cost of Discretion*, 29 J. FAM. L. 51 (1990–91).

12. Duncan Kennedy, *A Cultural Pluralist Case for Affirmative Action in Legal Academia*, 1990 DUKE L.J. 705, 729 (citing Baeza, *Telecommunications Reregulation and Deregulation: The Impact on Opportunities for Minorities*, 2 HARV. BLACKLETTER J. 7 (1985)).

13. OMI & WINANT, *supra* note 4, at 62. For an extended discussion of "common sense" in the construction of racial identities, see Stuart Alan Clarke, *Fear of a Black Planet: Race, Identity Politics, and Common Sense*, 21 SOCIALIST REV. No. 3–4, 37 (1991).

14. City of Richmond v. J. A. Croson Co., 488 U.S. 469, 505 (1989). For a critique of Justice O'Connor's decision in *Croson*, see Patricia J. Williams, *The Obliging Shell: An Informal Essay on Formal Equal Opportunity*, 87 MICH. L. REV. 2128 (1989).

15. *See, e.g.,* DERRICK BELL, FACES AT THE BOTTOM OF THE WELL: THE PERMANENCE OF RACISM (1992); *and* Gary Peller, *Race Consciousness*, 1990 DUKE L.J. 758.

16. *See generally* LEON KAMIN ET AL., NOT IN OUR GENES: BIOLOGY, IDEOLOGY, AND HUMAN NATURE (1984); Alan Almquist & John Cronin, *Fact, Fancy and Myth on Human Evolution*, 29 CURRENT ANTHROPOLOGY 520 (1988); *and* Bruce Bower, *Race Falls from Grace*, 140 SCI. NEWS 380 (1991).

17. *See* Richard C. Lewontin, *The Apportionment of Human Diversity*, 6 EVOLUTIONARY BIOLOGY 381, 397 (1972). *See generally* L. L. Cavalli-Sforza, *The Genetics of Human Populations*, 231 SCI. AM. 80 (Sept. 1974).

18. THOMAS F. GOSSETT, RACE: THE HISTORY OF AN IDEA IN AMERICA 342–47 (1975).

19. *See generally* STEPHEN JAY GOULD, THE MISMEASURE OF MAN (1981); WILLIAM STANTON, THE LEOPARD'S SPOTS: SCIENTIFIC ATTITUDES TOWARD RACE IN AMERICA 1815–59 (1960); *and* NANCY STEPAN, THE IDEA OF RACE IN SCIENCE: GREAT BRITAIN, 1800–1960 (1982).

20. GOSSETT, *supra* note 18, at 65–83. Charles Darwin proposed several of these axes, arguing at one point that "[w]ith civilized nations, the reduced size of the jaws from lessened use, the habitual play of different muscles serving to express different emotions, and the increased size of the brain from greater intellectual activity, have together produced a considerable effect on their general appearance in comparison with savages." *Id.* at 78 (quoted without attribution to a specific source). Darwin also supposed that the body lice of some races could not live on the bodies of members of other races, thus prompting him to suggest that "a racial scale might be worked out by exposing doubtful cases to different varieties of lice." *Id.* at 81. Leonardo da Vinci is another icon of intellectual greatness guilty of harboring ridiculous ideas regarding race. Da Vinci attributed racial differences to the environment in a novel manner, arguing that those who lived in hotter climates worked at night and so absorbed dark pigments, while those in cooler climates were active during the day and correspondingly absorbed light pigments. *Id.* at 16.

21. 260 U.S. 178 (1922).

22. *Id.* at 197.

23. *See* Barbara Jeanne Fields, *Slavery, Race and Ideology in the United States of America*, 181 NEW LEFT REV. 95–96 (1990).

24. Genocide Convention Implementation Act of 1987, 18 U.S.C. § 1093 (1988).

25. 481 U.S. 604 (1987).

26. *Id.* at 610, n.4.

27. *Id.* at 613.

28. Neil Gotanda, *A Critique of "Our Constitution Is Color-Blind,"* 44 STAN. L. REV. 1, 32 (1991) (citing Ruth Marcus, *FCC Defends Minority License Policies: Case Before High Court Could Shape Future of Affirmative Action*, WASH. POST, Mar. 29, 1990, at A8).

29. OMI & WINANT, *supra* note 4, at 61.

30. Cal. Stat. 175 (1855), *excerpted in* ROBERT F. HEIZER & ALAN J. ALMQUIST, THE OTHER CALIFORNIANS: PREJUDICE AND DISCRIMINATION UNDER SPAIN, MEXICO, AND THE UNITED STATES TO 1920, at 151 (1971). The recollections of "Dame Shirley," who resided in a California mining camp between 1851 and 1852, record efforts by the ascendant Anglos to racially denigrate Mexicans. "It is very common to hear vulgar Yankees say of the Spaniards, 'Oh, they are half-civilized black men!' These unjust expressions naturally irritate the latter, many of whom are highly educated gentlemen of the most refined and cultivated manner." L.A.K.S. CLAPPE, THE SHIRLEY LETTERS FROM THE CALIFORNIA MINES, 1851–1852, at 158 (1922), quoted in HEIZER & ALMQUIST, *supra* at 141.

31. T. J. FARNHAM, LIFE, ADVENTURES, AND TRAVEL IN CALIFORNIA 413 (1840), quoted in HEIZER & ALMQUIST, *supra* note 30, at 140.

32. *See generally* Robert A. Williams, *The Algebra of Federal Indian Law: The Hard Trail of Decolonizing and Americanizing the White Man's Indian Jurisprudence*, 1986 WIS. L. REV. 219.

33. *See* Nancy Leys Stepan, *Race and Gender: The Role of Analogy in Science, in* ANATOMY OF RACISM 38 (David Theo Goldberg ed., 1990).

34. REGINALD HORSMAN, RACE AND MANIFEST DESTINY: THE ORIGINS OF AMERICAN RACIAL ANGLO-SAXONISM 233 (1981) (citation omitted).

35. SYLVESTER MOWRY, THE GEOGRAPHY OF ARIZONA AND SONORA 67 (1863), *quoted in* RONALD TAKAKI, IRON CAGES: RACE AND CLASS IN NINETEENTH CENTURY AMERICA 163 (1990).

36. *See* Kimberlé Crenshaw, *Race, Reform, and Retrenchment: Transformation and Legitimation in Antidiscrimination Law*, 101 HARV. L. REV. 1331, 1373 (1988).

From the Editor:
Issues and Comments

A R E you persuaded by Richard Delgado's argument that racial insults are harmful enough to warrant legal sanction? Is the definition of "harm" itself a political question, one that elite groups will generally insist be resolved in ways that do not alter their prerogatives too greatly? Can the law do anything about "microaggressions"? Should it? Are jury trials inevitably affected by bias when the defendant is black and the victim white? If so, is that an argument for eliminating jury trials in such cases, or for insisting that the jury be, for example, at least 50 percent black? Is social science in general a promising avenue for those seeking to reform the legal system in a nonracist direction—or is social science itself a universalizing instrument that is likely only to reflect the needs and perspectives of the dominant group, and hence unlikely to serve the cause of social transformation? Does what we call race even exist, except in our heads—or, perhaps, as a means of constructing (or going along with) white superiority?

The reader seeking further discussion of the foundations of race may wish to reconsider Part II (on stories and narratives relating to race and racism) and to note how race, class, sex, and sexual orientation intersect (Part VI). A famous article by Charles Lawrence on unconscious racism is listed in the Suggested Readings, immediately following. See also the work of Stephen Carter, much of which is also noted in the Suggested Readings throughout this book. On an anticolonialist approach to subordination, see generally the work of Robert Williams, excerpted in this volume and listed in the Suggested Readings for Parts II and III, above.

Suggested Readings

Carter, Stephen L., *When Victims Happen to Be Black*, 97 YALE L.J. 420 (1988).

Grillo, Trina, *The Mediation Alternative: Process Dangers for Women*, 100 YALE L.J. 1545 (1991).

Haddon, Phoebe A., *Rethinking the Jury*, 3 WM. & MARY BILL OF RTS. J. 29 (1994).

Johnson, Sheri Lynn, *Cross-Racial Identification Errors in Criminal Cases*, 69 CORNELL L. REV. 934 (1984).

Johnson, Sheri Lynn, *Unconscious Racism and the Criminal Law*, 73 CORNELL L. REV. 1016 (1988).

Lawrence, Charles R., III, *The Id, the Ego, and Equal Protection: Reckoning with Unconscious Racism*, 39 STAN. L. REV. 317 (1987).

Nunn, Kenneth B., *Rights Held Hostage: Race, Ideology and the Peremptory Challenge*, 28 HARV. C.R.-C.L. L. REV. 63 (1993).

STRUCTURAL DETERMINISM

A NUMBER of Critical Race theorists focus on ways in which the entire structure of legal thought, or at least of major doctrines like the First Amendment, influences its content, always tending toward maintaining the status quo. Some of these authors believe that once we understand how our categories, tools, and doctrines influence us, we may escape their sway and work more effectively for liberation. Others, such as Derrick Bell, hold that even this insight will do little to free us, although working against oppression brings its own rewards.

Part V begins with a chapter by Richard Delgado and Jean Stefancic explaining how three principal tools that lawyers use in researching the law and in finding cases promote sameness and stagnation, inhibiting reform and innovation. In the next chapter, Delgado and Stefancic show how the First Amendment, a mainstay of liberal jurisprudence, is of little use to racial reformers but instead deepens minorities' predicament. Part V ends with Derrick Bell's "Serving Two Masters," nearly twenty years old but timely today, in which he points out that civil rights attorneys, by virtue of their status and position, often fail to represent the real interests of their clients, pursuing instead the search for high-flown and highly aspirational ideals that are never realized.

18 Why Do We Tell the Same Stories? Law Reform, Critical Librarianship, and the Triple Helix Dilemma

RICHARD DELGADO and JEAN STEFANCIC

A REMARKABLE sameness afflicts many scholarly articles, books, and doctoral dissertations. Most blame peer review, tenure and promotion requirements, and ivory-tower isolation. In law, additional restraints operate: stare decisis—the insistence that every statement be supported by a previous one—bar requirements, and the tyranny of the casebook.

Although a few legal innovators have managed to escape these constraints, an impartial observer casting an eye over the landscape of the law would conclude that most of our stories are very similar—variations on a theme of incremental reform carried out within the bounds of dominant Western tradition.

This chapter focuses on an additional, seldom noticed means by which this sameness is created and maintained—namely, professionally prepared research and indexing systems. We single out three of these in wide use today: the Library of Congress subject heading system, the *Index to Legal Periodicals,* and the West Digest System. These devices function like DNA; they enable the current system to replicate itself endlessly, easily, and painlessly. Their categories mirror precedent and existing law; they both facilitate traditional legal thought and constrain novel approaches to the law.

A scholar who works within one or more of these systems finds the task of legal research greatly simplified. Beginning with one idea, such systems quickly bring to light closely related ideas, cases, and statutes. The indexes are like a workshop full of well-oiled tools, making work easier. Relying on them exclusively, however, renders innovation more difficult; innovative jurisprudence may require entirely new tools, tools often left undeveloped or unnoticed because our attention is absorbed with manipulating old ones.[1]

A few legal innovators have risen to this challenge, aided, from time to time, by mavericks and reformers in the library science field. Computerized word-search strategies promise some hope of breaking the constraints imposed by older

42 STAN. L. REV. 207 (1989). Copyright © 1989 by the Board of Trustees of the Leland Stanford Junior University. Reprinted by permission.

systems, but even they promise only a partial solution. Nothing approaching a general solution is on the horizon.

The categories contained in current indexing systems are like eyeglasses we have worn a long time. They enable us to see better, but lull us into thinking our vision is perfect and that there may not be a still better pair. Even when we discover a better pair, it, like the old, again sets limits on what we see. This process is inherent in our condition. We move from one set of limitations to another, finding only slightly greater freedom in our new condition. The beginning of wisdom is to understand and, insofar as we may, work around our limitations.

Classification Systems in Legal Scholarship

The three principal classification systems in use in the legal world are the Library of Congress subject heading system, which describes library collections; various periodical indexes, including the *Index to Legal Periodicals*; and the West Digest System, which classifies legal decisions under various subject headings and "key numbers."

LIBRARY OF CONGRESS SUBJECT HEADINGS

The Library of Congress Subject Headings, now in its 11th edition, originated in 1898 when the Library of Congress adopted the List of Subject Headings for Use in Dictionary Catalogs as a basis for its own scheme. The first edition of the *Library of Congress Subject Headings* was published in parts between 1909 and 1914. Later editions, appearing at irregular intervals, add new headings, reflect changes in conceptualization, and assure consistency. The current edition contains 162,750 headings; its three volumes contain 4,164 pages.

The list of headings, which is continually revised, expands at the rate of approximately 8,000 headings each year. An editorial committee of the Library of Congress Subject Cataloging Division reviews proposals for new headings to determine whether the revision is warranted and congruent with the existing *Library of Congress Subject Headings* structure. Although most proposals originate in-house, catalogers at libraries that have a cooperative agreement with the Library of Congress may also propose changes. Readers may be intrigued to know that the primary authorities for validating new law subject headings are *Black's Law Dictionary* and *Current Law Index.*

Critics of the Library of Congress charge that its subject heading policy is conservative, excessively cost-conscious, and without a coherent philosophy or structure. Critics also charge that the Library of Congress's position of leadership magnifies these weaknesses because other libraries generally follow the Library of Congress's example. Other critics complain that the system of headings simply replicates majoritarian politics and thought and gives too little attention to new, marginal, or renegade ideas.

Impatience with the *Library of Congress Subject Headings* has led at least one other library system, that of Minnesota's Hennepin County, to produce its own subject heading list and make it available to other libraries. Hennepin's subject headings have been called both more current than *Library of Congress Subject Headings* and more sensitive to social and cultural changes.

LEGAL PERIODICAL INDEXES

A number of services currently index legal periodicals. The two principal ones, the *Index to Legal Periodicals* and *Current Law Index*, provide subject access, but they derive their headings from different sources. The *Index to Legal Periodicals* lists *Black's Law Dictionary* (published by West) and West's *Legal Thesaurus/Dictionary* as sources of authority for its subject headings.[2] *Current Law Index* is based on Library of Congress subject headings with modifications.[3] The Library of Congress lists *Black's Law Dictionary* and *Current Law Index* as principal sources used to establish authority.[4] The circle is nearly complete.[5]

THE WEST DIGEST SYSTEM

The West Digest System began as an aid to legal researchers. Prior to its inception there was no comprehensive or uniform indexing of state and federal cases. As a result, late 19th and early 20th century American scholars encountered a great deal of difficulty as they struggled with the unwieldy body of American law. Henry Terry aptly summarized the early quandary: "In substance our law is excellent, full of justice and good sense, but in form it is chaotic. It has no systematic arrangement which is generally recognized and used, a fact which greatly increases the labors of lawyers and causes unnecessary litigation."[6] Some scholars note that the inability of lawyers to follow the development of the law either nationally or locally threatened stare decisis because of the "enormous and unrestrained quantity" of competing reporters, which "discouraged research and inevitably led to a conflict among authorities."[7]

In 1876 the West Company published its first compilations of court reports, *The Syllabi.* By 1879 the company published a permanent edition, the *North Western Reporter,* which included judicial decisions of the Dakota Territory, Iowa, Michigan, Minnesota, Nebraska, and Wisconsin. Facing little competition, West blanketed the country with its seven regional reporters that came to be known as the National Reporter System. The system today covers states, the various federal courts, and some sets of statutes. West's great advantage was a uniform plan of headnotes and indexing in all its reporters. A 1983 article states that eight classification editors assign keynotes to cases; thirty-four general editors who work under them write headnotes and synopses. Change comes slowly: The topic "Labor" received a heading in the 1950s, and until recently West classified "Workers' Compensation" under "Master and Servant" law.[8]

Classification Systems and the Replication of Preexisting Thought: The Triple Helix Dilemma

Existing classification systems serve their intended purpose admirably: They enable researchers to find helpful cases, articles, and books. Their power is instrumental; once the researcher knows what he or she is looking for, the classification systems enable him or her to find it. Yet, at the same time, the very search for authority, precedent, and hierarchy in cases and statutes can create the false impression that law is exact and deterministic—a science—with only one correct answer to a legal question.[9]

Moreover, in many instances the researcher will not know what he or she is looking for. The situation may call for innovation. The indexing systems may not have developed a category for the issue being researched, or having invented one, have failed to enter a key item into the database selected by the researcher, thus rendering the system useless. The systems function rather like molecular biology's double helix: They replicate preexisting ideas, thoughts, and approaches. Within the bounds of the three systems, moderate, incremental reform remains quite possible, but the systems make foundational, transformative innovation difficult. Because the three classification systems operate in a coordinated network of information retrieval, we call the situation confronting the lawyer or scholar trying to break free from their constraints the triple helix dilemma.

To illustrate this dilemma, consider the range of listings found under the general heading of civil rights. Recently, scholars have begun to question basic premises in this area of law.[10] Some have challenged the utility of White-generated theory developed in White-dominated academic milieux.[11] Others have called into question key presuppositions of civil rights cases and statutes, observing that present legal remedies generally benefit Whites more than Blacks[12] and provide relief for Blacks only when they do not impose unacceptable costs on elite Whites.[13] They also cast doubt on such cherished beliefs as that Blacks are experiencing steady socio-economic gains,[14] that affirmative action enables many to move ahead in the workplace,[15] and that the foremost challenge facing the civil rights community is attacking individual and institutional racism through education, litigation, and progressive legislation.[16]

These writers have found current legal categorization schemes a hindrance more than a help. A glance at the standard categories shows why; each system bears a strong imprint of the incremental civil rights approach these writers decry. The *Index to Legal Periodicals* and *Decennial Digest*, for example, lead the reader to works on civil rights, employment discrimination, and school integration or desegregation, but contain no entry for hegemony or interest convergence. The *Index to Legal Periodicals* lacked an entry for critical legal studies until September 1987, nearly a decade after the movement began. The *Decennial Digest* contains entries on slums and miscegenation. To find cases on ghettos, one must look in the Descriptive Word Index under slums, which refers the searcher to public improvements under the topic municipal corporations. Another index contains an entry labeled, simply, races. None of the major indexes contains entries for legitimation, false consciousness, or many other themes of the "new" or critical race-remedies scholarship. Indeed, a researcher who confined himself or herself to the sources listed under standard civil rights headings would be unlikely to come in contact with these ideas, much less invent them on his or her own.

As an example of the channeling effect of current legal categorization schemes, consider the situation of Black women wishing to sue for job discrimination directed against them as Black women. Attorneys searching for precedent will find a large body of case and statutory law under the headings "race discrimination" and "sex discrimination." No category combines the two types of discrimination (although computer-assisted researchers can better approximate a cross-referencing system by combining the two categories in the same search). Because of the structure of the indexing systems, attorneys for Black women have filed suit under one category or the other, or sometimes both.[17] Recently, critics have pointed out that under this approach Black women will lose if the employer can show that it has a satisfactory record for hiring and promoting women generally (including White women) and similarly for hiring Blacks (including Black men). The employer will prevail even if it has been blatantly discriminatory against Black women because the legal classification schemes treat Black women like the most advantaged members of each group (White women and Black men, respectively), when they are probably the least advantaged.[18]

To correct this problem, legal scholars have recently created the concept of intersectionality and have urged that Black women's unique situation be recognized, named, and addressed.[19] Of course, more than the absence of an index category created the Black women's dilemma.[20] But until the lacuna was recognized and named, legal classification systems made it difficult to notice or redress. Reform now will require disaggregation of the current dichotomous classification scheme, creation of a more complex one, and reorganization of the relevant cases and statutes accordingly.

Word-based computer searches solve only part of the problem. Some key articles and cases dealing with concepts such as civil disobedience or legitimation do not refer to them by name; others that do are not included in standard legal databases.[21] The efficiency of word-based searches depends on the probability that the searcher and the court have used the same word or phrase for the concept in question. Computers may be excellent means of finding cases about cows that wander onto highways. They are less useful in finding cases that illustrate or discuss more complex or abstract concepts.[22] Word-based computer searches provide even less assistance to the researcher in coining a concept or word. They are most useful once someone has proposed the concept or word and an editor has entered the text containing it into the database. Finally, computerized research can "freeze" the law by limiting the search to cases containing particular words or expressions. Research should encourage browsing and analogical reasoning. Paradoxically, computer-assisted research can discourage innovation and law reform.

LEXIS, WESTLAW, and their users are now more sophisticated than in the early days when simple questions stumped the companies' demonstrators, but many of these problems remain. Ironically, a number of observers suggest adding subject indexing to the LEXIS and WESTLAW systems, thus interposing another human being's subjective judgment between researcher and text—the very thing that computer-assisted legal research was designed to replace.

Existing legal research systems thus tug the researcher toward the familiar, the conventional. The legal researcher quickly discovers preexisting ideas, arguments, and legal strategies and is rewarded for staying on familiar ground. Striking out on one's own is costly and inefficient. Courts, other scholars, and one's adversary will all frame the problem in common terms; the temptation to go along is almost irresistible. Stepping outside the framework is like abandoning a well-known and well-mapped coast for the uncharted sea. We never realize that we cannot embark on certain types of journeys armed only with conventional maps.

Preexisting legal thought thus replicates itself. The indexes put one set of ideas at the researcher's disposal; it becomes difficult to visualize another, or imagine that one could exist. Nevertheless, a few thinkers do manage to escape the trammels we have discussed and propose new ways of thinking about legal reality. The next section explores ways to achieve this innovation, including how to turn the existing classification systems to the advantage of the legal transformer.

How to Break the Circle

We can sometimes break the cycle of repetitive thought and scholarship and achieve genuine innovation. Just as in evolution, where organisms regularly appear with traits not present in their ancestors, each generation presents us with a few legal thinkers able to break free from the constraints of preexisting thought and offer striking and effective new approaches.[23]

Often, but not always, these thinkers will be individuals whose life experiences have differed markedly from those of their contemporaries.[24] They may be members of marginal groups, or persons who are in other ways separated from the mainstream.[25] In civil rights scholarship, one thinks of Derrick Bell, the innovative Black scholar whose work on interest-convergence, the usefulness of standard remedies, and parables of racial injustice is challenging the civil rights community to reexamine long-held assumptions.[26] We should heed these divergent individuals. Their ideas offer the possibility of legal transformation and growth. Like nature's mutant or hybrid, they offer the infusion of new material needed to retain the vitality of our system of thought.

Can others acquire the skill which some possess at transcending conventional legal categories and modes of thought? In a recent article, Richard Sherwin implies that "suspicion" may be an acquired ability which we can sharpen through experience.[27] We are less sanguine. One scholar suggests that creativity is neither widely nor predictably distributed among the human population, and that it is not easily acquired.[28] In law and politics innovative potential may be linked with "double consciousness"[29] or life experiences that in some way deviate from the norm.[30] The incentive to innovate may be stronger in persons for whom the current system does not work well. The pressures of a lawyer's or librarian's life may hinder creativity.[31] Law professors are not free of all those pressures—they have classes to teach, papers to grade, meetings to attend, and other minutiae of academic life. Perhaps we can only try to look beyond the conventional and applaud those who, often for unknown reasons, actually do so.

Our bondage offers a second route to transformation. Categories in the principal legal indexing systems are explicit. They exist externally, in printed and electronic media, as well as within our minds. If we examine them, we will see an outline of the structure of traditional legal thought. That structure will reveal what previous courts and writers have recognized and what indexers have faithfully recorded. By inspecting this record, we may gain a glimpse of the very conceptual framework we have been wielding in scrutinizing and interpreting our societal order. We may then inquire whether that framework is the only, or the best, means of doing so. We may turn that system on its side and ask what is missing.

Our earlier review of the way civil rights categories limit thought and innovation showed that open-minded inquiry is not easy. Yet, a skeptical examination of what exists may sometimes prompt a researcher to ask why something else does not exist. For example, a feminist study group recently explored a legal issue affecting women. Although the members knew of several cases that dealt with the problem, West indexers had created no category for it. Thus, the only way to find the cases was to know about and shepardize one or perform a word-based computer search employing as many descriptive terms and synonyms as possible. The feminists, sophisticated in ways of patriarchy and mindset, concluded from their experience that the oversight was not merely inadvertent, but rooted in the structure of male-dominated law. Less sophisticated users might have blamed themselves for not finding the right section of the Digest or concluded that the absence of a category was an isolated oversight, attributable perhaps to bibliographic lag, that would be cleared up in the next edition.

G O I N G beyond standard legal categories and conventional wisdom is difficult even when we are only looking for moderate, incremental reform that does little to tax one's imagination or the traditional legal system. Where one desires more fundamental change, the task is made more difficult by stare decisis, bar requirements, and the standardizing effect of law school casebooks. These forces set up a powerful, largely unconscious, preference for the familiar, rendering legal innovation difficult.

This chapter has focused on an additional barrier to legal transformation: the principal indexing and research systems. These systems confine thought to the familiar categories of traditional legal theory. They quickly and painlessly enable the researcher to locate books, articles, and cases within that tradition, but they are unlikely to bring to light transformative ideas and analogies. The principal indexing systems' ease and economy encourage an unconscious self-censorship of the mind that is difficult to elude, indeed even to recognize.[32]

We discussed two means by which we can sometimes escape the constraints of current legal categories, to examine the framework that underlies legal reality. These strategies enable us to discover the intricacies and limitations inherent in our framework, make allowances for them, and so view reality in a truer, fairer light. Yet, an expanded framework will in time become a further prison, requiring yet another struggle to break free. We can only hope to progress from one degree of nonfreedom to another, slightly less confining one. Vigilance and effort are required to achieve even these modest gains.

NOTES

1. The very rules of structure that enable editors and indexers to place an article or case into particular categories are themselves matters of interpretation, custom, and ultimately politics, which in time have come to seem natural and inevitable. *See* Steven M. Barkan, *Deconstructing Legal Research: A Law Librarian's Commentary on Critical Legal Studies*, 79 LAW LIBR. J. 617, 632–34 (1987); *see also* Basil B. Bernstein, *On the Classification and Framing of Educational Knowledge, in* 1 CLASS, CODES, AND CONTROL: TOWARDS A SOCIOLOGY OF LANGUAGE 202 (1971) (the way society selects and classifies public knowledge "reflects both the distribution of power and the principles of social control"); *Groups Challenge Library's Holocaust-Revisionist Titles*, 19 AM. LIBR. 640 (1988) (decisions to categorize material in one form or another, e.g., "straight" or with commentary, are ultimately political); Duncan Kennedy, *The Structure of Blackstone's Commentaries*, 28 BUFFALO L. REV. 209, 215–16 (1979) (all legal categories are essentially lies, artificial constructs designed to make things seem more orderly than they are, and yet, paradoxically, we cannot live without them).
2. INDEX TO LEGAL PERIODICALS: THESAURUS iv (1988).
3. 8 CURRENT LAW INDEX iii (1987); KENT OLSON & ROBERT BERRING, PRACTICAL APPROACHES TO LEGAL RESEARCH (1988) ("*CLI* uses Library of Congress subject headings instead of the more general Wilson headings.").
4. P. ENYINGI ET AL., CATALOGUING LEGAL LITERATURE 370 (2d ed. 1988).
5. Circularities are also rampant within particular systems. A 1988 search on LEGALTRAC of the term "sexual orientation" provided a 'see also' reference to "sexual deviation" which carried a 'see' reference from "sexual perversion." Under "sexual deviation" was a 'see also' reference to "sexual masochism." The University of San Francisco Law Library notified Information Access of these peculiarities, and the headings have since been revised. Printouts are on file with the authors. *See generally* Mary Dykstra, *Can Subject Headings Be Saved?*, Libr. J., Sept. 15, 1988, at 55; Mary Dykstra, *LC Subject Headings Disguised as a Thesaurus*, Libr. J., Mar. 1, 1988, at 42, 44–46.
6. Henry Terry, *Arrangement of the Law*, 15 U. ILL. L. REV. 61 (1920).
7. Thomas Woxland, *"Forever Associated with the Practice of Law": The Early Years of the West Publishing Company*, 5 LEGAL REFERENCE SERVICES Q., no. 1, 1985, at 123.
8. Jill Abramson et al., *Inside the West Empire: They Define American Jurisprudence—And Make Millions in the Process. Can They Keep It Up?*, AM. LAW., Oct. 1983, at 90 (current).
9. *See, e.g.*, William F. Birdsall, *The Political Persuasion of Librarianship*, LIBR. J., June 1, 1988, at 75 (classifications based on ideology are inevitably normative, but few indexers realize this); David Kairys, *Legal Reasoning, in* THE POL-

ITICS OF LAW: A PROGRESSIVE CRITIQUE 11 (1982) (legal reasoning basically normative).

10. *See, e.g.,* DERRICK BELL, AND WE ARE NOT SAVED (1987); Kimberlé Williams Crenshaw, *Race, Reform, and Retrenchment: Transformation and Legitimation in Antidiscrimination Law,* 101 HARV. L. REV. 1331 (1988); Richard Delgado, *Derrick Bell and the Ideology of Racial Reform: Will We Ever Be Saved?* (Book Review), 97 YALE L.J. 923 (1988); Alan David Freeman, *Legitimizing Racial Discrimination Through Antidiscrimination Law: A Critical Review of Supreme Court Doctrine,* 62 MINN. L. REV. 1049 (1978); Patricia J. Williams, *Alchemical Notes: Reconstructing Ideals from Deconstructed Rights,* 22 HARV. C.R.-C.L. L. REV. 401 (1987); Robert A. Williams, Jr., *Taking Rights Aggressively: The Perils and Promise of Critical Legal Theory for Peoples of Color,* 5 LAW & INEQUALITY 103 (1987).

11. Richard Delgado, *The Imperial Scholar: Reflections on a Review of Civil Rights Literature,* 132 U. PA. L. REV. 561 (1984).

12. *E.g.,* BELL, *supra* note 10, at 51–74; DERRICK A. BELL, JR., RACE, RACISM AND AMERICAN LAW 40–44 (1980).

13. BELL, *supra* at 40–44; Delgado, *supra;* Charles R. Lawrence III, *The Id, the Ego, and Equal Protection: Reckoning with Unconscious Racism,* 39 STAN. L. REV. 317 (1987).

14. *E.g.,* Delgado, *supra* note 10, at 930–32.

15. *Id.;* BELL, *supra* at 140–61; Freeman, *supra* note 10.

16. *E.g.,* BELL, *supra* at 51–74; Delgado, *supra* note 13; Lawrence, *supra; see* Mari J. Matsuda, *Looking to the Bottom: Critical Legal Studies and Reparations,* 22 HARV. C.R.-C.L. L. REV. 323 (1987).

17. *See* Kimberlé Crenshaw, *Demarginalizing the Intersection of Race and Sex: A Black Feminist Critique of Antidiscrimination Doctrine, Feminist Theory and Antiracist Politics,* 1989 CHI. LEGAL F. 139, 141–52.

18. *Id.* at 139–43.

19. *See generally id.*

20. Their political weakness and Congress's lack of foresight obviously contributed as well.

21. For a case dealing with concepts that are not referred to by name, see United States v. Berrigan, 283 F. Supp. 336 (D. Md. 1968), *aff'd sub nom.,* United States v. Moylan, F.2d 1002 (4th Cir. 1969) (Catholic priest convicted of dousing Selective Service files with blood in protest against Vietnam war, but the district court does not refer to civil disobedience by name). For articles dealing with concepts that are not referred to by name, see Robert C. Berring, *Full-Text Databases and Legal Research: Backing into the Future,* I HIGH TECH. L.J. 27, 48 (1986) ("The fact is that law involves ideas, and ideas are not directly correlated with particular words."); Steven Alan Childress, *The Hazards of Computer-Assisted Research to the Legal Profession,* 55 OKLA. B.J. 1531, 1533 (1984) (computers' focus on words grounds searches in language, rather than content, of an opinion); John O. Cole, *Thoughts from the Land of And,* 39 MERCER L. REV. 907, 924–26 (1988); Daniel P. Dabney, *The Curse of Thamus: An Analysis of Full-Text Document Retrieval,* 78 LAW LIBR. J. 5, 19 (1986).

Studies by the Norwegian Research Center for Computers and Law showed that 15 percent to 25 percent of failures to retrieve relevant documents were due to the fact that no single word or set of synonyms represented the idea sought by the researcher. Jon Bing, *Performance of Legal Text Retrieval Systems: The Curse of Boole*, 79 L. LIBR. J. 187, 193 (1987). For a discussion of articles and cases dealing with concepts that are referred to by name, but are not included in standard legal databases, see Virginia Wise, *Of* Lizards, *Intersubjective Zap, and Trashing: Critical Legal Studies and the Librarian*, 8 LEGAL REFERENCE SERVICES Q., nos. 1/2, 1988, at 7 (early critical legal studies materials often absent from databases).

22. For example, one author notes:

> [t]hat which goes unnamed may exert considerable influence over us, but because we have no words for it we cannot address it directly or deal with it. One example is battering. Only in the last couple of decades have we had a word for battering. It was going on long before then, but it did not functionally exist until it was given a common, agreed-upon name. Nobody talked about it. No one was called a batterer or a victim of battering. No statistics were gathered about it. No safe houses were set up to shelter its victims; no funding was set aside to study or treat it. Once it had a name, though, it became an acknowledged reality in our society. Individuals could say, "I've been battered," or "I've been a batterer." They could talk about their experience and thus validate it.

ANNE WILSON SCHAEF, WHEN SOCIETY BECOMES AN ADDICT 9 (1987).

Rita Reusch, *The Search for Analogous Legal Authority: How to Find It When You Don't Know What You're Looking for?*, 4 LEGAL REFERENCE SERVICES Q., no. 3, 1984, at 33.

23. Geneticist Richard Goldschmidt theorized that new types of organisms can arise suddenly as chance effects of major mutations, rather than gradually through the incremental changes posited by classical evolutionary theory. Goldschmidt called these new creatures "hopeful monsters," which may be an apt metaphor for the kind of thinker envisioned here. *See* STEPHEN JAY GOULD, THE PANDA'S THUMB 186–93 (1980) for a discussion of Goldschmidt. *See also* TRACY I. STORER & ROBERT L. USINGER, GENERAL ZOOLOGY 199–200 (4th ed. 1965).

24. *See* Richard Delgado, *Legal Storytelling for Oppositionists and Others: A Plea for Narrative*, 87 MICH. L. REV. 2411 (1989) (on role of peripheral groups in reforming law through telling of "counterstories").

25. *E.g., The Legal System and Homosexuality—Approbation, Accommodation, or Reprobation?*, 10 U. DAYTON L. REV. 445 (1985).

26. *See* D. Bell, *supra* note 10 (using narrative and parables to challenge racial myths); Derrick Bell, *Brown v. Board of Education and the Interest-Convergence Dilemma*, 93 Harv. L. Rev. 518 (1980) (asserting that interests of blacks are accommodated only where they converge with interests of whites); Derrick Bell, *The Supreme Court, 1984 Term—Foreword: The Civil Rights Chronicles*, 99 HARV. L. REV. 4 (1985).

27. Richard K. Sherwin, *A Matter of Voice and Plot: Belief and Suspicion in Storytelling*, 87 MICH. L. REV. 543, 550–52 (1988) (noting necessity of balancing rhetoricians' search for belief and community with deconstructionists' suspicion).

28. *See* Sir Cyril Burt, *Foreword* to ARTHUR KOESTLER, THE ACT OF CREATION 14–15 (1964).

29. W. E. BURGHARDT DU BOIS, THE SOULS OF BLACK FOLK 45 (1969).

30. *See* Delgado, *supra* note 24 (role of "outgroups" in telling "counterstories" and thus reforming law and legal culture).

31. For example, current law practice has increased the pressure to generate billable hours and to specialize. Mega-firms are replacing smaller ones, and much of law practice is becoming routinized.

32. Most progressive librarians are quick to recognize and condemn active censorship. *See* Ron Seely, *Censors Take More Liberty in Banning Books*, Wis. St. J., Sept. 25, 1988, at 1, col. 1 (discussing campaign to remove controversial books). But the kind of unconscious self-censorship we have been describing is much more difficult to detect and counter. The categories we use to screen and interpret reality seem natural and inevitable. We rarely question their adequacy or fairness.

19 Images of the Outsider in American Law and Culture: Can Free Expression Remedy Systemic Social Ills?

RICHARD DELGADO and JEAN STEFANCIC

CONVENTIONAL First Amendment doctrine is beginning to show signs of strain. Outsider groups and women argue that free speech law inadequately protects them against certain types of harm.[1] Further, on a theoretical level, some scholars are questioning whether free expression can perform the lofty functions of community-building and consensus-formation that society assigns to it.[2]

We believe that in both situations the source of the difficulty is the same: failure to take account of the ways language and expression work. The results of this failure are more glaring in some areas than others. Much as Newtonian physics enabled us to explain the phenomena of daily life but required modification to address the larger scale, First Amendment theory will need revision to deal with issues lying at its farthest reaches. Just as the new physics ushered in considerations of perspective and positionality, First Amendment thinking will need to incorporate these notions as well.

Our thesis is that conventional First Amendment doctrine is most helpful in connection with small, clearly bounded disputes. Free speech and debate can help resolve controversies over whether a school disciplinary or local zoning policy is adequate, over whether a new sales tax is likely to increase or decrease net revenues, or over whether one candidate for political office is a better choice than another. Speech is less able, however, to deal with systemic social ills, such as racism or sexism, that are widespread and deeply woven into the fabric of society. Free speech, in short, is least helpful where we need it most.

We choose racism and racial depiction as our principal illustration. Several museums have featured displays of racial memorabilia from the past. One exhibit recently toured the United States; *Time* reviewed the opening of another. Filmmaker Marlon Riggs produced an award-winning one-hour documentary, *Ethnic Notions*, with a similar focus. Each of these collections depicts a shock-

77 CORNELL L. REV. 1258 (1992). Copyright © 1992 by Cornell University. All rights reserved. Reprinted by permission.

ing parade of Sambos, mammies, coons, uncles—bestial or happy-go-lucky, watermelon-eating—African-Americans. They show advertising logos and household commodities in the shape of blacks with grotesquely exaggerated facial features. They include minstrel shows and film clips depicting blacks as so incompetent, shuffling, and dim-witted that it is hard to see how they survived to adulthood. Other images depict primitive, terrifying, larger-than-life black men in threatening garb and postures, often with apparent designs on white women.

Seeing these haunting images today, one is tempted to ask: "How could their authors—cartoonists, writers, filmmakers, and graphic designers—individuals, certainly, of higher than average education, create such appalling images?[3] And why did no one protest?" The collections mentioned focus on African-Americans, but the two of us, motivated by curiosity, examined the history of ethnic depiction for each of the four main minority subgroups of color—Mexicans, African-Americans, Asians, and Native Americans—in the United States. In each case we found the same sad story: Each group is depicted, in virtually every epoch, in terms that can only be described as demeaning or worse. In addition, we found striking parallels among the stigma-pictures that society disseminated of the four groups. The stock characters may have different names and appear at different times, but they bear remarkable likenesses and seem to serve similar purposes for the majority culture. We review this history in the first part of this chapter.

Our answer to the "How could they" question is, in brief, that those who composed and disseminated these images simply did not see them as grotesque. Their consciences were clear—their blithe creations did not trouble them. It is only today, decades later, that these images strike us as indefensible and shocking. Our much-vaunted system of free expression, with its marketplace of ideas, cannot correct serious systemic ills such as racism or sexism simply because we do not see them as such at the time. No one can formulate an effective contemporaneous message to challenge the vicious depiction; this happens only much later, after consciousness shifts and society adopts a different narrative. Our own era is no different. This is the dominant, overpowering lesson we draw from reviewing two centuries of ethnic depiction.

We call the belief that we can somehow control our consciousness despite limitations of time and positionality the *empathic* fallacy. In literature, the *pathetic* fallacy holds that nature is like us, that it is endowed with feelings, moods, and goals we can understand. The poet, feeling sad, implores the world to weep with him or her. Its correlate, which we term the *empathic* fallacy, consists of believing that we can enlarge our sympathies through linguistic means alone: By exposing ourselves to ennobling narratives, we broaden our experience, deepen our empathy, and achieve new levels of sensitivity and fellow-feeling—we can, in short, think, talk, read, and write our way out of bigotry and narrow-mindedness, out of our limitations of experience and perspective. As we illustrate, however, we can do this only to a very limited extent. Indeed, our system of free speech not only fails to correct the repression and abuse subjugated groups must face, but often deepens their predicament.

Images of the Outsider

A small but excellent literature chronicles the depiction in popular culture of each of the major minority subgroups of color—African-Americans, Mexicans, Native Americans, and Asians. Here, we summarize that history and draw parallels among the ways that society has traditionally depicted the four groups.

[*Ed.* The authors review history of popular depiction of blacks, Mexicans, Native Americans, and Asians over 200 years of U.S. history. They then continue as follows.]

The depiction of ethnic groups of color is littered with negative images, although the content of those images changes over time. In some periods, society needed to suppress a group, as with blacks during Reconstruction. Society coined an image to suit that purpose—that of primitive, powerful, larger-than-life-blacks, terrifying and barely under control. At other times, for example during slavery, society needed reassurance that blacks were docile, cheerful, and content with their lot. Images of sullen, rebellious blacks dissatisfied with their condition would have made white society uneasy. Accordingly, images of simple, happy blacks, content to do the master's work, were disseminated.

In every era, then, ethnic imagery comes bearing an enormous amount of social weight. Nevertheless, we sense that we are in control, that things need not be that way. We believe we can use speech, jiujitsu fashion, on behalf of oppressed peoples.[4] We believe that speech can serve as a tool of destabilization. It is virtually a prime tenet of liberal jurisprudence that by talk, dialog, exhortation, and so on we present each other with passionate, appealing messages that will counter the evil ones of racism and sexism, and thereby advance society to greater levels of fairness and humanity.[5]

Consider, for example, the current debate about campus speech codes. In response to a rising tide of racist incidents, many campuses have enacted, or are considering enacting, student conduct codes that forbid certain types of face-to-face insult. These codes invariably draw fire from free-speech absolutists and many campus administrators on the ground that they would interfere with free speech. Campuses, they argue, ought to be "bastions of free speech." Racism and prejudice are matters of "ignorance and fear," for which the appropriate remedy is more speech. Suppression merely drives racism underground, where it will fester and emerge later in even more hateful forms. Speech is the best corrective for error; regulation risks the spectre of censorship and state control. Efforts to regulate pornography, Klan marches, and other types of race-baiting often meet similar responses.

But modernist and postmodern insights about language and the social construction of reality show that reliance on countervailing speech that will, in theory, wrestle with bad or vicious speech is often misplaced. This is so for two in-terrelated reasons: First, the account rests on simplistic and erroneous notions of narrativity and change, and second, on a misunderstanding of the relation be-tween the subject, or self, and new narratives.

THE FIRST REASON—TIME WARP: WHY WE (CAN) ONLY CONDEMN THE OLD NARRATIVE

Our review of 200 years of ethnic depiction in the United States showed that we simply do not see many forms of discrimination, bias, and prejudice as wrong at the time. The racism of other times and places does stand out, does strike us as glaringly and appallingly wrong. But this happens only decades or centuries later; we acquiesce in today's version with little realization that it is wrong, that a later generation will ask "How could they?" about *us*. We only condemn the racism of another place (South Africa) or time. But that of our own place and time strikes us, if at all, as unexceptional, trivial, or well within literary license. Every form of creative work (we tell ourselves) relies on stock characters. What's so wrong with a novel that employs a black who . . . , or a Mexican who. . . ? Besides, the argument goes, those groups are disproportionately employed as domestics, are responsible for a high proportion of our crime, are they not? And some actually talk this way; why, just last week, I overheard . . .

This time-warp aspect of racism makes speech an ineffective tool to counter it. Racism is woven into the warp and woof of the way we see and organize the world[6]—it is one of the many preconceptions we bring to experience and use to construct and make sense of our social world.[7] Racism forms part of the domi-nant narrative, the group of received understandings and basic principles that form the baseline from which we reason. How could these be in question? Re-cent scholarship shows that the dominant narrative changes very slowly and resists alteration.[8] We interpret new stories in light of the old. Ones that devi-ate too markedly from our pre-existing stock are dismissed as extreme, coercive, political, and wrong. The only stories about race we are prepared to condemn, then, are the old ones giving voice to the racism of an earlier age, ones that so-ciety has already begun to reject. We can condemn Justice Brown for writing as he did in *Plessy v. Ferguson*, but not university administrators who refuse reme-dies for campus racism, failing to notice the remarkable parallels between the two.[9]

THE SECOND REASON: OUR NARRATIVES, OUR SELVES

Racial change is slow, then, because the story of race is part of the dominant nar-rative we use to interpret experience. The narrative teaches that race matters, that people are different, with the differences lying always in a predictable direc-tion.[10] It holds that certain cultures, unfortunately, have less ambition than oth-ers, that the majority group is largely innocent of racial wrongdoing, that the cur-rent distribution of comfort and well-being is roughly what merit and fairness dictate. Within that general framework, only certain matters are open for discussion: How different? In what ways? With how many exceptions? And what measures are due to deal with this unfortunate situation and at what cost to whites?[11] This is so because the narrative leaves only certain things intelligible; other arguments and texts would seem alien.

A second and related insight from modern scholarship focuses not on the role of narratives in confining change to manageable proportions, but on the relationship between our selves and those narratives. The reigning First Amendment metaphor—the marketplace of ideas—implies a separation between subjects who do the choosing and the ideas or messages that vie for their attention.[12] Subjects are "in here," the messages "out there." The pre-existing subjects choose the idea that seems most valid and true—somewhat in the manner of a diner deciding what to eat at a buffet.

But scholars are beginning to realize that this mechanistic view of an autonomous subject choosing among separate, external ideas is simplistic. In an important sense, we *are* our current stock of narratives, and they us. We subscribe to a stock of explanatory scripts, plots, narratives, and understandings that enable us to make sense of—to construct—our social world. Because we then live in that world, it begins to shape and determine *us*, who we are, what we see, how we select, reject, interpret, and order subsequent reality.[13]

These observations imply that our ability to escape the confines of our own preconceptions is quite limited. The contrary belief—that through speech and remonstrance alone we can endlessly reform ourselves and each other—we call the *empathic fallacy*. It and its companion, the pathetic fallacy, are both based on *hubris*, the belief that we can be more than we are. The empathic fallacy holds that through speech and remonstrance we can surmount our limitations of time, place, and culture, can transcend our own situatedness. But our examination of the cultural record, as well as postmodern understandings of language and personhood, both point to the same conclusion: The notion of ideas competing with each other, with truth and goodness emerging victorious from the competition, has proven seriously deficient when applied to evils, like racism, that are deeply inscribed in the culture. We have constructed the social world so that racism seems normal, part of the status quo, in need of little correction. It is not until much later that what we believed begins to seem incredibly, monstrously wrong. How could we have believed *that*?

True, every few decades an occasional genius will rise up and offer a work that recognizes and denounces the racism of the day. Unfortunately, they are ignored—they have no audience. Witness, for example, the recent "discovery" of long-forgotten black writers such as Charles Chesnutt, Zora Neale Hurston, or the slave narratives. Consider that Nadine Gordimer won the Nobel Prize after nearly 40 years of writing about the evils of apartheid; Harriet Beecher Stowe's book sold well, but only after years of abolitionist sentiment and agitation had sensitized her public to the possibility that slavery was wrong. One should, of course, speak out against social evils. But we should not accord speech greater efficacy than it has.

How the System of Free Expression
Sometimes Makes Matters Worse

Speech and free expression are not only poorly adapted to remedy racism, they often make matters worse—far from being stalwart friends, they can impede the cause of racial reform. First, they encourage writers, filmmakers, and other creative people to feel amoral, nonresponsible in what they do. Because there is a marketplace of ideas, the rationalization goes, another filmmaker is free to make an antiracist movie that will cancel out any minor stereotyping in the one I am making. My movie may have other redeeming qualities; besides, it is good entertainment and everyone in the industry uses stock characters like the black maid or the bumbling Asian tourist. How can one create film without stock characters?

Second, when insurgent groups attempt to use speech as an instrument of reform, courts almost invariably construe First Amendment doctrine against them. As Charles Lawrence pointed out, civil rights activists in the sixties made the greatest strides when they acted in defiance of the First Amendment as then understood.[14] They marched, were arrested and convicted; sat in, were arrested and convicted; distributed leaflets, were arrested and convicted. Many years later, after much gallant lawyering and the expenditure of untold hours of effort, the conviction might be reversed on appeal if the original action had been sufficiently prayerful, mannerly, and not too interlaced with an action component. This history of the civil rights movement does not bear out the usual assumption that the First Amendment is of great value for racial reformers.[15]

Current First Amendment law is similarly skewed. Examination of the many "exceptions" to First Amendment protection discloses that the large majority favor the interests of the powerful. If one says something disparaging of a wealthy and well-regarded individual, one discovers that one's words were not free after all; the wealthy individual has a type of property interest in his or her community image, damage to which is compensable even though words were the sole instrument of the harm. Similarly, if one infringes the copyright or trademark of a well-known writer or industrialist, again it turns out that one's action is punishable. Further, if one disseminates an official secret valuable to a powerful branch of the military or defense contractor, that speech is punishable. If one speaks disrespectfully to a judge, police officer, teacher, military official, or other powerful authority figure, again one discovers that one's words were not free; and so with words used to defraud, form a conspiracy, breach the peace, or untruthful words given under oath during a civil or criminal proceeding.

Yet the suggestion that we create new exception to protect lowly and vulnerable members of our society, such as isolated young black undergraduates attending dominantly white campuses, is often met with consternation: the First Amendment must be a seamless web; minorities, if they knew their own self-interest, should appreciate this even more than others.[16] This one-sidedness of free-speech doctrine makes the First Amendment much more valuable to the majority than to the minority.

The system of free expression also has a powerful after-the-fact apologetic function. Elite groups use the supposed existence of a marketplace of ideas to justify their own superior position.[17] Imagine a society in which all *A*s were rich and happy, all *B*s were moderately comfortable, and all *C*s were poor, stigmatized, and reviled. Imagine also that this society scrupulously believes in a free marketplace of ideas. Might not the *A*s benefit greatly from such a system? On looking about them and observing the inequality in the distribution of wealth, longevity, happiness, and safety between themselves and the others, they might feel guilt. Perhaps their own superior position is undeserved, or at least requires explanation. But the existence of an ostensibly free marketplace of ideas renders that effort unnecessary. Rationalization is easy: our ideas, our culture competed with their more easygoing ones and won. It was a fair fight. Our position must be deserved; the distribution of social goods must be roughly what fairness, merit, and equity call for. It is up to them to change, not us.

A free market of racial depiction resists change for two final reasons. First, the dominant pictures, images, narratives, plots, roles, and stories ascribed to, and constituting, the public perception of minorities are always dominantly negative. Through an unfortunate psychological mechanism, incessant bombardment by negative images inscribes those images on the souls and minds of minority persons. Minorities internalize the stories they read, see, and hear every day. Persons of color can easily become demoralized, blame themselves, and not speak up vigorously. The expense of speech also precludes the stigmatized from participating effectively in the marketplace of ideas.[18] They are often poor—indeed, one theory of racism holds that maintenance of economic inequality is its prime function[19]—and hence unlikely to command the means to bring countervailing messages to the eyes and ears of others.

Second, even when minorities do speak they have little credibility. Who would listen to, who would credit, a speaker or writer one associates with watermelon-eating, buffoonery, menial work, intellectual inadequacy, laziness, lasciviousness, and demanding resources beyond his or her deserved share?

Our very imagery of outsiders shows that, contrary to the usual view, society does not really want them to speak out effectively in their own behalf and, in fact, cannot visualize them doing so. Ask yourself: How do outsiders speak in the dominant narratives? Poorly, inarticulately, with broken syntax, short sentences, grunts, and unsophisticated ideas. Try to recall a single popular narrative of an eloquent, self-assured black (for example) orator or speaker. In the real world, of course, they exist in profusion. But when we stumble upon them, we are surprised: "What a welcome 'exception'!"

Words, then, can wound. But the fine thing about the current situation is that one gets to enjoy a superior position and feel virtuous at the same time. By supporting the system of free expression no matter what the cost, one is upholding principle. One can belong to impeccably liberal organizations and believe one is doing the right thing, even while taking actions that are demonstrably injurious to the least privileged, most defenseless segments of our society.[20] In time, one's actions will seem wrong and will be condemned as such, but paradigms change slowly. The world one helps to create—one in which denigrating depiction is good or at least acceptable, in which minorities are buffoons, clowns, maids, or Willie Hortons, and only rarely fully individuated human beings with sensitivities, talents, personalities, and frailties—will survive into the future. One gets to create culture at outsiders' expense. And, one gets to sleep well at night, too.

Racism is not a mistake, not a matter of episodic, irrational behavior carried out by vicious-willed individuals, not a throwback to a long-gone era. It is ritual assertion of supremacy, like animals sneering and posturing to maintain their places in the hierarchy of the colony. It is performed largely unconsciously, just as the animals' behavior is. Racism seems right, customary, and inoffensive to those engaged in it, while bringing psychic and pecuniary advantages. The notion that more speech, more talking, more preaching, more lecturing can counter this system of oppression is appealing, lofty, romantic—and wrong.

What Then, Should be Done? If Not Speech, What?

What can be done? One possibility we must take seriously is that *nothing* can be done—that race- and perhaps sex-based subjugation is so deeply embedded in our society, so useful for the powerful, that nothing can dislodge it. No less gallant a warrior than Derrick Bell has recently expounded his view of "Racial Realism": things will never get better, powerful forces maintain the current system of white-over-black supremacy. Just as the Legal Realists of the early years of this century urged society to cast aside comforting myths about the uniformity, predictability, and "scientific" nature of legal reasoning, legal scholars must do something similar today with respect to race. Reformers must labor for what they believe right with no certainty that their programs will ever prove successful. Holding out the hope that reform will one day bear fruit is unnecessary, unwise, and calculated only to induce despair, burn-out, and paralysis.

We agree with much of what Bell says. Yet we offer four suggestions for a program of racial reform growing out of our research and analysis. We do this while underscoring the limitations of our own prescriptions, including the near-impossibility of getting a society to take seriously something whose urgency it seems constitutionally unable to appreciate. First, society should act decisively in cases of racism that we do see, treating them as proxies for the ones we know remain unseen. Second, past mistreatment will generally prove a more reliable basis for remedial action (such as affirmative action or reparations) than future- or present-oriented considerations; the racism of the past is the only kind that we recognize, the only kind we condemn. Third, whenever possible we should employ and empower minority speakers of color and expose ourselves to their messages. Their reality, while not infallible and certainly not the only one, is the one we must heed if we wish to avoid history's judgment. It is likely to be the one society will adopt in 30 years.

Scholars should approach with skepticism the writings of those neoconservatives, including some of color, who make a practice of telling society that racism is ended.[21] In the sense we have described, there *is* an "essential" unitary minority viewpoint;[22] the others are wrong.[23] Finally, we should deepen suspicion of remedies for deep-seated social evils that rely on speech and exhortation. The First Amendment is an instrument of variable efficacy, more useful in some settings than others. Overextending it provokes the anger of oppressed groups and casts doubt on speech's value in settings where it is, in fact, useful. With deeply inscribed cultural practices that most can neither see as evil nor mobilize to reform, we should forthrightly institute changes in the structure of society that will enable persons of color—particularly the young—to avoid the worst assaults of racism. As with the controversy over campus racism, we should not let a spurious motto that speech be "everywhere free" stand in the way of outlawing speech that is demonstrably harmful, that is compounding the problem.

Because of the way the dominant narrative works, we should prepare for the near-certainty that these suggestions will be criticized as unprincipled, unfair to "innocent whites," wrong. Understanding how the dialectic works, and how the scripts and counterscripts work their dismal paralysis, may, perhaps, inspire us to continue even though the path is long and the night dark.

NOTES

1. *See, e.g.,* Richard Delgado, *Words That Wound: A Tort Action for Racial Insults, Epithets and Name-Calling,* 17 HARV. C.R.-C.L. L. REV. 133 (1982); Charles R. Lawrence III, *If He Hollers Let Him Go: Regulating Racist Speech on Campus,* 1990 DUKE L.J. 431; Catharine A. MacKinnon, *Not a Moral Issue,* 2 YALE L. & POL'Y REV. 321 (1984); Mari J. Matsuda, *Public Response to Racist Speech: Considering the Victim's Story,* 87 MICH. L. REV. 2320 (1989).

2. *See, e.g.,* Derrick Bell & Preeta Bansal, *The Republican Revival and Racial Politics,* 97 YALE L.J. 1609 (1988); Richard Delgado, *Zero-Based Racial Politics and an Infinity-Based Response: Will Endless Talking Cure America's Racial Ills?,* 80 GEO. L.J. 1879 (1992); Robert Justine Lipkin, *Kibitzers, Fuzzies and Apes Without Tails: Pragmatism and the Art of Conversation in Legal Theory,* 66 TUL. L. REV. 69 (1991).

3. *Cf.* ROBERT JAY LIFTON, THE NAZI DOCTORS (1986) (pointing out that German administrators and physicians who carried out atrocities were highly educated); I–III ELIE WIESEL, AGAINST SILENCE (1985) (same).

4. For the view that speech may serve this counter-hegemonic function, see Stephen M. Feldman, *Whose Common Good? Racism in the Political Community,* 80 GEO. L.J. 1835 (1992); Ed Sparer, *Fundamental Human Rights, Legal Entitlements, and the Social Struggle: A Friendly Critique of the Critical Legal Studies Movement,* 36 STAN. L. REV. 509 (1984).

5. For classic works on dialogism or the Republican revival, see Robert M.

Cover, *Foreword: Nomos and Narrative*, 97 HARV. L. REV. 4 (1983); Frank I. Michelman, *Foreword: Traces of Self-Government*, 100 HARV. L. REV. 4 (1986); Cass R. Sunstein, *Naked Preferences and the Constitution*, 84 COLUM. L. REV. 1689 (1984).

6. DERRICK BELL, AND WE ARE NOT SAVED: THE ELUSIVE QUEST FOR RACIAL JUSTICE (1987) (noting that racism is ubiquitous and discouragingly difficult to eradicate).

7. *See Symposium, Legal Storytelling*, 87 MICH. L. REV. 2073 (1989) (including articles by Ball, Bell, Delgado, Matsuda, and Williams on race and narrative).

8. *See generally* BELL, *supra* note 6 (arguing that racial progress is slow, and majority society is rarely receptive to pleas for justice). For another view of the prospects for reform, see Richard Delgado, *Derrick Bell and the Ideology of Law Reform: Will We Ever Be Saved?*, 97 YALE L.J. 923 (1988) (reform slow because: (1) mindsets of whites and blacks radically different, and (2) majoritarian positions are firmly rooted in white self-interest).

9. In Plessy v. Ferguson, 163 U.S. 537, 550–51 (1896), the Court failed to see any difference between requiring blacks to sit in a separate railroad car and a similar imposition on whites. For Brown, if blacks found that requirement demeaning, it was only because they chose to put that construction on it; the cars were equal, and the races had similar accommodations. *See also* Herbert Wechsler, *Toward Neutral Principles of Constitutional Law*, 73 HARV. L. REV. 1 (1959) (making similar criticism of *Brown v. Board of Education*: whites forced to associate with blacks were mistreated just as seriously as blacks denied the right to associate with whites—both were denied freedom of action).

In the campus-speech controversy, some argue that the right of a racist to hurl an ethnic insult must be balanced against the right of a person of color not to receive it. Who is to say which right (to speak—or not to be spoken to) is superior? Denying one right strengthens the other, but only at the expense of the first.

10. For a discussion of the hold that racism exercises on our psyches, see Charles A. Lawrence III, *The Id, the Ego, and Equal Protection: Reckoning with Unconscious Racism*, 39 STAN. L. REV. 317 (1987).

11. On the view that the cost of racial remedies is always placed on blacks or low-income whites, see Derrick Bell, Bakke, *Minority Admissions, and the Usual Price of Racial Remedies*, 67 CAL. L. REV. 3 (1979).

12. On the reigning marketplace conception of free speech, see Abrams v. United States, 250 U.S. 616, 630 (1919) (Holmes, J., dissenting); ALEXANDER MEIKLEJOHN, FREE SPEECH AND ITS RELATION TO SELF-GOVERNMENT (1948); JOHN MILTON, AREOPAGITICA (Michael Davis ed., 1965) (classic early statement). *See also* Stanley Ingber, *The Marketplace of Ideas: A Legitimating Myth*, 1984 DUKE L.J. 1 ("market" shown to favor entrenched structure and ideology).

13. *See* MILNER BALL, LYING DOWN TOGETHER: LAW, METAPHOR AND THEOLOGY 135 (1985); 1 & 2 PAUL RICOEUR, TIME AND NARRATIVE (1984–85). For modernist/postmodern expositions of this view, see, *e.g.*, PETER L. BERGER & THOMAS LUCKMAN, SOCIAL CONSTRUCTION OF REALITY (1967); NELSON GOODMAN, WAYS OF WORLDMAKING (1978).

14. Lawrence, *supra* note 1 at 466–67 (pointing out that courts construed First Amendment law narrowly, so as to uphold convictions of peaceful civil rights protestors; citing cases).

15. *Id.*

16. *See* LEE C. BOLLINGER, THE TOLERANT SOCIETY (1986) (racist speech must be protected—part of the price "we" pay for living in a free society).

17. On "triumphalism"—the view that conquerors always construct history so that they appear to have won fairly through superior thought and culture rather than by force of arms—see Richard Delgado, *Norms and Normal Science: Toward a Critique of Normativity in Legal Thought,* 139 U. PA. L. REV. 933 (1991); Martin, *College Curriculum Scrutinized in "Politically Correct" Spotlight,* DENVER POST, Jan. 25, 1992. For the view that many Enlightenment figures were genteel or not-so-genteel cultural supremacists, see BELL, *supra* note 6, at 26–51 (pointing out that the document's Framers calculatedly sold out the interests of African-Americans in establishing a union of free propertied white males).

18. *See* Buckley v. Valeo, 424 U.S. 1, 17–19 (1976).

19. This "economic determinist" view is associated with Derrick Bell, and earlier with Charles Beard.

20. The American Civil Liberties Union, for example, follows a policy of challenging virtually every campus speech code as soon as it is enacted. *See, e.g.,* DOE V. UNIVERSITY OF MICH., 721 F. Supp. 852 (E.D. Mich. 1989); U.W.M. Post, Inc. v. Regents, Univ. of Wis., 774 F. Supp. 1163 (E.D. Wis. 1991); Nadine Strossen, *Regulating Racist Speech on Campus: A Modest Proposal?* 1990 DUKE L.J. 484 (author is national president, A.C.L.U.).

21. *E.g.,* RICHARD RODRIGUEZ, HUNGER OF MEMORY (1982); *see also* STEPHEN CARTER, REFLECTIONS OF AN AFFIRMATIVE ACTION BABY (1991) (reciting less extreme statement of same position); THOMAS SOWELL, CIVIL RIGHTS: RHETORIC OR REALITY? (1984); SHELBY STEELE, THE CONTENT OF OUR CHARACTER: A NEW VISION OF RACE IN AMERICA (1990).

22. Essential, that is, to our own salvation.

23. On the debate about "essentialism" and whether the minority community contains one or many voices, see Angela P. Harris, *Race and Essentialism in Feminist Legal Theory,* 42 Stan. L. Rev. 581 (1990).

20 Serving Two Masters: Integration Ideals and Client Interests in School Desegregation Litigation

DERRICK BELL

In the name of equity, we . . . seek dramatic improvement in the quality of the education available to our children. Any steps to achieve desegregation must be reviewed in light of the black community's interest in improved pupil performance as the primary characteristic of educational equality. We define educational equity as the absence of discriminatory pupil placement and improved performance for all children who have been the objects of discrimination. We think it neither necessary, nor proper to endure the dislocations of desegregation without reasonable assurances that our children will instructionally profit.
—Coalition of black community groups in Boston

H O W should the term "client" be defined in school desegregation cases that are litigated for decades, determine critically important constitutional rights for thousands of minority children, and usually entail major restructuring of a public school system? How should civil rights attorneys represent the often diverse interests of clients and class in school suits? Do they owe any special obligation to class members who emphasize educational quality and who probably cannot obtain counsel to advocate their divergent views? Do the political, organizational, and even philosophical complexities of school desegregation litigation justify a higher standard of professional responsibility on the part of civil rights lawyers to their clients, or more diligent oversight of the lawyer-client relationship by bench and bar?

As is so often the case, a crisis of events motivates this long overdue inquiry. The great crusade to desegregate the public schools has faltered. There is increasing opposition to desegregation at both local and national levels (not all of which can now be simply condemned as "racist"), while the once vigorous support of federal courts is on the decline. New barriers have arisen—inflation makes the attainment of racial balance more expensive, the growth of black populations

85 YALE L.J. 470 (1976). Originally published in the Yale Law Journal. Reprinted by permission.

in urban areas renders it more difficult, an increasing number of social science studies question the validity of its educational assumptions.

Civil rights lawyers dismiss these new obstacles as legally irrelevant. Having achieved so much by courageous persistence, they have not wavered in their determination to implement *Brown v. Board of Education*[1] using racial balance measures developed in the hard-fought legal battles of the last few decades. This stance entails great risk for clients whose educational interests may no longer accord with the integration ideals of their attorneys. Now that traditional racial balance remedies are becoming increasingly difficult to achieve or maintain, there is tardy concern that racial balance may not be the relief actually desired by the victims of segregated schools.

School Litigation: A Behind-the-Scenes View[2]

Although *Brown* was not a test case with a result determined in advance, the legal decisions that undermined and finally swept away the "separate but equal" doctrine of *Plessy v. Ferguson*[3] were far from fortuitous. Their genesis can be found in the volumes of reported cases stretching back to the mid-19th century, cases in which every conceivable aspect of segregated schools was challenged. By the early 1930s, the NAACP, with the support of a foundation grant, had organized a concerted program of legal attacks on racial segregation. In October 1934, Vice-Dean Charles H. Houston of the Howard University Law School was retained by the NAACP to direct this campaign. According to the NAACP Annual Report for 1934, "the campaign [was] a carefully planned one to secure decisions, rulings and public opinion on the broad principle instead of being devoted to merely miscellaneous cases."[4] These strategies were intended to eliminate racial segregation, not merely in the public schools, but throughout society. The public schools were chosen because they presented a far more compelling symbol of the evils of segregation and a far more vulnerable target than segregated railroad cars, restaurants, or restrooms. Initially, the NAACP's school litigation was aimed at the most blatant inequalities in facilities and teacher salaries. The next target was the obvious inequality in higher education evidenced by the almost total absence of public graduate and professional schools for blacks in the South.

Thurgood Marshall succeeded Houston in 1938 and became Director-Counsel of the NAACP Legal Defense and Educational Fund (LDF) when it became a separate entity in 1939. Jack Greenberg, who succeeded Marshall in 1961, recalled that the legal program "built precedent," treating each case in a context of jurisprudential development rather than as an isolated private law suit.[5] Of course, it was not possible to plan the program with precision: "How and when plaintiffs sought relief and the often unpredictable course of litigation were frequently as influential as any blueprint in determining the sequence of cases, the precise issues they posed, and their outcome."[6] But as lawyer-publisher Loren Miller observed of *Brown* and the four other school cases decided with it, "There was more to this carefully stage-managed selection of cases for review than meets the naked eye."[7]

In 1955, the Supreme Court rejected the NAACP request for a general order requiring desegregation in all school districts, issued the famous "all deliberate speed" mandate, and returned the matter to the district courts. It quickly became apparent that most school districts would not comply with *Brown* voluntarily. Rather, they retained counsel and determined to resist compliance as long as possible.

By the late 1950s, the realization by black parents and local branches of the NAACP that litigation would be required, together with the snail's pace at which most of the school cases progressed, brought about a steady growth in the size of school desegregation dockets. Because of their limited resources, the NAACP and LDF adopted the following general pattern for initiating school suits. A local attorney would respond to the request of a NAACP branch to address its members concerning their rights under the *Brown* decision. Those interested in joining a suit as named plaintiffs would sign retainers authorizing the local attorney and members of the NAACP staff to represent them in a school desegregation class action. Subsequently, depending on the facts of the case and the availability of counsel to prepare the papers, a suit would be filed. In most instances, the actual complaint was drafted or at least approved by a member of the national legal staff. With few exceptions, local attorneys were not considered expert in school desegregation litigation and served mainly as a liaison between the national staff lawyers and the local community.

Named plaintiffs, of course, retained the right to drop out of the case at any time. They did not seek to exercise "control" over the litigation, and during the early years there was no reason for them to do so. Suits were filed, school boards resisted the suits, and civil rights attorneys tried to overcome the resistance. Obtaining compliance with *Brown* as soon as possible was the goal of both clients and attorneys. But in most cases, that goal would not be realized before the named plaintiffs had graduated or left the school system.

The civil rights lawyers would not settle for anything less than a desegregated system. While the situation did not arise in the early years, it was generally made clear to potential plaintiffs that the NAACP was not interested in settling the litigation in return for school board promises to provide better segregated schools. Black parents generally felt that the victory in *Brown* entitled the civil rights lawyers to determine the basis of compliance. There was no doubt that perpetuating segregated schools was unacceptable, and the civil rights lawyers' strong opposition to such schools had the full support of both the named plaintiffs and the class they represented. Charges to the contrary initiated by several Southern states were malevolent in intent and premature in time.

THE THEORY

The rights vindicated in school litigation literally did not exist prior to 1954. Despite hundreds of judicial opinions, these rights have yet to be clearly defined. This is not surprising. Desegregation efforts aimed at lunchrooms, beaches, transportation, and other public facilities were designed merely to gain access to those facilities. Any actual racial "mixing" has been essentially fortuitous; it was hardly part of the rights protected (to eat, travel, or swim on a nonracial basis). The strategy of school desegregation is much different. The actual presence of white children is said to be essential to the right in both its philosophical and pragmatic dimensions. In essence the arguments are that blacks must gain access to white schools because "equal educational opportunity" means integrated schools, and because only school integration will make certain that black children will receive the same education as white children. This theory of school desegregation, however, fails to encompass the complexity of achieving equal educational opportunity for children to whom it so long has been denied.

The NAACP and the LDF, responsible for virtually all school desegregation suits, usually seek to establish a racial population at each school that (within a range of 10 to 15 percent) reflects the percentage of whites and blacks in the district. But in a growing number of the largest urban districts, the school system is predominantly black. The resistance of most white parents to sending their children to a predominantly black school and the accessibility of a suburban residence or private school to all but the poorest renders implementation of such plans extremely difficult. Although many whites undoubtedly perceive a majority black school as ipso facto a poor school, the schools can be improved and white attitudes changed. All too little attention has been given to making black schools educationally effective. Furthermore, the disinclination of white parents to send their children to black schools has not been lessened by charges made over a long period of time by civil rights groups that black schools are educationally bankrupt and unconstitutional per se.[8] NAACP policies nevertheless call for maximizing racial balance within the district as an immediate goal while supporting litigation that will eventually require the consolidation of predominantly white surrounding districts.

The basic civil rights position that *Brown* requires maximum feasible desegregation has been accepted by the courts and successfully implemented in smaller school districts throughout the country. The major resistance to further progress has occurred in the large urban areas of both South and North where racially isolated neighborhoods make school integration impossible without major commitments to the transportation of students, often over long distances. The use of the school bus is not a new phenomenon in American education, but the transportation of students over long distances to schools where their parents do not believe they will receive a good education has predictably created strong opposition in white and even black communities.

The busing issue has served to make concrete what many parents long have sensed and what new research has suggested:[9] court orders mandating racial balance may be (depending on the circumstances) educationally advantageous, irrelevant, or even *disadvantageous*. Nevertheless, civil rights lawyers continue to argue that black children are entitled to integrated schools without regard to the educational effect of such assignments. That position might well have shocked many of the Justices who decided *Brown*, and hardly encourages those judges asked to undertake the destruction and resurrection of school systems in our large cities which this reading of *Brown* has come to require.

Troubled by the resistance and disruptions caused by busing over long distances, those judges have increasingly rejected such an interpretation of *Brown*. They have established new standards which limit relief across district lines[10] and which reject busing for intradistrict desegregation "when the time or distance of travel is so great as to either risk the health of children or significantly impinge on the educational process."[11] Litigation in the large cities has dragged on for years and often culminated in decisions that approve the continued assignment of large numbers of black children to predominantly black schools.

Lawyer-Client Conflicts: Sources and Rationale

CIVIL RIGHTS RIGIDITY SURVEYED

Having convinced themselves that *Brown* stands for desegregation and not education, the established civil rights organizations steadfastly refuse to recognize reverses in the school desegregation campaign—reverses which, to some extent, have been precipitated by their rigidity. They seem to be reluctant to evaluate objectively the high risks inherent in a continuation of current policies.

Many thoughtful observers now doubt that *Brown* can be implemented only by the immediate racial balancing of school populations. But civil rights groups refuse to recognize what courts in Boston, Detroit, and Atlanta have now made obvious: where racial balance is not feasible because of population concentrations, political boundaries, or even educational considerations, there is adequate legal precedent for court-ordered remedies that emphasize educational improvement rather than racial balance.

The plans adopted in these cases were formulated without the support and often over the objection of the NAACP and other civil rights groups. They are intended to upgrade educational quality, and, like racial balance, they may have that effect. But neither the NAACP nor the court-fashioned remedies are sufficiently directed at the real evil of pre-*Brown* schools: the state-supported subordination of blacks in every aspect of the educational process. Racial separation is only the most obvious manifestation of this subordination. Providing unequal and inadequate school resources and excluding black parents from meaningful participation in school policymaking are at least as damaging to black children as enforced separation.

Whether based on racial balance precedents or compensatory education theories, remedies that fail to attack all policies of racial subordination almost guarantee that the basic evil of segregated schools will survive and flourish, even in those systems where racially balanced schools can be achieved. Low academic performance and large numbers of disciplinary and expulsion cases are only two of the predictable outcomes in integrated schools where the racial subordination of blacks is reasserted in, if anything, a more damaging form.[12]

The literature in both law and education discusses the merits and availability of educational remedies in detail.[13] The purpose here has been simply to il-lustrate that alternative approaches to "equal educational opportunity" are pos-sible and have been inadequately explored by civil rights attorneys. Although some of the remedies fashioned by the courts themselves have been responsive to the problem of racial subordination, plaintiffs and courts seeking to implement such remedies are not assisted by counsel representing plaintiff classes. Much more effective remedies for racial subordination in the schools could be obtained if the creative energies of the civil rights litigation groups could be brought into line with the needs and desires of their clients.

CLIENTS AND CONTRIBUTORS

The hard-line position of established civil rights groups on school desegregation is explained in part by pragmatic considerations. These organizations are sup-ported by middle-class blacks and whites who believe fervently in integration. At their socioeconomic level, integration has worked well, and they are certain that once whites and blacks at lower economic levels are successfully mixed in the schools, integration also will work well at those levels. Many of these supporters either reject or fail to understand suggestions that alternatives to integrated schools should be considered, particularly in majority-black districts. They will be understandably reluctant to provide financial support for policies which they think unsound, possibly illegal, and certainly disquieting. The rise and decline of the Congress of Racial Equality (CORE) provides a stark reminder of the fate of civil rights organizations relying on white support while espousing black self-re-liance.[14]

Jack Greenberg, LDF Director-Counsel, acknowledges that fund-raising con-cerns may play a small role in the selection of cases. Even though civil rights lawyers often obtain the clients, Greenberg reports "there may be financial con-tributors to reckon with who may ask that certain cases be brought and others not."[15] He hastens to add that within broad limits lawyers "seem to be free to pur-sue their own ideas of right, . . . affected little or not at all by contributors."[16] The reassurance is double-edged. The lawyers' freedom to pursue their own ideas of right may pose no problems as long as both clients and contributors share a com-mon social outlook. But when the views of some or all of the clients change, a de-layed recognition and response by the lawyers is predictable.[17]

School expert Ron Edmonds contends that civil rights attorneys often do not represent their clients' best interests in desegregation litigation because "they an-swer to a minuscule constituency while serving a massive clientele."[18] Edmonds distinguishes the clients of civil rights attorneys (the persons on whose behalf suit is filed) from their "constituents" (those to whom the attorney must answer for his actions).[19] He suggests that in class action school desegregation cases the mass of lower-class black parents and children are merely clients. To define con-stituents, Edmonds asks, "[To] what class of Americans does the civil rights at-torney feel he must answer for his professional conduct?"[20] The answer can be determined by identifying those with whom the civil rights attorney confers as he defines the goals of the litigation. He concludes that those who currently have access to the civil rights attorney are whites and middle-class blacks who advocate integration and categorically oppose majority black schools.

Edmonds suggests that, more than other professionals, the civil rights attorney labors in a closed setting isolated from most of his clients. No matter how numerous, the attorney's clients cannot become constituents unless they have access to him before or during the legal process. The result is the pursuit of metropolitan desegregation without sufficient regard for the probable instructional consequences for black children. In sum, he charges, "A class action suit serving only those who pay the attorney fee has the effect of permitting the fee paying minority to impose its will on the majority of the class on whose behalf suit is presumably brought."[21]

The Resolution of Lawyer-Client Conflicts

Some civil rights lawyers, like their more candid poverty law colleagues, are making decisions, setting priorities, and undertaking responsibilities that should be determined by their clients and shaped by the community. It is essential that lawyers "lawyer" and not attempt to lead clients and class. Commitment renders restraint more, not less, difficult, and the inability of black clients to pay handsome fees for legal services can cause their lawyers, unconsciously perhaps, to adopt an attitude of "we know what's best" in determining legal strategy. Unfortunately, clients are all too willing to turn everything over to the lawyers. In school cases, perhaps more than in any other civil rights field, the attorney must be more than a litigator. The willingness to innovate, organize, and negotiate—and the ability to perform each with skill and persistence—are of crucial importance. In this process of overall representation, the apparent—and sometimes real—conflicts of interest between lawyer and client can be resolved.

Finally, commitment to an integrated society should not be allowed to interfere with the ability to represent effectively parents who favor education-oriented remedies. Those civil rights lawyers, regardless of race, whose commitment to integration is buoyed by doubts about the effectiveness of predominantly black schools should reconsider seriously the propriety of representing blacks, at least in those school cases involving heavily minority districts.

This seemingly harsh suggestion is dictated by practical as well as professional considerations. Lacking more viable alternatives, the black community has turned to the courts. After several decades of frustration, the legal system, for a number of complex reasons, responded. Law and lawyers have received perhaps too much credit for that response.[22] The quest for symbolic manifestations of new rights and the search for new legal theories have too often failed to prompt an assessment of the economic and political conditions that so influence the progress and outcome of any social reform improvement.

In school desegregation blacks have a just cause, but that cause can be undermined as well as furthered by litigation. A test case can be an important means of calling attention to perceived injustice; more important, school litigation presents opportunities for improving the weak economic and political position which renders the black community vulnerable to the specific injustices the litigation is intended to correct. Litigation can and should serve lawyer and client as a community-organizing tool, an educational forum, a means of obtaining data, a method of exercising political leverage, and a rallying point for public support.

But even when directed by the most resourceful attorneys, civil rights litigation remains an unpredictable vehicle for gaining benefits, such as quality schooling, which a great many whites do not enjoy. The risks present in such efforts increase dramatically when civil rights attorneys, for idealistic or other reasons, fail to consider continually the limits imposed by the social and political circumstances under which clients must function even if the case is won. In the closest of lawyer-client relationships this continual reexamination can be difficult; it becomes much harder where much of the representation takes place hundreds of miles from the site of the litigation.

Ultimately, blacks must provide an enforcement mechanism that will give educational content to the constitutional right recognized in *Brown*. Simply placing black children in white schools will seldom suffice. Lawyers in school cases who fail to obtain judicial relief that reasonably promises to improve the education of black children serve poorly both their clients and their cause.

In 1935, W.E.B. Du Bois, in the course of a national debate over the education of blacks which has not been significantly altered by *Brown*, expressed simply but eloquently the message of the coalition of black community groups in Boston with which this article began:

> [T]he Negro needs neither segregated schools nor mixed schools. What he needs is Education. What he must remember is that there is no magic, either in mixed schools or in segregated schools. A mixed school with poor and unsympathetic teachers, with hostile public opinion, and no teaching of truth concerning black folk, is bad. A segregated school with ignorant placeholders, inadequate equipment, poor salaries, and wretched housing is equally bad. Other things being equal, the mixed school is the broader, more natural basis for the education of all youth. It gives wider contacts; it inspires greater self-confidence; and suppresses the inferiority complex. But other things seldom are equal, and in that case, Sympathy, Knowledge, and the Truth, outweigh all that the mixed school can offer.[23]

Du Bois spoke neither for the integrationist nor the separatist, but for poor black parents unable to choose, as can the well-to-do of both races, which schools will educate their children. Effective representation of these parents and their children presents a still unmet challenge for all lawyers committed to civil rights.

NOTES

1. 347 U.S. 483 (1954).

2. The author was a staff attorney specializing in school desegregation cases with the NAACP Legal Defense Fund from 1960 to 1966. From 1966 to 1968

he was Deputy Director, Office for Civil Rights, U.S. Department of Health, Education and Welfare.

3. 163 U.S. 537 (1896).

4. J. GREENBERG, RACE RELATIONS AND AMERICAN LAW 34–35 (1959). For an account of the development of the NAACP's legal program, see Robert L. Rabin, *Lawyers for Social Change: Perspectives on Public Interest Law*, 28 STAN. L. REV. 207, 214–18 (1976).

5. *See* GREENBERG, *supra* note 4, at 37.

6. *Id.*

7. L. MILLER, THE PETITIONERS: THE STORY OF THE SUPREME COURT OF THE UNITED STATES AND THE NEGRO 334 (1966).

8. L. FEIN, THE ECOLOGY OF THE PUBLIC SCHOOLS: AN INQUIRY INTO COMMUNITY CONTROL 6 (1971):

> In effect, the liberal community, both black and white, was caught up in a wrenching dilemma. The only way, it appeared, to move a sluggish nation towards massive amelioration of the Negro condition was to show how terrifyingly debilitating were the effects of discrimination and bigotry. The more lurid the detail, the more guilt it would evoke, and the more guilt, the more readiness to act. Yet the same lurid detail that did, in the event, prompt large-scale federal programs, also reinforced white convictions that Negroes were undesirable objects of interaction.

9. As one author summarized the situation, "During the past 20 years considerable racial mixing has taken place in schools, but research has produced little evidence of dramatic gains for children and some evidence of genuine stress for them." N. ST. JOHN, SCHOOL DESEGREGATION OUTCOMES FOR CHILDREN 136 (1975). Some writers are more hopeful, *e.g.,* Meyer Weinberg, *The Relationship Between School Desegregation and Academic Achievement: A Review of the Research,* 39 LAW & CONTEMP. PROB. 241 (1975); others are more cautious, *e.g.,* Cohen, *The Effects of Desegregation on Race Relations,* 39 LAW & CONTEMP. PROB. 271 (1975); Epps, *The Impact of School Desegregation on Aspirations, Self-Concepts and Other Aspects of Personality,* 39 LAW & CONTEMP. PROB. 300 (1975).

10. In Milliken v. Bradley, 418 U.S. 717, 745 (1974), the Supreme Court held (5–4) that desegregation remedies must stop at the boundary of the school district unless it can be shown that deliberately segregative actions were "a substantial cause of interdistrict segregation."

11. Swann v. Charlotte-Mecklenburg Bd. of Educ., 402 U.S. 1, 30–31 (1971).

12. *See generally* Hawkins v. Coleman, 3766 F. Supp. 1330 (N.D. Tex. 1974) (disproportionately high discipline and suspension rates for black students in the Dallas school system found to be the results of "white institutional racism"). During the 1972–1973 school year, black students were suspended at more than twice the rate of any other racial or ethnic group. CHILDRENS DEFENSE FUND, SCHOOL SUSPENSIONS: ARE THEY HELPING CHILDREN? 12 (1975). The report suggests the figure is due in large part to the result of racial discrimination, insensitivity, and ignorance as well as to "a pervasive intolerance by school officials for all students who are *different* in any number of ways." *Id.* at 9. *See also* Winifred Green, *Separate and Unequal Again,* INEQUALITY IN EDUC., July 1973, at 14.

13. For a collection of sources, see D. Bell, *Waiting on the Promise of Brown*, 39 LAW & CONTEMP. PROB. 341, 352–66 & nn.49–119 (1975).

14. *See* A. MEIER & E. RUDWICK, CORE: A STUDY IN THE CIVIL RIGHTS MOVEMENT 1942–1968 (1973).

15. J. Greenberg, *Litigation for Social Change*, RECORD OF N.Y.C.B.A. 320, 349 (1974).

16. *Id.*

17. Professor Leroy Clark, a former LDF lawyer, is more critical than his former boss about the role of financial contributors in setting civil rights policy:

> [T]here are two "clients" the civil rights lawyer must satisfy: (1) the immediate litigants (usually black), and (2) those liberals (usually white) who make financial contributions. An apt criticism of the traditional civil rights lawyer is that too often the litigation undertaken was modulated by that which was "salable" to the paying clientele who, in the radical view, had interests threatened by true social change. Attorneys may not make conscious decisions to refuse specific litigation because it is too "controversial" and hard to translate to the public, but no organization dependent on a large number of contributors can ignore the fact that the "appeal" of the program affects fund-raising. Some of the pressure to have a "winning" record may come from the need to show contributors that their money is accomplishing something socially valuable.

Clark, *The Lawyer in the Civil Rights Movement—Catalytic Agent or Counter-Revolutionary?* 19 KAN. L. REV. 459, 469 (1971).

The litigation decisions made under the pressure of so many nonlegal considerations are not always unanimous. A few years ago, LDF decided not to represent the militant black communist Angela Davis. LDF officials justified their refusal on the grounds that the criminal charges brought against Davis did not present "civil rights" issues. The decision, viewed by staff lawyers as an unconscionable surrender to conservative contributors, caused a serious split in LDF ranks. A few lawyers resigned because of the dispute and others remained disaffected for a long period.

18. R. Edmonds, *Advocating Inequity: A Critique of the Civil Rights Attorney in Class Action Desegregation Suits*, 3 BLACK L.J. 176, 178 (1974). Edmonds is Director of the Center for Urban Studies, Harvard Graduate School of Education.

19. *Id.*

20. *Id.* at 179.

21. *Id.*

22. Blacks lost in Plessy v. Ferguson, 163 U.S. 537 (1896), in part because the timing was not right. The Supreme Court and the nation had become reactionary on the issue of race. As LDF Director-Counsel Greenberg has acknowledged:

> [Plaintiff's attorney in *Plessy*, Albion W.] Tourgée recognized [that the tide of history was against him] and spoke of an effort to overcome its effect by influencing public opinion. But this, too, was beyond his control. All the lawyer can realistically do is marshall the evidence of what the claims of history may be and present them to the court. But no matter

how skillful the presentation, *Plessy* and *Brown* had dynamics of their own. Tourgée would have won with *Plessy* in 1954. The lawyers who brought *Brown* would have lost in 1896.

Greenberg, *supra* note 15, at 334.

23. W.E.B. Du Bois, *Does the Negro Need Separate Schools?*, 4 J. NEGRO EDUC. 328, 335 (1935).

From the Editor:
Issues and Comments

A R E law and litigation a trap for the serious reformer, structures designed more to maintain the current system of class advantage than to challenge it? If the main tools of legal thought, as several of the authors argue, are calculated to produce at most incremental change, how is Derrick Bell—or Critical Race Theory, for that matter—possible? Is the very structure of human thought by which we attempt to understand the experience of the Other—namely, metaphor and analogy to something within our own experience—doomed to fail? Or can we somehow escape the "empathic fallacy," as Delgado and Stefancic put it, so as to understand and react fully to the plight of human beings unlike us in color and class condition? Can a lawyer represent a person of radically different background and class from her or his own?

For further analysis of our emotional and intellectual shortcomings and blindfolds in dealing with race, see the second section of Part II (on counterstories) and Parts VI and VII (on how perspective and group loyalties confine our ability to imagine and identify with others). See, as well, the Suggested Readings, immediately following, especially the selections by Banks (on the inadequacies of tort, or private, law redressing certain harms), Kennedy (on "celebratory" scholarship); and Williams (on how colonialist discourse permitted the slaughter of Indians and plunder of their lands).

Suggested Readings

Banks, Taunya Lovell, *Teaching Laws with Flaws: Adopting a Pluralistic Approach to Torts*, 57 MO. L. REV. 443 (1992).

Bell, Derrick A., Jr., *Does Discrimination Make Economic Sense? For Some—It Did and Still Does*, 15 HUM. RTS. 38 (Fall 1988).

Brown, Kevin, *The Legal Rhetorical Structure for the Conversion of Desegregation Lawsuits to Quality Education Lawsuits*, 42 EMORY L.J. 791 (1993).

Delgado, Richard, *Norms and Normal Science: Toward a Critique of Normativity in Legal Thought*, 139 U. PA. L. REV. 933 (1991).

Delgado, Richard, *Rodrigo's Third Chronicle: Care, Competition, and the Redemptive Tragedy of Race*, 81 CAL. L. REV. 387 (1993).

Delgado, Richard, *Shadowboxing: An Essay on Power*, 77 CORNELL L. REV. 813 (1992).

Freeman, Alan D., *Legitimizing Racial Discrimination Through Antidiscrimination Law: A Critical Review of Supreme Court Doctrine*, 62 MINN. L. REV. 1049 (1978).

Karst, Kenneth L., *Citizenship, Race, and Marginality*, 30 WM. & MARY L. REV. 1 (1988).

Kennedy, Randall L., *Race Relations Law and the Tradition of Celebration: The Case of Professor Schmidt*, 86 COLUM. L. REV. 1622 (1986).

Mensch, Elizabeth & Alan Freeman, *A Republican Agenda for Hobbesian America?*, 41 FLA. L. REV. 581 (1989).

powell, john a., *New Property Disaggregated: A Model to Address Employment Discrimination*, 24 U.S.F. L. REV. 363 (1990).

West, Cornel, *The Role of Law in Progressive Politics*, 43 VAND. L. REV. 1797 (1990).

Williams, Robert A., Jr., *Encounters on the Frontiers of International Human Rights Law: Redefining the Terms of Indigenous Peoples Survival in the World*, 1990 DUKE L.J. 660.

Williams, Robert A., Jr., *The Medieval and Renaissance Origins of the Status of the American Indian in Western Legal Thought*, 57 S. CAL. L. REV. 1 (1983).

PART VI

RACE, SEX, CLASS, AND THEIR INTERSECTIONS

O N E of the newer and more exciting and recent trends in Critical Race Theory has been the examination of race, sex, and class and how they interact in a system of oppression. Scholars are asking whether these elements are separate disadvantaging factors, and whether one of them is primary. They are asking whether black men and women stand on the same footing in confronting racism; whether black and white women are affected by patriarchy, unfair laws, and the danger of rape in the same way. A few of these scholars examine sexual orientation, and the relation of gays and lesbians of color to the broader minority community.

The three chapters of Part VI illustrate many of these issues. In the first, Rodrigo, Professor Richard Delgado's alter ego, explains how he got caught in the crossfire at a meeting of the Women's Law Caucus at his school. His experience leads him and "the professor" to analyze issues of race and sex, ending up with a new theory of social change and small groups. In the next chapter, Angela Harris provides the best explanation of gender essentialism and the way in which many black women take issue with the all-encompassing aspects of the white-dominated feminist movement.

The final chapter, by Professor Paulette Caldwell, recounts an employment discrimination case involving a black woman who wished to wear her hair in braids. She uses it as a springboard for discussing employment discrimination law's inadequacies in dealing with discrimination aimed at black women on account of their black womanhood or of some aspect of their personal identity or appearance.

21 Rodrigo's Sixth Chronicle: Intersections, Essences, and the Dilemma of Social Reform

RICHARD DELGADO

I W A S returning to my office from the faculty library one flight below, when I spied a familiar figure waiting outside my door.

"Rodrigo!" I said. "Its good to see you. Please come in."

I had not seen my young protégé in a while. A graduate of a fine law school in Italy, Rodrigo had returned to the United States recently to begin LL.M. studies at a well-known school across town in preparation for a career as a law professor. An African-American by birth and ancestry, the talented Rodrigo had sought me out over the course of a year to discuss Critical Race Theory and many other ideas. For my part, I had gratefully used him as a foil and a sounding board for my own thoughts.

"Have a seat. You look a little agitated. Is everything OK?" Rodrigo had been pacing my office while I was putting my books down and activating my voice mail. I hoped it was intellectual excitement and his usual high-pitched energy that accounted for his restless demeanor.

"Professor, I'm afraid I'm in some trouble. Do you have a few minutes? There's something I need to talk over with someone older and wiser."

"I'm definitely older," I said. "The other part I'm not sure about. What's happening?"

"There's a big feud going on in the Law Women's Caucus at my school. The women of color and the white members are going at it hammer and tongs. And like a dummy, I got caught right in the middle."

"You? How?" I asked.

"I'm not a member. I don't think any man is. But Giannina is an honorary member, as I think I mentioned to you last time. The Caucus has tried to keep its struggle quiet, but I learned about it from Giannina. And I'm afraid I really—how do you put it?—put my foot in the mouth."

"In your mouth," I corrected. Although Rodrigo had been born in the States and spent his early childhood here, he occasionally failed to use an idiom cor-

68 N.Y.U. L. REV. 639 (1993). Copyright © 1993 by the New York University Law Review. Reprinted by permission.

rectly, a difficulty I had observed with other foreigners. "Tell me more," I continued. "How did it happen? Is it serious?"

"It's extremely serious," said Rodrigo, leaping to his feet and resuming his pacing. "They were having a meeting down in the basement, where I went after class to pick up Giannina. We were going to catch the subway home, and I thought her meeting would be over by then. I stood at the door a minute, when a woman I knew motioned me in. That was my mistake."

"Are the meetings closed to men?"

"I don't think so. But I was the only man there at the time. They were talking about essentialism[1]—as I've learned to call it—and the organization's agenda. A woman of color was complaining that the group never paid enough attention to the concerns of women like her. Some of the white women were getting upset. I made the mistake of raising my hand."

"What did you say?"

"I only tried to help analyze some of the issues. I drew a couple of distinctions, or tried to anyway. Both sides got mad at me. One called me an imperial scholar, an interloper, a typical male, and a pest. I got out of there fast. And now, no one will talk to me. Even Giannina made me move out of the bedroom. I've been sleeping on the couch for the last three nights. I feel like a leper."

A quarrel between lovers! I had not had to deal with one of those since my sons were young. "I'm sure you and she will patch it up," I offered. "You'd better—the two of you owe me dinner, remember?"

Rodrigo was not cheered by my joke nor my effort to console him. "I may never have Giannina's companionship again," he said, looking down.

"These things generally get better with time," I said, making a mental note to address the point later. "It's part of life. But if talking about some of these issues would help, I'm game."

In Which Rodrigo and I Review the Essentialism Debate and Try to Understand What Happened at the Law Women's Caucus

"The debate about essentialism has both a political and a theoretical component," Rodrigo began. "That book (Rodrigo nodded in the direction of *Yearning: Race, Gender and Cultural Politics*,[9] by bell hooks, lying open on my desk) and those articles[3] pay more attention to the political dimension. But there's also a linguistic-theory component."

"You mean the early philosophical discussion about whether words have essences?" I asked, pausing a moment to offer Rodrigo a cup of steaming espresso. I pointed out the tray of ingredients and said, "Help yourself if it needs more cream and sugar."

"Exactly," Rodrigo replied, slurping his coffee. "The early antiessentialists attacked the belief that words have core, or central, meanings. If I'm not mistaken,

Wittgenstein was the first in our time to point this out.[4] In a way, it's a particularly powerful and persuasive version of the antinominalist argument."[5]

As always, Rodrigo surprised me with his erudition. I wondered how an Italian-trained scholar, particularly one so young, had managed to learn about Wittgenstein, whose popularity I thought lay mainly in the English-speaking world. "How did you learn about Wittgenstein?" I asked.

"He's popular in Italy," Rodrigo explained. "I belonged to a study group that read him. The part of his teaching that laid the basis for anti-essentialism was his attack on the idea of core meanings. As you know, he wrote that the meaning of a term is its use."[6]

"I haven't read him in a while," I added hastily. "But you mentioned that the controversy's political side seems to be moving into the fore right now, which seems true. And I gather it's this aspect of the essentialism debate that you wandered into at school."

"In its political guise," Rodrigo continued, "members of different outgroups argue about the appropriate unit of analysis—about whether the Black community, for example, is one community or many, whether gays and lesbians have anything in common with straight activists, and so on.[7] At the Law Women's Caucus, they were debating one aspect of this—namely, whether there is one, essential sisterhood, as opposed to many. The women of color were arguing that to think of the women's movement as singular and unitary disempowers them. They said that this view disenfranchises anyone—say, lesbian mothers, disabled women, or working-class women—whose experience and status differ from what they term 'the norm.' "[8]

"And the others, of course, were saying the opposite?"

"Not exactly," Rodrigo replied. "They were saying that vis-à-vis men, all women stood on a similar footing. All are oppressed by a common enemy, namely patriarchy, and ought to stand together to confront this evil."[9]

"I've read something similar in the literature," I said.

"I'm not surprised. In a way, the debate the Caucus was having recapitulates an exchange between Angela Harris, a talented Black writer, and Martha Fineman, a leading white feminist scholar."

"Those articles are on my list of things to read. In fact," I paused, ruffling through the papers on my littered desk, "they're right here. I skimmed this one and set this other one aside for more careful reading later. I have to annotate both for my editors."

"Then you have at least a general idea of how the political version goes," Rodrigo said. "It has to do with agendas and the sorts of compromises people have to make in any organization to keep the group working together. In the Caucus's version, the sisters were complaining that the organization did not pay enough attention to the needs of women of color. They were urging that the group write an amicus brief on behalf of Haitian women and take a stand for the mostly Black custodial workers at the university. While not unsympathetic, the Caucus leadership thought these projects should not have the highest priority."

"I see what you mean by recapitulation of the academic debate. Fineman and Harris argue over some of the same things. Not the specific examples, of course, but the general issues. Harris writes about the troubled relationship between Black women and other women in the broader feminist mainstream,[10] although she notes that many of the issues this relationship raises reappear in exchanges between straight and gay women, working- and professional-class minorities, Black women and Black men, and so on. She and others write of the way in which these relationships often end up producing or increasing disempowerment for the less influential group.[11] They point out that white feminist theorists, while powerful and brilliant in many ways, nevertheless base many of their insights on gender essentialism—the idea that women have a single, unitary nature. They point out that certain feminist scholars write as though women's experiences can be captured in general terms, without taking into account differences of race or class.[12] This approach obscures the identities and submerges the perspectives of women who differ from the norm. Not only does legal theory built on essentialist foundations marginalize and render certain groups invisible, it falls prey to the trap of over-abstraction, something the same writers deplore in other settings. It also promotes hierarchy and silencing, evils that women should, and do, seek to subvert."

"Much the same goes on within the Black community," I pointed out. "This community is diverse, many communities in one. Black neoconservatives, for example, complain that folks like you and me leave little room for diversity by disparaging them as sellouts and belittling their views as unrepresentative.[13] They accuse us of writing as though the community of color only has one voice—ours—and of arrogating to ourselves the power to make generalizations and declare ourselves the possessors of all socio-political truth."[14]

"I know that critique," Rodrigo replied. "It seems to me that they might well have a point, although it does sound a little strange to hear the complaint of being overwhelmed, smothered, spoken for by others, coming from the mouth of someone at Yale or Harvard."

"Like you at the Law Caucus, I found myself on the end of some stinging criticism. I have Randall Kennedy and Steve Carter, particularly, in mind. They write powerfully, and of course many in the mainstream loved their message—so much so that they neglected to read any of the replies. But let's get back to the feminist version, and what happened to you at the Law Women's meeting."

"Oh, yes. The discussion in many ways mirrored the debate in the legal literature and in that book." Rodrigo again pointed in the direction of the bell hooks book. "As you probably know, Harris's principal opponent in the anti-essentialism debate has been Martha Fineman, who takes Black feminists to task for what she considers their overpreoccupation with difference. Their focus on their own unique experience contributes to a 'disunity' within the broader feminist movement that she finds troubling. It's troubling, she says, because it weakens the group's voice, the sum total of power it wields. Emphasizing minor differences between young and old, gay and straight, and Black and white women is divisive, verging on self-indulgence. It contributes to the false idea that the individual is the unit of social change, not the group. It results in tokenism and plays into the hands of male power."[15]

"And the discussion in the room was proceeding along these lines?" I asked.

"Yes," Rodrigo replied. "Although I had the sense that things had been brewing for some time. As soon as some of the leaders expressed coolness toward the Black women's proposal for a day-care center, the level of acrimony increased sharply. A number of women of color said, 'This is just like what you said last time.' Some of the white women accused them of narrow parochialism. And so it went."

"Rodrigo, you might not know this because you've been out of the country for—what?—the last ten years?" Rodrigo nodded yes. "These issues are really heated right now. And they're not confined to feminist organizations. Many of the same arguments are being waged within communities of color. Latinos and Blacks are feuding. And, of course, everyone knows about Korean merchants and inner-city Blacks. Black women are telling us men about our insufferable behavior. We're always finishing sentences for them, expecting them to make coffee at meetings. Some of them with long memories recall how we made them march in the second row during the civil rights movement. We make the same arguments right back at them: 'Don't criticize, you'll weaken the civil rights movement, the greater evil is racism, we need unity, there must be common cause,' and so on. They're starting to get tired of that form of essentializing, and to point out our own chauvinism, our own patriarchal mannerisms and faults."

"Those are some of the things I got called at the meeting. It looks like I have company."

"We all need to think these things through. You and I could talk about it some more, if you think it would help. Can I offer you another cup of coffee?"

In Which Rodrigo Posits a Theory of Social Change and Explains the Role of Oppositional Groups in Bringing It About

RODRIGO LAYS OUT A NATURAL HISTORY OF SOCIAL IDEAS

"I think that virtually all revolutionary ideas start with an outsider of some sort," Rodrigo began. "We mentioned the reasons before. Few who operate within the system see its defects. They speak, read, and hear within a discourse that is self-satisfying. The primary function of our system of free speech is to effect stasis, not change. New ideas are ridiculed as absurd and extreme, and discounted as political, at first. It's not until much later, when consciousness changes, that we look back and wonder why we resisted so strongly."

"Revolutionaries always lead rocky lives. You'll see that too, Rodrigo, although I don't know if you classify yourself as one or not. All the pressure is in the direction of conforming, of doing what others do, in teaching, in scholarship, in fact in all areas of life."

Rodrigo shrugged off my counsel. "So, new ideas and movements come along relatively rarely. And when they do, they are beleaguered. For a long time, they garner little support. Then, for some reason, they acquire something like a critical mass. Society begins to pay attention. Now, the situation is in flux. The group now needs all the allies they can muster. They begin to make inroads and need to make more. They see that they are beginning to approach the point where they might be able to change societal discourse in a direction they favor."

"Including the power to define who is 'divisive,' " I added.

"That, too—especially that," Rodrigo said animatedly, seeing how my observation fit into the theory he was developing. He looked up with gratitude, then continued:

"At this point, they need all the help they can get. If they are you, they need Gary Peller and Alan Freeman.[16] If they are feminists, they need Cass Sunstein.[17] Earlier, they needed the religious right in their campaign against pornography. And so on. With a little growth in numbers, they may perhaps reach the point at which power begins to translate into knowledge. And knowledge, of course, is the beginning of social reform. When everyone knows you are right, knows you have a point, you are well on your way to victory."[18]

"And for this the group needs numbers."

"Right. With them, they can change the interpretive community.[19] They can remake the model of the essential woman, say, along lines that are genuinely more humane."[20]

RODRIGO AND I DISCUSS THE ROLE OF REFORMERS AND MALCONTENT GROUPS

"So, Rodrigo," I continued, "you are saying that new knowledge of any important, radical sort begins with a small group. This group is dissatisfied, but believes it has a point. It agitates, acquires new members, begins to get society to take it seriously. And it's at this point that the essentialism/anti-essentialism debate usually sets in?"

"Before it wouldn't arise. And later, when the large group is nearing its goals, it doesnt need the disaffected faction. So it's right at this mid-point in a social revolution—for example, the feminist movement—that we have debates like the one I got caught in the middle of."

"But you were saying before that the disaffected cell ought to sit out the revolution, as it were, and not just for its own good but for that of the wider society as well?"

"It should. And often such groups do, consciously or unconsciously. I'm just saying that when they do, it's usually not a bad thing."

"And this is because of your theory of knowledge, I gather, in which canonical thinking always gets to a point where it no longer works and needs a fundamental challenge?"

"And this, in turn, can only come from a disaffected group. Every new idea, if it has merit, eventually turns into a canon. And every canonical idea at some point needs to be dislodged, challenged, and supplanted by a new one."

"So maverick, malcontent groups are the growing edge of social thought."

"Not every one. Some are regressive—want to roll back reform."

"I can think of several that fit that bill," I said shuddering. "But you said earlier that the outsider has a kind of binocular vision that enables him or her to see defects in the bubbles in which we all live—to see the curvature, the limitations, the downward drift that eventually spells trouble. But earlier you used another metaphor. What was it?"

Rodrigo thought for a moment. "Oh, I remember. It was the role of hunger."

"I'd love for you to explain."

"It's like this." Rodrigo pushed aside his plate. "Change comes from a small, dissatisfied group for whom canonical knowledge and the standard social arrangements don't work. Such a group needs allies. Thus, white women in the feminist movement reach out to women of color; Black men in the civil rights movement try to include Black women, and so on. Eventually, the larger group makes inroads, changes the paradigm, begins to be accepted, gets laws passed, and so on."

"Can I take that plate?" I asked. Rodrigo passed it over, and I put it in the non-recyclable bin outside my office along with the other remnants of our snack. "This is what you argued before, so I assume you're getting to your theory about hunger."

"Correct. But you see, as soon as all this happens, the once-radical group begins to lose its edge. It enters a phase of consolidation, in which it is more concerned with defending and instituting reforms made possible by the new consensus, the new paradigm of Foucault's Knowledge/Power, than with pushing the envelope towards more radical change. The group is beginning to lose binocular vision, the special form of insight most outgroups have, about social inequities and imbalances."

"And so the reform movement founders?" I asked. "We've seen many examples of that. As you know, legal scholarship is now extremely interested in that question. Many in the left are trying to discover why all our best intentions fail, why the urge to transform society for the better always comes to naught."[21]

"I'm not sure I'd say the movement founders," Rodrigo interjected. "Rather, it enters into a different phase. I don't want to be too critical."

"But at any rate, it peters out," I said. "It loses vigor."

"But then, eventually, another group rises up to take its place. Often this is a disaffected subset of the larger group, the one that won reforms, that got the Supreme Court or Congress to recognize the legitimacy of its claims. It turns out that the reforms did not do much for the subgroup. The revolution came and went, but things stayed pretty much the same for it. So, it renews its effort."

"And that's what you meant by hunger?"

"In a way. Those who are hungry are most desperate for change. Human intelligence and progress spring from adversity, from a sense that the world is not supplying what the organism needs and requires. A famous American philosopher developed a theory of education based on this idea."

"I assume you mean John Dewey?"[22]

"Him and others. He was a sometime member of the school of American pragmatists. But his approach differed in significant respects from that of the other pragmatists like William James and Charles Peirce. One was this.[23] And so I'm thinking we can borrow from his theory to explain the natural history of revolutionary movements, applying what he saw to be true for individuals to larger groups."

"Where you think it holds as well?" I asked. "It's always dangerous extrapolating from the individual to the group."

"I think the observation does hold for groups, as well," Rodrigo replied. "But I'd be glad to be corrected if you think I am wrong. The basic idea is that groups that are victors become complacent. They lose their critical edge, because there is no need to have it. The social structure now works for them. If by intelligence, one means critical intelligence, we become dumber all the time. It's a kind of reverse evolution. Eventually society gets out of kilter enough that a dissident group rises up, its critical skills honed, its perception equal to that of the slave. It challenges the master by condemning the status quo as unjust, just as Giannina challenged me. Sometimes the injustices it points to are ones that genuinely need mending, and not just for the discontented group. Rather, they signal a broader social need to reform things in ways that will benefit everybody."[24]

I leaned forward; the full force of what Rodrigo was saying had hit me. "So, Rodrigo, you are saying that the history of revolution is, by its nature, iterative. The unit of social intelligence is small; reform and retrenchment come in waves. This fits in with what you were saying earlier about the decline of the West and the need for infusion of outsider thought. And, it dovetails with other currents under way in environmental thought,[25] economic thought[26]—and, as you mentioned, in American political philosophy. . . ."

NOTES

1. On essentialism, *see* generally BELL HOOKS, AIN'T I A WOMAN?: BLACK WOMEN AND FEMINISM (1981) (discussing inseparability of race and sex for Black women); BELL HOOKS, YEARNING: RACE, GENDER AND CULTURAL POLITICS (1991) (articulating radical cultural critique linked with concern for transforming oppressive structures of domination); BELL HOOKS & CORNEL WEST, BREAKING BREAD: INSURGENT BLACK INTELLECTUAL LIFE (1991) (scrutinizing dilemmas, contradictions, and joys of Black intellectual life); ELIZABETH V. SPELMAN, INESSENTIAL WOMAN: PROBLEMS OF EXCLUSION IN FEMINIST THOUGHT (1988) (showing how essentialism denies significance of heterogeneity for feminist theory and political activity); Trina Grillo & Stephanie M. Wildman, *Obscuring the Importance of Race: The Implications of Making Comparisons Between Racism and Sexism or Other -Isms*, 1991 DUKE L.J. 397 (discussing dangers of analogizing racism to other forms of discrimination); Angela P. Harris, *Race and Essentialism*

in Feminist Legal Theory, 42 STAN. L. REV. 581 (1990) (criticizing gender essentialism for failing to take into account Black women's experiences). As Rodrigo and the professor use the term, essentialism consists of treating as unitary a concept or group that, to some at least, contains diversity.

2. HOOKS, YEARNING, *supra* note 1.

3. *See* notes and text *supra.*

4. *See* LUDWIG WITTGENSTEIN, TRACTATUS LOGICO-PHILOSOPHICUS 9–25 (D. F. Pears & B. F. McGuinness trans., 2d ed. 1974) (1921) (developing idea that meaning of term or symbol lies in its use).

5. The antinominalist argument holds, in short, that words and terms do not correspond to permanent essences or things existing in a realm outside time. *See, e.g.,* 3 ENCYCLOPEDIA OF PHILOSOPHY 59–60 (P. Edwards ed., 1967) (Essence and Existence); 8 ENCYCLOPEDIA OF PHILOSOPHY, *supra* at 199–204 (on conceptualism, nominalism, and resemblance theories).

6. WITTGENSTEIN, *supra* note 4, at 10–25 (postulating that meaning of a word comes from its use; even terms like "chair" have no core meanings or necessary and sufficient conditions for their application).

7. *See, e.g.,* Harris, *supra* note 1 (criticizing gender essentialism).

8. *See* generally Kimberlé Crenshaw, *Demarginalizing the Intersection of Race and Sex: A Black Feminist Critique of Antidiscrimination Doctrine, Feminist Theory and Antiracist Politics*, 1989 U. CHI. LEGAL F. 139 (examining how tendency to treat race and gender as mutually exclusive categories of experience and analysis is perpetuated by a single-axis framework that is dominant in antidiscrimination law, feminist theory, and antiracist politics); Harris, *supra* note 1.

9. *See* Martha L. Fineman, *Challenging Law, Establishing Differences: The Future of Feminist Legal Scholarship*, 42 U. FLA. L. REV. 25, 36 (1990) (advocating unified stand by all women against patriarchy).

10. *See* Harris, *supra* note 1, at 585–604.

11. *See generally, e.g.,* Paulette Caldwell, *A Hair Piece: Perspectives on the Intersection of Race and Gender*, 1991 DUKE L.J. 365 (criticizing Rogers v. American Airlines, 527 F. Supp. 229 (S.D.N.Y. 1981), and legal system in general for failing to consider intersection between race and gender); Crenshaw, *supra* note 8.

12. *See* Harris, *supra* note 1, at 585–90, 595–605, 612–13 (mentioning Robin West and Catharine MacKinnon as examples).

13. *See generally, e.g.,* DINESH DSOUZA, ILLIBERAL EDUCATION (1991) (articulating neoconservative critique of Black and liberal politics); RICHARD RODRIGUEZ, HUNGER OF MEMORY (1982) (recounting experiences of Spanish-speaking student who pursues his education in English-speaking schools); SHELBY STEELE, THE CONTENT OF OUR CHARACTER (1990) (arguing that while there is racial insensitivity and some racial discrimination in our society there is also much opportunity); *see also* STEPHEN L. CARTER, REFLECTIONS OF AN AFFIRMATIVE ACTION BABY (1991) (articulating neoconservative critique of Black and liberal politics).

14. *Id. See also* Randall L. Kennedy, *Racial Critiques of Legal Academia*, 102 HARV. L. REV. 1745 (1989) (analyzing writings which examine effect of racial difference on distribution of prestige in legal academia).

15. *See* Fineman, *supra* note 9, at 39–43.

16. Viz., white authors who have written work supportive of Critical Race scholarship by academics of color. *See* generally Alan D. Freeman, *Legitimizing Racial Discrimination Through Antidiscrimination Law: A Critical Review of Supreme Court Doctrine*, 62 MINN. L. REV. 1049 (1978) (describing major developments in antidiscrimination law in 25-year period following Brown v. Board of Education, 347 U.S. 483 (1954), with emphasis on "victim's perspective"); Alan D. Freeman, *Racism, Rights, and the Quest for Equality of Opportunity: A Critical Legal Essay*, 23 HARV. C.R.-C.L. L. REV. 295 (1988) (commenting on racism and rights in response to minority critique of Critical Legal Studies movement); Gary Peller, *Race Consciousness*, 1990 DUKE L.J. 758 (exploring conflict between integrationist and Black nationalist images of racial justice, and its effect on current mainstream race reform discourse).

17. *See generally, e.g.*, FEMINISM & POLITICAL THEORY (Cass R. Sunstein ed., 1990) (providing a representative wide-ranging, yet unified, set of readings on feminist political thought); Cass R. Sunstein, *Pornography and the First Amendment*, 1986 DUKE L.J. 589 (arguing that pornography is low-value speech that can be regulated consistently with first amendment).

18. *See* MICHEL FOUCAULT, POWER/KNOWLEDGE: SELECTED INTERVIEWS AND OTHER WRITINGS 1972–77 (Colin Gordon ed. & Colin Gordon et al. trans., 1980). Michel Foucault, a well-known contemporary philosopher, wrote about the relation between structures of social control and what is regarded as knowledge. He believed that knowledge is often socially constructed—that is, a matter of consensus—and that what is regarded as true is as much a function of power and influence as objective truth.

19. "Interpretive community" is a commonly employed term in the theory of interpretation. It refers to the manner in which texts and words acquire a meaning in reference to a community of speakers who agree tacitly to employ them in particular ways. As Rodrigo employs it, he means that large numbers of people can sometimes change the way we *see* things, deploy words, and ascribe meanings to concepts such as women.

20. On the hope that this kind of radical reconstruction of womanhood can happen, *see generally* AMERICA'S WORKING WOMEN (Rosalyn Baxandall et al. eds., 1976) (offering collection of views on social change and reform).

21. *See generally* D. BELL, AND WE ARE NOT SAVED (1991) (providing new insights and suggesting more effective strategies in response to failed pledges for racial equality in past).

22. *See generally* JOHN DEWEY, EXPERIENCE AND EDUCATION (First Collier Books ed. 1963) (1938) (classic statement of progressive education which includes theory of inquiry learning, freedom, and learning through experiences); JOHN DEWEY, HOW WE THINK (1933) (articulating philosopher's approach to thought and action in relation to his program of American pragmatism).

23. Viz., Dewey's theory of education, a topic that he addressed much more fully than any other American philosopher of his period. He believed that understanding how the mind works and assimilates new material is essential to understanding how an individual adapts to her reality.

24. On the notion that reforms born of the struggle for racial justice often end up benefiting all, not just Blacks, *see* generally HARRY KALVEN, THE NEGRO

AND THE FIRST AMENDMENT (1965) (focusing on impact of the civil rights movement on first amendment).

25. On the idea that small is better, environmentally speaking, *see, e.g.,* KENNETH E. BOULDING ET AL., ENVIRONMENTAL QUALITY IN A GROWING ECONOMY 3–14 (Henry Jarrett ed., 1966) (criticizing society's obsession with production and consumption, and its lack of concern for future ramifications); ALDO LEOPOLD, A SAND COUNTY ALMANAC AND SKETCHES HERE AND THERE viii, ix, 199–226 (1949) (arguing for land ethic which examines land-use questions in terms of ethics and aesthetics, and not just as economic problems).

26. On the idea that government should be as small and nonintrusive as possible, *see generally* RICHARD A. EPSTEIN, FORBIDDEN GROUNDS: THE CASE AGAINST EMPLOYMENT DISCRIMINATION LAWS (1992) (arguing that economic and social consequences of antidiscrimination laws in employment should be focused on more than historical injustices).

22 Race and Essentialism in Feminist Legal Theory

ANGELA P. HARRIS

I N *Funes the Memorious*, Borges tells of Ireneo Funes, who was a rather ordinary young man (notable only for his precise sense of time) until the age of nineteen, when he was thrown by a half-tamed horse and left paralyzed but possessed of perfect perception and a perfect memory.

After his transformation, Funes

> knew by heart the forms of the southern clouds at dawn on the 30th of April, 1882, and could compare them in his memory with the mottled streaks on a book in Spanish binding he had only seen once and with the outlines of the foam raised by an oar in the Río Negro the night before the Quebracho uprising. These memories were not simple ones; each visual image was linked to muscular sensations, thermal sensations, etc. He could reconstruct all his dreams, all his half-dreams. Two or three times he had reconstructed a whole day; he never hesitated, but each reconstruction had required a whole day.[1]

Funes tells the narrator that after his transformation he invented his own numbering system. "In place of seven thousand thirteen, he would say (for example) *Máximo Pérez*; in place of seven thousand fourteen, *The Railroad*; other numbers were Luis Melián Lafinur, Olimar, sulphur, the reins, the whale, the gas, the caldron, Napoleon, Agustín de Vedia."[2] The narrator tries to explain to Funes "that this rhapsody of incoherent terms was precisely the opposite of a system of numbers. I told him that saying 365 meant saying three hundreds, six tens, five ones, an analysis which is not found in the 'numbers' *The Negro Timoteo* or *meat blanket*. Funes did not understand me or refused to understand me."[3]

In his conversation with Funes, the narrator realizes that Funes' life of infinite unique experiences leaves Funes no ability to categorize: "With no effort, he had learned English, French, Portuguese and Latin. I suspect, however, that he was not very capable of thought. To think is to forget differences, generalize, make abstractions. In the teeming world of Funes, there were only details, almost immediate in their presence."[4] For Funes, language is only a unique and private system of classification, elegant and solipsistic. The notion that language, made abstract, can serve to create and reinforce a community is incomprehensible to him.

"WE THE PEOPLE"

Describing the voice that speaks the first sentence of the Declaration of Independence, James Boyd White remarks:

> It is not a person's voice, not even that of a committee, but the "unanimous" voice of "thirteen united States" and of their "people." It addresses a universal audience—nothing less than "mankind" itself, located neither in space nor in time—and the voice is universal too, for it purports to know about the "Course of human events" (all human events?) and to be able to discern what "becomes necessary" as a result of changing circumstances.[5]

The Preamble of the United States Constitution, White argues, can also be heard to speak in this unified and universal voice. This voice claims to speak

> for an entire and united nation and to do so directly and personally, not in the third person or by merely delegated authority. . . . The instrument thus appears to issue from a single imaginary author, consisting of all the people of the United States, including the reader, merged into a single identity in this act of self-constitution. "The People" are at once the author and the audience of this instrument.[6]

Despite its claims, however, this voice does not speak for everyone, but for a political faction trying to constitute itself as a unit of many disparate voices; its power lasts only as long as the contradictory voices remain silenced.

In a sense, the "I" of Funes, who knows only particulars, and the "we" of "We the People," who know only generalities, are the same. Both voices are monologues; both depend on the silence of others. The difference is only that the first voice knows of no others, while the second has silenced them.

The first voice, the voice of Funes, is the voice toward which literature sometimes seems driven. Law, however, has not been much tempted by the sound of the first voice. Lawyers are all too aware that legal language is not a purely self-referential game, for "legal interpretive acts signal and occasion the imposition of violence upon others."[7] In their concern to avoid the social and moral irresponsibility of the first voice, legal thinkers have veered in the opposite direction, toward the safety of the second voice, which speaks from the position of "objectivity" rather than "subjectivity," "neutrality" rather than "bias." This voice, like the voice of "We the People," is ultimately authoritarian and coercive in its attempt to speak for everyone.

We are not born with a "self," but rather are composed of a welter of partial, sometimes contradictory, or even antithetical "selves." A unified identity, if such can ever exist, is a product of will, not a common destiny or natural birthright. Thus, consciousness is "never fixed, never attained once and for all";[8] it is not a final outcome or a biological given, but a process, a constant contradictory state of becoming, in which both social institutions and individual wills are deeply implicated. A multiple consciousness is home both to the first and the second voices, and all the voices in between. Mari Matsuda, while arguing that in the legal realm "[h]olding on to a multiple consciousness will allow us to operate both within the abstractions of standard jurisprudential discourse, *and* within the details of our own special knowledge,"[9] acknowledges that "this constant shifting of consciousness produces sometimes madness, sometimes genius, sometimes both."[10]

RACE AND ESSENTIALISM IN FEMINIST LEGAL THEORY

In feminist legal theory, the move away from univocal toward multivocal theories of women's experience and feminism has been slower than in other areas. In feminist legal theory, the pull of the second voice, the voice of abstract categorization, is still powerfully strong: "We the People" seems in danger of being replaced by "We the Women." And in feminist legal theory, as in the dominant culture, it is mostly white, straight, and socioeconomically privileged people who claim to speak for all of us.[11] Not surprisingly, the story they tell about "women," despite its claim to universality, seems to black women to be peculiar to women who are white, straight, and socioeconomically privileged—a phenomenon Adrienne Rich terms "white solipsism."[12]

Elizabeth Spelman notes:

[T]he real problem has been how feminist theory has confused the condition of one group of women with the condition of all.

. . . A measure of the depth of white middle-class privilege is that the apparently straightforward and logical points and axioms at the heart of much of feminist theory guarantee the direction of its attention to the concerns of white middle-class women.[13]

The notion that there is a monolithic "women's experience" that can be described independent of other facets of experience like race, class, and sexual orientation I refer to in this essay as "gender essentialism." A corollary to gender essentialism is "racial essentialism"—the belief that there is a monolithic "Black Experience," or "Chicano Experience." The source of gender and racial essentialism (and all other essentialisms, for the list of categories could be infinitely multiplied) is the second voice, the voice that claims to speak for all. The result of essentialism is to reduce the lives of people who experience multiple forms of oppression to addition problems: "racism + sexism = straight black women's experience," or "racism + sexism + homophobia = black lesbian experience." Thus, in an essentialist world, black women's experience will always be forcibly fragmented before being subjected to analysis, as those who are "only interested in race" and those who are "only interested in gender" take their separate slices of our lives.

Moreover, feminist essentialism paves the way for unconscious racism. Spelman puts it this way:

[T]hose who produce the "story of woman" want to make sure they appear in it. The best way to ensure that is to be the storyteller and hence to be in a position to decide which of all the many facts about womens lives ought to go into the story, which ought to be left out. Essentialism works well in behalf of these aims, aims that subvert the very process by which women might come to see where and how they wish to make common cause. For essentialism invites me to take what I understand to be true of me "as a woman" for some golden nugget of woman-ness all women have as women; and it makes the participation of other women inessential to the production of the story. How lovely: the many turn out to be one, and the one that they are is me.[14]

In a racist society like this one, the storytellers are usually white, and so "woman" turns out to be "white woman."

Why, in the face of challenges from "different" women and from feminist method itself, is feminist essentialism so persistent and pervasive? I think the reasons are several. Essentialism is intellectually convenient, and to a certain extent cognitively ingrained. Essentialism also carries with it important emotional and political payoffs. Finally, essentialism often appears (especially to white women) as the only alternative to chaos, mindless pluralism (the Funes trap), and the end of the feminist movement. In my view, however, as long as feminists, like theorists in the dominant culture, continue to search for gender and racial essences, black women will never be anything more than a crossroads between two kinds of domination, or at the bottom of a hierarchy of oppressions; we will always be required to choose pieces of ourselves to present as wholeness.

Modified Women and Unmodified Feminism: Black Women in Dominance Theory

Catharine MacKinnon[15] describes her "dominance theory," like the Marxism with which she likes to compare it, as "total": [T]hey are both theories of the totality, of the whole thing, theories of a fundamental and critical underpinning of the whole they envision."[16] Both her dominance theory (which she identifies as simply "feminism") and Marxism "focus on that which is most one's own, that which most makes one the being the theory addresses, as that which is most taken away by what the theory criticizes. In each theory you are made who you are by that which is taken away from you by the social relations the theory criticizes."[17] In Marxism, the "that" is work; in feminism, it is sexuality.

MacKinnon defines sexuality as "that social process which creates, organizes, expresses, and directs desire, creating the social beings we know as women and men, as their relations create society."[18] Moreover, "the organized expropriation of the sexuality of some for the use of others defines the sex, woman. Heterosexuality is its structure, gender and family its congealed forms, sex roles its qualities generalized to social persona, reproduction a consequence, and control its issue."[19] Dominance theory, the analysis of this organized expropriation, is a theory of power and its unequal distribution.

In MacKinnon's view, "[t]he idea of gender difference helps keep the reality of male dominance in place."[20] That is, the concept of gender difference is an ideology which masks the fact that genders are socially constructed, not natural, and coercively enforced, not freely consented to. Moreover, "the social relation between the sexes is organized so that men may dominate and women must submit and this relation is sexual—in fact, is sex."[21]

For MacKinnon, male dominance is not only "perhaps the most pervasive and tenacious system of power in history, but . . . it is metaphysically nearly perfect."[22] The masculine point of view is point-of-viewlessness; the force of male dominance "is exercised as consent, its authority as participation, its supremacy as the paradigm of order, its control as the definition of legitimacy."[23] In such a world, the very existence of feminism is something of a paradox. "Feminism claims the voice of women's silence, the sexuality of our eroticized desexualization, the fullness of 'lack,' the centrality of our marginality and exclusion, the public nature of privacy, the presence of our absence."[24] The wonder is how feminism can exist in the face of its theoretical impossibility.

In MacKinnon's view, men have their foot on women's necks, regardless of race or class, or of mode of production: "Feminists do not argue that it means the same to women to be on the bottom in a feudal regime, a capitalist regime, and a socialist regime; the commonality argued is that, despite real changes, bottom is bottom."[25] As a political matter, moreover, MacKinnon is quick to insist that there is only one "true," "unmodified" feminism: that which analyzes women *as women*, not as subsets of some other group and not as gender-neutral beings.

Despite its power, MacKinnon's dominance theory is flawed by its essentialism. MacKinnon assumes, as does the dominant culture, that there is an essential "woman" beneath the realities of differences between women—that in describing the experiences of "women" issues of race, class, and sexual orientation can therefore be safely ignored, or relegated to footnotes. In her search for what is essential womanhood, however, MacKinnon rediscovers white womanhood and introduces it as universal truth. In dominance theory, black women are white women, only more so.

Essentialism in feminist theory has two characteristics that ensure that black women's voices will be ignored. First, in the pursuit of the essential feminine, Woman leached of all color and irrelevant social circumstance, issues of race are bracketed as belonging to a separate and distinct discourse—a process which leaves black women's selves fragmented beyond recognition. Second, feminist essentialists find that in removing issues of "race" they have actually only managed to remove black women—meaning that white women now stand as the epitome of Woman. Both processes can be seen at work in dominance theory.

DOMINANCE THEORY AND THE BRACKETING OF RACE

MacKinnon repeatedly seems to recognize the inadequacy of theories that deal with gender while ignoring race, but having recognized the problem, she repeatedly shies away from its implications. Thus, she at times justifies her essentialism by pointing to the essentialism of the dominant discourse: "My suggestion is that what we have in common is not that our conditions have no particularity in ways that matter. But we are all measured by a male standard for women, a standard that is not ours."[26] At other times she deals with the challenge of black women by placing it in footnotes. For example, she places in a footnote without further comment the suggestive, if cryptic, observation that a definition of feminism "of coalesced interest and resistance" has tended both to exclude and to make invisible "the diverse ways that many women—notably Blacks and working-class women—have *moved* against their determinants."[27] In another footnote generally addressed to the problem of relating Marxism to issues of gender and race, she notes that "[a]ny relationship *between* sex and race tends to be left entirely out of account, since they are considered parallel 'strata,'"[28] but this thought simply trails off into a string cite to black feminist and social feminist writings.

Finally, MacKinnon postpones the demand of black women until the arrival of a "general theory of social inequality"; recognizing that "gender in this country appears partly to comprise the meaning of, as well as bisect, race and class, even as race and class specificities make up, as well as cross-cut, gender,"[29] she nevertheless is prepared to maintain her "colorblind" approach to women's experience until that general theory arrives (presumably that is someone else's work).

The results of MacKinnon's refusal to move beyond essentialism are apparent in the most tentative essay in *Whose Culture? A Case Note on Martinez v. Santa Clara Pueblo.*[30] Julia Martinez sued her Native American tribe, the Santa Clara Pueblo, in federal court, arguing that a tribal ordinance was invalid under a provision of the Indian Civil Rights Act guaranteeing equal protection of the laws. The ordinance provided that if women married outside the Pueblo, the children of that union were not full tribal members, but if men married outside the tribe, their children were full tribal members. Martinez married a Navajo man, and her children were not allowed to vote or inherit her rights in communal land. The United States Supreme Court held that this question was a matter of Indian sovereignty to be resolved by the tribe.[31]

MacKinnon starts her discussion with an admission: "I find *Martinez* a difficult case on a lot of levels, and I don't usually find cases difficult."[32] She concludes that the Pueblo ordinance was wrong, because it "did nothing to address or counteract the reasons why Native women were vulnerable to white male land imperialism through marriage—it gave in to them, by punishing the *woman*, the Native person."[33] Yet she reaches her conclusion, as she admits, without knowledge other than "word of mouth" of the history of the ordinance and its place in Santa Clara Pueblo culture.

MacKinnon has Julia Martinez ask her tribe, "Why do you make me choose between my equality as woman and my cultural identity?"[34] But she, no less than the tribe, eventually requires Martinez to choose; and the correct choice is, of course, that Martinez's female identity is more important than her tribal identity. MacKinnon states,

[T]he aspiration of women to be no less than men—not to be punished where a man is glorified, not to be considered damaged or disloyal where a man is rewarded or left in peace, not to lead a derivative life, but to do everything and be anybody at all—is an aspiration indigenous to women across place and across time.[35]

What MacKinnon does not recognize, however, is that though the aspiration may be everywhere the same, its expression must depend on the social historical circumstances. In this case, should Julia Martinez be content with struggling for change from within, or should the white government have stepped in "on her behalf"? What was the meaning of the ordinance within Pueblo discourse, as opposed to a transhistorical and transcultural feminist discourse? How did it come about and under what circumstances? What was the status of women within the tribe, both historically and at the time of the ordinance and at the present time, and was Martinez's claim heard and understood by the tribal authorities or simply ignored or derided? What were the Pueblo traditions about children of mixed parentage, and how were those traditions changing? In a jurisprudence based on multiple consciousness, rather than the unitary consciousness of MacKinnon's dominance theory, these questions would have to be answered before the ordinance could be considered on its merits and even before the Court's decision to stay out could be evaluated. MacKinnon does not answer these questions, but leaves the essay hanging with the idea that the male supremacist ideology of some Native American tribes may be adopted from white culture and therefore invalid.[36] MacKinnon's tentativeness may be due to not wanting to appear a white cultural imperialist, speaking for a Native American tribe, but to take up Julia Martinez's claim at all is to take that risk. Without a theory that can shift focus from gender to race and other facets of identity and back again, MacKinnon's essay is ultimately crippled. Martinez is made to choose her gender over her race, and her experience is distorted in the process.

DOMINANCE THEORY AND WHITE WOMEN AS ALL WOMEN

The second consequence of feminist essentialism is that the racism that was acknowledged only in brackets quietly emerges in the feminist theory itself—both a cause and an effect of creating "Woman" from white woman. In MacKinnon's work, the result is that black women become white women, only more so.

In a passage in *Signs I*, MacKinnon borrows a quote from Toni Cade Bambara describing a black woman with too many children and no means with which to care for them as "grown ugly and dangerous from being nobody for so long," and then explains:

> By using her phrase in altered context, I do not want to distort her meaning but to extend it. Throughout this essay, I have tried to see if women's condition is shared, even when contexts or magnitudes differ. (Thus, it is very different to be "nobody" as a Black woman than as a white lady, but neither is "somebody" by male standards.) This is the approach to race and ethnicity attempted throughout. I aspire to include all women in the term "women" in some way, without violating the particularity of any woman's experience. Whenever this fails, the state-

ment is simply wrong and will have to be qualified or the aspiration (or the theory) abandoned.[37]

I call this the "nuance theory" approach to the problem of essentialism: by being sensitive to the notion that different women have different experiences, generalizations can be offered about "all women" while qualifying statements, often in footnotes, supplement the general account with the subtle nuances of experience that "different" women add to the mix. Nuance theory thus assumes the commonality of all women—differences are a matter of "context" or "magnitude"; that is, nuance.

The problem with nuance theory is that by defining black women as "different," white women quietly become the norm, or pure, essential Woman. Just as MacKinnon would argue that being female is more than a "context" or a "magnitude" of human experience, being black is more than a context or magnitude of all (white) women's experience. But not in dominance theory.

For instance, MacKinnon describes how a system of male supremacy has constructed "woman":

> Contemporary industrial society's version of her is docile, soft, passive, nurturant, vulnerable, weak, narcissistic, childlike, incompetent, masochistic, and domestic, made for child care, home care, and husband care. . . . Women who resist or fail, including those who never did fit—for example, black and lower-class women who cannot survive if they are soft and weak and incompetent, assertively self-respecting women, women with ambitions of male dimensions—are considered less female, lesser women.[38]

In a peculiar symmetry with this ideology, in which black women are something less than women, in MacKinnon's work black women become something more than women. In MacKinnon's writing, the word "black," applied to women, is an intensifier: If things are bad for everybody (meaning white women), then they're even worse for black women. Silent and suffering, we are trotted onto the page (mostly in footnotes) as the ultimate example of how bad things are.

Thus, in speaking of the beauty standards set for (white) women, MacKinnon remarks, "Black women are further from being able concretely to achieve the standard that no woman can ever achieve, or it would lose its point."[39] The frustration of black women at being unable to look like an "All-American" woman is in this way just a more dramatic example of all (white) women's frustration and oppression. When a black woman speaks on this subject, however, it becomes clear that a black woman's pain at not being considered fully feminine is different qualitatively, not merely quantitatively, from the pain MacKinnon describes. It is qualitatively different because the ideology of beauty concerns not only gender but race. Consider Toni Morrison's analysis of the influence of standards of white beauty on black people in *The Bluest Eye*.[40] Claudia MacTeer, a young black girl, muses, "Adults, older girls, shops, magazines, newspapers, window signs—all the world had agreed that a blue-eyed, yellow-haired, pink-skinned doll was what every girl child treasured." Similarly, in the black community, "high yellow" folks represent the closest black people can come to beauty, and darker people are always "lesser. Nicer, brighter, but still lesser." Beauty is whiteness itself; and middle-class black girls

> go to land-grant colleges, normal schools, and learn how to do the white man's work with refinement: home economics to prepare his food; teacher education to instruct black children in obedience; music to soothe the weary master and entertain his blunted soul. Here they learn the rest of the lesson begun in those soft houses with porch swings and pots of bleeding heart: how to behave. The careful development of thrift, patience, high morals, and good manners. In short, how to get rid of the funkiness. The dreadful funkiness of passion, the funkiness of nature, the funkiness of the wide range of human emotions.
>
> Wherever it erupts, this Funk, they wipe it away; where it crusts, they dissolve it; wherever it drips, flowers, or clings, they find it and fight it until it dies. They fight this battle all the way to the grave. The laugh that is a little too loud; the enunciation a little too round; the gesture a little too generous. They hold their behind in for fear of a sway too free; when they wear lipstick, they never cover the entire mouth for fear of lips too thick, and they worry, worry, worry about the edges of their hair.[41]

Thus, Pecola Breedlove, born black and ugly, spends her lonely and abused childhood praying for blue eyes. Her story ends in despair and the fragmentation of her mind into two isolated speaking voices, not because she's even further away from ideal beauty than white women are, but because Beauty *itself* is white, and she is not and can never be, despite the pair of blue eyes she eventually believes she has. There is a difference between the hope that the next makeup kit or haircut or diet will bring you salvation and the knowledge that nothing can. The relation of black women to the ideal of white beauty is not a more intense form of white women's frustration: It is something other, a complex mingling of racial and gender hatred from without, self-hatred from within.

MacKinnon's essentialist, "color-blind" approach also distorts the analysis of rape that constitutes the heart of *Signs II*. By ignoring the voices of black female theoreticians of rape, she produces an ahistorical account that fails to capture the experience of black women.

MacKinnon sees sexuality as "a social sphere of male power of which forced sex is paradigmatic."[42] As with beauty standards, black women are victimized by rape just like white women, only more so: "Racism in the United States, by singling out Black men for allegations of rape of white women, has helped obscure the fact that it is men who rape women, disproportionately women of color."[43] In this peculiar fashion MacKinnon simultaneously recognizes and shelves racism, finally reaffirming that the divide between men and women is more fundamental and that women of color are simply "women plus." MacKinnon goes on to develop a powerful analysis of rape as the subordination of women to men, with only one more mention of color: "[R]ape comes to mean a strange (read Black) man knowing a woman does not want sex and going ahead anyway."[44]

This analysis, though rhetorically powerful, is an analysis of what rape means to white women masquerading as a general account; it has nothing to do with the experience of black women. For black women, rape is a far more complex experience, and an experience as deeply rooted in color as in gender.

For example, the paradigm experience of rape for black women has historically involved the white employer in the kitchen or bedroom as much as the strange black man in the bushes. During slavery, the sexual abuse of black women by white men was commonplace. Even after emancipation, the majority of working black women were domestic servants for white families, a job which made them uniquely vulnerable to sexual harassment and rape.

Moreover, as a legal matter, the experience of rape did not even exist for black women. During slavery, the rape of a black woman by any man, white or black, was simply not a crime.[45] Even after the Civil War, rape laws were seldom used to protect black women against either white or black men, since black women were considered promiscuous by nature. In contrast to the partial or at least formal protection white women had against sexual brutalization, black women frequently had no legal protection whatsoever. "Rape," in this sense, was something that only happened to white women; what happened to black women was simply life.

Finally, for black people, male and female, "rape" signified the terrorism of black men by white men, aided and abetted, passively (by silence) or actively (by "crying rape"), by white women. Black women have recognized this aspect of rape since the nineteenth century. For example, social activist Ida B. Wells analyzed rape as an example of the inseparability of race and gender oppression in *Southern Horrors: Lynch Law in All Its Phases*, published in 1892. Wells saw that both the law of rape and Southern miscegenation laws were part of a patriarchal system through which white men maintained their control over the bodies of all black people: "[W]hite men used their ownership of the body of the white female as a terrain on which to lynch the black male."[46] Moreover, Wells argued, though many white women encouraged interracial sexual relationships, white women, protected by the patriarchal idealization of white womanhood, were able to remain silent, unhappily or not, as black men were murdered by mobs. Similarly, Anna Julia Cooper, another nineteenth-century theorist, "saw that the manipulative power of the South was embodied in the southern patriarch, but she describes its concern with 'blood,' inheritance, and heritage in entirely female terms and as a preoccupation that was transmitted from the South to the North and perpetuated by white women."[47]

Nor has this aspect of rape become purely a historical curiosity. Susan Estrich reports that between 1930 and 1967, 89 percent of the men executed for rape in the United States were black;[48] a 1968 study of rape sentencing in Maryland showed that in all 55 cases where the death penalty was imposed the victim had been white, and that between 1960 and 1967, 47 percent of all black men convicted of criminal assaults on black women were immediately released on probation.[49] The case of Joann Little is testimony to the continuing sensitivity of black women to this aspect of rape. As Angela Davis tells the story:

Brought to trial on murder charges, the young Black woman was accused of killing a white guard in a North Carolina jail where she was the only woman inmate. When Joann Little took the stand, she told how the guard had raped her in her cell and how she had killed him in self-defense with the ice pick he had used to threaten her. Throughout the country, her cause was passionately supported by individuals and organizations in the Black community and within the young women's movement, and her acquittal was hailed as an important victory made possible by this mass campaign. In the immediate aftermath of her acquittal, Ms. Little issued several moving appeals on behalf of a Black man named Delbert Tibbs, who awaited execution in Florida because he had been falsely convicted of raping a white woman.

Many Black women answered Joann Littles appeal to support the cause of Delbert Tibbs. But few white women—and certainly few organized groups within the anti-rape movement—followed her suggestion that they agitate for the freedom of this Black man who had been blatantly victimized by Southern racism.[50]

The rift between white and black women over the issue of rape is highlighted by the contemporary feminist analyses of rape that have explicitly relied on racist ideology to minimize white women's complicity in racial terrorism.[51]

Thus, the experience of rape for black women includes not only a vulnerability to rape and a lack of legal protection radically different from that experienced by white women, but also a unique ambivalence. Black women have simultaneously acknowledged their own victimization and the victimization of black men by a system that has consistently ignored violence against women while perpetrating it against men. The complexity and depth of this experience is not captured, or even acknowledged, by MacKinnon's account.

MacKinnon's essentialist approach re-creates the paradigmatic woman in the image of the white woman, in the name of "unmodified feminism." As in the dominant discourse, black women are relegated to the margins, ignored or extolled as "just like us, only more so." But "Black women are not white women with color."[52] Moreover, feminist essentialism represents not just an insult to black women, but a broken promise—the promise to listen to women's stories, the promise of feminist method.

NOTES

1. JORGE LUIS BORGES, LABYRINTHS: SELECTED STORIES AND OTHER WRITINGS 59, 63–64 (D. Yates & J. Irby eds., 1964).
2. *Id.* at 64.
3. *Id.* at 65.
4. *Id.* at 66.
5. JAMES BOYD WHITE, WHEN WORDS LOSE THEIR MEANING 232 (1984).
6. *Id.* at 240.
7. Robert M. Cover, *Violence and the Word*, 95 YALE L.J. 1601, 1601 (1986); *see also* Robert Weisberg, *The Law-Literature Enterprise*, 1 YALE J.L. & HUMANITIES 1, 45 (1988) (describing how students of legal interpretation are ini-

tially drawn to literary interpretation because of its greater freedom, and then al-most immediately search for a way to reintroduce constraints).

8. Teresa de Lauretis, *Feminist Studies/Critical Studies: Issues, Terms, and Contexts, in* FEMINIST STUDIES/CRITICAL STUDIES 1, 8 (T. de Lauretis ed., 1986).

9. Mari J. Matsuda, *When the First Quail Calls: Multiple Consciousness as Jurisprudential Method,* 11 WOMENS RTS. L. REP. 7, 9 (1989).

10. *Id.* at 8.

11. *See, e.g.,* CATHARINE A. MACKINNON, *On Collaboration, in* FEMINISM UNMODIFIED 198, 204 (1987) ("I am here to speak for those, particularly women and children, upon whose silence the law, including the law of the First Amend-ment, has been built") [hereinafter FEMINISM UNMODIFIED].

12. Rich defines white solipsism as the tendency to "think, imagine, and speak as if whiteness described the world." ADRIENNE RICH, *Disloyal to Civi-lization: Feminism, Racism, Gynephobia, in* ON LIES, SECRETS, AND SILENCE 275, 299 (1979).

13. ELIZABETH V. SPELMAN, INESSENTIAL WOMAN: PROBLEMS OF EXCLUSION IN FEMINIST THOUGHT 3, 4 (1988).

14. *Id.* at 159.

15. In my discussion I focus on Catharine A. MacKinnon, *Feminism, Marx-ism, Method, and the State: An Agenda for Theory,* 7 Signs 515 (1982) [hereinafter MacKinnon, SIGNS I], and Catharine A. MacKinnon, *Feminism, Marxism, Method, and the State: Toward Feminist Jurisprudence,* 8 SIGNS 635 (1983) [here-inafter MacKinnon, SIGNS II], but I make reference to the essays in MACKINNON, FEMINISM UNMODIFIED, *supra,* note 11, as well.

16. MACKINNON, *Desire and Power, in* FEMINISM UNMODIFIED, *supra* note 11, at 46, 49.

17. *Id.* at 48.

18. MacKinnon, *Signs I, supra* note 15, at 516 (footnote omitted).

19. *Id.*

20. MACKINNON, *Desire and Power, supra* note 11, at 3.

21. *Id.* Thus, MacKinnon disagrees both with feminists who argue that women and men are really the same and should therefore be treated the same un-der the law, and with feminists who argue that the law should take into account women's differences. Feminists who argue that men and women are "the same" fail to take into account the unequal power relations that underlie the very con-struction of the two genders. Feminists who want the law to recognize the "dif-ferences" between the genders buy into the account of women's "natural differ-ence," and therefore (inadvertently) perpetuate dominance under the name of inherent difference. *See id.* at 32–40, 71–77.

22. MacKinnon, *Signs II, supra* note 15, at 638.

23. *Id.* at 639.

24. *Id.*

25. MacKinnon, *Signs I, supra* note 15, at 523.

26. MACKINNON, *On Exceptionality: Women as Women in Law, in* FEMI-NISM UNMODIFIED, *supra* note 11, at 70, 76.

27. MacKinnon, *Signs I, supra* note 15, at 518 & n.3.

28. *Id.* at 537 n.54.

29. MacKinnon, *supra* note 11, at 2–3.

30. MacKinnon, *Whose Culture? A Case Note on Martinez v. Santa Clara Pueblo, in* Feminism Unmodified, *supra* note 11, at 63.

31. Santa Clara Pueblo v. Martinez, 436 U.S. 49, 71–72 (1978).

32. MacKinnon, *Whose Culture? supra* note 30, at 66.

33. *Id.* at 68.

34. *Id.* at 67.

35. *Id.* at 68.

36. *Id.* at 69.

37. MacKinnon, *Signs I, supra* note 15, at 520 n.7.

38. *Id.* at 530. Yet, having acknowledged that black women have never been "women," MacKinnon continues in the article to discuss "women," making it plain that the "women" she is discussing are white.

39. *Id.* at 540 n.59. Similarly, in Feminism Unmodified, MacKinnon reminds us that the risk of death and mutilation in the course of a botched abortion is disproportionately borne by women of color, MacKinnon, *Not by Law Alone: From a Debate with Phyllis Schlafly, in* Feminism Unmodified, *supra* note 11, at 21, 25, but only in the context of asserting that "[n]one of us can afford this risk," *id.*

40. Toni Morrison, The Bluest Eye (1970).

41. *Id.* at 64.

42. MacKinnon, *Signs II, supra* note 15, at 646.

43. *Id.* at 646 n.22; *see also* MacKinnon, *A Rally Against Rape, in* Feminism Unmodified, *supra* note 11, at 81, 82 (black women are raped four times as often as white women); Diana Russell, Sexual Exploitation 185 (1984) (black women, who comprise 10 percent of all women, accounted for 60 percent of rapes reported in 1967).

Describing Susan Brownmiller, Against Our Will: Men, Women and Rape (1976), MacKinnon writes, "Brownmiller examines rape in riots, wars, pogroms, and revolutions; rape by police, parents, prison guards; and rape motivated by racism—seldom rape in normal circumstances, in everyday life, in ordinary relationships, by men as men." MacKinnon, *Signs II, supra* note 15, at 646.

44. MacKinnon, *Signs II, supra* note 15, at 653; *cf.* Susan Estrich, Real Rape 3 (1987) (remarking, while telling the story of her own rape, "His being black, I fear, probably makes my account more believable to some people, as it certainly did with the police."). Indeed. Estrich hastens to assure us, though, that "the most important thing is that he was a stranger." *Id.*

45. *See* Jennifer Wriggins, *Rape, Racism, and the Law,* 6 Harv. Womens L.J. 103, 118 (1983).

46. Hazel V. Carby, *"On the Threshold of Woman's Era": Lynching, Empire, and Sexuality in Black Feminist Theory, in* "Race," Writing, and Difference, 301, 309 (Henry L. Gates, Jr., ed., 1985).

47. Carby, *supra* at 306 (discussing Anna Julia Cooper, *A Voice from the South* (1892)). Carby continues:

By linking imperialism to internal colonization, Cooper thus provided black women intellectuals with the basis for an analysis of how patriar-

chal power establishes and sustains gendered and racialized social for-
mations. White women were implicated in the maintenance of this
wider system of oppression because they challenged only the parameters
of their domestic confinement; by failing to reconstitute their class and
caste interests, they reinforced the provincialism of their movement.

Id. at 306–07.

48. ESTRICH, *supra* note 44, at 107 n.2.

49. Wriggins, *supra* note 45, at 121 n.113. According to the study, "the average sentence received by Black men, exclusive of cases involving life imprisonment or death, was 4.2 years if the victim was Black, 16.4 years if the victim was
white." *Id.* I do not know whether a white man has ever been sentenced to death
for the rape of a black woman, although I could make an educated guess as to the
answer.

50. ANGELA DAVIS, WOMEN, RACE, AND CLASS 174 (1981).

51. For example, Susan Brownmiller describes the black defendants in publicized Southern rape trials as "pathetic, semiliterate fellows," BROWNMILLER,
supra note 43, at 237, and the white female accusers as innocent pawns of white
men, *see, e.g., id.* at 233 ("confused and fearful, they fell into line"). *See also*
DAVIS, *supra* note 50, at 196–99.

52. Barbara Omolade, *Black Women and Feminism, in* THE FUTURE OF DIF-
FERENCE 247, 248 (H. Eisenstein & A. Jardine eds., 1980).

23   A Hair Piece: Perspectives on the Intersection of Race and Gender

PAULETTE M. CALDWELL

I WANT to know my hair again, to own it, to delight in it again, to recall my earliest mirrored reflection when there was no beginning and I first knew that the person who laughed at me and cried with me and stuck out her tongue at me was me. I want to know my hair again, the way I knew it before I knew that my hair is me, before I lost the right to me, before I knew that the burden of beauty— or lack of it—for an entire race of people could be tied up with my hair and me.

I want to know my hair again, the way I knew it before I knew Sambo and Dick, Buckwheat and Jane, Prissy and Miz Scarlett. Before I knew that my hair could be wrong—the wrong color, the wrong texture, the wrong amount of curl or straight. Before hot combs and thick grease and smelly-burning lye, all guaranteed to transform me, to silken the coarse, resistent wool that represents me. I want to know once more the time before I denatured, denuded, denigrated, and denied my hair and me, before I knew enough to worry about edges and kitchens and burrows and knots, when I was still a friend of water—the rain's dancing drops of water, a swimming hole's splashing water, a hot, muggy day's misty invisible water, my own salty, sweaty, perspiring water.

When will I cherish my hair again, the way my grandmother cherished it, when fascinated by its beauty, with hands carrying centuries-old secrets of adornment and craftswomanship, she plaited it, twisted it, cornrowed it, finger-curled it, olive-oiled it, on the growing moon cut and shaped it, and wove it like fine strands of gold inlaid with semiprecious stones, coral and ivory, telling with my hair a lost-found story of the people she carried inside her?

Mostly, I want to love my hair the way I loved hers, when as granddaughter among grandsons I stood on a chair in her room—her kitchen-bed-living-dining room—and she let me know her hair, when I combed and patted it from the crown of her head to the place where her neck folded into her shoulders, caressing steel-gray strands that framed her forehead before falling into the soft, white, cottony temples at the border of her cheekbones.

1991 DUKE L.J. 365. Originally published in the Duke Law Journal. Reprinted by permission.

267

ON BEING THE SUBJECT OF A LAW SCHOOL HYPOTHETICAL

The case of *Rogers v. American Airlines*[1] upheld the right of employers to prohibit the wearing of braided hairstyles in the workplace. The plaintiff, a black woman, argued that American Airlines' policy discriminated against her specifically as a black woman. In effect, she based her claim on the interactive effects of racial and gender discrimination. The court chose, however, to base its decision principally on distinctions between biological and cultural conceptions of race. More importantly, it treated the plaintiff's claims of race and gender discrimination in the alternative and independent of each other, thus denying any interactive relationship between the two.

Although *Rogers* is the only reported decision that upholds the categorical exclusion of braided hairstyles,[2] the prohibition of such styles in the workforce is both widespread and longstanding. Protests surrounding recent cases in Washington, D.C., sparked national media attention. Nearly fifty women picketed a Hyatt Hotel, and black political leaders threatened to boycott hotels that prohibit black women from wearing braids. Several employees initiated legal action by filing complaints with federal or local fair employment practices agencies; most cases were settled shortly thereafter. No court has yet issued an opinion that controverts *Rogers*.

I discovered *Rogers* while reading a newspaper article describing the actual or threatened firing of several black women in metropolitan Washington, D.C., solely for wearing braided hairstyles. The article referred to *Rogers* but actually focused on the case of Cheryl Tatum, who was fired from her job as a restaurant cashier in a Hyatt Hotel under a company policy that prohibited "extreme and unusual hairstyles."

The newspaper description of the Hyatts grooming policy conjured up an image of a ludicrous and outlandishly coiffed Cheryl Tatum, one clearly bent on exceeding the bounds of workplace taste and discipline. But the picture that accompanied the article revealed a young, attractive black woman whose hair fell neatly to her shoulders in an all-American, common, everyday pageboy style, distinguished only by the presence of tiny braids in lieu of single strands of hair.

Whether motivated by politics, ethnic pride, health, or vanity, I was outraged by the idea that an employer could regulate or force me to explain something as personal and private as the way that I groom my hair. I resented the implication that I could not be trusted to choose standards appropriate for the workplace and that my right to work could be conditioned on my disassociation with my race, gender, and culture. Mostly, I marveled with sadness that something as simple as a black woman's hair continues to threaten the social, political, and economic fabric of American life.

My anger eventually subsided, and I thought little more about *Rogers* until a student in my course in Employment Discrimination Law asked me after class to explain the decision. I promised to take up the case when we arrived at that point in the semester where the issues raised by *Rogers* fit most naturally in the development of antidiscrimination law.

Several weeks passed, and the student asked about *Rogers* again and again (always privately, after class); yet I always put off answering her until some point later in the semester. After all, hair is such a little thing. Finally, while participating in a class discussion on a completely unrelated topic, the persistent one's comments wandered into the forbidden area of braided-hair cases. As soon as the student realized she had publicly introduced the subject of braided hair, she stopped in mid-sentence and covered her mouth in embarrassment, as if she had spoken out of turn. I was finally forced to confront what the student had obviously sensed in her embarrassment.

I had avoided private and public discussions about braided hair not because the student had asked her questions at the wrong point in the semester. Nor had I avoided the subject because cases involving employer-mandated hair and grooming standards do not illustrate as well as other cases the presence of deeply ingrained myths, negative images, and stereotypes that operate to define the social and economic position of blacks and women. I had carefully evaded the subject of a black woman's hair because I appeared at each class meeting wearing a neatly braided pageboy, and I resented being the unwitting object of one in thousands of law school hypotheticals.

WHY WOULD ANYONE WANT TO WEAR THEIR HAIR THAT WAY?

Discussing braided hairstyles[3] with students did not threaten me in places where I had become most assured. I was personally at ease in my professionalism after a decade of law practice and nearly as many years as a law professor. I had lost— or become more successful in denying—any discomfort that I once may have experienced in discussing issues of race and gender in the too few occasions in the legal profession devoted to their exploration. I had even begun to smart less when confronted with my inability to change being the only, or one of inevitably too few, blacks on the faculty of a traditionally white law school. But I was not prepared to adopt an abstract, dispassionate, objective stance to an issue that so obviously affected me personally; nor was I prepared to suffer publicly, through intense and passionate advocacy, the pain and outrage that I experience each time a black woman is dismissed, belittled, and ignored simply because she challenges our objectification.

Should I be put to the task of choosing a logical, credible, "legitimate," legally sympathetic justification out of the many reasons that may have motivated me and other black women to braid our own hair? Perhaps we do so out of concern for the health of our hair, which many of us risk losing permanently after years of chemical straighteners; or perhaps because we fear that the entry of chemical toxins into our bloodstreams through our scalps will damage our unborn or breast-feeding children. Some of us choose the positive expression of ethnic pride not only for ourselves but also for our children, many of whom learn, despite all of our teachings to the contrary, to reject association with black people and black culture in search of a keener nose or bluer eye. Many of us wear braids in the exercise of private, personal prerogatives taken for granted by women who are not black.

Responding to student requests for explanations of cases is a regular part of the profession of law teaching. I was not required, therefore, to express or justify the reasons for my personal decision to braid my hair in order to discuss the application of employment discrimination laws to braided hairstyles. But by legitimizing the notion that the wearing of any and all braided hairstyles in the workplace is unbusinesslike, *Rogers* delegitimized me and my professionalism. I could not think of an answer that would be certain to observe traditional boundaries in academic discourse between the personal and the professional.

The persistent student's embarrassed questioning and my obfuscation spoke of a woman-centered silence: She, a white woman, had asked me, a black woman, to justify my hair.[4] She compelled me to account for the presence of legal justifications for my simultaneously "perverse visibility and convenient invisibility."[5] She forced me and the rest of the class to acknowledge the souls of women who live by the circumscriptions of competing beliefs about white and black womanhood and in the interstices of racism and sexism.

Our silence broken, the class moved beyond hierarchy to a place of honest collaboration. Turning to *Rogers*, we explored the question of our ability to comprehend through the medium of experience the way in which a black woman's hair is related to the perpetuation of social, political, and economic domination of subordinated racial and gender groups; we asked why issues of experience, culture, and identity are not the subject of explicit legal reasoning.

To Choose Myself: Interlocking Figurations in the Construction of Race and Gender

SUNDAY. School is out, my exams are graded, and I have unbraided my hair a few days before my appointment at the beauty parlor to have it braided again. After a year in braids, my hair is healthy again: long and thick and cottony soft. I decide not to french roll it or twist it or pull it into a ponytail or bun or cover it with a scarf. Instead, I comb it out and leave it natural, in a full and big "Angela Davis" afro style. I feel full and big and regal. I walk the three blocks from my apartment to the subway. I see a white male colleague walking in the opposite direction and I wave to him from across the street. He stops, squints his eyes against the glare of the sun, and stares, trying to figure out who has greeted him. He recognizes me and starts to cross over to my side of the street. I keep walking, fearing the possibility of his curiosity and needing to be relieved of the strain of explanation.

MONDAY. My hair is still unbraided, but I blow it out with a hair dryer and pull it back into a ponytail tied at the nape of my neck before I go to the law school. I enter the building and run into four white female colleagues on their way out to a white female lunch. Before I can say hello, one of them blurts out, "It IS weird!" Another drowns out the first: "You look so young, like a teenager!"

The third invites me to join them for lunch while the fourth stands silently, observing my hair. I mumble some excuse about lunch and interject, almost apologetically, that I plan to get my hair braided again the next day. When I arrive at my office suite and run into the white male I had greeted on Sunday, I realize immediately that he has told the bunch on the way to lunch about our encounter the day before. He mutters something about how different I look today, then asks me whether the day before I had been on my way to a ceremony. He and the others are generally nice colleagues, so I half-smile, but say nothing in response. I feel a lot less full and big and regal.

TUESDAY. I walk to the garage under my apartment building, again wearing a big, full "Angela Davis" afro. Another white male colleague passes me by, not recognizing me. I greet him and he smiles broadly, saying that he has never seen me look more beautiful. I smile back, continue the chit chat for a moment more, and try not to think about whether he is being disingenuous. I slowly get into my car, buckle up, relax, and turn on the radio. It will take me about forty-five minutes to drive uptown to the beauty parlor, park my car, and get something to eat before beginning the long hours of sitting and braiding. I feel good, knowing that the braider will be ecstatic when she sees the results of her healing handiwork. I keep my movements small, easy, and slow, relishing in a rare, short morning of being free.

My initial outrage notwithstanding, *Rogers* is an unremarkable decision. Courts generally protect employer-mandated hair and dress codes, often according the greatest deference to ones that classify individuals on the basis of socially conditioned rather than biological differences. All in all, such cases are generally considered only marginally significant in the battle to secure equal employment rights.

But *Rogers* is regrettably unremarkable in an important respect. It rests on suppositions that are deeply imbedded in American culture—assumptions so entrenched and so necessary to the maintenance of interlocking, interdependent structures of domination that their mythological bases and political functions have become invisible, especially to those to whom their existence is most detrimental. *Rogers* proceeds from the premise that, although racism and sexism share much in common, they are nonetheless fundamentally unrelated phenomena—a proposition proved false by history and contemporary reality. Racism and sexism are interlocking, mutually reinforcing components of a system of dominance rooted in patriarchy. No significant and lasting progress in combatting either can be made until this interdependence is acknowledged, and until the perspectives gained from considering their interaction are reflected in legal theory and public policy.

Cases arising under employment discrimination statutes illustrate both the operation in law and the effect on the development of legal theory of the assumptions of race-sex correspondence and difference. These cases also demonstrate the absence of any consideration of either race-sex interaction or the stereotyping of black womanhood. Focusing on cases that involve black female plaintiffs, at least three categories emerge.

In one category, courts have considered whether black women may represent themselves or other race or gender discriminatees. Some cases deny black women the right to claim discrimination as a subgroup distinct from black men and white women.[6] Others deny black women the right to represent a class that includes white women in a suit based on sex discrimination, on the ground that race distinguishes them.[7] Still other cases prohibit black women from representing a class in a race discrimination suit that includes black men, on the ground of gender differences.[8] These cases demonstrate the failure of courts to account for race-sex intersection, and are premised on the assumption that discrimination is based on either race or gender, but never both.

A second category of cases concerns the interaction of race and gender in determining the limits of an employer's ability to condition work on reproductive and marital choices associated with black women.[9] Several courts have upheld the firing of black women for becoming pregnant while unmarried if their work involves association with children—especially black teenage girls. These decisions rest on entrenched fears of and distorted images about black female sexuality, stigmatize single black mothers (and by extension their children), and reinforce "culture of poverty" notions that blame poverty on poor people themselves. They also reinforce the notion that the problems of black families are attributable to the deviant and dominant roles of black women and the idea that racial progress depends on black female subordination.

A third category concerns black women's physical images. These cases involve a variety of mechanisms to exclude black women from jobs that involve contact with the public—a tendency particularly evident in traditionally female jobs in which employers place a premium on female attractiveness—including a subtle, and often not so subtle, emphasis on female sexuality. The latter two categories sometimes involve, in addition to the intersection of race and gender, questions that concern the interaction of race, gender, and culture.

The failure to consider the implications of race-sex interaction is only partially explained, if at all, by the historical or contemporary development of separate political movements against racism and sexism. Rather, this failure arises from the inability of political activists, policymakers, and legal theorists to grapple with the existence and political functions of the complex of myths, negative images, and stereotypes regarding black womanhood. These stereotypes, and the culture of prejudice that sustains them, exist to define the social position of black women as subordinate on the basis of gender to all men, regardless of color, and on the basis of race to all other women. These negative images also are indispensable to the maintenance of an interlocking system of oppression based on race and gender that operates to the detriment of all women and all blacks. Stereotypical notions about white women and black men are not only developed by comparing them to white men but also by setting them apart from black women.

THE *ROGERS* OPINION

The *Rogers* decision is a classic example of a case concerning the physical image of black women. Renee Rogers, whose work for American Airlines involved extensive passenger contact, charged that American's prohibition of braided hairstyles in certain job classifications discriminated against her as a woman in general, and as a black woman in particular.[10] The court did not attempt to limit the plaintiff's case by forcing her to proceed on either race or gender grounds, nor did it create a false hierarchy between the two bases by treating one as grounded in statutory law and the other as a "plus" factor that would explain the application of law to a subgroup not technically recognized as a protected group by law. The court also appeared to recognize that the plaintiff's claim was not based on the cumulative effects of race and gender.

However, the court treated the race and sex claims in the alternative only. This approach reflects the assumption that racism and sexism always operate independently even when the claimant is a member of both a subordinated race and a subordinated gender group. The court refused to acknowledge that American's policy need not affect all women or all blacks in order to affect black women discriminatorily. By treating race and sex as alternative bases on which a claim might rest, the court concluded that the plaintiff failed to state a claim of discrimination on either ground. The court's treatment of the issues made this result inevitable—as did its exclusive reliance on the factors that it insisted were dispositive of cases involving employee grooming or other image preferences.

The distinct history of black women dictates that the analysis of discrimination be appropriately tailored in interactive claims to provide black women with the same protection available to other individuals and groups protected by antidiscrimination law. The *Rogers* court's approach permitted it to avoid the essence of overlapping discrimination against black women, and kept it from applying the basic elements of antidiscrimination analysis: a focus on group history; identification of recurring patterns of oppression that serve over time to define the social and economic position of the group; analysis of the current position of the group in relation to other groups in society; and analysis of the employment practice in question to determine whether, and if so how, it perpetuates individual and group subordination.

The court gave three principal reasons for dismissing the plaintiff's claim. First, in considering the sex discrimination aspects of the claim, the court disagreed with the plaintiff's argument that, in effect, the application of the company's grooming policy to exclude the category of braided hairstyles from the workplace reached only women. Rather, the court stressed that American's policy was even-handed and applied to men and women alike.[11] Second, the court emphasized that American's grooming policy did not regulate or classify employees on the basis of an immutable gender characteristic.[12] Finally, American's policy did not bear on the exercise of a fundamental right.[13] The plaintiff's racial discrimination claim was analyzed separately but dismissed on the same grounds: neutral application of American's anti-braid policy to all races and absence of any impact of the policy on an immutable racial characteristic or of any effect on the exercise of a fundamental right.

The court's treatment of culture and cultural associations in the racial context bears close examination. It carefully distinguished between the phenotypic and cultural aspects of race. First, it rejected the plaintiff's analogy between all-braided and Afro, or "natural," hairstyles. Stopping short of concluding that Afro hairstyles might be protected under all circumstances, the court held that "an all-braided hairstyle is a different matter. It is not the product of natural hair growth but of artifice."[14] Second, in response to the plaintiff's argument that, like Afro hairstyles, the wearing of braids reflected her choice for ethnic and cultural identification, the court again distinguished between the immutable aspects of race and characteristics that are "socioculturally associated with a particular race or nationality."[15] However, given the variability of so-called immutable racial characteristics such as skin color and hair texture, it is difficult to understand racism as other than a complex of historical, sociocultural associations with race.

The court conceived of race and the legal protection against racism almost exclusively in biological terms. Natural hairstyles—or at least some of them, such as Afros—are permitted because hair texture is immutable, a matter over which individuals have no choice. Braids, however, are the products of artifice—a cultural practice—and are therefore mutable, i.e., the result of choice. Because the plaintiff could have altered the all-braided hairstyle in the exercise of her own volition, American was legally authorized to force that choice upon her.

In support of its view that the plaintiff had failed to establish a factual basis for her claim that American's policy had a disparate impact on black women, thus destroying any basis for the purported neutral application of the policy, the court pointed to American's assertion that the plaintiff had adopted the prohibited hairstyle only shortly after it had been "popularized" by Bo Derek, a white actress, in the film *10*.[16] Notwithstanding the factual inaccuracy of American's claim, and notwithstanding the implication that there is no relationship between braided hair and the culture of black women, the court assumed that black and white women are equally motivated (i.e., by the movies) to adopt braided hairstyles.

Wherever they exist in the world, black women braid their hair. They have done so in the United States for more than four centuries. African in origin, the practice of braiding is as American—black American—as sweet potato pie. A braided hairstyle was first worn in a nationally televised media event in the United States—and in that sense "popularized"—by a black actress, Cicely Tyson, nearly a decade before the movie *10*.[17] More importantly, Cicely Tyson's choice to popularize (i.e., to "go public" with) braids, like her choice of acting roles, was a political act made on her own behalf and on behalf of all black women.[18]

The very use of the term "popularized" to describe Bo Derek's wearing of braids—in the sense of rendering suitable to the majority—specifically subordinates and makes invisible all of the black women who for centuries have worn braids in places where they and their hair were not overt threats to the American aesthetic. The great majority of such women worked exclusively in jobs where their racial subordination was clear. They were never permitted in any affirmative sense of the word any choice so closely related to personal dignity as the choice—or a range of choices—regarding the grooming of their hair. By virtue of their subordination—their clearly defined place in the society—their choices were simply ignored.

The court's reference to Bo Derek presents us with two conflicting images, both of which subordinate black women and black culture. On the one hand, braids are separated from black culture and, by implication, are said to arise from whites. Not only do blacks contribute nothing to the nation's or the world's culture, they copy the fads of whites. On the other hand, whites make fads of black culture, which, by virtue of their popularization, become—like all "pop"—disposable, vulgar, and without lasting value. Braided hairstyles are thus trivialized and protests over them made ludicrous.

To narrow the concept of race further—and, therefore, racism and the scope of legal protection against it—the *Rogers* court likened the plaintiff's claim to ethnic identity in the wearing of braids to identity claims based on the use of languages other than English. The court sought refuge in *Garcia v. Gloor*, a decision that upheld the general right of employers to prohibit the speaking of any language other than English in the workplace without requiring employers to articulate a business justification for the prohibition.[19] By excising the cultural component of racial or ethnic identity, the court reinforces the view of a homogeneous, unicultural society, and pits blacks and other groups against each other in a battle over minimal deviations from cultural norms. Black women cannot wear their hair in braids because Hispanics cannot speak Spanish at work. The court cedes to private employers the power of family patriarchs to enforce a numbing sameness, based exclusively on the employers' whim, without the obligation to provide a connection to work performance or business need, and thus deprives employees of the right to be judged on ability rather than on image or sound.

Healing the Shame

Eliminating the behavioral consequences of certain stereotypes is a core function of antidiscrimination law. This function can never be adequately performed as long as courts and legal theorists create narrow, inflexible definitions of harm and categories of protection that fail to reflect the actual experience of discrimination. Considering the interactive relationship between racism and sexism from the experiential standpoint and knowledge base of black women can lead to the development of legal theories grounded in reality, and to the consideration by all women of the extent to which racism limits their choices as women and by black and other men of color of the extent to which sexism defines their experiences as men of subordinated races.

Creating a society that can be judged favorably by the way it treats the women of its darkest race need not be the work of black women alone, nor will black women be the exclusive or primary beneficiaries of such a society. Such work can be engaged in by all who are willing to take seriously the everyday acts engaged in by black women and others to resist racism and sexism and to use these acts as the basis to develop legal theories designed to end race and gender subordination.

Resistance can take the form of momentous acts of organized, planned, and disciplined protests, or it may consist of small, everyday actions of seeming insignificance that can nevertheless validate the actor's sense of dignity and worth—such as refusing on the basis of inferiority to give up a seat on a bus or covering one's self in shame. It can arise out of the smallest conviction, such as knowing that an old woman can transmit an entire culture simply by touching a child. Sometimes it can come from nothing more than a refusal to leave a grandmother behind.

NOTES

1. 527 F. Supp. 229 (S.D.N.Y. 1981).

2. *Rogers* relied on Carswell v. Peachford Hosp., 27 Fair Empl. Prac. Cas. (BNA) 698 (N.D. Ga. 1981) (1981 WL 224). In *Carswell*, the employer discharged the plaintiff for wearing beads woven into a braided hairstyle. The prohibition applied to jewelry and other items and was justified by safety precautions for employees working in a hospital for psychiatric and substance-abusing patients. Significantly, the court noted that the hospital did not categorically prohibit the wearing of either braided or Afro hairstyles.

3. According to Cheryl Tatum, the Hyatt's personnel manager, a woman, said: "I can't understand why you would want to wear your hair like that anyway. What would our guests think if we allowed you all to wear your hair like that?" Employers often rely on "customer preference" to justify the imposition of certain requirements on employees or to restrict, on the grounds of race or sex, the persons who can occupy certain jobs. This justification typically amounts to nothing more than the expression of the preferences of the employer or a subterfuge for the exploitation of the images of employees for economic advantage. *See* L. Binder, *Sex Discrimination in the Airline Industry: Title VII Flying High*, 59 CALIF. L. REV. 1091 (1971).

4. I know that the student intended no harm toward me. She, too, was disturbed by *Rogers*. She had come to law school later in life than many of her classmates and was already experiencing the prejudices of the labor market related to the intersection of gender and age. She seemed to sense that something in the underlying racism and sexism in *Rogers* would ultimately affect her in a personal way.

5. McKay, *Black Woman Professor—White University*, 6 WOMEN'S STUD. INT'L. F. 143, 144 (1983).

6. *See, e.g.,* DeGraffenreid v. General Motors Assembly Div., 413 F. Supp. 142, 145 (E.D. Mo. 1976) (Title VII did not create a new sub-category of "black women" with standing independent of black males).

7. *See, e.g.,* Moore v. Hughes Helicopter, Inc., 708 F.2d 475, 480 (9th Cir. 1983) (certified class includes only black females, as plaintiff black female inadequately represents white females' interests).

8. *See, e.g.,* Payne v. Travenol, 673 F.2d 798, 810–12 (5th Cir. 1982) (interests of black female plaintiffs substantially conflict with interests of black males, since females sought to prove that males were promoted at females' expense notwithstanding the court's finding of extensive racial discrimination).

9. *See* Chambers v. Girls Club of Omaha, 834 F.2d 697 (8th Cir. 1987).

10. Rogers v. American Airlines, Inc., 527 F. Supp. 229, 231 (S.D.N.Y. 1981). Rogers sued under the thirteenth amendment, 42 U.S.C. § 1981 (1988), and Title VII of the Civil Rights Act of 1964, 42 U.S.C. § 2000e (1988). The court disposed of the thirteenth amendment claim on the ground that the amendment prohibits practices that constitute badges and incidents of slavery. Unless the plaintiff could show that she did not have the option to leave her job, her claim could not be maintained. *Rogers,* 527 F. Supp. at 231. The court also noted that the Title VII and section 1981 claims were indistinguishable in the circumstances of the case and were, therefore, treated together. *Id.*

11. *Id.* at 231.

12. *Id.*

13. *Id.*

14. *Id.* at 232.

15. *Id.*

16. *Id.* at 232.

17. Tyson is most noted for her roles in the film *Sounder* (20th Century Fox 1972) and in the television special *The Autobiography of Miss Jane Pitman* (CBS Television Broadcast, Jan. 1974).

18. Her work is political in the sense that she selects roles that celebrate the strength and dignity of black women and avoids roles that do not.

19. Garcia v. Gloor, 618 F.2d 264, 267–69 (5th Cir. 1980); *cf.* Gutierrez v. Municipal Court, 838 F.2d 1031, 1040–41 (9th Cir.), *vacated,* 409 U.S. 1016 (1988).

From the Editor:
Issues and Comments

D O Y O U agree with Rodrigo that small groups who split off from the larger parent organization have nothing to apologize for, but are instead apt to represent the cutting edge of social change? Can a larger group, such as feminism, adequately represent the interests of a smaller subset of itself, such as black women, and if so, when and when not? Should smaller groups make strategic alliances with larger ones, even if the larger one does not represent its interests exactly? If a group—say, black women—has a practice (e.g., wearing hair in braids) that is more characteristic of it, more associated with identity, than that same practice is for white women or black men, how should courts treat the practice when it collides with a private company's rule? Should it receive more, or less, solicitude than a rule that disadvantages men or women in general?

Is there a union of all oppressed people, regardless of the means of their oppression, whether race, sex, class, sexual orientation, or something else? Or can we only speak of "oppressions"?

Part VII, which follows, treats many of these same problems and issues through the opposite lens—that of essentialism and antiessentialism; in that sense, the two parts represent a coherent whole and should be read together. On race and *class*, see the selections by Calmore, powell, and Ansley in the Suggested Readings, immediately following. On how race, class, and culture affect women as childbearers, see the excellent article by Ikemoto. On gays and lesbians of color, see the work of Kendall Thomas generally (especially his contribution to *Constructing Masculinity*, Maurice Berger/DIA Center, eds., forthcoming from Routledge, 1995). On the situation of non-black communities of color and their role in civil rights as U.S. demography changes rapidly, see the contributions of Lisa Ikemoto (on intergroup conflict), Robert Chang (on a radical Asian critique of law), and Michael Olivas (on Latinos) elsewhere in this book.

Suggested Readings

Ansley, Frances Lee, *Stirring the Ashes: Race, Class and the Future of Civil Rights Scholarship*, 74 CORNELL L. REV. 993 (1989).

Austin, Regina, *Black Women, Sisterhood, and the Difference/Deviance Divide*, 26 NEW ENG. L. REV. 877 (1992).

Calmore, John O., *Exploring the Significance of Race and Class in Representing the Black Poor*, 61 OR. L. REV. 201 (1982).

Crenshaw, Kimberlé Williams, *Demarginalizing the Intersection of Race and Sex: A Black Feminist Critique of Antidiscrimination Doctrine, Feminist Theory and Antiracist Politics*, 1989 U. CHI. LEGAL F. 139.

Davis, Adrienne D. & Stephanie M. Wildman, *The Legacy of Doubt: Treatment of Sex and Race in the Hill-Thomas Hearings*, 65 S. CAL. L. REV. 1367 (1992).

Gilmore, Angela D., *It Is Better to Speak*, 6 BERKELEY WOMEN'S L.J. 74 (1990–91).

Ikemoto, Lisa C., *Furthering the Inquiry: Race, Class, and Culture in the Forced Medical Treatment of Pregnant Women*, 59 TENN. L. REV. 487 (1992).

Karst, Kenneth L., *Citizenship, Race, and Marginality*, 30 WM. & MARY L. REV. 1 (1988).

powell, john a., *Race and Poverty: A New Focus for Legal Services*, CLEARINGHOUSE REV., Spec. Issue 1993, at 299.

Scales-Trent, Judy, *Black Women and the Constitution: Finding Our Place, Asserting Our Rights*, 24 HARV. C.R.-C.L. L. REV. 9 (1989).

Thomas, Kendall, *Beyond the Privacy Principle*, 92 COLUM. L. REV. 1431 (1992).

PART VII

ESSENTIALISM AND ANTIESSENTIALISM

W H A T is the black community, or community of color? Does it exist? Or are there in reality many partially overlapping, partially competing subcommunities? If the latter, who speaks for this community or communities? How should minority communities view what are conventionally seen as offenders, or criminals, in their midst—including their own youth? What are we to think of situations, like the Los Angeles insurrection, that apparently saw minority groups, such as Korean merchants and inner-city African-American youth, in conflict?

Commentators who address these issues are concerned with the appropriate unit for analysis: Is the black (or Chicano) community one or many? Do middle- and working-class people of color have different needs and concerns? Do all oppressed people have something in common, or speak in a single, distinctive "voice"?

Daniel Farber and Suzanna Sherry write that the minority community is not one, but several communities, and that racial militants and Critical Race scholars cannot and do not speak for all of them—indeed, no one voice can. Regina Austin explores the troubled relationship between "the black community" and its own offenders, arguing for a politics of identification that seeks to find the good, the strengths in what is commonly seen as criminal behavior, while resisting the aspects of youthful offending that are genuinely dangerous for the broader community of which the offenders are a part. Lisa Ikemoto shows that the narrative of interracial group conflict reveals more than a trace of white racism in the way such conflicts are constructed. Randall Kennedy takes leading CRT theorists to task for assuming too easily that there is such a thing as a unitary minority experience that they can call on and tap. Robert Chang writes that insufficient attention has been given to the legal needs and problems of Asian-American communities, indeed that Asians often are depicted as model minorities whom others should emulate. He calls for a new Critical Asian scholarship that will address these deficiencies. Finally, Robin Barnes points out how two leading African-American authors of radically different political persuasions nevertheless address issues in many of the same ways.

24 Telling Stories Out of School: An Essay on Legal Narratives

DANIEL A. FARBER and SUZANNA SHERRY

ONCE upon a time, the law and literature movement taught us that stories have much to say to lawyers, and Robert Cover taught us that law is itself a story. Instead of living happily ever after with that knowledge, some feminists and critical race theorists have taken the next logical step: telling stories, often about personal experiences, on the pages of the law reviews. By 1989, legal storytelling had risen to such prominence that it warranted a symposium in a major law review. Thus far, however, little or no systematic appraisal of this movement has been offered. We agree with the storytellers that taking the movement seriously requires engaging its ideas, and that it is time for a "sustained, *public* examination of this new form of legal scholarship."[1]

Before we begin, it may be helpful to say a few words about what we mean by legal storytelling. Reliance on case studies and other narratives is hardly new to legal scholarship. Based on our reading of the literature, however, we have identified three general differences between the new storytellers and conventional legal scholars. First, the storytellers view narratives as central to scholarship, while de-emphasizing conventional analytic methods. Second, they particularly value "stories from the bottom"—stories by women and people of color about their oppression. Third, they are less concerned than conventional scholars about whether stories are either typical or descriptively accurate, and they place more emphasis on the aesthetic and emotional dimensions of narration. These three differences combine to create a distinctive mode of legal scholarship. [*Ed.* But does it follow that *only* women and scholars of color can engage, or engage successfully, in this new form of scholarship? The authors next examine this "distinctiveness" claim.]

Storytelling in a "Different Voice"

The body of literature asserting that women and people of color have unique perspectives to contribute to legal scholarship is vast and growing rapidly. Feminist legal scholars who embrace this view often speak of women's "different voice," harkening back to Carol Gilligan's groundbreaking book, *In a Different Voice*.[2] Prominent scholars of color who believe that there is a distinctive "voice of color" have often denominated their own scholarship "critical race theory." Because different voice feminists and critical race theorists have much in common, we will refer to both groups collectively as "different voice" scholars, differentiating among them as necessary.

At this point, it may be helpful to explain our understanding of the concept of different voices. So far as we are aware, there is no serious disagreement that some differences exist between the average life experiences of white males and those of other groups. It is plausible to assume that these differences in experiences cause some variations in attitudes and beliefs, particularly in those areas most closely connected with the differences in experience. Thus, for example, it would not be surprising to discover that blacks and whites have different attitudes about school busing, or that men and women tend to disagree about what constitutes sexual harassment. Our understanding of the different voice thesis, however, is that it goes beyond assuming differences only in the average attitudes and beliefs of different groups. Instead, it also postulates that members of different groups have different methods of understanding their experiences and communicating their understandings to others. This becomes relevant to storytelling through the claim that abstract analysis and formal empirical research are less appropriate than stories for communicating the understandings of women and people of color.

It is sometimes difficult to sort out the various claims that different voice scholars make. They all seem to agree that women and people of color speak in distinct voices, and many insist further that the minority or female voice is best heard in, and uniquely suited to, legal storytelling. We find disagreement, however, on the source of the different voices. Some theorists suggest that gender and minority heritage in themselves create a unique perspective or different voice that would persist even in a completely egalitarian society. Others argue that it is the experience of oppression that creates the different perspective. Whatever the source, however, many different voice scholars also argue that traditional academic standards reflect a white male voice and therefore undervalue the work of women and people of color. Let us now consider the nature and source of the different voice.

FEMINISM

In 1982, Carol Gilligan published *In a Different Voice*, which asserted that men and women may approach moral questions differently. Since then, scholars in a variety of disciplines, including law, have suggested that women have a general world-view that differs in significant respects from that of men. Although the details differ, these scholars share a common description of the differences between male and female perspectives: Women are inherently both more connected to others and more contextual than men.[3]

Feminist legal scholars who have adopted the different voice perspective contrast women's contextual voice with the male voice of the law. For example, Lucinda Finley argues that law and legal reasoning reflect a male voice by emphasizing "rationality, abstraction, a preference for statistical and empirical proofs over experiential or anecdotal evidence," and "universal and objective thinking."[4] Martha Fineman describes how feminist legal theory can become "an exercise in the concrete."[5] Margaret Jane Radin suggests that feminism shares with pragmatism "a commitment against abstract idealism, transcendence, foundationalism, and atemporal universality; and in favor of immanence, historicity, concreteness, situatedness, contextuality, embeddedness, [and] narrativity of meaning."[6] The feminine voice is also portrayed as more empathic and emotional. It is important to note the breadth of these claims: Feminist "different voice" scholars do not suggest simply that women might have a different perspective on issues directly involving gender relations, but rather that women's unique perspective casts a different light on virtually all legal issues. These feminist scholars, including one of the authors of this article, have examined the implications of contextuality and connection in the context of a great variety of legal questions.[7]

Although rarely made explicit, the connection between this description of women's voice and the methodology of storytelling is obvious. If legal reasoning, especially "grand theory," is overly abstract, objective, and empirical, then the antidote is legal storytelling, which usually focuses on the narrator's experience of events. Stories supply both the individualized context and the emotional aspect missing from most legal scholarship. Thus "personal narrative" is described as a "feminist method."

Despite the widespread invocation of different voice theories, the existence of such a voice and its connection to legal storytelling are matters of dispute even within the feminist legal community.[8] Gilligan's work is highly controversial within her own discipline, and Gilligan herself rejects extreme claims of differences between men and women. Her later work suggests that the moral approaches of men and women form overlapping bell curves, and that fully mature individuals of either sex should be able to use both "voices."[9] Other researchers in the field have been unable to duplicate Gilligan's original findings, and many have criticized her methodology. If male and female styles of thought were radically different, one would expect more consistent empirical evidence of gender differences.

Some feminist legal scholars have condemned suggestions about women's different voice as both unsound and unwise, because they are likely to lead to further marginalization of women in economic and political spheres.[10] Others, whom Robin West describes as "radical" as opposed to "cultural" feminists, attribute women's different voice to the male foot on women's throats,[11] suggesting that "women's connection to others is the source of women's misery, not a source of value worth celebrating."[12] And any claim that women think differently is subject to a charge of "gender essentialism," which ascribes a unitary voice to women.[13]

Other scholars deny that the "voice" of context and connection is uniquely female. Joan Williams, for example, points out that the "feminine voice" is simply another in a long line of epistemological critiques of liberalism, and therefore hardly unique to women.[14] Margaret Jane Radin suggests that feminist jurisprudence shares much with pragmatism. Male and female scholars alike have lamented the lack of a "human voice" in the law, describing such a missing voice in terms very similar to those used by feminists. Thus Julius Getman praises Charles Black's use of the human voice in Black's article on segregation, which (unlike traditional scholarship) used real experiences of real people to illuminate legal theory.[15] Without recourse to feminism, Lynne Henderson observes that legal decisions are too frequently isolated from both experience and empathy.[16] Both Carol Rose and Robert Cover, among others, have eloquently described storytelling by other cultures and other voices, including those of white males.[17]

Finally, there is a great deal of uncertainty about the source of women's unique perspective, if it does indeed exist. The earliest discussions of women's voice suggested that differences were based on biology or on childrearing practices, and some scholars still adhere to this view. Several of them have taken this view to extremes; one even relies on a contrast between women's lunar biological cycles and the historical importance of the solar calendar to suggest that the latter was a method for consolidating male power. Recently, however, many feminist legal scholars have attributed women's different perspective to experiences of exclusion, discrimination, and marginalization.[18]

Thus, although some evidence exists that men and women possess different perspectives on the law, the weight of the evidence does not support either of the strong versions of the different voice thesis: (i) that the voices of men and women are so different that the former normally can neither understand nor evaluate the work of the latter, or (ii) that women are in a unique position to transform legal scholarship. At most, the empirical evidence suggests that women may write about or emphasize different aspects of the law than men, potentially providing a more complete vision of the legal system.

CRITICAL RACE THEORY

Because the feminist version of different voice theory is older and therefore better developed than the critical race theory version, we found arguments regarding the voice of color particularly difficult to evaluate. However debatable Gilligan's conclusions regarding women's different voice may be, critical race theory has not yet established a comparable empirical foundation. We know of no work on critical race theory that discusses psychological or other social science studies supporting the existence of a voice of color. Most critical race theorists simply postulate the existence of a difference, often citing feminist scholarship for support, and thus implicitly equate a male voice with a white voice. One scholar denies that the existence of a distinct voice of color can or need be proven, as it is solely a matter of authorial intent: Those who intend to speak in the voice of color do so.[19] The best evidence supporting the existence of a voice of color is said to be that minority "scholarship raises new perspectives—the perspectives of [minority] groups."[20] Thus far, however, there has been no demonstration of how those new perspectives differ from the various perspectives underlying traditional scholarship.[21]

Related to the lack of evidence for the existence of a distinct voice of color, we have found little exploration of the content of such a voice. Although descriptions of how women focus on context and connection may be vague, laden with impenetrable jargon, and sometimes even inaccurate, they are often detailed and rich with examples. In contrast, descriptions of the voice of color are less common in the literature, and again often piggyback on feminist scholarship. The voice of color is described as contextualized,[22] opposed to abstraction and detachment,[23] and "grounded in the particulars of . . . social reality and experience."[24] The most concrete description we could find is that the voice of color "rejects narrow evidentiary concepts of relevance and credibility."[25]

These rather vague descriptions fail to identify the content of a distinct voice of color. Because the few examples offered focus on racially charged issues such as affirmative action and hate speech regulations, they provide little insight into any broad differences between voices of color and supportive white voices. Indeed, Mari Matsuda suggests that "multiple consciousness," her term for the perspective of women of color, is accessible to everyone.[26] And Patricia Williams, a feminist often cited as one of the foremost voices of color, seemingly implies that the voice of color has at least entered into that of western humanity generally when she argues that "people of color have always been part of Western Civilization."[27] A recent book by an African scholar suggests that the commonality of African cultures is a white myth invented to dominate blacks.[28] Of course, the difficulty in describing the voice of color does not disprove its existence, but it does make analysis more difficult.

Finally, although many critical race theorists claim a special affinity between storytelling and the voice of color, the connection is unclear. Two separate links have been suggested. First, several critical race scholars note that minority cultures have a strong tradition of storytelling, as opposed to more formal types of literature.[29] Second, storytelling is said to be a method of communication that can convey new truths that "just cannot be said by using the legal voice."[30] Thus, Richard Delgado suggests that "counterhegemonic" storytelling is one cure for the prevailing racist mentality.[31] Indeed, Alex Johnson contends that white men do not tell stories because they would have to tell of their own dominance.[32]

These efforts to link stories with the voice of color are problematic. White men clearly *do* tell stories. In fact, many European cultures have rich storytelling traditions. Moreover, a number of critical race theorists themselves assert that dominant groups, as well as conservative members of minority groups,[33] tell their own stories, and that the difference between their stories and those of outsiders is simply that the former are more readily accepted.[34]

The problem, then, is to identify the distinctiveness of stories told in the voice of color. Like many recent feminist voices, the voice of color sometimes seems to be defined on the basis of content: It embodies a certain view of race or gender relations (and occasionally other hot political topics). This becomes most apparent when we examine critical race scholars' attempts to explain the source of the voice of color. While an occasional statement suggests that culturally in-grained differences account for the distinct voice, most critical race theorists at-tribute the voice of color to the "experience of domination" and "marginal sta-tus." Like the feminists who attribute women's distinctive voice to gender oppression, these scholars define the voice in political terms. Matsuda notes that outsider scholarship concerns itself with such issues as affirmative action, pornography, and hate speech regulation because those with a different voice "recognize that this has always been a nation of dominant and dominated, and that changing that pattern will require affirmative, non-neutral measures de-signed to make the least the most."[35] She also suggests that the purpose of story-telling is to demonstrate how the pain caused by racism outweighs the pain of ending it. Alex Johnson characterizes the voice of color as any voice that ad-dresses "the plight of people of color."[36] Jerome Culp describes the voice of color as "based not on color, but on opposition to racial oppression."[37] And Richard Delgado asserts that the purpose of storytelling is to "subvert" the status quo.[38] According to this view, then, the true voice of color belongs only to a subgroup of people of color who have certain political views.

In addition, it would be helpful to have a more complete explanation of how black law school professors—whose occupation confers social and economic priv-ilege, and who may come from privileged backgrounds similar to their white counterparts'—have a special claim to represent the views of poor blacks in ur-ban ghettos. Indeed, there is evidence that they do not fully share the views of most African Americans. Stephen Carter points out that while most critical race theorists are politically to the left of their academic colleagues, most studies show African Americans to be considerably more conservative than whites on many issues.[39] This suggests that perhaps only a minority of African Americans truly speak with a political voice of color. As Alex Johnson notes, critical race theorists may conflate race and socioeconomic class: "If one substitutes the word 'poor' or 'oppressed' for 'color' in much of the literature advocating the existence of the voice of color, or claiming to speak in that voice of color, the content of that literature would be, by and large, unchanged."[40] Ideology, then, may be as important as race or class in defining the speaker's "voice." For instance, many of the stories that feminists and critical race theorists tell about the hiring and promotion practices of law schools are similar to those told by white male criti-cal legal scholars.[41]

Because critical race theorists have not articulated their claims as fully as feminists have, their theories are more difficult to evaluate. Without a clearer conception of the "voice of color," it is difficult to assess the arguments on be-half of its existence. If those who argue the existence of fundamental cognitive differences between races or genders have the burden of proof, they clearly have failed to carry that burden. Even if they do not bear the burden of proof, we think there are sound reasons to reject such claims. If radical differences did exist, we would expect that empirical studies or at least everyday observations would consistently reveal some differences, even if the results were not all of the magnitude predicted by the theory. Moreover, the most clearly articulated claim of the proponents, that different voices are characterized by contextuality and concreteness, may well be true as a description of overlapping bell curves, but is clearly false if those traits are claimed to be the sole property of any single group. Finally, the argument for a unique voice of color is undermined by the inability of the proponents to agree on its attributes or on paradigm cases. For these reasons, the claim for fundamental group differences is not only unproven but implausible.

[*Ed.* The authors go on to state that while they "reject the strongest version . . . which postulates radical distinctions" among groups, they "accept as a working hypothesis a weaker version—that women and people of color can sometimes provide a perspective that is not easily accessible to white men."]

NOTES

1. Kathryn Abrams, *Hearing the Call of Stories*, 79 CAL. L. REV. 971, 977 (1991).

2. CAROL GILLIGAN, IN A DIFFERENT VOICE: PSYCHOLOGICAL THEORY AND WOMEN'S DEVELOPMENT (1982).

3. For an excellent recent survey of feminist scholarship and jurisprudence, see MARTHA MINOW, MAKING ALL THE DIFFERENCE: INCLUSION, EXCLUSION, AND AMERICAN LAW 193–214 (1990).

4. Lucinda M. Finley, *Breaking Women's Silence in Law: The Dilemma of the Gendered Nature of Legal Reasoning*, 64 NOTRE DAME L. REV. 886, 893–94 (1989); *see also* Mari J. Matsuda, *Liberal Jurisprudence and Abstracted Visions of Human Nature: A Feminist Critique of Rawls' Theory of Justice*, 16 N.M. L. REV. 613, 619 (1986) ("[A]bstraction is the first step down the road of androcentric ignorance.").

5. Martha L. Fineman, *Challenging Law, Establishing Differences: The Future of Feminist Legal Scholarship*, 42 FLA. L. REV. 25, 28 (1990).

6. Margaret Jane Radin, *The Pragmatist and the Feminist*, 63 S. CAL. L. REV. 1699, 1707 (1990).

7. For a recent overview, see MINOW, *SUPRA* note 3, at 211–12. For examples, see Leslie Bender, *Feminist (Re)torts: Thoughts on the Liability Crisis, Mass Torts, Power, and Responsibilities*, 1990 DUKE L.J. 848 (tort law); Mary Coombs, *Agency and Partnership: A Study of Breach of Promise Plaintiffs*, 2 YALE J. L. & FEMINISM 1 (1989) (contract law); Eric T. Freyfogle, *Context and Accommodation in Modern Property Law*, 41 STAN. L. REV. 1529, 1547–48 (1989) (water law); Kit Kinports, *Evidence Engendered*, 1991 U. ILL. L. REV. 413 (evidence law). *See also* Carrie Menkel-Meadow, *Mainstreaming Feminist Legal Theory*, 23 PAC. L.J. 1493, 1524–33 (1992) (citing feminist jurisprudence). One scholar has gone so far as to suggest that women have different perceptions of time, space, and causality. Ann C. Scales, *Feminists in the Field of Time*, 42 FLA. L. REV. 95, 122–23 (1990).

8. For an excellent summary of the debate, see Deborah L. Rhode, *The*

"No-Problem" Problem: Feminist Challenges and Cultural Change, 100 YALE L.J. 1731, 1784–89 (1991).

9. See Carol Gilligan et al., Epilogue: Soundings into Development, in MAKING CONNECTIONS 314, 317–18 (Carol Gilligan et al. eds., 1989); Carol Gilligan & Jane Attanucci, Two Moral Orientations, in MAPPING THE MORAL DOMAIN: A CONTRIBUTION OF WOMEN'S THINKING TO PSYCHOLOGICAL THEORY AND EDUCATION 73, 82–85 (Carol Gilligan et al. eds., 1988).

10. See, e.g., Cynthia Fuchs Epstein, Faulty Framework: Consequences of the Difference Model for Women in the Law, 35 N.Y.L. SCH. L. REV. 309 (1990); Joan C. Williams, Deconstructing Gender, 87 MICH. L. REV. 797, 813–21 (1989); Joan C. Williams, Dissolving the Sameness/Difference Debate: A Post-Modern Path Beyond Essentialism in Feminist and Critical Race Theory, 1991 DUKE L.J. 296, 310–11; Wendy W. Williams, The Equality Crisis: Some Reflections on Culture, Courts, and Feminism, 7 WOMEN'S RTS. L. REP. 175, 199–200 (1982).

11. Ellen C. DuBois et al., Feminist Discourse, Moral Values, and the Law—A Conversation, 34 BUFFALO L. REV. 11, 74–75 (1985) (remarks of Catharine A. MacKinnon); see also CATHARINE A. MacKINNON, FEMINISM UNMODIFIED 32–45 (1987) (arguing that an important factor in inequality is gender dominance or hierarchy, not whether men and women are different); Joan C. Williams, Domesticity as the Dangerous Supplement of Liberalism, 2 J. WOMEN'S HIST. 69, 71 (1991) (Gilligan describing how women are taught to behave).

12. Robin West, Jurisprudence and Gender, 55 U. CHI. L. REV. 1, 29 (1988).

13. Angela P. Harris, Race and Essentialism in Feminist Legal Theory, 42 STAN. L. REV. 581, 585 (1990). See generally ELIZABETH V. SPELLMAN, INESSENTIAL WOMAN: PROBLEMS OF EXCLUSION IN FEMINIST THOUGHT (1988).

14. Williams, Deconstructing Gender, supra note 10, at 805–06.

15. Julius G. Getman, Voices, 66 TEX. L. REV. 577, 584 (1988).

16. Lynne N. Henderson, Legality and Empathy, 85 MICH. L. REV. 1574, 1649–50 (1987).

17. Robert M. Cover, The Folktales of Justice: Tales of Jurisdiction, 14 CAP. U. L. REV. 179, 183–86 (1985) (Talmudic storytelling); Carol M. Rose, Property as Storytelling: Perspectives from Game Theory, Narrative Theory, Feminist Theory, 2 YALE J. L. & HUMAN. 37, 38 (1990) (Locke and Blackstone used storytelling).

18. See Finley, supra note 4, at 893–94; Sharon Elizabeth Rush, Understanding Diversity, 42 FLA. L. REV. 1, 21 (1990); Williams, Deconstructing Gender, supra note 10, at 844; Iris Marion Young, Polity and Group Difference: A Critique of the Ideal of Universal Citizenship, 99 ETHICS 250, 261 (1989).

19. Alex Johnson, Racial Critiques of Legal Academia: A Reply in Favor of Context, 43 STAN. L. REV. 137, 138, 160–61 (1990).

20. Rush, supra note 18, at 22. In response to a question at a colloquium about the evidence for a unique voice of color, Jerome Culp made a similar argument, noting that studies are unnecessary because black scholars know that their views are different, and this is apparent in their work. Jerome McCristal Culp, Jr., Remarks at Faculty Colloquium, University of Minnesota Law School (Apr. 7, 1992); see also Jerome McCristal Culp, Jr., Toward a Black Legal Scholarship: Race and Original Understandings, 1991 DUKE L.J. 39, 103 (suggesting that

"there are some common reference points for all blacks in thinking about the law and legal change").

21. See Randall L. Kennedy, *Racial Critiques of Legal Academia*, 102 HARV. L. REV. 1745, 1749 (1989) (arguing that these scholars do not persuasively support their claims that people of color are systematically excluded or that legal scholars of color produce a racially distinctive brand of scholarship). [*Ed. See* Chapter 27 for Kennedy's own discussion.]

22. Richard Delgado, *When a Story Is Just a Story: Does Voice Really Matter?*, 76 VA. L. REV. 95, 95 & n.1 (1990).

23. Mari J. Matsuda, When the First Quail Calls: Multiple Consciousness as Jurisprudential Method, Address at the Yale Law School Conference on Women of Color and the Law (Apr. 16, 1988), *in* 11 WOMEN'S RTS. L. REP. 7, 9 (1989).

24. Mari J. Matsuda, *Public Response to Racist Speech: Considering the Victim's Story*, 87 MICH. L. REV. 2320, 2324 (1989).

25. Matsuda, *supra* note 23, at 8. By contrast, in another article Matsuda argues that theories of racial inferiority should not be published unless supported by credible evidence. Matsuda, *supra* note 24, at 2365.

26. Matsuda, *supra* note 23, at 9.

27. Patricia Williams, *The Obliging Shell: An Informal Essay on Formal Equal Opportunity*, 87 MICH. L. REV. 2128, 2136 (1989).

28. KWAME ANTHONY APPIAH, IN MY FATHER'S HOUSE (1992).

29. *See, e.g.*, Derrick Bell, *The Final Report: Harvard's Affirmative Action Allegory*, 87 MICH. L. REV. 2382, 2394 (1989) (discussing African tradition of storytelling); Richard Delgado, *Storytelling for Oppositionists and Others: A Plea for Narrative*, 87 MICH. L. REV. 2411, 2435–37 (1989) (discussing African American, Mexican American, and Native American traditions of storytelling).

30. Finley, *supra* note 4, at 903.

31. Letter from Richard Delgado, Professor of Law, University of Wisconsin, to Kevin Kennedy, Editor-in-Chief, MICHIGAN LAW REVIEW (June 1, 1988).

32. Alex M. Johnson, Jr., *The New Voice of Color*, 100 YALE L.J. 2007, 2047 n.170 (1991); *see also* Robin D. Barnes, *Politics and Passion: Theoretically a Dangerous Liaison*, 101 YALE L.J. 1631, 1654–55 (1992) (reviewing STEPHEN L. CARTER, REFLECTIONS OF AN AFFIRMATIVE ACTION BABY (1992) and PATRICIA WILLIAMS, THE ALCHEMY OF RACE AND RIGHTS (1991)).

33. Richard Delgado, *Enormous Anomaly? Left-Right Parallels in Recent Writings About Race*, 91 COLUM. L. REV. 1547, 1551–52 (1991) (book review).

34. *See, e.g.*, Delgado, *supra* note 29, at 2412 (observing that the dominant group's stories remind the group that its "superior position is seen as natural"); Jerome McCristal Culp, Jr., *Posner on Duncan Kennedy and Racial Difference: White Authority in the Legal Academy*, 1992 DUKE L.J. 1095, 1098 n.8 (stating that the storytelling techniques of scholars of color "have been adopted by white scholars").

35. Matsuda, *supra* note 23, at 10.

36. Johnson, *supra* note 32, at 2016.

37. Culp, *supra* note 34, at 1097.

38. Delgado, *supra* note 29, at 2413.

39. Stephen L. Carter, *Academic Tenure and "White Male" Standards:*

Some Lessons from the Patent Law, 100 YALE L.J. 2065, 2077 (1991); *see also* Lee Sigelman & James S. Todd, *Clarence Thomas, Black Pluralism, and Civil Rights Policy*, 107 POL. SCI. Q. 231, 243–44 (1992) (arguing that "the civil rights establishment distances itself from a substantial portion of the black public" when it espouses racial preferences); *cf.* Deborah L. Rhode, *Feminist Critical Theories*, 42 STAN. L. REV. 617, 623 (1990) (noting that "contemporary survey research suggests that the vast majority of women do not experience the world in the terms that most critical feminists describe").

40. Johnson, *supra* note 32, at 2035.

41. For arguments made by white males against meritocratic standards that embody virtually all the arguments made by different voice theorists, see Duncan Kennedy, *A Cultural Pluralist Case for Affirmative Action in Legal Academia*, 1990 DUKE L.J. 705; Gary Peller, *Race Consciousness*, 1990 DUKE L.J. 758.

25 "The Black Community," Its Lawbreakers, and a Politics of Identification

REGINA AUSTIN

Distinction Versus Identification: Reactions to the Impact of Lawbreaking on "The Black Community"

There exists out there, somewhere, "the black community." It once was a place where people both lived and worked. Now it is more of an idea, or an ideal, than a reality. It is like the mythical maroon colony of the Isle des Chevaliers (for those of you who have read Toni Morrison's *Tar Baby*) or like Brigadoon (for those of you who are culturally deprived). "The black community" of which I write is partly the manifestation of a nostalgic longing for a time when blacks were clearly distinguishable from whites and concern about the welfare of the poor was more natural than our hairdos. Perhaps my vision of the " 'quintessential' black community" is ahistorical, transcendent, and picturesque. I will even concede that "the community's" infrastructure is weak, its cultural heritage is lost on too many of its young, and its contemporary politics is in disarray. I nonetheless think of it as "Home" and refer to it whenever I want to convey the illusion that my arguments have the backing of millions.

"The black community" of which I write is in a constant state of flux because it is buffeted by challenges from without and from within. (The same is true for "the dominant society," but that is another story.) There are tensions at the border with the dominant society, at the frontier between liberation and oppression. There is also internal dissension over indigenous threats to security and solidarity. "Difference" is as much a source of contention within "the community" as it is the factor marking the boundary between "the community" and everyone else. "The community's" struggles are made all the more difficult because there is no bright line between its foreign affairs and its domestic relations.

Nothing illustrates the multiple threats to the ideal of "the black community" better than black criminal behavior and the debates it engenders. There is no shortage of controversy about the causes, consequences, and cures of black

criminality. To the extent there is consensus, black appraisals of questionable behavior are often in accord with those prevailing in the dominant society, but
sometimes they are not. In any event, there is typically no unanimity within "the
community" on these issues.

For example, some blacks contend that in general the criminal justice system
is working too well (putting too many folks in prison),[1] while others maintain
that it is not working well enough (leaving too many dangerous folks out on the
streets). Black public officials and others have taken positions on both sides of the
drug legalization issue.[2] Black neighbors are split in cities where young black men
have been stopped and searched by the police on a wholesale basis because of gang
activity or drug trafficking in the area. Those with opposing views are arguing
about the fairness of evicting an entire family from public housing on account of
the drug-related activities of a single household member, the propriety of boycotting Asian store owners who have used what some consider to be excessive
force in dealing with suspected shoplifters and would-be robbers, and the wisdom
of prosecuting poor black women for fetal neglect because they consumed drugs
during their pregnancies.

Whether "the black community" defends those who break the law or seeks
to bring the full force of white justice down upon them depends on considerations
not necessarily shared by the rest of the society. "The black community" evaluates behavior in terms of its impact on the overall progress of the race. Black criminals are pitied, praised, protected, emulated, or embraced if their behavior has a
positive impact on the social, political, and economic well-being of black communal life. Otherwise, they are criticized, ostracized, scorned, abandoned, and be-
trayed. The various assessments of the social standing of black criminals within
"the community" fall into roughly two predominant political approaches.

At times, "the black community" or an element thereof repudiates those who
break the law and proclaims the distinctiveness and the worthiness of those who
do not. This "politics of distinction" accounts in part for the contemporary emphasis on black exceptionalism. Role models and black "firsts" abound. Stress is
placed on the difference that exists between the "better" elements of "the community" and the stereotypical "lowlifes" who richly merit the bad reputations
the dominant society accords them.[3] According to the politics of distinction, little enough attention is being paid to the law-abiding people who are the lawbreakers' victims. Drive-by shootings and random street crime have replaced
lynchings as a source of intimidation, and the "culture of terror" practiced by
armed crack dealers and warring adolescents has turned them into the urban
equivalents of the Ku Klux Klan.[4] Cutting the lawbreakers loose, so to speak, by
dismissing them as aberrations and excluding them from the orbit of our concern
to concentrate on the innocent is a wise use of political resources.

Moreover, lawless behavior by some blacks stigmatizes all and impedes collective progress. For example, based on the behavior of a few, street crime is
wrongly thought to be the near exclusive domain of black males; as a result, black
men of all sorts encounter an almost hysterical suspicion as they negotiate pub-

lic spaces in urban environments[5] and attempt to engage in simple commercial exchanges.[6] Condemnation and expulsion from "the community" are just what the lawbreakers who provoke these reactions deserve.

In certain circumstances the politics of distinction, with its reliance on traditional values of hard work, respectable living, and conformity to law, is a perfectly progressive maneuver for "the community" to make. Deviance confirms stereotypes and plays into the hands of an enemy eager to justify discrimination. The quest for distinction can save lives and preserve communal harmony.

On the downside, however, the politics of distinction intensifies divisions within "the community." It furthers the interests of a middle class uncertain of its material security and social status in white society. The persons who fare best under this approach are those who are the most exceptional (i.e., those most like successful white people). At the same time, concentrating on black exceptionalism does little to improve the material conditions of those who conform to the stereotypes. Unfortunately, there are too many young people caught up in the criminal justice system to write them all off or to provide for their reentry into the mainstream one or two at a time.[7] In addition, the politics of distinction encourages greater surveillance and harassment of those black citizens who are most vulnerable to unjustified interference because they resemble the lawbreakers in age, gender, and class. Finally, the power of the ideology of individual black advancement, of which the emphasis on role models and race pioneers is but a veneer, is unraveling in the face of collective lower-class decline. To be cynical about it, an alternative form of politics may be necessary if the bourgeoisie is to maintain even a semblance of control over the black masses.

Degenerates, drug addicts, ex-cons, and criminals are not always "the community's" "others." Differences that exist between black lawbreakers and the rest of us are sometimes ignored and even denied in the name of racial justice. "The black community" acknowledges the deviants' membership, links their behavior to "the community's" political agenda, and equates it with race resistance. "The community" chooses to identify itself with its lawbreakers and does so as an act of defiance. Such an approach might be termed the "politics of identification."

In fact, there is not one version of the politics of identification but many. They vary with the class of the identifiers, their familiarity with the modes and mores of black lawbreakers, and the impact that black lawbreaking has on the identifiers' economic, social, and political welfare. The most romanticized form of identification prompts emulation among the young and the poor; the dangers and limitations such identification holds for them are fairly well known. Still, lawbreakers do have something to contribute to black political discourse and practice. In the 1960s segments of the black middle class identified with black criminals as sources of authentic "blackness." The young, new bourgeoisie extracted a style from lawbreaker culture and turned it into the trappings of a political militancy that still has currency today. I will evaluate the pros and cons of this effort. I will also consider black female lawbreakers, with whom there is little identification, and suggest why there ought to be more.

The politics of identification envisioned in this chapter is one that demands recognition of the material importance of lawbreaking to blacks of different socioeconomic strata, however damaging such recognition may be to illusions of black moral superiority. Moreover, the politics of identification described herein would have as an explicit goal the restoration of some (but not all) lawbreakers to good standing in the community by treating them like resources, providing them with opportunities for redemption, and fighting for their entitlement to a fair share of the riches of this society.

In Vogue: Bourgeois Identification as Militant Style

The urban poor are not the only segment of "the community" that can be seduced by the élan of black male lawbreakers. At times the black middle class has also bought into the quixotic view of the black criminal as race rebel.

During the late 1960s, black male lower-class and deviant cultures provided a source of up-to-date signs and symbols for the antiassimilationists. Leather jackets, big Afros, and "talking trash" were de rigueur for upwardly mobile yet nationalistic black college students. It is not clear what prompted this wave of identification. It may have been guilt about having escaped the ghetto, fear of losing the moral superiority associated with being black and oppressed, indignation over the supplicant role the southern civil rights movement seemingly encouraged blacks to play, or a desire to extract concessions from a white society scared to death of black lawbreakers and any impersonators with similar styles of dress, speech, and carriage.[8]

This is not the place for a full-blown critique of the black nationalism movement of the 1960s.[9] Some of its aspects undoubtedly ought not be repeated if a similar surge of lawbreaker identification should overtake the middle class anytime soon. The movement was fiercely misogynistic.[10] The predominant leadership style was marked by masculine bravado and self-aggrandizement. The movement's bourgeois brand of racial animosity, or "acting out," was easily indulged and domesticated with bribes. The benefits the nationalists won from the dominant society inured disproportionately to those who now make their living providing governmental services to other minority people or acting as intermediaries between the white managements of private enterprises and their minority employees and customers.[11] Ironically, these bureaucrats supply images of bourgeois success that obscure the economic inequality that produces the disgruntlement they are paid to redirect.

The movement did not maximize opportunities for lower-status blacks to speak and act on their own behalf. In adopting the lawbreakers' style and using it to advance their own interests, the middle class preempted any claim that the style was the spontaneous and well-justified reaction of less-well-off folks to specific material conditions that warranted the society's direct attention. The identification temporarily lent an aura of respectability to those who earned their deviant status by virtue of actually breaking the law. But when the movement died, or was killed, the real lawbreakers and others on the bottom of the status hierarchy found themselves outsiders again.[12]

In general, the "newly materializing" black militant bourgeoisie of the 1960s did not go very far in incorporating the concerns of lawbreakers into their demands or in adopting the more aggressive practices of criminals as the praxis of their movement. Others did. The Black Panthers, for example, employed black turtlenecks, leather jackets, berets, dark glasses, and shotguns as the accoutrements of militancy and attracted the attention of young northern urban blacks with their "belligerence and pride" and their outspokenness on issues of relevance to ghetto residents.[13] The Panthers specifically addressed the role white police officers played in black neighborhoods as well as the status of black criminal defendants and prisoners. They called for the release of "all black men held in federal, state, county and city prisons and jails" on the ground that "they had not received a fair and impartial trial."[14] (No mention was made of incarcerated women.) Their close observation of white cops as they arrested black citizens on the street highlighted the problem of police brutality. The Panthers' posturing and head-on clashes with the authorities, however, provoked repression and government-instigated internal warfare. This in turn caused the Panthers to squander resources on bail and attorneys that might have been better spent on "Serve the People" medical clinics and free breakfasts for children. Such service activities stood a better chance of mobilizing grassroots support among ordinary blacks and overcoming neighborhood problems than did the Panthers' attempts at militaristic self-defense and socialist indoctrination.

Despite the shortcomings of the black militancy of the 1960s, identification with black lawbreakers still has something to contribute to political fashion and discourse. That blacks are once again fascinated with the outspoken nationalist leader Malcolm X illustrates this. Even the most bourgeois form of identification represents an opening, an opportunity, to press for a form of politics that could restore life to the ideal of "the black community" by putting the interests of lawbreakers and their kin first. Drawing on lawbreaker culture would add a bit of toughness, resilience, bluntness, and defiance to contemporary mainstream black political discourse, which evidences a marked preoccupation with civility, respectability, sentimentality, and decorum. Lawbreaker culture supports the use of direct words and direct action that more refined segments of society would find distasteful. It might also support a bit of middle-class lawbreaking.

There is nothing that requires militant black male leaders to be selfish, stupid, shortsighted, or sexist. There is certainly nothing that requires militant black leaders to be men. As sources of militant style, women lawbreakers set a somewhat different example from the men. Furthermore, it is impossible to understand what lawbreakers can contribute to the substance of a politics of identification without considering women who break the law.

298   REGINA AUSTIN

Justifying Identification Where There Is None Now: Female Lawbreakers and the Lessons of Street Life

Black men do not have a monopoly on lawbreaking. Black women too are engaged in a range of aggressive, antisocial, and criminal conduct that includes prostitution, shoplifting, credit card fraud, check forgery, petty larceny, and drug dealing.[15] But unlike her male counterpart, the black female offender has little or no chance of being considered a rebel against racial, sexual, or class injustice. There is seemingly no basis in history or folklore for such an honor. The quiet rebellions slave women executed in the bedrooms of their masters and the kitchens of their mistresses are not well known today. Thus, the contemporary black female lawbreaker does not benefit from an association between herself and her defiant ancestors who resorted to arson, poisoning, and theft in the fight against white enslavement.

Aggressive and antisocial behavior on the part of black male lawbreakers is deemed compatible with mainstream masculine gender roles and is treated like race resistance, but the same sort of conduct on the part of black females is scorned as being unfeminine. Women are not supposed to engage in violent actions or leave their families to pursue a life of crime. Women who do such things may be breaking out of traditional female patterns of behavior, but their departures from the dictates of femininity are attributed to insanity or lesbianism without any basis in psychology or sociology.[16] No consideration is given to the structural conditions that make violence a significant factor in the lives of lower-class women and that suggest that their physical aggression is not pathological. Conversely, forms of deviance associated with feminine traits like passivity and dependency are dismissed as collaboration with the white/male enemy. Black male lawbreaking also backfires, but black female criminals are not given the benefit of the doubt the males enjoy, either because the hole the women dig for themselves is more readily apparent or because their defiance of gender roles is treated as deviance of a higher order.

What most blacks are likely to know about the degradation and exploitation black women suffer in the course of lawbreaking and interacting with other lawbreakers provides no basis for identifying with them. Take the lot of black streetwalkers, for example. Minority women are overrepresented among street prostitutes and as a result are overrepresented among prostitutes arrested and incarcerated.[17] Black and brown women are on the corner rather than in massage parlors or hotel suites in part because of the low value assigned to their sexuality. Many street prostitutes begin their careers addicted to cocaine, heroin, or both or develop addictions thereafter; drug habits damage their health, impair their appearance (and thereby their earnings), and increase their physical and mental vulnerability. Finally, streetwalkers encounter violence and harassment from pimps, johns, police officers, assorted criminals, and even other women in the same line of work.

Prostitution is but one form of criminal activity a woman in street life might be employed in at any particular time. Less is known about lawbreaking of a non-sexual nature. The exploitation, manipulation, and physical jeopardy associated with street prostitution are also experienced by female lawbreakers who are members of male-affiliated female gangs and criminal networks. These networks, which once were quite prevalent, consist of loosely affiliated households or pseudofamilies made up of a male head and one or more females, sometimes referred to as "wives-in-law." In such collectives the male hustlers hustle the females. In return for giving money, assistance in criminal endeavors, affection, and loyalty to "their men," the women get protection, tight controls on their sexual dalliances, and the privilege of competing with other females for attention. Try as they might to break out of traditional gender roles with aggressive criminal or antisocial behavior, the female members of traditional girl gangs and networks sink deeper into the optionlessness of low-status, low-income female existence. That hardly makes them fitting candidates for admiration or emulation.

There is accordingly much for which respectable black women can rebuke black females who participate in crime and seemingly little with which respectable women can identify. Hierarchy will not crumble, however, if the wicked do not get a shot at upending the righteous. Where community depends upon challenging the social, economic, and political stratification produced by traditional mainstream values, vice must have some virtue.

In the black vernacular, "the streets" are not just the territory beyond home and work, nor merely the place where deviants ply their trades. More figuratively, they are also a "source of practical experience and knowledge necessary for survival."[18] The notion of a politics of identification suggests that "the streets" might be the wellspring of a valuable pedagogy for a vibrant black female community if straight black women had more contact with and a better understanding of what motivates black women in street life. Black women from the street might teach straight black women a thing or two about "heroine-ism" if straight women let themselves be taught.

Identification with black street women will be difficult for many in "the community" but not impossible, if we take the women on their own terms as we do the men. What can possibly be wrong with wanting a job that pays well, is controlled by the workers, provides a bit of a thrill, and represents a payback for injustices suffered? To be sure, street women will not accomplish their goals on any sustained basis through lawbreaking. But that does not mean that they should abandon their aspirations, which, after all, are not so very different from those of many straight black women who battle alienation and boredom in their work lives. Street women may be correct in thinking that some kind of risk taking will provide an antidote for a fairly common misery.

Street life is public life. It entails being "Out There," aggressive and brazen, in a realm normally foreclosed to women. Operating on the streets takes wisdom, cunning, and conning. The ways of black women should be infused into black political activism, and young black women should be allowed to be militant political leaders, just like their male counterparts. The search for political styles and points of view should extend broadly among different groups and categories of black women, including lesbians, adolescent mothers, rebellious employees, and lawbreakers immersed in street life. In a real black community, everyone would be a resource, especially those whom the dominant society would write off as having little or nothing to contribute. That, in essence, is what a politics of identification is all about.

And finally, street women accept the justifiability of engaging in illegal conduct to rectify past injustices and to earn a living. This may prove to be the hardest lesson for straight black women to learn—and the most valuable.

"Bringing It Home": A Legal Agenda for a Politics of Identification

The politics of identification delineated in this chapter recognizes that blacks from different classes have different talents and strengths to contribute to "a revitalized black community." In general, this politics of identification would blend the defiance, boldness, and risk taking that fuel street life with the sacrifice, perseverance, and solidity of straight life. Taking a leaf from the lawbreakers' style manual, it would confront the status quo with a rhetoric that is hard-nosed, pragmatic, aggressive, streetwise, and spare. In recognition of the struggles of street women, it would foster a public life that is inclusive of deviants and allows both females and males to play an equal role. In order to have an impact on the material conditions that promote black criminal behavior, it would draw its praxis from the informal economic activity of bridge people who straddle the street and straight worlds. In this way, a politics of identification would promote a critical engagement between lawbreakers and the middle class in order to move some of the lawbreakers beyond the self-destruction that threatens to bring the rest of us down with them.

The laws of the dominant society are not intended to distinguish between members of "the black community" who are truly deserving of ostracism and those who are not yet beyond help or hope. In addition, it is unlikely that the standards by which "the community" differentiates among lawbreakers can be codified for use by the legal system because of the informal, customary process by which the standards develop. Still, one of the goals of a legal agenda tied to a politics of identification would be to make the legal system more sensitive to the social connection that links "the community" and its lawbreakers and affects black assessments of black criminality.[19]

"The community" acknowledges that some, but not all, lawbreakers act out of a will to survive and an impulse not to be forgotten, and it admires them for this even though it concludes that their acts ought not to be emulated. In recognition of this, the legal program of a politics of identification would advocate changes in the criminal justice system and in other institutions of the dominant society in order to increase the lawbreakers' chances for redemption. "To redeem" is not only "to atone" but also "to rescue," "ransom," "reclaim," "recover," and "release."[20] Thus, redemption may be actively or passively acquired. The lawbreakers need both types of redemption. They need challenging employment that will contribute to the transformation of their neighborhoods and earn them the respect of "the community."[21] They also need to be freed from the material conditions that promote deviance and death. If persuasion, argument, and conflict within the law fail to prompt the dominant society to reallocate resources and reorder priorities, then a jurisprudence that aims to secure redemption for lawbreakers must acknowledge that activity outside the law, against the law, and around the law may be required.

The development of the informal economy in poor black enclaves is crucial to the lawbreakers' redemption and the revitalization of "the black community." The jurisprudential component of a politics of identification would make an issue of the fact that the boundary between legal economic conduct and illegal economic conduct is contingent. It varies with the interests at stake, and the financial self-reliance or self-sufficiency of the minority poor is almost never a top priority. A legal praxis associated with a politics of identification would find its reference points in the "folk law" of those black people who, as a matter of survival, concretely assess what laws must be obeyed and what laws may be justifiably ignored. It would investigate the operations of the informal economy, which is really the illegitimate offspring of legal regulation. It would seek to stifle attempts to criminalize or restrict behavior merely because it competes with enterprises in the formal economy. At the same time, it would push for criminalization or regulation where informal activity destroys communal life or exploits a part of the population that cannot be protected informally. It would seek to legalize both informal activity that must be controlled to ensure its integrity and informal activity that needs the imprimatur of legitimacy in order to attract greater investment or to enter broader markets. Basically, then, a politics of identification requires that its legal adherents work the line between the legal and the illegal, the formal and the informal, the socially (within "the community") acceptable and the socially despised, and the merely different and the truly deviant.

Working the line is one thing. Living on or near the line is another. All blacks do not do that, and some folks who are not black do. Though the ubiquitous experience of racism provides the basis for group solidarity,[22] differences of gender, class, geography, and political affiliations keep blacks apart. These differences may be the best evidence that a single black community no longer exists. Only blacks who are bound by shared economic, social, and political constraints, and who pursue their freedom through affective engagement with each other, live in real black communities. To be a part of a real black community requires that one go Home every once in a while and interact with the folks. To keep up one's membership in such a community requires that one do something on-site. A politics of identification is not a way around this. It just suggests what one might do when one gets there.

NOTES

1. In the District of Columbia, a black defendant charged with murder was reportedly acquitted because some members of the jury were convinced that there were already enough young black men in prison. Barton Gellman & Sari Horwitz, *Letter Stirs Debate After Acquittal*, WASH. POST, Apr. 22, 1990, at A1. On the role that racism continues to play or that blacks think it plays in the criminal justice system, see Sam Roberts, *For Some Blacks, Justice Is Not Blind to Color*, N.Y. TIMES, Sept. 9, 1990, at D5. *See generally Developments in the Law—Race and the Criminal Process*, 101 HARV. L. REV. 1472 (1988) (discussing recent developments in race-related criminal law issues).

2. See Kurt L. Schmoke, *An Argument in Favor of Decriminalization*, 18 HOFSTRA L. REV. 501 (1990); *Drug Legalization—Catastrophe for Black Americans: Hearing Before the House Select Comm. on Narcotics Abuse and Control*, 100th Cong., 2d Sess. 5–13, 19–21 (1988) (presenting the testimony of the mayor of Hartford in favor of legalization and that of the mayors of Newark and Philadelphia and the president of the National Medical Association against). *See generally A Symposium on Drug Decriminalization*, 18 HOFSTRA L. REV. 457 (1990) (discussing the pros and cons of the decriminalization of illegal drugs).

3. *See* ELIJAH ANDERSON, STREETWISE: RACE, CLASS, AND CHANGE IN AN URBAN COMMUNITY 66–69 (1990) (recounting the derision voiced by working- and middle-class blacks toward members of the "underclass").

4. *See* Philippe Bourgois, *In Search of Horatio Alger: Culture and Ideology in the Crack Economy*, 16 CONTEMP. DRUG PROBS. 619, 631–37 (1990). Based on his ethnographic research in Spanish Harlem, Bourgois maintains that "upward mobility in the underground economy requires a systematic and effective use of violence against one's colleagues, one's neighbors, and to a certain extent, against oneself." *Id.* at 632. "Individuals involved in street activity cultivate the culture of terror in order to intimidate competitors, maintain credibility, develop new contacts, cement partnerships, and, ultimately, have a good time." *Id.* at 634. *See also* CARL S. TAYLOR, DANGEROUS SOCIETY 66–67 (1990) (noting that gangs use violence to discipline members and earn the respect of others).

5. *See* Elijah Anderson, *Race and Neighborhood Transition, in* THE NEW URBAN REALITY 99, 112–16, 123–24 (Paul E. Peterson ed., 1985); Lawrence Thomas, *Next Life, I'll Be White*, N.Y. TIMES, Aug. 13, 1990, at A15.

6. *See The Jeweler's Dilemma*, THE NEW REPUBLIC, Nov. 10, 1986, at 18; Jane Gross, *When "By Appointment" Means Keep Out*, N.Y. TIMES, Dec. 17, 1986, at B1.

7. It was estimated that on any given day in mid-1989, 23 percent of black males between the ages of 20 and 29 were in prison, in jail, or on probation or parole, compared with 10.4 percent of Hispanic males and 6.2 percent of white males. MARK MAUER, YOUNG BLACK MEN AND THE CRIMINAL JUSTICE SYSTEM: A GROWING NATIONAL PROBLEM 3 (1990). Given that young black men are continually being admitted and released from the criminal justice system, the proportion of those actually processed in the course of the year probably exceeded one-quarter of the population. *Id.* According to the Sentencing Project, in 1990 the incarceration rate for black males was 3,370 per 100,000, compared with only 681 per 100,000 in South Africa. The American rate was five times higher than that

of South Africa. *See* Fox Butterfield, *U.S. Expands Its Lead in the Rate of Imprisonment*, N.Y. TIMES, Feb. 11, 1992, at A16.

8. *See, e.g.,* Henry Louis Gates, Jr., *"Jungle Fever" Charts Black Middle-Class Angst*, N.Y. TIMES, June 23, 1991, at B20; Jennifer Jordan, *Cultural Nationalism in the 1960s: Politics and Poetry, in* RACE, POLITICS, AND CULTURE 29, 32–33 (Adolph Reed, Jr., ed., 1986).

9. For an especially critical, class-conscious analysis of black radicalism in the 1960s, see Adolph Reed, Jr., *The "Black Revolution" and the Reconstitution of Domination, in* RACE, POLITICS, AND CULTURE, *supra* note 8, at 61.

10. *See* MICHELE WALLACE, INVISIBILITY BLUES: FROM POP TO THEORY 18–22 (1990); PAULA GIDDINGS, WHEN AND WHERE I ENTER: THE IMPACT OF BLACK WOMEN ON RACE AND SEX IN AMERICA 314–24 (1984) (dubbing the 1960s "The Masculine Decade"); HARRY BRILL, WHY ORGANIZERS FAIL: THE STORY OF A RENT STRIKE (1971) (examining the leadership style of the black militant male organizers of a rent strike).

11. NATIONAL RESEARCH COUNCIL COMMITTEE ON THE STATUS OF BLACK AMERICANS, A COMMON DESTINY: BLACKS AND AMERICAN SOCIETY 169 (Gerald D. Jaynes & Robin M. Williams, Jr., eds., 1989).

12. Barrio gangs underwent a similar elevation of status during the Chicano Movement of the late 1960s and a decline thereafter. *See* Joan W. Moore, *Isolation and Stigmatization in the Development of an Underclass: The Case of Chicano Gangs in East Los Angeles*, 33 SOC. PROBS. 1 (1985).

13. HERBERT H. HAINES, BLACK RADICALS AND THE CIVIL RIGHTS MAINSTREAM, 1954–1970 56–57 (1988). Unfortunately, the Panthers' "bad nigger shtick" also delighted white radicals, the media, and the "brothers off the block" who did not allow their Panther membership to deter them from continuing their normal criminal activity. *See generally* OFF THE PIGS! THE HISTORY AND LITERATURE OF THE BLACK PANTHER PARTY (G. Louis Heath ed., 1976) (offering a negative assessment of the Panthers' activities, including their involvement in ordinary crime).

14. REGINALD MAJOR, A PANTHER IS A BLACK CAT 292 (1971) (quoting the Black Panther Party Platform and Program (Oct. 1966)).

15. BETTYLOU VALENTINE, HUSTLING AND OTHER HARD WORK 23, 126–27 (1978); ELEANOR M. MILLER, STREET WOMAN 6, 35 (1986).

16. Karlene Faith, *Media, Myths and Masculinization: Images of Women in Prison, in* TOO FEW TO COUNT: CANADIAN WOMEN IN CONFLICT WITH THE LAW 181 (Ellen Adelberg & Claudia Currie eds., 1987).

17. *See* Priscilla Alexander, *Prostitution: A Difficult Issue for Feminists, in* SEX WORK: WRITINGS BY WOMEN IN THE SEX INDUSTRY 184, 196–97 (Frédérique Delacoste & Priscilla Alexander eds., 1987); Gloria Lockett, *Leaving the Streets, in* SEX WORK, *supra* at 96, 96–97.

18. EDITH A. FOLB, RUNNIN' DOWN SOME LINES 256 (1980).

19. John Griffiths has sketched out a "family model" for the criminal process that would include black people's interest in punishment with the possibility of redemption. John Griffiths, *Ideology in Criminal Procedure or A Third "Model" of the Criminal Process*, 79 YALE L.J. 359 (1970).

20. WEBSTER'S THIRD NEW INTERNATIONAL DICTIONARY 1902 (1981). In black Christian theology, for example, redemption refers to more than repentance

and deliverance from one's sins. OLIN P. MOYD, REDEMPTION IN BLACK THEOLOGY 15–59 (1979). In talking about redemption, black worshipers are not just thinking about heaven, but about "deliverance and rescue from [the] disabilities and constraints" of this world while they are still in it. *Id.* at 53. Redemption is "salvation from woes, salvation from bondage, salvation from oppression, salvation from death, and salvation from other states and circumstances in the here and now," *id.* at 44, "that destroy the value of human existence." *Id.* at 38. Redemption, then, entails both a pay back and a pay out. *Id.* at 38 (*quoting* Donald Daniel Leslie, *Redemption, in* ENCYCLOPAEDIA JUDAICA (1971)).

21. Elliott Currie, *Crime, Justice, and the Social Environment, in* THE POLITICS OF LAW 294, 307 (David Kairys ed., rev. ed. 1990).

22. *See* DIANA FUSS, ESSENTIALLY SPEAKING: FEMINISM, NATURE AND DIFFERENCE 90–93 (1989) (describing the use of essentialism in the writings of Afro-American literary critics).

26 Traces of the Master Narrative in the Story of African American/Korean American Conflict: How We Constructed "Los Angeles"

LISA C. IKEMOTO

M A N Y who have written about Los Angeles see the dynamics of race in the terrible events that took place on April 29 to May 1, 1992. Some blamed Black racism for what happened; others found fault with the behavior of Korean merchants. Others, more perceptively, blamed our society's system of white-over-colored supremacy for pitting the two outsider groups against one another, setting the stage for the conflict that exploded on those fateful days. I agree with this latter position, but my aim in this chapter is slightly different. It is to explore how we analyzed, explained, came to understand, and gave meaning to "Los Angeles." How and why did we construct the story of that conflict as we did?

During the early aftermath of the civil disorder in Los Angeles, the notion of Korean American/African American conflict emerged as a focal point in explanations for "Los Angeles." Examination of this construct reveals that Korean Americans, African Americans, and those apparently outside the "conflict" used concepts of race, identity, and entitlement in ways that described conflict as inevitable. Further interrogation suggests that despite the absence of obvious whiteness in a conflict described as intergroup, culturally embedded white supremacy (racism) provides the operative dynamic. I use "master narrative" to describe white supremacy's prescriptive, conflict-constructing power, which deploys exclusionary concepts of race and privilege in ways that maintain intergroup conflict. I try here to give my sense of the dynamic that lies beneath the surface of the stories that emerged. I do not assume a unilateral "master hand," although at times I may use that image to evoke a sense of control felt but not seen, and of contrivance. When I assert that I write with the goal of revealing the hand of the master narrative in social discourse, I mean that I will point to traces of white su-

66 S. CAL. L. REV. 1581 (1993). Copyright © 1993 by the Southern California Law Review, Inc. Reprinted by permission.

premacy as evidence of that narrative. And in telling of a master narrative, I may take the role of narrator and impose my own hand.

In questioning the concepts of race used to describe a Korean American/ African American conflict, I note that the master narrative defines race and racial identity oppositionally. Here, a Black/African American racial identity is located in opposition to an Asian/Korean American identity, a strategy that merges ethnicity, culture, gender, and class into race.[1] With respect to African Americans, the master narrative tells us that Asians are Koreans who are merchants and crime victims. The assumption that Asians are foreign intruders underlies this description. With respect to Asian Americans, the narrative tells us that African Americans are Blacks who are criminals who are poor. All of these identities replicate the dominant society's understandings of blackness and Asianness.

Although the conflict as constructed does not directly speak of dominant white society, it arranges the various racial identities so as to preserve the authority of whiteness and devalue difference. The differences between Blacks and Asians emerge as a tale of relative nonwhiteness. When racial identity is constructed oppositionally, conflict becomes inevitable, coalition unimaginable, and both groups are publicly debilitated and exposed.

I begin by locating myself with regard to the constructed African American/Korean American conflict. As I do so, I recognize categories that are being imposed and ones that I am claiming. I am a Sansei woman, a person of color who has experienced oppression as an Asian female, not as a Korean or African American, a third-generation Asian American of Japanese descent, not a person who has lived as an immigrant, a woman writing of a story in which few have talked about gender. I grew up in a Los Angeles suburb. I was teaching in the Midwest when the uprising in Los Angeles occurred. Viewing the events from a physical distance, I felt both removed and personally traumatized.

I write aware that I do not know what really happened in "Los Angeles." I doubt it took place only in Los Angeles, and I assert that whatever occurred began long before April 1992. I am conscious that the major news outlets have mediated my picture and experience of Los Angeles, and I wonder to what extent those who lived the uprising relied on the same media accounts to interpret their experiences. I write as one who deploys "Los Angeles" as an ironic, iconic metaphor for the stories of social disorder and racial conflict used to explain what happened there. These stories give birth to "Los Angeles" as a metaphor but are in turn swallowed by it as the events in Los Angeles become part of the master narrative.

Traces of White Supremacy

Consider the thesis: The stories of intergroup conflict came from the master narrative of white supremacy. Those Korean and African Americans who participated in the storytelling spoke and acted from the imposed experience of racism.[2] I am not saying that the Korean American or African American communities or anyone told the conflict constructing stories in a consciously strategic way.[3] Rather, I am acknowledging that we interpret our experiences by referring to familiar stories about the world.[4]

If you live within a society pervaded by racism, then racism prescribes your experience. Racism is so much a part of our experience that we cannot always recognize those moments when we participate.[5] As a corollary, if you experience racism as one marginalized by it, then you use racism to explain your relations with other groups and their members. Racism operates, in part, through stories about race. These stories both filter and construct our reality.[6]

Now consider the stories of conflict.

Claims of Entitlement

"The pie is only so big, and everybody wants a piece, and they're fighting over it."

"[J]ust twenty-three percent of the blacks said they had more opportunities than recently arrived immigrants. Twice that many whites said they had more opportunities than new immigrants."

"People here are out of jobs and yet they allow foreign people to come over and take work away from people born here in America. . . . [T]hey can come over and get loans and open up businesses, but no one will lend any money to us."

"These businesses belong to people who have exploited, abused and disrespected black people."

"I respect the different cultures . . . but they are here in America now, and they're doing business in our community."

"We didn't do anything wrong," said [Bona Lee], who came to Los Angeles from Korea two decades ago. "We worked like slaves here."

"I left Korea because America is a good country, a free country, and to get rich."

"This is not an act of aggression. This is just saying, 'Leave us alone and let us get back to business.' "

As the above sub-stories show, one common explanation circulated during the aftermath of the uprisings that had to do with competition between Korean Americans and African Americans for a too small piece of the economic pie. The issue became one of entitlement. In the fray, many different claims to entitlement were made. Some complained that Korean Americans had, in effect, cut in line. The premise was that African Americans have been waiting in line for a longer time, and that more recent arrivals must go to the back.

This story is more complex than it first appears. To begin, there is the image of the breadline and the use of a first-in-time principle to claim entitlement. The breadline image evokes a picture of hierarchy. At issue is whether Korean Americans or African Americans must stand further back in line or lower in the hierarchy. The image also admits that both Korean Americans and African Americans are outgroups dependent on the will and leftovers of a dominant group. It presupposes deprivation by social and political forces beyond our control. And it assumes that the competition must occur among those forced to stand in line, not between those making the handouts and those subject to those handouts.

The use of the first-in-time principle echoes traditional property law[7] and suggests that the process of keeping outgroups in line has commodified status as well as goods.[8] In part, this story asserts that Korean Americans do not understand the plight of Blacks in America, and that if they did they would wait their turn. This assertion assumes knowledge of the history of white oppression of Blacks stemming from, but not limited to, the practice and laws of slavery. It also expresses the idea that more recently arrived immigrants do not understand because they are less "American." Ultimately, the first-in-time principle both denies and reifies the truth—that African Americans have been first in time, but last in line since the practice of slavery began in the American colonies.[9]

A closely related entitlement claim was that Korean American merchants were not giving back to the Black community. African Americans charged Korean merchants with failure to hire Blacks, rudeness to Black customers, and exploitive pricing. The claim draws a boundary around the Black community as the in-group, relative to the Korean outsiders who can gain admission only by purchasing it—by giving back value. Jobs and respect are the local currency. The claim also elaborates upon the breadline image in a telling way. It describes the Black community as the in-group with the authority to set the standards for admission, yet, by claiming victimhood status for the Black community, it places the Black community behind Korean Americans in the breadline. This simultaneously excuses the resulting end-of-the-line position of African Americans and delegitimizes the relatively better place of Korean Americans.

Korean American merchants responded, in part, by casting themselves as actors in the "American Dream"—Koreans working hard to support their families, survive as immigrants, and succeed as entrepreneurs. By doing so, they bring enterprise to the poorest neighborhoods. Claiming entitlement by invoking the American Dream recharacterizes the breadline. One's place in the line is not, according to this claim, the inevitable plight of those marginalized by the dominant society; it is changeable for those who pursue the Dream. Those left standing at the end of the line deserve their fate. The American Dream counters the "American Nightmare"—the history of racial oppression—that the claims of Black community entitlement invoke. For many, "Los Angeles" represents the death of the American Dream.

Racial Positioning

Another story of conflict, intertwined with that of competition, is concerned with racial hierarchy. And, while it expressly racializes Korean American and African American identity, it also implies an important story about whiteness.

African Americans and others who complained about Korean merchants took a nativist position. The first-in-time principle describes Korean Americans not only as immigrants and therefore later in time but also as foreigners and therefore less American.[10] Nativism simultaneously calls for assimilation and assumes that Asians are less assimilable than other races. Characterizing Koreans as rude, clannish, and exploitive, with little or no effort made to learn Korean culture, calls up longstanding anti-Asian stereotypes.[11] The charge that Koreans do not understand the plight of Blacks implies that "real" Americans would. The implication that Blacks are real Americans strikes an odd note in this context since the norm-making dominant society has usually defined the real American as white.[12] Perhaps the real irony is the duality of the un-American charge. Excluding Koreans from the category of American suggests that Koreans are not also subject to racial oppression, while simultaneously racializing Korean identity. The master hand does double duty here. It collapses ethnicity into race, thus including Korean Americans within the racial conflict; and it defines ethnicity as "foreignness," to describe Korean Americans as outside the racial hierarchy.

I noted that usually the dominant society takes the nativist position. When African Americans made nativist charges, they positioned themselves as whites relative to Asians. When Korean Americans responded by placing themselves within the American Dream—a dream produced and distributed by the dominant society—they positioned themselves as white. Their belief in an American Dream and their hope to be independent business operators positioned them as white relative to Blacks. The rule underlying this racial positioning is white supremacy. Racial positioning would not be coherent, could not take place, but for racism. In other words, I have used "positioned" as an active verb, with Korean Americans and African Americans as actors, but here I sense a master hand positioning Korean Americans and African Americans as objects.

The stories of conflict are not about ordinary, marketplace competition. Nor do they tell of empowering community. Instead, they plot relative subordination, subordinated domination, subordinating storytelling. In doing so, the stories of race and conflict flatten our understanding of racial identity.

Constructed Identities and Racial Pairing

The stories of conflict have filtered largely through the major media; other stories have been filtered out. Media-selected images and words both represent and reinforce the constructed conflict. The stories described above were told in words. The stories addressed here were also told with pictures. The latter,

I suspect, will prove more memorable and therefore more significant in the construct of conflict. Recall, for a moment, the much-photographed Latasha Harlins and Soon Ja Du, gangmember looters, and armed Korean storeowners.[13] These images have merged into the African American/Korean American conflict plotted by the master narrative. They operate by informing and reinforcing the identities created for conflict. The result: Shoplifter, looter, and gangmember images are reinforced as the operative aspects of African American identity; crime-victim, gun-toting merchant, and defender-of-property images emerge as the Korean American character types.[14] Thus, apparently race-neutral categories—criminals and property-owning crime victims—become part of African American and Korean American racial identities.

Racializing identity has another effect; it submerges class and gender. According to the constructed identities, "Korean Americans" are merchants. "African Americans" are not simply criminals, but are most likely poor, because shoplifting and looting are considered crimes of poverty. And both gun-toting merchants and gangmember looters are probably typified as male.[15] These identities describe class and gender as characteristics of race, not effects of racism. The construct of conflict defines African American and Korean American identities in opposition to each other. It neatly positions Korean Americans as white, relative to Blacks. In other words, in black-white conflicts, blackness would be similarly criminalized and whiteness would be accorded victim status. This conclusion does not require a leap of logic or faith. Rodney King and Latasha Harlins emerged as the two main symbols of racial injustice during the events surrounding the uprising. The Rodney King verdict became representative, in part, of white oppression of Blacks. Once the uprising began, many invoked the name "Latasha Harlins" to recall the sentence issued in *People v. Soon Ja Du.* "Latasha Harlins" came to represent (white) systemic, race-based injustice even while it reinforced the sense of African American/Korean American conflict and goaded many to target Korean-owned stores for looting and vandalism. For purposes of defining racial injustice, "Korean" became provisionally identified with whiteness. Racial pairing not only creates racial differences, but it also makes racial difference a source of inevitable conflict. The primary model for identifying bases for positive relations between groups is that of sameness/difference—the assumption that there are either samenesses or differences and that we should identify and focus on sameness and overlook difference. The underlying assumption is that difference can only lead to contention. Positive relations between Blacks and Asians become impossible because there are only apparent racial differences. "Black" now suggests the possibility of conflict with Asian, and "Asian" with Black.

Racial pairing also essentializes race. The essentialized understanding of race occurs via a syllogism: The stories of conflict construct African American identity in opposition to Korean American identity. In the context of intergroup conflict with African Americans, the oppositional Asian is Korean; all Asians are Korean. This syllogism silently strips Korean identity of ethnic and cultural content, making "Korean" interchangeable with "Asian." It is important that "Korean" has been defined in the context of conflict with African Americans. So, it is probably more accurate to say that the syllogism concludes: All Asians are Korean for purposes of intergroup conflict. Further, the constructed Korean American/Asian identity—economically successful minorities, hardworking, entrepreneurs[16]—reinforces its opposite, constructed blackness. "It is no accident . . . that immigrant populations (and much immigrant literature) understood their 'Americanness' as an opposition to the resident black population."[17]

The media-reinforced construct makes racial identity not only flat, but also transparent. The stories of conflict have given many the sense that they know about Korean Americans and African Americans. "Korean American" and "African American" invoke a whole set of conclusions that do not follow from a personal or group history or from Korean American or African American experience, but from the construct of conflict. For those who are both object and subject of the conflict, the essentialized racial identities filter out the possible bases of understanding. What is perceived as Korean rudeness may reinforce the experience African Americans have had—race-based rejection. In responding negatively to "Korean Americans," African Americans may be rejecting imposed blackness. In addition, many of the comments made by both African Americans and Korean Americans to reporters indicated that the speaker not only lacked understanding of the culture, experience, or history of the other group but also rejected the need to try—the other group was the one that had an obligation to conform in some way. For example, in response to claims of bigotry by Black customers, Korean storeowners often asserted that they had businesses to run, thereby suggesting that good business practice did not include recognizing local concerns. Or consider African Americans who discounted the Korean cultural practice of not touching strangers by asserting "this is America." The construct of conflict not only filters out personal experience, group history, and culture, but deems them irrelevant.

Distancing Stories, Symbols of Disorder

Consider the effect of the stories of conflicts: The notion of a Korean American/African American conflict locates the causes of the uprisings in problems originating within and bounded by communities of color. At the same time, the rubric of race and racism used to describe the conflict is legalistic; it focuses on intent and attributes racism to wrong-minded individuals. This denies the possibility of embedded, culture-wide racism. It makes race fungible and independent of the history of racial subordination in the United States. And it distances the problem of intergroup conflict from the dominant society; the problem is defined as one of race. This distance distinguishes race from whiteness.

The constructed conflict created a great sense and desire for distance. Even as the uprising and the events surrounding it enraged, demoralized, inspired, and traumatized me, I also felt safe and fortunate in viewing it all from afar. When I acknowledged my lack of physical proximity as my good fortune, I removed myself from those more directly affected. It was not my problem. Since the conflict was specifically cast as African American/Korean American, that I am Japanese and not Korean American made this conclusion easier to reach. I used the categories deployed in this construct to opt out. I can, to the extent that I opt out, sympathize with victims and condemn villains. This may make me well-meaning. But it protects me from participation, which is harder to accomplish, more difficult to bear, but may reduce the sense that the conflict is confined to two specific groups. I could not opt out entirely. I was affected—perhaps because I identify as a person of color and as an Asian American, more inclusive descriptors that place me within the conflict.

At first, I wanted to deny that intergroup conflict was a significant problem. I wanted to say that the problem was economic. That may have been an effort to reject the submerging, essentializing effects of imposed racial identity. I may have been resisting the sense of inevitable unresolvable conflict that flows from my experience and understanding of race. I know that others denied race as the problem. Perhaps they did so because they know that not every person intentionally discriminates. Some described the problem as specific to Los Angeles. But "Los Angeles" is not located in Southern California. As I have been arguing, it is part of the master narrative. Each of us creates and locates it somewhere else to make it unique, episodic—i.e., not integral to American functioning—and, above all, "not my fault." Racial distancing enables each of us to say, "It was really too bad. But fundamentally, it is not my problem."

Symbols of Disorder, or Why Multiculturalism Won't Work

The constructed Korean American/African American conflict has become, for many, the racial conflict of the moment. The symbolized conflict is not only that between Korean Americans and African Americans. It is the potential for conflict among the (too) many groups of racial minorities. To the extent that the apparent Korean American/African American conflict contributes to the conclusion that a multiracial/multicultural[18] society is doomed to conflict, it displaces white supremacy as the central race issue. That displacement, in turn, may strengthen the distinction between whiteness and race.

The stories of conflict also describe interracial tension as representative and key to broader social disorder. Because the constructed identities conflate other forms of problematized status with race, intergroup conflict implicates underclass and failure to assimilate. One result is that whiteness becomes symbolic of order and race becomes symbolic of disorder. Thus, while Latasha Harlins and Rodney King became symbols of systemic racial injustice, "Los Angeles" has become a metaphor for the failure of racial diversity.

It is difficult to escape the constructs I describe. To the extent that we interpret our experience from within the master narrative, we reinforce our own subordination. We must also compete for space with the master narrative. That is where the master hand tailors stories about identity and conflict to the situation—African American/Korean American relations, Los Angeles, Latasha Harlins and Soon Ja Du, Rodney King—in ways that make Asianness the subordinator of Blackness and vice versa, and in ways that isolate the conflict from whiteness. Whether Korean and other Asian Americans can counter racism may depend, finally, on our ability to claim identities outside the master narrative.

Conflict—the real world kind, I mean—can be bloody, misguided, and wholly tragic. It behooves us always to try to understand how and why bloodshed breaks out as it does. But the very narratives and stories we tell ourselves and each other afterwards, in an effort to explain, understand, excuse, and assign responsibility for conflict, may also be, in a sense, the source of the very violence we abhor. I have identified a number of ways the "master narrative" works itself out in the stories by which we constructed "Los Angeles." This master narrative is at one and the same time lulling, disturbing, provocative, and always powerfully apologetic. Understanding how we assemble reality unjustly, apologetically, and in status-quo-preserving ways may enable us, with effort, to disassemble it—and perhaps, one day, to define difference as a basis for coalition and fairness.

NOTES

1. Compare the conflict constructed from the Clarence Thomas confirmation hearings. The fact that both Clarence Thomas and Anita Hill are African American had the effect of submerging race to gender in dominant culture's account of the conflict. This reinforces the point that existing categories inadequately describe the experience of oppression. *See* Kimberlé Crenshaw, *Whose Story Is It Anyway? Feminist and Antiracist Appropriations of Anita Hill, in* RACE-ING JUSTICE, EN-GENDERING POWER: ESSAYS ON ANITA HILL, CLARENCE THOMAS, AND THE CONSTRUCTION OF SOCIAL REALITY 402 (Toni Morrison ed., 1992); Adrienne D. Davis & Stephanie M. Wildman, *The Legacy of Doubt: Treatment of Sex and Race in the Hill-Thomas Hearings*, 65 S. CAL. L. REV. 1367, 1378–84 (1992).

2. For an elaboration of the effects of imposed "truth," see MICHEL FOUCAULT, *Truth and Power, in* POWER/KNOWLEDGE: SELECTED INTERVIEWS & OTHER WRITINGS 1972–1977 (Colin Gordon ed., 1980).

3. I do acknowledge that some, for commercial, political, or other reasons, consciously and tactically construct stories. For purposes of this chapter, the media are the primary storymaker. It is important to remember, however, that while print, television, and radio media may have commercial motives, to some extent the stories are part and parcel of mainstream culture.

4. Richard Delgado & Jean Stefancic, *Images of the Outsider in American Law and Culture: Can Free Expression Remedy Systemic Social Ills?*, 77 CORNELL L. REV. 1258, 1277–82 (1992); *see generally* PETER L. BERGER & THOMAS LUCKMAN, THE SOCIAL CONSTRUCTION OF REALITY: A TREATISE IN THE SOCIOLOGY OF KNOWLEDGE (1966).

5. *See* JOEL KOVEL, WHITE RACISM: A PSYCHOHISTORY 211–12 (1984) describing "metaracism":

Metaracism is a distinct and very peculiar modern phenomenon. Racial degradation continues on a different plane, and through a different agency: those who participate in it are not racists—that is, they are not racially prejudiced—but metaracists, because they acquiesce in the larger cultural order which continues the work of racism.

6. *See* Trina Grillo & Stephanie M. Wildman, *Obscuring the Importance of Race: The Implication of Making Comparisons Between Racism and Sexism (Or Other -Isms)*, 1991 DUKE L.J. 397, 397 (illustrating the use of "filter" to explain how personal experience shapes one's worldview.)

7. *See* Symposium, *Time, Property Rights, and the Common Law*, 64 WASH. U. L.Q. 661 (1986) for a recent evaluation of this principle. Historically, the first-in-time principle has been racialized. *See, e.g.*, Johnson v. M'Intosh, 21 U.S. (8 Wheat.) 543, 573–74 (1823) (holding valid a land patent taken from the United States because the United States' claim derived from the (white) European "discovery" of America. The Court reached its conclusion, in part, by distinguishing between mere "occupancy" made by Native American nations and "ultimate dominion" asserted by the European nations.)

8. For valuable discussion on the link between property rights and status, see Joseph William Singer, *Sovereignty and Property*, 86 Nw. U. L. REV. 1, 40–51 (1991). *See also* DERRICK BELL, AND WE ARE NOT SAVED, 135 (1989) (where the fictional character Geneva Crenshaw, recalling the fate of the Black Reparations Foundation and its leader, Goldrich, stated, "Goldrich planned to raise the actual status of blacks as compared with their white counterparts, and that is why in the Chronicle he was more condemned than canonized.").

9. *See* Bakke v. Regents of Univ. of Cal., 438 U.S. 265, 400 (1978) (Marshall, J., dissenting) ("The experience of Negroes in America has been different in kind, not just in degree, from that of other ethnic groups. It is not merely the history of slavery alone but also that a whole people were marked as inferior by the law. And that mark has endured."); *see also* DERRICK BELL, FACES AT THE BOTTOM OF THE WELL (1992) (discussing "Racial Realism"). For discussion of the history of racism and the historical origins of Western concepts of race, see Christina Delacampagne, *Racism and the West: From Praxis to Logos*, in ANATOMY OF RACISM 83 (David Theo Goldberg ed., 1990); David Theo Goldberg, *The Social Formation of Racism Discourse in* ANATOMY OF RACISM, *supra* at 295.

10. Immigration and naturalization laws at various times have defined "American" in similarly exclusive ways. SUCHENG CHAN, ASIAN AMERICANS: AN INTERPRETIVE HISTORY 45–61 (1991) (describing anti-Asian laws, including exclusive immigration and naturalization laws); YUJI ICHIOKA, THE ISSEI: THE WORLD OF THE FIRST GENERATION JAPANESE IMMIGRANTS, 1885–1924, at 210–54 (1988) (describing the struggle for naturalization rights, Alien Land Law litigation, and the 1924 Immigration Act); RONALD TAKAKI, STRANGERS FROM A DIFFERENT SHORE: A HISTORY OF ASIAN AMERICANS 99–112, 271–73, 419–20 (1989) (discussing anti-Chinese laws, including the Chinese Exclusion Act of 1882 and People v. Hall, the Asiatic Exclusion League activities against Korean immigrants, and the Immigration Act of 1965).

11. TAKAKI, *supra* note 10, at 101, 105. *See also* Richard Delgado & Jean Stefancic, *Norms and Narratives: Can Judges Avoid Serious Moral Error?*, 69 TEX. L.

REV. 1929, 1943–46 (1991) (discussing the Chinese Exclusion Cases and the Japanese Internment Cases as judicial expressions of anti-Asian stereotypes).

12. ROGER DANIELS, THE POLITICS OF PREJUDICE 65–68 (1977).

13. *See* People v. Super. Ct. (Soon Ja Du), 7 Cal. Rptr. 2d 177, *modified*, 5 Cal. App. 4th 1643a (1992). The print media devoted extensive space to presenting verbal descriptions of the Soon Ja Du case and the events during the uprising. It is, however, the photographic and video images that have proved the most memorable and defining. A store security camera recorded Soon Ja Du shooting Latasha Harlins and the preceding confrontation. The television media replayed this video many times. Television camera crews filmed two Korean men firing weapons in defense of their store, and people, including Black men, looting stores and other businesses during the uprising. These videos were broadcast on the television news and published as photos in newspapers across the nation.

14. *See, e.g.,* IRA REINER, GANGS, CRIME AND VIOLENCE IN LOS ANGELES: FINDINGS AND PROPOSALS FROM THE DISTRICT ATTORNEY'S OFFICE at iv (1992). The study reports that "the police have identified almost half of all Black men in Los Angeles County between the ages of 21 and 24 as gang members." *Id.* The fact that the police made these identifications should raise questions about the finding. The report itself admits that the "number is so far out of line with other ethnic groups that careful, professional examination is needed to determine whether police procedures may be systematically over-identifying Black youths as gang members." *Id. See also* Stephen Braun & Ashley Dunn, *View of Model Multiethnic City Vanishes in Smoke*, L.A. TIMES, May 1, 1992, at A1 ("Each new graphic televised image— . . . angry black assailants, frightened Korean merchants guarding their shuttered markets with guns—threatened to reinforce the long-held fears and prejudices gnawing at the city's populace, worried community leaders and race relations experts said Thursday.").

15. *See, e.g.,* REINER, *supra* note 14, at 118–19.

16. *See* TAKAKI, *supra* note 10, at 474–84 (discussing the harmful effects of the Myth of the Model Minority).

17. TONI MORRISON, PLAYING IN THE DARK 47 (1992). For a case illustrating how Asians as relative whites were deployed against Blacks, see Gong Lum v. Rice, 275 U.S. 78 (1927).

18. Stuart Alan Clarke, *Fear of a Black Planet: Race, Identity Politics, and Common Sense*, 21 SOCIALIST REV. 37, 40–41 (illustrating how some have racialized "multiculturalism" so as to present it as a threat to democratic principles. "In this context, it is unsurprising that the 'multicultural threat' is pictured most compellingly in the public imagination as a black threat."). *Id.* at 41.

27 Racial Critiques of Legal Academia

RANDALL L. KENNEDY

MATSUDA AND CLAIMS OF RACIAL DISTINCTIVENESS— ESSENTIALISM IN THE RANKS OF CRITICAL RACE THEORY

Professor Mari Matsuda's criticisms of legal academia[1] are generally congruent with those articulated by Professors Bell and Delgado. She, too, maintains that the allocation of academic prestige is distorted by an illicit racial hierarchy that favors whites over blacks. In contrast to Bell and Delgado, however, who emphasize the racial exclusion theme that is prevalent in racial critiques, Matsuda emphasizes the theme of racial distinctiveness. She argues that by the exclusions imposed by existing practices, legal academia loses the sensibilities, insights, and ideas that are the products of racial oppression. She insists that, because of their minority status and the experience of racial victimization that attaches to that status, people of color offer valuable and special perspectives or voices that, if recognized, will enrich legal academic discourse. "Those who have experienced discrimination," she writes, "speak with a special voice to which we should listen."[2] "The victims of racial oppression," she asserts, "have distinct normative insights."[3] "Those who are oppressed in the present world," she avers, "can speak most eloquently of a better one."[4]

But what, as a function of race, is "special" or "distinct" about the scholarship of minority legal academics? Does it differ discernibly in ways attributable to race from work produced by white scholars? If so, in what ways and to what degree is the work of colored intellectuals different from or better than the work of whites?

Matsuda's answers to these questions are revealing, though what they reveal is undoubtedly at odds with what she intends to display. She writes that readers "will delight in the new insights gleaned from writers previously unknown,"[5] that "[t]he new voices will emphasize difference,"[6] and that "[t]he outsiders' different knowledge of discrimination . . . is concrete and personal"[7] and will force readers "to confront the harsh edge of realism."[8] Yet, at least with respect to legal scholarship, she fails to show the newness of the "new knowledge" and the difference that distinguishes the "different voices."

102 HARV. L. REV. 1745 (1989). Copyright © 1989 by the President and Fellows of Harvard College. Reprinted by permission.

In the course of building her argument, she refers to a broad range of cultural expression: Speeches by Frederick Douglass, writings by W.E.B. Du Bois, poetry by Pauli Murray, music by John Coltrane, essays by Audrey Lorde, novels by James Weldon Johnson and Ishmael Reed, and the oral memoirs of Japanese-Americans detained in American concentration camps during World War II. She counsels legal academics to look to these and other sources that embody insights offered by people who have been oppressed. She includes within the ranks of such people legal academics of color. But their work is virtually non-existent among the prominent examples of the cultural expression she champions. Like Delgado, she offers little detailed advocacy in favor of particular works of legal scholarship that have supposedly been wrongly overlooked.

Matsuda claims that the racial status of minority scholars uniquely deepens and sharpens their analysis of racism and their resolve to end it. She suggests, in other words, that victimization breeds certain intellectual and moral virtues.[9] She writes, for instance, that "Black Americans, because of their experiences, are quick to detect racism, to distrust official claims of necessity, and to sense a threat to freedom."[10] When closely scrutinized, however, this line of distinction blurs and erodes.

This is not to say that Matsuda's assertions are wholly incorrect. For example, some black Americans undoubtedly do display certain moral and intellectual virtues derived from experience with racial oppression. But Matsuda's proposition distorts reality by ignoring significant tendencies that run counter to the ones she acknowledges. She notes that some black Americans displayed laudable solicitude for Japanese-Americans whom the United States government confined in internment camps during World War II. She suggests that that solicitude stemmed from an empathy grounded in blacks' experience with racism. But what about the passivity with which *most* blacks—like *most* whites—responded to the internment of Japanese-Americans? Significantly, neither the NAACP nor any other predominantly black organization submitted an amicus curiae brief to the Supreme Court in *Korematsu v. United States*[11] or the other cases challenging the government's internment policy.

The mere experience of racial oppression provides no inoculation against complacency. Nor does it inoculate the victims of oppression against their own versions of prejudice and tyranny. One need only consider, for example, the phenomena of free blacks owning slave blacks,[12] or lighter-skinned Negroes shunning darker-skinned Negroes,[13] or the participation by substantial numbers of blacks in the subjugation of other people of color both domestically and internationally.[14] Matsuda refers to Martin Luther King, Jr., and the Civil Rights Movement in the course of suggesting that rebellion has been the natural, inevitable response of those who have experienced racial oppression. Under many circumstances, however, oppression is as likely to breed docility as resistance.[15] King himself repeatedly emphasized that breaking their own habitual acquiescence to racist oppression would constitute one of the heaviest burdens blacks would have to overcome in their struggle for greater freedom.[16]

The negative side of the idyllic portrait Matsuda paints should indicate that the relationship between thought, experience, and racial status is not nearly so predictable as she suggests. Moreover, internalization of color prejudice, acquiescence to subordination, and indifference or hostility toward others victimized by racism cannot be dismissed as the idiosyncratic responses of relatively few people of color.[17] These behaviors and forms of consciousness constitute central aspects of the complex way in which racial minorities have responded to conditions in the United States and are thus clearly relevant to any attempt to derive theories based upon that response.

Matsuda's analysis is marred by both her tendency to homogenize the experience of persons of color and her tendency to minimize the heterogeneity of opinions held and articulated by persons of color.

Because, in Matsuda's view, the experience of racial oppression is a profoundly significant, if not decisive, determinant of intellectual work, it would seem important for her to focus on the actual experience of colored scholars. Matsuda, however, simply *presumes* that any scholar of color will have undergone the experience—the initiation into racial victimhood—that she deems so important. In her analysis, racial status and the experience of racial victimization are fastened together inextricably and unambiguously, creating a vestment that comes in one size and is apparently supposed to fit all people of color. Matsuda is aware, to some degree, of questions raised by her emphasis on racial as opposed to other social determinants of thought and conduct. She thus rejects the suggestion that economic class affiliation may have equal if not more influence than race on cultural expression and political viewpoint. Racial perspective, she writes, "cuts across class lines. . . . There is something about color that doesn't wash off as easily as class."[18] To some extent, that proposition serves as a useful antidote to the belief, propounded by social thinkers of varying political stripes, that the integrative forces of the modern world would dissolve racial, ethnic, nationalistic, religious, and other parochial attachments.[19] Not only do racial and other ascriptive loyalties continue to organize a great deal of social, political, and intellectual life throughout the world; in many areas such loyalties have intensified. It is also true, however, that racial groups are not monolithic and that social divisions generate differences in interests and consciousness within racial groups. Matsuda's analysis wraps in one garment of racial victimization the black law professor of middle-class upbringing with a salary of $65,000 and the black, unemployed, uneducated captive of the ghetto. In the overwhelming majority of cases, however, these two social types will inhabit radically dissimilar social universes;[20] worlds as different as those evoked by Andrea Lee on the one hand and John Edgar Wideman on the other.[21] Even during the eras of slavery and de jure segregation, the structure and experience of racial oppression often varied along class lines *within* black communities. There are, moreover, other important cross-cutting variables, largely ignored by Matsuda, that diversify the experiences of persons of color, including gender, region, and differing group affiliations within the catch-all category "people of color."

M Y C E N T R A L objection to the claim of racial distinctiveness propounded by Professor Matsuda and others of like mind can best be summarized by observing that it *stereotypes* scholars. By stereotyping, I mean the process whereby the particularity of an individual's characteristics are denied by reference to the perceived characteristics of the racial group with which the individual is associated. This is the process that, in its grossest form, produces the statement "they all look alike to me." In the past, negative images of colored groups prevented or diminished appreciation for the particular characteristics of individual colored intellectuals. The work of Negro intellectuals, for instance, was (and in many contexts probably still is) prejudged according to expectations governed by the perception that Negroes as a group lack certain valued capacities. Professor Matsuda's stereotyping is of a very different sort insofar as she perceives colored groups in a uniformly favorable light and spreads that favorable perception over all the colored intellectuals or artists whom she discusses. Matsuda's analysis, like Delgado's, lacks any discussion that hints of any dissatisfaction with work produced by people of color. Matsuda thus substitutes for the traditional, i.e., *negative*, stereotype a *positive* stereotype. But as Louis Lusky once noted, "*any* stereotype results in a partial blindness to the actual qualities of individuals, and consequently is a persistent and prolific breeding ground for irrational treatment of them."[22]

[*Ed.* A second portion of Professor Kennedy's critique appears in Part X, below.]

NOTES

1. *See* M. Matsuda, *Affirmative Action and Legal Knowledge*, 11 HARV. WOMEN'S L.J. 1 (1988); M. Matsuda, *Looking to the Bottom*, 22 HARV. C.R.-C.L. L. REV. 323 (1987).

2. Matsuda, *Looking to the Bottom*, *supra* note 1, at 324.

3. *Id.* at 326.

4. *Id.* at 346.

5. Matsuda, *Affirmative Action and Legal Knowledge*, *supra* note 1, at 5.

6. *Id.* at 8.

7. *Id.*

8. *Id.* at 9.

9. The intuition behind this idea has a long, distinguished, but ultimately disappointing history. Marx, for instance, suggested that capitalism would provide the schooling that would instruct the proletariat of the necessity for communist revolution. "Not in vain," he wrote, "does [the proletariat] go through the harsh but hardening school of labour." K. Marx, *Alienation and Social Classes*, *in* THE MARX-ENGELS READER, 172–73 (R. Tucker 2d ed. 1978); *cf.* V. Lenin, *What Is to Be Done*, *in* THE LENIN ANTHOLOGY 50 (R. Tucker ed., 1972). As Lenin wrote:

> The history of all countries shows that the working class, exclusively on its own effort, is able to develop only trade union consciousness. . . . The theory of socialism, however, grew out of the philosophic, historical, and

economic theories elaborated by educated representatives of the propertied classes, by intellectuals. By their social status the founders of modern scientific socialism, Marx and Engels, themselves belonged to the bourgeois intelligentsia.

Id. at 24–25.

10. Matsuda, *Looking to the Bottom, supra* note 1, at 360; *see also* Harlon L. Dalton, The Clouded Prism, 22 HARV. C.R.-C.L.L. REV. 435–41 1987; R. Delgado, *The Imperial Scholar*, 132 U. PA. L. REV. 561, 573–74 (1984).

11. 323 U.S. 214 (1944). *See generally* P. IRONS, JUSTICE AT WAR (1983); E. Rostow, *The Japanese-American Cases—A Disaster*, 54 YALE L.J. 489 (1945).

12. Here, of course, I do not refer to free blacks who rescued slave relatives or friends by buying them. In some of these instances, rescuers were prevented by state law from freeing their "slaves." Rather, I refer to the appreciable number of free blacks in the South who, internalizing one of the reigning ideas of their society, bought slaves for profit and convenience. *See* I. BERLIN, SLAVES WITHOUT MASTERS: THE FREE NEGRO IN THE ANTEBELLUM SOUTH 274–75 (1974); M. JOHNSON & J. ROARK, BLACK MASTERS: A FREE FAMILY OF COLOR IN THE OLD SOUTH (1984).

13. For an examination of this issue in a present-day setting, see S. LEE & L. JONES, UPLIFT THE RACE: THE CONSTRUCTION OF "SCHOOL DAZE" 85, 94–95 (1988).

14. *See generally* B. NALTY, STRENGTH FOR THE FIGHT: A HISTORY OF BLACK AMERICANS IN THE MILITARY (1986). For a particularly strong antidote to sentimentality about the effects of racist oppression on Negro Americans, see W. TERRY, BLOODS: AN ORAL HISTORY OF THE VIETNAM WAR BY BLACK VETERANS (1984).

15. *See* B. MOORE, INJUSTICE: THE SOCIAL BASES OF OBEDIENCE AND REVOLT (1978).

16. *See, e.g.,* M. KING, STRIDE TOWARD FREEDOM 20–25 (Perennial Library ed. 1964). According to King, a striking fact about the Negro community in Montgomery, Alabama, prior to the famous bus boycott of 1955–1956

> was the apparent passivity of the majority of the uneducated. . . . [The] largest number accepted [segregation] without apparent protest. Not only did they seem resigned to segregation per se; they also accepted the abuses and indignities which came with it. . . . Their minds and souls were so conditioned to the system of segregation that they submissively adjusted themselves to things as they were.

Id. at 21–22.

17. For an insightful discussion of the broad range of adaptations that people of color and other marginalized groups have exhibited in the midst of oppressive social environments, see G. ALLPORT, THE NATURE OF PREJUDICE 142–64 (25th anniversary ed. 1988). In a chapter titled "Traits Due to Victimization," Allport discusses, among other things, denial of membership in the disparaged group, withdrawal, pacificity, clowning, strengthening in-group ties, self-hatred, militancy, and enhanced striving. *See id.* at 142–61.

18. Matsuda, *Looking to the Bottom, supra* note 1, at 360–61.

19. The classic statement is by Karl Marx and Friedrich Engels, who be-

lieved that with the coming of capitalism "[a]ll fixed, fast-frozen relations, with their train of ancient and venerable prejudices and opinions, are swept away. . . . All that is solid melts into air. . . ." *Manifesto of the Communist Party, in* THE MARX-ENGELS READER, *supra* note 9, at 476.

20. As Professor William Julius Wilson states:

> Unlike more affluent blacks, many of whom continued to experience improved economic opportunity even during the recession period of the 1970s, the black underclass has evidenced higher unemployment rates, lower labor-force participation rates, higher welfare rates, and, more recently, a sharply declining movement out of poverty. The net effect has been a deepening economic schism in the black community.

W. WILSON, THE DECLINING SIGNIFICANCE OF RACE 142 (2d ed. 1980).
See also J. Hochschild, *Race, Class, Power, and the American Welfare State, in* DEMOCRACY AND THE WELFARE STATE 163–64 (A. Gutmann ed., 1988) ("although all blacks continue to operate at a disadvantage . . . some operate at a much greater disadvantage than others. . . . The problem of race in the United States is, in sum, not really one problem.").

21. *Compare* A. LEE, SARAH PHILLIPS (1984) (evoking the texture of life of upper-middle-class black characters), *with* J. WIDEMAN, HIDING PLACE (1981) (evoking the texture of life of lower-class black characters).

22. Lusky, *The Stereotype: Hard Core of Racism,* 13 BUFFALO L. REV. 450, 451 (1964) (emphasis in original); *see also* S. Sontag, *The Third World of Women,* 40 PARTISAN REV. 180, 186 (1973) ("Women should work toward an end to all stereotyping of any kind, positive as well as negative, according to people's sexual identity."

28 Toward an Asian American Legal Scholarship: Critical Race Theory, Post-Structuralism, and Narrative Space

ROBERT S. CHANG

OF THE different voices in which I speak, I have been most comfortable with the one called silence. Silence allowed me to escape notice when I was a child. I could become invisible, and hence safe.

Yet now I find myself leaving the safety of my silence. I wonder if this is wise. I teach legal writing; I want to teach substantive law.[1] I have been told that engaging in nontraditional legal scholarship may hurt my job prospects, that I should write a piece on intellectual property, where my training as a molecular biologist will lend me credibility.

I try to follow this advice, but my mind wanders. I think about the American border guard who stopped me when I tried to return to the United States after a brief visit to Canada. My valid Ohio driver's license was not good enough to let me return to my country. He asked me where my passport was. I told him that I did not have one and that it was my understanding that I did not need one, that a driver's license was sufficient. He told me that a driver's license is not proof of citizenship. We were at an impasse. I asked him what was going to happen. He said that he might have to detain me. I looked away. I imagined the phone call that I would have to make, the embarrassment I would feel as I told my law firm in Seattle that I would not be at work the next day, or maybe even the day after that—until I could prove that I belonged. I thought about my naturalization papers, which were with my parents in Ohio. I thought about how proud I had been when I had become a citizen.

Before then, I had been an alien. Being a citizen meant that I belonged, that I had the same rights as every other American. At least, that is what I used to believe. Things have happened since then that have changed my mind. Like the time I was driving in the South and was refused service at a service station. Or the time I was stopped in New Jersey for suspicion of possessing a stolen vehi-

81 CAL. L. REV. 1244 (1993). Copyright © 1993 by Asian Law Journal and California Law Review. Copyright © 1994 by Asian Law Journal. Reprinted by permission.

cle. At first, it was just two cops. Then another squad car came. Four big (white) policemen for one small (Asian) man, in a deserted parking lot—no witnesses if it came to that. Perhaps they were afraid that I might know martial arts, which I do, but I am careful never to let them know. When my license and registration checked out, they handed back my papers and left without a word. They could not even say that one word, "Sorry," which would have allowed me to leave that incident behind. I might have forgotten it as a mistake, one of those unpleasant things that happen. Instead, I have to carry it with me because of the anger I feel, and because of the fear—fear of the power that certain people are able to exercise over me because of this (contingent) feature that makes me different. No matter how hard I scrub, it does not come clean. No matter how hard I try, and I do try, I can never be as good as everyone else. I can never be white.

These are the thoughts that intrude when I think about intellectual property. I try to push them away; I try to silence them. But I am tired of silence.

And so, I raise my voice.

PROFESSOR Jerome Culp raised his voice when he proclaimed boldly to the legal academy that it was in "an African-American Moment," a time "when different and blacker voices will speak new words and remake old legal doctrines."[2] He also cautioned that "[t]hose in the legal academy who cannot speak the language of understanding will be relegated to the status of historical lepers alongside of Tory Americans and Old South Democrats."[3] It remains to be seen whether his prophecy will come true. The mainstream legal academy has largely ignored his proclamation and the work of other critical race scholars, if frequency of citation is to be taken as a measure of attention, and some legal scholars have condemned the methods of critical race scholarship.

Nevertheless, the time has come to announce another such moment, an Asian American Moment. This Moment is marked by the increasing presence of Asian Americans in the legal academy who are beginning to raise their voices to "speak new words and remake old legal doctrines."[4] This Moment brings new responsibilities for Asian American legal scholars. This Moment brings new challenges. This Moment also brings us hope.

Many people remain unaware of the violence and discrimination that have plagued Asian Americans since their arrival in this country. Moreover, those who know the history often fail to make the connection between the history and the problems that continue to plague Asian Americans today. The philosopher George Santayana said that "[p]rogress, far from consisting in change, depends on retentiveness. . . . Those who cannot remember the past are condemned to repeat it."[5] When I look at certain recent events, such as the rise in the incidence of hate crimes directed toward Asian Americans, or the rhetoric of the official English movement and of politicians such as Patrick Buchanan, or even the uproar caused by the sale of the Rockefeller Center and the Seattle Mariners to Japanese investors, I question how much progress we have made. I wonder if Santayana is right, because when I look at those events, I see a replay of the past, variations on the tired theme of anti-Asian sentiment.

Violence against Asian Americans

Anti-Asian sentiment has historically expressed itself in violent attacks against Asian Americans. The killing of Vincent Chin in Detroit is one variation on this theme. Chin was the Chinese American killed in 1982 by Detroit autoworkers Ronald Ebens and Michael Nitz. Ebens, according to one witness, said "that it was because of people like Chin—Ebens apparently mistook him for a Japanese—that he and his fellow employees were losing their jobs." The two men pleaded guilty to manslaughter and were each given three years' probation and fines of $3,780. They did not serve a single day in jail for the killing of Vincent Chin.

When criticized for the light sentence, Judge Kaufman defended himself in a letter to a newspaper:

> He said that in Michigan, sentences are tailored to the criminal and not just to the crime. According to him, since Ebens and Nitz had no previous criminal record, were longtime residents of the area, and were respectably employed citizens, he thought there was no reason to suspect they would harm anybody again. Hence, the light sentences.[6]

Following efforts by several California congressmen and a Detroit-based community organization, the United States Justice Department brought federal civil rights charges against the two men. During the initial federal civil rights trial, Ebens was found guilty and sentenced to twenty-five years; Nitz was acquitted. Ebens' conviction was overturned on appeal. When his case was retried, it was moved to Cincinnati upon a motion for change of venue. Ebens was ultimately acquitted. The change in venue may have played an important role in this acquittal. Cincinnati residents and jurors had little exposure to Asian Americans; they were also unfamiliar with the level of anti-Asian sentiment then rampant in Detroit.[7]

I relate this story not to point out a miscarriage of justice—others have done so more eloquently than I ever could. And I understand that our judicial system is not perfect. Instead, I tell the story to begin developing the thesis that the killing of Vincent Chin is not an isolated episode. Violence stems from, and is causally related to, anti-Asian feelings that arise during times of economic hardship and the resurgence of nativism.[8]

Another variation on the theme of anti-Asian sentiment is the killing of Navroze Mody. Mody was an Asian Indian who was beaten to death in 1987 in Jersey City by a gang of eleven youths. The gang did not harm Mody's white friend. No murder or bias charges were brought; three of the assailants were convicted of assault, while one was convicted of aggravated assault.

To understand the significance of this attack, it must be placed in context.

Asian Indians were the fastest-growing immigrant group in New Jersey; many settled in Jersey City. Racially motivated hostilities increased with the growth of the Asian Indian community and the transformation of Jersey City as Asian Indians opened shops and restaurants. Earlier in the month that Navroze Mody was killed, a Jersey City gang called the Dotbusters had published a letter in the *Jersey Journal* saying that they "would 'go to any extreme' to drive Indians from Jersey City."[9] Violence against Asian Indians began the next day, leading up to and continuing after the killing of Mody. One community leader said that "the violence worked. . . . People moved out, and others thinking of moving here from the city moved elsewhere."[10]

These recent events read in some ways like a page from the book of history. They resemble other racially motivated incidents of the past, such as what happened in 1877 in Chico, California. While attempting to burn down all of Chico's Chinatown, white arsonists murdered four Chinese by tying them up, dousing them with kerosene, and setting them on fire. The arsonists were members of a labor union associated with the Order of Caucasians, a white supremacist organization which was active throughout California. The Order of Caucasians blamed the Chinese for the economic woes suffered by all workers.

The Chinese Massacre of 1885 also took place in the context of a struggling economy and a growing nativist movement. In Rock Springs, Wyoming, a mob of white miners, angered by the Chinese miners' refusal to join their strike, killed twenty-eight Chinese laborers, wounded fifteen, and chased several hundred out of town. A grand jury failed to indict a single person.[11]

I could go on, but my point is not merely to describe: I seek to link the present with the past. In linking these late-nineteenth-century events with present events, I may seem to be drawing improper associations by taking events out of context. In fact, I am doing the reverse: placing present events into context to show that today's rising incidence of hate crimes against Asian Americans, like the violence of the past, is fostered by a climate of anti-Asian sentiment spurred by economic troubles and nativism. As Professor Stanley Fish said in a different context, "I am arguing for a match at every level, from the smallest detail to the deepest assumptions. It is not simply that the books written today bear some similarities to the books that warned earlier generations of the ethnic menace: they are the same books."[12] Fish was discussing books, but there is, of course, a sometimes unfortunate link between words and deeds.

Nativistic Racism

The words accompanying the violent deeds of the present also grow out of the resurgence of nativism. This resurgence is apparent in some of the arguments marshalled against multiculturalism and in the official English movement. Some politicians have used the rhetoric of nativism to great effect, gaining support among segments of the population.

Nativism, with its message of America first, has a certain allure. Indeed, to

326 ROBERT S. CHANG

reject its message seems unpatriotic. However, present-day nativism is grounded in racism, and thus, is inconsistent with American values. In this way, it differs from the nativism that first swept this country in the 1840s; that nativism included anti-Catholic and anti-European strains. Present-day nativism also differs from the traditional paradigm of racism by adding an element of "foreign."

Nativistic racism lurks behind the spectre of "the Japanese 'taking over,' " which appeared when Mitsubishi Corporation bought a 51% share of the Rockefeller Center and when Nintendo purchased "a piece of America's national pastime." The first problem with the notion of "the Japanese taking over" is that "the Japanese" did not buy Rockefeller Center; nor did "Japan" buy a piece of America's national pastime. In both instances, private corporations made the investments. The second problem is that there is "an outcry when the Japanese buy American institutions such as Rockefeller Center and Columbia Pictures, but not when Westerners do."[13] Moreover, the notion of the Japanese "taking over" is factually unsupported. As of January 1992, in the midst of the clamor about the Japanese buying out America, Japanese investors owned less than 2% of United States commercial property.[14]

Similarly, in 1910, three years before California passed its first Alien Land Laws (prohibiting aliens ineligible for citizenship from owning real property), Japanese Americans, aliens and citizens, controlled just 2.1 percent of California's farms.[15] Nevertheless, the Japanese Americans were perceived to be a threat of such magnitude that a law was passed "to discourage further immigration of Japanese aliens to California and to call to the attention of Congress and the rest of the country the desire of California that the 'Japanese menace' be crushed."[16] The law was tailored to meet this aim by limiting its ambit to aliens ineligible for citizenship. In this way, European interests were protected.

The climate of anti-Asian sentiment, still present today, hurts Asian Americans because, as the death of Vincent Chin has demonstrated, many non-Asian Americans persist in thinking of Asian Americans as foreign. It is this sense of "foreignness" that distinguishes the particular type of racism aimed at Asian Americans.

The Model Minority Myth

This history of discrimination and violence, as well as the contemporary problems of Asian Americans, are obscured by the portrayal of Asian Americans as a "model minority." Asian Americans are portrayed as "hardworking, intelligent, and successful." This description represents a sharp break from past stereotypes of Asians as "sneaky, obsequious, or inscrutable."

But the dominant culture's belief in the "model minority" allows it to justify ignoring the unique discrimination faced by Asian Americans. The portrayal of Asian Americans as successful permits the general public, government officials, and the judiciary to ignore or marginalize the contemporary needs of Asian Americans.

An early articulation of the model minority theme appeared in *U.S. News & World Report* in 1966:

> At a time when Americans are awash in worry over the plight of racial minorities—
>
> One such minority, the nation's 300,000 Chinese-Americans, is winning wealth and respect by dint of its own hard work.
>
> In any Chinatown from San Francisco to New York, you discover youngsters at grips with their studies. . . .
>
> Still being taught in Chinatown is the old idea that people should depend on their own efforts—not a welfare check—in order to reach America's "promised land."
>
> Visit "Chinatown U.S.A." and you find an important racial minority pulling itself up from hardship and discrimination to become a *model* of self-respect and achievement in today's America.[17]

This "model minority" theme has become a largely unquestioned assumption about current social reality.

At its surface, the label "model minority" seems like a compliment. However, once one moves beyond this complimentary facade, one can see the label for what it is—a tool of oppression which works a dual harm by (1) denying the existence of present-day discrimination against Asian Americans and the present-day effects of past discrimination, and (2) legitimizing the oppression of other racial minorities and poor whites.

That Asian Americans are a "model minority" is a myth. But the myth has gained a substantial following, both inside and outside the Asian American community. The successful inculcation of the model minority myth has created an audience unsympathetic to the problems of Asian Americans. Thus, when we try to make our problems known, our complaints of discrimination or calls for remedial action are seen as unwarranted and inappropriate. They can even spark resentment. For example, Professor Mitsuye Yamada tells a story about the reactions of her Ethnic American Literature class to an anthology compiled by some outspoken Asian American writers:

> [One student] blurted out that she was offended by its militant tone and that as a white person she was tired of always being blamed for the oppression of all the minorities. I noticed several of her classmates' eyes nodding in tacit agreement. A discussion of the "militant" voices in some of the other writings we had read in the course ensued. Surely, I pointed out, some of these other writings have been just as, if not more, militant as the words in this introduction? Had they been offended by those also but failed to express their feelings about them? To my surprise, they said they were not offended by any of the Black American, Chicano or Native American writings, but were hard-pressed to explain why when I asked for an explanation. A little further discussion revealed that they "understood" the anger expressed by the Blacks and Chicanos and they "empathized" with the frustrations and sorrow expressed by the Native Americans. But the *Asian* Americans??

> Then finally, one student said it for all of them: "It made me angry. *Their* anger made *me* angry, because I didn't even know the Asian Americans felt oppressed. I didn't expect their anger."[18]

This story illustrates the danger of the model minority myth: it renders the oppression of Asian Americans invisible. This invisibility has harmful consequences, especially when those in positions of power cannot see:

> To be out of sight is also to be without social services. Thinking Asian Americans have succeeded, government officials have sometimes denied funding for social service programs designed to help Asian Americans learn English and find employment. Failing to realize that there are poor Asian families, college administrators have sometimes excluded Asian-American students from Educational Opportunity Programs (EOP), which are intended for *all* students from low-income families.[19]

In this way, the model minority myth diverts much-needed attention from the problems of many segments of the Asian American community, particularly the Laotians, Hmong, Cambodians, and Vietnamese who have poverty rates of 67.2 percent, 65.5 percent, 46.9 percent, and 33.5 percent, respectively. These poverty rates compare with a national poverty rate of 9.6 percent.

In addition to government officials, this distorted view of the current status of Asian Americans has infected at least one very influential member of the judiciary and legal academy. At a recent conference of the Association of American Law Schools, Judge Posner asked two rhetorical questions: "Are Asians an oppressed group in the United States today? Are they worse off for lacking sizable representation on the faculties of American law schools?"[20] His questions are rhetorical because he already has answers, with figures to back them up: "In 1980, Japanese-Americans had incomes more than 32 percent above the national average income, and Chinese-Americans had incomes more than 12 percent above the national average; Anglo-Saxons and Irish exceeded the average by 5 percent and 2 percent, respectively." He also points out that "in 1980, 17.8 percent of the white population aged 25 and over had completed four or more years of college, compared to 32.9 percent of the Asian-American population."

The unspoken thesis in Judge Posner's comments, which has been stated by other proponents of meritocracy, is "that, when compared to Whites, there are equal payoffs for qualified and educated racial minorities; education and other social factors, but not race, determine earnings."[21] If Posner is right, Asian Americans should make as much as their white counterparts, *taking into account* "education and other social factors, but not race." Yet when we look more carefully at the statistics, we find some interesting anomalies which belie the meritocratic thesis.

First, Posner's reliance on median family income as evidence for lack of discriminatory effects in employment is misleading. It does not take into account that Asian American families have more workers per household than do white families; in fact, "more Asian American women are compelled to work because the male members of their families earn such low wages."[22] Second, the use of national income averages is misleading because most Asian Americans live in locations which have both higher incomes and higher costs of living. Wage disparities become apparent when geographic location is considered. Third, that Asian Americans have a higher percentage of college graduates does not mean that they have economic opportunities commensurate to their level of education. Returns on education rather than educational level provide a better indicator of the existence of discrimination. Many Asian Americans have discovered that they, like other racial minorities, do not get the same return for their educational investment as do their white counterparts.

A closer look, then, at Japanese Americans, Posner's strongest case, reveals flaws in his meritocratic thesis when individual income, geographic location, educational attainment, and hours worked are considered. In 1980, Japanese American men in California earned incomes comparable to those of white men, but "they did so only by acquiring more education (17.7 years compared to 16.8 years for white men twenty-five to forty-four years old) and by working more hours (2,160 hours compared to 2,120 hours for white men in the same age category)."[23] The income disparities for men from other Asian American groups are more glaring.

Thus, the answer to Posner's first question is yes—Asian Americans are an oppressed group in America. To accept the myth of the model minority is to participate in the oppression of Asian Americans.

In addition to hurting Asian Americans, the model minority myth works a dual harm by hurting other racial minorities and poor whites who are blamed for not being successful like Asian Americans. "African-Americans and Latinos and poor whites are told, 'look at those Asians—anyone can make it in this country if they really try.' " This blame is justified by the meritocratic thesis supposedly proven by the example of Asian Americans. This blame is then used to campaign against government social services for these "undeserving" minorities and poor whites and against affirmative action. To the extent that Asian Americans accept the model minority myth, we are complicitous in the oppression of other racial minorities and poor whites.

This blame and its consequences create resentment against Asian Americans among African Americans, Latinos, and poor whites. This resentment, fueled by poor economic conditions, can flare into anger and violence. Asian Americans, the "model minority," serve as convenient scapegoats, as Korean Americans in Los Angeles discovered during the 1992 riots. Many Korean Americans "now view themselves as 'human shields' in a complicated racial hierarchy," caught between "the racism of the white majority and the anger of the black minority."[24] The model minority myth plays a key role in establishing a racial hierarchy which denies the oppression of Asian Americans while simultaneously legitimizing the oppression of other racial minorities and poor whites.

IMMIGRATION AND NATURALIZATION

In 1882, the United States government passed the first of a series of Chinese exclusion acts, specifically targeting Chinese by severely restricting Chinese immigration. These acts culminated in the Geary Act of 1892, an act called the most draconian immigration law of all time. This Act remained in force for over fifty years. To enforce these exclusionary immigration laws, the government set up a special immigration station in 1910 near San Francisco. Here, hundreds of would-be immigrants were detained for months and were often sent back to China. The Angel Island facility, like Alcatraz Prison nearby, was intended to be escape-proof.

The detainment of Chinese immigrants on Angel Island and the discriminatory treatment they received created a sense of alienation and powerlessness not only in the detainees but also in those Chinese already in the United States. The detainees were treated like animals or commodities, forced to live in squalid, cramped quarters. The number of persons of Chinese ancestry dropped from 107,488 in 1890 to 61,639 in 1920. As their numbers dwindled, most Chinese remained within the security and familiarity of ethnic enclave Chinatowns, while others repatriated. The decline in numbers can also be partially attributed to the gender imbalance that hindered family formation.

Immigration laws were soon passed which directly attacked the development of existing Chinese communities in the United States. When it appeared that more Chinese women were immigrating, a new immigration law was passed in 1924:

> One of the law's provisions prohibited the entry of aliens ineligible for citizenship. "The necessity [for this provision]," a congressman stated, "arises from the fact that we do not want to establish additional Oriental families here." This restriction closed tightly the gates for the immigration of Chinese women. "We were beginning to repopulate a little now," a Chinese man said bitterly, "so they passed this law to make us die out altogether."[25]

This provision crippled the development of a stable Chinese American community; and in conjunction with antimiscegenation laws in many states, it effectively emasculated an entire generation of male Chinese immigrants. Men in other Asian American groups underwent similar experiences, although the strategies employed were different.

These discriminatory measures remained largely in effect until the passage of the 1952 McCarran-Walter Act, which permitted the naturalization of Asian immigrants and set token immigration quotas. These quotas, based on national origins quotas established in 1921 and codified in the 1924 National Origins Act, were not changed until 1965 when the McCarran-Walter Act was amended to abolish the national origins system as well as the Asiatic barred zone. The 1965 amendments profoundly affected the development of Asian America.

The 1965 amendments permitted my family to emigrate to the United States from Korea. As an immigrant, I entered this country in the historical context which I have set forth. To an extent, I inherited that legacy of discrimination. I am bound by the still-present stereotype of Asian Americans as "aliens," those who do not belong here and whose presence here is not desired. My colleague at the law school mistakes me for the "copy boy." Those were not his words, but his question as to whether I was "doing copying for the faculty" made me feel very small. When I am stopped by the police for suspicion of possessing a stolen vehicle, their actions and my reactions take place in the context of a history of nonresponsiveness to and active harassment of Asian Americans by police. Maybe it was the kind of car I was driving. Maybe it was the color of my car. Maybe, just maybe, it was the color of my skin.

I find myself in internal and external conflict when I talk about these things. The internal conflict comes from my being an immigrant, and as one I sometimes wonder if I have a right to complain. This point was brought home to me in an anonymous student evaluation after my first year of teaching in law school: "Leave the racist comments out. Go visit Korea if you don't like it here. We need to unite as a country not drive wedges between us."[26] I wonder if this student is right.

However, in the same way that I inherit a legacy of discrimination against Asian Americans, I also inherit a legacy of struggle, a struggle that belongs to both foreign-born and American-born Asian Americans. Early Asian immigrants were not politically insular, as popular American history has painted them. It is our responsibility to bring our forebears back from the silence in which they have been placed. We must recognize that the early Asian immigrants were brave enough to raise their voices. We can do no less.

DISFRANCHISEMENT

When I joined the faculty at my former school, the Dean told me that I could participate in faculty meetings. On the first Tuesday of September, I felt proud to attend my first faculty meeting. I did not know then that it would be the last one I would attend that semester. As issues came up for decision, I voted, just like the other faculty members. It was only after the meeting that I was told that, as a legal writing instructor, I was not allowed to vote. My face turned red. I did not return.

The Dean had not lied to me when he told me that I was allowed to participate in faculty meetings; we simply differed in our interpretation of "participation." From my perspective, the Dean's notion of "participation" was impoverished because I included "meaningful" as part of my definition of "participation."

To an outside observer, it might appear that I stopped going because I did not care about faculty meetings. But when you listen to my story, you will understand that this is not so.

SYSTEMIC disfranchisement—whether at the level of faculty meetings or national elections—discourages many Asian Americans from participating in the political process. This political silence has been attributed to cultural differences and lack of cohesion. These reasons, however, are largely myths created to prevent the enfranchisement of Asian Americans. The low voter registration figures can be attributed to several specific barriers that prevent Asian Americans from participating in a meaningful manner.

The greatest historical barrier to Asian American participation in the political process was that Asian Americans could not become naturalized and could therefore not vote since only citizens had that right. Some states even prohibited American-born Asians from voting. This historical exclusion has an inertia that carries into the present. Yet the dominant culture, and in particular the legislature and judiciary, do not understand because they are largely unaware of this pattern of formally excluding Asian Americans.

Two current apportionment policies dilute Asian American voting strength: (1) the splitting of the Asian American population in an area into several voting districts, and (2) the establishment of at-large election systems in areas of high Asian American population. Attempts to redress Asian American vote dilution are hindered by a United States Supreme Court decision which requires that a minority group "be able to demonstrate that it is sufficiently large and geographically compact to constitute a majority in a single-member district."[27] One problem with this requirement is that it excludes Asian Americans, many of whom are geographically dispersed, at times involuntarily, through the will of the government.

Another formal mechanism that prevents greater voter participation among Asian Americans is the use of English-only ballots. Congress, recognizing the problems with English-only ballots, amended the Voting Rights Act in 1975 and again in 1982 to provide language assistance to "language minorities." However, these measures did not take into account the distinct problems facing Asian Americans. Congress, in establishing that a language minority must constitute at least five percent of the voting age population, did not consider the diversity of languages and cultures among Asian Americans. Thus, even if the Asian American population in a given political subdivision were greater than the requisite five percent, no single Asian American language minority constituted a large enough group to benefit from the Act's provisions. As a result, no Asian American groups were able to claim the status of a "language minority" under that amendment.

This did not change until the voices of Asian Americans spoke our distinct problems into existence. Because Asian Americans were unable to constitute language minorities for the purposes of the 1982 Voting Rights Act, members of the community began to voice concerns and to protest the 1982 Act. Many participated in Roundtable Conferences on Civil Rights sponsored by the United States Commission on Civil Rights. Their efforts led to the 1992 amendment to the Voting Rights Act, which led to the enfranchisement of many Asian Americans.

Achieving enfranchisement is only the first step toward meaningful political participation and social change. The next step is to elect legislators and appoint public officials who will address and respond to the unique needs of Asian Americans. In legislative halls, executive agencies, and judicial chambers, the law is made and implemented, but Asian Americans, perhaps more so than other disempowered groups, have not yet been able to enter these domains in a significant way. Nevertheless, the voting rights example shows how legal reform can be brought about when Asian Americans participate in the political process and give voice to our oppression and our needs.

THE JAPANESE AMERICAN INTERNMENT AND REDRESS

Although it is difficult to determine when exactly the redress movement began, it did not receive national attention until the 1978 Japanese American Citizens League (JACL) national convention. In 1978, the JACL adopted redress as its priority issue and sought a "$25,000 compensation figure plus the creation of a Japanese American Foundation to serve as a trust for funds to be used for the benefit of Japanese American communities throughout the country."[28] The national attention came when Senator S. I. Hayakawa, in an interview during the convention that was carried by newspapers nationwide, called the JACL's demand for redress "absurd and ridiculous."[29] The media attention that followed gave Japanese Americans their first opportunity "to talk publicly about what they experienced during World War II."[30]

Initial reactions to the movement were mixed, both within and without the Japanese American community. Within the Japanese American community, many rejected redress on the ground that no amount of money could compensate for their suffering. Others saw it as a form of welfare, while others thought that it was best not to reopen past wounds. Many were shocked a "model minority" should make such demands.

However, in 1980, the government began to respond to demands for redress with the congressional establishment of the Commission on Wartime Relocation and Internment of Civilians. The Commission held hearings in several cities, at which more than 750 Japanese American internees testified about their experiences. To many, telling their stories provided a much-needed catharsis. The stories also provided a compelling moral force to the claims of redress. One survivor related how he had felt before he was evacuated:

> I went for my last look at our hard work. . . . Why did this thing happen to me now? I went to the storage shed to get the gasoline tank and pour the gasoline on my house, but my wife . . . said don't do it, maybe somebody can use this house; we are civilized people, not savages.[31]

Others described the conditions in the camps. One survivor commented, "I was too young to understand, but I do remember the barbed wire fence from which my parents warned me to stay away. I remember the sight of high guard towers. I remember soldiers carrying rifles, and I remember being afraid."[32] All evacuees were given numbers; the numbering process was a particularly disheartening experience. The internment left a scar on the Nisei; it has become a "point of reference" in their lives.

The Commission released its findings in 1982, concluding that "Executive Order 9066 and the internment that it sanctioned resulted from 'race prejudice, war hysteria, and a failure of political leadership.' "[33] The Commission further presented five recommended remedies. These included a recommendation that an official apology be issued and that each surviving internee be given $20,000. The Commission's report and recommendations as well as the work of Japanese American congressmen paved the way for the redress bill, which was passed by the House in September 1987 and by the Senate in April 1988. The government began making payments on October 9, 1990.

Professor Chan comments that "[t]he redress movement has been a prime example of how Asian American elected officials have worked hand in hand with community activists toward a common end."[34] But this "end" did not come about until the "model minority" broke its silence, demonstrating the power of narrative through testimony about the injustice of the internment camps.

NOTES

1. I was teaching legal writing when I wrote this chapter; I now teach contracts. I have, to an extent, gotten my wish.

2. Jerome M. Culp, Jr., *Toward a Black Legal Scholarship: Race and Original Understandings*, 1991 DUKE L.J. 39, 40.

3. *Id.* at 41.

4. *Id.* at 40.

5. 1 GEORGE SANTAYANA, THE LIFE OF REASON 284 (2d ed. 1922).

6. SUCHENG CHAN, ASIAN-AMERICANS: AN INTERPRETIVE HISTORY 177 (1991). Professor Chan notes that "[a] number of newspaper editorials pointed out that, in essence, the message Judge Kaufman was imparting to the public was that in the state of Michigan, as long as one was employed or was going to school, a license to kill cost only $3,000." *Id.*

7. *See id.* at 178; U.S. COMMISSION ON CIVIL RIGHTS, CIVIL RIGHTS ISSUES FACING ASIAN AMERICANS IN THE 1990s 26 (1992) ("Whereas Detroit in the early 1980s was the scene of a massive campaign against foreign imports, especially those from Japan, a campaign that inflamed anti-Asian sentiments in that city, there had not been the same type of campaign in Cincinnati.").

8. Nativism is the

> intense opposition to an internal minority on the grounds of its foreign (i.e., "un-American") connections. Specific nativistic antagonisms may, and do, vary widely in response to the changing character of minority irritants and the shifting conditions of the day; but through each separate hostility runs the connecting, energizing force of modern nationalism. While drawing on much broader cultural antipathies and ethnocentric judgments, nativism translates them into a zeal to destroy the enemies of a distinctively American way of life.

Juan F. Perea, *Demography and Distrust: An Essay on American Languages, Cultural Pluralism, and Official English*, 77 MINN. L. REV. 269, 278 (1992) (quoting JOHN HIGHAM, STRANGERS IN THE LAND 4 (2d ed. 1988)).

9. Al Kamen, *When Hostility Follows Immigration: Racial Violence Sows Fear in New Jersey's Indian Community*, WASH. POST, Nov. 16, 1992, at A1, A6.

10. *Id.* at A6.

11. Paul Crane & Alfred Larson, *The Chinese Massacre*, 12 ANNALS OF WYOMING 47, 47–49 (1940).

12. Stanley Fish, *Bad Company*, 56 TRANSITION 60, 63 (1992).

13. Ronald E. Yates, *Ishihara's Essays on Japan-US Ties Still Hit the Mark*, CHI. TRIB., Apr. 19, 1992, at C3 (quoting SHINTARO ISHIHARA, THE JAPAN THAT CAN SAY NO: WHY JAPAN WILL BE FIRST AMONG EQUALS (1991)).

14. *See Don't Reject Japanese Pitch*, USA TODAY, Jan. 29, 1992, at 10A. This editorial also points out that, in other countries, United States businesses own "everything from England's Jaguar to corners near Russia's Red Square." *Id.* British investors actually own much more of the United States than do Japanese investors. See Mike Meyers, *Enduring U.S.-Japanese Rivalry Has Roots That Precede World War II*, STAR TRIB. (Minneapolis), Dec. 8, 1991, at 1A.

15. Edwin E. Ferguson, *The California Alien Land Law and the Fourteenth Amendment*, 35 CALIF. L. REV. 61, 77 (1947).

16. *Id.* at 62.

17. *Success Story of One Minority Group in U.S.*, U.S. NEWS & WORLD REP., Dec. 26, 1966, at 73, 73, *reprinted in* ROOTS: AN ASIAN AMERICAN READER 6 (Amy Tachiki et al. eds., 1971) (emphasis added).

18. Mitsuye Yamada, *Invisibility Is an Unnatural Disaster: Reflections of an Asian American Woman, in* THIS BRIDGE CALLED MY BACK: WRITINGS BY RADICAL WOMEN OF COLOR 35, 35 (Cherríe Moraga & Gloria Anzaldúa eds., 1981).

19. RONALD TAKAKI, STRANGERS FROM A DIFFERENT SHORE 478 (1989).

20. Richard A. Posner, *Duncan Kennedy on Affirmative Action*, 1990 DUKE L.J. 1157, 1157 (revised text of speech delivered on January 4, 1991, at Association of American Law Schools convention).

21. Henry Der, *Asian Pacific Islanders and the "Glass Ceiling"—New Era of Civil Rights Activism?: Affirmative Action Policy, in* THE STATE OF ASIAN PACIFIC AMERICA, A PUBLIC POLICY REPORT: POLICY ISSUES TO THE YEAR 2020 215, 219 (LEAP Asian Pac. Am. Pub. Policy Inst. and UCLA Asian Am. Studies Ctr. eds., 1993) (discussing and discrediting the meritocratic thesis).

22. CHAN, *supra* note 6, at 169.

23. TAKAKI, *supra* note 19, at 475.

24. *See* Seth Mydans, *Giving Voice to the Hurt and Betrayal of Korean-Americans*, N.Y. TIMES, May 2, 1993, § 4, at 9 (interviewing Angela Oh, Korean American attorney and president of the Southern California Korean American Bar Association).

25. TAKAKI, *supra* note 19, at 235 (alteration in original). A portion of this law that excluded wives of American citizens was repealed in 1930. *Id.*

26. Anonymous student evaluation, Spring 1993 (copy on file with author).

27. Thornburg v Gingles, 478 U.S. 30, 50 (1986).

28. John Tateishi, *The Japanese American Citizens League and the Struggle for Redress, in* JAPANESE AMERICANS: FROM RELOCATION TO REDRESS 191, 191 (Roger Daniels et al. eds., rev. ed. 1991). The redress issue had been raised within the JACL as early as the 1970 JACL convention in Chicago, but differing views prevented the JACL from reaching a single, coherent position. *Id.*

29. *Id.* at 192. This same Senator S. I. Hayakawa made the following comment in 1971 about the relocation and internment:

All the people I know have a very positive attitude towards it. The ones I know in Chicago say, "We would have never gone to Chicago, if it hadn't been for the wartime relocation. We would have all been hung along a little strip of the Pacific coast and would have never discovered San Francisco, or New York, or Chicago, Omaha, or Minneapolis, where the Japanese are scattered all over the place. So this really gave us a chance to really become Americans instead of residents of Little Tokyo in Los Angeles."

An Interview with S. I. Hayakawa, President of San Francisco State College, in ROOTS, *supra* note 17, at 19, 21.

30. Tateishi, *supra* note 28, at 192. Before then, many Japanese Americans remained silent because they had "been infused with a philosophy that stresses: 'Let's make the most of a bad situation and push ahead,' " and had "internalized the subtle ways in which the larger society reminds one to stay in his place." Isao Fujimoto, *The Failure of Democracy in a Time of Crisis: The War-Time Internment of the Japanese Americans and its Relevance Today, in* ROOTS, *supra* note 17, at 207, 207.

31. COMMISSION ON WARTIME RELOCATION AND INTERNMENT OF CIVILIANS, PERSONAL JUSTICE DENIED 132 (1982) (quoting John Kimoto).

32. *Id.* at 176 (quoting George Takei).

33. CHAN, *supra* note 6, at 174.

34. *Id.*

29 Politics and Passion: Theoretically a Dangerous Liaison

ROBIN D. BARNES

[*Ed.* In the course of reviewing Stephen Carter's *Reflections of an Affirmative Action Baby* (1991) and Patricia Williams's *The Alchemy of Race and Rights* (1991), the author comments as follows on issues of diversity and multiculturalism.]

T H E footage of the vote taken on the floor of the United States Senate following the Judiciary Committee hearings last fall will be forever emblazoned in my mind. Viewers of Justice Clarence Thomas' confirmation process witnessed a prime example of white male domination. Every member of the Judiciary Committee was a white man. Indeed, the Senate itself was all white and ninety-eight percent male. Of course, the Senate is hardly the only bastion of white male privilege. Of the nearly 150 appointments to the U.S. Courts of Appeals by Presidents Nixon, Ford, Reagan, and Bush, ninety-seven percent were white and ninety-three percent were white men. No women of color were appointed.

One of the principal challenges to this pattern of white male domination is the diversity movement. This movement began on the theory that we can eventually have greater equality and justice in the world than has existed under centuries of white male domination. The movement is a natural outgrowth of affirmative action. It is also an independent justification for affirmative action, for it urges that the previously excluded be brought into positions of power not simply to remedy discrimination, but also to provide those institutions the benefit of the participation of all segments of society. Diversifying power, then, is one of the greatest benefits of affirmative action.

While the impact of diversity upon institutions of power has not been studied seriously, mounting anecdotal evidence suggests that diversity proponents are correct. Legislative and judicial diversity may have real consequences for some Americans. Take, for example, legislative differentiation between penalties for the possession of powdered cocaine versus crack-cocaine. Recently, five African-

101 Yale L.J. 1631 (1992). Originally published in the Yale Law Journal. Reprinted by permission of The Yale Law Journal Company and Fred B. Rothman & Company.

American defendants challenged a Minnesota statutory scheme that provided for 48 months imprisonment for crack possession and 12 months imprisonment for cocaine possession. According to the plaintiffs, because 96.69 percent of those charged with crack possession were Black, and 79.6 percent of those charged with cocaine possession were white, the statutes had a discriminatory impact on Blacks. An African-American woman, Judge Pamela Alexander, ruled that the state had made an insufficient showing with respect to the pharmacological differences between the two forms of cocaine to justify the disparate impact of the sanctions on African Americans.[1] While Judge Alexander's race did not determine the outcome of the decision, her experiences as a Black American undoubtedly heightened her sensitivity to the possible disparate impact.

I have seen the impact of diversity in the hiring of law school faculty as well. Not long ago I witnessed the process of filling a long-term adjunct position at a high-ranking law school. Three white male members of the hiring committee, all good liberals, had a white male friend that they honestly believed would have filled the position well. No doubt he would have. But for the fact that two women also sat on the committee, the friend might have received the position immediately, without any fuss. However, the women insisted that the committee hold the position open for a while to consider women and persons of color, and ultimately prevailed. While these white male faculty members are guilty of no malice, what almost occurred would have been totally exclusionary, regardless of motive or intent. Had these women—both beneficiaries of affirmative action—not been members of this committee, they would not have been able to negotiate for what men often take for granted, the mere *opportunity* for inclusion.

Of course, to accept the diversity rationale one must also accept the notion that Blacks and women have distinctive perspectives directly linked to their race and gender. Carter criticizes this notion, but he also seems to accept it, if only to a limited extent. He says, "[W]e should love and value us, black people in all of our diversity: rich, poor, gay, straight, religious, secular, left, right. For it is none of these distinctions that define our blackness; what defines us, rather, is the society's attitude toward us—all of us are black before we are anything else. . . ."[2]

Nevertheless, some continue to deny experiential knowledge. Critics of this approach advance two main arguments. The first questions the source and/or nature of unique minority perspectives. It challenges the view that "people of color have a distinctive voice, a vision of the world, that is not being represented in the [lily-white] places where vital decisions are being made,"[3] by asking who has this special voice, where does it come from, and how did they get it?[4] The second asserts that any theory of essentialism limits scholars of color and makes them fungible commodities, ultimately hurting minority intellectuals. Academicians who believe that racial minorities provide unique perspectives have been characterized as, at best, romanticizing the notion that skin color manifests a particular social consciousness, and, at worst, engaging in militarizing discourse to advance hidden political agendas that ostensibly include passing off second-rate scholarship as meritorious.[5]

I understand diversity's proponents to be arguing that racial minorities have, at the very least, a dual perspective. On the one hand, we can see how "old-fashioned American values" foster success in this society. On the other hand, we also recognize the extent to which we, and/or countless members of our socially subordinated group, are being pushed to the edge to observe this success from the periphery.[6] If whites, particularly white men, have witnessed firsthand the extent to which they, and/or members of their socially elevated group, are being pushed over others toward center stage and receiving greater access to positions of power, they are not writing narratives describing these experiences. Unsurprisingly, those who are excluded are writing such narratives. Particularly in the university setting, diversity of people, viewpoints, and experiences in both scholarship and presence allows for more opportunities to influence decisionmaking. The opportunity for scholars, from the United States and abroad, to encounter other perspectives lies at the heart of academic freedom.

As Williams argues: "It's important to hire [blacks] because the presence of blacks within, as opposed to without, the bell jar of a given community changes the dynamic forever."[7] Carter also recognizes that "we do have background and experiences and visions that it is important to share."[8] Carter describes having unifying relationships with his Black students.[9] Carter only mentions his Black students, and the reason, I think, speaks for itself. Racism per se is encountered under predictable circumstances in the inner city, but as we attempt to move away from that boundary and into the mainstream many would agree with Carter's statement: "Racism has done more than touch me. It has helped to shape me, just as the modern diversity movement would insist."[10]

Unfortunately, while recognizing the influence of racism in shaping consciousness, Carter singles out for criticism individuals who have responded to it. For example, he criticizes the Harvard student protest upon Derrick Bell's brief departure. When protesting students demanded a person of color to teach a civil rights course formerly taught by Derrick Bell, their actions did not, to my mind, express disdain for Jack Greenberg (a leading white civil rights lawyer and instructor), his commitment to social and political equality, or his competency as litigator.[11] Members of Harvard's student body, alongside some of its affirmative action babies, simply wanted to voice their desire for Derrick Bell's distinct perspective on civil rights.

One of the more controversial issues raised by those who dissent from the minority viewpoint school is the emphatic rejection of theories that treat Blacks as a monolith. This argument notes that Blacks have varying religious, sexual, and political orientations, and myriad education and income levels. It questions whether, in light of these differences, a shared skin color can make us all the same. The answer, of course, is that it cannot. Many Arab Americans and Mexican Americans have dark brown skin, and ostensibly their world perspectives differ from those of American slaves' descendants.

But while skin color alone means nothing, the shared experience that accompanies that skin color has great significance. Even middle-class Blacks, many of whom operate in environments that are largely white, are aware of and share many of those experiences. How is it that, unrelentingly, four generations of women—my grandmother, my mother, myself, and my daughter—no matter what era we have lived through, region we have settled in, or life chances we have received, have all experienced almost identical treatment at each stage of our lives? Black Americans read, hear, and observe the experiences of other Blacks and think of corresponding incidents in their own lives and the lives of their families.

Although Williams and Carter adopt somewhat different attitudes toward the racial distinctiveness thesis, one of the most remarkable features of these two books is the extent to which both authors, one explicitly and the other implicitly, provide strong evidence of a distinct shared perspective. I suspect that Pat Williams and Stephen Carter have much in common in terms of life experiences and "advantages." Yet they interpret their own experiences, and those of others, in very different ways. They reach radically different conclusions and use very different language. Despite these differences, a strong commonality binds the two, a commonality that must stem from race. In distinct ways, both Williams and Carter tell stories about being outsiders.

Williams recounts that a couple of years ago, during the holidays in New York City, she was pressing her "round brown face" up to the pane of glass at the door of a Benetton's store."[12] She wanted to enter and look at a sweater for her mother. She remembers having a pink wad of rubber burst in her face as the gum-chewing-boy-clerk refused to buzz her in, past the locked door, at one o'clock in the afternoon. He told her that the store was closed. She could plainly see that other customers, all white, were shopping around for sweaters for *their* mothers. Williams was enraged. She made a large poster describing the incident and taped it to the store's window after its actual closing. She describes the experience as devaluing, a removal not only from "the market but from the pseudo-spiritual circle of psychic and civic communion."[13]

Carter also depicts outsider experiences. For instance, he describes himself as young, ambitious, and ready to prove himself in high school. He writes that during his senior year he received a phone call from an academic counselor informing him that he had won a National Achievement Scholarship for college, designated for high-achieving Black students.[14] According to the caller, acceptance of this award would preclude his receiving a National Merit Scholarship, designated for the highest-achieving students of any race. The recipients of this second scholarship, for which he and his white friends were competing, had yet to be announced. The caller responded to his questions about preclusion by stating that "people who get National Achievement Scholarships are never good enough to get National Merit Scholarships."[15] Carter accepted the award only to discover, a short time later, that his standardized test scores were higher and grades comparable to those of white students who received what Carter assesses to be the more prestigious scholarship. As one who despises everything that implies that Blacks cannot compete with whites intellectually, Carter notes that "I still wish the National Merit Scholarship people had given me the chance to prove it."[16]

Carter, throughout much of the book, describes the span of his career as a continuum along similar lines. He lashes out at being labeled. He complains of being boxed in, expected to provide the sideshow for the benefit of others: see the jig-a-boo dance the civil rights or neoconservative shuffle; he is among the best jigs we know.

Peering into the Benetton window, Williams saw her personhood excluded from the realm of visibility. Carter sees himself as an intellectual who has been placed into a box that others peer into—once they discover the color of his skin they attach whatever label they deem appropriate.[17] He describes this as a threat to his individuality since he believes that it is now uncommon to look beyond skin color. Race is used as a proxy for whatever is convenient and consistent with the labeler's own political agenda.

Both authors share an awareness that, notwithstanding their individual characteristics, to outside observers they are first, last, and always Blacks. This shared racial consciousness between two such dissimilar authors is itself a deeply powerful argument for the diversity movement, and, ultimately, for affirmative action.

NOTES

1. *See* State v. Russell, 477 N.W.2d 886 (Minn. 1991) (affirming trial court decision).

2. STEPHEN L. CARTER, REFLECTIONS OF AN AFFIRMATIVE ACTION BABY 204 (1991).

3. Stephen L. Carter, *I Am an Affirmative Action Baby*, N.Y. TIMES, Aug. 5, 1991, at 13.

4. *See, e.g.,* Randall Kennedy, *Racial Critiques of Legal Academia,* 102 HARV. L. REV. 1745, 1778–87, 1801–07 (1989).

5. CARTER, *supra* note 2, at 33.

6. Kennedy, *supra* note 4, at 1767, 1769–70.

7. PATRICIA J. WILLIAMS, THE ALCHEMY OF RACE AND RIGHTS 101 (1991).

8. CARTER, *supra* note 2, at 203.

9. *Id.* at 99–100.

10. *Id.* at 75–76.

11. *Id.* at 41–44.

12. *See* WILLIAMS, *supra* note 7, at 44–46.

13. Id. at 71.

14. CARTER, *supra* note 2, at 47–69.

15. *Id.* at 49.

16. *Id.* at 69. In fact, after the publication of his book Carter revealed that he had misremembered the incident and that he had not been precluded from consideration for the National Merit Scholarship upon accepting the National Achievement Scholarship. Instead, he was considered for, and failed to win, a National Merit Scholarship. *See* Stephen L. Carter, *"Best Black" Syndrome: My Bitter Memory; Somehow, for Twenty Years, I Was Haunted by a Slight That Never Happened,* WASH. POST, Oct. 13, 1991, at C5.

17. According to Carter, several labels have been affixed to Black professionals, among them: "CAUTION: BLACK LEFT-WING ACTIVIST, HANDLE WITH CARE OR BE ACCUSED OF RACISM," "CAUTION: BLACK NEOCONSERVATIVE, PROBABLY A NUT CASE," "WARNING! AFFIRMATIVE ACTION BABY! DO NOT ASSUME THAT THIS INDIVIDUAL IS QUALIFIED!" CARTER, *supra* note 2, at 2.

From the Editor: Issues and Comments

A R E Kennedy and Farber and Sherry right that left-leaning racial reformers do not speak for all of the minority community? And if so, what follows from this— should they cease speaking, merely moderate their claims, or speak even more strenuously so as to convince those (few?) in their communities who remain unconvinced? Should minority communities demonstrate solidarity by embracing their own offenders as much as possible—or should they distance themselves from those offenders and call for swift, harsh punishment? Is the notion of group conflict between minorities a myth, constructed by the white press to serve the purposes of elite whites, and in particular to discredit the multicultural movement? Is focus on distinctness, and a small unit of analysis, debilitating for the cause of racial reform—or does genuine reform spring mainly from small, relatively homogeneous groups?

For further impressive commentary on essentialism and minority communities, see the book by Stephen Carter in the Suggested Readings, following. See also the article there by Gerald Torres on the decline of the universalist ideal and its replacement by local, or "plural," justice.

Suggested Readings

Austin, Regina, *Black Women, Sisterhood, and the Difference/Deviance Divide*, 26 NEW ENG. L. REV. 877 (1992).

Calmore, John O., *Exploring the Significance of Race and Class in Representing the Black Poor*, 61 OR. L. REV. 201 (1982).

CARTER, STEPHEN, REFLECTIONS OF AN AFFIRMATIVE ACTION BABY (1991).

Haney López, Ian, *Community Ties, Race, and Faculty Hiring: The Case for Professors Who Dont Think White*, 1 RECONSTRUCTION No. 3, 1991, at 46.

Scales-Trent, Judy, *Commonalities: On Being Black and White, Different, and the Same*, 2 YALE J.L. & FEMINISM 305 (1990).

Scarborough, Cathy, *Conceptualizing Black Women's Employment Experiences*, 98 YALE L.J. 1457 (1989).

Torres, Gerald, *Critical Race Theory: The Decline of the Universalist Ideal and the Hope of Plural Justice—Some Observations and Questions of an Emerging Phenomenon*, 75 MINN. L. REV. 993 (1991).

VIII

CULTURAL NATIONALISM AND SEPARATISM

A THEME that recurs insistently in much Critical Race writing is the idea of cultural nationalism. Nationalism, almost a defining motif of the movement, insists that people of color can best promote their own interest through separation from the American mainstream. Nationalists hold that black and brown communities should develop their own schools, colleges, businesses, and security forces. Some believe that preserving diversity will benefit not just minority communities but the majority-race one as well. Rooted in W.E.B. Du Bois's philosophy and the Black Panther and Muslim movements of the 1960s and 1970s, cultural nationalism retains enormous vitality today in left and Critical movements.

Part VIII begins with an excerpt from *Rodrigo's Chronicle,* by Richard Delgado, in which "Rodrigo," the author's alter ego, puts forward his audacious assessment of Western culture, including his view that the dominant culture needs the ideas and talents of people of color more than the other way around. Following are a portion of Richard Delgado's *Michigan Law Review* article rejecting the role-model argument for affirmative action and a portion of an article by Alex Johnson explaining the theory of cultural nationalism. Finally, law and education specialist Kevin Brown puts forward the case for Afrocentric immersion schools for black youth, analyzing some of the legal and policy problems these schools present. (An important related article by Robert Cottrol and Raymond Diamond, on arming and defending the black community appears in Part III.)

30 Rodrigo's Chronicle

RICHARD DELGADO

Introduction: Enter Rodrigo

"Excuse me, Professor, I'm Rodrigo Crenshaw. I believe we have an appointment."

Startled, I put down the book I was reading and glanced quickly first at my visitor, then at my desk calendar. The tall, rangy man standing in my doorway was of indeterminate age—somewhere between twenty and forty—and, for that matter, ethnicity. His tightly curled hair and olive complexion suggested that he might be African American. But he could also be Latino, perhaps Mexican, Puerto Rican, or any one of the many Central American nationalities that have been applying in larger numbers to my law school in recent years.

"Come in," I said. "I think I remember a message from you, but I seem not to have entered it into my appointment book. Please excuse all this confusion," I added, pointing to the pile of papers and boxes that had littered my office floor since my recent move. I wondered: Was he an undergraduate seeking admission? A faculty candidate of color like the many who seek my advice about entering academia? I searched my memory without success.

"Please sit down," I said. "What can I do for you?"

"I'm Geneva Crenshaw's brother. I want to talk to you about the LSAT, as well as the procedure for obtaining an appointment as a law professor at an American university."

As though sensing my surprise, my visitor explained: "Shortly after Geneva's accident, I moved to Italy with my father, Lorenzo, who was in the Army. After he retired, we remained in Italy, where he worked as a civilian at the same base where he had been serving. I finished high school at the base, then attended an Italian university, earning my law degree last June. I've applied for the LL.M. program at a number of U.S. law schools, including your own. I want to talk to you about the LSAT, which all the schools want me to take, and which, believe it or not, I've never taken. I'd also like to discuss my chances of landing a teaching position after I earn the degree."

[Ed. Rodrigo and the Professor next discuss the LSAT, affirmative action, and the law school hiring market. They then continue their conversation as follows.]

101 YALE L.J. 1357 (1992). Originally published in the Yale Law Journal. Reprinted by permission of The Yale Law Journal Company and Fred B. Rothman & Company.

In Which Rodrigo Begins to Seem a Little Demented

"A recent article [Rodrigo said] pointed out that nearly three-fourths of articles on equality or civil rights published in the leading journals during the last five years were written by women or minorities.[1] Ten years ago, the situation was reversed: minorities were beginning to publish, but their work was largely ignored.[2] The same is true in other areas as well. Critical legal studies and other modernist and postmodern approaches to law are virtually the norm in the top reviews. Formalism has run its course."

"Perhaps," I said. "You don't see many articles in the classic vein today. In fact, I haven't seen one of those plodding, case-crunching, 150-page blockbusters with 600 footnotes in a top journal for a while."

"No one believes that way of writing is useful anymore. Some are writing chronicles. Others are writing about storytelling in the law, narrative theory, or 'voice' scholarship. The feminists are writing about changing the terms of legal discourse and putting women at the center. Even 'mainstream' writers—the serious ones, at any rate—have moved beyond mere doctrinal analysis to realms such as political theory, legal history, and interdisciplinary analysis. There is a whole new emphasis on legal culture, perspective, and on what some call 'positionality,' as well as a renewed focus on the sociopolitical dimension of judging and legal reasoning."

"I'm not up on all these postmodern approaches, Rodrigo," I said quickly, "although I have read your friend and countryman Antonio Gramsci who, as you say, got into trouble with the authorities.[3] I find his work quite helpful. And I gather that the current ferment in American law is one of the reasons why you are thinking of returning here for your graduate degree?"

"In part. But I was mainly responding to your earlier question about the irony of multiculturalism. However progressive certain mainstream scholars may be in their writing and analysis, the institutions they control still exclude and oppress minorities by manipulating the status quo and refusing to challenge their own informal expectations. The irony is that the old, dying order is resisting the new, rather than welcoming it with open arms."

Hmm. I thought of the words of a Bob Dylan song,[4] but instead asked: "And just who, or what, do you think this new order is, Rodrigo?"

"Well, let me put it this way," Rodrigo explained. "You've heard, I assume, of double consciousness?"

"Of course. It's W.E.B. Du Bois' term.[5] It refers to the propensity of excluded people to see the world in terms of two perspectives at the same time—that of the majority race, according to which they are demonized, despised, and reviled, and their own, in which they are normal. Lately, some—particularly feminists of color—have invented the term 'multiple consciousness' to describe their experience."

"And you know that many members of minority groups speak two languages, grow up in two cultures?"

"Of course, especially our Hispanic brothers and sisters; for them, bilingualism is as much an article of faith as, say, Martin Luther King and his writings are for African Americans."

"And so," Rodrigo continued, "who has the advantage in mastering and applying critical social thought? Who tends to think of everything in two or more ways at the same time? Who is a postmodernist virtually as a condition of his or her being?"

"I suppose you are going to say us—people of color."

Rodrigo hesitated. "Remember that I have been sitting in Italian law libraries all these years, reading and learning about legal movements in the United States secondhand. I suppose it looks different to you here."

"It has scarcely been a bed of roses," I replied dryly.[6] "The old order, as you put it, has not welcomed the new voices with any great warmth, although I must agree that the law reviews seem much more open to them than my faculty colleagues. And your notion that it is we—persons of color—who have the edge in mastering critical analysis would strike most of my majority-race colleagues as preposterous. If double consciousness turns out to be an advantage, they'll either deny it exists or insist that they can have it too.[7] Aren't you just trying to invert the hierarchy, placing at the top a group that until now has occupied the bottom— and isn't this just as wrong as what the others have been doing to us?"

Rodrigo paused. "I see your point. But maybe this way of looking at things seems harsh only because it is so unfamiliar. In my circles everyone talks about the decline of Western thought, so finding evidence of it in law and legal scholarship doesn't seem so strange. I'm surprised it does to you. Are you familiar with the term 'false consciousness?' "[8]

"Yes, of course," I said (with some irritation—the impudent pup!). "It's a mechanism whereby oppressed people take on the consciousness of the oppressor group, adjusting to and becoming parties to their own oppression. And I suppose you think I'm laboring under some form of it?"

"Not you, Professor. Far from it. But when you rebuked me a moment ago, I wondered if you weren't in effect counseling *me* to internalize the views of the majority group about such things as hierarchy and the definition of a 'troublemaker.' "

"Perhaps," I admitted. "But my main concern is for you and your prospects. If you want to succeed in your LL.M. studies, not to mention in landing a professorship at a U.S. law school, perhaps you had better 'cool it' for a while. Criticizing mainstream scholarship is one thing; everyone expects that from young firebrands like you. But this business about a more general 'decline of the West'— that's out of our field, frowned on as flaky rhetoric, and nearly impossible to support with evidence. Even if you did have evidence to support your claims, no one would want to listen to you."

"Yes, I suppose so," admitted Rodrigo. "It's not the story you usually hear. If I had told you that I'm returning to the United States because it's the best country on earth, with rosy prospects, a high quality of life, and the fairest political system for minorities, your countrymen would accept that without question. No one would think of asking me for documentation, even though that is surely as much an empirical claim as its opposite."

"You're right," I said. "The dominant story always seems true and unexceptionable, not in need of proof. I've written about that myself, along with others.[9] And you and I discussed a case of it earlier when we talked about minority hiring. But tell me more about your thoughts on the West."

"Well, as I mentioned, my program of studies at Bologna centered on the history of Western culture. I'm mainly interested in the rise of Northern European thought and its contribution to our current predicament. During my early work I had hoped to extend my analysis to law and legal thought."

"I think I know what you will say about legal thought and scholarship. Tell me more about the big picture—how you see Northern European thought."

"I've been studying its rise in the late Middle Ages and decline beginning a few decades ago. I'm interested in what causes cultures to evolve, then go into eclipse. American society, even more than its European counterparts, is in the early stages of dissolution and crisis. It's like a wave that is just starting to crest. As you know, waves travel unimpeded across thousands of miles of ocean. When they approach the shore, they rise up for a short time, then crest and lose their energy. Western culture, particularly in this country, is approaching that stage. Which explains, in part, why I am back."

I had already switched off my telephone. Now, hearing my secretary's footsteps, I stepped out into the hallway to tell her to cancel my appointments for the rest of the afternoon. I had a feeling I wanted to hear what this strange young thinker had to say undisturbed. When I returned, I saw Rodrigo eyeing my computer inquiringly.

Returning his gaze to me, Rodrigo went on: "I'm sure all the things I'm going to say have occurred to you. Northern Europeans have been on top for a relatively short period—a mere wink in the eye of history. And during that time they have accomplished little—except causing a significant number of deaths and the disruption of a number of more peaceful cultures, which they conquered, enslaved, exterminated, or relocated on their way to empire. Their principal advantages were linear thought, which lent itself to the development and production of weapons and other industrial technologies, and a kind of messianic self-image according to which they were justified in dominating other nations and groups. But now, as you can see"—Rodrigo gestured in the direction of the window and the murky air outside—"Saxon-Teuton culture has arrived at a terminus, demonstrating its own absurdity."

"I'm not sure I follow you. Linear thought, as you call it, has surely conferred many benefits.[10] And is it really on its last legs? Aside from smoggy air, Western culture looks firmly in control to me."

"So does a wave, even when it's cresting—and you know what happens shortly thereafter. Turn on your computer, Professor," Rodrigo said, pointing at my new terminal. "Let me show you a few things."

For the next ten minutes, Rodrigo led me on a tour of articles and books on the West's economic and political condition. His fingers fairly danced over the keys of my computer. Accessing databases I didn't even know existed, he showed me treatises on the theory of cultural cyclicity, articles and editorials from *The Economist, Corriere della Sera*, the *Wall Street Journal*, and other leading newspapers, all on our declining economic position; material from *The Statistical Abstract* and other sources on our increasing crime rate, rapidly dwindling fossil fuels, loss of markets, and switch from a production- to a service-based economy with high unemployment, an increasingly restless underclass, and increasing rates of drug addiction, suicide, and infant mortality. It was a sobering display of technical virtuosity. I had the feeling he had done this before and wondered how he had come by this proficiency while in Italy.

Rodrigo finally turned off the computer and looked at me inquiringly. "A bibliography alone will not persuade me," I said. "But let's suppose for the sake of argument that you have made a prima facie case, at least with respect to our economic problems and to issues concerning race and the underclass. I suppose you have a theory on how we got into this predicament?"

"I do," Rodrigo said with that combination of brashness and modesty that I find so charming in the young. "As I mentioned a moment ago, it has to do with linear thought—the hallmark of the West. When developed, it conferred a great initial advantage. Because of it, the culture was able to spawn, early on, classical physics, which, with the aid of a few borrowings here and there, like gunpowder from the Chinese, quickly enabled it to develop impressive armies. And, because it was basically a ruthless, restless culture, it quickly dominated others that lay in its path. It eradicated ones that resisted, enslaved others, and removed the Indians, all in the name of progress. It opened up and mined new territories—here and elsewhere—as soon as they became available and extracted all the available mineral wealth so rapidly that fossil fuels and other mineral goods are now running out, as you and your colleagues have pointed out."

"But you are indicting just one civilization. Haven't all groups acted similarly? Non-linear societies are accomplishing at least as much environmental destruction as Western societies are capable of. And what about Genghis Khan, Columbus, the cruelties of the Chinese dynasties? The Turkish genocide of the Armenians, the war machine that was ancient Rome?"

"True. But at least these other groups limited their own imperial impulses at some point."

"Hah! With a little help from their friends," I retorted.

"Anyway," continued Rodrigo, "these groups produced valuable art, music, or literature along the way. Northern Europeans have produced next to nothing—little sculpture, art, or music worth listening to, and only a modest amount of truly great literature. And the few accomplishments they can cite with pride can be traced to the Egyptians, an African culture."[11]

"Rodrigo, you greatly underestimate the dominant culture. Some of them may be derivative and warlike, as you say. Others are not; they are creative and humane. And even the ones you impeach have a kind of dogged ingenuity for which you do not give them credit. They have the staying and adaptive powers to remain on top. For example, when linear physics reached a dead end, as you pointed out, they developed relativity physics. When formalism expired, at least some of them developed Critical Legal Studies, reaching back and drawing on existing strands of thought such as psychoanalysis, phenomenology, Marxism, and philosophy of science."

"Good point," admitted Rodrigo a little grudgingly, "although I've already pointed out the contributions of Gramsci, a Mediterranean. Fanon and your Critical Race Theory friends are Black or brown. And Freud and Einstein are, of course, Jews. Consider, as well, Cervantes, Verdi, Michelangelo, Duke Ellington, the current crop of Black writers—non-Saxons all."

"But Northern Europeans, at least in the case of the two Jewish giants," I interrupted.

"True, people move," he countered.

"Don't be flip," I responded. "Since when are the Spanish and Italians exempt from criticism for 'Western' foibles? What about the exploitive capacity of the colonizing conquistadors? Wasn't the rise of commercial city-states in Renaissance Italy a central foundation for subsequent European cultural imperialism? Most ideas of Eurocentric superiority date to the Renaissance and draw on its rationalist, humanist intellectual, and artistic traditions."

"We've had our lapses," Rodrigo conceded. "But theirs are far worse and more systematic." Rodrigo was again eyeing my computer.

Wondering what else he had in mind, I continued: "What about Rembrandt, Mozart, Shakespeare, Milton? And American popular culture—is it not the envy of the rest of the world? What's more, even if some of our Saxon brothers and sisters are doggedly linear, or, as you put it, exploitive of nature and warlike, surely you cannot believe that their behavior is biologically based—that there is something genetic that prevents them from doing anything except invent and manufacture weapons?" Rodrigo's earnest and shrewd retelling of history had intrigued me, although, to be honest, I was alarmed. Was he an Italian Louis Farrakhan?[12]

"The Saxons do all that, plus dig up the earth to extract minerals that are sent to factories that darken the skies, until everything runs out and we find ourselves in the situation where we are now." Then, after a pause: "Why do you so strongly resist a biological explanation, Professor? Their own scientists are happy to conjure up and apply them to us.[13] But from one point of view, it is they whose exploits—or rather lack of them—need explaining."

"I'd love to hear your evidence."

"Let me begin this way. Do you remember that famous photo of the finish of the hundred-meter dash at the World Games this past summer? It showed six magnificent athletes straining to break the tape. The first two finished under the world record. All were Black."

"I do remember."

"Black athletes dominated most of the events, the shorter ones at any rate. People of color are simply faster and quicker than our white brothers and sisters. Even the marathon has come to be dominated by people of color. And, to anticipate your question, yes I do believe the same holds true in the mental realm. In the ghetto they play 'the dozens'[14]—a game that requires throwaway speed. The dominant group has nothing similar. And take your field, law. Saxons developed the hundred-page linear, densely footnoted, impeccably crafted article—saying, in most cases, very little. They also brought us the LSAT, which tests the same boring, linear capacities they developed over time and that now exclude the very voices they need for salvation. Yet you, Matsuda, Lawrence, Torres, Peller, and others toss off articles with ridiculous ease—critical thought comes easy for you, hard for them. I can't, of course, prove your friends are genetically inferior; it may be their mindset or culture. But they act like lemmings. They go on building factories until the natural resources run out, thermonuclear weapons when their absurdity is realized and everyone knows they cannot be used, hundred-page law review articles that rehash cases when everyone knows that vein of thought has run dry—and they fail even to sense their own danger. You say they are adaptive. I doubt it."

"Rodrigo," I burst in. "You seriously misread the times. Your ideas on cultural superiority and inferiority will obviously generate resistance, as you yourself concede. Wait till you see how they respond to your hundred-yard-dash example; you're sure to find *yourself* labeled as racist. Maybe we both are—half the time I agree with you. But even the other things you say about the West's predicament and its need for an infusion of new thought—things I strongly agree with—will fall on deaf ears. All the movement is the other way. This is a time of retrenchment. The country is listening to the conservatives, not to people like you and me."

"I know," said Rodrigo. "I've been reading about that retrenchment. We do get the *New York Times* in Italy, even if it comes a few days late."

"And so you must know about conservative writers like Allan Bloom, Thomas Sowell, Glenn Loury, Roger Kimball, Shelby Steele, E. D. Hirsch, and Dinesh D'Souza and the tremendous reception they have been receiving, both in popular circles and in the academy?"

"Yes. I read D'Souza on the flight over, in fact. Like the others, he has a number of insightful things to say. But he's seriously wrong—and hardly represents the wave of the future, as you fear."

"They certainly represent the present," I grumbled. "I can't remember a period—except perhaps the late 1950's—when I have seen such resistance to racial reform. The public seems tired of minorities, and the current Administration is no different. The backlash is apparent in the university setting as well: African-American studies departments are underfunded and the exclusionary Eurocentric curriculum is making a comeback."

"But it's ordinary, natural—and will pass," Rodrigo responded. "In troubled times, a people turns to the past, to its own more glorious period. That's why these neoconservative writers are popular—they preach that the culture need not change direction to survive, but only do the things it did before, harder and more energetically."

"What our psychologist friends call 'perseveration,' " I said.

"Exactly. In my studies, I found that most beleaguered people do this, plus search for a scapegoat—a group they can depict as the source of all their troubles."

"An old story," I agreed ruefully. "D'Souza, for example, places most of the blame for colleges' troubles at the doorstep of those demanding minorities who, along with a few deluded white sympathizers, have been broadening the curriculum, instituting Third World courses, hiring minority professors, and recruiting 'unqualified' students of color—all at the expense of academic rigor and standards.[15] He says the barbarians—meaning us—are running the place[16] and urges university administrators to hold the line against what he sees as bullying and a new form of racism."[17]

"Have you ever thought it curious," Rodrigo mused, "how some whites can see themselves as victimized by us—a pristine example of the sort of post-modern move they profess to hate. I suppose if one has been in power a long time, any change seems threatening, offensive, unprincipled, and wrong. But reality eventually intervenes. Western culture's predicament runs very deep—every indicator shows it. And, there are straws in the wind, harbingers of hopeful change."

"Rodrigo, I'll say this for you—you've proposed a novel approach to affirmative action. Until now, we've struggled with finding a moral basis for sustaining what looked like breaches of the merit principle, like hiring a less qualified person over a more qualified person for racial reasons. But you're saying that white people should welcome nonwhites into their fold as rapidly as possible out of simple self-interest—that is, if they want their society to survive. This is something that they are not accustomed to hearing, to put it mildly. Do you have any support for *this* assertion?"

"Turn on your computer again, Professor. This won't take but a minute."

I obliged him, and was treated to a second lightning display of technological wizardry as Rodrigo showed me books on Asian business organization, Eastern mysticism, Japanese schooling, ancient Egyptian origins of modern astronomy and physics, and even on the debt our Founding Fathers owed the Iroquois for the political ideas that shaped our Constitution. He showed me articles on the Japanese computer and automobile industries, the seemingly more successful approach that African and Latino societies have taken to family organization and the treatment of their own aged and destitute, and even the roots of popular American music in Black composers and groups.

"It's only a beginning," Rodrigo said, switching off my computer. "I want to make this my life's work. Do you think anyone will listen to me?"

NOTES

1. Richard Delgado, *The Imperial Scholar Revisited: How to Marginalize Outsider Writing, Ten Years Later,* 140 U. PA. L. REV. 1349 (1992); *see also* Alex M. Johnson, Jr., *The New Voice of Color,* 100 YALE L.J. 2007 (1991).

2. Richard Delgado, *The Imperial Scholar: Reflections on a Review of Civil Rights Literature,* 132 U. PA. L. REV. 561 (1984).

3. *See* ANTONIO GRAMSCI, LETTERS FROM PRISON (Lynne Lawner ed. & trans., 1973).

4. "You know, they rejected Jesus, too. / I said, 'you're not Him.' " BOB DYLAN, *115th Dream, on* BRINGING IT ALL BACK HOME (Columbia/CBS Records 1965).

5. W.E.B. DU BOIS, THE SOULS OF BLACK FOLK 16–17 (1903); *see also* RALPH ELLISON, INVISIBLE MAN (1952). For contemporary explications of double consciousness, see BELL HOOKS, FEMINIST THEORY: FROM MARGIN TO CENTER (1984).

6. *E.g.,* Derrick Bell, *The Price and Pain of Racial Perspective,* THE JOURNAL (Stanford Law School), May 9, 1986, at 5.

7. Randall L. Kennedy, *Racial Critiques of Legal Academia,* 102 HARV. L. REV. 1745 (1989) (questioning whether a single minority "voice" exists or, if it does, whether it is limited to blacks).

8. *See* GEORG LUKÁCS, HISTORY AND CLASS CONSCIOUSNESS (Rodney Livingstone trans., 1971); Duncan Kennedy, *Antonio Gramsci and the Legal System* 6 A.L.S.A. FORUM 32 (1982).

9. I thought of the recent spate of writing on narrativity and the way in which law's dominant stories change very slowly. If legal culture does resist insurgent thought until it is too late—until it has lost the power to transform us—what does this bode for Rodrigo? *See, e.g.,* GRAMSCI, *supra* note 3.

10. I thought of countless examples. Just that morning I had read about a new medical breakthrough developed at an American research university. Only two weeks ago I had my car rebuilt by a mechanic who (I hope) was well versed in linear thought. The day before I had baked a batch of brownies following a 10-step recipe.

11. MARTIN BERNAL, BLACK ATHENA I (1987); MARTIN BERNAL, BLACK ATHENA II (1991).

12. I thought of recent writings condemning the sin of "essentialism." *E.g.,* Angela P. Harris, *Race and Essentialism in Feminist Legal Theory,* 42 STAN. L. REV. 581 (1990). The writings of early anthropologists (and a few latter-day pseudo-scientists) purporting to find race-based differences in intellectual endowment also came to mind. *See infra.*

13. *See, e.g.,* Stephen J. Gould, The Mismeasure of Man 30–72 (1981); NANCY STEPAN, THE IDEA OF RACE IN SCIENCE (1982); Richard Delgado et al., *Can Science Be Inopportune?* 31 UCLA L. REV. 128 (1983).

14. A game involving rapid-fire repartee, in which the objective is to insult or wound one's antagonist more often, elegantly, and completely than he or she is able to insult you.

15. Dinesh D'Souza, Illiberal Education 2–23 (listing areas of liberal excess in admissions policy in class, and on campus); 94–122 (criticizing Afrocentric curricular reforms); 124–56 (decrying university hate-speech rules).

16. *Id.* at 256–57 (activists set the agenda, timorous administrators usually go along).

17. *Id.* at 51 (white and Asian students see themselves as victims); 131 (white students feel "under attack"); 84 (academics feel intimidated); 146, 152–56 (censorship); 200 (complaints of truculent minority students).

31 Affirmative Action as a Majoritarian Device: Or, Do You Really Want to Be a Role Model?

RICHARD DELGADO

H A V E you ever noticed how affirmative action occupies a place in our system of law and politics far out of proportion to its effects in the real world? Liberals love talking about and sitting on committees that define, oversee, defend, and give shape to it.[1] Conservatives are attached to the concept for different reasons: they can rail against it, declare it lacking in virtue and principle, and use it to rally the troops.[2] Affirmative action is something they love to hate. The program also generates a great deal of paper, conversation, and jobs—probably more of the latter for persons of the majority persuasion than it has for its intended beneficiaries. Yet, despite its rather meager accomplishments and dubious lineage, a number of us have jumped on the bandwagon, maybe because it seemed one of the few that would let us on.

But should we? Lately, I have been having doubts, as have other writers of color.[3] Scholars of color have grown increasingly skeptical about both the way in which affirmative action frames the issue of minority representation and the effects that it produces in the world. Affirmative action, I have noticed, generally frames the question of minority representation in an interesting way: Should we as a society admit, hire, appoint, or promote some designated number of people of color in order to promote certain policy goals, such as social stability, an expanded labor force, and an integrated society? These goals are always forward-looking; affirmative action is viewed as an instrumental device for moving society from state *A* to state *B*.[4] The concept is neither backward-looking nor rooted in history; it is teleological rather than deontological. Minorities are hired or promoted not because we have been unfairly treated, denied jobs, deprived of our lands, or beaten and brought here in chains. Affirmative action neatly diverts our attention from all those disagreeable details and calls for a fresh start. Well, where are we now? So many Chicano bankers and chief executive officers, so many

89 MICH. L. REV. 1222 (1991). Originally published in the Michigan Law Review. Reprinted by permission.

black lawyers, so many Native American engineers, and so many women physicians. What can we do to increase these numbers over the next ten or twenty years? The system thus bases inclusion of people of color on principles of social utility, not reparations or *rights*. When those in power decide the goal has been accomplished, or is incapable of being reached, what logically happens? Naturally, the program stops. At best, then, affirmative action serves as a homeostatic device, assuring that only a small number of women and people of color are hired or promoted. Not too many, for that would be terrifying, nor too few, for that would be destabilizing. Just the right small number, generally those of us who need it least, are moved ahead.[5]

Affirmative action also neatly frames the issue so that even these small accomplishments seem troublesome, requiring great agonizing and gnashing of teeth. Liberals and moderates lie awake at night, asking how far they can take this affirmative action thing without sacrificing innocent white males. Have you ever wondered what that makes *us*—if not innocent, then . . . ? Affirmative action enables members of the dominant group to ask, "Is it fair to hire a less-qualified Chicano or black over a more-qualified white?"[6] This is a curious way of framing the question, as I will argue, in part because those who ask it are themselves the beneficiaries of history's largest affirmative action program. This fact is rarely noticed, however, while the question goes on causing the few of us who are magically raised by affirmative action's unseen hand to feel guilty, undeserving, and *stigmatized*.[7]

Affirmative action, as currently understood and promoted, is also ahistorical. For more than 200 years, white males benefited from their own program of affirmative action, through unjustified preferences in jobs and education resulting from old-boy networks and official laws that lessened the competition.[8] Today's affirmative action critics never characterize that scheme as affirmative action, which of course it was. By labeling problematic, troublesome, ethically agonizing a paltry system that helps a few of us get ahead, critics neatly take our eyes off the system of arrangements that brought and maintained them in power, and enabled them to develop the rules and standards of quality and merit that now exclude us, make us appear unworthy, dependent (naturally) on affirmative action.

Well, if you were a member of the majority group and invented something that cut down the competition, made you feel good and virtuous, made minorities grateful and humble, and framed the "minority problem" in this wondrous way, I think you would be pretty pleased with yourself. Moreover, if you placed the operation of this program in the hands of the very people who brought about the situation that made it necessary in the first place, society would probably reward you with prizes and honors.

Please do not mistake what I am saying. As marginalized people we should strive to increase our power, cohesiveness, and representation in all significant areas of society. We should do this, though, because we are entitled to these things and because fundamental fairness requires this reallocation of power. We should reformulate the issue. Our acquiescence in treating it as "a question of standards" is absurd and self-defeating when you consider that we took no part in creating those standards and their fairness is one of the very things we want to call into question.[9]

Affirmative action, then, is something no self-respecting person of color ought to support. We could, of course, take our own program, with our own goals, our own theoretical grounding, and our own managers and call it "Affirmative Action." But we would, of course, be talking about something quite different. My first point, then, is that we should demystify, interrogate, and destabilize affirmative action. The program was designed by others to promote their purposes, not ours.

The Role Model Argument

Consider now an aspect of affirmative action mythology, the role model argument, that in my opinion has received less criticism than it deserves. This argument is a special favorite of moderate liberals, who regard it as virtually unassailable. Although the argument's inventor is unknown, its creator must have been a member of the majority group and must have received a prize almost as large as the one awarded the person who created affirmative action itself. Like the larger program of which it is a part, the role model argument is instrumental and forward-looking. It makes us a means to another's end. A white-dominated institution hires you not because you are entitled to or deserve the job. Nor is the institution seeking to set things straight because your ancestors and others of your heritage were systematically excluded from such jobs. Not at all. You're hired (if you speak politely, have a neat haircut, and, above all, can be trusted) not because of your accomplishments, but because of what others think you will do for them. If they hire you now and you are a good role model, things will be better in the next generation.

Suppose you saw a large sign saying, "ROLE MODEL WANTED. GOOD PAY. INQUIRE WITHIN." Would you apply? Let me give you five reasons you should not.

REASON NUMBER ONE.   Being a role model is a tough job, with long hours and much heavy lifting.[10] You are expected to uplift your entire people. Talk about hard, sweaty work![11]

REASON NUMBER TWO.   The job treats you as a means to an end. Even your own constituency may begin to see you this way. "Of course Tanya will agree to serve as our faculty advisor, give this speech, serve on that panel, or agree to do us *X*, *Y*, or *Z* favor, probably unpaid and on short notice. What is her purpose if not to serve us?"

REASON NUMBER THREE.   The role model's job description is monumentally unclear. If highway workers or tax assessors had such unclear job descriptions, they would strike. If you are a role model, are you expected to do the same things your white counterpart does, in addition to counseling and helping out the community of color whenever something comes up? Just the latter? Half and half? Both? On your own time, or on company time? No supporter of the role model argument has ever offered satisfactory answers to these questions.

REASON NUMBER FOUR.   To be a good role model, you must be an assimilationist,[12] never a cultural or economic nationalist, separatist, radical reformer, or anything remotely resembling any of these. As with actual models (who walk down runways wearing the latest fashions), you are expected to conform to prevailing ideas of beauty, politeness, grooming, and above all responsibility. If you develop a quirk, wrinkle, aberration, or, heaven forbid, a vice, look out![13] I have heard more than once that a law school would not hire *X* for a teaching position because, although *X* might be a decent scholar and good classroom teacher, he was a little exuberant or rough around the edges and thus not good role model material. Not long ago, Margaret Court, the ex–tennis star and grand dame of English tennis officialdom, criticized Martina Navratilova as a poor role model for young tennis players. Martina failed Court's assessment not because she served poorly, wore a wrinkled tennis uniform, displayed bad sportsmanship, or argued with the referees. Rather, in Court's opinion, Martina was not "straight," not "feminine" enough, and so could not serve as a proper role model.[14] Our white friends always want us to model behavior that will encourage our students and proteges to adopt majoritarian social mores; you never hear of them hiring one of their number because he or she is bilingual, wears dashikis, or is in other ways culturally distinctive.

REASON NUMBER FIVE   (the most important one). The job of role model requires that you *lie*—that you tell not little, but big, whopping lies, and that is bad for your soul. Suppose I am sent to an inner city school to talk to the kids and serve as role model of the month. I am *expected* to tell the kids that if they study hard and stay out of trouble, they can become a law professor like me.[15] That, however, is a very big lie: a whopper. When I started teaching law sixteen years ago, there were about thirty-five Hispanic law professors, approximately twenty-five of which were Chicano. Today, the numbers are only slightly improved.[16] In the interim, however, a nearly complete turnover has occurred. The faces are new, but the numbers have remained the same from year to year. Gonzalez leaves teaching; Velasquez is hired somewhere else. Despite this, I am expected to tell forty kids in a crowded, inner city classroom that if they work hard, they can each be among the chosen twenty-five. Fortunately, most kids are smart enough to figure out that the system does not work this way. If I were honest, I would advise them to become major league baseball players, or to practice their hook shots. As Michael Olivas points out, the odds, pay, and working conditions are much better in these other lines of work.[17]

Recently, the California Postsecondary Commission, concerned about the fate of minorities in the state's colleges and universities,[18] had its statisticians compile a projection for all young blacks starting public school in California that year. That number was about 35,000. Of these, the statisticians estimated that about one half would graduate from high school, the rest having dropped out. Of those completing high school, approximately one out of nine would attend a four-year college. Of that number, about 300 would earn a bachelor's degree. You can form your own estimate of how many of this group, which began as 35,000, will continue on to earn a law degree. Thirty? Fifty? And of these, how many will become law professors? My guess is one, at most. But I may be an optimist.

Suppose I told the ghetto kids these things, that is, the truth. And, while I am at it, told them about diminishing federal and state scholarship funds that formerly enabled poor kids to go to college, about the special threat to assistance for minority college students, and about a climate of increasing hostility, slurs, and harassment on the nation's campuses. Suppose I told them, in short, what the system is really like, how the deck is stacked against them. What would happen? I would quickly be labeled a poor role model and someone else sent to give the inspiring speech next month.

Why Things Are the Way They Are
and What Can Be Done

The role model theory is a remarkable invention. It requires that some of us lie and that others of us be exploited and overworked. The theory is, however, highly functional for its inventors. It encourages us to cultivate non-threatening behavior in our own people. In addition, it provides a handy justification for affirmative action, which, as I have pointed out, is at best a mixed blessing for communities of color.

As with any successful and popular program, I think we need only examine the functions served by the role model argument to see why our white friends so avidly embrace it. Demographers tell us that in about ten years, Caucasians will cease to be the largest segment of California's population. In approximately sixty years, around the year 2050, the same will happen nationally. While this radical demographic shift is occurring, the population also will be aging. The baby boomers, mostly white, will be retired and dependent on social security for support. These retirees will rely on the continuing labor of a progressively smaller pyramid of active workers, an increasing proportion of them of color. You see, then, why it is essential that we imbue our next generation of children with the requisite respect for hard work. They must be taught to ask few questions, pay their taxes, and accept social obligations, even if imposed by persons who look different from them and who committed documented injustices on their ancestors.

If you want the job of passing on *that* set of attitudes to young people of color, go ahead. You will be warmly received and amply rewarded. But you do not have to be a role model. You can do other more honorable, authentic things. You can be a mentor.[19] You can be an "organic intellectual,"[20] offering analysis and action programs for our people. You can be a matriarch, a patriarch, a legend, or a pro-vocateur.[21] You can be a socially committed professional who marches to your own drummer. You can even be yourself. But to the ad, ROLE MODEL WANTED, the correct answer, in my view, is: NOT ME!

NOTES

1. Almost every major law review has devoted space to the treatment, usu-ally sympathetic and from a liberal standpoint, of affirmative action. *See, e.g.,* sources noted in R. Delgado, *The Imperial Scholar: Reflections on a Review of Civil Rights Literature,* 132 U. PA. L. REV. 561, 562 n.3 (1984); *see also* L. TRIBE, AMERICAN CONSTITUTIONAL LAW 1521–44, 1565–71 (2d ed. 1988) (discussion of affirmative action, or "benign" classification, in areas of race and sex).

2. *See, e.g.,* Abram, *Affirmative Action: Fair Shakers and Social Engi-neers,* 99 HARV. L. REV. 1312 (1986); L. Graglia, *Special Admission of the "Cul-turally Deprived" to Law School,* 119 U. PA. L. REV. 351 (1970); *see also* S. Carter, *The Best Black and Other Tales,* RECONSTRUCTION, Winter 1990, at 6 (middle-of-the-road criticism of affirmative action as psychologically deleterious to its pur-ported beneficiaries).

3. *E.g.,* D. BELL, AND WE ARE NOT SAVED: THE ELUSIVE QUEST FOR RACIAL JUSTICE 140–61 (1987); Carter, *supra* note 2; R. Delgado, Book Review, *Derrick Bell and the Ideology of Racial Reform: Will We Ever Be Saved?* 97 YALE L.J. 923, 923–24, 933 (1988).

4. Delgado, *supra* note 1, at 570 ("The past becomes irrelevant; one just asks where things are now and where we ought to go from here, a straightforward social-engineering inquiry of the sort that law professors are familiar with and good at.").

5. *See* BELL, *supra* note 3, at 140–61.

6. For a poignant recounting of a talented black's encounter with this at-titude, see Carter, *supra* note 2.

7.. *See id.;* R. Kennedy, *Racial Critiques of Legal Academia,* 102 HARV. L. REV. 1745, 1795–96, 1801–07, 1817–18 (1989).

8. R. Delgado, *Approach-Avoidance in Law School Hiring: Is the Law a WASP?* 34 ST. LOUIS U. L.J. 631, 639 (1990).

9. On the absurdity of using current standards to judge challenges to those very standards, see R. Delgado, *When A Story Is Just a Story: Does Voice Really Matter?* 76 VA. L. REV. 95, 100–02 (1990); R. Delgado, *Brewer's Plea: Critical Thoughts on Common Cause,* 44 VAND. L. REV. 1, 8–10 (1991) [hereinafter *Brewer's Plea*].

10. For a dreary picture of such a life, see R. Delgado, *Minority Law Profes-sors' Lives: The Bell-Delgado Survey,* 24 HARV. C.R.-C.L. L. REV. 349, 369 (1989) (reporting survey results and concluding: "It is impossible to read the . . . returns without being acutely conscious of the pain and stress they reflect. Large num-bers of minority law professors are overworked, excluded from informal informa-tion networks and describe their work environment as hostile, unsupportive, or openly or subtly racist."); C. Pierce, *Unity in Diversity: Thirty-Three Years of*

Stress, Solomon Carter Fuller Lecture, Am. Psychiatric Assn. Meeting, Wash., D.C. (May 12, 1986) (on file with author) (same).

11. Pierce, *supra* note 10; *see also* R. Brooks, *Life After Tenure: Can Minority Law Professors Avoid the Clyde Ferguson Syndrome?* 20 U.S.F. L. REV. 419 (1986) (overwork and overcommitment produce serious risk of early death for professionals of color in high-visibility positions).

12. On assimilationism, see *Brewer's Plea, supra* note 9. On black nationalism and separatism, see BELL, *SUPRA* note 3, at 215–35, and D. BELL, RACE, RACISM AND AMERICAN LAW 47–51 (2d ed. 1980).

13. On the intense scrutiny that role models encounter, see Brooks, *supra* note 11, and Delgado, *supra* note 10.

14. Downey, *She Succeeds as a person, as an Athlete,* L.A. TIMES, July 16, 1990, at C1, col. 2.

15. Most minority law professors of color (if we are honest) know we got our positions either by luck—by being in the right place at the right time—or as a result of student pressure and activism. This, of course, is not what our majority-race friends and supervisors want us to say to our proteges and communities.

16. Telephone interview with Michael Olivas, Professor of Law, University of Houston, Director, Institute of Higher Education Law and Governance (Sept. 1990). Professor Olivas is a member of various Association of American Law Schools and other professional committees that track the numbers of professors of color in law teaching. For current figures, see Lempinen, *A Student Challenge to the Old Guard,* STUDENT LAW., Sept. 1990, at 12, 15 (citing 1990 figure from Olivas of 51 Latino faculty members).

17. Interview with Michael Olivas, *supra* note 16. Olivas has recounted this story to several professional groups and committees, where it has always been greeted with dismay. The message is clear. Even if true, one should not say such things!

18. Address by Manning Marable, University of Colorado (Sept. 1990), reporting apparently unpublished results of the Commission's survey. *See Why All the Dropouts?* (editorial), L.A. TIMES, Dec. 27, 1985, Part II, at 4, col. 1.

19. *I.e.,* one who tells aspiring young persons of color *truthfully* what it is like to practice your profession in a society dominated by race.

20. Attributed to Italian Criticalist Antonio Gramsci, the term refers to a people's intellectual who operates in a nonhierarchical fashion and places his or her talents at the service of social reform.

21. In recent times, the most inspired (and maligned) example of most of these things is Derrick Bell, whose imaginative chronicles and acts of nonviolent resistance at Harvard (including a sit-in in his own office and, later, teaching his own classes while on unpaid leave) have galvanized us all.

32 Bid Whist, Tonk, and *United States v. Fordice:* Why Integrationism Fails African-Americans Again

ALEX M. JOHNSON, JR.

Introduction

The seminal race relations issue facing our society today is how to promote successful integration while respecting the differences that still separate the races. In *United States v. Fordice,*[1] the Supreme Court found de facto discrimination in Mississippi's post-secondary educational system, but rejected an effort by African-American plaintiffs to obtain funding for publicly supported historically black colleges and universities in Mississippi equal to that afforded Mississippi's predominantly white colleges. As a result of *Fordice,* it appears that these historically black colleges will be merged into Mississippi's white colleges, all under the guise of "integration." Indeed, *Fordice* is the logical and compelling end to the line of cases that began with *Brown v. Board of Education* and its explicit adoption of integrationism.

This chapter argues that *Fordice* was erroneously decided for a variety of reasons having nothing to do with the body of traditional, incremental constitutional scholarship that typically addresses such questions as whether the Supreme Court followed or departed from precedent in deciding a particular case. Similarly, this analysis of *Fordice* is not premised on some meta-normative theory as to whether the Court should take an originalist or nonoriginalist position on racial discrimination and equal protection issues. Instead, the chapter argues that the Supreme Court's decision in *Fordice* is wrong as a matter of social policy because it is built upon a premise of integrationism, first articulated in *Brown,* that has failed our society. Simply put, *Fordice* is wrong because *Brown* was a mistake.

As in *Brown,* the integrationism articulated by the *Fordice* Court is seriously flawed because it conflates the process of integration with the ideal of integration.[2] Both the 1954 and the 1992 Courts failed to recognize and appreciate the

81 CAL. L. REV. 1401 (1993). Originally published in the California Law Review. Reprinted by permission.

social realities that preclude the attainment of meaningful integration through simple judicial or legislative fiat. Only by acknowledging and accommodating the reality of the unique and separate African-American culture or *nomos* will the *process* of integration ever move forward to accomplish the *ideal* state of integration sought by *Brown* and its progeny.[3] The ideal of integration can only be achieved by respecting this unique culture through the maintenance and operation of *separate* institutions that allow African-Americans to join together "in collective associations which have . . . educational and social dimensions."[4]

Otherwise, as is currently the case, the courts are embracing a social reality that does not exist: a society in which race is viewed as an irrelevant characteristic. From this base assumption, courts then reach the similarly wrongheaded conclusion that race is not a relevant or permissible characteristic in the implementation of an educational system. *Fordice* will generate more harm than good. One's racial identity is constitutive of one's personal identity. The "ideal society" can be achieved only through a transitive stage in which racial differences are truly respected and treated in a way similar to the way we currently treat religious differences. While the contention that separate black colleges should be supported and maintained may at first glance seem inconsistent with traditional notions of integration, it is only by providing choice—even if that choice legitimates predominantly or historically black colleges—that African-Americans will be afforded equal opportunity in our educational system.

Given this society's past and present, the only appropriate result in *Fordice* should have been the maintenance, at an improved funding level, of predominantly or historically black colleges, while at the same time preserving equal opportunity for African-Americans to attend predominantly white educational institutions. It is only by providing this choice that African-American students will be afforded equal opportunity in our post-secondary educational institutions. By permitting the elimination of historically black colleges, the Court in *Fordice* prevented African-American students from selecting *when* integration should occur. It is only when those students are sufficiently mature, confident, and equipped to enter the predominantly white society that meaningful integration will occur.

"Forced" integration of the type mandated by *Fordice*, if not doomed to failure, will certainly be less successful than the "voluntary" integration that occurs when individuals are given the choice whether and when to integrate. In the end, *Fordice* severely retards progress toward integration as envisioned in our ideal society.

The Hidden Costs Generated by Integrating College Campuses

I start with the assumption that the continued popularity of predominantly or historically black colleges proves that they are providing a valuable service to our society. Their popularity persists despite an environment in which funding is problematic and in which African-Americans have the opportunity to matriculate, for example, at either Morehouse College or the University of Georgia. The colleges fill a unique niche in our educational system and thus should be maintained.

The cost of *Fordice*, which eliminates choice for African-American students, is difficult to quantify. It is best measured in two interrelated ways: first, by examining the personal costs that will be incurred by African-Americans forced to attend predominantly white colleges in lieu of black colleges; second, by examining what integration costs the African-American community and majoritarian society. Most African-Americans who choose to attend predominantly white institutions of higher education are making an important choice. They are subjecting themselves to alien institutions in which their minority status puts them at a degree of risk not faced by white students.[5] The resulting dynamic significantly impacts them, the community from which they come, and the community into which they are being integrated.

The personal costs incurred by African-Americans are caused by the loss of choice provided to African-American students who have, to that point, been "sheltered" in the African-American community. The students are forced into a hostile environment whether they are ready for it or not.[6] This hostile environment has a detrimental effect on African-American students' performance at college.

> The racial dynamic—arising out of occasional blatant racism, recurrent subtle remarks or unconscious behavior, and an ever-present white norm that is the foundation of institutional racism—conspires to create a cognizable injury to black students in predominantly white schools. It alters students' conditions of education just as courts have recognized racial harassment on the job alters conditions of employment. Racism adds to the stress and anxiety that diminish any person's ability and desire to excel in an academic environment, especially one leading to a professional world known to contain further racial roadblocks to career advancement and hospitable working conditions. The racial dynamic to which black students are subjected at predominantly white colleges contributes to stress that has a detrimental effect on personal well-being as well as academic performance.[7]

Those not ready for immersion into that hostile environment in which overt and covert racist acts become a daily part of their educational experience may choose not to go to college:

> Tamla Moore, a sophomore at a predominantly black school, lives at home with her unemployed parents. Asked whether she would attend a white college if her school closes, she said, "I just got out of high school, and I don't want to go through all that racial tension again. . . ."
>
> Moore recalled with relief that, at her school, she does not face incidents such as the time a white student smeared what looked like blood on his face and told their high school principal that blacks had beaten him.[8]

In light of accounts like these, is it any mystery that many African-Americans choose to attend predominantly or historically black colleges, even though these schools have allegedly "inferior" facilities and are underfunded, when the alternative is to attend an institution in which learning takes place in a hostile environment? The only mystery is why any African-American would choose to attend a predominantly white college when a predominantly or historically black college is available.

Beyond individual costs, *Fordice* imposes costs on both the African-American community and majoritarian society. *Fordice* forces all African-Americans—nationalists, integrationists, and desegregationists alike—into an environment in which only integrationists may be ready and capable of competing.[9] More importantly, it forces desegregationist African-Americans, who envision their successful integration into mainstream white culture at some point in their lives, to make college their point of integration irrespective of their desires. Finally, it forces those nationalists who would choose not to integrate to forgo their nationalist philosophy or forgo publicly financed higher education.

This "cost" is directly related to the fact that, although integration as a process leads to the admission of African-Americans to formerly all-white institutions, integration as an ideal has failed to eliminate inequalities and racism. The integration ideal will continue to fail because predominantly white colleges mask norms that create an environment in which African-Americans are considered "them" or the "other."

> [M]any white[] [students] tend to think that racism has largely disappeared, at least in any form that could serve as an impediment to opportunity and achievement. White students have a very hard time understanding how their predominantly white campuses can seem hostile to people of color; how their campus social life is a distinctly "white culture," even when the major institutions within it are not explicitly labeled the "white student union," "white student newspaper," or "white debating club." It does not occur to most white students that their indifference or hostility to the Martin Luther King national holiday, for example, is evidence of attitudes on racial issues that differ tremendously from their black colleagues. It does not occur to most white students that the major, campus-sponsored concerts of white music groups constitute distinctly *white* cultural events.[10]

In other words, it does not occur to white students that there is a unique African-American *nomos* worthy of their respect.

Tonk and Bid Whist

The popular card games of Bid Whist and Tonk are African-American versions of the card games Bridge and Poker, respectively. Indeed, some will no doubt argue that Tonk and Bid Whist are mere derivations of Bridge and Poker, perhaps the two most preeminent card games in America. What is revealing is that African-Americans continue to play card games (Tonk and Bid Whist) that are strikingly similar to Bridge and Poker in most respects, but remarkably different in others, while continuing to play Bridge and Poker.[11]

As a student or a faculty member, I have had intimate contacts with African-American students at eight post-secondary institutions. None of these institutions is predominantly or historically African-American, but each of them has a discrete, identifiable minority population. The one universal characteristic of each institution's African-American population was that the African-American students played Bid Whist and Tonk. Indeed, recalling my undergraduate days at Princeton, Bid Whist served as the major social event and recreational activity at the Third World Center at which minority students congregated.

Bid Whist served as an ice-breaker or entree into the social community that gathered at institutions such as the Third World Center on various campuses on the East Coast. As a member of an African-American drama group during my sophomore year at Princeton, I had occasion to travel to numerous other colleges at which we performed. What I remember so vividly about that time of my life were the numerous Bid Whist games played at these foreign institutions before and after the performances. New acquaintances and friendships were established through these card games. (A lot can be learned about the character of an individual across a card table.) Moreover, it was not uncommon to receive flyers from African-Americans at other predominantly white institutions inviting students (whom I presume were African-Americans, although they were not designated as such) to play in upcoming Bid Whist "tournaments" at the host school.

Furthermore, these two card games, especially Bid Whist, served as a great social segregator among African-Americans. At the time I went to college (1971–75), African-American students could be divided roughly into three categories: (1) nationalists, who wanted very little to do with white students; (2) desegregationists, who clearly "identified" with the African-American community, but also felt comfortable interacting with white students; and (3) assimilationists, those African-American students who did not "identify" with other African-Americans and made a conscious choice not to interact with other African-Americans, in favor of socializing exclusively with whites.[12]

"Identifying" with the African-American community is a term of art which requires some explanation. "Identifying" does not mean identifying oneself as an African-American to whites and other African-Americans. To the contrary, the first part of "identifying" is the visual identification and recognition of an individual as an African-American.[13] The second and much more difficult part of "identifying" is dependent upon whether an individual who is visibly African-American under the rule of recognition, or who acknowledges her African-American heritage under the rule of descent,[14] chooses to acknowledge this status by acknowledging the presence—and thus the shared subordinated experience—of other African-Americans. It is as simple as one African-American saying hello to another African-American as they pass each other on a predominantly white campus, even though they may never have seen each other before, and even though neither would do the same—that is, say hello—if the other party was not an African-American.

Another aspect of "identifying" that deserves mention is its transcendence of class lines. For example, it was common to see upper-middle-class African-American students speak to and acknowledge the presence of an African-American janitor at Princeton. From that simple gesture of acknowledging another African-American's presence, a gesture that takes place in a myriad number of ways millions of times a day, one African-American can determine whether another African-American is willing to talk to or be seen with other African-Americans.

Tonk and Bid Whist were frequently used as methods to demarcate nationalists and desegregationists, who "identify," from assimilationists, who may not. This is not to say that every African-American student who fell into the first two categories knew how to play Tonk and Bid Whist, but a significant percentage of the African-American students who were nationalists or desegregationists played both games. Of course, it is probably also true that a fair number of assimilationist students could play Tonk or Bid Whist and had encountered these two games at some point in their lives. However, if they were familiar with these uniquely African-American card games, they typically refused to play them with other African-Americans.

My point is simply this: now that the reader has some familiarity with the significance of Tonk and Bid Whist in, at least, the African-American college community, the obvious question is why is there a need for such African-Americanized versions of card games given the existence and popularity of their counterparts, Poker and Bridge? Furthermore, why is it that Tonk and Bid Whist serve the unique identifying and uniting roles that I have addressed above?

The continued existence and use of Tonk and Bid Whist to separate nationalists and desegregationists, on the one hand, from assimilationists, on the other hand, illustrates the necessity and continued use of predominantly or historically black colleges. Nationalists would naturally rather play Tonk and Bid Whist, games associated with and unique to the African-American community, than any type of card game that is associated with mainstream white culture, which they explicitly reject. Desegregationists would continue to play Tonk and Bid Whist with other African-Americans for a lot of different reasons, including the fact that, having learned these unique games and having an audience comprised of people who also know how to play them (i.e., nationalists and other desegregationists), it is easier to continue to play Bid Whist and Tonk even if some or most African-Americans also know how to play Poker and Bridge.

Assimilationists, on the other hand, would refuse to play or even learn how to play, because Tonk and Bid Whist represent something to which they philosophically object: the existence of a separate and unique African-American community that stands apart from the mainstream culture or community. For the assimilationist African-American, Poker or Bridge serves as a vehicle to integrate society because those games are played not solely with other African-Americans but primarily with whites. The assimilationist African-American would meet and compete with the whites on the their terms, with their games, and under their rules.

There is, however, a more compelling and substantive reason why nationalists and desegregationists continue to play these games while assimilationists refuse to do so. Tonk and Bid Whist continue to be played because they symbolize African-Americans' unique and subordinated status in this society. The games neatly capture the position of African-Americans in today's society, potentially on the precipice of true integration. Like many other social institutions found in the African-American community, Bid Whist and Tonk mirror, to a large extent, their counterpart institutions in white society. There is no question that such white counterpart institutions served as models for their original African-American analogues. However, due to the historically segregated nature of American society, African-American institutions developed and evolved separately over time. They maintained their necessary elements, discarded unnecessary elements, and, most importantly, added those elements that make the institutions successful in the African-American community.[15] Tonk and Bid Whist are no doubt like this—derived from card games played by whites but subtly changed to make the game more attractive to African-Americans.[16]

Bid Whist and Tonk, like many other African-American institutions, are maintained because they are ours: they provide us with a safe harbor for the preservation of the idiopathic rules, customs, and norms that developed in our community while we were kept separate from whites by law. This safe harbor also allows those who choose not to fully embrace the norms of white society to retain a place in an African-American community in which confrontation between African-American norms and conflicting white norms never takes place. Moreover, this safe harbor protects African-American culture, because when the assimilationist version of integration occurs African-American culture is typically not merged into majoritarian culture but obliterated by it—leaving no trace of what was once a unique cultural vehicle.

This cultural destruction explains why nationalists choose to play Tonk and Bid Whist: the games do not require the sublimation or supplantation of African-American values by those of the mainstream white community. Desegregationists continue to play Bid Whist and Tonk for two reasons. First, Bid Whist and Tonk serve as important learning tools whose lessons will be utilized by the African-American when interaction with the dominant white community is desired. For example, the similarities between these African-American games and Poker and Bridge allow the African-American to easily take up those white counterparts if and when she *chooses* to do so. Second and more importantly, desegregationists continue to play Tonk and Bid Whist—both before entering the white community and after their "successful integration" into that larger community—because Tonk and Bid Whist represent their heritage and are constitutive of their basic identity.

In order to integrate properly into society, African-Americans, like other ethnic groups, must proceed on their own terms from a position of strength and solidarity. The African-American community and the dominant white community cannot become one through forced integration, because that process reflects no choice and has the effect of locking African-Americans into inferior positions in society. Indeed, if anything is to be learned from this country's history, it is that people truly become a part of America's melting pot only when they enter the mix voluntarily, from a position of strength rather than from one of weakness.

What separates this view of integration, which is premised on diversity and tolerance, from segregationism, which is premised on racial domination and superiority, is that it looks forward to a time when people will attain the idealized state of one community. Its goal is positive, but it recognizes that the ideal vision of integration cannot be mandated by either legislative or judicial fiat. This vision of integrationism is different from the brand embodied by *Fordice*. It rejects assimilationism and argues that integration is not a cultural one-way street in which African-Americans must absorb white norms in order to be assimilated into American society. Rather, when integration does occur, African-Americans should have as much influence on whites as whites have on African-Americans.

The assimilationist version of integrationism, premised on traditional liberalism, presupposes a homogeneous community in which all the members of society inhabit one cultural community. However, the continued existence of Tonk and Bid Whist demonstrate that African-Americans have developed their own community with norms that must be respected and internalized in the larger pluralistic society. The problem with *Fordice* is that, in its quest for equality through an assimilationist version of integration, it does not respect this separate culture. It forces African-Americans to abandon Tonk and Bid Whist in favor of Poker and Bridge.

NOTES

1. 112 S. Ct. 2727 (1992).

2. In the context of education, the process/ideal dichotomy of integration has even more significance. The integration of schools is part of the process by which the ideal society is ultimately achieved. Integration itself serves a dual role. First, it is the method or mechanism of implementation by which the ideal racially harmonized society is achieved. Its secondary, albeit no less important, role is that of metric, measuring whether the ideal society has been achieved. These two roles of integration are often conflated.

3. One definition of *nomos* has been provided by Professor Weinreb:

> Greek philosophy made a crucial distinction between *physis* . . . and *nomos*. The usual translation of *physis*, from which we get the word "physics" and its cognates, is "nature"; and the translation of *nomos* is "convention." "Physis," however, had normative significance that ordinarily our references to nature specifically exclude. And although "nomos" was dependent in some way on human will, it was not whatever was posited, merely as such. *Nomos* referred to the ways of the community, as established but also, more significantly, as valid. Nevertheless it was not unalterable, and it was the *nomos* of a particular community.

Lloyd L. Weinreb, *What Are Civil Rights?* Soc. Phil. & Pol'y, Spring 1991, at 1, 2. The concept of *nomos* is elaborated *infra*.

4. Richard A. Wasserstrom, *Racism, Sexism, and Preferential Treatment: An Approach to the Topics*, 24 UCLA L. REV. 581, 605, 609 (1977). Moreover, pursuant to my conception of the ideal society, racial differences are either viewed positively under the philosophy of diversity or simply allowed pursuant to the philosophy of tolerance. As a result, in certain institutions like post-secondary schools, racial differences are not only maintained, they are exploited and reinforced.

5. I say "most" because some African-Americans, especially those whom I have characterized as integrationist, may not experience the same hostile or alien environment when they attend a predominantly white institution. These African-American students are fortunate in the sense that the predominantly white college campus poses no threat or challenge to them or their identity, oftentimes because they grew up and went to school in an "integrated," predominantly white environment. For example, consider STEPHEN L. CARTER, REFLECTIONS OF AN AFFIRMATIVE ACTION BABY 47–48 (1991), reviewing his own high school days:

> My father taught at Cornell, which made me a Cornell kid, a "fac-brat," and I hung out with a bunch of white Cornell kids in a private little world where we competed fiercely (but only with one another—no one else mattered!) for grades and test scores and solutions to brain teasers. We were the sort of kids other kids hated: the ones who would run around compiling lists of everyone else's test scores and would badger guidance counselors into admitting their errors in arithmetic (no computers then) in order to raise our class ranks a few notches. . . . (No one had yet told me that standardized tests were culturally biased against me.) Like the rest of the fac-brats, I yearned for the sobriquet "brilliant," and tried desperately to convince myself and everyone else who would listen that I had the grades and test scores to deserve it.

Of course, these integrationist African-Americans are not the ones harmed by *Fordice*—it is nationalist and desegregationist African-Americans who bear the burden most heavily. By "nationalist," I mean those who want very little to do with whites. I use the term "desegregationist" to refer to those African-Americans who "identify" with other African-Americans, yet feel comfortable interacting with whites.

6.

> The hostility, or at least puzzlement, one hears among many white students toward distinctly black cultural centers, student groups, and social events arises from white students' lack of recognition that the overwhelmingly white campuses themselves are in some sense large white cultural centers—ones in which black students are likely to have difficulty feeling at home. Thus, white students' assertions that they only want all people treated the same, without the separatism of institutions such as black cultural centers, are often experienced by minority students as demands that they assimilate into white-dominated institutions and culture. That white norm extends even into the classroom.

Darryl Brown, Note, *Racism and Race Relations in the University*, 76 VA. L. REV. 295, 315 (1990).

7. *Id.* at 324–25 (footnotes omitted).

8. Mary Jordan, *Mississippi, An Integration Uproar*, WASH. POST, Nov. 17, 1992, at A14.

9. While one might make the argument that integrationist African-Americans are also detrimentally affected by *Fordice,* at least to the extent that they are foreclosed from experiencing the *nomos* of the African-American community as expressed in predominantly black colleges, the likelihood that this putative injury rivals that imposed on nationalist and desegregationist African-Americans is remote and far-fetched.

10. Brown, *supra* note 6, at 314–15 (footnote omitted).

11. One of the nation's leading bridge players is Second Circuit Court of Appeals Judge Amalya Kearse, an African-American. This fact was relayed to me by my former colleague Lynn Baker, a former Kearse clerk.

12. Throughout the chapter, I have referred to the doctrine of integration and the philosophy of integrationism. However, in my tripartite definition of African-American students who attended colleges in 1971–75, I have characterized these students as "nationalists," "desegregationists," and lastly, "assimilationists." I have not characterized any of these students as "integrationists" because I believe that the concept of integration and integrationism means different things for those applying the definition in majoritarian culture and those on whom it is applied. Thus, it is my contention that many majoritarian integrationists actually propose a method of integration which favors and produces "assimilationist" African-American students. In contrast, I contend that in an ideal society, African-American students who are "desegregationists" will or should be the norm.

13. For an in-depth discussion of the phenomenon of "passing," see Cheryl I. Harris, *Whiteness as Property*, 106 HARV. L. REV. 1707, 1710–14 (1993). Although it is possible that certain African-Americans may "pass" as white, under the rule of recognition, the overwhelming majority of African-Americans are easily identifiable as African-Americans: "Any person whose Black-African ancestry is visible is Black."

14. The rule of descent: "Any person with a known trace of African ancestry is Black, notwithstanding that person's visual appearance. . . ." *Id.* at 1710–14 (discussing passing and rule of descent).

15. In this respect, these two card games, Tonk and Bid Whist, have followed the development and achieved the unique status of African-American churches with their emotional preaching style and the extensive use of spirituals. In other words, although the origins of both the African-American churches and card games may be traced to majoritarian models, these derivations are now imbued with unique attributes reflective of their community.

16. Tonk, for example, is largely a game of luck in which the player's strategy plays a smaller role than it does in Poker. Also, given the small amount of money involved in each hand, Tonk is accessible to all African-Americans and not simply those with substantial resources, as is rarely the case in Poker. Tonk is not structured as a progressive gambling game in which the "pot" to be won may vary significantly in any given game. Similarly, because Bid Whist is relatively simple compared to Bridge, almost everyone in the African-American com-

munity who chooses to play, can play. Moreover, most Bid Whist is played under so-called "rise and fly" rules, meaning that the team losing one hand has to rise and fly (leave the table) so that the next team can sit down and challenge the winners. This allows for a very fast turnover on the tables so that the interaction among the teams is quite good. In these respects, the game is more social and less competitive than Bridge.

33 African-American Immersion Schools: Paradoxes of Race and Public Education

KEVIN BROWN

IMMERSION schools provide educators with the opportunity to develop teaching strategies, techniques, and materials that take into account the influence of the dominant American and the African-American cultures on the social environment and understandings of African-Americans. Educators can formulate strategies and teach techniques to African-American students to help them overcome racial obstacles. Immersion schools also provide educators with an opportunity to reduce the cultural conflict between the dominant American culture, which is enshrined in the traditional public education program, and African-American culture. This conflict is a primary reason for the poor performance of African-Americans in public schools.

Since education is an acculturating institution, concern about the influence of culture in determining the appropriate educational techniques and strategies is understandable. Educators are necessarily drawn to the influence of culture on the attitudes, opinions, and experiences of individuals. In contrast, the Supreme Court's interpretation of the Equal Protection Clause requires that government make decisions by abstracting people from the social conditions that influence them. While education requires that culture—as a molder of people—be taken into account, law views individuals as self-made. While our legal system may not be blind to the influence of culture on individuals, it tends to assume that individuals choose to be influenced by their culture. For education, cultural influences are important. For law, they are not.

Because of the interplay between the differing frameworks of law and education, there is no good solution to the legal problem posed by the establishment of immersion schools. Any resolution will lead to a striking paradox. There are three conceivable methods of resolving the legal conflict concerning the establishment of immersion schools. The first is to justify immersion schools by viewing them as racially neutral because they are open to all, while ignoring that they are structured to appeal to African-Americans. This conceptualization produces two para-

78 IOWA L. REV. 813 (1993). Originally published in the Iowa Law Review. Reprinted by permission.

doxes. First, it calls for labeling schools designed for African-Americans as race-neutral. Second, it implies that the impact of culture on individual African-Americans is chosen. The justification for immersion schools, however, rests on the fact that African-Americans are not free to choose the influence which cultural ideology—both dominant and African-American—exerts on their lives.

Second, courts can invalidate immersion schools as violating the Equal Protection Clause. This amounts to a declaration that African-American students experience equal treatment in schools which are not immersion schools. However, education in schools that are not immersion schools remains inadequate because it does not address influences of culture on the social environment created by the dominant culture and the educational experience of African-Americans.

The third resolution would be for courts to uphold the decisions of educators to establish immersion schools because they survive strict scrutiny. In order for this to happen, proponents of the schools must provide compelling justifications for their racially motivated decisions. This will force courts to conclude that the deplorable social and educational conditions of African-Americans in traditional school systems constitute those compelling justifications. However, the use of statistics to support this proposition itself reinforces derogatory beliefs about African-Americans. One motivation for establishing immersion schools is to provide black students with strategies to overcome society's presumption that blacks are incompetent. Yet in order to provide the compelling interest for this kind of education, proponents of immersion schools must attempt to provide a factual basis that works to justify the presumption of black incompetence. This resolution, therefore, reinforces one of the very problems that makes immersion schools necessary.

Comparison of Voluntary Immigrants and Involuntary Minorities

A group's cultural understanding of public education influences both the students' and the communities' attitudes and strategies regarding education. Two historical forces helped shape the cultures of ethnic minority groups in their dominant host society: their initial terms of incorporation into that society and their pattern of adaptive responses to discriminatory treatment by members of the dominant group after their incorporation.[1]

Voluntary immigration to a country with the purpose of searching for a better life provides an ethnic group with a reference point for understanding their economic, social, political, and educational experiences in that country. Voluntary immigrants generally move to their host country hoping for greater economic opportunities and more political freedom than was probable at home. Therefore, they tend to compare their economic, social, political, and educational situations in their host country to what they left behind. Generally, this comparison allows them to develop a positive comparative framework for interpreting their conditions in their host country. Many voluntary immigrants who do not believe they are better off exercise the option of returning to their native land.

Voluntary immigrants also come with their native culture intact. Their cultures have not evolved in response to discrimination experienced in America. As a result, cultural and language differences between voluntary immigrants' native culture and the dominant American culture, as enshrined in public schools, are not oppositional. Voluntary immigrants see the cultural differences between themselves and dominant group members as something they must overcome to achieve their goals for a better life. This goal of finding a better life, after all, is what brought them to their host country originally.

Both voluntary immigrants and involuntary minorities frequently face prejudice and discrimination in American society and public education. When confronted with this discrimination, voluntary immigrants tend to interpret the economic, political, and social barriers they face as temporary. They believe they can overcome these problems in time, with hard work and more education. Voluntary immigrants also tend to interpret prejudice and discrimination in their host country as a result of being foreigners. They view prejudice and discrimination as the price they must pay for the benefits they enjoy. Therefore, they have a greater degree of trust of, or at least acquiescence towards, members of the dominant group and the institutions they control.

This cultural story also influences the view voluntary immigrants have toward public education. By viewing the obstacles they face as flowing from their lack of knowledge about their host country, education becomes an important element in the strategy of getting ahead. Even though voluntary immigrants know that their children may suffer from prejudice and discrimination in public schools, voluntary immigrants tend to view this as a price of the benefit derived from being in the new country. Opportunities for education in the United States also aid this positive educational comparison, as opportunities far exceed those available in their native land.

Voluntary immigrants come to their host country to improve their economic, political, and social conditions. This starkly contrasts with the situation of involuntary minorities who were brought into their present society through slavery, conquest, or colonization. Without the voluntary aspect of their original incorporation, involuntary minorities differ from voluntary immigrants in their perceptions, interpretations, and responses to their situation. Unlike voluntary immigrants, involuntary minorities cannot refer to a native homeland to generate a positive comparative framework for their condition. Instead, they compare themselves to the dominant group. Since the dominant group is generally better off, the comparative framework of involuntary minorities produces a negative interpretation of their condition. Their cultural interpretation leads to resentment. Minorities perceive themselves as victims of institutionalized discrimination perpetuated against them by dominant group members. As a result, involuntary minorities distrust members of the dominant group and the institutions they control.

Involuntary minorities respond to prejudice and discrimination differently from the way voluntary immigrants do. Involuntary minorities are not in the position of being able to understand prejudice or discrimination as a result of their status as foreigners. In their view, the prejudice and discrimination they experience in society and school relates to their history as members of a victimized group. Unlike immigrants, involuntary minorities do not view their current condition as temporary.

Cultural differences between involuntary minorities and the dominant group also arise after the former becomes an involuntary minority. Recall that the Africans brought to America came from a collection of diverse cultural groups. These culturally diverse groups forged much of their unifying culture within America itself. In order to live with subordination, involuntary minorities developed coping mechanisms. These responses are often perceived as oppositional to those of the dominant group. The historical interactions of blacks and whites in this country have led to an oppositional character in the cultures of the two races.[2] Many elements of the African-American culture started out as responses to conditions of oppression and subordination. The African-American culture is more at odds with the dominant American culture enshrined in public schools than the native culture brought to this country by voluntary immigrants.

Cultural differences also function as boundary-maintaining mechanisms which differentiate involuntary minorities from their oppressors, namely, dominant group members. These cultural differences give involuntary minorities a sense of social identity and self-worth. Adopting the cultural frame of reference of the dominant group can be threatening to the involuntary minority's identity and security, as well as the group's solidarity. As a result, involuntary minorities are less likely to interpret differences between them and dominant group members as differences to overcome; rather, they are differences of identity to be maintained.

Thus, involuntary minority students often face the dilemma of choosing between academic success and maintaining their minority cultural identity. Furthermore, there is a fear that, even if they did act like members of the dominant group, involuntary minority students still might not gain acceptance. This could result in the worst of all possible situations: losing the support of the minority group and not gaining acceptance by the dominant group.

Cultural Conflict between African-American Culture and Public School Culture

This reference to African-American culture does not presuppose that African-American culture is somehow better or worse than dominant American culture, only that it is different. Nor does this reference to culture rest upon the idea that all African-American school children share an undifferentiated black culture. Certainly there are geographic, religion, class, color, and gender

variations that affect the attitudes and behaviors of individual blacks. Some social scientists argue that the academic problems of African-Americans are attributable to the fact that more are from the lower class or underclass. For these
social scientists, a racial-cultural conflict no longer exists.[3] However, research
generally shows that at any given socio-economic class level black students, on
average, do poorer than their white counterparts.[4] Race appears to exert its own
unique influence on the school experiences and outcomes of black children un-
explainable by other socio-economic factors.[5]

Even though individual minority members may react very differently to their
individual educational situation, ethnic groups are able to develop a cultural response that influences the collective interpretation of the group's educational experience. This cultural interpretation influences the overall success of members
of their community in public schools. A number of educational researchers have
examined how cultural misunderstandings between teachers and students result
in conflict, distrust, hostility, and school failure for many African-American students.[6] Some of these misunderstandings stem from black students' perceptions
that certain behaviors and understandings are characteristic of white Americans,
and hence inappropriate for them.[7] Further, teachers and administrators generally
are reluctant to discuss race and race-related issues. The color-blind philosophy
of educators is, in part, linked to uneasiness in discussing race, lack of knowledge
of the African-American culture, and fears that open consideration of differences
might incite racial discord.

My reaction to reading *Huck Finn* in my junior literature class illustrates the
racial cultural conflict.[8] As a middle-class black child, whose parents both possessed master's degrees in education from Indiana University, I shared much in
common with my white teachers and classmates. Nevertheless, a racial cultural
conflict existed between my interpretation of our class reading *Huck Finn* and the
interpretation of my English literature teacher. My teacher and I were both interpreting *Huckleberry Finn*, but we were interpreting it from the understanding
of radically different cultures. Use of the word "nigger" by whites is offensive to
African-Americans, even if written in a so-called "literary classic." Understanding *The Adventures of Huckleberry Finn* from an African-American cultural
perspective led me to believe that it was not a literary classic, but rather an offensive and racist book. Consequently, the interpretation of my teacher's requirement that the class read the book, especially out loud, was that the exercise was
insulting and degrading to all African-Americans, including me.[9] My objecting to
the reading of *Huckleberry Finn* was, therefore, a rebellion against an act of racial
subordination. My teacher, however, was perceiving my actions from a completely different set of cultural ideas. Rather than viewing her actions as insulting, she saw my actions as both biased and asking for "special treatment" because
I was interjecting race into what she understood as a racially neutral situation
(i.e., reading a classic literary book).

The cultural experience and the interpretation of traditional education in
public schools by involuntary minorities is different from that of voluntary im-

migrants. Ignoring or undervaluing the culture of involuntary minorities is likely to have far more negative consequences for their education than for voluntary immigrant groups. One researcher, for example, examined the performance of high achieving African-American students. She noted that they were forced to develop a raceless persona to succeed in the public schools.[10]

Proponents of immersion schools reject the assumption that the traditional assimilationist education is either value-neutral or embodies the appropriate education for African-Americans.[11] Traditional education programs fail to take into account both the unique social environment of African-Americans created by the dominant culture and the influence of African-American culture on the educational experience of blacks. As a result, traditional educational programs, even when formally denominated multicultural, incorporate the Anglo-American cultural bias of our society.

Proponents of immersion schools often cite the negative educational statistics of African-Americans. The Detroit School Board, for example, argued that the need for male academies was due, in part, to the failure of the traditional coeducational program.[12] The school board pointed to statistics which show the poor academic performance of African-American males and their high dropout rates.[13] These statistics documented the failure of the traditional educational program. Many of those who objected to the exclusion of females from these academies did so because they felt that the condition of African-American females within educational institutions was just as deplorable as that of the males.[14]

Poor educational performance among African-Americans results from an improperly designed structure of education. Proponents cite statistics to demonstrate the educational crisis of African-Americans, not to demonstrate the inabilities of African-Americans. These statistics focus on the flawed nature of the traditional educational approach as it is applied to African-Americans. That flawed approach results in African-Americans shaping themselves to fit within the negative expectations that flow from the dominant social construction of African-Americans.[15] As a result, traditional public education is not the solution to the racial obstacles African-Americans encounter. Rather, it is one of those obstacles.

In a sense, immersion schools represent a traditional approach by African-Americans to make education in racially separate schools more responsive to the needs and interests of African-American students.[16] Immersion schools have their roots in the long-standing debate regarding separate versus integrated education for African-Americans. This debate has a history that is two centuries old. It is part of a much larger debate about the general social, political, and economic condition of blacks in this country. The issue of whether the educational interests of black children are better served in separate institutions, as opposed to racially mixed schools, was first addressed by the black community of Boston, Massachusetts. in the 1780s and 1790s. This debate also flared up in some of the state constitutional conventions after the Civil War and during the discussions of the Blair Education Bill in the 1880s.

While the threads of the debate about immersion schools are traceable to earlier times, the place in which to begin this most recent chapter is a special issue of *Ebony* magazine, published in August 1983. The issue introduced the African-American community to Walter Leavy's provocative question: Is the black male an endangered species?[17] To emphasize the deteriorating condition of the African-American male, Leavy pointed to the homicide rates, the high rates of imprisonment, an increase in the rate of suicide, the infant mortality rate, and a decrease in life expectancy. The crisis of the African-American male was brought to the attention of mainstream America with proposals by a few public school systems to establish African-American male classrooms or academies. These proposals have raised one of the most controversial educational issues of the 1990s. Proposals for such education surfaced in a number of cities, including Miami, Baltimore, Detroit, Milwaukee, and New York.

The legality of race- and gender-segregated schools limited to African-American males, however, is open to serious questions.[18] The Ujamaa Institute, an immersion school in New York City that opened in September 1992, is coeducational. The Milwaukee School System, on advice of counsel, abandoned its original proposal to establish an all–black male school and instead established immersion schools that include females. In *Garrett v. Board of Education*,[19] a federal district court in August 1991 granted a preliminary injunction against the Detroit School Board's proposal for male academies. The American Civil Liberties Union of Michigan and the National Organization of Women Legal Defense and Education Fund represented the plaintiffs. The plaintiffs ignored the race-based decision making that motivated the adoption of proposals for those schools. They only challenged the gender based exclusion. The district court enjoined the implementation of the male academies, concluding that the Detroit plan would violate state law as well as Title IX, the Equal Educational Opportunities Act, and the Fourteenth Amendment.[20]

New York, Detroit, and Milwaukee have, however, gone forward and now operate schools with a focus on the culture and heritage of African-Americans. Enrollment at these schools is formally open to anyone in the respective school system who wishes to apply. Immersion schools experiment with creative teaching techniques directed toward the learning and socialization styles of African-Americans. These schools also provide special mentoring and tutoring programs for students and faculty development programs for teachers.

Educators may be in the process of reshaping and redefining public education to fit the specific social environmental needs of African-American children. In the past, a number of African-American scholars have argued that black children are systematically miseducated in the traditional educational program. Educational initiatives in immersion schools may represent the beginning of an effort to address the inappropriateness of the traditional education program when applied to African-Americans. This deficiency flows from an improper conceptualization of the educational needs of African-Americans. The traditional educational program that purports to be value-neutral may actually be detrimental to the educational interest of many African-Americans.

The experimental programs that immersion schools employ are attempts to reduce the cultural conflicts existing between their African-American students and the dominant American culture enshrined in the traditional educational program. If successful, immersion schools could redefine the African-American cultural interpretation of the educational experience. Additionally, immersion schools allow educators the opportunity to teach strategies to help African-Americans deal with the ever present hassle of being black.

The Significance of Immersion Schools

The dominating logic which motivated educational reform for African-Americans in the 1960s, 1970s, and early 1980s originated during a time when both legal and political forces in America were attempting to desegregate public education. With the termination of school desegregation decrees, the pro-integrationist policies of the school desegregation era will likely become relics of an increasingly distant past. Many educators will begin to approach African-American educational issues with the realization that racial separation in public schools and American society is here to stay. For education officials, the reform logic behind the desegregation era could become passé. The acceptance of long-term segregation in public schools may exert a tremendous influence on educational reform for African-Americans. The desire to develop standardized educational programs across racial and ethnic lines, including multicultural programs, could become anachronistic. This will inexorably lead to more attempts to redesign the education of African-American youth.

Purpose of Afrocentric Curriculum

The incorporation of Afrocentric curricular materials into the educational process is one of the primary strategies immersion schools employ to accomplish their goals. The use of Afrocentric curricular materials in urban school systems is on the rise. School systems in Atlanta, Detroit, Indianapolis, New Orleans, Portland, and Washington, D.C., have approved their use.[21]

An Afrocentric curriculum is an emerging educational concept and educators will determine what passes as truly Afrocentric over the course of time. In general, an Afrocentric curriculum teaches basic courses by using Africa and the socio-historical experience of Africans and African-Americans as its reference points. An Afrocentric story places Africans and African-Americans at the center of the analysis. It treats them as the subject rather than the object of the discussion. However, this perspective is not a celebration of black pigmentation. An Afrocentric perspective does not glorify everything blacks have done. It evaluates, explains, and analyzes the actions of individuals and groups with a common yardstick, the liberation and enhancement of the lives of Africans and African-Americans.

An Afrocentric curriculum provides black students with an opportunity to study concepts, history, and the world from a perspective that places them at the center. Such a curriculum infuses these materials into the relevant content of various subjects, including language arts, mathematics, science, social studies, art, and music. Students are provided with both instruction in the relevant subject and a holistic and thematic awareness of the history, culture, and contributions of people of African descent. For example, from an Afrocentric perspective the focal point of civilization is the ancient Egyptian civilization (known as "Kemet" or "Said") as opposed to Ancient Greece. Therefore, Egypt, not Greece, is the origin of basic concepts of math and science. This is done to show African-American students that they can maintain their cultural identity and still succeed in their studies.

Nowhere is the implication of Afrocentric education more profound and more controversial than in the context of American history. From an Afrocentric, perspective American history is a tale about the historic struggle of blacks against the racial oppression and subjugation of Africans and their descendants. The presentation of American history from an Afrocentric, rather than an Anglocentric, perspective leads to different conclusions about the heritage of African-Americans within the United States. A brief look at the slavery experiences of African-Americans illustrates the difference and illuminates the educational strategies behind such a presentation.

From the Afrocentric perspective, the focus on slavery centers around what African-Americans and their ancestors did to resist the institution of slavery. What is important about captivity (slavery) was the struggle by the captives (slaves) against their oppressors. It is important to note that the captives did not sink into helplessness, apathy, and demoralization, rather, they struggled to survive, both spiritually and physically. Thus, while unable successfully to challenge the system of captivity frontally, the captives waged a many-sided struggle against their captors. The events that represent this struggle are infinite. There were uncounted rebellions and personal acts of defiance (including suicides) by Africans on ships of captivity during the "Middle Passage." Some of these courageous individuals showed that they would rather die than submit to captivity. There were countless insurgency actions by freedom fighters led by known revolutionary figures such as Jemmy, Nat Turner, Toussaint Louverture, Gabriel Prosser, and Denmark Vesey, along with unknown revolutionary figures. There were countless assassinations and poisonings of the captors by the captives. Major fires set in many American cities, such as Charleston, Albany, Newark, New York, Savannah, and Baltimore, were suspected of being set by blacks intent upon overthrowing the yoke of captivity. There was the work of blacks, such as Harriet Tubman, Elijah Anderson, and John Mason, who assisted others out of the most severe form of captivity—slavery. There were also countless individual acts of self-liberation and protest by the captives, including their refusal to submit to work or performing the work in a haphazard fashion.

An Afrocentric perspective would conceptualize the genesis of the Civil

War as an effort to hold the Union together as opposed to a movement to free the black captives. The massive movement of individual captives to free themselves by heading toward Union army camps when the war broke out forced the Union government to address the issue of their freedom. This perspective would also emphasize that Lincoln's Emancipation Proclamation was more of a military document than a humanitarian one. It excluded from its provisions the "loyal" slave states of Missouri, Kentucky, Delaware, and Maryland, the anti-Confederate West Virginia Territory, and loyal areas in certain other Confederate states. As a consequence, nearly one million black people whose masters were considered loyal to the Union were, theoretically, unaffected by the Proclamation. Their freedom was not legally secured until the Thirteenth Amendment was ratified almost three years later. From an Afrocentric perspective, Lincoln is not the great emancipator of the black captives. Rather, the great emancipators are those African-American ancestors who made freedom their personal responsibility.

The Anglocentric focus on slavery, however, presents the struggle against racial oppression as primarily one orchestrated and waged by abolitionist whites, such as the Quakers, William Garrison, and John Brown with occasional assistance from blacks like Frederick Douglass and Harriet Tubman. This perspective emphasizes twin goals of the Civil War as holding the Union together and eradicating slavery. President Lincoln is seen as leading the charge to reverse years of racial bigotry. The Anglocentric perspective treats the Emancipation Proclamation as both a humanitarian and military necessity. An Anglocentric perspective of slavery converts slaveholders, such as George Washington and Thomas Jefferson, into saviors because of their personal concern with the institution of slavery and their private acts of manumission. In fact, many whites who opposed slavery did so not for what slavery did to blacks but because of its negative impact on the work ethic and morality of whites. Nevertheless, these individuals are considered champions of the interests of slaves.

Presenting the story of slavery from an Afrocentric point of view shows African-Americans that they are descendants of over seventeen generations of people who struggled against racial subordination in America. It demonstrates graphically to African-American youth that they must take charge of their own liberation. It is only when blacks commit themselves to this task that their condition will improve.

The Anglocentric perspective, however, portrays whites as active parties in the abolition of slavery. Their efforts in overcoming the racial bigotry of other whites are praised. The Anglocentric perspective intends to foster feelings of loyalty for the country by showing how America overcame its own atrocities. This perspective portrays blacks as passive and submissive to the racial domination of slavery. Presenting only this view to African-American school children may lead to a sense of disempowerment. This perspective projects the view that, as in the time of slavery, improvements in the conditions of African-Americans must await the beneficence or enlightenment of whites.[22]

Paradoxes Resulting from the Legal
Analysis of Immersion Schools

On racial and educational grounds, then, a powerful case can be made for immersion schools. Yet, the abstract, highly individualistic nature of the legal system bodes ill for their future. Each of the three resolutions of the legal conflict involving the establishment of immersion schools will result in a paradox. First, in justifying immersion schools, courts can ignore that immersion schools appeal to African-Americans and view them as racially neutral, since they are open to all. What to some (many, most) would appear to be racially motivated decision making actually would be deemed an educational decision which happens to have a racial overtone. In effect, this would cause immersion schools, designed for African-Americans, to be labelled race-neutral. In addition, such a conceptualization of immersion schools reinforces the notion that the impact of culture on individual African-Americans is primarily a matter of choice because enrollment is a matter of choice. But the justifications for immersion schools flow from a belief that the impact of culture is not a matter of choice. As a result, the primary justifications for the schools evaporate.

Second, courts can invalidate immersion schools from the perspective that they violate the Equal Protection Clause. In an effort to uphold the Equal Protection Clause's requirement of equal treatment, courts would be confining African-Americans to an educational situation that cannot take account of the disparate social environment created for them by the conflicting influences of African-American and dominant Anglo-American cultures. Such a result amounts to a declaration that the public schools treat African-American students equally even though they are receiving an inappropriate education. By forcing African-Americans to remain in educational institutions insensitive to their social environment and the cultural conflicts that exist for them, courts sanction inequality for African-American students through the guise of equality.

The third resolution is for courts to uphold the decision of educators to establish immersion schools because it survives strict scrutiny. Upholding immersion schools for this reason will force proponents to provide reasons that make their race-based decision making compelling. This will require proponents to paint the most negative picture about the plight of African-Americans. The more miserable the condition of African-Americans is portrayed, the better the chances of establishing the compelling interest needed to justify immersion schools. In providing objective evidence about the negative condition of African-Americans, however, proponents legitimate derogatory beliefs about African-Americans. As a result, the need to supply legal justification will force proponents of immersion schools to argue the reasonableness of the social construction of African-Americans in our dominant culture. Since one of the primary justifications for immersion schools is the negative social construction of African-Americans, this solution reinforces the problem which makes the solution necessary.

In short, there is no solution to this problem that will not lead to a paradox.

A paradox is unavoidable because public education is an acculturating institution. Culture necessarily influences the attitudes, opinions, and experiences of individuals in public schools. Law, by contrast, attempts to make decisions by abstracting those decisions from the social conditions that influence them. While education focuses on the impact of culture in molding the person, law focuses on the concept of individuals who choose what and how they want to be. For education, culture is important. For law, it is not. It is the interplay of these different cognitive frameworks that creates the contradiction in any solution to the problem of soundly educating African-Americans.

NOTES

1. John U. Ogbu, *Immigrant and Involuntary Minorities in Comparative Perspectives, in* MINORITY STATUS AND SCHOOLING: A COMPARATIVE STUDY OF IMMIGRANT AND INVOLUNTARY MINORITIES 3, 3–33 (Margaret A. Gibson & John Ogbu eds., 1991).

2. Due to the conflicts between the dominant American cultural heritage and perspective and Afrocentric cultural heritage and perspective, the two cultures cannot be integrated without some personality dislocation. ROBERT STAPLES, INTRODUCTION TO BLACK SOCIOLOGY 68 (1976).

3. Pierre L. VanDen Berghe, *A Review of Minority Education and Caste: The American System in Cross-Cultural Perspective,* 24 COMP. EDUC. REV. 126, 126–30 (1980); George Clement Bond, *Social Economic Status and Educational Achievement: A Review Article,* 12 ANTHROPOLOGY & EDUC. Q., 227–57 (1981).

4. Ogbu, *Immigrant and Involuntary Minorities in Comparative Perspectives, in* MINORITY STATUS AND SCHOOLING, supra note 1, at 3, 5–6.

5. John U. Ogbu, *Class Stratification, Racial Stratification and Schooling, in* CLASS, RACE AND GENDER IN AMERICAN EDUCATION 164 (L. Weis ed., 1988) (arguing that poor performance of blacks in education is due to racial stratification rather than to class differences).

6. *See, e.g.,* Reuben M. Baron et al., *Social Class, Race and Teacher Expectations, in* TEACHER EXPECTANCIES 251–69 (Jerome B. Dusek ed., 1985); COMM. ON POLICY FOR RACIAL JUSTICE, VISIONS OF A BETTER WAY: A BLACK APPRAISAL OF PUBLIC SCHOOLING 16–17 (1989) (discussing research revealing that teachers' gross stereotyping as well as their inaccurate, negative, and rigid expectations of black and low-income children form the groundwork for self-fulfilling prophecies of academic failure).

7. Ogbu, *Immigrant and Involuntary Minorities in Comparative Perspectives, in* MINORITY STATUS AND SCHOOLING, supra note 1, at 3, 27.

8. Law school academics also can experience cultural conflict in their legal academies. *See, e.g.,* Pierre Schlag, *The Problem of the Subject,* 69 TEX. L. REV. 1627, 1679–83 (1991) (describing the experience of young liberal thinkers in American law schools whose political and cultural maturation was influenced by the Civil Rights movement and the Vietnam War, as well as the counter culture). These individuals found themselves as members of a law faculty and were being groomed to think and act like the very people against whom they were fighting. *Id.*

9. In my high school, students received grades in their classes every six

weeks. For the six week period that preceded reading *Huck Finn*, my grade in English was a "B." For the six week period that we read *Huck Finn*, it was a "D." During the time the class read *Huck Finn*, an antagonistic relationship developed between my English teacher and me that continued during the remainder of the time I was in her class. Even though my English grade improved to an "A" for the six week grading period after reading *Huck Finn*, the antagonism in our relationship did not lessen. At the end of the third grading period, my English teacher was given the opportunity to send six of her students to another English class with a different teacher. Needless to say, I was one of those transferred.

10. Signithia Fordham, *Racelessness as a Factor in Black Students' School Success: Pragmatic Strategy or Pyrrhic Victory?*, 58 HARV. EDUC. REV. 54, 55 (1988) (discussing the impact of race on scholarly black students).

11. For a discussion of the philosophy of leading Afrocentric educators on the influence of culture in determining the educational strategies for African-Americans, see INFUSION OF AFRICAN AND AFRICAN AMERICAN CONTENT IN THE SCHOOL CURRICULUM: PROCEEDINGS OF THE FIRST NATIONAL CONFERENCE, OCTOBER 1989 (A. G. Hilliard III et al. eds., 1990).

12. [Memorandum of Law in Opposition to Plaintiffs' Motion for Temporary Restraining Order and Preliminary Injunction] at 15, Garrett v. Board of Educ., 775 F. Supp. 1004 (E.D. Mich. 1991) (No. 91–73821).

13. *Id.* at 3–4. According to an article in *Newsweek* magazine that discussed the Milwaukee plan for separate schools for African-American males, black men, who account for 6 percent of the U.S. population, represent 46 percent of state prison inmates. Barbara Kantrowitz, *Can the Boys Be Saved?*, NEWSWEEK, Oct. 15, 1990, at 67. In addition, among black men who are in their 20s, 23 percent are incarcerated or on probation or parole. *Id.*

14. *See, e.g.*, Garrett v. Board of Educ., 775 F. Supp. 1004, 1006 (E.D. Mich. 1991).

15. *See* Langston Hughes, *Theme for English B, in* THE LANGSTON HUGHES READER 108–09 (1958).

16. *See, e.g.*, CARNEGIE COMM'N ON THE FUTURE OF HIGHER EDUC., FROM ISOLATION TO MAINSTREAM: PROBLEMS OF THE COLLEGES FOUNDED FOR NEGROES 11 (1971) (praising historically black colleges for providing educational opportunities for blacks and enhancing the general quality of life of black Americans).

17. Walter Leavy, *Is the Black Male an Endangered Species?*, EBONY, Aug. 1983, at 41. There have been debates and discussions about the survivability and viability of the African-American male. *See generally* BLACK MEN (Lawrence E. Gary ed., 1981); YOUNG, BLACK, AND MALE IN AMERICA; AN ENDANGERED SPECIES (Jewelle Gibbs et al. eds., 1988).

18. The Supreme Court has addressed the issue of gender segregation in both public education and public university education. Mississippi Univ. for Women v. Hogan, 458 U.S. 718 (1982). In *Hogan*, the Court struck down the state's single sex admission policy for its school of nursing at the Mississippi University for Women. *Id.* at 730. The Court noted that the proffered justification for the exclusion, providing a remedial haven for women from the hierarchy of domination in the man's world of higher education, was unpersuasive. *Id.* at 731. They viewed excluding men from a school of nursing as perpetuating the stereotyped view of nursing as exclusively a woman's job. *Id.* at 729–30.

The issue of gender-segregated education in public schools was addressed by the Court in Vorchheimer v. School Dist. of Philadelphia, 430 U.S. 703 (1977) (per curiam). An evenly divided Court upheld an otherwise coeducational school system's maintenance of sexually segregated high schools for high academic achievers. *Id.* at 703.

19. 775 F. Supp. 1004 (E.D. Mich. 1991).

20. The district court specifically noted it "[was] not presented with the question of whether the Board can provide separate but equal public school institutions for boys and girls." *Garrett*, 775 F. Supp. at 1006 n.4.

21. *See* Peter Schmidt, *Educators Foresee 'Renaissance' in African Studies*, EDUC. WK., Oct. 18, 1989, at 8.

22. Professor Derrick Bell, for example, argues that the Supreme Court's school desegregation cases can be understood as balancing the interests of black rights against white interests and choosing the latter. *See* Derrick Bell, Brown *and the Interest-Convergence Dilemma, in* SHADES OF BROWN: NEW PERSPECTIVES ON SCHOOL DESEGREGATION 91, 91–106 (Derrick Bell ed., 1980). *See generally* DERRICK BELL, AND WE ARE NOT SAVED (1987).

From the Editor:
Issues and Comments

D O Y O U agree that black schools are an essential aspect of black identity, and that role modeling (as it is usually understood) simply plays into the hands of integrationist forces? Is Rodrigo right in arguing that Western civilization is in eclipse and that Western industrialist nations, like the United States, need an infusion of minority ideas at least as much as minorities need access to majority society? If so, is this a better basis for affirmative action—namely, majoritarian self-interest—than the usual ones? Is cultural nationalism a mere stage, necessary perhaps for psychic and spiritual salvation for blacks and other minorities, but something that should be discarded as communities of color become self-sufficient? Is cultural nationalism racism in reverse? Will Afrocentric immersion schools help—or hurt—black schoolchildren, perhaps by disabling them from functioning in the broader society? If immersion schools could confer even greater benefits on young black males by being unisex, would it be constitutional to exclude young women and girls—and would it be wise? In Part III, Robert Cottrol and Raymond Diamond argue for arming the black community as a response to inadequate police protection and even abuse at the hands of white police. Is this the logical extension of cultural nationalism? If so, is it to be cheered or deplored?

See also the articles in Parts VII and XI, particularly those by Monica Evans, Lisa Ikemoto, and Regina Austin, on insurrection and criminality in communities of color.

Suggested Readings

Aleinikoff, T. Alexander, *A Case for Race-Consciousness*, 91 COLUM. L. REV. 1060 (1991).

Austin, Regina, *Sapphire Bound!*, 1989 WIS. L. REV. 539.

BELL, DERRICK A., JR., AND WE ARE NOT SAVED: THE ELUSIVE QUEST FOR RACIAL JUSTICE (1987).

Calmore, John O., *Critical Race Theory, Archie Shepp, and Fire Music: Securing an Authentic Intellectual Life in a Multicultural World*, 65 S. CAL. L. REV. 2129 (1992).

Evans, Monica J., *Stealing Away: Black Women, Outlaw Culture and the Rhetoric of Rights*, 28 HARV. C.R.-C.L. L. REV. 263 (1993).

Lâm, Maivân Clech, *The Kuleana Act Revisited: The Survival of Traditional Hawaiian Commoner Rights in Land*, 64 WASH. L. REV. 233 (1989).

López, Gerald P., *The Idea of a Constitution in the Chicano Tradition*, 37 J. LEGAL EDUC. 162 (1987).

Peller, Gary, *Race Consciousness*, 1990 DUKE L.J. 758.

LEGAL INSTITUTIONS, CRITICAL PEDAGOGY, AND MINORITIES IN THE LAW

IN ADDITION to tackling such substantive issues as hate speech, the critique of race and sex, and American Indian law reform, CRT writers have taken a lively interest in the politics and fairness of the institutions where they work—law schools, law firms, and the bar. Part IX begins with Derrick Bell's sly, probing "Chronicle of the DeVine Gift," in which he examines head-on the tired excuse that white-dominated institutions cannot hire minority lawyers and professors because "the pool is so small." His parable explores what would happen if a school found itself deluged with spectacularly credentialed blacks willing to teach there. Next, Richard Delgado examines the domination of civil rights writing and discourse by influential whites. Then, Jerome Culp, an original and exciting writer, addresses the place of autobiography and personal experience in framing legal questions, issues, and classroom teaching. What can a black man say that a majority-race scholar cannot—or is unlikely to—say? This part concludes with Deborah Waire Post's reflections on her own choice with respect to her biracial identity and how that choice shapes her perspective as a black lawyer and teacher.

Each of these chapters emphasizes themes that the reader will already find familiar from earlier sections of this book: the qualification hurdle and how it can be seen differently from different perspectives; the marginalization of outsider ideas and the energetic insistence of outsider writers that they be heard; the legitimacy (indeed, necessity) of grounding theories and strategies in the personal; the ubiquity of the white perspective in legal case law; the way empathy often fails, but nevertheless is urgently needed; and the necessity of establishing true diversity if society is to prosper.

34 The Civil Rights Chronicles: The Chronicle of the DeVine Gift

DERRICK BELL

I T W A S a major law school, one of the best [my friend Geneva Crenshaw began], but I do not remember how I came to teach there rather than at Howard, my alma mater. My offer, the first ever made to a black, was the culmination of years of agitation by students and a few faculty members. It was the spring of my second year. I liked teaching and writing, but I was exhausted and considered resigning, although more out of frustration than fatigue.

I had become the personal counselor and confidante of virtually all of the black students and a goodly number of the whites. The black students needed someone with whom to share their many problems, and white students, finding a faculty member willing to take time with them, were not reluctant to help keep my appointment book full. I liked the students, but it was hard to give them as much time as they needed. I also had to prepare for classes—where I was expected to give an award-winning performance each day—and serve on every committee at the law school on which minority representation was desired. In addition, every emergency concerning a racial issue was deemed "my problem." I admit that I wanted to be involved in these problems, but they all required time and energy. Only another black law teacher would fully understand what I had to do to make time for research and writing.

So, when someone knocked on my door late one afternoon as I was frantically trying to finish writing final exam questions, I was tempted to tell the caller to go away. But I didn't. And, at first, I was sorry. The tall, distinguished man who introduced himself as DeVine Taylor was neither a student nor one of the black students' parents, who often dropped by when they were in town just to meet their child's only black teacher.

Mr. Taylor, unlike many parents and students, came quickly to the point. He apologized for not making an appointment, but explained that his visit concerned a matter requiring confidentiality. He showed me a card and other papers identifying him as the president of the DeVine Hair Products Co., a familiar name in many black homes and one of the country's most successful black

99 HARV. L. REV. 4 (1985). Copyright © 1985 by The Harvard Law Review Association.

businesses. I recognized Mr. Taylor's face and told him that I knew of his business, even if I did not use his products.

"You may also know," Mr. Taylor said, "that my company and I have not been much involved in this integration business. It seems to me that civil rights organizations are ready to throw out the good aspects of segregation along with the bad. I think we need to wake up to the built-in limits of the 'equal opportunity' that liberals are always preaching. Much of it may be a trick that will cost us what we have built up over the years without giving us anything better to take its place. Personally, I am afraid they will integrate me into bankruptcy. Even now, white companies are undercutting me in every imaginable way.

"But," he interrupted himself with a deep sigh, "that is not why I am here. You have heard of foundations that reward recipients based on their performance rather than on their proposals. Well, for some time my company has been searching for blacks who are truly committed to helping other blacks move up. We have located and helped several of these individuals over the years by providing them with what we call 'the DeVine Gift.' We know of your work and believe that you deserve to be included in that group. We want to help you to help other blacks, and we can spend a large amount of money in that effort. For tax and other business reasons, we cannot provide our help in cash. And we do not wish anyone to know that we are providing the help."

It was clear that he was serious, and I tried to respond appropriately. "Well, Mr. Taylor, I appreciate the compliment, but it is not clear how a black hair products company can be of assistance to a law teacher. Unless"—the idea came to me suddenly—"unless you can help me locate more blacks and other minorities with the qualifications needed to become a faculty member at this school."

Mr. Taylor did not look surprised. "I was a token black in a large business before I left in frustration to start my own company. I think I understand your problem exactly, and with our nationwide network of sales staff, I think we can help."

When I was hired, the faculty promised that although I was their first black teacher, I would not be their last. This was not to be a token hire, they assured me, but the first step toward achieving a fully integrated faculty. But subsequent applicants, including a few with better academic credentials than my own, were all found wanting in one or another respect. My frustration regarding this matter, no less than my fatigue, was what had brought me to the point of resignation prior to Mr. Taylor's visit.

With the behind-the-scenes help from the DeVine Gift, the law school hired its second black teacher during the summer, a young man with good credentials and some teaching experience at another law school. He was able to fill holes in the curriculum caused by two unexpected faculty resignations. The following year, we "discovered," again with the assistance of Mr. Taylor's network, three more minority teachers—a Hispanic man, an Asian woman, and another black woman. In addition, one of our black graduates, a law review editor, was promised a position when he completed his judicial clerkship.

We now had six minority faculty members, far more than any other major *white law school. I was ecstatic, a sentiment that I soon learned was not shared by many of my white colleagues. I am usually more sensitive about such things, but I so enjoyed the presence of the other minority faculty members, who eased the burdens on my time and gave me a sense of belonging to a "critical mass," that I failed to realize the growing unrest among some white faculty members.*

Had we stopped at six, perhaps nothing would have been said. But the following year, Mr. Taylor's company, with growing expertise, recruited an exceptionally able black lawyer. His academic credentials were impeccable. The top student at our competitor school, he had been a law review editor and had written a superb student note. After clerking for a federal court of appeals judge and a U.S. Supreme Court Justice, he had joined a major New York City law firm and was in line for early election to partnership. I am not sure how they did it, but the DeVine people discovered that he had an unrealized desire to teach, and an application followed. He would be our seventh minority faculty member and, based on his record, the best of all of us.

When the Dean came to see me, he talked rather aimlessly for some time before he reached the problem troubling him and, I later gathered, much of the faculty. The problem was that our faculty would soon be twenty-five percent minority. "You know, Geneva, we promised you we would become an integrated faculty, and we have kept that promise—admittedly with a lot of help from you. But I don't think we can hire anyone else for a while. I thought we might 'share the wealth' a bit by recommending your candidate to some of our sister schools whose minority hiring records are far less impressive than our own."

"Mr. Dean," I said as calmly and, I fear, as coldly as I could, "I am not interested in recruiting black teachers for other law schools. Each of the people we have hired is good, as you have boasted many times. And I can assure you that the seventh candidate will be better than anyone now on the faculty without regard to race."

"I admit that, Geneva, but let's be realistic. This is one of the oldest and finest law schools in the country. It simply would not be the same school with a predominantly minority faculty. I thought you would understand."

"I'm no mathematician," I said, "but twenty-five percent is far from a majority. Still, it is more racial integration than you want, even though none of the minorities, excluding perhaps myself, has needed any affirmative action help to qualify for the job. I also understand, even if tardily, that you folks never expected that I would find more than a few minorities who could meet your academic qualifications; you never expected that you would have to reveal what has always been your chief qualification—a white face, preferably from an upper-class background."

To his credit, the Dean remained fairly calm throughout my tirade. "I have heard you argue that black law schools like Howard should retain mainly black faculties and student bodies, even if they have to turn away whites with better qualifications to do so. We have a similar situation; we want to retain our image as a white school just as you want Howard to retain its image as a black school."

"That is a specious argument, Dean, and you know it. Black schools have a special responsibility to aid the victims of this country's long-standing and continuing racism. Schools like this one should be grateful for the chance to change their all-white image. And if you are not grateful, I am certain the courts will give you ample reason to reconsider when this latest candidate sues you to be instated in the job he has earned and is entitled to receive."

The Dean was not surprised by my rather unprofessional threat to sue. "I have discussed this at length with some faculty members, and we realize that you may wish to test this matter in the courts. We think, however, that there are favorable precedents on the issues that such a suit will raise. I do not want to be unkind. We do appreciate your recruitment efforts, Geneva, but a law school of our caliber and tradition simply cannot look like a professional basketball team."

He left my office after that parting shot, and I remember that my first reaction was rage. Then, as I slowly realized the full significance of all that had happened since I received the DeVine Gift, the tears came and kept coming. I cried and cried at the futility of it all. Through those tears, over the next few days, I completed grading my final exams. Then I announced my resignation as well as the reasons for it.

When I told the Seventh Candidate that the school would not offer him a position and why, he was strangely silent, only thanking me for my support. About a week later, I received a letter from him—mailed not from his law firm but, according to the postmark, from a small, all-black town in Oklahoma.

> Dear Professor Crenshaw:
>
> Until now, when black people employed race to explain failure, I, like the black neoconservative scholars, wondered how they might have fared had they made less noise and done more work. Embracing self-confidence and eschewing self-pity seemed the right formula for success. One had to show more heart and shed fewer tears. Commitment to personal resources rather than reliance on public charity, it seemed to me, is the American way to reach goals—for blacks as well as for whites. Racial bias is not, I thought, a barrier but a stimulant toward showing them what we can do in the workplace as well as on the ball field, in the classroom as well as on the dance floor.
>
> Now no rationale will save what was my philosophy for achievement, my justification for work. My profession, the law, is not a bulwark against this destruction. It is instead a stage prop illuminated with colored lights to mask the ongoing drama of human desolation we all suffer, regardless of skills and work and personal creed.
>
> You had suggested I challenge my rejection in the courts, but even if I won the case and in that way gained the position to which my abilities entitled me, I would not want to join a group whose oft-stated moral commitment to the meritocracy has been revealed as no more than a hypocritical conceit, a means of elevating those like themselves to an elite whose qualifications for their superior positions can never be tested because they do not exist.
>
> Your law school faculty may not realize that the cost of rejecting me is ex-

posing themselves. They are, as Professor Roberto Unger has said in another context, like a "priesthood that had lost their faith and kept their jobs."[1]

But if I condemn hypocrisy in the law school, I must not condone it in myself. What the law school did when its status as a mainly white institution was threatened is precisely what even elite colleges faced with a growing number of highly qualified Asian students are doing: changing the definition of merit. My law firm and virtually every major institution in this country would do the same thing in a similar crisis of identity. I have thus concluded that I can no longer play a role in the tragic farce in which the talents and worth of a few of us who happen to get there first is dangled like bait before the masses who are led to believe that what can never be is a real possibility. When next you hear from me, it will be in a new role as avenger rather than apologist. This system must be forced to recognize what it is doing to you and me and to itself. By the time you read this, it will be too late for you to reason with me. I am on my way.

Yours,
The Seventh Candidate

This decision, while a shock, hardly prepared me for the disturbing letter that arrived a few days later from DeVine Taylor, who evidently had read my well-publicized resignation.

Dear Geneva,

Before you received the DeVine Gift, your very presence at the law school posed a major barrier to your efforts to hire additional minority faculty. Having appointed you, the school relaxed. Its duty was done. Its liberal image was assured. When you suggested the names of other minorities with skills and backgrounds like your own, your success was ignored and those you named were rejected for lack of qualifications. When the DeVine Gift forced your school to reveal the hidden but no less substantive basis for dragging their feet after you were hired, the truth became clear.

As a token minority law teacher, Geneva, you provided an alien institution with a facade of respectability of far more value to them than any aid you gave to either minority students or the cause of black people. You explained your resignation as a protest. But you should realize that removing yourself from that prestigious place was a necessary penance for the inadvertent harm you have done to the race you are sincerely committed to save.

I am happy to see that the DeVine Gift has served its intended purpose. I wish you success in your future work.

DeVine Taylor

"A devastating note," I murmured. Geneva had seemed to relive rather than simply retell her Chronicle. She was so agitated by the time she finished that she seemed to forget I was there and began to pace the room. She said something about the foolishness of accepting a teaching position at a school where she would be so vulnerable. For my part, I was more worried about the current state of Geneva's health than about her Chronicle. I tried to reassure her.

"I think that most minorities feel exposed and vulnerable at predominantly white law schools. And I know that most black teachers run into faculty resistance when they seek to recruit a second nonwhite faculty member. Of course, these teachers continue to confront the qualifications hurdle; they never reach the problem you faced. Our question, however, is whether the Supreme Court would view the law school's rejection of a seventh eminently qualified minority candidate as impermissible racial discrimination. At first glance," I said, "the Dean's confidence in favorable precedents was not justified. Although the courts have withdrawn from their initial expansive reading of title VII, even a conservative Court might find for your seventh minority candidate, given his superior credentials."

"Remember," Geneva cautioned, "the law school will first claim that its preference for white applicants is based on their superior qualifications. I gather the cases indicate that the employer's subjective evaluation can play a major role in decisions involving highly qualified candidates who seek professional level positions."

"That is true," I conceded. "Generally, courts have shown an unwillingness to interfere with upper-level hiring decisions in the 'elite' professions, including university teaching. Under current law, if there are few objective hiring criteria and legitimate subjective considerations, plaintiffs will only rarely obtain a searching judicial inquiry into their allegation of discrimination in hiring."

"In other words," Geneva summarized, "this would not be an easy case even if the plaintiff were the first rather than the seventh candidate."

"I think that is right, Geneva," I replied. "Many of the decisions that the Court let stand went against plaintiffs alleging discriminatory practices, although some held in their favor."

"Do you think, then," Geneva asked, "that our seventh candidate has no chance?"

"No," I answered. "The Court might surprise us if the record shows that the plaintiff's qualifications are clearly superior to those of other candidates. It would be a very compelling situation, one not likely to occur again soon, and the Supreme Court just might use this case to reach a 'contradiction-closing' decision.

Geneva was getting anxious. "So are you now ready to predict what the Supreme Court would do in this case?"

Like most law teachers, I am ready to predict judicial outcomes even before being asked, but recalling what Geneva believed was at stake, I thought it wise to review the situation more closely. "Weighing all the factors," I finally said, "the Dean's belief that his law school will prevail in court may be justified after all."

"I agree," Geneva said. "And we have not yet considered the possibility that even if the Court found that our candidate had the best paper credentials, the law school might have an alternative defense."

"That is true," I said. "The law school might argue that even if its rejection of the seventh candidate was based on race, the decision was justified. The school will aver that its reputation and financial well-being are based on its status as a 'majority institution.' The maintenance of a predominantly white faculty, the school will say, is essential to the preservation of an appropriate image, to the recruitment of faculty and students, and to the enlistment of alumni contributions. With heartfelt expressions of regret that 'the world is not a better place,' the law school will urge the Court to find that neither title VII nor the Constitution prohibits it from discriminating against minority candidates when the percentage of minorities on the faculty exceeds the percentage of minorities within the population. At the least, the school will contend that no such prohibition should apply while most of the country's law schools continue to maintain nearly all-white faculties."

"And how do you think the Court would respond to such an argument?" Geneva asked.

"Well," I answered, "given the quality of the minority faculty, courts might discount the law school's fears that it would lose status and support if one-fourth of its teaching staff were nonwhite."

Geneva did not look convinced. "I don't know," she said. "I think a part of the Dean's concern was that if I could find seven outstanding minority candidates, then I could find more—so many more that the school would eventually face the possibility of having a fifty percent minority faculty. And the courts would be concerned about the precedent set here. What, they might think, if other schools later developed similar surfeits of super-qualified minority job applicants?"

"Well," I responded, "the courts have hardly been overwhelmed with cases demanding that upper-level employers have a twenty-five to fifty percent minority work force, particularly in the college and university teaching areas. But perhaps you are right. A recent Supreme Court case involving skilled construction workers suggests that an employer may introduce evidence of its hiring of blacks in the past to show that an otherwise unexplained action was not racially motivated.[2] Perhaps, then, an employer who has hired many blacks in the past may at some point decide to cease considering them. Even if the Court did not explicitly recognize this argument, it might take the law school's situation into account. In fact, the Court might draw an analogy to housing cases in which courts have recognized that whites usually prefer to live in predominantly white housing developments."

"I am unfamiliar with those cases," Geneva said. "Have courts approved ceilings on the number of minorities who may live in a residential area?"

"Indeed they have," I replied. "Acting on the request of housing managers trying to maintain integrated developments, courts have tailored tenant racial balance to levels consistent with the refusal of whites to live in predominantly black residential districts. The Second Circuit, for example, allowed the New York City Housing Authority to limit the number of apartments it made available to minority persons whenever 'such action is essential to promote a racially balanced community and to avoid concentrated racial pockets that will result in a segregated community."[3] The court feared that unless it allowed the housing authority to impose limits on minority occupancy, a number of housing developments would reach the 'tipping point'—the point at which the percentage of minorities living in an area becomes sufficiently large that virtually all white residents move out and other whites refuse to take their places.[4]

"The analogy is not perfect," I concluded, "but the 'tipping point' phenomenon in housing plans may differ little from the faculty's reaction to your seventh candidate. Both reflect a desire by whites to dominate their residential and nonresidential environments. If this is true, the arguments used to support benign racial quotas in housing may also be used to support the law school's employment decision."

Geneva disagreed. "I do not view the law school's refusal to hire the seventh candidate as in any way 'benign.' The school's decision was unlike the adoption of a housing quota intended to establish or protect a stable, integrated community before most private discrimination in the housing area was barred by law. The law school did not respond to a 'tipping point' resulting from the individual decisions of numerous parties whom the authorities cannot control. The law school instead imposed a 'stopping point' for hiring blacks and other minorities, regardless of their qualifications. School officials, whose actions are covered by title VII, arbitrarily determined a cut-off point."

"Don't get trapped in semantics," I warned Geneva. "A housing quota that is 'benign' seems quite 'invidious' to the blacks who are excluded by its operation. They are no less victims of housing bias than are those excluded from neighborhoods by restrictive covenants. Yet at least in some courts, those excluded by benign quotas have no remedy. In our case, the law school could argue that the seventh candidate should likewise have no remedy: he has made—albeit involuntarily—a sacrifice for the long-run integration goals that so many find persuasive in the housing sphere.

"In other words," Geneva said, "if and when the number of blacks qualified for upper-level jobs exceeds the token representation envisioned by most affirmative action programs, opposition of the character exhibited by my law school could provide the impetus for a judicial ruling that employers have done their 'fair share' of minority hiring. This rule, while imposing limits on constitutionally required racial fairness for the black elite, would devastate civil rights enforcement for all minorities. In effect, the Court would formalize and legitimize the subordinate status that is already a de facto reality."

"Indeed," I said, "affirmative action remedies have flourished because they offer more benefit to the institutions that adopt them than they do to the minorities whom they are nominally intended to serve. Initially, at least in higher education, affirmative action policies represented the response of school officials to the considerable pressures placed upon them to hire minority faculty members and enroll minority students. Rather than overhaul admissions criteria that provided easy access to offspring of the upper class and presented difficult barriers to all other applicants, officials chose to 'lower' admissions standards for minority candidates. This act of self-interested beneficence had unfortunate results. Affirmative action now 'connotes the undertaking of remedial activity beyond what normally would be required. It sounds in *noblesse oblige*, not legal duty, and suggests the giving of charity rather than the granting of relief.' At the same time, the affirmative action overlay on the overall admissions standards admits only a trickle of minorities. These measures are, at best, 'a modest mechanism for increasing the number of minority professionals, adopted as much to further the self-interest of the white majority as to aid the designated beneficiaries.' "[5]

"There is one last point," I told Geneva. "Some courts have been reluctant to review academic appointments, because 'to infer discrimination from a comparison among candidates is to risk a serious infringement of first amendment values.' "[6]

"In other words," Geneva said, "the selection of faculty members ascends to the level of a first amendment right of academic freedom."

"I am afraid so," I nodded, "and the law schools' lawyers will certainly not ignore Justice Powell's perhaps unintended support for this position given in his *Bakke* opinion, in which he discussed admissions standards in the context of a university's constitutional right of academic freedom.[7] He acknowledged that ethnic diversity was 'only one element in a range of factors a university properly may consider in attaining the goal of a heterogeneous student body.' Given the importance of faculty selection in maintaining similar aspects of this form of academic freedom, it would seem only a short step to a policy of judicial deference to a school's determination that a successful minority recruiting effort was threatening to unbalance the ethnic diversity of its faculty."

"You say all this to make what point?" Geneva asked.

"Just this. Your school's affirmative action program had not contemplated the DeVine Gift. Because the Gift enabled you to recruit outstanding minority candidates for every faculty vacancy, the Gift thus rendered possible what was not supposed to happen. The faculty's opposition to your seventh candidate was based on an unconscious feeling that it had been double-crossed. Had the seventh candidate been the first, the faculty would have gladly accepted him. It might even have hired him if you had recognized its fear of becoming a predominantly minority faculty and agreed to limit your recruitment drive. But with no end in sight to the flow of qualified minority applicants, the faculty determined to call a halt."

"You assume," Geneva said, "that any faculty would react as mine did to an apparently endless flow of outstanding minority faculty prospects. But I would wager that if the Chronicle of the DeVine Gift were presented to white law teachers in the form of a hypothetical, most would insist that their faculties would snap up the seventh candidate in an instant."

"What you are seeking," I said, "is some proof that a faculty *would* respond as yours did, and then some explanation as to *why*. The record of minority recruitment is so poor as to constitute a prima facie case that most faculties *would* reject the seventh candidate. And most black law teachers would support this view. Their universal complaint is that after predominantly white faculties have

hired one or two minority teachers, the faculties lose interest in recruiting minorities and indicate that they are waiting for a minority candidate with truly outstanding credentials. Indeed, as long as a faculty has one minority person, the
pressure is off, and the recruitment priority simply disappears."

"No one, of course, can prove *whether* a given faculty would react as mine
did," Geneva said, "but for our purposes, the more interesting question is why a
faculty would if it did. You would think that whites would be secure in their sta-
tus-laden positions as tenured members of a prestigious law school faculty. Why,
then, would they insist on a predominantly white living and working environment? Why would they reject the seventh candidate?"

"Initially," I replied, "it is important to acknowledge that white law teachers
are not bigots in the red-neck, sheet-wearing sense. Certainly, no law teacher I
know consciously shares Ben Franklin's dream of an ideal white society or accepts the slave owner's propaganda that blacks are an inferior species who, to use
Chief Justice Taney's characterization, 'might justly and lawfully be reduced to
slavery for his benefit.'[8] Neither perception flourishes today, but the long history
of belief in both undergirds a cultural sense of what Professor Manning Marable
identifies as the 'ideological hegemony' of white racism. Marable asserts that all
of our institutions of education and information—political and civic, religious
and creative—either knowingly or unknowingly 'provide the public rationale to
justify, explain, legitmize or tolerate racism.' Professor Marable does not charge
that ideological hegemony is the result of a conspiracy, plotted and executed with
diabolical cunning.[9] Rather, it is sustained by a culturally ingrained response by
whites to any situation in which whites are not in a clearly dominant role. It explains, for example, the 'first black' phenomenon in which each new position or
role gained by a black for the first time creates concern and controversy as to
whether 'they' are ready for this position, or whether whites are ready to accept
a black in this position."

"Putting it that way," Geneva responded, "helps me to understand why the
school's rejection of my seventh candidate hurt me without really surprising me.
I had already experienced a similar rejection on a personal level. When I arrived,
the white faculty members were friendly and supportive. They smiled at me a lot
and offered help and advice. When they saw how much time I spent helping minority students and how I struggled with my first writing, they seemed pleased.
It was patronizing, but the general opinion seemed to be that they had done well
to hire me. They felt good about having lifted up one of the downtrodden. And
they congratulated themselves for their affirmative action policies. But were
these policies to continue for three generations, who knew what might happen?

"Then, after I became acclimated to academic life, I began receiving invitations to publish in the top law reviews, to serve on important commissions, and
to lecture at other schools. At that point, I noticed that some of my once-smiling
colleagues now greeted me with frowns. For them, nothing I did was right: my articles were flashy but not deep, rhetorical rather than scholarly. Even when I published an article in a major review, my colleagues gave me little credit; after all,

students had selected the piece, and what did they know anyway? My popularity with students was attributed to the likelihood that I was an easy grader. The more successful I appeared, the harsher became the collective judgment of my former friends."

"I think many minority teachers have undergone similar experiences," I consoled Geneva. "Professor Richard Delgado thinks that something like 'cognitive dissonance' may explain the shift:

> At first, the white professor feels good about hiring the minority. It shows how liberal the white is, and the minority is assumed to want nothing more than to scrape by in the rarefied world they both inhabit. But the minority does not just scrape by, is not eternally grateful, and indeed starts to surpass the white professor. This is disturbing; things weren't meant to go that way. The strain between former belief and current reality is reduced by reinterpreting the current reality. The minority has a fatal flaw. Pass it on.[10]

The value of your Chronicle, Geneva, is that it enables us to gauge the real intent and nature of affirmative action plans. Here, the stated basis for the plan's adoption—'to provide a more representative faculty and student body'—was pushed to a level its authors never expected it to reach. The influx of qualified minority candidates threatened, at some deep level, the white faculty members' sense of ideological hegemony and caused them to reject the seventh candidate. Even the first black or the second or the third no doubt threatens the white faculty to some extent. But it is only when we reach the seventh, or the tenth, that we are truly able to see the fear for what it is. Get my point?"

NOTES

1. Roberto Unger, *The Critical Legal Studies Movement*, 96 HARV. L. REV. 563, 675 (1983).

2. *See* Furnco Constr. Corp. v. Waters, 438 U.S. 567, 579–80 (1978).

3. Otero v. New York City Hous. Auth., 484 F.2d 1122, 1140 (2d Cir. 1973).

4. For explanations and examinations of the "tipping point" phenomenon, see ANTHONY DOWNS, OPENING UP THE SUBURBS 68–73 (1973); Bruce Ackerman, *Integration for Subsidized Housing and the Question of Racial Occupancy Controls*, 26 STAN. L. REV. 245, 251–66 (1974); and Note, *Tipping the Scales of Justice: A Race-Conscious Remedy for Neighborhood Transition*, 90 YALE L.J. 377, 379–82 (1980).

5. Derrick Bell, *Bakke, Minority Admissions and the Usual Price of Racial Remedies*, 67 CALIF. L. REV. 3, 8 (1979).

6. Leiberman v. Gant, 630 F.2d 60, 67 (2d Cir. 1980).

7. *See* Regents of the Univ. of Cal. v. Bakke, 438 U.S. 265, 311–12 (1978).

8. Dred Scott v. Sandford, 60 U.S. (19 How.) 393, 407 (1857).

9. Manning Marable, *Beyond the Race-Class Dilemma*, THE NATION, Apr. 11, 1981, at 428.

10. Letter from Richard Delgado to Linda Greene (Apr. 24, 1985) (copy on file at Harvard Law School Library).

35

"The Imperial Scholar" Revisited: How to Marginalize Outsider Writing, Ten Years Later

RICHARD DELGADO

T E N years ago I wrote an article, *The Imperial Scholar: Reflections on a Review of Civil Rights Literature*,[1] that became one of the more controversial pieces of its time. It has been cited more than fifty times, as often without approval as with. Even as sympathetic a coreligionist as Derrick Bell describes the article as "an intellectual hand grenade, tossed over the wall of the establishment as a form of academic protest."[2]

In it, I showed that an inner circle of twenty-six scholars, all male and white, occupied the central arenas of civil rights scholarship to the exclusion of contributions of minority scholars. When a member of this inner circle wrote about civil rights issues he cited almost exclusively to other members of the circle for support. I argued that this exclusion of minority scholars' writings about key issues of race law caused the literature dealing with race, racism, and American law to be blunted, skewed, and riddled with omissions. Among the reasons for the curious citation practices I discovered were (1) the mistaken belief that minority authors who write about racial issues are not objective, (2) the mainstream writers' need to remain in control, thus ensuring that legal change does not occur too quickly, and (3) the sense of personal satisfaction resulting from being at the forefront of a powerful social movement.

I concluded that article by urging minority students and teachers to question insistently and to improve upon the unsatisfactory scholarship produced by the inner circle, and by encouraging white liberal authors to redirect their energies towards other areas. Although the article provoked a storm when it appeared, many of its premises and assertions seem commonplace today.

I now address the "second generation" question: What happens when a group of insurgent scholars gains admission, gets inside the door, earns the credibility and credentials that warrant consideration by mainstream scholars? Are these new scholars promptly granted equal standing, integrated fully into the conver-

140 U. Pa. L. Rev. 1349 (1992). Copyright © 1992 University of Pennsylvania Law Review.

sations, colloquies, footnotes, and exchanges that constitute legal-academic discourse on issues of race and equality? Or, are they still marginalized, muffled, and kept in limbo—to be seen, perhaps, but not heard?

To focus the inquiry, I limit my examination to two groups of insurgent scholars, Critical Race Theorists and radical feminists. These scholars were barely beginning to make themselves heard, were still marginal to the mainstream discourse, at the time *The Imperial Scholar* was written. Currently, members of these groups teach at the top law schools and publish in the best law reviews. Their work is subject to commentary by distinguished colleagues and critics in top reviews, and their controversies are covered by the *New York Times* and *The Nation.* Even if not in the living room, they are plainly somewhere "inside the door." What reception are they receiving?

Abandonment of the Field

Most civil rights writing published in the top law reviews these days is written by women and minorities. As new writers have entered the field, established ones have either reduced their production or left the field entirely. What Judge Wyzanski called the "minstrel show"[3]—black rights being enforced and interpreted by white men—is finally coming to an end. Part of the abandonment is simply due to increasing age: some of the great names of ten years ago have died or retired. Others are moving into the golden part of their careers in which heavily documented and supported scholarship can give way to "reflections," opinion pieces, and musings that rely not on the careful analysis and painstaking research of traditional articles but on the strength of a reputation built by such analysis and research. The aging of the inner circle alone, however, does not account for the entire shift in the demographics of authorship on race or gender and the law.

Rather, many inner-circle writers have moved to other fields. Perhaps they do not see race and women's issues as the urgent topics they were in the 1960s and 70s. It may be, as well, that as the recognition of female and minority voices increases, some members of the inner circle find their efforts neither as necessary nor as productive as they once were. When a middle-class, white male scholar sees articles written by outsider scholars published in the top law reviews, he may well ask himself why he should continue writing about those same issues, with which he has a much more tenuous connection. Perhaps he wrote, in part, out of generosity or a sense of social obligation. Now that others have taken up the torch, his efforts may seem less necessary.

The field of civil rights has not been given over entirely to minority and feminist scholars, however. Nor am I arguing that it should be. For one thing, white males are affected to some degree by issues of racial justice. Moreover, we certainly do not need ghettoization; the cross-fertilization resulting from integrated scholarship can be as beneficial as recognition of long-neglected voices.

Those Who Stayed

The original inner-circle scholars who continue to write about civil rights can be divided into three subgroups according to their treatment of the new scholarship.

THE UNCONVERTED

A few from the original group of writers continue to ignore the new voices of color and the feminists. This practice leads to many of the scholarly deficiencies I noted several years ago, deficiencies extending far beyond failure to give recognition when it is due. A recent article on the right to an abortion, for example, slights feminist analysis and describes the woman's interest as lacking any constitutional or moral foundation. The writer frames the issue as the right to destroy third-party life, cites mainly male authorities, and gives short shrift to feminist commentators, mentioning but three in passing footnotes.

Others do cite the new literature but opt for the most familiar, and perhaps safest, versions. This results in a softened and incomplete picture of the debate about liberalism's defects. The impression that could be received from reading these otherwise impressive works is that the liberal system of law and politics that has reigned since the 1930s is largely intact and that the challengers are doing little more than raising variations on a familiar theme.

THE LATTER-DAY IMPERIALISTS

There comes a time when most scholars can no longer ignore the work being done by previously excluded writers. Then, two possible responses exist. One is thoughtful inclusion of the previously excluded work. The other is limited, grudging, or calculated acceptance, coupled with resort to an arsenal of mechanisms to reduce its impact. The old-line, inner-circle scholars have employed three types of mechanisms to lessen the threat of insurgent scholarship; newcomers to the field have developed even more.[4]

Mechanism one: Oh yes, before I forget: The afterthought. One way to acknowledge outsider scholarship without fully assimilating it is to cite it at the end of a string citation. In the main text the author can continue to rely on the familiar list of friends and acquaintances, saving reference to critical scholarship for a footnote, frequently of the "see generally" or "see also" variety. This approach allows the author to show that he is familiar with the new work, while avoiding fully accounting for it in his analysis. The approach also conveys the message that minority or feminist writing is deservedly obscure, and thus worthy only of passing mention.

Mechanism two: The stereotypical dismissal. An established author can dismiss a troublesome radical by caricaturing her or appealing to the reader's pre-existing assumptions about her writings without treating those writings seriously. Alternatively, the author can merely call the new voices utopian, daring, "interesting," or not really doing law. These approaches enable the writer to avoid confronting what the Criticalist is saying. The teeth of the criticism are thus drawn, and it emerges in more innocuous form than if it had remained unmentioned.

Mechanism three: I'm so hip. The Establishment writer cites to his familiar inner circle for 95 percent of his article. Then, for a proposition or section that cries out for citation to a Critical Race Theorist or feminist, the author will cite to one: Gee, aren't I hip! The author appears to be recognizing and assimilating outsider scholarship while actually doing little to integrate it into his own. For example, a scholar writing or teaching about developments in evidence law considers feminist thought only in connection with his treatment of rape. He writes the rest of his article or teaches the rest of his course as he has always done—linearly, hierarchically, and with little thought to its impact on women or the poor.

THOSE ON THE ROAD TO DAMASCUS

Some original inner-circle authors have accepted and incorporated the writings of the Critical Race Theorists and feminists. Instead of dismissing their writings or ignoring them outright, the mainstream author engages their propositions or ideas in a forthright manner. When an author raises an issue from outsider scholarship and takes the time to discuss his agreement or disagreement with it, he is recognizing its validity and relevance; it is not simply brushed aside or ignored.

This thoughtful treatment of outsider scholarship encourages expansion of the civil rights canon, which in turn recognizes the current condition of civil rights scholarship. In that sense, it constitutes an awareness on the part of these members of the inner circle that civil rights writing has not really been composed of two separate strains but rather of parallel traditions that must inevitably lose their Euclidean separateness and become one integrated tradition.

The New Generation: *The Imperial Scholar* Updated

Since I wrote *The Imperial Scholar* ten years ago, however, newcomers have arrived on the scene. Many of these are white; most are males; some have brought reputations achieved in other areas of the law. As with the old-line group, a few of the new scholars are relatively egalitarian in their scholarship, citing Critical Race Theorists and radical feminists about as frequently as one might fairly expect. The most fascinating, the neo-imperialist scholars, have deployed an almost baroque variety of ways to minimize, marginalize, co-opt, soften, miss the point of, selectively ignore, or generally devalue the new insurgent writers.

Mechanisms four and five: The hero, the zero. As with the original inner-circle scholars, the new majority-race writers have their heroes and zeroes.

Duncan Kennedy, Alan Freeman, Alex Aleinikoff, and Gary Peller cite the new voices appropriately, sometimes agreeing and sometimes taking issue with them. Others, however, either ignore the insurgent scholars or treat their work diffidently. One author offers two "special interest" references, one for feminists and one for Critical Race Theorists. In an article on slavery and slave law, another only once cites to Bell's *Race, Racism and American Law,* a standard work, and at no time mentions Leon Higginbotham's well-regarded history, *In the Matter of Color.* A third wrote a stinging footnote chastising a number of the new-voice authors for dangerous reliance on notions of class-based harm and redress. Unlike some, this author at least cited oppositional scholars for a proposition, if only to attack it.

Mechanism six: "Yeah, yeah"; no need to tell me more. Many of the new writers in the field of civil rights cite work by women and minorities as perfunctorily as the old-timers do, but with a difference. That difference consists of citing an early page of an article or book—for example, page 3, not 403. When an author does this regularly, it raises the suspicion that he has not bothered to read the entire article or book, but has merely leafed through the article's preface or introduction in search of a general proposition he can cite with a minimum of effort. The author discharges his obligation to refer to the new voices but avoids the hard work of reading the entire piece and dealing with it seriously. Women will recognize this treatment as a conversational gambit many men use—interruption. The male listens to a woman's opening words, then bursts in to finish her sentence, saying "Yeah, yeah. I get it; no need to go on . . . now, what do you think about *my* idea?"

Mechanism seven: "I know": The facile (and safe) translation. This mechanism translates a novel, hard-edged, and discomfiting thesis by an outside writer so that it becomes familiar, safe, and tame. Often the translation forces the thesis into liberal-legalist terms that were intended to be avoided. For example, some scholars translate MacKinnon's work on pornography into an intriguing First Amendment question. MacKinnon does not consider pornography a First Amendment question, but a near-crime, a civil rights offense against women. Once translated into a First Amendment framework her proposal loses much of its urgency and original character.

Mechanism eight: "I loved Dan's idea." A number of the new writers show familiarity with ideas feminists and Critical Race Theory scholars have been proposing, but either forget where they heard them or cite a derivative source—a critic, or a majority-race commentator—to summarize outsider views. This approach corresponds to another experience familiar to most women: co-optation. A woman proposes an idea; no one in the group reacts. Twenty minutes later, a male restates and puts forward the same suggestion, which immediately wins widespread praise and thereafter becomes "Dan's idea."

Mechanism nine: "I know just how you must have felt": Co-optation of others' experience. Some of the new writers make an effort to identify with the stories and accounts the outsider narrativists are offering, but in a way that co-opts or minimizes these stories. The majority-race author draws a parallel between something in the experience of the outsider author and something that happened to him. There is nothing wrong with using analogies and metaphors to deal with the experience of others, for that is how we extend our sympathies. If, however, we analogize to refocus a conversation or an article towards ourselves exclusively, something is wrong, especially if the experience to which we liken another's is manifestly less serious. For example, the author of one article on campus racial harassment observes that everyone experiences "insulting" or "upsetting" speech at one time or another, so what is so special about the racist version?

Mechanism ten: "Pure poetry": How poignant, touching, or moving—Placing outsider writing on a pedestal. Some writers of majority race praise the new writing for its passionate or emotional quality. The writing is so personal, so colorful, so poetic, so "moving." This approach can marginalize outsider writing by placing it in a category of its own. Women and minority writers feel more deeply than we; they have "soul." The writing is evaluated as a journal of the author's individual thoughts and feelings, not as an article that delivers uncomfortable insights and truths about society and injustice.

Mechanism eleven: Assimilation/co-optation—"We have been saying this all along." This mechanism dismisses the feminists and Critical Race Theorists as saying little new; we have been making the same points about brotherhood, equality, and civility for hundreds, if not thousands, of years. Plato, Aquinas, Austin, Unger, and any favorite male author urged that society be arranged justly and that all should be treated with respect. Yet one might argue that earlier authorities wrote inadequately and spoke poorly to our condition because that condition persists today. If outsider voices are addressing new or old grievances in new ways, one ought not dismiss what they are saying merely because someone else previously said something remotely similar.

Mechanism twelve: "She wrote just one" (and I'll cite it, too). Some of the mainstream authors treat the new voices as though each of them had written exactly one article or book. Susan Estrich is cited for her book on rape, Mari Matsuda for *Looking to the Bottom*, Derrick Bell for *And We Are Not Saved*, me for *The Imperial Scholar.* Each of these writers has written many works, arguably of comparable merit to the one cited. Routinized, stereotypical citation to one work gives the impression the author wrote only the one. It also conveys the message that insurgent writers can only write one work, probably an anomaly, the result of a gigantic effort or internal convulsion that they are capable of producing only once in a lifetime.

Mechanism thirteen: The all-purpose citation. The author has a flash of insight, into the way constitutional equality works, for example. Midway through the article it dawns on the author that he had better cite a minority. What better place to do so than for the proposition that (1) racism is terrible, (2) discrimination still exists, or (3) we all must work really hard at dealing with it.

"At the Margin": Why We Always Fail to Recognize New Stories

Even though the new voices are finding their way into the pages of the top reviews and journals, they are not being quickly and easily integrated into the conversations and dialogues of traditional legal scholarship. Some of the resistance may be intentional and mean-spirited. Some may also be the product of inflexibility and an unwillingness to entertain new positions.

But most mainstream legal writers are neither mean-spirited nor lazy. I think the most likely explanation for most of the mechanisms I have detailed lies elsewhere. Legal scholarship is currently radically transforming itself. A subtler yet audacious form of legal writing has appeared, with roots in postmodernism, critical thought, and narrative theory. The authors, format, and authorities cited are radically different from those that came before. If not a full-fledged paradigm shift, something similar seems to be happening. As sociologists of knowledge have pointed out, such a shift occurs only when the costs of resisting it become unacceptable compared to the gains of adopting the new approach.[5]

A second, related explanation applies insights from narrative theory.[6] As many have pointed out, reality comes to us not as a given but in terms of narratives, mindsets, or stories—interpretive structures by which we construct and come to terms with the world of reality. Each of us is the product of a large number of such understandings, or "stories," by which we reduce the diversity of daily life to manageable proportions. In a sense, we are our stock of stories and they us. When a feminist or Critical Race Theorist offers a radically new story, we evaluate it in terms of the one we currently hold. If it seems too different, we are apt to reject it as extreme, coercive, political, harsh, or untrue.

Both mechanisms lead to a melancholy truth. We postpone confronting novelty and change until they acquire enough momentum that we are swept forward. We take seriously new social thought only after hearing it so often that its tenets and themes begin to seem familiar, inevitable, and true. We then adopt the new paradigm, and the process repeats itself. We escape from one mental and intellectual prison only into a larger, slightly more expansive one. Each jail-break is seen as illegitimate. We reject new thought until, eventually, its hard edges soften, its suggestions seem tame and manageable, and its proponents are "elder states-persons," to be feared no longer. By then, of course, the new thought has lost its radically transformative character. We reject the medicine that could save us until, essentially, it is too late.

NOTES

1. Richard Delgado, *The Imperial Scholar: Reflections on a Review of Civil Rights Literature*, 132 U. PA. L. REV. 561 (1984).

2. *Quoted in* Jon Wiener, *Law Profs Fight the Power*, 249 NATION 246, 246 (1989).

3. Western Addition Community Org. v. NLRB, 485 F.2d 917, 940 (D.C. Cir. 1973) (Wyzanski, J., dissenting), *rev'd sub nom.* Emporium Capwell Co. v. Western Addition Co., 420 U.S. 50 (1975).

4. Joanna Russ found a similar tendency to rely on a few recurring mechanisms for suppressing insurgent writing. Her classic, JOANNA RUSS, HOW TO SUPPRESS WOMEN'S WRITING (1983), examines the techniques literary scholars have used throughout recent times to belittle literature by women.

5. The classic work describing this phenomenon is THOMAS KUHN, THE STRUCTURE OF SCIENTIFIC REVOLUTIONS (2d ed. 1970).

6. For descriptions of narrative theory, see ON NARRATIVE (W.J.T. Mitchell ed., 1981); 1 & 2 PAUL RICOEUR, TIME AND NARRATIVE (1984–85); Robin West, *Jurisprudence as Narrative: An Aesthetic Analysis of Modern Legal Theory*, 60 N.Y.U.L. REV. 145 (1985).

36 Autobiography and Legal Scholarship and Teaching: Finding the Me in the Legal Academy

JEROME McCRISTAL CULP, JR.

I S T A R T many of my law school courses with a description of myself. "I am," I say slowly, "the son of a poor coal miner." The reason I do so says much about the difference in how blacks and whites approach the issue of legal scholarship and teaching. Being black, I cannot stop, at least in the short run, being an anomaly to many people. I can only hope to shape the way in which that anomaly is understood. I define myself as a poor coal miner's son both to claim a past rooted in the history of my parents' struggle and to define a future rooted in the contrasting nature of a different experience. I am saying to my black students that they too can engage in the struggle to reach a position of power and influence, and to my white students that black people have to struggle. But in the strange times in which we live it is not easy for a black law professor to claim a history without creating disbelief among students.

Perhaps my ability to convey who I am has changed, and therefore I am saying who I am with a different emphasis or cadence. But for some reason students hear what I say differently now than they did six years ago when I first started teaching at my present law school. Black and white students no longer believe that I have a father who is a coal miner. They think that I am telling an exaggerated story to take advantage of them in the repartee between teacher and student. I think they say to themselves: "He is not really a son of a poor coal miner. He is something else, or he would not be a law professor."[1]

Henry Louis Gates, English professor and literary theorist, has noted that black Americans approach the subject of what they write differently from other groups. He suggests that for many of the most famous black American writers, autobiography is done at the beginning, rather than at the end, of their literary careers.[2] This is true of Frederick Douglass and Malcolm X;[3] Thomas Sowell and Booker T. Washington;[4] Maya Angelou and Michele Wallace;[5] and Claude Brown.[6]

77 VA. L. REV. 539 (1991). Originally published in the Virginia Law Review. Reprinted by permission.

There is a reason for this use of autobiography by black writers. Black people feel the need to justify who they are and to describe where they come from as part of the description of where they want to go.[7] In order to be considered a poet, Phillis Wheatley had to prove to a group of white observers that she had written her poetry. The attestation by these white observers, in a preface to Ms. Wheatley's poems, tells of her recent emigration to this country as an "uncultivated Barbarian from Africa."[8] The work that begins this forwardlooking approach to autobiography by black intellectuals is the autobiography of Frederick Douglass, who felt compelled to include the words "written by himself" in the subtitle of his first autobiography. Douglass, like Wheatley, wanted to claim a legitimacy that black people in his era could not claim.

Black critics (both inside and outside the legal academy) of racial perspectives in the law have also used their autobiography to convince their audience. We learn much of the autobiography of Stephen Carter, Glenn Loury, Thomas Sowell, and Shelby Steele in their own words and images. When Stephen Carter and Shelby Steele tell us of experiences in their past, where being African-American was used to limit their ambitions, they use their lives as proof. These writers know that their autobiographies are a form of proof (not definitive, but proof nonetheless), a way of defeating those who see them only as just the best black. Despite criticism and doubts about the existence of black perspectives, black writers have a need to tell a story, whether or not it is free. This story is autobiographical. White writers also tell their story, but it is not often as consciously autobiographical, particularly early in their academic careers.[9]

I was unconsciously forced by white students, who would ask for my curriculum vitae, to use my own truncated autobiography. Typically on the first day of class, some student raises a question that includes, "Where did you go to law school?" I understand that question to be, "What gives *you* the right to teach this course to *me?*" I did not even realize that the question was being asked every year until a white colleague heard the question and became upset for me. When I answer that question, I give a long response that includes a description of an undergraduate education at the University of Chicago, and graduate and legal training at Harvard University. For most students, this biography is sufficient. It reduces the discomfort they feel about having a black law professor. That is not, however, the biographical information I want them to remember. My autobiographical statement—that I am the son of a poor coal miner—has informational content that has a transformative potential much greater than my curriculum vitae. *Who we are* matters as much as what we are and what we think. It is important to teach our students that there is a "me" in the law, as well as specific rules that are animated by our experiences.

Because black professors of law often enter law in order to create and sustain societal change, it should not surprise us that black professors of law use their autobiographies in a number of ways to illuminate their teaching and scholarship. Black law professors, of course, are not just their autobiographies; we must communicate material, teach students how to read cases, and perform all the other tasks required of other professors. But many black law professors believe, and most convey the impression, that who we are influences our examination of the law. White colleagues use our racial autobiographies to confirm or, occasionally, to test their views of the world; we use our autobiographies in various ways to define the contours of our teaching and scholarship. Almost all black law professors are forced to write, teach, or speak their concerns about race. Neither our colleagues, nor our own interest in racial justice, will permit us to forget that we are black professors of law.

Putting a Me into Legal Scholarship

Professor Patricia Williams has been an innovator in legal scholarship. She writes about her own experiences and uses them to transform the debate about law. When Professor Williams describes the differences between the needs of blacks and whites in contractual situations by using her experience in renting an apartment in New York, she shows why for blacks there can be a need for formality that whites often do not experience. Her experiences as a black woman are central to the transformative power of that debate. It is, of course, beneficial that Professor Williams is a lawyer and a former litigator, but more importantly, her unique perspective and experiences enhance both her legal analysis and the truth of what she says. When we read her words, we read a contemporary embodiment of racial and legal experiences. Her approach to legal scholarship is different for the very reason that some legal teachers do not appreciate it as scholarship or recognize it as an effective pedagogical tool.

In order to change the most basic and fundamental notions about the world, it is first necessary to alter the terms of the debate. Professor Williams requires us to see the world through her eyes; her words will not permit us the freedom to ignore her reality. This is good lawyering and good scholarship. The most basic job of a lawyer is to convey a story that puts her client's perspective in its best light; no scholar who fails to create a new intellectual world can hope to be successful. Professor Williams impels us to listen to her history precisely because without that pressure too many of us who read and teach the law will ignore that history. We all start with mythic structures about the world, but for most of us who teach the law these mythic structures do not include black men or women. Patricia Williams gives us new mythic structures to use in our efforts to include these two groups.

When I started teaching law at Rutgers Law School, a white colleague and friend said that one of the things that he found most disquieting about contemporary legal scholarship was the extent to which it was personal. He found that the efforts of radical and critical writers to use their personal histories in legal discourse were destructive of law. "Everything that they are saying could be said in a less personal way," he concluded. I never asked him the question that I will pose here, but I think I know the answer he would give. The question is, "Why is the personal not also legal?" After all, cases (at least in our federal courts) usually involve some personal experience to which the law will be applied. The answer I think I would have received is that law should not be too influenced by the personal aspects of a litigant's experience. Law has to treat rich and poor, pretty and ugly, black and white alike.

The problem for those of us who are black in the legal academy is that it does not seem possible to find a neutral place to observe how race interacts with legal decisionmaking. When the United States Supreme Court acknowledges the validity of a sociological study that reveals a correlation between a victim's race and a likelihood of a jury imposing the death penalty,[10] yet concludes that courts cannot consider this study, because to do so would require judges to examine too many conflicting concerns, black people are reminded that American law has consistently made such injurious decisions. If we are to persuade the next Supreme Court, or Congress, of the tragedy of this perspective on race and the death penalty, then it is important that the experiences of blacks be included in the discourse. When we leave out the personal in the realm of the law, what is left out is the truth of the experiences of black people in American society. Indeed, to the extent that we permit the personal to be included, we often leave out the reality of being black. For example, the Supreme Court does not believe it is reversible error in a death penalty case (involving a white defendant) for a defense attorney to have not called a black professional who would have testified as a character witness, because the defense attorney feared that the blackness of the character witness would harm his client's case.[11] The only conclusion that we can take from this case is that the stigma attached to blackness is simply a cross that black (and some white) people must bear.

My answer to my former colleague, and continued friend, is that by ignoring the experiences of black people we are limiting our vision of law to one that reflects a white male perspective. It is not possible to think neutrally about these questions; we either include or ignore black people in the world that is created by our individual assumptions. By leaving out the personal, as my colleague suggests, we simply replace our personal stories with mythic assumptions about race.

Whenever one raises the question of including the personal, especially the personal experiences of people of color, one hears the response by many that color does not and cannot matter to legal discourse. "Truth is color blind" is the unstated, but assumed, premise that undergirds the discussion in this area. One sees this premise played out on the undergraduate level in the truly chaotic discussion of what the "canon" ought to be in basic history and English courses. The defenders of the current canon combat the onslaught of black and other concerns with nonsensical arguments that the current canons have apolitical and transhistorical content.[12] They contend that if black concerns and literary works are to be included in the canon they have to earn their way, no doubt the old-fashioned way, through some neutral process. Because it is easy to prove that those who invented the canons in history and English did so partly for political purposes, it is not possible to defend the current canons on such grounds.[13] Indeed, what ought to frighten us is that so many leaders with significant educational backgrounds would believe that such a defense of educational structure makes sense.

Finding the Me in Tort Law

Every year I begin my torts class with a hypothetical from my past. As an undergraduate at the University of Chicago, I asked my girlfriend to accompany me to Evanston, Illinois. We got off the train from downtown Chicago with our very long and newly hip Afros and began walking around Evanston. Near the train station we saw an old white woman. As my girlfriend and I approached the woman, she began to shake. The closer we came to her the more she shook. As I write about this incident, I can remember the beauty of that former girlfriend's face but not her name. But I remember as clearly as I can taste my last cup of coffee the old white woman turning her back and assuming a pseudo-fetal posture as we approached her. I could read that situation as clearly as any other: for the old white woman, the black revolution had come to Evanston. She saw us not as the well-dressed black college students that we were, but as mythic black revolutionaries. In her mind, she knew we were Black Panthers who had come to Evanston to do her harm.

I ask my class whether it would have been an assault for me to lean over and to whisper "boo" to that old woman. I then add that I thought about doing so and pause, for only a second, before saying that I did not say anything. This is not the pause that refreshes. Indeed my comment changes for all time the impression some have of me. Many white students no longer see me as the affable black person in front of the room, but understand that I have some anger that some interpret as black radicalism. One student asked me how I could have thought of saying anything to this old white woman, who was captured by her racial past. "That could have been my grandmother," another white student added. I did not respond that this was exactly the reaction I wanted. I would not say "boo" to an old white woman who feared my blackness, but I posed the hypothetical to alter the assumptions that we make about the relationships between people and the trade-offs imposed by the law. It is dangerous for a black person to make an old woman or white students face the deeply embedded racism in our society. The old woman is likely to charge an assault of some kind and the students are likely to see such actions as the imposition of politically connected concerns. I must, however, first be able to think dangerous thoughts before they can become reality, and I want the class to think about how much of tort law is socially constructed custom.

Black students who are forced to listen to hypotheticals that are seldom, if ever, from their racial perspective are often invigorated by a hypothetical that permits them to be the person who is claiming a right to be black and free. They generally understand these situations; they have been there before. My hypothetical includes a discussion of what tort liability exists for me if I knowingly say anything that will create in the old white woman an apprehension of intentional and immediate bodily injury. This discussion makes my class aware that I am black; it prompts questions about how race influences the construction of law and legal doctrine. I try to impress on them that they should understand why this case is not governed primarily by tort law in the real world. I also try to show them that there are other rules that limit my actions and require me to censor myself. I hope that my students understand that silence is imposed on me and all black people, and that I say things in many ways to my class and colleagues, even when I do not verbalize them. By raising an explicit racial situation, I hope to free my black students to include their experiences in the classroom, and to inform the non-black students that other ways of looking at issues are possible and necessary.

Autobiography and the Faculty

Some of my colleagues and I have discussed the usefulness, appropriateness, and efficacy of Derrick Bell's strike against Harvard Law School. Professor Bell requested a leave without pay from his job as a Professor of Law until Harvard Law School hire a tenured woman of color. I was struck by Dean Robert Clark's reaction to Professor Bell's strike, and by the fact that none of my white colleagues reacted to it as I did. Dean Clark's response, as Dean of Harvard Law School, was that Professor Bell's action was not "an appropriate or effective way to further the goal of increasing the number of minorities and women on the faculty."[14] How is it possible for Dean Clark to define what is appropriate? I do some things that I know my colleagues find inappropriate. Some of them would like me to dress differently, for example, eliminating the shorts I wear in good weather on days when I do not teach. I choose not to listen to criticisms about either my dress or my autobiography. Criticisms of this sort are made on everyone, particularly those who are different, but I have chosen to adopt only some of the qualities that a "good" black professor of law should adopt.

These criticisms have a different quality in the context of challenging the existing order in law schools. I have seen many things in my almost ten years in law school teaching. Faculty have been abusive to students and to each other. I have noticed faculty skating close to and over the edge of sexual harassment. Faculty have been heard to call each other fool, racist, incompetent, and idiot, and to engage in, or threaten, physical combat with each other. I have taught at three very good law schools, but I have yet to see or hear of a dean who publicly challenged a faculty member's shortcomings, whether personal or professional. I have never heard of a law school dean chastising a faculty colleague publicly for racial or other allegations of discrimination, though I know of deans who should have been chastised for their own racial insensitivity. If deans, including the small number of nonwhite ones, do not label such actions publicly as inappropriate, then how is it justified to label a strike by a faculty member against his perception of racism as inappropriate? It is only possible to claim that something is inappropriate if Dean Clark has a model of appropriate behavior for black law faculty. It seems that, for Dean Clark, what is appropriate behavior for black faculty is to accept our tenured positions in appreciative silence. The autobiography that Dean Clark requires of Derrick Bell, Professor of Law, is that of supporter of the current order in law schools. Dean Clark argues that Harvard "is a university, not a lunch counter in the [1960s'] South."[15] Professor Bell contends that his autobiography teaches him that most white institutions, including Harvard Law School, are very similar to lunch counters of the 1960s' South.[16] Black law professors have a different autobiography, which we use more and more frequently. We do not always use it better than our white colleagues, but certainly no worse.

An anonymous colleague put a copy of one of Shelby Steele's recent writings in my faculty mailbox after an acrimonious faculty meeting about an affirmative action issue. Professor Steele has become the darling of neo-liberal opinionmakers in the pages of the *Atlantic*, the *New York Times*, PBS's *Frontline* program, and ABC's *Nightline* program for his view that although racial bigotry exists, and is ugly and dangerous, the black middle class are free to prosper despite racial animosity. Professor Steele has come to the conclusion that racism does not handicap the lives of people like him, who are tenured faculty with graduate degrees and comfortable salaries. By placing that article anonymously in my box my colleague was saying to me: "You are not a black professor of law, you are a professor of law who happens to be black; your blackness does not influence in any important way your present. Be appropriately appreciative of the blessings your position bestows on you." I understand Professor Steele's and my colleague's desire for this to be my autobiographical present, but it is not. I do my students, both black and white, a disservice if I permit my colleagues to rewrite my autobiography in ways that I believe to be incorrect. I have struggled in my own way, as hard as I could, against the racial oppression that exists in America. It has not eroded to the point where it does not continue to impact my life. I do not ask my colleagues always to consider my concerns and injuries, but I do ask that they not always assume a silent present for me.

Autobiography also influences my white colleagues. I believe I disquiet my colleagues when I raise issues about the composition of our student body or our faculty or what we teach, because it raises issues about their own autobiographies. My white colleagues think I am saying to them, "How did you get here?" They would like me to join them in a conspiracy of silence that claims a common and simple autobiography. I will not.

All of us have autobiographies that help us understand the world and put it into order. I am reminded of the white law professors who were not at the very top of their class, who were not editor-in-chief of their law review, and who did not clerk for the most prestigious judge.[17] Some of these colleagues are the most ardent supporters of narrow notions of "meritorious," credential-based appointments to their faculties. They oppose even the weakest form of affirmative action, including the simple requirement that appointment committees look at black and minority candidates outside of the above-mentioned, elite criteria. Whenever I see this reaction, I am convinced that my colleagues believe in those standards because they are insecure about their own autobiographies. This insecurity seems to be misplaced. The pool of people who end up being the best teachers, scholars, and law professors is not limited to those with excellent credentials; the notion that we must defend our autobiographies by creating a myth that law faculties are limited to the narrowest band of people with the highest credentials is a false statement about who makes up the legal academy. In my opinion, there are various reasons (some good and some bad) for my colleagues, both black and white, to believe in the narrowest credential-based hiring. But it is also true that some of my colleagues defend their autobiographies by defending standards that were not applied to their appointments.

When I raise autobiographical concerns, some of my colleagues complain that I am attempting to privilege my autobiography. They say to me: "If we deal with your autobiography, we ignore our histories. Our parents suffered discrimination and hardship, but we do not think it important to mention it, and neither should you." True diversity, they claim, would not look at race or sex, but at other ethnic and cultural concerns that are not included in the current debate for political reasons.[18] They are correct that such claims are by definition political, but what these law professors will not admit is that it is not possible to be apolitical. It is possible to have a legal curriculum that does not worry about racism, but that decision is political. I do not think the autobiographies of my colleagues are unimportant, but they have to use their autobiographical pasts in their own ways in their teaching and scholarship.

I am willing to admit that I would like to privilege my story if my colleagues in legal education will admit that they tell a story in their teaching and scholarship. The real question is which story will be told. Their real problem with me is not that they have no autobiographies, but that they do not want to use their real ones, and wish I would not use mine either. The very question they have raised is wrong. The challenge I pose for all my colleagues and students is how to permit some of the experiences of black people into the discussion of what is law. The story I tell includes white people and black people. Unfortunately, the story most of us tell in our scholarship and teaching excludes black autobiographies.

It is not possible to tell the whole truth of our lives in the classroom or in our scholarship. Reality is not a novel or an autobiography, where all of the unimportant details are culled by the author offstage so that we can digest "truth" in simple bites. As teachers and legal scholars, we are the authors of our present and our past. We define what is irrelevant and relevant. Black people, because of who they are, know the power of full autobiography. It echoes more explicitly in our lives. I can demonstrate that being the son of a poor black coal miner influences who I am and how I perceive the legal system about which I teach. The hard question for those of us in legal teaching is what that autobiography we teach will look like.

There are many truths we can tell about the law; few of them include black people and their concerns. Part of my task as a black professor of law is to insure that black people are included in the mythic structures of legal discourse. Black law professors cannot escape that task. We tell a tale of blackness and the law by our being and through our teaching and scholarship. I choose to convey an autobiography that includes my blackness and my struggles in my past and present. I can only hope that my students and colleagues will listen to my story, attempt to understand it, and accept it as a valid part of legal discourse.

NOTES

1. Some of my students think that I have exaggerated my past and certainly, from some perspectives, I have. For a discussion of the extent to which all autobiographies are lies, see T. ADAMS, TELLING LIES IN MODERN AMERICAN AUTOBIOGRAPHY 1–16 (1990). Others may believe that my autobiography, like all autobiographies, is unimportant and irrelevant to the objectivity inherent in the law. In its general sense, I reject that notion of objectivity.

2. HENRY LOUIS GATES, *Introduction*, in BEARING WITNESS: SELECTIONS FROM AFRICAN AMERICAN AUTOBIOGRAPHY IN THE TWENTIETH CENTURY (1991).

3. F. DOUGLASS, NARRATIVE OF THE LIFE OF FREDERICK DOUGLASS, AN AMERICAN SLAVE, WRITTEN BY HIMSELF (B. Quarles ed., 1967) (1845); A. HALEY & MALCOLM X, THE AUTOBIOGRAPHY OF MALCOLM X (1964).

4. T. SOWELL, BLACK EDUCATION: MYTHS AND TRAGEDIES (1969); B. T. WASHINGTON, UP FROM SLAVERY: AN AUTOBIOGRAPHY (1901).

5. M. ANGELOU, I KNOW WHY THE CAGED BIRD SINGS (1969); M. WALLACE, BLACK MACHO AND THE MYTH OF THE SUPERWOMAN (1978) (The author writes her autobiography through an account of the Black Power movement, an exploration of myths that surround black men and black women, and a call for black women to define and write their own history.).

6. C. BROWN, MANCHILD IN THE PROMISED LAND (1965).

7. To some extent all writing is autobiographical. We normally distinguish between good and bad writing by making a distinction between what rings true and what sounds false. In that sense all good writing, fictional and nonfictional, is autobiographical, but there is a difference between white and black writers. White autobiography, meaning those works that are officially classified as autobiography, is done at the end of a writer's career. It has a self-congratulatory tone and reflects over a completed life. Black autobiography is different. It looks not backward over a completed career, but forward to what the black writer is doing and intends to do in the future.

8. *Preface to* P. WHEATLEY, POEMS ON VARIOUS SUBJECTS, RELIGIOUS AND MORAL (1773), *in* THE POEMS OF PHILLIS WHEATLEY 48 (J. Mason ed. 1966). This proof was enough to convince our most illustrious forefather, Thomas Jefferson, that Phillis Wheatley had written the poetry, but it proved nothing about the intellect of black people because the poetry was bad. Jefferson stated:

> Misery is often the parent of the most affecting touches in poetry.— Among the blacks is misery enough, God knows, but no poetry. Love is the peculiar [gift] of the poet. Their love is ardent, but it kindles the senses only, not the imagination. Religion indeed has produced a Phyllis Whately [sic]; but it could not produce a poet.

T. JEFFERSON, NOTES ON THE STATE OF VIRGINIA 143 (W. Peden ed., 1954) (J. Stockdale, ed. 1787) (footnote omitted).

9. The lone exception is the writing of feminist legal scholars. *See, e.g.,* S. ESTRICH, REAL RAPE (1987); R. Austin, *Sapphire Bound!,* 1989 WIS. L. REV. 539. Among legal scholars, however, minority women have been more likely to use autobiography than nonminority women, and women use autobiography more than men.

10. McCleskey v. Kemp, 481 U.S. 279 (1987).

11. Burger v. Kemp, 483 U.S. 776 (1987).

12. A. BLOOM, THE CLOSING OF THE AMERICAN MIND 95–97 (1987).

13. P. NOVICK, THAT NOBLE DREAM 311–14 (1988).

14. Daly, *Harvard Law Students Demand Diverse Faculty,* WASH. POST, Apr. 25, 1990, at 3, col. 1.

15. A. Flint, *Bell at Harvard: A Unique Activism,* BOSTON GLOBE, May 7, 1990, at 4, col. 6.

16. *Id.*

17. A majority in the legal profession and a significant minority in even the "best" law schools do not have these credentials. See M. Olivas, *Latino Faculty at the Border,* CHANGE, May–June 1988, at 6, 7.

18. My colleagues often contend that race is not real diversity and that other criteria are just as or more useful. *See, e.g.,* R. POSNER, THE PROBLEMS OF JURISPRUDENCE 458 (1990) (Diversity in the judiciary is important but it should not be based upon sexual or racial politics. Other criteria, including religion, health backgrounds, and hobbies, are as important as gender and race.).

37 Reflections on Identity, Diversity, and Morality

DEBORAH WAIRE POST

W H E N I was growing up in Auburn, New York, people referred to me as "one of the Post girls." I never thought to question the label. Although it did not describe me completely, it provided most of the information needed to place me within the social landscape of our town. In fact, I never really thought about describing myself in any other way until I left home and people began to ask me "What are you, anyway?"

After twenty or more years of being asked "What are you?", if I remain ambivalent about the answer, it is not because of any confusion about my identity, but because I am uncertain about the politics of choosing a particular descriptive term. I was a very small child when I rejected the idea of identifying myself as a mulatto. In college I struggled with the choice between the more traditional "negro" and the more unfamiliar and radical terminology "black." Today we are asked to abandon "black" for "African-American," and I find myself as intransigent in my use of "black" as my grandparents' generation was in the use of "colored."

Over the years the question "What are you?" has lost its sting. It no longer makes me angry. I recognize it as a question which asks me to identify myself in social and cultural terms. The danger hidden in the question "What are you?" is found in the motives of the asker, a danger that has not diminished over the years. It is this danger that gives my answer a moral and ethical dimension.

My decision to identify myself as a black person is not exclusively a matter of descent, although my father's grandfathers were a runaway slave and a free black man who fought in the Civil War. Nor is it simply a matter of residence, although that I grew up in a black neighborhood surely played a part in the creation of my sense of identity. It is not a matter of skin color, although there has never been a question about my being a person of color. Some might argue that I am black because whites will not let me be anything else. I prefer to believe that I am who I am, a black woman, because I made an ethically and morally correct choice with respect to my identity.

A few years ago, I began spending summers with a white woman friend who married a black man. It became a running joke with her children that my arrival

6 BERKELEY WOMEN'S L.J. 136 (1990–91). Originally published in the Berkeley Women's Law Journal. Reprinted by permission.

would herald the beginning of an intense course in black history and culture. I expected the boys to grumble. I did not expect an emotional confrontation with their mother. Why, she asked me, did I think of myself as black when my mother was white? Didn't I see that she was hurt when I encouraged her children to ignore their white identity? If they were to choose to be black, she explained, they would be rejecting her culture. If they rejected her culture, they rejected her.

I fell back on an easy answer. I told her that they did not have a choice. She accepted the truth of what I said when her eldest son was called "nigger" for the first time.

I recently read an article in a philosophy journal which used the question "But would that still be me?" to explore the idea of race, gender, and ethnicity as sources of "ethical identity."[1] The author, Anthony Appiah, uses "ethics" and "ethical" in several ways in the essay. He alludes to the "ethical project of composing one's life," where ignoring social reality, the centrality of race and gender, is a form of self-deception. Self-deception is "inauthentic" and therefore unethical behavior. He distinguishes between the different ethical consequences which flow from what are arguably qualitatively different denials of identity. A rejection that takes the form of a lack of participation in the life of the community is defined as inauthenticity. Active concealment of identity, a more serious transgression, is dishonesty.

The ethical nature of identity hinges on the "centrality" of the particular characteristic or attribute. I assume that "centrality" refers to the emotional and psychological significance of a source of identity. The centrality of a socially constructed source of identity like gender, race, or ethnicity cannot be separated from culture or politics. Approaching the problem of ethical identity from the perspective of a social scientist rather than as a philosopher, I would argue that the most significant source of identity for individuals is that which defines the purpose and direction of their lives. Individuals experience oppression as a struggle for dignity and self-respect, and that struggle provides meaning for their lives. When the rationale for oppression is tied to social status, to membership in a particular social category, the fate and the identities of the individual and the group are linked.

But it was the stories my father told me about his own part in the struggle that made the greatest impression on me. He told me about the time he spit in the face of a white dowager who leaned over my carriage and exclaimed "My, what a cute little pickaninny." He told me about the time the Ku Klux Klan burned a cross on the hill at the top of our street and all the black men in the neighborhood marched up to meet them armed with guns and makeshift weapons. The KKK disappeared in the night and never resurfaced, at least not in their Klan guise.

The existence of a shared struggle generates a normative construct, an imperative that makes rejection of membership in the group unethical and immoral. Most simply stated, ethical identity is a concept which describes a set of loyalty norms. My father used his stories to teach me what it means to be black in America, the responsibilities that go with my identity, my role in the struggle. He gave me my ethical identity as a black person.

Gender became a part of my ethical identity while I was in law school. In the legal profession, gender bias is the dominant experience of all women, black and white. I had been prepared for the discrimination I would face as a black person. I was singularly unprepared for the attacks on my dignity and my competence which are the product of the hostility of men towards women in this profession.

I learned in my very first year in law school how dangerous it is to be a woman in an environment where men rule—men who are faculty and men who are students. I learned how easy it is for women to adopt the attitudes of men, to internalize the value system which teaches them to hate themselves and other women.

I do not know any women in law teaching who are not feminists, whether they call themselves that or not. We all recognize gender as a political issue because power is distributed or withheld on the basis of gender. Economic resources are allocated on the basis of gender. I am a feminist because people use gender as a basis for deciding whether or not I will be allowed to pursue my vocation as a teacher and a scholar.

Opposition creates an environment in which it is possible for members of the affected groups to strengthen or even to create a community. I am part of a community of women, white and black. The stories of my white female colleagues are my stories, for we are engaged in a common struggle. The sense of community among women is built on shared experiences. Here, too, I recognize social borders created by sentiments of affinity and external estrangement. It is the sense of community which gives loyalty norms, the ethics of identity, their power. Abandoning a concept or idea may be unprincipled. Abandoning people who depend on you or are members of your community is immoral.

Among the educated, particularly in elite institutions like law schools, overt expression of gender and race bias is socially unacceptable. As a result, the status norms of neutrality and objectivity have become the instruments of exclusion. These status norms can be used to silence as well as to exclude women and minorities. Presented with a choice expressed as a conflict between professional standards and political opinions, between virtue and unprincipled partisanship, women and minorities are compelled to choose between competing loyalties.

It was early in the morning and I was on my way to the faculty library. I saw a white woman colleague approaching and I braced myself to be cheerful and pleasant. This was the woman who brought me into law teaching. She had been more like a sister than a friend. Lately our relationship had become strained. Being friends had become extremely hard work. I said hello and she walked by without responding. I felt as if I had ceased to exist.

My friend was on the Promotion and Tenure Committee that considered my application for retention. Personal loyalties and the norms of ethical identity collided with status norms and institutional loyalty.

I was advised by a senior member of the faculty that retention review was pro forma if you had an article accepted for publication. Then the review process began and the rules seemed to change. No. That is wrong. The rules did not change. I concluded that the Committee had applied the standards reserved for black faculty members. The only other black on the faculty had been reviewed for retention, not once, but every year for five years until he was tenured.

The Committee never heard of the law review in which my article would be published. My female colleague and friend pointed out to the Committee the respectable position of that law review on a list of "most frequently cited" law reviews. (A male colleague who received tenure that year had his only law review article in a law review that was not even on the list.) Members of the Committee raised questions about the use of terms like "values" and "social structure" in my article. My friend painstakingly marked every mention of values and norms in a book co-authored by the same male colleague who received tenure.

She never wavered in her defense of me, but, in our personal relationship, I felt the erosion of her confidence in me. She lived up to her ethical obligation, an ethic which flowed from our friendship and from the identity we shared as women. I am not sure whether, in the end, she thought she had done the right thing. I think of our friendship and each of us individually as casualties in a cultural conflict.

The normative preferences, the values, and the aesthetics of the professional are defined by the dominant culture. The standards which are used by those who occupy the status of a professional do not exist outside of or apart from the culture of which they are a part. "Merit" is culturally defined and every meritocracy is influenced by politics. The mythic attributes of the "true" professional, neutrality and objectivity, are used to bludgeon those who question the fairness of the process by which others are excluded from the profession.

Many of us, women, blacks, and people of color, have fought hard to achieve professional status. Charges that one of us is behaving in an "unprofessional" manner can be devastating. It is an attack on the individual's reputation, on his or her judgment and integrity. It suggests that the guilty party does not really "belong" in that professional status, undermines his or her credibility, and creates a fear that the privileges may indeed be withdrawn. Our ability to demystify and demythologize the process is the only effective defense against that kind of assault.

The Diversity Ideal in Academia: The Politics of Identity

W.E.B. Du Bois described his first awareness of racism as the realization that he was a "problem" for white people.[2] His initial response was to beat them at their own game, to achieve academically and professionally. What Du Bois ultimately discovered, what all black people have discovered, is that it is risky to play a game with opponents who can change the rules at any time.

Although *The Souls of Black Folk* was written almost 80 years ago, black people, people of color, and women remain "problems" for the most enlightened institutions in our society, the law schools and universities where we teach. We are a problem even for the individuals and the institutions which have embraced the ideal of diversity, for administrations which wrestle with the problem of recruiting and retaining minorities and women. Task force after task force examines the problem. Reports are issued, remedies are proposed.

Anyone who has been in academia for a while has seen countless examples of the way in which these "objective" criteria are manipulated to obtain tenure for those individuals who are well-liked and to deny tenure to those who are unpopular for one reason or another. People can be unpopular because of their personalities or politics, but the issues which concern me here are gender and ethnicity. Unconscious and conscious racism and gender bias eat away like acid at the integrity of the hiring and tenure processes.

Racism creates a profound skepticism about the abilities of blacks, a skepticism which is perpetuated even in the solutions which are proposed to cure one of the symptoms of racism: the absence in meaningful numbers of black people in law teaching. The idea that black law professors need some remedial help with scholarship is absurd. The problem is not ours. The problem is institutional. We exist in an environment where the decision not to write is eminently rational. We realize that our scholarship is suspect because our areas of interest are unacceptable, that average work, work comparable to that of our peers, is unacceptable. We cannot afford to make mistakes because everything we do is scrutinized with such attention to detail and minutiae that it would paralyze most creative people.

As long as we define the "problem" as something external to the white males who are the decision-makers in our institutions, as long as we ignore the biases of those who administer the process and the manipulability of the criteria of selection, the problem will not go away. As it currently stands, the institutional position condemns racism and sexism without seeking to eradicate them. Instead, it offers extra assistance to people of color and women so that they can compete and occasionally succeed on an unequal playing field.

I understand the frustration of faculty of good will whose colleagues are openly racist or sexist.

I heard the frustration in the voice of a white male who asked, "What can we do about our racist colleagues?" I don't think he was listening when I answered: Admonish them for their conduct. Confront them and tell them that their behavior is inappropriate. Develop standards which make it clear that certain behavior is unacceptable. Even as I spoke I realized nothing would be done. Confrontation is divisive.

Perhaps the realization that the "standards" we are asked to meet are not standards at all has given some of us the courage to pursue our own interests in our own way. If women and people of color have been a problem in the past, they are even more so now. The struggle for diversity has expanded beyond a head count of people of color and women. It now embraces the idea that different styles of scholarship and teaching have a place in our institutions. "Counter-hegemonies" are abroad in the land and the "problem" is being redefined as a failure or refusal to assimilate.[3]

The Struggle for Diversity: The Politics of Identity

As I stand before a class of law students in which there are far too few students of color, I sometimes experience a feeling of total frustration, a kind of battle fatigue. I am diminished in the eyes of my women and minority students who perceive the difference in the amount of respect I receive from students as compared to my white male counterparts. I am diminished by the unreasonable demands of my white male students who think that because I am different from their white male teachers I am deficient in some respect. The subtle demands for conformity from the former are well-intentioned; the demands from the latter are less benign.

The greatest challenge in teaching is overcoming the obstacles to learning which students construct out of their racism and their gender bias. Their hostility finds expression in the classroom in subtle but disruptive ways: the noise level, the inattention, the answers which verge on disrespect. Even when students are attentive and interested, male colleagues who critique our teaching often focus on the issue of control in the classroom.

If half of the current battle for diversity is acclimating students to a different style of teaching—teaching our students in spite of themselves—the other half is educating our well-meaning colleagues whose preference for existing models of scholarship and teaching cause them to trivialize our work. Even those who believe in the value of diversity are prone to habits of mind and unconscious assumptions which devalue other cultures or which assume the superiority of white male models of scholarship.

Style or manner of expression can be a product of gender or cultural differences. The dominant culture includes notions of the appropriate choice of style. In a social setting, a style which is associated with women is often appropriate. It can make the difference between a successful event and one which is a dismal failure. Conversely, this "feminine" style has no place in the classroom, in faculty meetings, or in scholarship because it is distracting.

Two years ago, I raised objections to certain practices used by our Academic Policy Committee in deciding petitions for academic probation. In the course of a very heated discussion, the Chair, a tenured white male and a long-time warrior in the area of civil rights, looked directly at me and said, "I can't understand you when you are emotional."

The style of discourse which I employ, one which includes emotion, personal anecdotes, digressions (in which I attempt to reconnect ideas that have been separated out for instructional purposes), and a style of delivery that is animated and full of gestures and which removes the physical distance between me and the student, is seen by some as distracting. It is thought to be inappropriate in a setting that demands discipline, structure and control, the use of dispassionate discourse, and linear logic. The male model assumes an antithetical relationship between certain kinds of style and knowledge that corresponds roughly to the false dichotomy drawn in Western culture between emotion and reason.

A critique of style has become one of the major weapons in the hands of those opposed to diversity. It is used successfully by evaluators who pretend that value judgments are not being made about the ideas which are promoted in the scholarship, that the objectification of standards of scholarship makes them value neutral, and that the ideas or political positions of scholars are irrelevant. The cultural preferences which currently dominate legal scholarship leave women and people of color open to attacks which trivialize their work. The theoretical or pedagogical strategies which they employ are dismissed or ignored.

It is not perversity which informs my choice as a black woman to continue using a style which leaves me open to attack by those who claim to be the arbiters of quality and intellectual rigor. It is a commitment to the principle of diversity and to the idea that all of us, including white males, will be impoverished by rejection of ideas, interests, styles, and beliefs merely because they are different. The abandonment of cultural differences does not increase understanding; it diminishes in a very real way the possibility of understanding. We gain nothing if we contract the universe of possibilities with respect to intellectual discourse or human interaction.

Ethical Identity and the Diversity Ideal

The struggle for equality began with an argument which denied the differences between men and women, between blacks and whites. Today, a different paradigm of equality is being offered. In it, the struggle for equality embraces differences and demands equality, not in spite of, but because of, those differences. The struggle for equality has a cultural dimension. We no longer want to emulate those who control our institutions. We no longer want to talk like them, write like them, or teach like them. Blacks are "reinventing difference," reconstructing cultures which have been decimated by the pressure to assimilate. Women are turning stereotypes on their heads, using gender difference as a vehicle for the reconstruction of society.

"I'm Black and I'm Proud" may have begun as a taunt thrown in the face of white America, a defense against the psychological assault of racism, but the slogans of activists like Stokely Carmichael and H. Rap Brown altered our aesthetics and strengthened our sense of identity. Ours was a form of cultural nationalism.[4] We rediscovered our cultural traditions and rejected the myth that black culture was a "ghetto" culture. The expression of our culture became an affirmation of self. Today, the scholarship or pedagogy of black women and men can be an affirmation of self.

The battle for cultural dominance did not begin with the creation of something called "critical race theory." The clarion call of diversity would not have been heard if the ethos of cultural relativism had not been instilled in so many white students in the Sixties. These students, dissatisfied with the more repressive aspects of white middle-class culture, sought out courses in anthropology. They learned not to use the word "primitive" to describe other cultures. They learned something about the extensiveness of cultural plagiarism by the West— the extent to which ideas, music, and art had been borrowed from other "inferior" cultures. In some respects, while black youths like me were busy rediscovering our culture, these white students were inventing their own. Today, cultural relativism has several new names in legal academia: diversity, multivocality, intersectional analysis, critical race theory, and feminist theory. It exists because there are men and women of good faith who learned to embrace rather than shrink from the ideal of true diversity.

With diversity has come the introduction of the counter-hegemonies—the cultural preferences, aesthetics, and taxonomies that exist in groups marginalized by the existing social order. The power of counter-hegemonies is their ability to reclassify social categories. They offer alternatives to existing and dominant systems of classifications.

For example, in the current controversy over the regulation of hate speech, women and people of color have drawn on counter-hegemonic models to criticize the classification of hate speech as a protected category of speech. They have also exposed and criticized the values that form the basis for the dominant culture's classifications of protected speech. In doing so, they have reclassified the venom spewed by bigots from protected speech to unprotected speech, assimilating it to other unprotected categories of speech like defamation, obscenity, and fighting words.

The most important and valuable contribution of counter-hegemonies is the solutions they offer. They are more radical or revolutionary than the theories which expose and attack the political ideology that is embedded in our law and reproduced by our legal system. For example, *Brandenburg v Ohio* and *National Socialist Party v Skokie*, the Klan and Nazi Party cases, legitimized speech which advocates the subjugation, oppression, or persecution of people of color, women, Jews, and gays and lesbians.[5] In response, some of us have questioned the meaning of the term "political" in such a system of classification, where the speech of the Klan and of Nazis receives protection.

The power of the counter-hegemonies which have been unleashed in our society can be measured in the intensity of the reaction to them in academia today. Those who sought to segregate the intellectual efforts of blacks and women have sounded a battle cry over the canons of literature and the intellectual impoverishment of the American student. For those who wish to maintain the status quo, counter-hegemonies have a disruptive effect.

Cultural politics have erupted into open warfare. In the past, the struggle sometimes seemed like guerrilla warfare fought by isolated and fanatical adherents who risked everything despite the cost. Now that battle is being waged in the open. To borrow two phrases from a recent article by Henry Louis Gates, it is the "forces of oppression" against the "returning repressed who have challenged the traditional curriculum."[6] I would modify his very apt description only to recognize the significant role that the majority scholars who are allies of diversity play in this battle.

The most serious and credible attack on diversity and cultural relativism comes from those who argue that relativism carried to its logical extreme renders us unable to make moral choices or that it disables political movements which advocate radical social change. If there are no absolute values, we will be unable to ascertain the difference between good and evil, or, in the case of scholarship, the difference between excellence and ineptitude. If we abandon reason and objectivity, we will be unable or unwilling to continue the fight against oppression and injustice.

These criticisms ignore that cultural relativism is itself a moral choice. It is a choice which affirms human dignity and the principle of equality. Cultural relativism is resisted not because it makes cynics of us all, but because it compels uncomfortable value choices. These choices involve the recognition and accommodation of difference. These are choices which threaten to alter the power structure of our society.

NOTES

1. Anthony Appiah, *"But Would That Still Be Me?" Notes on Gender, "Race," Ethnicity, as Sources of Identity*, 87 J. PHILOSOPHY 493 (Oct. 1990).

2. W.E.B. DU BOIS, THE SOULS OF BLACK FOLK 43 (New American Library, 1969) (1903).

3. "Counter-hegemonies" refers to the cultures of subordinated or marginalized groups in society.

4. See generally FRANTZ FANON, THE WRETCHED OF THE EARTH (Grove, 1965) (1961).

5. Brandenburg v Ohio, 395 U.S. 444 (1969); NATIONAL SOCIALIST PARTY V. SKOKIE, 432 U.S. 43 (1977).

6. HENRY LOUIS GATES JR., *Whose Canon Is It Anyway?* NY TIMES MAGAZINE 44 (Feb. 26, 1989).

From the Editor: Issues and Comments

W H Y does the professor think that Geneva's colleagues resisted hiring the seventh candidate of color even though he was as well, if not better, credentialed than the first six to be hired? And does the Chronicle reveal the hollowness of the merit argument—questioning as it does that blacks would be hired even if they had an extraordinary amount of merit? Has the "new," or Critical, civil rights scholarship been accepted over the past decade? If it has, is this a refutation of Bell's argument? What are the advantages of the autobiographical approach to writing and teaching? Does it have any dangers and risks? To what extent is ethnicity—or blackness—a matter of personal choice, a decision to be, or not to be, black? What costs and benefits accrue to one who decides to be black?

For additional discussions of the role of persons of color in academia or the legal profession, see the chapters by Grillo and Wildman (in Part XII), Caldwell (Part VI), Kennedy (Parts VII and X), Russell (Part XI), and Montoya (Part XI). Important articles by Bell and Edmonds, Crenshaw, Espinoza, and Haney López, among others, are listed in the Suggested Readings, immediately following.

Suggested Readings

Ansley, Frances Lee, *Race and the Core Curriculum in Legal Education*, 79 CAL. L. REV. 1511 (1991).

Banks, Taunya Lovell, *Teaching Laws with Flaws: Adopting a Pluralistic Approach to Torts*, 57 MO. L. REV. 443 (1992).

Barnes, Robin D., *Black Women Law Professors and Critical Self-Consciousness: A Tribute to Professor Denise S. Carty-Bennia*, 6 BERKELEY WOMEN'S L.J. 57 (1990–91).

Bell, Derrick A., Jr., *The Final Report: Harvard's Affirmative Action Allegory*, 87 MICH. L. REV. 2382 (1989).

Bell, Derrick & Erin Edmonds, *Students as Teachers, Teachers as Learners*, 91 MICH. L. REV. 2025 (1993).

Carter, Stephen L., *Academic Tenure and White Male Standards: Some Lessons from the Patent Law*, 100 YALE L.J. 2065 (1991).

Crenshaw, Kimberlé Williams, *Foreword: Toward a Race-Conscious Pedagogy in Legal Education*, 11 NAT'L BLACK L.J. 1 (1989).

Culp, Jerome McCristal, Jr., *Posner on Duncan Kennedy and Racial Difference: White Authority in the Legal Academy*, 41 DUKE L.J. 1095 (1992).

Culp, Jerome McCristal, Jr., *Toward a Black Legal Scholarship: Race and Original Understandings*, 1991 DUKE L.J. 39.

Culp, Jerome McCristal, Jr., *You Can Take Them to Water but You Can't Make Them Drink: Black Legal Scholarship and White Legal Scholars*, 1992 U. ILL. L. REV. 1021.

Delgado, Richard, *The Imperial Scholar: Reflections on a Review of Civil Rights Literature*, 132 U. PA. L. REV. 561 (1984).

Delgado, Richard, *Minority Law Professors' Lives: The Bell-Delgado Survey*, 24 HARV. C.R.-C.L. L. REV. 349 (1989).

Espinoza, Leslie G., *The LSAT: Narratives and Bias*, 1 J. GENDER & L. 121 (1993).

Greene, Linda S., *Serving the Community: Aspiration and Abyss for the Law Professor of Color*, 10 ST. LOUIS U. PUB. L. REV. 297 (1991).

Haney López, Ian, *Community Ties, Race, and Faculty Hiring: The Case for Professors Who Don't Think White*, 1 RECONSTRUCTION No. 3, 1991, at 46.

Harris, Angela P., *On Doing the Right Thing: Education Work in the Academy*, 15 VT. L. REV. 125 (1990).

Lawrence, Charles R., III, *The Word and the River: Pedagogy as Scholarship as Struggle*, 65 S. CAL. L. REV. 2231 (1992).

López, Gerald P., *Training Future Lawyers to Work with the Politically and Socially Subordinated: Anti-Generic Legal Education*, 91 W. VA. L. REV. 305 (1989).

CRITICISM AND SELF-ANALYSIS

SOMETIMES a movement's themes and distinctive contours will emerge most clearly in the crucible of criticism, both external and internal. Part X begins with an excerpt of a famous article by Harvard law professor Randall Kennedy, a leading civil rights scholar. Kennedy, an African American, takes three of the leading Critical Race Theory writers to task for exaggerating the importance of race and elevating a writer's race virtually to a requirement of "standing." And in the next chapter, Leslie Espinoza, writing in the *Harvard Law Review*, takes issue with Randall Kennedy's critique of CRT, likening much of it to the donning of a mask. Alan D. Freeman, a sympathetic white scholar who has contributed important Critical work, expresses doubts about some of CRT's bleak perspectives on the possibility of racial change. In an excerpt from his review of Derrick Bell's casebook he wonders whether readers and law students will not be left enervated, discouraged from working for racial justice because of the hopelessness of many of Bell's analyses. In the final chapter, Richard Delgado argues that criticism from at least one quarter—from some of the new black neoconservative writers—is not particularly damaging to the movement or to the cause of racial justice, and that many of the themes of the Critical left and of the new right coincide.

38 Racial Critiques of Legal Academia

RANDALL L. KENNEDY

T H I S chapter analyzes recent writings that examine the effect of racial difference on the distribution of scholarly influence and prestige in legal academia. These writings articulate two interrelated theses. The first—the exclusion thesis—is the belief that the intellectual contributions of scholars of color are wrongfully ignored or undervalued. A decade ago, Professor Derrick Bell expressed this concern, protesting what he viewed as the undue extent to which "white voices have dominated the minority admissions debate."[1] Subsequently, Professor Richard Delgado criticized what he described as "white scholars' systematic occupation of, and exclusion of minority scholars from, the central areas of civil rights scholarship."[2] More recently, Professor Mari Matsuda decried what she perceives as "segregated scholarship."[3] Although the legal academic establishment has been the main target of commentators who seek to delineate illicit racial hierarchy in the organization of legal scholarship, the Critical Legal Studies (CLS) Movement, the major bulwark of leftism in legal academic culture, has also been criticized for being "imperialistic"[4] and for "silencing" scholars of color.[5]

The second tenet of the writings I analyze is the racial distinctiveness thesis: the belief (1) that minority scholars, like all people of color in the United States, have experienced racial oppression; (2) that this experience causes minority scholars to view the world with a different perspective from that of their white colleagues; and (3) that this different perspective displays itself in valuable ways in the work of minority scholars. Bell expresses one version of the distinctiveness thesis when he writes that "[r]ace can [be an important positive qualification] in filling a teaching position intended to interpret . . . the impact of racial discrimination on the law and lawyering."[6] Delgado asserts that important race-based differences exist that distinguish the race-relations law scholarship of whites from that of people of color, differences involving choice of topics, tenor of argument, and substantive views.[7] Matsuda insists that "those who have experienced discrimination speak with a special voice to which we should listen,"[8] that "the victims of racial oppression have distinct normative insights,"[9] and that "[t]hose who are oppressed in the present world can speak most eloquently of a better one."[10]

102 HARV. L. REV. 1745 (1989). Copyright © 1989 by The Harvard Law Review Association. Reprinted by permission.

The exclusion thesis and the distinctiveness thesis intersect in the idea that the value of intellectual work marked by the racial background of minority scholars is frequently either unrecognized or underappreciated by white scholars blinded by the limitations of their own racially defined experience or prejudiced by the imperatives of their own racial interests.

T H E writings by Professors Derrick Bell, Richard Delgado, and Mari Matsuda have placed on scholarly agendas questions that have heretofore received little or no attention, questions that explore the nature and consequences of racial conflict within legal academia. Before then, some of the most provocative studies of the history and sociology of legal academia emerged from the legal realist and CLS movements.[11] Like certain proponents of legal realism and current advocates of CLS, proponents of racial critiques are insurgent scholars seeking to transform society, including, of course, the law schools. Unlike previous academic rebels, however, the proponents of racial critiques tap as their primary sources of emotional and intellectual sustenance an impatient demand that all areas of legal scholarship show an appreciation for the far-reaching ways in which race relations have impinged upon every aspect of our culture and a resolute insistence upon reforming all ideas, practices, and institutions that impose or perpetuate white racist hegemony. Thus inspired, they have succeeded in making "the race question" a burning issue for a substantial number of persons in legal academia.

At the same time, the writings . . . reveal significant deficiencies—the most general of which is a tendency to evade or suppress complications that render their conclusions problematic. Stated bluntly, they fail to support persuasively their charges of racial exclusion or their insistence that legal academic scholars of color produce a racially distinctive brand of valuable scholarship. My criticism of the Bell/Delgado/Matsuda line of racial critiques extends farther, however, than their descriptions of the current state of legal academia. I also take issue with their politics of argumentation and with some of the normative premises underlying their writings. More specifically, . . . I challenge: (1) the argument that, on intellectual grounds, white academics are entitled to less "standing" to participate in race-relations law discourse than academics of color; (2) the argument that, on intellectual grounds, the minority status of academics of color should serve as a positive credential for purposes of evaluating their work; (3) explanations that assign responsibility for the current position of scholars of color overwhelmingly to the influence of prejudiced decisions by white academics.

The Cultural Context of Racial Critiques

Racial critiques of legal education mirror anxieties that haunt our culture, anxieties that stem from the problematic relationship between knowledge and power. Racial critiques exemplify a development that Louis Wirth memorably described over three decades ago:

In the light of modern thought and investigation much of what was once taken for granted is declared to be in need of demonstration and proof. The criteria of proof themselves have become subjects of dispute. We are witnessing not only a general distrust of the validity of ideas but of the motives of those who assert them.[12]

Like the sociology of knowledge, and various Marxist and feminist analyses of culture, the racial critiques make critical reflection on the relationship between knowledge and power a central topic of concern. Unlike these kindred strains of analysis, however, racial critiques are primarily rooted in the history of American race relations.

Two related aspects of this history are particularly relevant for understanding the origins of the racial critiques. First, of all the many racially derogatory comments about people of color, particularly Negroes, none has been more hurtful, corrosive, and influential than the charge that they are intellectually inferior to whites.[13] In the age of slavery, the image of Negro intellectual inferiority became entrenched in the minds of pro-slavery and anti-slavery whites alike[14] and helped to rationalize the denial of educational resources to blacks. Throughout the century following the abolition of slavery, efforts by blacks to participate equally in American intellectual culture continued to encounter the skepticism of those who held a low opinion of the intellectual capacity of Negroes and the opposition of those who believed that educated Negroes posed a special menace to a well-ordered society. As students, teachers, and writers in the humanities, sciences, and professions, Negroes confronted exclusionary color bars in every imaginable context. W. S. Scarborough, an accomplished Negro scholar of Greek and Latin, found that there simply was no place for him in academia in late nineteenth–century America, "not even at the predominantly Negro Howard University, where the white members of the Board of Trustees took the position that the chair in classical languages could be filled only by a Caucasian."[15]

Alongside invidious discrimination perpetrated by individuals or private organizations was discrimination authorized or compelled by government.[16] In considering racial critiques of legal academia, one must remember that the struggle against de jure segregation was primarily one against segregation in *education*, and that prior to *Brown v. Board of Education*[17] the desegregation of state law schools was a major locus of controversy.[18] Also of particular relevance, given the claims of the racial critique literature, is that although the overt forms of racial domination described thus far were enormously destructive, *covert* color bars have been, in a certain sense, even more insidious. After all, judgments based on expressly racist criteria make no pretense about evaluating the merit of the individual's work. Far more cruel are racially prejudiced judgments that are rationalized in terms of meritocratic standards.[19] Recognizing that American history is seeded with examples of intellectuals of color whose accomplishments were ignored or undervalued because of race[20] is absolutely crucial for understanding the bone-deep resentment and distrust that finds expression in the racial critique literature.

Many white academics manifested the same racist attitudes in their intellectual work as in their institutional practices. For example, Ulrich B. Phillips' apologetic account of slavery[21] and William A. Dunning's pejorative portrayal of Reconstruction[22]—both of which were enormously influential and long considered to constitute sound scholarly learning—reflected the limitations of a culture in which whites believed that racial minorities were simply unfit to participate as equals in the cultural, social, or political life of the nation.[23] These same cultural assumptions have affected legal scholarship as well.[24] There was a time, not so long ago, when articles and notes in law reviews *defended* segregation,[25] questioned the legality and desirability of the fifteenth amendment,[26] and even condoned (albeit with qualifications) the practice of lynching.[27] Although we now inhabit a very different political, social, and cultural environment, it is useful to question—as the racial critiques invite us to do—whether racial prejudices continue to affect to some degree the governance and scholarship of legal academia.

A 1983 B O Y C O T T of a race-relations law course at Harvard Law School indicated the continuing potency of some of these sentiments. The boycotted course was taught by Jack Greenberg, a white civil rights attorney who was then the Director-Counsel of the NAACP Legal Defense Fund (LDF), and Julius Chambers, a prominent black civil rights attorney.[28] The boycott dramatized a variety of objections, including primarily a dissatisfaction with Harvard's failure to add more minority professors to its faculty; of sixty-four full-time faculty members, only two were persons of color.[29] Chambers' participation in the course was seen as unresponsive to this concern since he was a practicing attorney who clearly was not interested in an academic career. Moreover, some protesters felt affronted by Greenberg's long-standing position as Director-Counsel of the LDF, the nation's leading private organization devoted to civil rights litigation. They viewed him as the archetypal white liberal who facilitates black advancement in society at large but retards it in his immediate environment by exercising authority in a way that precludes the development of black leadership. Furthermore, in the view of at least some of the boycotters, that the course involved race-relations law made the racial background of the professor especially relevant. In addition to the special insight a minority instructor was presumed to provide, some boycotters and their supporters believed that with respect to race-relations law, it could safely be assumed there would exist a substantial pool of suitably qualified minority teachers.

The boycott was harshly criticized by a broad array of observers.[30] At the same time, some academics supported, or at least defended it. Arguing that race should be a consideration in matching instructors to course offerings, Harvard Law School Professor Christopher Edley, Jr., maintained that "[r]ace remains a useful proxy for a whole collection of experiences, aspirations and sensitivities. . . . [W]e teach what we have lived. . . ."[31] Similarly, Professor Derrick Bell argued that "[r]ace can create as legitimate a presumption as a judicial clerkship in filling a teaching position intended to interpret . . . the impact of racial discrimination on the law and lawyering."[32] Racial background can properly be considered a credential, he observed, because of "[t]he special and quite valuable perspective on law and life in this country that a black person can provide."[33]

One reason why many black intellectuals feel moved to assert proprietary claims over the study of race relations and the cultural history of minorities is the perceived need to react defensively to the enhanced ability of whites, because of racial privilege, to exploit popular interest in these subjects. Even at the height of popular interest in the Black Power Movement, the conditioned reflexes of many editors and publishers produced a veritable bonanza for white commentators. Moreover, the privileging of whites in cultural enterprise is pervasive. James Baldwin once wrote that "[i]t is only in his music . . . that the Negro in America has been able to tell his story."[34] The color line, however, has cast long shadows over that area of cultural accomplishment as well. In the 1950s, for instance, when "rhythm and blues" played a major role in transforming the sensibilities of many young whites, the color bar prevented black musicians from capitalizing fully on the popularity of a genre they had done much to establish; instead, white cultural entrepreneurs typically reaped the largest commercial rewards—a pattern still visible today, albeit in less dramatic form.

Given the pervasiveness and tenacity of racial prejudice in American culture, it is readily imaginable that current practice and discourse in legal academia could be tainted by biases of the sort that some commentators claim to have identified. There is a considerable difference, however, between plausible hypotheses and persuasive theories. What separates the two is testing. . . .

Race, Standing, and Scholarship

In *The Imperial Scholar*, Professor Delgado asks the question: "what difference does it make if the scholarship about the rights of group *A* [i.e., people of color] is written by members of group *B* [i.e., whites]."[35] He answers this question by applying to the world of scholarship juridical concepts of standing "which in general insist that *B* does not belong in court if he or she is attempting, without good reason, to assert the rights of, or redress the injuries to *A*."[36] Elaborating upon this analogy he writes:

> [I]t is possible to compile an *a priori* list of reasons why we might look with concern on a situation in which the scholarship about group A is written by members of group B. First, members of group B may be ineffective advocates of the rights and interests of persons in group A. They may lack information; more important, perhaps, they may lack passion, or that passion may be misdirected. B's scholarship may tend to be sentimental, diffusing passion in useless directions, or wasting time on unproductive breast-beating. Second, while the B's might advocate effectively, they might advocate the wrong things. Their agenda may differ from that of the A's; they may pull their punches with respect to remedies, especially where remedying A's situation entails uncomfortable consequence for B. Despite the best of intentions, B's may have stereotypes embedded deep in their

psyches that distort their thinking, causing them to balance interests in ways inimical to A's. Finally, domination by members of group B may paralyze members of group A, causing the A's to forget how to flex their legal muscles for themselves.[37]

Delgado argues that "[a] careful reading of [race-relations law scholarship by white academics] suggests that many of the above mentioned problems and pitfalls are not simply hypothetical, but do in fact occur."[38] They occur, Delgado suggests, because white scholars have not suffered the analogue to "injury in fact."[39] Without the suffering that comes from being a person of color in a society dominated by whites, white scholars cannot see the world from the victim's perspective, and will, to that extent, be prevented from creating scholarship fully attuned to the imperatives of effective struggle against racial victimization. They presumably have neither the information required for such a task, first-hand experience as a victim of white racism, nor the motivation generated by victimization, the drive to rescue oneself and one's people from subjugation.

Delgado need not resort to standing doctrine in order to object to ignorant, sloppy, misleading, or sentimental scholarship. He looks to standing doctrine for assistance because that doctrine underscores the importance of a party's *status*. Standing is a status-based limitation on the ability of a party to invoke the jurisdiction of a court. It is a limitation that, in theory, looks not to the substance of a given party's argument but to the relationship of the party to the injury prompting litigation. Delgado is similarly concerned with status. He does not identify the body of work to which he objects solely on the basis of perceived intellectual deficiencies. Rather, he identifies and criticizes "imperial scholarship" largely by reference to the ascribed racial characteristics of its authors.

Concepts of status-based standing in the intellectual arena have a long and varied history.[40] Professor Delgado's ideas, in other words, are by no means isolated. Some commentators have argued that within the subject area embraced by black studies, white intellectuals have no standing whatsoever. Others have contended that while there are some race-related subjects white intellectuals can usefully investigate, there are others that whites should avoid because of their racial status.[41] A related position is that while white scholars can perhaps contribute significantly to the study of people of color, they cannot realistically aspire to be *leading* figures.[42]

Delgado does not contend that white scholars should be precluded altogether from participating in discourse on race-relations law. He leaves the distinct impression, though, that readers should view white commentators as suspect. Moreover, he argues that white academics should, on their own, quietly leave the field. "The time has come," Delgado writes, "for white liberal authors . . . to redirect their efforts and to encourage their colleagues to do so as well. . . . As these scholars stand aside, nature will take its course [and] the gap will quickly be filled by talented and innovative minority writers and commentators."[43]

The concept of race-based standing functions to achieve two overlapping but discrete goals. One is to redistribute on racial lines academic power—jobs, promotions, and prestige. The standing analogy is well-suited to accomplish this end; it provides a device for excluding or disadvantaging white scholars to the benefit of scholars of color. A second goal is to promote those best able to provide useful analyses of racial issues. It seems to be implicitly argued that race-based standing furthers this purpose because the intellectual shortcomings of analyses provided by white academics are sufficiently correlated with their racial background that "whiteness" can appropriately serve as a proxy for these shortcomings. Seen in this light, placing restrictions on white scholars pursuant to the concept of race-based standing is not simply a device for protecting the market position of scholars of color; it is a device that advances a broader social interest.

There are a variety of problems with Delgado's conception of racial standing and the way he articulates it. First, his criticism of "[d]efects in Imperial Scholarship" is itself problematic. According to Delgado, scholars of color and white scholars typically differ in articulating justifications for affirmative action. He suggests that scholars of color characteristically justify affirmative action as a type of reparations, while the white authors in the "inner circle" "generally make the case on the grounds of utility or distributive justice."[44] He contends that this theoretical divergence stems from racially conditioned differences in perspective and deems the reparations theory analytically superior to its competitors.[45] He writes that justifications of affirmative action based on utilitarian or distributive-justice theories are "sterile."[46] These theories, he says, enable "the writer to concentrate on the present and the future and overlook the past . . . rob[bing] affirmative action programs of their moral force."[47] Delgado, however, offers no persuasive reason for labeling as "sterile" the theories he derides. Although Delgado criticizes liberal writers for "overlook[ing] the past,"[48] a fair reading of their work belies that charge. In an article that Delgado singles out for criticism,[49] Professors Kenneth Karst and Harold Horowitz advocate the implementation of affirmative action, expressly stating that "[i]n order to prevent past discrimination from acting as a psychological inhibitor of present aspirations, we need to see large numbers of black, Chicano, Native American and other minority faces in every area of our society."[50] Contrary to Delgado's assertions, they do acknowledge the nation's long and brutal history of racial oppression. They suggest, however, that appeals to that history alone may not suffice as a convincing rationale for racial preferences. They therefore articulate and refine alternative and supplementary justifications—a course that should hardly be objectionable to advocates of affirmative action.[51]

Delgado also argues that scholarship by white scholars is preoccupied with procedure. He complains that many of the articles of "imperial scholarship" that he listed

> were devoted, in various measures, to scholarly discussions of the standard of judicial review that should be applied in different types of civil rights suits. Others were concerned with the relationship between federal and state authority in antidiscrimination law, or with the respective competence of a particular decisionmaker to recognize and redress racial discrimination. One could easily conclude

that the question of who goes to court, what court they go to, and with what standard of review, are the burning issues of American race-relations law.[52]

These issues, of course, are not the only ones important to understanding race-relations law. And if Delgado's point is simply that the body of work he reviews dwells unduly upon procedural and legalistic issues to the exclusion of extra-legal studies, including sociology, history, and psychology—I agree with him, at least in part.[53] But if he means to say what his language most plausibly suggests, I must demur in astonishment because race-relations law, like every other field of law, is vitally shaped by answers to questions involving jurisdiction,[54] institutional competence,[55] and standards of judicial review.[56]

A second and far more troubling problem with Delgado's conception of racial standing involves his linkage of white scholars' racial background to the qualities in their work that he perceives as shortcomings.[57] On the one hand, he concedes that there are at least some white scholars who produce work that transcends the failings he notes.[58] On the other hand, there are an appreciable number of scholars of color whose work is marked by the features that Delgado associates with white academics.[59] Against this backdrop, it is unclear what is "white" about the intellectual characteristics to which Delgado objects.

If the tables were turned—if a commentator were to read articles by twenty-eight scholars of color, describe deficiencies found in some of them, acknowledge that some black scholars produced work that avoided these pitfalls, but nonetheless conclude that manifestations of these flaws were attributable to the *race* of the twenty-eight authors—there would erupt, I suspect (or at least hope), a flood of criticism. Part of the criticism would stem from concerns over accuracy: using race as a proxy would rightly be seen as both over- and underinclusive. However, a deeper concern would likely arise, stemming from the peculiar place of race in American life. There are many types of classification that negate individual identity, achievement, and dignity. But racial classification has come to be viewed as paradigmatically offensive to individuality. We often resort to proxies with no feeling of moral discomfort, knowing that they will yield results of varying degrees of inaccuracy. But the use of *race* as a proxy is specially disfavored because, even when relatively accurate as a signifier of the trait sought to be identified, racial proxies are especially prone to misuse. By the practice of subjecting governmentally imposed racial distinctions to strict scrutiny, federal constitutional law recognizes that racial distinctions are particularly liable to being used in a socially destructive fashion. Two features of Delgado's analysis are thus deeply worrisome: first, the casualness with which he uses negative racial stereotypes to pigeonhole white scholars, and second, the tolerance, if not approbation, of that aspect of his critique.

Implicit in Delgado's conception of standing is a belief that one reason why white scholars produce deficient race-relations scholarship is that they are "outsiders" to the colored communities that are deeply affected by such law. But that same logic puts into doubt the position of scholars of color; after all, they could be said to be "outsiders" to white communities affected by race-relations law.

Apart from that difficulty, moreover, is the problematic assumption that the mere status of being an "outsider" is intellectually debilitating. Being an outsider or "stranger" may *enhance* opportunities for gathering information and perceiving certain facets about a given situation. As Professor Patricia Hill Collins has noted, the stranger's salutary "composition of nearness and remoteness, concern and indifference" suggests that he may "see patterns that may be more difficult for those immersed in the situation to see."[60] Tocqueville, Lord Bryce, and Gunnar Myrdal are examples of insightful outsiders. Professor Collins adds to this list the work of certain black feminists, noting that "for many Afro-American female intellectuals, 'marginality' has been an excitement to creativity."[61] The point here is not that an outsider is necessarily or even presumptively insightful; to make such an assertion would simply replicate in reverse Delgado's error of assigning to a given social status too much determinative influence on thought. Rather, the point is that distance or nearness to a given subject—"outsiderness" or "insiderness"—are simply social conditions; they provide opportunities that intellectuals are free to use or squander, but they do not in themselves determine the intellectual quality of scholarly productions; *that* depends on what a particular scholar makes of his or her materials, regardless of his or her social position.

Widespread application of Delgado's conception of intellectual standing would be disastrous. First, it would likely diminish the reputation of legal scholarship about race relations. Already, the field is viewed by some as intellectually "soft." To restrict the field on a racial basis would surely—and rightly—drive the reputation of the field to far lower depths. By requesting that white scholars leave the field or restrict their contributions to it, Delgado seems to want to transform the study of race-relations law into a zone of limited intellectual competition.

Second, widespread application of Delgado's conception of standing would likely be bad for minority scholars. It would be bad for them because it would be bad for *all* scholars. It would be bad for all scholars because status-based criteria for intellectual standing are anti-intellectual in that they subordinate ideas and craft to racial status. After all, to be told that one lacks "standing" is to be told that no matter what one's message—no matter how true or urgent or beautiful—it will be ignored or discounted because of *who* one is. Furthermore, as is so often the case in our society, the negative consequences of misconceived policy will fall with particular harshness upon racial minorities. Accepting the premises of race-based standing will tend to fence whites out of certain topics to the superficial advantage of black scholars. But acceptance might also tend to fence blacks out of certain subjects. If inferences based on sociological generalities permit us to use presumptions that disadvantage white scholars in relation to blacks in race-relations law, why should we not indulge a reverse set of presumptions in, say, antitrust, corporate finance, or securities regulation? Both presumptions would be improper because scholars should keep racial generalizations in their place, including those that are largely accurate. Scholars should do so by evaluating other scholars as individuals, without prejudgment, no matter what their hue. Scholars should, in other words, inculcate what Gordon Allport referred to as "habitual open-mindedness," a skeptical attitude toward all labels and categories that obscure appreciation of the unique features of specific persons and their work.

E V A L U A T I V E judgments linked to the race of authors should be seen as illegitimate if the purpose of evaluation is to reach a judgment about a given piece of work. Perhaps in some situations race can serve as "a useful proxy for a whole collection of experiences, aspirations and sensitivities."[62] But for purposes of evaluating a novel, play, law review article, or the entire written product of an individual, there is no reason to rely on such a proxy because there exists at hand the most probative evidence imaginable—the work itself.

Another negative aspect of the racial standing doctrine is illuminated by an essay by Richard Gilman significantly titled *White Standards and Black Writing*.[63] In this essay, Gilman declared that, as a white man, he was disqualified from evaluating certain forms of "black writing" that were autobiographical and polemical. Discussing Eldridge Cleaver's *Soul on Ice,* Gilman maintained that it was a book "not subject . . . to approval or rejection by those of us who are not black."[64] Ironically, although Gilman was undoubtedly attempting to react sympathetically, the conclusion he reached actually cast *Soul on Ice* into a cultural ghetto, one in which "black" writing could be read by whites but not critically evaluated by them. More troubling still is the route by which Gilman reached his conclusion. Voicing an extreme version of the racial distinctiveness thesis, he averred that "[t]he black man doesn't feel the way whites do, nor does he think as whites do. . . . [B]lack suffering is not of the same kind as ours."[65] Apart from its extraordinary racialism, that claim is also ironic because at the very moment Gilman confesses ignorance, he tells readers that blacks neither think nor even suffer the way that whites do.

Illuminating in a different way is an article by Professor Alan Freeman.[66] Freeman's earlier article *Legitimizing Racial Discrimination Through Antidiscrimination Law*[67] articulated one of the most useful concepts we have for analyzing the jurisprudence of race relations—the distinction between the "victim" and the "perpetrator" perspective.[68] Yet, after having contributed creatively to the development of a critical, anti-racist approach to race-relations law, Freeman stated, in the course of responding to racial critiques of CLS:

> My personal commitment is to participate in the development of answers [to problems posed by the continuing presence of racist ideas and practices in American culture]. My whiteness is of course an inescapable feature of that participation. I have tried hard to listen, to understand, to gain some empathetic connection with victims of racist practice. I have no illusion of having crossed an uncrossable gap; yet I believe I can make a contribution. It is true that I am not compelled by color to participate in this struggle; I could stop any time, but I haven't.[69]

The most interesting facet of this poignant statement is the note of apology with which Freeman writes that he is not "compelled by color" to participate in the struggle against racism. This comment was probably prompted by Professor Matsuda's suggestion that people of color, because of their race, are stronger partisans in this struggle because of their supposedly *compelled* commitment.[70] Both Freeman and Matsuda are mistaken, however, in believing that a person's racial status compels him to contribute to struggles against racism. Frederick Douglass did not have to join the abolitionist movement, thereby putting himself at risk; plenty of other blacks chose not to. Rather, he joined and contributed mightily to that movement by virtue of his own volition. Harriet Tubman was not compelled by her color to perform her remarkably heroic feats on the Underground Railroad. She may have considered herself obligated by her racial kinship to other slaves to pursue the career she followed. But feelings of subjective compulsion are themselves elements of personal character. After all, most runaway slaves avoided putting themselves at risk of re-enslavement, and some did little or nothing to aid those whom they had left behind in bondage.

Participation in struggles against racial tyranny or any other sort of oppression is largely a matter of choice, an assertion of will. That is why we honor those who participate in such struggles. Such individuals are admirable precisely because they choose to engage in risky and burdensome conduct that was avoidable. Many people of color have *chosen* to resist racial oppression; many others have not. The same holds true for whites. There is, then, no reason for Professor Freeman to feel apologetic, embarrassed, or deficient simply because he is a white person who seeks to contribute in the intellectual arena to struggles against racial inequality. There is reason, however, to be apprehensive about a style of thought that induces unwarranted feelings of guilt or inadequacy and that exalts "necessity" over choice.

[*Ed.* Another installment of Kennedy's critique appears in Part VII of this volume.]

NOTES

1. D. Bell, Bakke, *Minority Admissions, and the Usual Price of Racial Remedies*, 67 CALIF. L. REV. 1, 4 n.2 (1979). Illustrating the basis of his concern as it applied to legal academia in the immediate aftermath of Regents of the University of California v. Bakke, 438 U.S. 265 (1978), Professor Bell observed:

> At least five "mainstream" law reviews [*Columbia Law Review, Santa Clara Law Review, Southwestern Law Review, Virginia Law Review,* and *University of Chicago Law Review*] have published symposia or workshop papers on the minority admissions issue. All papers published on the issue from these five symposia or conferences were by white scholars. Many of them support minority admissions programs, but support or opposition is less important than the seeming irrelevance of minority views on the subject. As one symposium coordinator responded to my expressed concern that none of the major papers at his conference would be presented by minorities: "We tried to obtain the best scholars we could get." Although candor requires acknowledgment that few mi-

nority academics have national reputations or are frequently published in the major law reviews, this admission largely reflects the exclusion of minorities from the professions.

Id.

See also D. BELL, *Minority Admissions as a White Debate, in* RACE, RACISM AND AMERICAN LAW § 7.12.1, at 445–48 (2d ed. 1980) (arguing that minorities had been excluded from participation in the *Bakke* litigation).

2. R. Delgado, *The Imperial Scholar: Reflections on a Review of Civil Rights Literature,* 132 U. PA. L. REV. 561, 566 (1984).

3. M. Matsuda, *Affirmative Action and Legal Knowledge: Planting Seeds in Plowed-Up Ground,* 11 HARV. WOMEN'S L.J. 1, 2–4 & n.12 (1988).

4. *See* R. Delgado, *The Ethereal Scholar: Does Critical Legal Studies Have What Minorities Want?,* 22 HARV. C.R.-C.L. L. REV. 301, 307 (1987).

5. *See* H. Dalton, *The Clouded Prism,* 22 HARV. C.R.-C.L. L. REV. 435, 441 (1987).

6. D. Bell, *A Question of Credentials,* HARV. L. REC., Sept. 17, 1982, at 14, col. 1; *see also* Bell, *Minority Admissions as a White Debate, supra* note 1, at 445 n.2 (noting that, in the decisive opinion in *Bakke,* "Justice Powell cited ten law review articles, all of which were written by well-known white professors," a fact that, according to Bell, suggests that "prestige counted for more than minority viewpoint in Justice Powell's selections").

7. *See* Delgado, *The Imperial Scholar, supra* note 2, at 566–73.

8. M. Matsuda, *Looking to the Bottom: Critical Legal Studies and Reparations,* 22 HARV. C.R.-C.L. L. REV. 323, 324 (1987).

9. *Id.* at 326.

10. *Id.* at 346.

11. *See, e.g.,* K. Llewelyn, *Some Realism About Realism,* 44 HARV. L. REV. 1222 (1931); Keyserling, *Social Objectives in Legal Education,* 33 COLUM. L. REV. 437 (1933); D. KENNEDY, LEGAL EDUCATION AND THE REPRODUCTION OF HIERARCHY, (1983); A. Konefsky & H. Schlegel, *Mirror, Mirror on the Wall: Histories of American Law Schools,* 95 HARV. L. REV. 833 (1982); M. Tushnet, *Truth, Justice and the American Way: An Interpretation of Public Law Scholarship in the Seventies,* 57 TEX. L. REV. 1307 (1979).

Studies focusing on the gender question in legal academia have emerged around the same time as the racial critiques. *See, e.g.,* C. Menkel-Meadow, *Excluded Voices: New Voices in the Legal Profession Making New Voices in the Law,* 42 U. MIAMI L. REV. 29 (1987); M. Minow, *Feminist Reason: Getting It and Losing It,* 38 J. LEGAL EDUC. 47 (1988); D. Rhode, *Perspectives on Professional Women,* 40 STAN. L. REV. 1163 (1988); D. Rhode, *The "Woman's Point of View,"* 38 J. LEGAL. EDUC. 39 (1988); A. Scales, *The Emergence of Feminist Jurisprudence,* 95 YALE L.J. 1373 (1986); C. Weiss & L. Melling, *The Legal Education of Twenty Women,* 40 STAN. L. REV. 1299 (1988); West, *Jurisprudence and Gender,* 55 U. CHI. L. REV. 1 (1988); Williams, *Deconstructing Gender,* 87 MICH. L. REV. 797 (1989).

12. L. Wirth, *Preface* to K. MANNHEIM, IDEOLOGY AND UTOPIA at xiii (1954).

13. *See, e.g.,* S. GOULD, THE MISMEASURE OF MAN (1981); J. HALLER, JR., OUTCASTS FROM EVOLUTION: SCIENTIFIC ATTITUDES OF RACIAL INFERIORITY, 1859–1900 (1971); L. KAMIN, THE SCIENCE AND POLITICS OF IQ (1974); W. STAN-

TON, THE LEOPARD'S SPOTS: SCIENTIFIC ATTITUDES TOWARD RACE IN AMERICA, 1815–1859 (1960); J. Howard & R. Hammond, *Rumors of Inferiority: The Hidden Obstacles to Black Success*, NEW REPUBLIC, Sept. 9, 1985, AT 17.

14. *See generally* G. FREDRICKSON, THE BLACK IMAGE IN THE WHITE MIND (1971); W. JORDAN, WHITE OVER BLACK: AMERICAN ATTITUDES TOWARD THE NEGRO, 1550–1812 (1968). Robert Allen notes that, in the North, free blacks censured white abolitionists who "set a double standard of achievement which strongly suggested black inferiority. Thus, whites who expected less of black pupils in the classroom or who accepted shoddy performances by black ministers and teachers, were themselves subjected to stringent criticism." R. ALLEN, RELUCTANT REFORMERS: RACISM AND SOCIAL REFORM MOVEMENTS IN THE UNITED STATES 37 (Anchor Books ed. 1975).

15. J. Franklin, *The Dilemma of the American Negro Scholar, in* SOON, ONE MORNING 70 (H. Hill ed., 1963).

16. On the eve of the Supreme Court's decision in Brown v. Board of Education, 347 U.S. 483 (1954), eighteen jurisdictions made segregated public schools mandatory, while four permitted but did not require segregation. *See* R. Leflar & W. Davis, *Segregation in the Public Schools—1953*, 67 HARV. L. REV. 377, 378 n.3 (1954).

17. 347 U.S. 483 (1954).

18. *See, e.g.*, Sweatt v. Painter, 339 U.S. 629, 636 (1950) (ordering the admission of a Negro plaintiff to the University of Texas Law School); Sipuel v. Board of Regents, 332 U.S. 631, 632–33 (1948) (ordering the state to provide equal law school facilities to a Negro plaintiff); Missouri ex. rel. Gaines v. Canada, 305 U.S. 337, 348–52 (1938) (ordering the state to furnish legal education within the state to a Negro plaintiff since it furnished legal education within the state to white citizens); Pearson v. Murray, 169 Md. 478, 489, 182 A. 590, 594 (1936) (ordering the admission of a Negro plaintiff to the only law school in the state). *See generally* R. KLUGER, SIMPLE JUSTICE (1975); M. TUSHNET, THE NAACP'S LEGAL STRATEGY AGAINST SEGREGATED EDUCATION, 1925–1950 (1987).

19. In his history of desegregation in major-league baseball, Jules Tygiel notes that on the eve of Jackie Robinson's dramatic breakthrough in 1946, "[s]ome baseball 'experts' argued that the absence of blacks in the majors stemmed from their lack of talent, intelligence, and desire." J. TYGIEL, BASEBALL'S GREAT EXPERIMENT: JACKIE ROBINSON AND HIS LEGACY 32 (1983). More recently, some observers have ascribed the absence of black managers in professional baseball to a lack of administrative ability. *See, e.g.*, P. Gammons, *The Campanis Affair*, SPORTS ILLUSTRATED, Apr. 20, 1987, at 31 (describing the controversy that erupted when the vice-president of the Los Angeles Dodgers professional baseball team stated that the reason that baseball had no black manager is that blacks "may not have some of the necessities" to hold such positions); see also H. Edwards, *The Collegiate Athletic Arms Race: Origins and Implications of the "Rule 48" Controversy, in* FRACTURED FOCUS: SPORT AS A REFLECTION OF SOCIETY 30–33 (R. Lapchick ed., 1986) (giving statistics indicating a dearth of blacks in managerial positions in college and professional sports).

20. *See, e.g.*, K. MANNING, BLACK APOLLO OF SCIENCE (1983) (delineating in moving detail the ways in which Ernest Just's achievements as a biologist were

minimized and undermined by racism in the American scientific community between approximately 1910 and 1940). As a white colleague noted soon after Just's death, " '[a]n element of tragedy ran through all Just's scientific career due to the limitations imposed by being a Negro in America.' " *Id.* at 329 (quoting F. Lillie, II SCIENCE 95 (1942)). The social history of intellectuals of color is a neglected subject in dire need of the sort of careful, detailed study that is exemplified by Professor Manning's work.

21. *See* U. PHILLIPS, AMERICAN NEGRO SLAVERY (1918).

22. *See* W. DUNNING, RECONSTRUCTION, POLITICAL AND ECONOMIC, 1865–1877 (A. Hart ed., 1907). For a brief discussion of the baneful influence of such accounts of Reconstruction on judicial decisionmaking in race-relations cases, see R. Kennedy, *Reconstruction and the Politics of Scholarship*, 98 YALE L.J. 521, 527–28 (1989).

23. *See* G. FREDRICKSON, *supra* note 14, at xii–xiii; R. LOGAN, THE BETRAYAL OF THE NEGRO 359–92 (new enlarged ed. 1965); C. VANN WOODWARD, THE STRANGE CAREER OF JIM CROW 67–109 (3d rev. ed. 1974).

24. *See* R. Kennedy, *The Tradition of Celebration*, 86 COLUM. L. REV. 1622, 1622–23 (1986).

25. *See, e.g.,* S. S. Field, *The Constitutionality of Segregation Ordinances*, 5 VA. L. REV. 81 (1917); Note, *Constitutionality of Segregation Ordinances*, 16 MICH. L. REV. 109 (1917); Comment, *Unconstitutionality of Segregation Ordinances*, 27 YALE L.J. 393 (1918).

26. *See* A. Machen, *Is the Fifteenth Amendment Void?*, 23 HARV. L. REV. 169 (1910).

27. *See* C. Bonaparte, *Lynch Law and Its Remedy*, 8 YALE L.J. 335 (1899). In his article, Future United States Attorney General Charles Bonaparte wholly ignored the use of lynching as a device for reinforcing the ideology and practice of white supremacy. *See* M. BELKNAP, FEDERAL LAW AND SOUTHERN ORDER 1–26 (1987).

28. The LDF is an organization mainly devoted to the protection and enlargement of blacks' rights through recourse to litigation. Its accomplishments include: Shelley v. Kraemer, 334 U.S. 1 (1948), which invalidated state court enforcement of a racially restrictive covenant; Brown v. Board of Educ., 347 U.S. 483 (1954), which invalidated de jure segregation in public schools; and the virtual abolition of capital punishment in the decade prior to 1976. *See* R. KLUGER, *supra* note 18; M. MELTSNER, CRUEL & UNUSUAL: THE SUPREME COURT AND CAPITAL PUNISHMENT (1973); M. TUSHNET, *supra* note 18; C. VOSE, CAUCASIANS ONLY (1959); E. Muller, *The Legal Defense Fund's Capital Punishment Campaign*, 4 YALE L. & POL'Y REV. 158 (1985).

Jack Greenberg succeeded Thurgood Marshall as the Director-Counsel of LDF and guided its operation until 1983. He has distinguished himself both as an advocate, participating in scores of cases before the Supreme Court, including *Brown*, and as a scholar. *See, e.g.,* J. GREENBERG, RACE RELATIONS AND AMERICAN LAW (1959); J. Greenberg, *Capital Punishment as a System*, 91 YALE L.J. 908 (1982). See generally J. KAUFMAN, BROKEN ALLIANCES: THE TURBULENT TIMES BETWEEN BLACKS AND JEWS IN AMERICA 85–123 (1988) (providing a biographical portrait of Greenberg).

Julius Chambers has long been one of the nation's leading civil rights attorneys. Among the several cases he has argued before the Supreme Court are: Swann v. Charlotte-Mecklenburg Bd. of Educ., 402 U.S. 1 (1971); Albermarle Paper Co. v. Moody, 422 U.S. 405 (1975); and Patterson v. McLean Credit Union, No. 87–107 (U.S. filed Oct. 5, 1987). At the time of the boycott at Harvard, he served as President of LDF and in 1983 succeeded Greenberg as Director-Counsel. *See generally* Carroll, *Rights Unit's New Leader*, N.Y. TIMES, June 13, 1984, at A17, col. 1.

29. In an open letter to the Harvard Law School community, the Third World Coalition stated that it advocated boycotting the course taught by Greenberg and Chambers because of:

(1) the extremely low number of Third World professors at the Law School, (2) the appropriateness of a Third World instructor to teach the Constitutional Law and Minority Issues course, (3) the availability of qualified Third World legal professionals to teach this course in particular and teach at the Law School in general, and (4) the inadequate efforts of Harvard Law School to find these professionals and the biased criteria it uses to judge prospective Third World faculty candidates.

Letter from the Third World Coalition to the Harvard Law School Community (May 24, 1982) (on file at the Harvard Law School Library).

30. *See, e.g., Blind Pride at Harvard*, N.Y. TIMES, Aug. 11, 1982, at A22, col. 1 (editorial); R. Kennedy, *On Cussing Out White Liberals*, NATION, Sept 4, 1982, at 169, 171; *see also* Race as a Problem in the Study of Race Relations Law (unpublished compilation of materials on the Greenberg-Chambers controversy) (on file at the Harvard Law School Library). Critics of the boycott included Carl Rowan, *see id.* at 76, Max Freedman, *see* compilation, *supra* at 97, Bayard Rustin, *id.* at 73, and the NORTH CAROLINA DAILY NEWS, *id.* at 89.

31. C. Edley, *The Boycott at Harvard: Should Teaching Be Colorblind?*, WASH. POST, Aug. 18, 1982, at A23, col. 3.

32. Bell, *A Question of Credentials, supra* note 6, at 14, col. 1.

33. *Id.*

34. J. BALDWIN, NOTES OF A NATIVE SON 24 (1949).

35. Delgado, *The Imperial Scholar, supra* note 2, at 566.

36. *Id.* at 567.

37. *Id.* (citation omitted).

38. *Id.*

39. *See id.* at 567–69. The Supreme Court has held that in order to invoke the power of a federal court, a litigant must show "injury in fact," which means that he must " 'show that he personally has suffered some actual or threatened injury as a result of the putatively illegal conduct of the defendant.' " Valley Forge Christian College v. Americans United for Separation of Church and State, Inc., 454 U.S. 464, 472 (1982) (quoting Gladstone Realtors v. Village of Bellwood, 441 U.S. 91, 99 (1979)). *See generally* L. TRIBE, AMERICAN CONSTITUTIONAL LAW § 3–16, at 114–29 (2d ed. 1988) (discussing "injury in fact" requirement for standing in federal court).

It is interesting that proponents of the racial critique unqualifiedly embrace a rather narrow conception of standing. After all, that conception has long been criticized as an unfair impediment to judicial relief needed by politically weak persons or groups, including, of course, racial minorities. *See, e.g.*, Fallon, *Of Justiciability, Remedies and Public Law Litigation*, 59 N.Y.U. L. REV. 1 (1984); B. Meltzer, *Deterring Constitutional Violations by Law Enforcement Officials*, 88 COLUM. L. REV. 247, 295–313 (1988); G. Nichol, *Abusing Standing: A Comment on* Allen v. Wright, 133 U. PA. L. REV. 635 (1985); S. Winter, *The Metaphor of Standing and the Problem of Self-Governance*, 40 STAN. L. REV. 1371 (1988).

40. Scholars of color are not alone in giving vent to the urge to oust "outsiders" from discussions on topics over which the purported "owners" of the field assert proprietary claims. Mary McCarthy reports that in the early 1960s when she engaged in debate over Hannah Arendt's *Eichmann in Jerusalem* (1964), some Jewish intellectuals made her feel "like a child with a reading defect in a class of normal readers—or the reverse. It [was] as if *Eichmann in Jerusalem* had required a special pair of Jewish spectacles to make its 'true purport' visible." M. MC-CARTHY, *The Hue and the Cry*, in THE WRITING ON THE WALL AND OTHER LITERARY ESSAYS 55 (1970). Commenting on some of the broader issues raised by the debate over *Eichmann in Jerusalem*, Daniel Bell asked whether one can "exclude the existential person as a component of the human judgment." D. Bell, *The Alphabet of Justice: Reflection on* Eichmann in Jerusalem, 30 PARTISAN REV. 417, 428 (1963). Answering in a curiously ambiguous fashion, he replied that "[i]n this situation, one's identity as a Jew, as well as *philosophe*, is relevant." *Id.*

A fate similar to McCarthy's has befallen some men who have sought to contribute to feminist studies. In an essay strikingly similar to *The Imperial Scholar*, Elaine Showalter expressed skepticism regarding male literary critics who apply feminist literary criticism, doubt about their ability to think and "speak" in an authentically feminist way, and apprehension about the consequences of their work for women feminist critics. *See* E. Showalter, *Critical Cross-Dressing: Male Feminists and the Woman of the Year*, in MEN IN FEMINISM 116 (A. Jardine & P. Smith eds., 1987); *see also* A. Jardine, *Men in Feminism: Odor di Uomo or Compagnons de Route?* in MEN IN FEMINISM, *supra* at 60 ("[O]ur male allies should issue a moratorium on talking about feminism/women/femininity/female sexuality/feminine identity/etc.").

Perhaps the most dismal chapters in the history of the concept of intellectual standing were supplied by the Nazis who contrasted "the access to authentic scientific knowledge by men of unimpeachable Aryan ancestry with the corrupt versions of knowledge accessible to non-Aryans." R. Merton, *Insiders and Outsiders: A Chapter in the Sociology of Knowledge*, 78 AM. J. SOC. 9, 12 (1972). In a fascinating article, Michael H. Kater recently observed that after the Nazis discovered that the great jazz musician Benny Goodman was Jewish, they "forbade the importation of records with any 'Jewish content' whatsoever." M. Kater, *Forbidden Fruit? Jazz in the Third Reich*, 94 AM. HIST. REV. 11, 21 (1989). Ironically, "[t]he fact that nothing was ever said about blacks was probably due to the confusion by Nazi experts as to which jazzmen were to be considered black." *Id.*

41. *See, e.g.*, Blauner & Wellman, *Toward the Decolonization of Social Research*, in THE DEATH OF WHITE SOCIOLOGY 328–29 (J. Ladner ed. 1973).

> We do not argue that whites cannot study Blacks and other non-whites today; our position is rather that, in most cases, it will be preferable for

minority scholars to conceive and undertake research on their communities and group problems. . . . There are certain aspects of racial phenomena . . . that are particularly difficult—if not impossible—for a member of the oppressing group to grasp empirically and formulate conceptually. These barriers are existential and methodological as well as political and ethical. We refer here to the nuances of culture and group ethos; to the meaning of the oppression and especially psychic reactions; to what is called the Black, the Mexican-American, the Asian and the Indian experience. . . . Today the best contribution that white scholars could make toward [study on race relations] is not first hand research but the facilitation of such studies by people of color.

Id.

42. In the preface to his biography of Zora Neale Hurston, Robert Hemenway writes that while he attempts to show why Hurston "deserves an important place in American literary history," he makes no attempt to produce a "definitive" work about her. "[T]hat book remains to be written," he suggests, "and by a black woman. . . ." R. HEMENWAY, ZORA NEALE HURSTON xx (1977). Professor bell hooks writes that "[a]s a black female literary critic, I have always appreciated [Hemenway's] statement. . . . By actively refusing the position of 'authority,' Hemenway encourages black women to participate in the making of Hurston scholarship and allows for the possibility that a black woman writing about Hurston may have special insight." B. HOOKS, TALKING BACK 46 (1989).

43. Delgado, *The Imperial Scholar, supra* note 2, at 577. Delgado does not specify why he addresses white liberals as opposed to whites generally. I interpret him as signifying a belief that, among whites, only liberals and radicals would even consider the proposal he advocates.

44. *Id.* at 569.

45. *See id.* at 569–73.

46. *See id.* at 570.

47. *Id.* According to Delgado, recourse to utilitarian or distributive-justice justifications facilitates avoidance of history:

[U]npleasant matters like lynch mobs, segregated bathrooms, Bracero programs, migrant farm labor camps, race-based immigration laws, or professional schools that, until recently, were lily white. The past becomes irrelevant; one just asks where things are now and where we ought to go from here, a straightforward social-engineering inquiry of the sort that law professors are familiar with and good at.

Id.

48. *See id.*

49. *See id.* at 569 n.43 (citing K. Karst & H. Horowitz, *Affirmative Action and Equal Protection*, 60 VA. L. REV. 955 (1974)).

50. Karst & Horowitz, *supra* note 49, at 966. Delgado also singled out F. Michelman, *The Supreme Court, 1968 Term—Foreword: On Protecting the Poor Through the Fourteenth Amendment*, 83 HARV. L. REV. 7, 13 (1969), as representative of distributive-justice rationales for increasing minority representation. *See* Delgado, *The Imperial Scholar, supra* note 2, at 569 n.44. In his *Foreword*, however, Michelman did not address himself specifically to racial issues

but instead to the broader problem of poverty—a problem that, in my view, highlights the moral and practical limits of reparative appeals to history as the basis for racial preferences as opposed, say, to nonracial preferences intended to break the grip of entrenched class oppression.

51. For other efforts to ground affirmative action on bases other than appeals to history, see O. Fiss, *Groups and the Equal Protection Clause*, 5 PHIL. & PUB. AFF. 107, 147–70 (1976); and C. Sullivan, *The Supreme Court, 1986 Term—Comment: Sins of Discrimination: Last Term's Affirmative Action Cases*, 100 HARV. L. REV. 78, 96–98 (1986).

52. Delgado, *The Imperial Scholar, supra* note 2, at 568–69 (footnotes omitted).

53. *See* R. Kennedy, *Martin Luther King's Constitution: Montgomery*, 98 YALE L.J. 999, 1004 (1989).

54. *See, e.g.,* Dred Scott v. Sandford, 60 U.S. 393 (1857) (holding that Negroes lack federal citizenship and are thus precluded from invoking federal judicial protection); Cherokee Nation v. Georgia, 30 U.S. 1 (1831) (holding that the Supreme Court lacked jurisdiction to adjudicate a dispute because the Cherokee Nation was not a "foreign" state).

55. *See, e.g.,* Giles v. Harris, 189 U.S. 475 (1903) (holding that the Court's inability to enforce an order requiring black voter registration precluded granting requested relief).

56. *See, e.g.,* San Antonio Indep. School Dist. v. Rodriguez, 411 U.S. 1 (1973) (applying rational basis scrutiny to school funding system that discriminates on basis of wealth).

57. This is the flip side of the problem arising from the positive stereotyping of work by minority academics.

58. *See* Delgado, *The Imperial Scholar, supra* note 2, at 569.

59. *See* text *supra.*

60. P. Collins, *Learning from the Outsider Within: The Sociological Significance of Black Feminist Thought*, SOC. PROBS., Dec. 1986, at S15.

61. *Id.* at S14.

62. Edley, *supra* note 31, at A23, col. 3.

63. R. GILMAN, *White Standards and Black Writing, in* THE CONFUSION OF REALMS 3 (1969).

64. *Id.* at 9. Gilman goes on to write:

I know this is likely to be misunderstood. We have all considered the chief thing we should be working toward is that state of disinterestedness, of "higher" truth and independent valuation, which would allow us, white and black, to see each other's minds and bodies free of the distortions of race, to recognize each other's gifts and deficiencies as gifts and deficiencies, to be able to quarrel as the members of an (ideal) family and not as embattled tribes. We want to be able to say without self-consciousness or inverted snobbery that such and such a Negro is a bastard or a lousy writer.

. . . .

But we are nowhere near that stage and in some ways we are moving farther from it as polarization increases.

Id.

450 RANDALL L. KENNEDY

65. *Id.* at 5.

66. Freeman, *Racism, Rights, and the Quest for Equality of Opportunity,* 23 HARV. C.R.-C.L. L. REV. 295 (1988).

67. 62 MINN. L. REV. 1049 (1978).

68. *See id.* at 1052.

69. Freeman, *supra* note 66, at 299.

70. *See* Matsuda, *Looking to the Bottom, supra* note 8, at 348. Illustrating her point, Matsuda says, for instance, that while "[w]hites became abolitionists out of choice; blacks were abolitionists out of necessity." *Id.* at 348 n.110 (quoting W. MARTIN).

39 Masks and Other Disguises: Exposing Legal Academia

LESLIE G. ESPINOZA

PART of the burden of being twelve years old, at least in the California public schools of 1964, was having to write "career reports." I dutifully produced three papers. The first, on being a secretary, was my pre-marriage hope. The second, on being an airline stewardess, was my wishful fantasizing. The third, on being a nurse, was my most ambitious dream. Yet despite the career reports, my belief was that I would be a housewife. My fear was that I would be a beautician like all the other working women in my extended family.

Could that twelve-year-old possibly be the same person who is now a law professor? At twelve I understood the limits of my expectations. At thirty-seven, I cannot forget who I was supposed to be. There is a little voice whispering in the back of my mind, always questioning my elaborate disguise of acculturation. I am, of course, not the only person in costume. Professor Randall Kennedy in his article criticizing CRT[1] clothes himself in the dominant discourse of the legal academy. Kennedy disputes the validity of Critical Race Scholarship by dressing himself in the attire of rigor and merit. Because Kennedy is black, his article relieves those in power in legal academia of concern about the merits of race-focused critiques of their stewardship, and it does so on the "objective" basis of scholarly methodology. For those outsiders in legal academia, however, stories of hard work and unbiased judgment do not sound the same or sell as well when hawked by a minority.

For many, Kennedy's piece inadvertently exposes the reality behind the myths of academia. The exposition will likely exacerbate confrontation between majority and minority legal academics; this is both its danger and its promise. Confrontation may undermine the personal struggle of legal scholars of color to integrate themselves into the law school world. It may also empower minorities by forcing us to identify and destroy the hidden barriers to our participation in the legal academy.

The Failure of Kennedy's Critique: Expectations Unchallenged

Kennedy's critique fails because he assumes the rationality and validity of the status quo. Outwardly, he neither defends the legal academy as it is nor directly attacks the substance of the racial critiques. He takes a "neutral" stance, arguing for improved scholarly methodology. But although Kennedy focuses on three named scholars—Richard Delgado, Derrick Bell, and Mari Matsuda—the implication of his article is that all Critical Race Scholarship is suspect and nonrigorous. He counterposes the well-worn arguments traditionally offered to explain the sorry state of the integration of law schools. He fails, however, to meet his own standard of objective, scholarly analysis in support of his counterarguments. Kennedy relies on the symbolic power of the dominant discourse as a substitute for evidence and analysis.

Kennedy deliberately chose a critique of the critics' methodology to shield himself from the charge that he was attacking minority scholarship on the merits. For example, Kennedy disputes the thesis of racial exclusion elaborated in Delgado's 1984 article, *The Imperial Scholar: Reflections on a Review of Civil Rights Literature.*[2] Delgado observes that frequently cited majority scholars, when arguing for affirmative action and minority civil rights, did not cite and were apparently uninformed by minority scholarship.[3] As a result, the analysis used by these majority scholars led them to propose racial remedies that were inadequate.[4] Kennedy does not dispute that minority civil rights and race scholarship exists, nor does he dispute that majority scholars generally have not cited these works.[5] Instead, Kennedy argues that Delgado does not attempt to prove that any of the minority race and civil rights scholarship is worth citing.[6] What Kennedy implies in his article is that he, Randall Kennedy, does not find any minority scholarship worth citing—a critique that is at once suspect, because Kennedy offers no indication that he has even read the legal scholarship in question,* and profound, because it exposes his assumptions. Kennedy is as blind to the early minority legal scholarship as the majority scholars cited by Delgado in 1984.

Kennedy's preoccupation with the *process* of argumentation demonstrates the same avoidance of the substantive issues that Critical Race scholars have all along attributed to whites. Delgado in *Imperial Scholar* writes about more than the politics of citation; he writes about the politics of law.[7] Citation practices are merely one small window through which to view the workings of legal structures—from scholarship to judicial doctrine. Delgado identifies some of the invisible barriers to production and recognition of minority scholarship. By not explicitly entertaining the possibility that Delgado could be right, notwithstanding possible failures of proof, Kennedy validates the belief that majority scholars do in fact cite only the best works—those most salient and worthy of comparison or critique. Kennedy does not consider that majority scholars might also cite the most conveniently found, prestigiously placed, familiar, and similar works.[8] Subtle barriers create a cycle of exclusion.

The second example of Kennedy's attempt to obscure the import of his critique is his view on the hiring of minority law professors. Rather than rely on methodology, as he does in his critique of Delgado, here Kennedy relies on mythology. Kennedy disputes Bell's argument of race-based exclusion and suggests that there may not be enough candidates: "Considerable evidence suggests that at present, distressingly few black candidates attain the qualifications typically required for admission to elite law school faculties. . . ."[9] This "considerable evidence" is journalist David Kaplan's unscientific compilation of the impressions of a handful of white deans for the *National Law Journal*.[10] Stating that he "know[s] of no study that systematically compares the credentials of white and minority candidates,"[11] Kennedy fails to acknowledge the ready availability of American Association of Law School (AALS) statistics on the credentials of new law faculty hires, both majority and minority. Kennedy also ignores the work of Michael Olivas, professor of law and director of the Institute for Higher Education at the University of Houston. Reviewing the AALS data, Olivas found the credentials of majority and minority candidates hired to law school faculties to be comparable.[12] In addition, he has compared the traditional credentials of Latino law faculty with those of all new law professors and found that the traditional qualifications of Latino professors were as good as, and in some categories superior to, those of the new law faculty pool.[13]

The actual credentials of the vast majority of white law professors belie the "quality" excuse offered by law schools in their persistent unwillingness to hire minorities. Contrary to Kennedy's enumeration of typical threshold qualifications, AALS statistics indicate that two-thirds of all new professors do not have law review experience and that most do not have advanced degrees, non-teaching experience, or a published article.[14] The alleged shortage of minorities with traditional credentials, therefore, does not explain why one-third of all law schools have no minority professors and one-third have only one.

More important, Kennedy's focus on elite law schools misleads the reader into thinking that racial exclusion from the *broad* professoriat is justified. Because faculty at the elite schools will be the most select, the profile of the "traditional" candidate at these law schools may be used to generalize about the profiles of all law school faculty. Law faculties are in fact filled with majority candidates who look on paper surprisingly like "unqualified" minority candidates. That most law faculty, minority and majority, do not have traditional credentials exposes the myth that a particular resumé is necessary to be a law professor.

Finally, Kennedy relies on the rhetoric of individuality in his critique of Matsuda. Matsuda urges identification and nurturances of a minority voice that offers a new perspective on legal issues.[15] Kennedy does not deny the possible existence of such a voice. He worries, however, that claims of racial distinctiveness may reinforce racial generalizations and thereby undermine the promotion of equality. In Kennedy's view, minorities are individuals and should be judged by a standard of merit that is blind to race and background.[16] The very existence of Kennedy's piece, however, serves as a counterpoint to his thesis that race does not count in the assessment of scholarship. Kennedy contends that minorities should not be assumed by virtue of their experience to have a unique insight or message about the way the world works,[17] yet his own article was considered important, and worthy of publication, primarily because he is black. The unspoken legitimation of Kennedy's critique is based on his blackness.

The Pain of Kennedy's Critique: Expectations Revealed

Kennedy's assumptions wound deeply because they mirror the personal, ongoing battle against racist doubts that we carry on in our own minds. Kennedy does not deny the propositions in the minority works he critiques; rather, he "[s]tate[s] bluntly [that] they fail *to support persuasively* their claims of racial exclusion."[18] By shifting the burden to minority scholars to defend the quality of their work, he compounds the effects of the exclusion and reinforces the assumption of its inadequacy.

Likewise, Kennedy is easily satisfied with cursory, anecdotal evidence of the "pool" problem that allegedly keeps law schools from hiring minority faculty candidates. Does his own little voice leave him predisposed to accept the assertions of a few law deans? In the struggle with self-doubt, is Randall Kennedy like me? The twelve-year-old, now adult, wonders: *my life is so surprising to me, so unexpected. It makes two things easier to believe: there are very few others like me, and because there are so few, my success must be a mistake, an aberration.*

The value of Kennedy's piece is that it moves the personal disjuncture between expectations and experience into the public arena. Racism disempowers us by infecting individual consciousness with self-doubt.[19] Race-conscious scholarship breaks our isolation. We express our own perceptions of the profound effect of racism and recognize the manifestations of racism identified by other scholars. Kennedy's article may be a spur to this process. His transparent invocation of the dominant discourse reveals its hollowness, demanding response.

The danger of Kennedy's article is that it may reinforce assumptions of inadequacy. With the Kennedy imprimatur on traditional conceptions of merit, minorities may be further excluded from faculties and scholarly recognition. Kennedy potentially provides the universal citation in the minds of tenure and promotion committees seeking to dismiss minority scholarship as uncompelling or as theoretically misdirected. The law school power structure may discount intellectual efforts that do not conform to preconceived notions of what legal scholarship should speak to and look like. For the minority scholar, therefore, Kennedy's article increases the risk of writing racial critiques.

Minority scholars struggle to find a place in a world to which they were not invited and in which they did not anticipate living. The twelve-year-old knew where she belonged. The adult may fight for and follow a different path. The stigma of prejudice, however, leaves a residue of self-doubt in the adult, no matter what her achievements. For many minorities, the personal struggle to quiet the little voice never ends. Kennedy's experience notwithstanding, the dominant discourse seldom inspires in minorities a belief that opportunity will be equal or that individual merit will be fairly assessed. Our experience is too much to the contrary. Yet, although disbelieved, the discourse hauntingly reinforces the earlier certainty of existing social structure, the gnawing little voice. *If the world is really a place that will judge me as an individual and welcome me for my objective accomplishments, why is it that I feel excluded and experience prejudice?*[20] *The little voice must be right. I was meant to be a secretary, housewife, or beautician.*

Minority scholars battle with their own socialized self-perceptions, constructed at an early age and reinforced in the institution. It is painful to feel excluded and disturbing to perceive the world differently from those whose discourse dominates. It is difficult not to internalize the sense of otherness as a personal failing. The knowledge that we may depart from expectations is the first triumph. The prerequisite to this victory, however, is the identification of those expectations and the social construct they represent. Critical Race Scholarship is one vehicle through which minorities in law understand and reconcile the world as predicted, the world as experienced, and the world as dreamed.

The strength of Critical Race Scholarship is its identification of the commonality of minority experience. It is a shared courage to be different. In the battle to adapt, to quiet the little voice and to appear to "belong," the easiest garment to wear is the one without distinctiveness. Minority legal scholars, in order to get where they are, have spent a lifetime disguising their difference, hoping that the difference will not disqualify them from achievement.[21] To explore that difference, to acknowledge it, is to be vulnerable. Kennedy's call for individualism reinforces exclusion by delegitimating the commonality of the experience of otherness many minorities feel with other minorities and express in their scholarship. Although there is much individual divergence, focusing on the individual before we recapture that which is our shared difference would result in a cacophony of voices unrecognized, indecipherable, and overwhelmed by the dominant discourse.

NOTES

1. R. Kennedy, *Racial Critiques of Legal Academia*, 102 HARV. L. REV. 1745 (1989).

2. R. Delgado, *The Imperial Scholar: Reflections on a Review of Civil Rights Literature*, 132 U. PA. L. REV. 561 (1984).

3. *See id.* at 562–63.

4. Delgado cites specific works of majority scholars. *See id.* at 568 (criticizing the factual naiveté and insularity of majority scholars); *id.* at 571 (criticizing majority scholars for failing to confront issues of guilt and reparation and for not advocating remedies that might "encroach too much on middle or upper-class prerogatives"). Delgado uses the pre–*Imperial Scholar* minority scholarship throughout his critique of majority civil rights work. *See id.* at 562 n.2, 569 n.45, 572 n.60, 576 n.76. Minority scholars justified affirmative action as reparations

for past discrimination and argued for substantive remedies. *Id.* at 569 n.45. Majority scholars, on the other hand, posed alternative utility-based or distributive justice rationales for affirmative action, leading, Delgado argues, to procedural remedies that are inadequate. *See id.* at 568–72.

5. *See* Kennedy, *supra* note 1, at 1771.

6. *See id.* at 1774 ("Delgado fails to shoulder the essential burden of championing on substantive grounds specific works that deserve more recognition than they have been given.").

Id. The author here cites a lengthy list of pre–*Imperial Scholar* writing by scholars of color.

7. Kennedy recognizes the breadth of the critique: "[T]he sociology of citation focuses attention on . . . the political economy of scholarly recognition." *Id.* at 1771.

8. Many of the minority scholarly articles in the 1970s were published in the BLACK LAW JOURNAL, which is not carried by either Lexis or Westlaw. The scholars who wrote these articles were not invited to present their work at the more prestigious symposia on affirmative action. *See* D. Bell, *Bakke, Minority Admissions, and the Usual Price of Racial Remedies,* 67 CALIF. L. REV. 3, 4 n.2 (1979). They did not trade reprints with scholars in the inner circle because they were not part of it. For an exposition of how interacting with diverse scholars enriches knowledge, see M. Matsuda, *Affirmative Action and Legal Knowledge: Planting Seeds in Plowed-up Ground,* 11 HARV. WOMEN'S L.J. 1, 3–8 (1988).

9. Kennedy, *supra* note 1, at 1762.

10. *See id.* at 1762 n.71 (citing D. Kaplan, *Hard Times for Minority Profs,* NAT'L L.J., Dec 10, 1984, at 28, col. 1).

11. *Id.*

12. *See* M. Olivas, *Latino Faculty at the Border,* CHANGE, May–June 1988, at 6, 7.

13. There are 5860 full-time law teachers in the United States, only 47 of whom are Latino. Of the 47, 32 percent were law review members, 28 percent held judicial clerkships, and 28 percent had an advanced degree. Of the total pool of 313 law teachers hired in 1988–1989, only 24 of whom were Latino, 36 percent were law review members and 11 percent had advanced degrees. *Id.*

14. *See* Memorandum from Betsy Levin to Deans of Member and Fee Paid Schools at 17, Association of American Law Schools (May 26, 1988) (on file at the Harvard Law School Library).

15. *See* Matsuda, *supra* note 8, at 13; M. Matsuda, *Looking to the Bottom: Critical Legal Studies and Reparations,* 22 HARV. C.R.-C.L. L. REV. 323, 324–26 (1987).

16. Kennedy, *supra* note 1, at 1796–97.

17. *Id.* at 1801–04.

18. *Id.* at 1749 (emphasis added).

19. *See* R. Delgado, *Words That Wound: A Tort Action for Racial Insults, Epithets, and Name-Calling,* 17 HARV. C.R.-C.L. L. REV. 133, 137 (1982) ("The psychological responses to [racial slurs] consist of feelings of humiliation, isolation, and self-hatred. Consequently, it is neither unusual nor abnormal for stigmatized individuals to feel ambivalent about their self-worth and identity.");

C. Lawrence, *The Id, the Ego, and Equal Protection: Reckoning with Unconscious Racism*, 39 STAN. L. REV. 317, 318 (1987) ("We were all victims of our culture's racism. We had all grown up on *Little Black Sambo* and *Amos and Andy*.").

20. *See* R. Delgado, *The Bell-Delgado Survey*, 24 HARV. C.R.-C.L. L. REV. 349, 369 (1989) ("It is impossible to read the survey returns without being acutely conscious of the pain and stress they reflect. Large numbers of minority law professors are overworked, excluded from informal information networks and describe their environment as hostile, unsupportive, or openly or subtly racist.").

> I know now that once I longed to be white
> How? you ask.
> Let me tell you the ways.
> when I was growing up, people told me
> I was dark and I believed my own darkness
> in the mirror, in my soul, my own narrow vision
> . . . .
> when I was growing up, I was proud
> of my English, my grammar, my spelling
> fitting into the group of smart children
> smart Chinese children, fitting in,
> belonging, getting in line
> . . . .
> I know now that once I longed to be white.
> How many more ways? you ask.
> Haven't I told you enough?

N. Wong, *When I was Growing Up*, in THIS BRIDGE CALLED MY BACK: WRITINGS BY RADICAL WOMEN OF COLOR 7, 7–8 (C. Moraga & G. Anzaldúa eds., 1981).

40 Derrick Bell—Race and Class: The Dilemma of Liberal Reform

ALAN D. FREEMAN

A L L too often, one greets the newest edition of a law school text with something less than enthusiasm. Typically, the "new" edition is the "old" book, with a few new cases and articles and footnotes jammed into the old form, which maintains the structure, analytic framework, and perspective of the original edition. Derrick Bell could easily have gotten away with the typical ploy. He had already produced an exciting and unconventional book,[1] rich in material on the historical and social context of legal developments, refreshingly insistent in its unabashed quest for racial justice. Instead of merely replicating a previous success, however, Bell has written a new book,[2] drawing on the strengths of the earlier edition while offering a new form, a new perspective, and a basis for a serious critical appraisal of civil rights law.

If one goes no further than the summary table of contents, the book looks rather conventional, what one would expect from a civil rights text. There is a fifty-page historical chapter, followed by eight substantive chapters, dealing with interracial sex and marriage, public facilities, voting rights, administration of justice, protests and demonstrations, education, housing, and employment. A mere glance at the detailed table of contents, however, suggests that there is something different about this book. One sees topic headings such as "The Principle of the Involuntary Sacrifice," "Reserved Racial Representation," "Racial Interest-Convergence Principles," "Minority Admissions as a White Strategy," and "Employment and the Race-Class Conflict." In these sections as well as in ones with more conventional names, Bell introduces, develops, and amplifies a number of themes that run through the book.

A major theme is that there is one and only one criterion for assessing the success or failure of civil rights law—results. Bell's approach to legal doctrine is unabashedly instrumental. The only important question is whether doctrinal developments have improved, worsened, or left unchanged the actual lives of American blacks (the book focuses almost exclusively on black/white relationships because it is in that context that most of the doctrine has developed). Bell eschews the realm of abstract, ahistorical, normative debate; he focuses instead on the relationships

90 YALE L.J. 1880 (1981). Reprinted by permission of the Yale Law Journal Company and Fred B. Rothman & Company from The Yale Law Journal.

between doctrine and concrete change, and the extent to which doctrine can be manipulated to produce more change. With respect to voting rights, for example, Bell offers three prerequisites to effective voting—access to the ballot, availability of political power, motivation to participate in the political process[3]—and then argues for recognition of aggregate voting rights and affirmative action in filling electoral positions.[4] Similarly, with respect to education, the issue for Bell is not desegregation, if that implies integration as the remedial goal, but how to obtain effective education for black children, with or without busing or racial balance.[5] In its instrumentalism and result orientation, the new book resembles the first edition, although many arguments have been developed further. The critical perspective of the new book, however, sets a strikingly different tone from that of the old one.

The problem addressed by Bell confronts everyone currently teaching civil rights law who is committed to achieving measurable, objective, substantive results: these results have for the most part not been achieved, and legal doctrine has evolved to rationalize the irrelevance of results. In 1973, when Bell's first edition came out, one could, despite the Burger Court, look with optimism at civil rights litigation. Perhaps the Court was going to dismantle the rights of the accused and soften the First Amendment, but it was remaining firm on civil rights. Decisions like *Swann*,[6] *Wright*,[7] and *Griggs*[8] not only allayed fears, but actually contributed to a spirit of utopianism. Since then, and beginning in 1974, we have experienced, among other Supreme Court cases, *Milliken v. Bradley*,[9] *Pasadena Board of Education v. Slangler*,[10] *Beer v. United States*,[11] *City of Mobile v. Bolden*,[12] *International Brotherhood of Teamsters v. United States*,[13] *Washington v. Davis*,[14] *Warth v. Seldin*,[15] and *Village of Arlington Heights v. Metropolitan Housing Development Corp.*[16]

It is tempting to regard these decisions as aberrations, as cases that could just as easily have "gone the other way," with better legal argument or incremental changes in judicial personnel (a fantasy becoming even more remote in the current political environment). Bell could, consistently with his result orientation, have simply offered new legal arguments or ways of distinguishing the worst cases, and seized on the few deviant decisions, however ambiguous their reasoning, as substantial sources of hope. The alternative approach is to try to put the doctrinal developments in perspective by asking what could have been expected from modern civil rights law, in whose interest the enterprise really functioned anyway, and whether what has actually happened is in fact more consistent with fundamental patterns of American society than what was once expected.

From the very beginning of the book, Bell develops such an alternative perspective. In the preface he suggests:

> We have witnessed hard-won decisions, intended to protect basic rights of black citizens from racial discrimination, lose their vitality before they could be enforced effectively. In a nation dedicated to individual freedom, laws that never should have been needed face neglect, reversal, and outright repeal, while the discrimination they were designed to eliminate continues in the same or a more sophisticated form.[17]

The historical chapter not only provides background information but also argues that what we have just gone through is best understood as a "Second Reconstruction," perhaps less successful than the first. Bell's discussion of the Emancipation Proclamation leads him to offer some generalizations intended to echo throughout the book:

> First, blacks are more likely to obtain relief for even acknowledged racial injustice when that relief also serves, directly or indirectly, to further ends which policymakers perceive are in the best interests of the country. Second, blacks as well as their white allies, are likely to focus with gratitude on the relief obtained, usually after a long struggle. Little attention is paid to the self-interest factors without which no relief might have been gained. Moreover, the relief is viewed as proof that society is indeed just, and that eventually all racial injustices will be recognized and remedied. Third, the remedy for blacks appropriately viewed as a "good deal" by policymaking whites often provides benefits for blacks that are more symbolic than substantive; but whether substantive or not, they are often perceived by working class whites as both an unearned gift to blacks and a betrayal of poor whites.[18]

Moreover, Bell takes serious issue with the liberal myth of "the civil rights crusade as a long, slow, but always upward pull that must, given the basic precepts of the country and the commitment of its people to equality and liberty, eventually end in the full enjoyment by blacks of all rights and privileges of citizenship enjoyed by whites."[19]

In support of this alternative perspective, Bell marshals a diverse array of sources. In the historical chapter, he cites historian Edmund Morgan for the view that "slavery for blacks led to greater freedom for poor whites,"[20] and develops that view a few pages later into a principle of "involuntary sacrifice" of blacks.[21] He uses a quotation from Justice Holmes about the powerlessness of law to define a notion of "democratic domination."[22] In a wonderfully inside-out (and somewhat ironic) treatment of Herbert Wechsler's famous "neutral principles" argument, Bell suggests that Wechsler may have been normatively wrong but descriptively all-too accurate:

> To the extent that this conflict is between "racial equality" and "associational freedom," used here as a proxy for all those things whites will have to give up in order to achieve a racial equality that is more than formal, it is clear that the conflict will never be mediated by a "neutral principle." If it is to be resolved at all, it will be determined by the existing power relationships in the society and the perceived self-interest of the white elite.[23]

Bell is not at all hesitant in citing and taking advantage of the work of more radical critics. W.E.B. Du Bois is cited for his perception that the *Brown* decision would not have been possible "'without the world pressure of communism'" and the self-perceived role of the United States as leader of the "Free World."[24] Lewis Steel is quoted for his perception that doctrinal changes in the law governing sit-ins and demonstrations were attributable to the fact that blacks ceased to be "'humble supplicants seeking succor from White America'" and became more militant, with the resultant decisions amounting to a "'judicial concession to white anxieties.'"[25] From Frances Piven and Richard Cloward comes the perception that "the poor gain more through mass defiance and disruptive protests than by organizing for electoral politics and other more acceptable reform policies," and that the latter kind of activity actually undermines effectiveness.[26] And I discovered myself cited for the proposition that "the probable long-term result of the civil rights drive based on integration remedies will result in the bourgeoisification of some blacks who will be, more or less, accepted into white society," with the great mass of blacks remaining in a disadvantaged status,[27] and quoted at some length for my own perceptions about the ideology of antidiscrimination law.[28]

In the last chapter of the book, Bell offers three generalizations about employment discrimination law that, he suggests, are equally applicable to other areas of antidiscrimination law:[29]

1. Employment discrimination laws will not eliminate employment discrimination.
2. Employment discrimination laws will not help millions of nonwhites.
3. Employment discrimination laws could divide those blacks who can from those who can not benefit from its protection.

Generalizations like these, in the context of this book, trigger a realization in the reader that a significant line has been crossed between the two editions of *Race, Racism and American Law*. That line represents the difference between teaching students to *do* civil rights law and teaching them *about* the unhappy history of modern civil rights law. It is not that the doctrinal materials are missing. To the extent that arguments remain available, one can find them in the book, or find the materials from which to formulate one's own. In many instances, doctrinal developments have already played themselves out to depressing conclusions. In at least one instance in which Bell ends a chapter in the second edition on a tentative and limited note of optimism, a subsequent Supreme Court case has reached the depressing conclusion.[30]

Despite the presence of doctrinal materials, the book in its dominant tone is impatient with legal doctrine and despairing; the book reflexively yet almost unwillingly offers legal arguments unlikely ever to be accepted. For some, Bell's emphasis will be regarded as merely cynical; others will find it realistic. At this point, my first serious issue reappears. What is one supposed to do in teaching this course? The simplest, but perhaps too facile, answer is: tell the truth. Yet if the truth seems so hopeless and dismal, and the generation of more legal argument so pointless, then one is dealing with something other than the usual law school enterprise of helping students to fashion a measure of craft, skill, and insight to deal with the needs and hopes of social life.

The dissonance becomes more striking when one considers the students who typically take a course in civil rights law. Based on my own eight years of teaching the course, I can report that the students who elect it tend to be the most committed to the goal of seeking social justice through law, the most believing in the possibility of such an outcome. Thus, one finds oneself not only offering a cynical perspective on one of the most idealistic areas of legal endeavor, but sharing that perspective with the students most likely to carry on with the endeavor in the future. One must let those students know that civil rights doctrine depends on and gains its legitimacy through a number of presuppositions. The world depicted in the doctrine is one of autonomous and responsive law, shared values (for example, individualism, color-blindness), monolithic whiteness or blackness (that is, no class structure), and gradual yet linear progress. To question these presuppositions is to suggest the gap between the mythical world of legal doctrine and the real world in history—where law is relatively autonomous at best and responsive to power more than to powerlessness, where values are contradictory, conflicting, and bound up with patterns of domination and hierarchy, where class relationships exist alongside racial ones, and where cyclical failure is as plausible as linear progress. Then what?

A number of teaching strategies are possible. One is simply to promote the self-conscious manipulation of legal doctrine to achieve whatever results one can. This approach emphasizes "playing the law game" but refuses to accord the game any legitimacy other than in utilizing the forms of argument the players must adopt. Along with this approach comes the frank recognition that structural change will not come through litigation (or legislation, given the current political process) and that all one can do is win occasional cases and improve the lives of some people.

A second strategy would extend the first and call for maximal politicization of the doctrinal activity—pushing the legal forms for explicitly political reasons to reveal contradictions and limits, promote public awareness, and even win cases. A variant of the second strategy would take off from the Piven and Cloward insight about mass movements and seek to promote legal activity that maximizes the force and protects the integrity of large, noisy, disruptive political activity, which is the real method of extracting concessions from power.

In some fashion, however, each of these strategies preserves the myths of liberal reform. To avoid these myths, one must simultaneously consider civil rights doctrine as immersed in social and historical reality. Such an approach assumes that negative, critical activity that self-consciously historicizes areas of legal doctrine like civil rights law will lead both to more self-aware and effective employment of legal forms and to a more realistic appraisal of the comparative utility of mechanisms for social change. The issue is not one for legal teaching alone; its implications are precisely parallel for both practice and scholarship. Yet it is one thing to call for—and show the need for—the historicization of civil rights law, and quite another to write the history. The task of unmasking, of exposing presuppositions, of delegitimizing, is easier than that of offering a concrete historical account to replace what is exposed as inadequate.

NOTES

1. D. Bell, Race, Racism and American Law (1st ed. 1973).
2. D. Bell, Race, Racism and American Law (2d ed. 1980).
3. *Id.* at 155.
4. *Id.* at 197–206.
5. *Id.* at 411–31.
6. Swann v. Charlotte-Mecklenburg Bd. of Educ., 402 U.S. 1 (1971).
7. Wright v. Council of Emporia, 407 U.S. 451 (1972).
8. Griggs v. Duke Power Co., 401 U.S. 424 (1971).
9. 418 U.S. 717 (1974).
10. 427 U.S. 424 (1976).
11. 425 U.S. 130 (1976).
12. 446 U.S. 55 (1980).
13. 431 U.S. 324 (1977).
14. 426 U.S. 229 (1976).
15. 422 U.S. 490 (1975).
16. 429 U.S. 252 (1977).
17. Bell, *supra* note 2, at xxiii.
18. *Id.* at 7. *See also* 230, 266–67, 303–04.
19. *Id.* at 8.
20. *Id.* at 25.
21. *Id.* at 29–30.
22. *Id.* at 127, 231.
23. *Id.* at 435.
24. *Id.* at 412.
25. *Id.* at 303.
26. *Id.* at 306.
27. *Id.* at 565.
28. *Id.* at 658–59.
29. *Id.* at 657.

30. Bell devotes a section to "voter dilution" cases in the Fifth Circuit, finding some basis for the most cautious of optimism for some voters in that circuit. *See id.* at 181–86. The principal case relied on was reversed by the Supreme Court in 1980. *See* City of Mobile v. Bolden, 446 U.S. 55 (1980), *rev'g* Bolden v. City of Mobile, 571 F.2d 238 (1978).

41 Beyond Criticism—Synthesis? Left-Right Parallels in Recent Writing about Race

RICHARD DELGADO

Introduction

Much recent writing about race and civil rights falls squarely within what I might call the classic-liberal mode. This writing, generally highly normative and rights-based in nature but cautiously incremental in scope and ambition, criticizes Supreme Court opinions, decries our recent inattention to the plight of women and persons of color, and urges a renewed commitment to racial justice. It accepts the dominant paradigm of civil rights scholarship and activism, and urges that we work harder—litigate more furiously, press for new legislation, exhort each other even more fervently than ever before—within that paradigm.

Recently, however, some scholars—particularly ones of color—have begun to find fault with civil rights strategies of the sort the liberals have been defending and promoting. At the same time, a group of black neoconservatives have been raising questions from the right. This chapter argues that, in many ways, the critique from the right and that from the left converge. Operating from different perspectives and widely divergent premises, the left- and right-leaning scholars come to many of the same conclusions both about what is wrong with the liberal civil rights program that has been this country's legacy since the Warren Court years and about the appropriate response.

I take four books as illustrations—Shelby Steele's *The Content of Our Character*,[1] Patricia Williams' *The Alchemy of Race and Rights*,[2] Stephen Carter's *Reflections of an Affirmative Action Baby*,[3] and Derrick Bell's *And We Are Not Saved*.[4] My guiding assumption is that ordinarily the left and the right do not agree on much. When they do, it behooves us to take note. Their common target, liberalism, may be in for hard times. Moreover, the areas where the critiques coincide, like circles cast by different flashlights, may be ones in which we may see more readily the flaws in our treatment of America's most intractable problem: Race.

91 COLUM. L. REV. 1547 (1991). Originally published in the Columbia Law Review. Reprinted by permission.

What the Left and the Right Are Saying About Race

Moderate liberals in think tanks, government, academia, and civil rights organizations should take note: Both the Critical left and the New right are finding fault with the strategies and ways of framing problems that have been our stock in trade for years. The criticisms are wide-ranging; they are more than disagreements over matters of detail or timing.

"TO BE SURE": WHAT THE CRITS AND THE NEOCONSERVATIVES DISAGREE ABOUT

The parallels should not obscure the many respects in which the two Critical and two neoconservative authors disagree. The neoconservatives emphasize individual agency and volition much more than the two leftist writers. Carter, for example, writes:

> Consequently change, if change there is to be, is in our hands—and the only change for which we can reasonably hope will come about because we commit ourselves to battle for excellence, to show ourselves able to meet any standard, to pass any test that looms before us, in short, to form ourselves into a vanguard of black professionals who are simply too good to ignore.[5]

All four authors rely on personal experience and storytelling, but the leftist writers use these tools to draw a message about social power or relations: Their minds run toward sociology and social theory.[6] The two more conservative authors use narrative and personal experience to draw lessons about black and white mindset; the science for which they feel the most affinity is psychology.[7]

The four authors show the same division regarding their prescriptions for our racial ills. Carter and Steele believe that racial progress will come only when black people change their attitudes and way of relating to white society, work harder, and resolve to "beat whitey" at his own game.[8] The two Critical writers are much more doubtful about the payoff for black resolve. Both see hidden barriers—Bell in material,[9] Williams in structure-of-thought factors[10]—that are likely to impede black success.

The authors place widely different premiums on individual versus collective effort[11] and make different uses of history. The leftist authors tend to see blacks' current problems as continuations of the past.[12] The conservatives are more present- and future-oriented:[13] If we set aside dimmed expectations and wounded self-images stemming from centuries of mistreatment, we will be able to take advantage of today's ostensibly improved racial climate.[14]

And, finally, the two sets of writers assign different valences and locations to hatred. For the neoconservatives, the main problem is that blacks hate themselves;[15] for the Criticalists, whites hate blacks and are unwilling to afford them their fair share of America's bounty.[16] All these differences, of course, shape the two groups' thinking on the nature of and cure for America's racial predicament.

The four authors, then, are manifestly not saying the same things. But on one level they are: They are all finding serious fault with (a) the racial status quo; and (b) the current system of civil rights laws and policies by which that status quo is maintained and (sometimes) permitted to evolve. I now examine a series of ways in which the attacks coincide on a critique of liberalism.

LEFT-RIGHT PARALLELS AND THE CRITIQUE OF LIBERAL LEGALISM

Despite their differences, the two groups of authors share deep dissatisfaction with the moderate-liberal civil rights policies this nation has been pursuing since the days of *Brown v. Board of Education*. This dissatisfaction often results in striking parallels with respect to the goals to which people of color ought to aspire, the means by which we should strive to reach these goals, the ways in which our racial problems are framed, and the role of law in advancing or retarding the search for racial justice.

PROBLEM FRAMING.   Both sets of writers have a vision of the search for racial justice, and law's role in it, that differs sharply from the conventional one. Many C.R.T. writers believe that civil rights law was never designed to help blacks. Derrick Bell's interest-convergence formula holds that whites will advance the cause of racial justice only when doing so coincides with their own self-interest.[17] Writers on the right, particularly Steele, sound a similar theme when they write that racial programs are aimed mainly at assuaging white guilt and constitute justice "on the cheap"—enabling whites to say they are doing something for blacks when they are doing very little.[18] Some Critical writers see civil rights law as a sort of societal safety valve that assures that racial reform occurs at just the right rate of speed. (Too much reform would be terrifying, too little might lead to disruption.) Similarly, writers on the right hold that a prime function of affirmative action is to offer whites "innocence"—the assurance that they are guiltless with respect to past transgressions and that little more need be done.

Both sets of writers argue that antidiscrimination law often makes matters worse. Crits point out that periodic victories—*Brown v. Board of Education*, the 1964 Civil Rights Act—are trumpeted as proof that our system is fair and just, but are then quickly stolen away by narrow judicial construction, foot-dragging, and delay.[19] The celebrations assure everyone that persons of color are now treated fairly in virtually every area of life—housing, education, jobs, and voting. With all that, if blacks are still not achieving, well, what can be done? Writers on the right echo this charge when they point out that affirmative action stigmatizes its intended beneficiaries, assists those least in need of help, and does little to remedy the structural sources of poverty and misery.[20] Williams, a Criticalist, writes that law teaches us not to know what we know—to ignore and falsify our own lives.[21] Similarly, conservatives such as Carter and Steele write that law falsifies our experience by denying us agency—by teaching us that we are weak, victimized, inferior, and must rely on preferences and handouts to get ahead.[22]

NEED FOR A BETTER CIVIL RIGHTS STRATEGY AND GOALS.   Not only do the two groups of writers concur on much of what is amiss with the current civil rights vision, they agree on at least the general contours of a new one. For the neoconservatives, this task will entail a heavy dose of antiessentialism and recognition of intragroup differences.[23] Not all blacks are the same; indeed, it is the essence of racism to believe so. Thus, any new strategy must take account of a complex, fragmented racial reality in which middle-class blacks, working-class blacks, and black entrepreneurs have differing goals and needs. There can be no single civil rights agenda, no single solution, no "party line."[24]

Writers on the far left, too, insist on the need to "name [our own] reality"[25]—formulate our own vision—but for them, that means freedom from the mental shackles of white-coined culture and mindset. For Williams, the grammar and concepts of race are pernicious, laid down long ago in an era in which blacks were property, were inferior, were denied an education or even, in some cases, the right to form a family.[26] Bell writes that the Constitution and entire body of race-reform statutes and case law are infected with racism and must be replaced. For both sets of authors, therefore, the dominant narratives and stories animating current civil rights law are wrong. They require wholesale revision; their defects cannot be fixed by a small amendment or change of focus.

TACTICS AND MEANS.   Not only do the four writers agree that there are fundamental flaws in our civil rights vision, they also demonstrate a surprising amount of agreement over (i) means for advancing a new vision and (ii) means that have failed and should be rejected. For example, writers on the left have exposed tokenism and other grudging, trickle-down approaches to racial justice, such as the "role model" argument.[27] For their part, conservatives find affirmative action demeaning and urge that we reject handouts in favor of individual and collective efforts to defeat the system by doing it one better.[28] Both sets of authors want to ensure that the individual is not nullified. Steele portrays affirmative action as a form of redemption—whites give blacks (almost any blacks) a few slots to free whites from any taint of a racist past.[29] For Carter, the only thing that matters is that the beneficiary be recognizably "black"—that is, conform to whites' idea of what a person of color should be like.[30] This approach denies black individuality, a charge Williams echoes when she complains of affirmative action's tendency to be satisfied with numbers rather than genuine representative diversity.[31]

Both groups reject white idealism and generosity as reliable wellsprings for advancing the cause of black justice.[32] The leftists urge mobilization, disruption, and subversive storytelling to fuel change.[33] The conservatives also reject whites' altruism and the magical helping hand, but offer a different alternative—work hard, make money, open a business, get a professional degree.[34] Then you will have something better and more reliable than good will: You will have entered the system on a basis of equality and respect.[35]

Both are distrustful of high-flown liberal discourse and academic writing praising equality, equal respect, and equal citizenship.[36] Both use stories, irony, and humor to puncture self-serving majoritarian myths built around such ideas.[37] Both point out that concepts such as "race," "racism," and "discrimination" are constructed by groups to serve their own purposes.[38] Both advocate storytelling by persons of color, although for slightly differing reasons. Critical writers encourage black people to tell and retell stories of their own oppression as an antidote to disabling self-doubt and hatred. Through recounting terrible tales of torture, rape, and spirit-murder, we gain healing: we realize that our current low estate is not our fault.[39] The conservative writers use storytelling for a different reason—to encourage their brothers and sisters to make use of what opportunities are now open to them, to stop thinking of themselves as victims, and to forge ahead fearlessly.[40]

Among the former, Williams tells of being taught in law school to combat raw power with images of powerlessness, to clothe victims in "utter, bereft[] naiveté," to "give voice to those whose voice had been suppressed . . . [by arguing] that they [have] no voice."[41] This is one of Steele's favorite themes: The victim binds himself to his victimization, comes to believe that prospects can only be improved by social means, not by individual initiative.[42] Steele says we need to break this dependency, jettison affirmative action, which encourages reliance on entitlements,[43] and emphasize deracinated programs that attack poverty in general, not black poverty.[44] Williams, on the other hand, advocates expanding our system of civil rights, including affirmative action, and offers stories and parables to explain how such a system might, at least at times, embolden and empower persons of color.[45]

Both sides are urging novel alignments. Crits are questioning the utility of the black-left coalition that has persisted over the years;[46] one (this author) has even urged that the nonwhite poor consider aligning themselves with the progressive wing of the Republican Party.[47] Steele and Carter seem open to this suggestion. Carter devotes nearly fifteen pages of his book to laying out ways in which moderate Republicans might strike up a liaison with at least a segment of the black community.[48]

PERSISTENCE OF RACISM; UNLIKELIHOOD OF RELIEF.   Finally, both groups agree that racism persists in our society, in the face of liberalism's optimistic claims of progress and forecasts of a rosy future. Williams, for example, notes ironically that she is considered nonblack for purposes of inclusion in mainstream society, but black for purposes of exclusion. She records a horrifying series of mistreatments at the hands of students, colleagues, and store clerks.[49] The two conservative writers also describe racist incidents they have suffered or witnessed—Carter, for example, recounts discrimination he suffered in the Boy Scouts, on a city bus, and at the hands of high school counselors and passing motorists—but nevertheless declines to call these "serious."[50] Steele recounts racial categorization in a vignette describing a road trip with his college debate team, but with a reverse twist: His middle-class identity is presumed to override his blackness. Because Steele was a high-achieving member of his team, his coach, a university

English professor, felt comfortable recounting his own racist treatment of a black renter.[51]

The two conservatives argue that current race-relations mechanisms, especially affirmative action, perpetuate racist attitudes and stereotypes. Derrick Bell goes even further: These effects, which might seem inadvertent, in fact confer a benefit on white elite groups, and hence will continue.[52] For both groups, civil rights and affirmative action are premised on, and inscribe even more deeply, white power and black helplessness. In that sense they serve to perpetuate the existing racial hierarchy.

Conclusion

Critical and neoconservative writers, while differing in a number of respects, nevertheless join in a wide-ranging attack on the current liberal civil rights vision, methods, and ideology. All four writers, like Critical theorists and neoconservatives generally, are impatient with incrementalism and token representation. Both groups share the belief that our much-vaunted system of racial justice is not working and perhaps was never intended to do so. In an era, like ours, hostile to racial reform, liberalism will thus be unable to look to many theoreticians of color for support.

Unless liberalism is able radically to transform itself, it will likely continue to weaken. What will replace it as a civil rights strategy? My guess is nothing. Society's need for legitimacy will assure that a few blacks ascend, while opposition to spending and mass programs will guarantee that most fall further and further behind. Conditions for change like those present in the 1960s are missing. The white leadership is timid or indifferent; the white middle- and blue-collar classes are frankly hostile to racial reform. There is little pressure at the international level for the United States to transform itself. In time, these conditions may change; in particular, demographic shifts will one day begin to add special urgency. But if I am right, in the short run liberalism will continue to decline, and nothing coherent will replace it, while conditions for blacks and other people of color will worsen. Race, our most enduring problem, is likely to remain, for now, as intractable as ever.

NOTES

1. SHELBY STEELE, THE CONTENT OF OUR CHARACTER: A NEW VISION OF RACE IN AMERICA (1990).

2. PATRICIA J. WILLIAMS, THE ALCHEMY OF RACE AND RIGHTS (1991).

3. STEPHEN L. CARTER, REFLECTIONS OF AN AFFIRMATIVE ACTION BABY (1991).

4. DERRICK BELL, AND WE ARE NOT SAVED: THE ELUSIVE QUEST FOR RACIAL JUSTICE (1987).

5. CARTER, *supra* note 3, at 60; *accord* STEELE, *supra* note 1, at 173 ("There

will be no end to despair and no lasting solution to any of our problems until we rely on individual effort within the American mainstream—rather than collective action against the mainstream—as our means of advancement.").

6. Williams uses the tools of literary criticism, deconstruction, and "psychoanalysis." *See* WILLIAMS, *supra* note 2, at 202–14; *see also* BELL, *supra* note 4, at 140–61 (Ch. 6—The Chronicle of the DeVine Gift—showing how social homeostasis operates to maintain white ascendancy at a law school, even when diligent affirmative action surprisingly produced an abundance of superbly qualified black teaching candidates).

7. *See* STEELE, *supra* note 1, at 40–45 (describing childhood experience to illustrate expansion and deepening of individuals' "innate capacity for insecurity"); CARTER, *supra* note 3, at 55–58 (describing how affirmative action causes whites to expect all blacks to be intellectually inferior); *infra* text (experience of affirmative action demeaning and stigmatizing).

8. *See* CARTER, *supra* note 3, at 58–62, 94–95, 227–35 (urging blacks to toughen up, abjure victim mentality and take advantage of opportunities now open to them); STEELE, *supra* note 1, at 127–65 (same).

9. For examples of Bell's material determinism, *see* BELL, *supra* note 4, at 26–50 (Constitution supports white-over-black supremacy); *id.* at 140–61 (white society will not tolerate black progress beyond a certain point); *id.* at 215–58 (same); *infra* text (interest-convergence formula).

10. *See* WILLIAMS, *supra* note 2, at 55–79 (language and mindset determine how we see racial events); *id.* at 146–65 (blacks and whites see formality and rights in radically different ways).

11. Conservatives naturally place more emphasis on individual effort, initiative or "character," Criticalists on destabilization tactics and mass actions. *See, e.g.,* BELL, *supra* note 4, at 5 (destabilization); *id.* at 215–35 (collective action); *id.* at 239–58 (same).

12.

If, moreover, racism is artificially relegated to a time when it was written into code, the continuing black experience of prejudice becomes a temporal shell game manipulated by whites. Such a refusal to talk about the past disguises a refusal to talk about the present. If prejudice is what's going on in the present, then aren't we, the makers and interpreters of laws, engaged in the purest form of denial? Or, if prejudice is a word that signified only what existed "back" in the past, don't we need a new word to signify what is going on in the present? Amnesia, perhaps?

WILLIAMS, *supra* note 2, at 103. *See also* BELL, *supra* note 4, at 26–50 (Black Americans' current status stems in part from political decisions made at Constitutional Convention).

13.

Supporters of preferences cite a whole catalogue of explanations for the inability of people of color to get along without them: institutional racism, inferior education, overt prejudice, the lingering effects of slavery and oppression, cultural bias in the criteria for admission and employment. All of these arguments are most sincerely pressed, and some of them are true. But like the best black syndrome, all of the arguments entail the assumption that people of color cannot at present compete on the same playing field with people who are white. I don't believe this for an instant. . . .

CARTER, *supra* note 3, at 69.

14. *See, e.g., id.* at 32–34, 94–95, 232–33; STEELE, *supra* note 1, at 28, 31, 39, 46–54, 66, 73, 173–74.

15. *See, e.g.,* CARTER, *supra* note 3, at 12–20, 31 (racial preferences make blacks doubt themselves and their abilities); STEELE, *supra* note 1, at 33 (cultivation of victim-role); *id.* at 46–48, 117–19, 152 (internalized fear that inferiority whites teach might be real).

16. *See, e.g.,* BELL, *supra* note 4, at 26–51 (basic constitutional thought consigns blacks to inferior status); *id.* at 51–74 (majority race uses civil rights laws and civil rights "breakthroughs" to continue oppression of blacks).

17. *See, e.g.,* Derrick Bell, Brown v. Board of Education *and the Interest-Convergence Dilemma*, 93 HARV. L. REV. 518 (1980); BELL, *supra* note 4, at 51–74 (civil rights laws benefit majority race at least as much as blacks).

18. *See* STEELE, *supra* note 1, at 1–21 (Ch. 1—I'm Black, You're White, Who's Innocent?), 77–92 (Ch. 5—White Guilt).

19. *See* BELL, *supra* note 4, at 25–50, 51–74, 140–61, 215–35 (civil rights law colonizes blacks, enables whites to maintain control, and ensures racial progress is slow and measured).

20. *See, e.g.,* CARTER, *supra* note 3, at 11–20, 71–72, 80; STEELE, *supra* note 1, at 14, 33, 52–54, 115.

21. *See, e.g.,* WILLIAMS, *supra* note 2, at 80–88.

22. *See* CARTER, *supra* note 3, at 24–25, 53–54, 232–33; STEELE, *supra* note 1, at 33–35, 37–39, 115–19, 152.

23. *See* CARTER, *supra* note 3, at 40 (asserting that those who believe blacks have same views make category mistake of biology implying ideology); STEELE, *supra* note 1, at 72 ("most dangerous threat to black identity is not . . . [white racism] . . . but the black who insists on his or her own individuality"). Both conservatives go further, urging that intragroup differences are healthy or a positive good. *See* CARTER, *supra* note 3, at 99–253 (Pts. II, III—need for black dissenters); STEELE, *supra* note 1, at xi, 23, 30, 93–109, 113 (community contains more than lower-income activists). For further articulation of this "anti-essentialist" message, see Randall L. Kennedy, *Racial Critiques of Legal Academia*, 102 HARV. L. REV. 1745, 1778–1807 (1989). *But see* STEELE, *supra* note 1, at 4–5 (race identity sometimes transcends class differences).

24. *See* CARTER, *supra* note 3, at 99–191 (Pt. II—need for black dissenters); *cf.* STEELE, *supra* note 1, at xi ("Whatever I do or think as a black can never be more than a variant of what all people do and think.").

25. This term was coined by Kimberlé Crenshaw; *see* K. Crenshaw, *Race, Reform, and Retrenchment*, 101 HARV. L. REV. 1331, 1336, 1349 (1988).

26. *See* WILLIAMS, *supra* note 2, at 11, 40, 49, 119–20, 162 (visions of white as superior metaphor over blackness); *see also supra* note 17 and accompanying text (civil rights law responds to white needs).

27. *See, e.g.,* Richard Delgado, *Affirmative Action as a Majoritarian De-*

vice: Or, Do You Really Want to Be a Role Model?, 89 MICH. L. REV. 1222, 1223 n.5 (1991) ("The role model argument . . . holds that affirmative action is justified in order to provide communities of color with exemplars of success, without which they might conclude that certain social roles and professional opportunities are closed to them.").

28. *See* CARTER, *supra* note 3, at 58–62, 228–31 (beating them at their own game).

29. *See* STEELE, *supra* note 1, at 86–92, 115 (affirmative action is device to achieve cosmetic diversity); *see also* CARTER, *supra* note 3, at 34 (discussing the "deceptive rubric of diversity"); *cf.* WILLIAMS, *supra* note 2, at 116–17 (exploring nullification of individual when "social text is an 'aesthetic of uniformity' ").

30. *See* CARTER, *supra* note 3, at 34 ("The ideals of affirmative action have become conflated with the proposition that there is a black way to be—and the beneficiaries of affirmative action are nowadays supposed to be people who will be black the right way.").

31. *See* WILLIAMS, *supra* note 2, at 103, 121.

32. *See, e.g.,* CARTER, *supra* note 3, at 67–69, 71–72 (rejecting affirmative action and handouts); STEELE, *supra* note 1, at 9, 39, 113 (same); *supra* text (Bell's interest-convergence formula, distrust of white idealism as staunch support for black justice); *see also* DERRICK BELL, RACE, RACISM AND AMERICAN LAW 3, 305 (2d ed. 1980) (discussing the futility in relying on the "moral sense of the white race").

33. *See, e.g.,* BELL, *supra* note 4, at 245–58 (discussing "the ultimate civil rights strategy"); BELL, *supra* note 32, at 279–361 (Ch. 6—Potentials of Protest, Parameters of Protection—including discussion of "Creative Disorder and the Courts"); Richard Delgado, *Storytelling for Oppositionists and Others: A Plea for Narrative*, 87 MICH. L. REV. 2411 (1989) [hereinafter *Oppositionists*].

34. *See* CARTER, *supra* note 3, at 88–89 ("[T]he proper goal of all racial preferences is opportunity. . . . So justified, the benefit of racial preference carries with it the concomitant responsibility not to waste the opportunity affirmative action confers.").

35. STEELE, *supra* note 1, at 173 (stressing need for individual effort); *accord* CARTER, *supra* note 3, at 60 (advocating development of a "vanguard of black professionals who are simply too good to ignore"); *see also* STEELE, *supra* note 1, at 108–09 ("Hard work, education, individual initiative, stable family life, [and] property ownership" are means by which black Americans must advance.).

36. *See, e.g.,* CARTER, *supra* note 3, at 73–75 (describing incident in which a conventional liberal tried to convince Carter that he was a deprived victim of "systemic" racism when Carter felt no such disadvantage).

37. On the use of counter-narratives and stories to debunk or jar self-serving majoritarian myths, *see Oppositionists, supra;* STEELE, *supra* note 1, at 127–48 (telling stories of campus radicals who demand orthodoxy, magnify grievances and pretend there has been no racial progress in last 25 years).

38. STEELE, *supra* note 1, at 28–35; WILLIAMS, *supra* note 2, at 65–66.

39. *See Oppositionists, supra* note 33, at 2435–37.

40. Carter recounts a conversation he had with an older student during his first year at law school at Yale. The older student tries to persuade Carter that he

has been disadvantaged by racism; Carter disagrees, pointing out that racism helped fuel him, helped him to succeed. The student wants Carter to focus on the obstacles, but Carter prefers laying the past to rest and making the most of the opportunities now present. *See* CARTER, *supra* note 3, at 73–75.

Steele recounts his own reaction to a professor's racist story. Steele responded defensively instead of seizing the opportunity to show the professor (his debate coach) his "blindness." *See* STEELE, *supra* note 1, at 103–06.

> Seeing myself as a victim meant that I clung all the harder to my racial identity, which, in turn, meant that I suppressed my class identity. This cut me off from all the resources my class values might have offered me. In those values, for instance, I might have found the means to a more dispassionate response, the response less of a victim attacked by a victimizer than of an individual offended by a foolish old man. As an individual, I might have reported this professor to the college dean. Or, I might have calmly tried to reveal his blindness to him, and possibly won a convert.

Id. at 105.

41. *See* WILLIAMS, *supra* note 2, at 155–56.

42. *See* STEELE, *supra* note 1, at 14–15.

43. *See id.* at 90, 158 (eliminating racism may require collective action at times, but betterment results only from individual initiatives); *see also* CARTER, *supra* note 3, at 60, 88–89 (change in our hands).

44. *See* STEELE, *supra* note 1, at 124, 172–75.

45. *See* WILLIAMS, *supra* note 2, at 164.

46. Bell's entire book can be seen as an impeachment of liberalism; *see, e.g.,* BELL, *supra* note 4, at 51–74 (civil rights litigation has benefited whites more than blacks).

47. *See* Richard Delgado, *Zero-Based Racial Politics: An Evaluation of Three Best-Case Arguments on Behalf of the Nonwhite Underclass*, 78 GEO. L.J. 1929, 1940–45 (1990); *see also* BELL, *supra* note 4, at 53–59 (Chronicle of the "Conservative Crusader," implying that a conservative Court might, paradoxically, advance cause of racial justice more than earlier liberal ones).

48. *See* CARTER, *supra* note 3, at 154–68.

49. *See* WILLIAMS, *supra* note 2, at 10, 21–24, 44–51, 71 -72, 80–91, 96–97, 214–15.

50. *See* CARTER, *supra* note 3, at 71–95 (Ch. 4—Racial Justice on the Cheap).

51. *See* STEELE, *supra* note 1, at 104.

52. The most stark expression is his "interest-convergence" formula.

From the Editor:
Issues and Comments

H O W does the "New," or Critical, race theory differ from liberal or conservative thought on race reform? Are the neoconservatives of color and the race-Crits really in as much agreement over the inadequacies of liberalism as Delgado implies? Is Bell's bleak scenario enervating, or is stone-cold-sober realism the only starting point for effectively reforming a society where race and caste matter?

Does Randall Kennedy have a point when he argues that *anyone*, including whites of good will, can write and act effectively on behalf of black causes? In addition to the chapters contained in Part X, Kennedy's attack spurred numerous responses. Some, noted in the Suggested Readings immediately following, are by Ball, Barnes, Cook, Delgado ("Brewer's Plea" and "Mindset and Metaphor"), and Alex Johnson. CRT authors who have parted with Critical Legal Studies (a left-leaning movement of the 1970s and 1980s) include Dalton, Delgado ("Ethereal Scholar"), and Matsuda ("Reparations"), all listed in the Suggested Readings, as well as Patricia Williams (see the third section of Part II).

Suggested Readings

Ball, Milner S., *The Legal Academy and Minority Scholars*, 103 HARV. L. REV. 1855 (1990).

Barnes, Robin D., *Race Consciousness: The Thematic Content of Racial Distinctiveness in Critical Race Scholarship*, 103 HARV. L. REV. 1864 (1990).

Chang, Robert S., *Toward an Asian American Legal Scholarship: Critical Race Theory, Post-Structuralism, and Narrative Space*, 81 CAL. L. REV. 1241 (1993).

Cook, Anthony E., *Beyond Critical Legal Studies: The Reconstructive Theology of Dr. Martin Luther King, Jr.*, 103 HARV. L. REV. 985 (1990).

Dalton, Harlon L., *The Clouded Prism*, 22 HARV. C.R.-C.L. L. REV. 435 (1987).

Delgado, Richard, *Brewers Plea: Critical Thoughts on Common Cause*, 44 VAND. L. REV. 1 (1991).

Delgado, Richard, *Critical Legal Studies and the Realities of Race—Does the Fundamental Contradiction Have a Corollary?*, 23 HARV. C.R.-C.L. L. REV. 407 (1988).

Delgado, Richard, *The Ethereal Scholar: Does Critical Legal Studies Have What Minorities Want?*, 22 HARV. C.R.-C.L. L. REV. 301 (1987).

Delgado, Richard, *The Inward Turn in Outsider Jurisprudence*, 34 WM. & MARY L. REV. 741 (1993).

Delgado, Richard, *Mindset and Metaphor*, 103 HARV. L. REV. 1872 (1990).

Delgado, Richard, *On Telling Stories in School: A Reply to Farber and Sherry*, 46 VAND. L. REV. 665 (1993).

Freeman, Alan D., *Racism, Rights, and the Quest for Equality of Opportunity: A Critical Legal Essay*, 23 HARV. C.R.-C.L. L. REV. 295 (1988).

Johnson, Alex M., Jr., *The New Voice of Color*, 100 YALE L.J. 2007 (1991).

474

Johnson, Alex M., Jr., Racial Critiques of Legal Academia: *A Reply in Favor of Context,* 43 STAN. L. REV. 137 (1990).

Matsuda, Mari J., *Looking to the Bottom: Critical Legal Studies and Reparations,* 22 HARV. C.R.-C.L. L. REV. 323 (1987).

Peller, Gary, *The Discourse of Constitutional Degradation,* 81 GEO. L.J. 313 (1992).

powell, john a., *Racial Realism or Racial Despair?,* 24 CONN. L. REV. 533 (1992).

Tushnet, Mark, *The Degradation of Constitutional Discourse,* 81 GEO. L.J. 251 (1992).

CRITICAL RACE FEMINISM

O N E of the newest, and most exciting, areas of Critical Race writing is what could be called Critical Race Feminism. In addition to writing about intersectionality (Part VI) and antiessentialism (Part VII)—two areas of obvious concern to women of color—they have been addressing such subjects as the woman as outlaw, the social construction of women of color, and women's reproductive rights.

Part XI begins with Lisa Ikemoto's impressive study of society's treatment of women in their childbearing role, showing how a trio of unholy forces combines to render women, especially ones of color, subject to intrusive surgical and legal demands, all supposedly in the interest of the fetus and the next generation. Jennifer Russell then describes in graphic detail how she felt on learning that even the acquisition of high social and professional status did not insulate her from being reminded that she was a "Gorilla in Your Midst." Monica Evans, in a brilliant flip, shows how black women have managed to capitalize on their invisibility, marginalization, and "outlaw" status to provide safe places for black revolution to take hold. Next, Adrien Wing and Sylke Merchán issue a chilling prediction: that the experience of Muslim women raped during the current Bosnian conflict will parallel that of early black family culture, subjected to brutal mistreatment at the hands of white masters, and that many of the same breakdowns and pathologies will again occur. Part XI closes with Margaret Montoya's *Máscaras, Trenzas, y Greñas* (Masks, Braids, and Messy Hair), in which she weaves the multiple strands of her own outsider identity into a jurisprudential and personal framework that can give feminists of color the means to survive in an alien world and also the strength to go on.

42 The Code of Perfect Pregnancy: At the Intersection of the Ideology of Motherhood, the Practice of Defaulting to Science, and the Interventionist Mindset of Law

LISA C. IKEMOTO

Thou shalt obey doctor's orders . . .
Thou shalt not partake of alcohol or drugs potentially harmful to the
    fetus . . .
Thou shalt do whatever the state deems necessary during pregnancy to
    produce a healthy baby . . .
Thou shalt be a Good Mother.

THESE commands issue from the Code of Perfect Pregnancy, which is ostensibly premised on the social good of "fetal interests." There is no Code of Perfect Pregnancy in the strictly legal sense. However, there is outstanding the idea and practice of controlling women with regard to conception, gestation, and childbirth in ways that express dominant cultural notions of motherhood. The "Code" has long roots in the way that patriarchy has constructed women as mothers and as wombs. What is new is that increasingly these subordinating social norms are being institutionalized as legal duties. The result is the regulation of pregnant women.

I use "Code of Perfect Pregnancy" not only to describe the subtext of recent cases and statutes that there "ought to be a law" to control the behavior of pregnant women, and not only to invoke the more apparently normative, historically based social code of good motherhood, but also to suggest other meanings of the word "Code." "Code" can refer to a restricted, controlled form of communica-

53 OHIO ST. L.J. 1205 (1992). Originally published in the Ohio State Law Journal. Reprinted by permission.

tion, one used to limit access to power to the few who hold the key. Because the Code defines motherhood, it excludes only women.

Further, the Code operates by institutionalizing the dilemma of disempowerment. Under the Code, women bear the responsibility of "motherhood," but are not deemed entitled to the authority to define it. The Code is double-edged. It operates by distinguishing between good mothers and bad mothers, incorporating some women into the subordinating ideology while subtracting from their power to claim alternative norms by making them moral exemplars to other women.

According to other fronts of patriarchy, motherhood is color-coded, class-coded, and culture-coded. Women of color, those who live in poverty, and those made outsiders by virtue of cultural or religious practices are stigmatized by the dominant society and are never presumed good mothers, as are white middle- and upper-class women. In addition, even while outsider women are subject to the white-middle-class-good-mother standard, direct and indirect state actions expressing patriarchal norms deprive these women of the material, political, and social resources to conform to the Code. The Code says that these women do not and cannot have the key to opening the door of "good motherhood" or defining pregnancy in other terms.

A "Code" word is also a masked word, a word that has another function. In the past few years "fetal protection policy," "forced cesarean," "court-ordered hospital detention," "fetal abuse," and "fetal personhood" have become familiar terms. They are part of the new vocabulary being formed by the Code of Perfect Pregnancy. Jennifer Johnson, Kimberly Hardy, Pamela Rae Stewart, Angela Carder, Jessie Mae Jefferson, Ayesha Madyun, and Brenda Vaughn have become familiar names. These are some of the women deemed punishable at law by the Code. Certain phrases have also become familiar: "A child has the right to be born sound and healthy"; "Eleven percent of the babies born in hospitals test positive for drugs. There is a serious problem that can be addressed by punishing women who use drugs during pregnancy"; and "There must be something wrong with a mother who would not submit to surgery in order to insure the health of her child." These stories of the Code tell of an inevitable maternal-fetal conflict, of the sacrifice and submission of good mothers, and the selfishness and willfulness of bad mothers. More specifically, the Code speaks of protecting fetal interests from bad mothers. Yet the stories say little or nothing about the lack of access to prenatal care for poor women, or the dearth of addiction treatment for pregnant women, or the high miscarriage rate among imprisoned women, or the very conservative nature of the male-dominated mainstream obstetrical practice, or the religious and cultural integrity of women whose medical decisions differ from the doctor's, or the physical and emotional impact of pregnancy on women who feel their powerlessness. The Code inserts the qualifier "but . . . in order to protect the fetus" after any mention of these facts. Within the Code, "but" has the job of denying social reality. Denying social reality makes it possible to escape the necessity of explaining how the subordination of women protects fetal interests and why less restrictive alternatives need not be used.

Because social reality is patriarchically constructed, patriarchal assumptions about gender, race, class, and culture implicitly shape the stories. Those assumptions are the social facts not put into words but present in the Code. The effect of the Code then is to direct the power of the state at women along race, class, and culture lines in the name of "protecting fetal interests." I try to reveal the denial of social reality and the failure of explanation, and to show that the concept of "fetal interests" serves not to protect fetuses, but to enforce subordination. Accordingly, I begin the process of challenging the stories of the Code by locating their roots largely in the historically based, socially constructed ideology of motherhood, in its late-nineteenth and early-twentieth-century form. I describe the developing regulatory scheme in terms of the ideology of motherhood in its current form. In doing so, I take heed of the particular effects of the Code—it devalues women of color, poor women, and culturally stigmatized women as mothers. I also follow the call of others to challenge the ways in which normative theories are formed and expressed,[1] to locate and thus dislocate the floors and ceilings of the stories that require regulation of women as childbearers and that devalue motherhood along patriarchal lines. I also show that the Code of Perfect Pregnancy is the result of three particular manifestations of the dominant, authoritarian culture—the ideology of motherhood, the practice of defaulting to science, and the interventionist mindset of law.

The Ideology of Motherhood During the Late Nineteenth and Early Twentieth Centuries

The ideology of motherhood[2] has a very particular and complex form, drawn along patriarchal lines of race, class, and culture. In that sense the ideology may be as old as patriarchy. The Good Mother ideology begins on an essentialist note. It goes something like this. By biology, women are mothers. It is women who have the capacity to carry the conceptus, give birth to the baby, and nurse the child through infancy. This premise then supports the norm that women should have the primary responsibility for childrearing and, concomitantly, that certain characteristics—nurturing, tenderness, compassion, and selflessness—are natural to good mothers. Further, the female reproductive system signifies that women are naturally suited to the role of producing a sound, healthy next generation by giving birth, milk, and moral guidance.

During the late nineteenth and early twentieth centuries it became particularly clear that the ideology defined motherhood in ways that make women buffers against social disorder. During the early industrial and Victorian periods the world became increasingly divided between the private and public spheres.[3] The private sphere was where virtue, morality, and tradition were founded. White middle- and upper-class women were confined to the private sphere and to the duty of maintaining virtue, morality, and tradition largely by inhabiting the "good mother" role. More specifically, motherhood, as an institution, had the charge of transmitting social rules. Good mothers were responsible for conceiving, giving birth to, and raising children who would grow up to contribute to the social order and not detract from it. Motherhood as a calling was fulfilled by individuals who were noble, benign, and self-sacrificing.

Social problems, then, could be explained as a failure in the private sphere—the failure to sustain motherhood as an institution, and the failure of individual women to meet the standards of the calling. As a result, fear of social disorder has often been expressed by regulating women as mothers. That is, society responds to problems in ways that elaborate upon the ideology of motherhood. One traditional way of regulating women is fairly straightforward—by promulgating laws that restrict women to the private sphere roles of mother and wife.

In *Bradwell v. Illinois*,[4] the Illinois Supreme Court denied Myra Bradwell's application for a license to practice law because she was a woman. "That God designed the sexes to occupy different spheres of action, and that it belonged to men to make, apply, and execute the laws, was regarded as an almost axiomatic truth."[5] The idea that women could participate in the making and administering of laws was dismissed "rather as abstract speculation than as an actual basis for action."[6] In Justice Bradley's now infamous concurring opinion, he supported the court's judgment by referring to the private sphere/public sphere distinction as fact. The state, he asserted, can restrict women to the private sphere by declaring them unsuited for responsibilities in the public. Justice Bradley's opinion not only makes express the idea that the state could restrict women to the roles of wife and mother, but asserts that the state should do so for the good of society:

> [T]he civil law, as well as nature herself, has always recognized a wide difference in the respective spheres and destinies of man and woman. . . . The constitution of the family organization, which is founded in the divine ordinance, as well as in the nature of things, indicates the domestic sphere as that which properly belongs to the domain and functions of womanhood. . . . The paramount destiny and mission of woman are to fulfill the noble and benign offices of wife and mother.[7]

The family is important to society. Women, as wives and mothers, are key to maintaining the "family institution." Because society has an interest in women as wives and mothers, women can be regulated as such. So the syllogism goes.

The United States Supreme Court restated this syllogism in *Muller v. Oregon*.[8] The Court upheld state restrictions on working hours for women, while striking down similar restrictions for men.

> Even though all restrictions on political, personal and contractual rights were taken away, . . . it would still be true that [woman] is so constituted that she will rest upon and look to them for protection; that her physical structure and a proper discharge of her maternal functions—having in view not merely her own health, but the well-being of the race—justify legislation to protect her. . . . The limitations . . . are not imposed solely for her benefit, but also largely for the benefit of all.[9]

The Court relied on two physical distinctions—lack of strength relative to man and the ability to give birth. As a matter of ideology, these biological distinctions signify woman's cultural function—producing and nurturing children in order to ensure the future well-being of the race. As a matter of cultural practice reflected in law, the economic freedom of women can be restricted to protect the unborn child and society.

Further, the footnotes to the *Muller* opinion and the original "Brandeis brief" offered four justifications for restricting the workday for women: "(a) the physical weakness and difference of women relative to men, (b) her maternal functions, (c) the rearing and education of children, [and] (d) the maintenance of the home. . . . [Each justification is] so important and so far reaching that the need for such reduction need hardly be discussed."[10] The first reason listed arguably protects the woman's interests.[11] But the other three speak of the ideology of motherhood and of protecting the interests of others, not those of the woman. The message is clear: Although women are responsible for the next generation, they are not entitled to make certain choices, to take certain risks that men can take, because women lack the ability to make decisions necessary for protecting the next generation. Hence, even though women bear the broad responsibility of motherhood, they are not entitled to the authority to define it.

A less direct way of maintaining social order is to impose laws that treat women who do not fit the norms as deviants, as the cause of disorder. In the late nineteenth and early twentieth centuries many church and political figures feared that industrialization was destroying the established order. Lecturers and editorial writers preached that the power of the family as an instrument of control was waning, resulting in a future of moral and physical degeneracy. During the late nineteenth century this fear expressed itself as the Social Purity Movement. Supporters crusaded against prostitution, alcohol, and pornography. The movement united a wide variety of interests by highlighting the idea that reinstating the family as the primary vehicle of social control would save America, and that preserving true womanhood and good motherhood would achieve that rescue.

As an example, the Social Purity Movement's crusade against prostitution expressed in various ways the idea that, for the good of society, women must remain in their private-sphere roles of wife and mother. Social mores cast prostitutes as "fallen," weak women who in betraying the norms had placed social order in jeopardy. Prostitutes contributed to social disorder in a variety of ways, including supposedly spreading syphilis.[12] Because prostitutes were presumed to be both morally and intellectually inferior, and because both types of inferiority were believed hereditary, prostitutes tainted the race by having substandard children.[13] Furthermore, prostitution contributed to the corruption of minors.

Patriarchy devalued nonstandard motherhood in at least three ways during the late nineteenth and early twentieth centuries. First, it operated on a class basis by presuming that the "Good Mother" model, derived from middle- and upper-class values and experiences, should apply regardless of class. Second, it used negative stereotypes of recent immigrants to devalue motherhood on ethnic lines. Third, it offered race-based mother models for women of color that truncated their roles or that described women of color as "natally dead."[14]

The three examples I used earlier rest on the public sphere/private sphere distinction. But that public/private construct described the life of middle- and upper-class women. Economic necessity generally mandated that poor women and women of color worked outside the home. So these women were held to a Good Mother standard that had little to do with their economic reality. Not surprisingly, the use of state power described in *Bradwell, Muller,* and by the Social Purity crusaders—disallowing access to public sphere power, imposing economic restrictions, and blaming and prosecuting "bad" women, all for social good and to enforce the ideology—fell most heavily on non-privileged women. These women were least able to comply with expectations of round-the-clock caretaking, nurturing, and moral guidance. The denial of their economic reality put the focus on their personal traits. It also set economic standards for motherhood, thus commodifying it, making good mothering something one could buy.

The ideology also devalued motherhood on racial lines. It defined mothering roles for Black women in subordinated positions within white households. Black women could be nannies and wet nurses. They were trusted with performing the physical tasks of motherhood, but not the moral duty of inculcating children with proper values. Thus, it was assumed that they should and could leave their own children at home in order to care for white children. The children of Native American women were sent to boarding schools in large part so they could not learn from their mothers.[15] Because racial stereotypes described Black women and Native American women as more like animals than rational beings, it was said that they would not feel the pain of these racially and economically forced separations as "normal" women would. They were considered "natally dead." But at the same time they were blamed for failing to meet the Good Mother standard and hence for reproducing social problems.

The late-nineteenth and early-twentieth-century version of the ideology forecasts the current regulation of pregnant women. It explains why women as mothers can be held responsible for social problems. It describes a Good Mother model that speaks from a particular class, race, and ethnic experience and then universalizes that model as a standard that should apply in disregard of other particular realities. And it devalues motherhood on race, class, and cultural lines.

The Current Ideology:
The Regulation of Pregnant Women

Today, the ideology of motherhood is most clearly expressed in law with restrictions that speak to women's biological capacity to conceive and bear children, not with laws confining women to the private sphere. However, while these laws and proposals most directly affect women's reproductive liberty and the twin values of bodily integrity and decisional autonomy, they also speak to our larger understanding of liberty, integrity, and autonomy. This effect in turn solidifies assumptions of subordination and prevents liberating ideology. Second, over the past century, these laws have begun to take the shape of an increasingly comprehensive regulatory scheme. There is not yet a Code per se. But there is a growing sense that there ought to be one. Third, the law is invading a set of choices not regulated before and it is doing so largely in the name of "fetal interests" and social good. These are the current code words for subordination. Finally, the ideology now defines good motherhood largely by negative example, and the devalued mother continues to be drawn on race, class, and culture lines.

Reproductive liberty can serve as the starting point for analysis. It is often described in terms of the procreative process: Conception, gestation, and childbirth. Until recently, attempts to regulate the woman as childbearer have been aimed primarily at controlling choices surrounding conception. That is, regulations have taken the form of state laws that restrict a woman's ability to determine whether to conceive, how to conceive, and whether to terminate the pregnancy. These regulations elaborate upon the ideology of motherhood by stating preferences about who should and who should not become pregnant and hence become mothers.

In the past few years, however, state regulations have emphasized a different question: To what extent can the state restrain a woman during pregnancy? The regulation of pregnancy has been premised on a singular construct: the maternal-fetal conflict. This oppositional description of pregnancy frames the legal issue in either/or terms and suggests that there must be a winner and a loser. Hence, the legal issue becomes whether the state should protect maternal or fetal interests. The use of the construct of conflict to the exclusion of all other descriptions of pregnancy also precludes women from defining pregnancy and the choices surrounding it for themselves. And the ideology of motherhood invests certain "choices" with greater moral weight. This proscribes the social and political reality of choice. And it justifies legal intervention to prevent "bad" choices and punish "bad" mothers.

[Ed. The author next reviews recent legal developments regulating contraception, abortion, sterilization, surrogate motherhood, forced cesareans and delivery, forced prenatal treatment, and punishment for the crime of being a bad gestator. She then continues as follows.]

THE COMPLETELY REGULATED WOMAN

Margery Shaw has probably suggested the most extensive regulatory scheme.[16] She has categorized a vast array of potential legal duties into time periods: before conception, early in pregnancy, during mid-pregnancy, and after viability. Many of these time periods would give rise to indirect state regulation. A child born with a defect may have a cause of action in tort against its mother for breaching these duties. However, Shaw also indicates that direct state regulation might be an appropriate way of enforcing several of these duties.

As an example of a duty beginning before conception, Shaw proposes that "[t]he only suggested remedy [for women born with phenylketonuria] is to return the women to a low phenylalaline diet before they become pregnant and rigorously monitor them throughout pregnancy."[17] She would require involuntary prenatal testing in some cases. "If the courts decide to mandate prenatal diagnosis in selected cases where there is a significant risk of a very burdensome disease that would cause the child severe pain and suffering and early death, there are precedents available."[18] For women whose amniocentesis indicates that the fetus has such a disease, Shaw prescribes selective abortion. "[I]t could be argued that the fetus should be 'allowed to die' if it is suffering a fatal disease."[19] After viability, "the state could order fetal therapy and choose a method of birth in the interests of the fetus if such intervention posed little or no harm to the mother."[20] Finally, she proposes fetal abuse statutes that would authorize courts to "compel parents and prospective parents to enter alcohol and drug abuse rehabilitation programs, and, in the extreme, to take 'custody' of the fetus to prevent mental and physical harm."[21]

LAW AND IDEOLOGY

The above-cited proposals would continue the trend toward forced intervention. They also continue two parallel stories. One is the current version of the ideology of motherhood. In the 1990s, we can laugh at the century-old medical theory of "prenatal impressions." According to this theory, a woman must avoid all "shocking, painful or unbeautiful sights," all intellectual stimulation, angry, or lustful thoughts, and also her husband's alcohol- or tobacco-tainted breath in order to prevent her baby from being deformed or stunted in the womb. We know better now. But the premise behind the prenatal impressions theory is the same as the premise behind current and proposed regulation of pregnant women: Women are childbearers, first and foremost. As such, their lives can be restricted in extraordinary ways. The ideology has established the premise of subordination; it leaves only the medical facts in dispute. If we accept, as did nineteenth-century society, that the brain and the fetus compete for energy and phosphates so that a pregnant woman's mental efforts deprive the fetus of nutrients, then mental activity can be discouraged by preventing access to higher education. If we accept, as we did in the mid-twentieth century, that weight gain will harm the developing child, then pregnant women can be ordered to diet. If we accept that a patient's doctor may choose the principle of physician control rather than patient choice because it is medically safer, then a pregnant woman can be forced to submit to cesarean delivery. If we accept using experimental in-utero surgery to correct a fetal defect, then courts can order surgery against the woman's will. This is the practice of justifying regulation by defining women as the perfecting agents of society and as mere vessels for the next generation.

The second story is both inextricably linked to the old and entirely new. The new and proposed regulation of pregnant women treats women as wombs as a matter of law. Aristotle believed that the male, during intercourse, implanted the fetal form into the female. The female role in reproduction was merely to provide the material.[22] Aristotle was a philosopher. He has been influential as such—but the Greek state never enacted his theory into statutory law. In 1870, J. L. Holbrook wrote, it was "as if the Almighty, in creating the female sex, had taken the uterus and built up a woman around it."[23] J. L. Holbrook was a doctor. He may have patronized his women patients, and as a professor he may have influenced his students to do the same, but he never issued a court order. In 1981, the state of Georgia took temporary custody of the fetus carried by Jessie Mae Jefferson. It was so ordered by the Georgia Supreme Court. The second story is the regulatory scheme.

Although the scope of the proposed regulatory scheme varies, the proposals are all premised on the idea that maternal interests must be weighed against fetal ones. Balancing tests all imply that one set of interests can be subordinated to the other. Here, consistent with cultural practice and with legal precedent, the interests of the woman are subordinated to those of another—the fetus. The balancing test says that preventing harm to the fetus justifies restrictions on the woman's decisional autonomy and invasions of her bodily integrity. In the case of proposed preconception duties, the woman's rights would be subordinated to a nonexistent being. The potential for grave harm to the might-be fetus, according to this argument, outweighs the woman's liberty interests.

The balancing test also expresses the corollary notion that regulation of women as childbearers will yield positive results for the rest of society. For one thing, it saves money. Prenatal care and therapy cost less than treating children born with defects. It also produces more money. Children born without defects will presumably have a better chance at being productive members of society. Another good is that forcible therapy preserves the integrity of the medical profession. It allows doctors to do what they think is best. It also allows them to forestall the legal liability posed by fetal defect or injury. And forcible therapy allows us to put costly advances in science and technology to use, so that we can justify our investment. Technology has a sort of momentum of its own.

In short, for the sake of the next generation, and for that of society as a whole, the state can regulate women as childbearers. If cultural practice remains consistent, that regulation will continue to fall disproportionately on poor women of color. This prediction is based not only on precedent but also on common sense. Enforcing the regulatory scheme requires monitoring and reporting. Women using public health facilities and public monies are subject to that monitoring and are more likely to be reported to authorities. It is poor women of color who are most likely to have contact with government agencies and use public hospitals.

Poor women of color are reported at disproportionately higher rates for drug use. It seems logical to conclude that poor women of color will be reported for other behavior at disproportionately higher rates. Private physicians who generally treat white middle- and upper-class women, on the other hand, are not likely to oppose their patients, whose continued patronage they want to preserve. The doctors are more likely to respect these patients as individuals.

The regulatory scheme, expanded to restrict choices implicated by continued gestation as well as those surrounding conception, includes both direct and indirect state intervention. As discussed, these interventions subtract from the bodily integrity and decisional autonomy of the woman. To the extent that the state invokes the parens patriae power to prevent harm to the fetus, the state subordinates the interests of the woman to those of the fetus. To the extent that the state regulates pregnant women to promote public health, safety, and morals—an exercise of the police power—it subordinates the interests of the woman to those of the rest of society. In either case, when the state regulates women as childbearers, it legislates the ideology of motherhood. Furthermore, it eliminates the possibility of self-definition.

The ideology, in regulatory form, creates two other effects that run across the direct-indirect organizational line: devaluing women as persons and devaluing them as mothers. Both of these effects describe women in terms other than humanist. That is, both effects are reductionist.

These regulations devalue women as persons by characterizing women as wombs. These laws treat women not as persons but as fetal containers, wombs surrounded by resources in human shape. The part of the ideology articulated through these regulations is that of women as mothers raising their children to contribute to the social order. They are means to an end. Now, in order to give these children a head start, their mothers are made guarantors that they will begin life with sound minds and bodies. It is women, as individuals, who bear this responsibility. It is women, as a group, who are devalued by the experience of childbearing under law.

These regulations also devalue some women as mothers. Regulations that infringe on women by race and class express the part of the ideology that motherhood as an institution has the charge of transmitting social rules, as well as moral and cultural values. Some women, according to these laws, are unfit to accomplish this task. Because they depart from the norm, they are likely to breed disorder.

When reviewed with a critical eye, the motherhood ideology as a regulatory scheme discloses the current social concerns. Social concerns have been translated by ideology into fears of woman-bred disorder, points at which women have failed as buffers. Many of the laws express a faith that the road to social order lies in genetic determinism. Many of the laws also reveal the influence of pro-life doctrines. And many of the laws, especially indirect regulations, reflect the fear generated by the war on drugs. In terms of history, the cultural practice of using women as buffers against disorder is an old one, but its current expression—state regulation of pregnant women—is new.

The Practice of Defaulting to Science and the Interventionist Mindset of Law

The regulation of pregnant women is an elaboration of the ideology of motherhood and an unprecedented use of state power. The extension of state power raises the question—why has the regulatory scheme expanded to restrict choices implicated by pregnancy? Many have noted that the sphere of activity protected from state intervention is shrinking. But, state regulation premised on the socially constructed ideology of motherhood is the key. It focuses the heavy power of the state on women. This regulation allows the state to present its restrictions on women as natural and the idea of self-definition for women as unnatural. This regulation gives the regulatory scheme its shape and character.

There are, however, other forces propelling the formation of a regulatory scheme at this time. In this section, I explain the regulation of pregnant women as the intersection of the motherhood ideology and of two other forces. One I call defaulting to science. It is the practice of letting developments in science and technology define the issues in a way that creates an imperative to use these developments. The other force is an interventionist mindset of law. This is a willingness that stems from a failure to consider alternatives, to use state power in a way that restricts individual choice and self-definition.

Defaulting to science is another way of saying that we equate, without thinking about it, science with progress. New developments in science and technology are being used in many cases simply for the sake of using them. We default to science when we assume that if the technology is there, we should use it, and then we act on this assumption without critical evaluation of the wisdom of acting.

In obstetrics, the practice of defaulting to science took shape during the late nineteenth and early twentieth centuries, the time when medical professionals acquired their status and influence. It was a time when physician participation in childbirth became standard. As technology for intervention became available, it raised the question of whether it should be used. But that question was not addressed at the outset. As the means of medical intervention became available, physicians simply used them as a matter of course. By assuming that the new science or technology should be used, physicians simultaneously created an imperative for its use.

History shows that the use of forceps and anesthesia in the delivery room became standard for reasons that had little to do with reducing maternal and infant mortality. Hospital births became common, and physicians used technology to intervene simply because the equipment was available. When physicians participated in home births, they intervened because they felt pressured in the presence of others to do something, to "perform." And some physicians, if pressed for time and other patients were waiting, used forceps, anesthesia, or both to direct labor into patterns under their control.

As the means of physician control became available, the experts constructed a need for it. They characterized childbirth as a process where harm might occur but for the use of forceps, episiotomies, ergot, anesthesia, and cesarean sections. One of the first results of physician participation in reproduction was a changed understanding of childbirth, from a natural but risky event, to a pathology.[24] Similarly, as the means for intervention in fetal development become available, pregnancy is coming to be understood as a pathology. It is being characterized as a process where harm might occur but for the imposition of medical treatment and behavior restrictions on the pregnant woman. Science provides the reason for, as well as the means of, taking control.

When we default to science, we cede control to the experts and institutions who have the technology. Physicians exercise control by prescribing both the problem—potential risks during pregnancy—and the solution, namely taking control of the biological processes. Science, the need for information, and technology developed by science become one and the same. But by assuming necessity, we fail to consider fully the consequences of ceding control. When courts order forcible medical treatment, and when judges and legislatures create legal sanctions for certain behavior for the ostensible reason of preserving fetal health, they may consider that imposing control over the biological processes of pregnancy means taking control of the pregnant woman's body, but they fail to consider that imposing control over a woman because she is pregnant means defining women as fetal carriers and devaluing them as individuals. That consideration is not subject to "scientific" proof. It is, however, fast becoming a political truth.

Scientific "truth" determines how we perceive and treat human beings—medically, socially, and politically. Modern science presents human life as "a system of 'organized complexity' whose driving force is the molecular structure of the gene."[25] The greatest single truth derived from our rapidly increasing knowledge of fetal development is that fetal life is complex and physically vulnerable to its environment. That "truth" provides a rationale for regulating pregnant women—it is environmental quality control. The scientific description of human life as biologically determined provides the rationale for elevating the importance of fetal life.

Science and technology also shape our understanding of pregnancy. As forceps and the episiotomy transformed the understanding of childbirth from natural event to pathology, technology such as the sonogram has changed the literal picture of pregnancy. The earlier model for the woman-fetus relationship was interdependence. Law followed this model. Unborn fetuses had very few legal interests at law. Now, doctors regard the fetus as a separate patient, and the law recognizes the fetus as a being with independent interests.

The important point is that once the two-patient model is accepted, conflict is assumed to be inevitable. This conflict is a cultural construct, not the result of "pure science." Relationships in our society are only dimly understood in terms of power and subordination. It is as if relationships characterized by domination and subordination are inevitable and unchangeable. They are more often described in terms of conflict and a balance of interests. It is true that our package of values includes the equality principle, which seems to acknowledge the need to eliminate subordination. But the equal protection doctrine is more often valued as a means of addressing only the obviously harmful results of subordination.[26] Hierarchy, not liberation, is the presumably immutable starting point in describing relationships. This cultural understanding prescribes the perception that in a woman-fetus relationship, the woman is in a position of power relative to the fetus, which in turn must be protected in order to prevent harm caused by the woman's abuse of that power. Since it is easier to perceive a power relationship and conflict between identifiably separate interests, the two-patient model enhances the construct of conflict.[27] But the model is being accepted with little consideration being given to the potential harm of describing pregnancy as the source of conflict.

Generally, the effect of using a two-patient model for pregnancy is that attention shifts to the fetus. This may have the good of promoting fetal health, but in some situations it detracts from the woman's interests. Where petitions for court-ordered medical treatment are sought, judges usually grant the petition. The decision to grant the petition appears almost reasonable if one considers the information received and the setting in which the judge must make a decision. The doctor informs the judge that she has the ability to prevent harm to the fetus or to correct a defect. Allowing the doctor to prevent harm seems like a humane response, one that is reinforced by the cultural practice of assuming that if we have the science, we should use it. It is also reinforced by the perception that the fetus is an innocent bystander, threatened by the other patient's noncooperation. Where child neglect petitions are sought, the doctor testifies that the pregnant woman had the ability to prevent the harm by not drinking or by not taking controlled substances. Again, the fetus is seen as victim. This response is reinforced by the assumption that if we have the information, we should act on it. Scientifically acquired information translates too quickly into additional rights or duties when we default. It is only a secondary thought that, in order to prevent the fetal harm or repair the defect, the woman's interests must be considered. As the cases indicate, many assign the woman's interests little weight.

THE INTERVENTIONIST MINDSET OF LAW

The interventionist mindset of law consists of a readiness to use state power to address perceived moral problems by regulating the individual. Like the assumption that science is progress, the interventionist mindset is accompanied by a failure critically to evaluate the wisdom of so acting. Many have commented on effects of this mindset—the regulatory state and the devaluation of individual rights. Consider now the impetus for using state power to address social problems as the moral failure of certain individuals or groups, as a twentieth-century mindset. The regulation of pregnant women is one result of this mindset. The labeling of pregnant women as "good mothers" and "bad mothers" signifies the sense of righteousness behind the regulation.

The interventionist mindset of law occurs as call and response. During the nineteenth century, there was a fairly clear line between the private and the public spheres. Family and church provided a broad moral authority. State power was generally reserved for maintaining public order and safety. Law might be used to defend the moral authority of the family, and it might do so by reinforcing narrow gender roles for women, as in *Bradwell and Muller*. But issues such as procreation, childrearing, education, and the transmission of values were regarded as family matters, not appropriate for state regulation. They were private, not in the constitutional sense, but by social function.

During the twentieth century, as the socializing authority of family and church has decreased, the law has become more salient. The state is now regulating behavior that used to be considered a private sphere matter. For example, criminal law during most of the nineteenth century moved away from using law to address moral issues as the influence of the Puritan ethic waned. During the earlier part of the century law was used to address issues that are more universally understood as crime without reference to a time-bound moral code—crimes against property or crimes resulting in bodily harm or death.[28] The use of law as social management began in the late nineteenth century. The regulation of female prostitutes was part of this trend, as was *Muller v. Oregon*.[29] That decision provides a striking example. The Supreme Court held that states could restrict the working hours of women because "healthy mothers are essential to vigorous offspring."[30] Ironically, this decision was rendered during the *Lochner*[31] era, a time when freedom of contract was considered essential to a free society. Liberty for men apparently depended on regulation of women.[32]

The current regulation of pregnant women continues to use law as social management. "Healthy babies" have become a social concern and a political issue. Women who give birth to unhealthy babies are the perceived problem. Law is used to address the issue by directly and indirectly restricting the choices of pregnant women. A moral appeal, unenforceable at law, to a woman as mother is no longer considered sufficient or politic. Women, perhaps due to feminism, have acquired some authority to define themselves without reference to their biological capacity to bear children. The Code describes this transformation as a failure of motherhood as a private sphere institution. Thus, a call is made to bolster the moral responsibility with fetal rights and maternal duties.

The interventionist mindset, then, is partly a failure to consider alternatives—alternative ways of understanding the problem, and alternatives to using regulation as a solution. The call to regulation has become an automatic response to social disorder. Underlying that response is the assumption that the social disorder is attributable to a particular individual or group, such that regulating those persons will solve the problem. That is, the mindset includes a preconceived approach to solving social problems. First, formulate the problem as the behavior of certain individuals, then use law to restrict the problematic behavior.

One reason regulation has appeal as a solution is that it is cheap. Regulation is cheap because it assigns responsibility for a problem to a particular group of persons. It assumes that they must pay or change. It focuses on their behavior, but does not look to the social, political, and economic context in which the behavior occurs. Regulation allows us to avoid anything but superficial evaluation of a problem. The interventionist mindset lets us perceive the victims of social problems as the cause. Otherwise, we might have to consider the possibility that illegal drug use, crime, and poverty are manifestations of bigger problems that might require bigger, more expensive, more inconvenient solutions. Some of these solutions might actually require the reallocation of resources, the equitable distribution of power.

Another reason regulation is appealing is that it is easy. Regulation is tangible proof that the state has done something. However, what is taken for proof that the problem has been solved is often little more than the regulation itself. Part of the mindset is a failure to review the effects of the regulation. We assume that regulation must be positive, neglecting to consider its effects on the individual, on the group, and on society as a whole.

CONVERGING FORCES: THE IDEOLOGY OF MOTHERHOOD, THE PRACTICE OF DEFAULTING TO SCIENCE, THE INTERVENTIONIST MINDSET OF LAW

The regulation of pregnant women is converging at the intersection of the ideology of motherhood, the practice of defaulting to science, and the interventionist mindset of law. A synergy among these forces exists that makes it difficult to attribute specific parts and moments of the regulatory scheme to any one force. I simply want to evoke some sense of the dynamic in play.

The ideology of motherhood focuses the power of the state on women, and does so in a way that categorizes women as mothers. Science as authority provides a neutral-sounding rationale for using state power. The readiness to use state power to subordinate, rather than to liberate, enhances the standardizing and punitive power of the motherhood ideology.

For example, when physician participation in childbirth became standard, the doctor gained control of the birth process. And obstetrics, the science of pregnancy, gained the authority to raise questions about medical intervention and answer them affirmatively. Obstetrics became a participant in the ongoing project of defining women as childbearers because of the practice of defaulting to science. The ideology is co-opting.

When we assume that science is neutral and disinterested, that it is apolitical and has authority only as a source of truth, we become blind to another truth—that knowledge is power. When we recognize science as truth and authority, we institutionalize it. The practice of defaulting to science has become canon. And when we fail to understand that institutions in a power-imbalanced world perpetuate hierarchy, we cede the autonomy of those marginalized by the hierarchy to those who control the institutions. By giving the institution of science the authority to raise questions and to answer them, we subtract from the ability of the individual to do so. We remove the individual from the dialogue. Thus, when obstetricians raise the question of whether or not to perform cesareans and obstetricians decide to perform them, then the notion that good mothers should consent to surgical intervention is added to the ideology.

The norm requires respect from individuals. When a woman acts or chooses in a way that defies that expectation, her act or choice is devalued. Because we default to science, when obstetrics speaks, we assume the message is rational. When obstetricians say a purse-string operation is necessary to prevent miscarriage, we assume consent to the operation is the rational choice of every woman. The woman who refuses consent, who defies the "truth" that her refusal endangers the fetus despite her doctor's concern, must be thinking irrationally. In ideological terms, the woman has failed to listen to reason, and her decision is self-ish; a woman who makes a selfish choice is an unnatural mother.

With regard to the regulation of pregnant women that is not imposed as medical treatment, but is more clearly punitive in nature, authority still issues from the institution of science. That is, scientifically acquired knowledge about fetal development, about the effects of drugs, alcohol, and other toxins and behaviors, provides the reason for directing state power at women. It casts the use of power in a reasonable light. It contributes to the normative, conformist, fault-imposing character of authority in a hierarchical state. The indirect regulations also result when the ideology of motherhood is applied in conjunction with the authority of science.

The interventionist mindset reinforces the notion inherent in the motherhood ideology that "the problem" defined by science is attributable to women, not to the institutions of power. In response to the call to law, women who defy the norm are sanctioned by the state. The irrationality of the response is not obvious, however, because the process of responding with regulation is apparently neutral. The process of applying neutral-sounding formulae shifts attention to the structure of the process rather than to its substance and results. It seems rational to find that the state's interest in protecting potential or fetal life outweighs the woman's interest in autonomy when one does not have to think about how those interests were identified and assigned a weight.

The Universal Standard of Good Motherhood and the Complex of Devalued Motherhood Models

The Good Mother tends to be used as a universal standard. It is applied to all women in a way that ignores the social reality in which they live. The regulatory approach constrains us to talk in terms of fetal rights and maternal duties. It permits no exploration of conflicts resulting from the unequal distribution of political power and social goods. The regulatory approach does not require those applying the standard to remember that poor people have little access to prenatal care or that certain medical procedures violate religious convictions. Nor does it take into account that some patient decisions originate from fear and misunderstanding perpetrated by the medical professionals, that persons addicted to drugs or alcohol cannot simply stop, and that pregnant women are seldom admitted to substance abuse rehabilitation centers. This approach does not require those applying the standard to explore how they have experienced race, class, and gender, or how the experience of subordinating might lead them to assume that certain women will be good mothers and certain women will not. Nor does the use of "fetal rights" reflect the wrongs suffered by women when regulation is imposed. In other words, the universal standard does not allow us to look beyond "bad mothers" for the "real" causes of social problems.

The result is a regulatory scheme that tells women to be good, to act selflessly, to protect children, and to ensure a healthier, more economically productive future for society. In terms revealed by explicating the general standard, the regulatory scheme tells women to subordinate their own interests to those identified by others as more important. The possibility that their failure as individuals is a conclusion imposed by the dominant culture is not admissible. Those who cannot be good given their social reality, or those who cannot be perceived as good given the cultural stigmas attached by those who control the standard, are blamed for the problems.

The ideology of motherhood has a very particular form. First, it distinguishes between white middle- and upper-class women, and women oppressed by race, poverty, cultural elitism, heterosexism, etc. White middle- and upper-class women are part of the sector that defines the norms. Thus, these women are the Good Mothers. Even the white middle- and upper-class women who defy the norms are not necessarily Bad Mothers under the ideology. The "bad" label is generally reserved for members of outgroups. Thus, those who defy the norm are usually considered Good Mothers gone astray.

The ideology holds outgroup women to the Good Mother standard and, at the same time, to often contradictory and always devalued models of motherhood particular to women of color, poor women, women who are lesbian, and women from other outgroups. There is a complex of devalued mother models working against outsider women.

Outgroup members are presumptively not Good Mothers. But they are presumed to fit within one or more of the devalued mother models. An outgroup woman can never completely conform to the Good Mother model because of her race, class, culture, or other orientation. Even the outsider who conforms to that extent is never a Good Mother. She will still be devalued. Some may say that she is extraordinary because she overcame her race or class, but not because she overcame racism, classism, cultural elitism, or heterosexism, to become a Good Mother. But the indicator of her outgroup status will not be part of her achievement.

A member of an outgroup who does not conform to the Good Mother standard to the extent that she is not privileged may still be a Good Black Mother, or a Good Welfare Mother, or a Good Hispanic Mother, or a Good Asian Mother, but under the ideology, those models are not quite as good as the Good Mother. Thus, there is a Good Black Mother model, but there is no such thing as valued Black motherhood. The devalued goodness of these models confirms the superiority and justifies the privilege of the ingroup.

Those women who cannot conform to any of the good mother standards are the Bad Mothers. That is, their noncompliance is presumptively willful and morally incorrect. These women are not bad mothers simply because they have failed to fit existing Good Mother models, but also because they do fit existing Bad Mother models. They confirm the expectations of failure that justify white middle-class privilege.

These devalued mother models operate in even more complex ways. If an outgroup woman conforms to a good outgroup mother model, she may overcome her presumed potential for bad motherhood, but not necessarily. Thus, Black women are perfectly acceptable as surrogate gestators for white women's children. That is one Good Black Mother model. However, she may still be regarded as only capable of raising her own children to be juvenile delinquents. When Black women raise "good" children, the children are more often than not regarded as extraordinary; they are said to be extraordinary because they have overcome the blackness of their mothers, not because of what they have achieved in the presence of racism.[33]

This is not a conclusion. It is the beginning, I hope, of a continuing project. It is time to break the Code.

NOTES

1. See bell hooks, *Feminism: A Transformational Politic*, in THEORETICAL PERSPECTIVES ON SEXUAL DIFFERENCE 185, 186 (Deborah L. Rhode ed., 1990) ("Emphasizing paradigms of domination that call attention to woman's capacity to dominate is one way to deconstruct and challenge the simplistic notion that man is the enemy, woman the victim; the notion that men have always been the oppressors. Such thinking enables us to examine our role as women in the perpetuation and maintenance of systems of domination."); CATHARINE A. MACKINNON, TOWARD A FEMINIST THEORY OF THE STATE 244 (1989) ("The first step is to claim women's concrete reality. . . . The next step is to recognize that male forms of power over women are affirmatively embodied as individual rights in law."); Richard Delgado, *Storytelling for Oppositionists and Others: A Plea for Narrative*, 87 MICH. L. REV. 2411, 2413–14 (1989) ("Ideology—the received wisdom—makes current social arrangements seem fair and natural. . . . The cure is storytelling. . . .").

2. I use the term "ideology" loosely. At the least, "ideology" refers to what Richard Delgado calls "the received wisdom." It is an attempt to explain and justify the social reality. Delgado, *supra* note 1, at 2415.

3. Ellen DuBois, *The Radicalism of the Woman Suffrage Movement: Notes Toward the Reconstruction of Nineteenth-Century Feminism*, in WOMEN, THE LAW AND THE CONSTITUTION 266, 266–69 (Kermit L. Hall ed., 1987); Nadine Taub & Elizabeth Schneider, *Perspectives on Women's Subordination and the Role of Law*, in THE POLITICS OF LAW 118–24 (D. Kairys ed., 1982).

4. 83 U.S. (16 Wall.) 130 (1872).

5. *Id.* at 132.

6. *Id.*

7. *Id.* at 141.

8. 208 U.S. 412 (1908).

9. *Id.* at 422.

10. *Id.* at 420, n.1.

11. In 1973, the Court condemned this type of "romantic paternalism." *See* Frontiero v. Richardson, 411 U.S. 677, 684 (1973).

12. Kay Ann Holmes, *Reflections by Gaslight: Prostitution in Another Age*, in WOMEN, THE LAW AND THE CONSTITUTION 367 (Kermit L. Hall ed., 1987).

13. LINDA GORDON, WOMAN'S BODY, WOMAN'S RIGHT: A SOCIAL HISTORY OF BIRTH CONTROL IN AMERICA 121–22 (1976).

14. TONI MORRISON, PLAYING IN THE DARK 21 (1992).

15. EVELYN C. ADAMS, AMERICAN INDIAN EDUCATION: GOVERNMENT SCHOOLS AND ECONOMIC PROGRESS 54–58 (1971);

16. *See* Margery Shaw, *Conditional Prospective Rights of the Fetus*, 5 J. LEGAL MED. 63 (1984).

17. *Id.* at 85.

18. *Id.* at 87.

19. Id.

20. *Id.* at 88.

21. *Id.* at 100.

22. NANCY TUANA, THE WEAKER SEED: THE SEXIST BIAS OF REPRODUCTIVE THEORY IN FEMINISM AND SCIENCE 147, 150 (1989).

23. BARBARA EHRENREICH & DEIRDRE ENGLISH, FOR HER OWN GOOD 120 (1979).

24. In "Kuhnsian" terms, once childbirth-as-pathology became accepted as a paradigm, novel means of physician intervention in the childbirth process were readily accepted and, as stated, justified as necessary. They merely confirmed the paradigm. And at the most, new means of intervention such as the use of anesthetics required a reformulation of the paradigm. Physician control, then, may be described as a micro-version of what Kuhn calls "normal science." THOMAS S. KUHN, THE STRUCTURE OF SCIENTIFIC REVOLUTIONS 23–30 (2d ed. 1970).

25. STANLEY ARONOWITZ, SCIENCE AS POWER 15 (1988).

26. See Richard Delgado, *When a Story is Just a Story: Does Voice Really Matter?*, 76 VA. L. REV. 95, 102–03 (1990) (describing civil rights in the purview of the dominant discourse as "the study of communities in conflict; its objective is the management of tension").

27. I am not saying that the construct of conflict began recently, only that recent developments in the scientific and social understanding of pregnancy have expanded and sharpened the construct. The debate through the centuries about whether a fertilized ovum contained a soul suggests a maternal-fetal conflict. *See* John T. Noonan, Jr., *An Almost Absolute Value in History*, in THE MORALITY OF ABORTION 1–59 (John T. Noonan, Jr., ed., 1970) (presenting the Christian humanist perspective on the philosophical debates over the legality of abortion through western history).

28. LAWRENCE M. FRIEDMAN, A HISTORY OF AMERICAN LAW 257–58, 508–10 (1973); KERMIT L. HALL, THE MAGIC MIRROR: LAW IN AMERICAN HISTORY 185–88 (1989).

29. 208 U.S. 412 (1908). *See* David L. Faigman, *"Normative Constitutional Fact-Finding": Exploring the Empirical Component of Constitutional Interpretation*, 139 U. PA. L. REV. 541 (1991) (identifying *Muller* as the beginning of sociological jurisprudence).

30. *Muller*, 208 U.S. at 421.

31. Lochner v. New York, 198 U.S. 45 (1905).

32. *See* Faigman, *supra* note 29, at 561. Faigman points out that "*Lochner* and *Muller* are consistent in that they embrace a similar theory of human rela-

tions, a theory made explicit in *Lochner* but left unstated in *Muller.* This theory, generally associated with Social Darwinism as popularized in the works of Herbert Spencer, dictated that freedom of contract was to be protected against legislative intrusion except in certain categories of cases," such as women and children. *Id.*

33. *See, e.g.,* BOYZ IN THE HOOD (Columbia Pictures, 1991).

43 On Being a Gorilla in Your Midst, or, The Life of One Blackwoman in the Legal Academy

JENNIFER M. RUSSELL

S O M E W H E R E out there in the wilderness is a dispossessed white male whose privation was caused by my appointment to the law faculty. Chances are, he is the same white male from whom I earlier misappropriated an entitlement when New Jersey's third largest law firm hired me as an associate attorney, when the United States Securities & Exchange Commission hired me as a staff attorney, and when New York University Law School accepted me as a member of the class of 1984. My undergraduate enrollment at Queens College of the City University of New York probably did not disinherit this white male, since even in its heyday Queens College never stood among that group of elite institutions to which the white male seeks a coveted admission. Queens College notwithstanding, my achievements, academic and professional, will forever enjoy only a presumption of theft. That perceived rapaciousness is just one of the many dilemmas I confront as a gorilla in your midst.

I had never equated maternity with a loss or diminution of self. But as our society at-large persisted in its demand for my exclusive mothering of my newborn son, I felt a great urgency to preserve and [re]claim the pre-maternal selves I had come to know and value greatly—my scholarly self, my teacher self, my student self, my lawyer self, my career self and so on. Faced with the possible extinction of my many non-mothering selves, within weeks of my son's birth I unofficially returned to my office (officially, I was still on maternity leave) eager to function as colleague, teacher and legal scholar. There, in my office at the law school, I could strut my stuff on familiar, safe territory.

So I thought until one morning a nostril-flaring beast with blood-shot eyes, menacing canines and mauler hands ambushed me as I negotiated my way through the law school. It was a gorilla whose hairy bulk occupied the cover of the *National Geographic* magazine that had been placed anonymously in my mailbox. I stopped dead in my tracks. My heart raced and sank in one simultaneous beat. I harbored no doubts about the loud, unambiguous message conveyed: "Claim no membership to the human race. You are not even a sub-species. You are of a different species altogether. A brute. Animal, not human." It was a time-worn message communicated to persons who are not white. Similarly degrading messages have been sent to those who are not male. How ironic that it would be delivered to me at a time when I most needed all the complexities of my humanity embraced.

I reached for the magazine, picked it up, removed my other mail and replaced the magazine in my mailbox. Those flaming eyes separated by those flaring nostrils steadily gazed at me. I was overtaken by a wave of empathy. How did such a gentle, now-endangered creature become a signifier for crass, cruel messages? My empathy lasted a fleeting moment. I wiped the hand that had touched the magazine on my clothing; at least, I thought, I should not be defiled physically. For the remainder of the day, I sought refuge behind the closed door of my office.

For several days the gorilla peered out at me, watching my comings and goings from the vantage point of my mailbox, which I purposely avoided. Finally, my secretary, upon returning to the office after an extended absence, quietly disposed of the magazine. Her actions indicated to me that she too understood its message. Unaware that I had been in and out of the law school building during her absence, she assumed her interception of the message had been successful and said nothing to me about the magazine. She comforted me in a way that was calculated not to alert me to the offense, and for her tact I am grateful.

I was hurt and enraged by the gorilla message. But my token status as the first blackwoman law professor at the University counseled against any public expression of my pain and anger. I am to look on the bright side and accept the gorilla message as one more opportunity for character building and fortification (that never-ending task). Only through silent introspection am I to affirm my worth and self-esteem.

Given the demands of a professional career as a teacher and a legal scholar, it is almost inevitable that the law school becomes an important venue for the pursuit of meaningful associations that are both ego-nurturing and identity-affirming. It has never been my understanding, however, that a healthy self-esteem could flourish in environments punctuated by acts of hostility, including those of an anonymous nature.

In fairness, I must acknowledge the one-time appearance of the gorilla messenger. But even in the absence of other similarly crude emissaries, the reality is that blackwomen can only expect to have dysfunctional relationships in the legal academy.

The presence of the blackwoman faculty member is a daily reminder that the law school as an institution has been adjudicated a practitioner of racial and gender discrimination, an immoral act of rank order. Her presence symbolizes the institution's contrition. Her presence also evokes an ugly history of subordination from which white males (and females), directly and indirectly, purposely and fortuitously, benefited. Presented daily with such a burdensome history, many colleagues of the blackwoman faculty member are awash in guilt and shame. The need for self-preservation causes some to resort to discrete, unwitnessed acts of animosity. Others, obviously conflicted, inconsistently grant and deny her their friendship. Most consciously have to remind themselves that she is their equal. Otherwise, the tendency is to assume her inferiority, to believe that her appointment was unmerited, and was thus nothing more than a grant of their grace.

There are consequences flowing from a clemency appointment. In the parlance of the appointments process, the blackwoman is a "diversity candidate" to be contrasted against the "stellar candidate." It means that post-appointment she will be treated like an intellectual waif. She cannot legitimately claim any special competence or expertise in any subject or field. Her considered judgments regarding course coverage, teaching methodology, examination and grading can be challenged with impunity. Brave colleagues can query of her: "So, how does it feel not knowing whether you were appointed to our faculty because of affirmative action or because of your qualifications?"

Through it all, the blackwoman scholar must appear neither hypersensitive nor paranoid. Her white male (and female) colleagues will quickly note the occurrence of facially similar events involving themselves to discredit what she knows to be the truth. The blackwoman scholar must be mindful, too, that oftentimes the touted congeniality of the faculty in actuality amounts to little more than cold civility among colleagues. How then can she—a gorilla in their midst—expect more?

The Academy speaks of "diversity" because it worries about its ability to recognize the stellar candidate who appears in the guise of a blackwoman. The Academy's history justifies that worry, although some believe that any invocation of the incongruities in generations past (and present) is nothing more than a cheap claim to a so-called "victim status." Yet, life for the blackwoman ain't never been no set of crystal stairs. So, just as the Academy is about to slip into a habitual state of collective amnesia, the language of "diversity" awakens it (most times reluctantly) to face up to the haunting reality of blackness and femaleness and to its exclusionary practices premised on those attributes. The language of "diversity" forces the Academy to make an accounting of its racist and sexist proclivities.

The problem is that the language of "diversity" insufficiently moves the Academy beyond mere recognition that something regrettable occurred (or is occurring). Confronting past horrors is psychologically and fiscally exhausting; it leaves the Academy feeling that whatever happened, no matter how unfortunate, the egregious happening is nonetheless irremediable or politically uncorrectable. This false sense of helplessness produces a linguistic as well as a cognitive shift. Rather than speak of "diversity," the Academy talks about "merit" as if the two are bi-polar considerations. The discourse then maunders over whether the Academy can afford to sacrifice "merit" for the sake of "diversity."

As if to substantiate the Academy's misgivings about "diversity," out in the wilderness of the non-academic world roams a white male with all of his star qualities, but allegedly without his due. He is a caricature with whom many sympathize; he is accorded most favored person status. Deep in the wilderness of the Academy there is an exceptional blackwoman; however, her just deserts remain contested. She is constructed as a gorilla. Does anyone in the Academy care that she might be in harm's way?

44 Stealing Away: Black Women, Outlaw Culture and the Rhetoric of Rights

MONICA J. EVANS

Steal away, steal away, steal away to Jesus;
Steal away, steal away home,
I ain't got long to stay here.
My Lord calls me; He calls me by the thunder,
The trumpet sounds within-a my soul,
I ain't got long to stay here.

T H E African-American spiritual *Steal Away* is located within the tradition of escape songs, a series of codes embedded in music and sung by slaves to alert each other to the time for escape from bondage to freedom. Slaves sang these songs under the very noses of their captors, who were unable to hear in the music any force that might subvert their own authority.

Escape songs present a dialectic of power, deceit and identity. By appearing to live out the identity of beasts of burden, loyal and unintelligent, lowing to each other in soothing, unpolitical tones, slaves were able to carve out time and space for resistance and could formulate their escape plans in the very presence of their captors. The marginality of slaves made it possible for them to effect their escape from a destructive culture and to construct their own identities.[1]

Steal Away is especially powerful in its use of theft imagery as a means of redemption. The song calls upon slaves to "steal," that is, to break the law in order to reclaim themselves. By stealing away, slaves took it upon themselves to subvert, by means of deceit, theft and disruption, the oppressive institutions of the prevailing social order. Theft, disorder and deceit, images we are trained to accept as incompatible with the law, nevertheless provided slaves and their descendants with a positive alternative to oppression. One hundred thirty years after emancipation, "stealing away" continues to describe African-American culture and, by extension, all communities of color that construct cultural identities as outlaws in a radical and positive alternative to oppression and exclusion.

Consider, for a moment, black women as shapers and transmitters of a positive, outlaw culture, through which black women develop and formalize strategies for coping with the terrifying exclusion of blacks from the protection of mainstream law. Consider outlaw culture as a historical and continuing response of African-American communities to the dominant culture, with specific emphasis on the role of African-American women in shaping that response. Outlaw culture forms a basis for African-American women to present themselves to a dominant legal and social culture that currently represents African-American women, if at all, in overwhelmingly negative terms. Might we not reconceptualize outlaw culture in positive terms and offer that concept as an alternative to the prevailing representation of black women in law, society and popular culture?

My use of outlaw culture as a constructively subversive norm is quite different from the concept of outlaw culture usually (and stereotypically)[2] represented in popular media, traditional legal systems, and even race discourse.[3] "Outlaw" means outside the purview of mainstream law, that is, outside of the law's regard and protection. This state of being on the outside is both a matter of fact—imposed by dominant legal discourse that silences, marginalizes and constructs black life as dangerous and deviant—and a matter of choice, in the sense that black communities often place themselves in deliberate opposition to mainstream cultural and legal norms when those norms ill serve such communities. "Outlaw culture" refers to a network of shared institutions, values and practices through which subordinated groups "elaborate an autonomous, oppositional consciousness."[4]

Outlaw culture is in constant motion, taking on different nuances in different contexts. Like the African-American community as a whole, outlaw culture is always in the process of making and re-making itself. Outlaw culture refers to the process by which African-Americans shift within and away from identities in response to mainstream legal systems and dominant culture. It describes a conscious and subconscious series of cultural practices constituting life at the margins. Marginality is thus a strategy for carving out spaces in which to maneuver and resist.

Outlaw culture is born of, but is not limited by, exclusion from mainstream norms and protections. It derives its power from deception; it embodies practices and codes that have significance in African-American communities at odds with the appearance of these practices and codes in mainstream society. The deception has multiple locations across a broad spectrum. In some instances, deception takes the form of aggression or even defiance. In other instances, deception locates itself in apparent *non*-aggression and in compliance with the law. The aggressive aspect of a young urban black man often masks a sense of vulnerability to physical abuse by police, or the knowledge that neither the police nor the legal system will provide aid when he is in need and will in many instance deploy violence against him.[5] On the other end of the spectrum, the extreme respectability of church ladies and clubwomen often provides protective coloring to mask a subversive political agenda. Critical race scholarship has been instrumental in revealing that law may act as an instrument of subordination as well as one of empowerment. In the sense of empowerment, outlaw culture involves defining and redefining one's relationship to law, acting insubordinate when necessary, and manifesting scrupulous adherence to law and order when useful.

Outlaw culture is not limited to young urban black males or relentlessly proper black church- and clubwomen. Rather, it cuts across temporal, political and class lines, providing a means for African-American communities to become themselves by constantly positioning themselves as "Other" and by subverting prevailing norms that are destructive to African-American communities. Outlaw culture is the means by which we engage in critique. Outlaw culture, rather than obstructing black empowerment, both interrogates mainstream culture and affirms African-American culture.

African-American Women and Outlaw Culture

The history of black stability and empowerment is inextricably linked with subversion, and black women have been an important source of subversive outlaw activity. The term "contraband" provides a striking example. In mainstream discourse, that word refers to illegal drugs, and often is associated with black urban culture. But "contrabands" have an antecedent reference to slaves who took it upon themselves—often with the aid of that most prominent of outlaw women, Harriet Tubman—to disrupt existing legal norms of property, and to explode the boundaries of a destructive culture.

The Montgomery bus boycott derived its impetus from Rosa Parks' subversion of a legally sanctioned apartheid system. And Carol Moseley Braun recently became the first African-American woman elected to the United States Senate in part because of her persistent critique of the Senate Judiciary Committee's outrageous mistreatment of Professor Anita Hill. Moseley Braun's very presence in the Senate is a disruption of implicit traditions embedded in the definition of a senator.

Harriet Tubman engaged in stealing away to freedom and self-definition. Such an assertion seems odd because it concedes, albeit in a very limited way, that what is being stolen is the self. Does this suggest that Harriet Tubman was in fact chattel—since chattel, and not fully realized selves, are the proper objects of theft? Clearly not. Rather, she used the concept of stealing away as a means of reclaiming herself, her family and the Underground Railroad passengers in her care. By stealing away, she denied the very commodification of her self that the institution of slavery sought to impose, and that the term stealing implies. In converting the notion of stealing for her own benefit, Harriet Tubman subverted the legal structure that demanded adherence from her. She was an outlaw in the truest sense.

The idea of Harriet Tubman as an outlaw, one standing outside of law as an act of resistance and self-definition, raises complex issues concerning the definitions of criminality and femininity by which black women are bound and that black women internalize. The concept of an outlaw woman is itself contradictory. In traditional notions of outlawry, an outlaw is a masculine metaphor. The qualities associated with outlaws—defiance, independence and rebelliousness—are closely associated with masculine concepts, invoking images of Jesse James, Butch Cassidy, Robin Hood and Rambo.

Sandra Rosado is another woman of color standing in opposition to law as a means of definition and redemption. Ms. Rosado's story is an intersectional examination of race, womanhood and lawbreaking. She stands outside the boundaries of law while calling into question the legitimacy of mainstream legal discourses in which the core experiences and aspirations of women of color are unable to find expression.

Sandra Rosado is a twenty-year-old Afro-Latina woman who lives with her brother Angel and her mother, Cecilia Mercado, in New Haven, Connecticut. Mrs. Mercado receives payments under the Aid to Families with Dependent Children (AFDC) program, more commonly referred to as "welfare." Ms. Rosado worked part-time in a community center, and, prior to government sanctions, she set aside her wages in a savings account earmarked for college. Unfortunately, Ms. Rosado's accumulation of approximately $4,900 for college exceeded the asset limits imposed by state welfare eligibility rules. As a result, state officials required Ms. Rosado to spend down her savings account balance in order to preserve her mother's eligibility for future welfare payments. Instead of spending the money on college tuition, Rosado was forced[6] to spend the money on clothes and perfume. Additionally, federal officials demanded that Mrs. Mercado return the approximately $9,300 she received in welfare payments while Ms. Rosado's money was in the bank. In May 1992, the Connecticut Supreme Court ruled against Mrs. Mercado's appeal of the repayment order.[7] Officials close to the case indicate that a waiver of the repayment order is unlikely.

Sandra Rosado's story is one example of what Patricia Hill Collins calls a "controlling image."[8] In shifting the national conversation away from the underlying skewed priorities that legitimize unfair power arrangements and perpetuate the underclass, welfare cheat rhetoric avoids examining the possibility that social ills implicate a flaw in the predatory individualism of the capitalist marketplace. In welfare queen rhetoric, it is lower-class, loose dark women who bring low the American dream. Feminist and race-critical scholarship posits law as a series of stories particularly reflecting the experiences of the narrator and selectively taking from history and culture in order to shape the narrative. The process of legal narrative is an epistemological enterprise of transforming local narrative into universal, neutral fact. The power of legal narrative to disregard or render insignificant the stories of those traditionally outside the law has been well, although far from exhaustively, explored.

In one sense, the decision at state and federal levels to pursue the Rosado matter as a case of welfare cheating was animated by an official incapacity to move beyond the perspective of controlling imagery. Sandra Rosado, coming within the purview and regard of law only to be condemned as a flouter of law, is clearly not within the category of persons whose stories reflect reality or fact. She is within a category of persons—women, people of color, young people—who are outsiders and whose stories lack the power to create fact. It is not what Sandra Rosado has done, but what she is, that makes her an outlaw.

In a larger sense, Sandra Rosado's story raises questions of representation and agency. What it means to be a young, unmarried and unpropertied woman of color is in great measure a function of the prevailing imagery and representations of young, working-class black women. This prevailing imagery tells us that Sandra Rosado *must* be a cheat. It also tells us that she is not an agent; she is not in the category of persons that the prevailing imagery recognizes as having access to capital, knowledge or the power of self-governance that derives from both of these resources. The dominant imagery of self-empowered capital-acquirers has nothing to do with Sandra Rosado. The image of the man who bucks the odds and pulls himself up by his bootstraps is just that—(1) an image (2) of a man.[9]

Sandra Rosado explodes the categories designated to her by the master narrative. She is a young woman who "stole away" from state-created dependency and from legal rules that could only hurt her. Saving money for college in violation of welfare rules and in violation of the rules preventing access to knowledge is the "insubordination" of an outlaw, kicking against the legal system that perpetuates her subordination.

CLUBWOMEN AS OUTLAWS

Unlike Harriet Tubman and Sandra Rosado, who quite literally broke the law, the clubwomen's outlawry stands in stark contrast to their very law-abiding natures. They would, presumably, wince at the idea of being outlaws. The clubwomen were part of the national black women's activist movement of the late nineteenth and early twentieth centuries.[10] The black women's clubs initially organized around issues of abolition, then around post-slavery relief programs providing basic food, clothing and shelter for emancipated and escaped slaves. The clubwomen later focused on education and social welfare programs.[11] Meetings were given to fund-raising, political writing[12] and discussion. State and regional clubs were united at the national level under the banner The National Association of Colored Women. The clubs shared strategies for black women's suffrage, racial parity and promulgation of moral and religious values. They united under the motto "Lifting As We Climb," which stood for clubwomen's focus on collective action and responsibility.[13] It was not enough for clubwomen individually to succeed; clubwomen shared a sense that they were representatives of their race and their gender so that their goals were unfulfilled to the extent that any member of their community was left behind.

In addition to political associations, African-American women formed literary clubs, sewing circles, "colored" YMCAs, and altar guilds. While there were some distinctions among the associations in terms of focus, they shared a common focus of "benevolent societies," organized around principles of social and religious uplift. The clubwomen were deeply religious and very proper. My mother (who was a child at the time) remembers that when the Twilight Social and Civic Improvement Club of West Baden, Indiana, met at Little Mother's house, the women always prefaced meetings with a prayer from St. Paul's epistle to the Philippians. Clubwomen "worked diligently throughout the years to battle racism, poverty and discrimination. The clubs provided a protective environment which encouraged the black women . . . to meet and seek solutions to the social problems of the black community."[14]

Clubwomen founded schools, orphanages, old age homes and other social institutions for black children and for the aged in an era in which public commitment and funding for black institutions were virtually non-existent. They carved out cultural institutions outside the purview of mainstream law, thereby providing an educational and social welfare structure where the law refused to do so and establishing an infrastructure that furthered the goals of race and gender equality.

While Harriet Tubman and Sandra Rosado disregarded certain laws that objectified and controlled them, clubwomen believed in adherence to the law and social order. Nonetheless, in several important aspects they were not bound by the dichotomies that governed mainstream social order. For instance, the division between public and private spheres did not hold meaning for clubwomen in certain contexts.[15] A clubwoman could not bring about public civic improvement if she was lacking in private morality, or if her home did not reflect the values she sought to bring to public spaces. For clubwomen, good mothering, education, religious devotion and family life all constituted political activity.

EDUCATED CLASS

An outlaw culture desperately needs an educated class of people for its survival. First, knowledge of the dominant law is important for strategy: one must know when to adhere to law and when to resist or oppose it. Having a body of educated participants provides the basic unit of citizenship in the larger culture. In the decades following *Brown v. Board of Education*, it has become apparent that the relationship between education and upward mobility for African-Americans remains contested. However, it is indisputable that without access to mainstream education African-Americans are unable even to maintain the status quo. Education gives outlaw culture the language with which to speak to and translate for the larger culture. The educated class acquires knowledge of the law through its liaisons to the larger culture and transmits this knowledge through a network of schools, churches and clubs that form the infrastructure of the African-American community.

Finally, it is not coincidence that clubwomen provided an educational structure and a knowledge of the law. Historically, black men have not been trusted by mainstream culture to be educated because education is a means of empowerment. Accordingly, empowered black males, already perceived as a physically and sexually aggressive force, pose an unacceptable threat to dominant norms of racial purity and intellectual superiority. Black women must fill the void, therefore, by absorbing and passing on vital information about mainstream law in an era in which looking at a white woman the wrong way or failing to observe de jure and de facto segregation laws could cost a black man his life or subject a black woman to rape and degradation.

UNDERGROUND RAILROAD

Outlawry also demands an ongoing underground railroad. An outlaw is someone whom the law declares may be trespassed against at will. Therefore, an outlaw needs a network of people who will provide help and harbor to the most vulnerable members of the culture.

Life without help or harbor for the outlaw may be inevitable in the dominant culture. However, such a condition is unlikely to flourish within the "safe spaces" in the African-American community where outlaws are invisible to the dominant gaze. Patricia Hill Collins identifies several locations of "relatively safe discourse"[16] where blacks speak freely "in order to articulate a self-defined standpoint."[17] She names black women's relationships with one another, both in informal friendships and in black women's organizations, as one such focal point for the nurturing of black women's consciousness.

Other focal points of African-American consciousness are located within the infrastructure that clubwomen provided. Churches, schools, orphanages, social outings and club meetings all provided what Professor Collins calls safe spaces. They are what I think of as safe houses on the underground railroad, places of harbor for fugitives from the dominant culture or lines behind which contrabands seek and find safety. In transforming the concept of the political, clubwomen converted their schools and "homeplaces" into spheres in which they could resist hegemonic representations of black women. In this sense the homeplace formed a situs of radical political activity.

Patricia Hill Collins' and bell hooks' references to "safe spaces" and "homeplaces" as sites wherein to resist cultural hegemony raise the issue of particular members of the culture who are vulnerable to dominant oppression. When I think of cultural hegemony and imperialism, I think of home and schools—the places children inhabit—as the most important sites of resistance. The most pernicious act of imperialism does not consist of the occupation of territory or the exploitation of resources. Rather, it is the co-opting of the representation of the indigenous self. This co-opting is most effectively done by engaging children as accomplices. I think of the Hitler Youth, whose loyalty and trust were co-opted and converted from their parents and family to the Nazi party. I think of the constant attacks on bilingual education and the message transmitted to children whose native language and culture are devalued and suppressed. I think of the generations of black children calling their "smart" classmates "Oreos"—children who learn early that white defines smartness—and who, through the pervasive negative imagery of black life, continue to scrub their skin raw in the hope that the blackness will wash off. I think of all the children of color who are subtly and not-so-subtly encouraged to repudiate the cultural legacies of their mothers and fathers.

Home and school were two sites of intense club activity. Providing places to revel in their culture, to resist negative representations of their culture, and to support each other in locating and defining the self within their culture was a transformative political act of the clubwomen. Thus, the clubwomen provided help, harbor and access to knowledge of the law. In so doing, they developed deliberate strategies for coping with their outsider status, transforming banditry into a culture of positive response to exclusion.

The elitism and class distinctions that informed much of the clubwomen's values have been widely criticized for replicating the very systems of oppression against which the clubwomen fought. What has been largely obscured is the extent to which the clubwomen's Victorian aspirations also contained a subversive political dimension—what Professor Higginbotham refers to as a "politics of respectability." The clubwomen's respectability was conservative, yet it expressed an outlaw sensibility at several levels.

The radical nature of the clubwomen's respectability must be viewed in light of the historical context of the clubs. Unlike those of their white counterparts, black women's clubs were formed with an emphasis on challenging representations of African-Americans as uneducated and morally unworthy of full participation as citizens in American society.

A response to societal views of black women as loose, immoral and sexually available provided much of the impetus behind clubwomen's respectability, which, in turn, led them to embrace a Victorian sexuality. This aggressive respectability of clubwomen was part of a method to define black women in opposition to negative representations of black female sexuality. Clubwomen, especially those of the middle class, challenged the prevailing stereotype by presenting themselves as largely de-sexualized, well-educated and hyper-respectable Victorian ladies.

Furthermore, respectability involved the political act of reclaiming the integrity of black men as well as black women. Typical excuses for the assertion that blacks were not entitled to full participation in American life were their illiteracy, lack of education and incapacity for moral behavior. Clubwomen exposed the racism behind such supposedly race-neutral objections by focusing their efforts on eradicating illiteracy and by taking on a system of moral values. Both efforts would create a critical mass of educated and hyper-moral blacks. If whites still rejected blacks' participation in society, it would have to be for some reason other than the supposedly race-neutral excuses offered. Clubwomen's respectability was thus a strategy for exposing the duplicity of a racist society by forcing white racism into the open. It provided a moral imperative that was the impetus and justification for further civil rights work. "Never give them a reason" is a maxim that resounded in my own upbringing and that underlay much of the clubwomen's politics of respectability.

Respectability and aspiration to Victorian values also provided a means of denying white patriarchy its presumptive access to black women's bodies. Little Mother told her great-grandson that one impetus for the establishment of the clubs was "to teach young Negro women that they do not have to submit to white men's advances . . . and to guide young Negro women into fruitful adulthood by establishing a value system which recognizes and protects their integrity."[18] The respectability and Victorian value system were components of a strategy for coping with exclusion from agency regarding one's body.

Even today, in stark contrast to the popular understanding of African-American culture(s), there is a deep Victorian and conservative streak that runs through many black communities.[19] My own upbringing—in terms of compulsory church attendance, parental discipline and teachings on sexuality—was far more strict than that of most of my white friends and colleagues. There are no conservatives like black conservatives.[20]

There was a sense of "beating them at their own game" that informed much of the respectability of the clubwomen and embodied a subversive element. Going farther than the white oppressors—acting more "ladylike," using crisper speech and disapproving of "low-class" behavior more than their white counterparts—was a means of appropriating and subverting the practices employed by white women. It was also a way of saying "we are better at following your rules than you are." A principal area in which clubwomen were committed to beating white women at their own game was the appropriation of values of "true" womanhood and motherhood in opposition to conventional wisdom that black women were suitable for neither.

The clubwomen's respectability thus reveals itself as subversive in its deployment of Victorian sensibilities as an aspect of the politics of self-identity. The clubwomen's privileging of respectable behavior and middle-class mores provided a locus for contesting the negative imagery of black women, and for reforming for themselves, for the dominant society, and for their race the institutions of womanhood, motherhood and sexuality as they are practiced by black women.

Implications for the Larger Culture:
Outlaw Culture and the Rhetoric of Rights

Looking to black women and outlaw culture would prove useful as a means of informing our understanding of rights and relationships. Rather than adopting an ethic of care and relationships to replace rights as an organizing principle of jurisprudence, I propose that scholars turn to those women and communities of women who embody an outlaw culture as a source of guidance for constructing lives at the margins of rights.

Outlaw culture involves the practice of shifting in and out of identities. Outlaw culture is an extraordinarily complex but/and intersection of life outside the purview of law that still holds law to its promises. As Martin Luther King pointed out, a promise broken is still a promise.[21] Like Dr. Martin Luther King, Jr., outlaw culture does not abandon the concept of rights: outlaws still have a claim upon the legal system to the extent that the system is centered on the discourse of rights. Women in outlaw culture have also built a rich life in the absence of rights. Therefore, outlaws are an appropriate and particularly helpful model of how to simultaneously hold on to rights and hold the nation to its promise of rights while using other, non-rights epistemologies for self-definition.

Clubwomen did not reject the notion of rights. As influential members of their communities asserting leadership positions in churches and schools, clubwomen fiercely asserted their right to control the educational and charitable services that they organized and oversaw. Black women were involved in the struggle for civil rights qua rights at every level. They thus can teach us alternative ways to think about rights. Stepping out of binary thinking can free us to imagine paradigms other than the rights/autonomy paradigm or the ethics of care/relationships paradigm. While clubwomen engaged in a struggle for rights, their concept of the self and the rights to which the self is entitled was not conflated with the idea of atomistic individualism. They did not define their mission in terms of a self-interested utility maximization as an autonomy-based rights discourse might. Rather, as their motto indicates, they lived out the relationship between rights and responsibilities by "lifting as we climb." For clubwomen, the struggle for rights was incoherent unless it simultaneously nurtured communal relationships that were predicated on a responsibility for uplifting the race. Engagement with rights, as part of the process of self-definition, was contextualized within home, family and community life. A truly defined self and a truly cultured person was one who had the ability to see his or her continuity with the larger community of family, church, school and race.

Clubwomen simultaneously occupied spheres of rights and relationships. This multidimensional existence—the "constant shifting of consciousness"—is described by critical scholars as multiple consciousness or, sometimes, intersectionality. This dualistic existence, far from being an incoherent contradiction, was a source of life and protective cover for the clubwomen as outlaws. Clubwomen who were outlaws, both as a normative matter and as a description of reality, were not either/or people. Their outlook is helpful in advancing a jurisprudence that moves beyond the polarities of rights versus relationships.

The ultimate irony of looking to outlaw culture is the paradox of looking to extra-legal communities as a source of jurisprudence. Outlaw communities show us how a rights discourse could function without consigning us to disconnected, atomistic autonomous spheres. They also teach us that constructing communities and rules on an ethic of care and interconnectedness need not entail a wholesale abandonment of rights.

There are at least two formidable (albeit self-engendered and therefore not insurmountable) obstacles to a jurisprudence informed by black women's outlaw culture. The first lies in the difficulty of moving out of the box, out of binary thinking. For a culture reared upon the tenet "You can't have it both ways" (I have always wondered why not), this is a daunting hurdle. The second is that the white male legal establishment must be able to place its sense of cultural and gender superiority aside and do that which white males find very difficult: learn how to learn from the (outlaw) cultural practices of African-American women.

Mainstream society is not accustomed to looking to the cultural practices of African-American women for any positive models. However, in a society where autonomous individualism and traditional rights discourse have not produced the goods promised, mainstream culture would do well to turn to the values that animate other communities. Perhaps the wily, audacious descendants of black club-women have something besides an outstretched palm to offer mainstream America.[22] Perhaps we can wonder, as does poet and critic Maya Angelou, "what if all the vitality and insouciance and love of life of black America were openly included in the national psyche?"[23]

The clubwomen, Harriet Tubman, Rosa Parks, Little Mother, Sandra Rosado, and all of the African-American women who in their own way resist the forces that would define, limit and misrepresent them are wily, audacious outlaws. With their constancy, African-American women have constructed a culture of opposition and a carefully honed wit to win.[24] We can teach you much.

NOTES

1. For a discussion of the relationship between power and identity, see generally Martha Minow, *Identities*, 3 YALE J. L. & HUMAN. 97 (1991); Lucie E. White, *Subordination, Rhetorical Survival Skills, and Sunday Shoes: Notes on the Hearing of Mrs. G.*, 38 BUFF. L. REV. 1, 45 (1990).

2. The stereotypical representation of black urban culture as an outlaw culture renders invisible the contributions of African-American women in shaping a cohesive society and in transmitting values of stability and empowerment within African-American communities. Representations of crack-ridden neighborhoods and welfare queens obscure the role of outlaw culture as an instrument of communal empowerment.

Outlaw culture has been and remains a tool for what bell hooks calls "decolonization" of black women's minds. *See* BELL HOOKS, YEARNING: RACE, GENDER AND CULTURAL POLITICS 41–49 (1991).

3. *Reconstruction*, a journal of opinion and commentary on African-American culture, recently published an article by Professor Mark Naison in which he notes the emergence of an "outlaw culture" among low-income black urban youth, a group that has "rejected African-American communal norms in favor of the predatory individualism of the capitalist marketplace." Mark Naison, *Outlaw Culture and Black Neighborhoods*, 1 RECONSTRUCTION 4, 128 (1992). *But see* Regina Austin, *"The Black Community," Its Lawbreakers, and a Politics of Identification*, 65 S. CAL. L. REV. 1769 (1992) (discussing, inter alia, the development of black women's gangs and the identity politics associated with urban outlaw communities). Even here, however, the discussion must avoid using men's gangs as the referent by which to evaluate the phenomenon of women's gangs. Conflating women's gangs with men's gangs obscures the differing functions served by women's lawbreaking activities.

4. White, *supra* note 1, at 48.

5. This sense of vulnerability has a firm foundation in American history. In 1987 the Supreme Court put us on notice that black life may be trespassed

against with lesser penalties than those imposed for trespass against white life. The Supreme Court has stated that the fact that murderers of whites are 4.3 times more likely to receive the death penalty than murderers of blacks is not sufficient to demonstrate that a death penalty sentence constituted arbitrary state action in violation of the Fourteenth Amendment or was cruel and unusual punishment contrary to the Eighth amendment. McCleskey v. Kemp, 481 U.S. 279 (1987).

6. AFDC restrictions on accumulation of assets also place limitations on the type of items on which Ms. Rosado's account could be spent down, militating against the acquisition of investment-type assets and in favor of non-durable, non-appreciating goods. Thus, Ms. Rosado's expenditures on clothes and perfume were not only reasonable within AFDC restrictions, but were for all practical purposes dictated by those restrictions.

7. *See* Mercado v. Commissioner of Income Maintenance, 607 A.2d 1142, 1146 (Conn. 1992).

8. *See* PATRICIA HILL COLLINS, BLACK FEMINIST THOUGHT: KNOWLEDGE, CONSCIOUSNESS, AND THE POLITICS OF EMPOWERMENT 67–90 (1991).

9. My first conscious realization of the power of cultural myths to drive my own imagination came as I was reading a United Negro College Fund advertisement in the New York City subway in the mid-1970s. The ad pictured a black woman wearing a white lab coat, peering into a microscope. The caption read, "Why do you assume that the scientist who finds a cure for cancer will be a man? Or white?" Even though I was already in high school, that was the first time it had occurred to me that someone other than a white man could be the one to find a cure for cancer. Prevailing representations of society's scientists, doctors and whiz-kids were at that time, and continue to be, almost universally white and male. Even those of us who are neither get seduced by the imagery.

10. *See, e.g.,* CYNTHIA NEVERDON-MORTON, AFRO-AMERICAN WOMEN OF THE SOUTH AND THE ADVANCEMENT OF THE RACE, 1885–1925 (1989); ANNE FIROR SCOTT, NATURAL ALLIES: WOMEN'S ASSOCIATIONS IN AMERICAN HISTORY (1991); Evelyn Brooks Higginbotham, *African-American Women's History and the Metalanguage of Race,* 17 SIGNS 251 (1992); Evelyn Brooks Higginbotham, *In Politics to Stay: Black Women Leaders and Party Politics in the 1920s, reprinted in* WOMEN, POLITICS AND CHANGE 199 (1990) [hereinafter Higginbotham, *In Politics to Stay*]; Anne Firor Scott, *Most Invisible of All: Black Women's Voluntary Associations,* 56 J. S. HIST. 3 (1990).

11. *See* SCOTT, NATURAL ALLIES, *supra* note 10, at 45–57.

12. My great-grandmother served as a ghostwriter of speeches for Herbert Hoover in his candidacy for President. This was not an unusual function of black clubwomen. While the black vote, especially in the wake of women's suffrage, was an important one for Republican candidates, then as now candidates for national office were reluctant to be seen as overly friendly to black interests. The use of black ghostwriters for political speeches was an important campaign strategy and provided avenues for overtly political activity for clubwomen who wrote on race and women's issues. For a discussion of black women's organizations in Republican party politics, see Higginbotham, *In Politics to Stay, supra* note 10, at 199–248.

13. *See, e.g., id.* at 205.

14. A Brief History of the Indiana State Federation of Colored Women's Clubs, Inc. 2 (1987).

15. For a discussion of black women's clubs and their repudiation of the public/private dichotomy, see generally Eileen Boris, *The Power of Motherhood: Black and White Activist Women Redefine the "Political"*, 2 Yale J. L. & Feminism 25 (1989).

16. Collins, *supra* note 8, at 95 (1991).

17. *Id.* at 96.

18. Conversation between Maxwell Sparks and Bessie Carter Jones, retold to me in New York (Feb. 5, 1991). Maxwell Sparks is my cousin and a great-grandson of Bessie Carter Jones.

19. This conservatism has both personal (for example, church and family values) and political elements (with respect to alliance with particular political parties). But feminism's admonition "the personal is political" operates here as well, and cautions that it is not a simple (or perhaps wise) matter of distinguishing between social (that is, personal) versus political conservatism in black communities. The 1992 presidential campaign debate over "family values" involved textured and interlocking systems of political as well as private conservatism. These interlocking systems act upon black communities and produce a black conservatism that is very difficult to categorize as either personal or political.

20. This appears to be a fairly well-kept secret: the true conservatives are often located in black communities. The emergence of black neo-conservatives such as Clarence Thomas and Shelby Steele has caused consternation and confusion among the traditional left. The confusion derives in part from longstanding assumptions that blacks who engaged in and benefited from the civil rights struggle would hold political views similar to white liberals. The confusion also derives from the cynical thoroughness with which the political right has linked liberal programs and the Democratic party with special favors for blacks.

Mari Matsuda asserts: "When you are on trial for conspiracy to overthrow the government for teaching the deconstruction of law, your lawyer will want black people on your jury [on the theory that black jurors are more likely to understand that people in power sometimes abuse law for their own ends]." Mari J. Matsuda, *Looking to the Bottom: Critical Legal Studies and Reparations*, 22 Harv. C.R.-C.L. L. Rev. 323, 323 (1987). I am not sure I would agree. It depends on the black juror. Not all black jurors recognize the hegemonic and subordinative dimensions of law; others, having internalized racist imagery, may be more willing than whites to render an adverse judgment in the scenario Professor Matsuda posits. There are some black people whom I would just as soon strike (from the jury, that is). If, as critical scholars assert, race is a coalition constantly in the process of being made and re-made, then Professor Matsuda's statement must be qualified in light of the different meanings that may attach to the term "black juror" at different times and in different circumstances.

21. Dr. Martin Luther King, Jr., I Have a Dream, Keynote Address of the March on Washington, D.C., for Civil Rights (August 28, 1963), *in* A Testament of Hope: The Essential Writings of Martin Luther King, Jr., 217 (James M. Washington ed., 1986).

22. Regina Austin, *Sapphire Bound!*, 1989 Wis. L. Rev. 539, 555.

23. Irvin Molotsky, *Poet of the South for the Inauguration*, N.Y. TIMES, Dec. 5, 1992, at A8.

24. As constructors of creative responses to exclusion, outlaws embody a poem by Edwin Markham that my mother often recited:

He drew a circle that shut me out—
Heretic, rebel, a thing to flout.
But Love and I had the wit to win:
We drew a circle that took him in!

EDWIN MARKHAM, *Outwitted, in* POEMS OF EDWIN MARKHAM 18 (Charles L. Wallis ed., Harper & Brothers 1950) (1913).

45 Rape, Ethnicity, and Culture: Spirit Injury from Bosnia to Black America

ADRIEN KATHERINE WING and SYLKE MERCHÁN

T H E recent armed conflict in the former Yugoslav republic of Bosnia-Herzegovina has brought the issue of systematic, wide-spread rapes of civilian women in times of war to the attention of the world community. Rape, which is pervasive in Bosnia, constitutes an injury not only to the individual victim but to the society as a whole. The combination of the physical and psychological effects of rape inflicts a "spirit injury" upon the victim. Patricia Williams defines spirit injury as the "disregard for others whose lives qualitatively depend on our regard."[1] It leads to the slow death of the psyche, of the soul, and of the identity of the individual. Spirit injury on a group level is the cumulative effect of individual spirit injuries, which leads to the devaluation and destruction of a way of life or of an entire culture. Spirit injury is "as devastating, as costly, and as psychically obliterating [to the victim] as robbery or assault; indeed they are often the same."[2] This chapter examines the situation of Bosnian Muslim spirit injury by developing a model that draws upon the experience of Black Americans during slavery and thereafter.

Rape manifests itself as a tool of the powerful over the subordinated.[3] A victim of rape may experience short-term and long-term physical and psychological effects which parallel those of post-traumatic stress disorder.[4] The physical manifestations of rape include personal injuries, pain, sleep anomalies, appetite disturbances, infection, and pregnancy. Short-term psychological effects of rape include anger, anxiety, depression, fear, and fixation on the rape. Long-term consequences for women may include mistrust, negative attitudes toward men, chronic depression, and fear of being left alone. Varying combinations of these physical and psychological effects might appear in different cultures. The consequences of rape are particularly severe in traditional, patriarchal societies, where the rape victim is often perceived as soiled and unmarriageable, thus becoming a target of societal ostracism.

Ethnicity and culture complicate the analysis of the crime of rape. How rape

25 COLUM. HUM. RTS. L. REV. 1 (1993). Originally published in the Columbia Human Rights Law Review. Reprinted by permission.

516

is viewed in any society is inextricably linked to the respective ethnic and cultural characteristics of both the perpetrator and the victim. Rape committed by someone of the same cultural or ethnic group may not be regarded in the same manner as if committed by someone from a different group. In America, for instance, the ultimate punishable rape has been the rape of a White woman by a Black man.[5]

The most dramatic occurrence of rape against those of different cultural, ethnic, and religious backgrounds takes place during war. Rapes on a mass scale were recorded during the battles of ancient Greece and the Crusades. Rapes were an issue during the United States Civil War and the Vietnam War. Yugoslavs complained of rapes committed by Josef Stalin's Red Army soldiers at the end of World War II. During the Nuremberg Trials, evidence indicated that Nazi Germany also used rape as a routine weapon of terror. The Japanese government has only recently acknowledged the kidnapping of 70,000 to 200,000 Korean, Chinese, and Filipino women during World War II for the purpose of sexual servitude as "comfort women." The rape of 200,000 to 400,000 Bengali women took place during the time period of Bangladesh's declaration of independence from West Pakistan in 1971, resulting in an estimated 25,000 pregnancies. Rape is thus another powerful tool in the arsenal of weapons used by one warring nation to conquer another nation.

If the long-term spirit injuries associated with mass rape are not confronted in the current Bosnian Muslim context, that society will suffer the same prognosis as the Black American culture—falling prey to a chronic festering spirit injury that has yet to be treated by American society. This spirit injury has been a contributing factor to the ravaging of Black American culture, more than one hundred years after the end of de jure slavery. Thus, even if the Bosnian conflict were resolved quickly, the disease of spirit injury, resulting from the systematic rapes of Bosnian Muslim women, may only appear to be in remission. In reality, the disease may be silently metastasizing like a cancer—waiting for an immunologically compromised moment to reappear. A resulting relapse may be terminal.

The Bosnian Conflict

The current crisis in the former Yugoslavia began in 1990 when the Yugoslav republics of Slovenia and Croatia voted to change their mode of governance from communist to non-communist. The Yugoslav republics of Macedonia and Bosnia-Herzegovina followed suit in November 1990 by ejecting their communist leaders from power. In June 1991, Slovenia and Croatia declared independence and received diplomatic recognition from the United States, the members of the European Community and other countries. In contrast to the other Yugoslav republics, voters in Serbia and Montenegro elected to maintain their communist government under their leader Slobodan Miloševic. In the summer of 1991, rumors spread that Croatia and Serbia had been negotiating about dividing Bosnia-Herzegovina up between them.

Bosnia-Herzegovina does not contain one predominant ethnic or religious group. Of the pre-war population of 4.4 million inhabitants, approximately eighteen percent are Croats who are Roman Catholic, approximately thirty-one percent are Serbs who are Orthodox Christian, and approximately forty-four percent are Muslim. In late February 1992, the Croat and Muslim populations of Bosnia-Herzegovina voted in favor of independence. Bosnia's Serbian politicians had previously held a referendum in November 1991 in which the Serbs declared their desire to remain as part of Yugoslavia, that is, as part of a Serb-controlled country. Despite intermittent peace negotiations, fighting broke out and escalated in Bosnia-Herzegovina between Bosnian Muslims and Bosnian Serb militia. The Serbs have successfully seized almost all of the territory of Bosnia and effectively held Bosnia's capital of Sarajevo under siege for many months.

During this period, an alarming number of rapes were committed by the armed troops against the female civilian population. Although the rapes were perpetrated by and against all sides, the majority were inflicted by Serbian forces against Bosnian Muslim women—as many as 60,000, resulting in 25,000 pregnancies. These assaults have been part of a campaign of ethnic cleansing, the goal of which is to forcibly and permanently relocate the bulk of the Muslim population by any means necessary, including rape, murder, and terrorism. The Serbian policy of ethnic cleansing is, in effect, a euphemism for a policy designed to consolidate the acquisition of territory by aggression and conquest. Thus, by terrorizing the Bosnian Muslim civilian population, the Serbs have been, in essence, fighting a war of attrition—the greater the number of Muslims who can be convinced to leave their homes "voluntarily," the easier it is for the Serbs to acquire and expand their territory into Bosnia-Herzegovina. [*Ed.* The author reviews international human rights provisions related to the punishment of rape, then continues as follows.]

RAPE AS A SPIRIT INJURY IN MUSLIM CULTURE

Beyond the international legal questions looms the issue of the long-term spiritual impact of the Serbian actions on the Bosnian Muslim population. If the systematic rapes of the female Muslim population by Serbs go unpunished, the long-term consequences of the Serbs' actions will constitute much more than mere criminal rape and the creation of hundreds or thousands of "mixed" children. If the war ends merely in a negotiated peace settlement without addressing the long-term spirit injury issues of the Bosnian conflict, the current actions of the Serbs will result in irreparable harm to the entire Bosnian Muslim population. "We need to see it [spirit injury] as a cultural cancer; we need to open our eyes to see the spiritual genocide it is wreaking."[6] By acknowledging spirit injury as a crime, this profound problem will be addressed at "the conceptual, if not the punitive level of a capital moral offense."[7]

In order fully to comprehend the long-term ramifications of the Serbs' systematic wide-spread rape of Bosnian Muslim women, it is necessary to understand the gender roles in Islamic society. In Muslim culture, religion and custom are intertwined. For many Muslims the honor of the family is of paramount concern and the chastity and purity of women is central to that honor. If female chastity and purity are not maintained, great dishonor falls upon the entire family. Traditionally, a woman who cannot prove her virginity on her wedding night could potentially be subject to annulment of her marriage, her impurity affecting her entire family's honor. Once married, a wife is judged in her new family primarily by her ability to bear sons, preferably within one year after the wedding. Since the father's line is continued through the birth of sons, a wife who does not bear sons may find herself divorced or replaced by another wife.[8] In contrast, Islamic religion and Muslim culture do not impose any limits on male sexuality, which is viewed as uncontrollable.

Historically, the *sharia*, the Islamic law found in the Koran and other sources, has governed the daily lives of Muslims.[9] Since the *sharia* forbids intermarriage by Muslim women, in many Muslim societies such intermarriage between Muslim women and non-Muslim men is prohibited by Islamic law. In Bosnia, however, there appears to have been a somewhat more liberal attitude in the Muslim community toward this type of intermarriage. Yet it must be noted that these intermarriages are voluntary unions of men and women from different ethnic backgrounds. It should come as no surprise that under these deeply held Islamic religious and cultural precepts the Serb-instigated, systematic rape of Muslim women constitutes not merely a physical injury but a spiritual injury on the very culture of the Bosnian Muslims. The removal of purity, chastity, and virginity from the unmarried rape victims literally makes them unmarriageable, and brings shame and disgrace to the entire family group. The violation perpetrated upon married women makes it impossible for many of them to stay in their marriages. Because of the great emphasis on honor in Muslim culture, the rape of a Muslim woman is a complete affront to her honor, and it is nearly impossible for Muslim culture to reconcile the rape with the concept of honor. Thus, the shame keeps many women from coming forward, forcing them to live with untreated spiritual damage. The spiritual injury is of course exponentially worse when the victim conceives a child as a result of the rape. For nine months, the Muslim woman knows she is carrying a child that is not only the product of rape but is also a non-Muslim child.

The systematic rape of Muslim women in Bosnia could potentially result in the complete destruction of the Muslim social fabric. Because of the centrality of the concept of honor, the rape of one female member of a family can bring shame and disgrace to not only her immediate family, but also the entire extended family. Thus, that family will not command the same position of respect in the community. This change in one family's social position will then affect the social ordering of that community, as another family may step into the vacuum left by the family of the rape victim. As a consequence, the systematic violation of Muslim women will destabilize the social ordering in Bosnia to the extent that the population will be fragmented and diminished, allowing for easy manipulation of the remaining inhabitants. This phenomenon of destabilizing and destroying the social order of an entire population group constitutes group spirit injury. A substantial part of the definition of the self is dependent upon how the self is perceived and judged by external society. Thus, if the surrounding society has a low opinion of a particular person, that particular person is also very likely to develop a low opinion of him- or herself. Thus, with the cumulative effect of the individual and group shame, disgrace and loss of dignity, the entire culture will become devalued and fragmented. It is very likely that the social fabric that holds the society together and gives it guidance and strength will break down, especially when faced with the long-term prospects of either rebuilding a new Bosnia in some enclave or remaining perpetual refugees. Because the cumulative effect of this spirit injury is so pervasive, it will take the Muslim population generations to recover from this ordeal, if they ever recover at all.

Fate of Black America and Bosnia

The experience of Black America during and after slavery creates a model for assessing the potential gravity of spirit injury to the Bosnian Muslims. The impact that the rapes and resulting forced miscegenation have had on Black American culture provides the basis for evaluation of the similar symptoms exhibited in the Bosnian context. The breakdown in the social fabric of the Black American population has taken place partially as a result of the untreated spirit injury resulting from these assaults. This spirit injury has metastasized in the Black American culture generations after the abolition of slavery. The systematic rape of the Bosnian Muslim women may similarly disrupt and alter the social ordering of that entire population for generations, if it is not treated.

HISTORY OF SLAVERY AND MISCEGENATION

The majority of rapes has always been committed by people of one ethnic/racial group against women of that same group. Yet in the United States, the history of rape has focused principally on the rape of one group, White females, by men from a different ethno-racial group, namely Blacks.[10] This history is invidious and exemplified by the societal reaction to the widely publicized Central Park jogger case. In that incident, a White investment banker was brutally attacked and gang-raped in New York's Central Park by a group of Black American and Hispanic youths. A few days later, a Black American woman was brutally raped, stripped and her dead body left in Fort Tyron Park, Upper Manhattan. This equally disturbing and violent attack was barely mentioned by the media, being reported merely as "[a]nother woman raped and strangled to death."[11] The treatment of Black rape victims by the media as somehow less worthy of outrage and sympathy can be traced to its roots in the American history of slavery. Rape was a critical weapon of slavery.[12] The law expressly provided in many jurisdictions for the death or castration of a Black man who raped a White woman.[13] The rape of a Black woman by a White man, however, was not treated as a crime,[14] since one could not legally rape one's property. The offspring of these interracial unions became slaves for the most part, expanding the master's property. The rape of a slave by another slave was not even contemplated by the law. The rape of Black women during slavery was thus an "institutional crime, part and parcel of the white man's subjugation of a people for economic and psychological gain."[15]

In the post-slavery period, the rape statutes became race neutral on their face; however, the reality remained the same. The only convictions obtained were in circumstances in which a White woman alleged that a Black man had raped her.[16] Allegations of rape involving Black men and White women often ended in the lynching and castration of the alleged Black rapist.[17] While lynchings were used as a sword of retribution against accused Black rapists, the assaults on Black women remained unavenged. Black women, and particularly those who worked as domestics and sharecroppers, found themselves unprotected by the law from their White male employers. Their Black fathers, brothers and husbands could do very little if anything to prevent such attacks or avenge them.

Much like the Bosnian Muslims, these rapes not only resulted in a physical violation of the rape victims but also inflicted an individual spirit injury on those victims. As the property, first, of her slave master, and second, of the Black man, the Black woman had no way to control her own sexuality. As a result, she suffered from diminishing self-esteem and an increasing loss of dignity, creating the spirit injury. On a group level women, men and children were all affected by the rapes: the women have experienced humiliation and loss of dignity caused by the rapists; the men in that they could do nothing to prevent these assaults on "their" women; and by the children born from these attacks in that they were the visible products of sexual assault and a constant reminder of the violations to the rest of the community. This sense of loss of control over their own circumstances creates a group spirit injury in that an entire population perceives itself as somehow having a lesser status than the rest of the society.

Symptoms of Spirit Injury: Black America and Bosnia

While the history of rape and miscegenation in Black America is distinct from the current situation affecting Bosnia in many respects, there are several comparable symptoms of spirit injury.

RAPE AS DEFILEMENT

In both Black America and Bosnia, one symptom of spirit injury has manifested itself as a sense of defilement. "A fundamental part of ourselves and of our dignity is dependent upon the uncontrollable, powerful, external observers who constitute society."[18] If society places a low value on certain of its members, they in turn will perceive themselves as having a lesser worth in that society. Thus, if a rape victim is viewed by her society as soiled by the rape, she will likely suffer a great loss of dignity, which will contribute to her spirit injury.

In Black America, the raped women often felt debased as individuals; this debasement manifested itself in how they related toward Black men, White men, their families, and their cultural group. They knew they were raped not only as individual women but also as members of a subordinated group of Black slaves whose men could not protect them. A modern version of this symptom of spirit injury could be seen as partially manifesting itself today in Black American society as evidenced by the breakdown of the traditional family structure. The ongoing sense of defilement within the culture may be one of many contributing factors to the deterioration in family structure.[19]

In the Bosnian case, many women may exhibit similar symptoms of defilement. As discussed above, honor is a central concept in Muslim culture. The rape of a woman results in the total loss of honor to that woman and her family. In her culture the woman is now regarded as defiled and no longer attractive as a prospective spouse and mother. Thus, it will be difficult for many of the Bosnian rape victims to find Muslim men willing to marry them. Similarly, already married rape victims may find it difficult to remain in their marriages. Based on the Black American experience, it can be postulated that in the Bosnian case this spirit injury will extend into the future, affecting the Bosnian Muslim women's ability to relate to Serbian and Bosnian Muslim men, their families, and their cultural group. Many of these women will remain single and possibly be ostracized by their own families. These women will have to find employment to support themselves because they can no longer rely on support from the extended family structure. Married women might not be able to resume their marriages after the war, becoming single women in need of jobs. If these women can be integrated into a post-war economy, they are likely to enter the work force at low paying positions with little prospect of advancement. Many will not possess the necessary skills to earn money sufficient for survival. In order to support themselves, these women may turn to prostitution, thus becoming further dishonored and defiled. The most likely result will be a lower standard of living for them than they had prior to the war. Thus, these women will not only receive physical injury from the rapes but also an economic injury, further contributing to the severity of their spirit injury.

RAPE AS SILENCE

Many Bosnian and Black women have internalized the spirit injuries that have resulted from their sense of defilement, by suffering in silence. This silence may convey a false sense of good health. In actuality, there is a chronic, festering wound which needs treatment. Due to a sense of shame, Black women in slavery who had been raped by White men often did not tell anyone about the crime. In addition, their silence enhanced the possibilities of day to day survival for their male relatives, who could be killed or lynched if they stood up to White men. The silence of a Black woman also decreased the possibility of rejection from any Black men who might feel the woman had been defiled. Silence, moreover, avoided contributing to the Black men's ongoing sense of emasculation by White society. In a world where White men had the ultimate control over Black lives, silence concerning interracial rape provided a comfort zone in which some Black men could at least feel they had some control—over Black female sexuality.

In Bosnia, many women will not admit their own rape to avoid rejection from their spouses, family, and culture. If the Bosnian war is ended through a peace settlement, one can extrapolate that, to avoid stigmatization, many women will pretend that they were not raped. They will hide the truth in an attempt to retain some modicum of dignity within their ruptured lives. This silence internalizes the untreated spirit injury, but does not cure it. Ultimately, ignoring the symptoms allows the illness to worsen, perhaps leading to metastasis and a terminal condition.

RAPE AS EMASCULATION

Both Black American and Bosnian Muslim cultures view the rape of women as a sign of the emasculation of men. Psychologically, this complete domination of the woman's body can create a sense of emasculation in many men. The rapes constitute a spirit injury because they show that Bosnian Muslim men cannot protect the Bosnian Muslim women, just as Black American men could not protect Black American women from victimization by their White slave masters.

The systematic rape of Black women during and after slavery has had a very profound impact on Black American culture as a whole, because the slightest actions could bring the most severe consequences. The Black man could be accused of raping or attempting to rape a White woman without a sexual assault actually having to occur.[20] The consequences of being accused of raping a White woman were extremely severe, such as castration and lynching. The Black woman could be raped merely because of the color of her skin and her status as the property of the slave master as well as of the Black man.

One result of the emasculation spirit injury in Black American culture is that Black American women, who have had to be physically and spiritually strong to survive, are seen as emasculating matriarchs and loud mouth "sapphires."[21] Because of their strength, they are often viewed as the cause rather than the victims of the Black American family's problems.

Similarly in the Bosnian case, the slightest action can lead to the most severe consequences. The Bosnian Muslim women are the targets of rape by Serbs solely on account of their ethnicity. Thus, there is nothing a Muslim woman can do in order to prevent the rape or take steps to control her own destiny, such as changing her behavior, since the rape is motivated primarily by ethnic hatred. The men also are powerless to prevent this assault on their women. They have to stand by helplessly and watch their wife, mother, or daughter be brutalized and raped in front of their eyes.

As in Black American culture, where the rapes have resulted in the emasculation of some Black American men, the emasculation of the Bosnian Muslim men through the rapes could also lead to the women in that culture having to be physically and emotionally strong to survive the ordeal and assume many of the functions within the family that were formerly performed by men. One might extrapolate that in the future many Muslim women will lead increasingly independent lives, due to their sense of defilement and rejection. Their status may be viewed as emasculating some Muslim men, making the women, in effect, Bosnian Sapphires.

RAPE AS TRESPASS

In both Black America and Bosnia, rape can be seen as trespass on the "property" rights of men. Traditionally, though this has changed somewhat in modern times, women were regarded as the property of either their fathers or their husbands. The rape of a woman thus constituted damage to the property of one man by another.

In slavery, White males held a legal property interest in Blacks as slaves. As property, Black women could be used for sexual pleasure and controlled by White men. Black men, also being property, had no control over their daughters and wives because their owners held legal title to them.[22] A de facto property interest in Black American women continued after slavery in which some White men felt free to rape Black American women with impunity. Black American men knew they could be lynched and castrated if they attempted to protect the women.[23]

Therefore, Black women, who were considered mere chattel, had no control over their own destiny, nor over their sexuality. Whether they were raped by a White or a Black man, the resulting children would add to the slave owner's pool of available slaves. Thus, in general, the White slave master did not consider the rape of a Black woman to be a crime. Although aware that the Black woman was the property of the White slave owner to be disposed of at the master's whim, the Black man also perceived himself as having a property interest in the Black woman. Thus, when the Black woman was raped by the White man, this violation constituted a trespass on the Black man's property. Yet, being a property interest of the White man himself, the Black man could do nothing to rectify or remedy this trespass.[24]

In Bosnia, the rapes may also be seen as a de facto trespass against Muslim men. Because Muslim society is a patriarchal society, the women are viewed as belonging to men. Thus the Serbian policy of systematic mass rape of Bosnian Muslim women is a trespass on the property of the Muslim man. Similar to the Black American man during slavery, the Bosnian Muslim man is also powerless to remedy this trespass.

It is possible that the Serbian men intended these attacks as an attack on the honor of Muslim men, who are unable to protect their women. In the future, this spirit injury may cause the Bosnian men to reject their tarnished "property."

RAPE AS POLLUTION

In Bosnia and Black America there are individuals who might view the cross-cultural rape as a deliberate attempt at ethnic pollution.[25] In the African American setting, some Black Americans have viewed their heritage as having been polluted. During slavery, the product of a rape became the property of the master, capable of being sold for a higher price due to the mixture of White blood. Such slaves became house slaves, who were treated better than the darker, unmixed field hands. This genetic dilution of the group has called into question the whole identity of some Black Americans.[26]

This forced miscegenation in slavery, among other factors, has today resulted in the lightening of the Black American population. Most Black Americans in the United States are living proof because their skin tones are lighter than their African heritage would have made them. After slavery, better treatment of light-skinned Black Americans took place within the Black American community itself. In the post-Black-power-movement period, it has also meant darker Black Americans looking down on lighter ones as "too White."

In the Bosnian case, many Bosnian Muslims view the mixed children resulting from rape as a deliberate attempt by the Serbs to pollute the Bosnian group. Because the rape victims will be considered polluted by many people in the Bosnian Muslim community, the resulting child is thus also considered polluted. The mixing of ethnicity may be accepted in a cross-cultural marriage. However, this would be a consensual union between a man and a woman of different ethnic backgrounds, a union that is motivated by love and respect. The rape of Bosnian Muslim women, on the other hand, is a completely involuntary act on the part of the women, and is motivated primarily by ethnic hatred on the part of the men. Thus, it is possible that within the Bosnian Muslim community a hierarchy of ethnic purity could develop.

Many children have been and will be born as a result of the wide-spread rapes. These children may be seen by many as polluted and undesirable, and thus will find it difficult to be accepted in the society. These children are viewed as different from the numerous mixed children that result from consensual cross-cultural marriages. The mere existence of these children will serve as a constant reminder to the Bosnian Muslim women of the shame, humiliation, and injury inflicted upon them by the rape, and their utter helplessness to prevent or stop the rape. These children will also serve as a reminder to the Bosnian Muslim men that they were unable to prevent this humiliation to their wives, mothers, and daughters. Furthermore, these children will serve as a constant reminder to all Bosnian Muslims of their inability to prevent these atrocities. The result will be a long-lasting spirit injury.

Conclusion

In 1945, Ivo Andrić, a Nobel prize–winning Serbian author, wrote: "One sometimes wonders whether the spirit of the majority of the Balkan peoples has not been forever poisoned and that perhaps they will never again be able to do anything other than suffer violence, or inflict it."[27] For nearly fifty years, it appeared that the disease of spirit injury had been completely cured as Serbs, Croats, and Muslims lived together. Unfortunately, the Serbian campaign of ethnic cleansing shows that the disease was merely in remission and Andric's fears were well founded. Bosnian rape as a form of ethnic cleansing illustrates a new manifestation of poisoning of the spirit. The physical and psychological injuries inflicted by the Serbs affect not only individuals but the Bosnian Muslim community as a whole. Rape constitutes an international law violation as well as a spirit injury in Muslim culture. The prognosis for the Muslims in the future can be extrapolated from the progression of the disease in another population group— Black America, whose history of forced miscegenation provides a model for evaluating the potential spirit injury to Bosnian Muslims. In both groups, the spirit injury of rape displays the following symptoms: defilement, silence, loss of sexuality, emasculation, trespass, and "pollution." These manifestations in Black America have contributed to the chronic suffering of the group. Without treatment, the prognosis for the Bosnian Muslim culture, exhibiting similar symptoms, is equally bleak.

The cure will depend on the commitment of the transnational community. As Karl Jaspers wrote, "[t]here exists a solidarity among men [and women] as human beings that makes each co-responsible for every wrong and every injustice in the world, especially for crimes committed in his presence or with his knowledge. If I fail to do whatever I can to prevent them, I too am guilty."[29] Ultimately, to prevent further relapses, triumph over the disease will necessitate not only a short-term treatment regimen for the immediate symptoms but also implementation of long-term preventive measures. For the sake of the ancestors, the victims, their children, and grand-children, we must not fail in using legal remedies to uplift and heal the spirit of the Bosnian people.

NOTES

1. Patricia Williams, *Spirit-Murdering the Messenger: The Discourse of Fingerpointing as the Law's Response to Racism*, 42 U. MIAMI L. REV. 127, 129 (1987).

2. *Id.* at 129.

3. SUSAN BROWNMILLER, AGAINST OUR WILL: MEN, WOMEN, AND RAPE 175 (1975).

4. Gail Elizabeth Wyatt, *The Sociocultural Context of African American and White American Women's Rape*, 48 J. SOC. ISSUES 77, 87 (1992).

5. Although the death penalty for rape was outlawed in Coker v. Georgia, 433 U.S. 584 (1977), Black men convicted of raping White women still receive the harshest penalties. Gary LaFree, *The Effect of Sexual Stratification by Race on Official Reactions to Rape*, 45 AM. SOC. REV. 842, 852 (1980); Jennifer Wriggins, *Rape, Racism, and the Law*, 6 HARV. WOMEN'S L.J. 103, 113–16 (1983).

6. Williams, *supra* note 1, at 155.

7. *Id.*

8. Elizabeth H. White, *Legal Reform as an Indicator of Women's Status in Muslim Nations, in* WOMEN IN THE MUSLIM WORLD 52, 58 (Lois Beck & Nikki Keddie eds., 1978). While polygamy is legal in many Muslim countries, it is not

in Bosnia. Bosnians converted to Islam under the 14th century Ottoman occupation; however, they did not adopt polygamy or the Turkish language from their occupiers. Arthur Kaptainis, *It's Getting a Bit Late for Yugoslav Quiz*, GAZETTE (Montreal), July 7, 1993, at D3, *available in* Lexis, Nexis Library, Current File.

9. The *sharia* constitutes a comprehensive code of conduct governing both public and private actions. It includes laws regarding criminal actions, torts, contracts, trusts and estates, and family law. The *sharia* restricts polygamy to four wives. It also allows women to obtain a divorce, but only upon proving certain limited grounds. Upon divorce, it provides for the financial maintenance of the wife. Abdullahi An-Naim, *The Rights of Women and International Law in the Muslim Context*, 9 WHITTIER L. REV. 491, 495 (1987).

10. Mann & Selva, *The Sexualization of Racism: The Black as Rapist and White Justice*, 3 W.J. BLACK STUD. 168 (1979).

11. Sam Roberts, *When Crimes Become Symbols*, N.Y. TIMES, May 7, 1989, at A4.

12. Brownmiller, *supra* note 3, at 165. *See also* ANGELA Y. DAVIS, WOMEN, RACE AND CLASS 24–27 (1981); BELL HOOKS, AIN'T I A WOMAN: BLACK WOMEN AND FEMINISM 24–27 (1981).

13. *See, e.g.,* Alabama Code of 1852 (mandates death penalty for slave or free Black convicted of rape of a White woman); Mississippi 1857 Statute (death penalty for a slave convicted of raping a White woman under 14 years of age); Tennessee 1858 Law (rape of a White woman by Black/Mulatto constituted penalty of death by hanging); Arkansas Code of 1938 (death penalty for Blacks/Mulattos convicted of assault with intent to commit rape of a White woman); Pennsylvania Code of 1700 (rape of a White woman by Black man results in death penalty); Kansas Compilation of 1855 (Black/Mulatto convicted of rape or attempted rape of a White woman was to be castrated at his own expense).

14. BROWNMILLER, *supra* note 3, at 176.

15. Wriggins, *supra* note 5, at 118.

16. *Id.* at 106.

17. *Id.* at 107.

18. Williams, *supra* note 1, at 151.

19. *See, e.g., Endangered Family*, NEWSWEEK, Aug. 30, 1993, at 17.

20. *See, e.g.,* BROWNMILLER, *supra* note 3, at 245–48 (the Emmett Till case).

21. Sapphire was the name of a character on the long-running Amos & Andy radio show (1930s to 1950s) created by two whites. *See* Regina Austin, *Sapphire Bound*, 1989 WIS. L. REV. 539. Austin defines a sapphire as a Black bitch, tough, emasculating, strident, and shrill. *Id.* at 540. BELL HOOKS, *supra* note 12, at 85–86; P. Scott, *Debunking Sapphire: Towards a Non-Racist and Non-Sexist Social Science, in* ALL THE WOMEN ARE WHITE, ALL THE BLACKS ARE MEN, BUT SOME OF US ARE BRAVE 85 (G. Hull et al. eds., 1982).

22. BROWNMILLER, *supra* note 3, at 177. The patriarchal institutions of both marriage and slavery merged. Even the most enlightened observers, including male slaves, did not view female slaves as having their own sexual rights and bodily integrity. *Id.*

23. The family lore of Professor Wing is that one great uncle killed a White man who raped the great uncle's sister in Georgia. The entire family had to leave the South and change the spelling of the family name to avoid the lynching of her

uncle. It is the "almost White" blue-eyed product of that rape, an old man now, who tells the tale upon prodding. This is a repressed spirit injury in the Wing family, which only the writing of this chapter has brought to light. *See infra* note 25.

24. *See generally* Wriggins, *supra* note 5.

25. Professor Wing's own family history illustrates the long-term impact of this forced miscegenation on Black Americans in terms of the breakdown of identity. The author is fortunate in that since the person who committed the forced miscegenation was a famous Southerner, she was able to trace her family history. General Beauregard, the Southern general who fired on Fort Sumter, had a relationship with the author's great-great-grandmother which resulted in the birth of her great-grandmother and so on down the line. To this day, the fact that General Beauregard was the slave master, and that the White blood dates back to France and General Beauregard, is a source of pride among some members of her family. To others, including the author, the fact of General Beauregard's rape is the greatest source of shame and spirit injury to them.

26. Professor Wing faces this every time she travels to Africa and says she is Black. Since she is light skinned, the Africans say she is not Black because Black means dark. She has to go through a lengthy explanation about how Black Americans got lighter, and has to justify her identity every time she goes there.

27. David Wood, *Experts Discount Conventional Wisdom, See Hope for Balkans*, HOUS. CHRON., May 30, 1993, at A33.

28. KARL JASPERS, THE QUESTION OF GERMAN GUILT 32 (E. B. Ashton trans., Caprixorny Books 1961) (1947), *quoted in* Louis René Beres, *After the Gulf War: Prosecuting Iraqi Crimes under the Rule of Law*, 24 VAND. J. TRANSNAT'L L. 487, 503 (1991).

46 *Máscaras, Trenzas, y Greñas:*[*] Un/masking the Self While Un/braiding Latina Stories and Legal Discourse

MARGARET E. MONTOYA

O N E of the earliest memories from my school years is of my mother braiding my hair, making my *trenzas.* In 1955, I was seven years old. I was in second grade at the Immaculate Conception School in Las Vegas, New Mexico. Our family home with its outdoor toilet was on an unpaved street, one house from the railroad track. I remember falling asleep to the earthshaking rumble of the trains.

We dressed in front of the space heater in the bedroom we shared with my older brother. Catholic school girls wore uniforms. We wore blue jumpers and white blouses. I remember my mother braiding my hair and my sister's. I can still feel the part she would draw with the point of the comb. She would begin at the top of my head pressing down as she drew the comb down to the nape of my neck. "Don't move," she'd say as she held the two hanks of hair, checking to make sure that the part was straight. Only then would she begin, braiding as tightly as our squirming would allow, so the braids could withstand our running, jumping, and hanging from the monkey bars at recess. "I don't want you to look *greñudas,*" my mother would say. ["I don't want you to look uncombed."]

Hearing my mother use both English and Spanish gave emphasis to what she was saying. She used Spanish to talk about what was really important: her feelings, her doubts, her worries.[1] She also talked to us in Spanish about gringos, Mexicanos, and the relations between them. Her stories were sometimes about being treated outrageously by gringos, her anger controlled and her bitterness implicit. She also told stories about Anglos she admired—those who were egalitarian, smart, well-spoken and well-mannered.

Sometimes Spanish was spoken so as not to be understood by Them. Usually, though, Spanish and English were woven together. *"Greñuda"* was one of many words encoded with familial and cultural meaning. My mother used the word to

[*]"Masks, braids, and uncombed, messy hair."

17 HARVARD WOMEN'S L.J. 185 (1994). Copyright © 1994 by the President and Fellows of Harvard College. Reprinted by permission of the Harvard Women's Law Journal.

admonish us, but she wasn't warning us about name-calling: *"greñuda"* was not an epithet that our schoolmates were likely to use. Instead, I heard my mother saying something that went beyond well-groomed hair and being judged by our appearance—she could offer strategies for passing *that* scrutiny. She used the Spanish word, partly because there is no precise English equivalent, but also because she was interpreting the world for us.

The real message of *"greñudas"* was conveyed through the use of the Spanish word—it was unspoken and subtextual. She was teaching us that our world was divided, that They-Who-Don't-Speak-Spanish would see us as different, would judge us, would find us lacking. Her lessons about combing, washing and doing homework frequently relayed a deeper message: be prepared, because you will be judged by your skin color, your names, your accents. They will see you as ugly, lazy, dumb and dirty.

As I put on my uniform and as my mother braided my hair, I changed; I became my public self. My *trenzas* announced that I was clean and well cared for at home. My *trenzas* and school uniform blurred the differences between my family's economic and cultural circumstances and those of the more economically comfortable Anglo students. I welcomed the braids and uniform as a disguise which concealed my minimal wardrobe and the relative poverty in which my family lived.

As we walked to school, away from home, away from the unpaved streets, away from the "Spanish" to the "Anglo" part of town, I felt both drawn to and repelled by my strange surroundings. I wondered what Anglos were like in their big houses. What did they eat? How did they furnish their homes? How did they pass the time? Did my English sound like theirs? Surely their closets were filled with dresses, sweaters and shoes, *apenas estrenados*. [*Ed.* Hardly worn.]

I remember being called on one afternoon in second grade to describe what we had eaten for lunch. Rather than admit to eating *caldito* (soup) *y tortillas*,[2] partly because I had no English words for those foods, I regaled the class with a story about what I assumed an "American" family would eat at lunch: pork chops, mashed potatoes, green salad, sliced bread, and apple pie. The nun reported to my mother that I had lied. Afraid of being mocked, I unsuccessfully masked the truth, and consequently revealed more about myself than I concealed.

Our school was well integrated because it was located in a part of town with a predominantly Latino population. The culture of the school, however, was overwhelmingly Anglo and middle class. The use of Spanish was frowned upon and occasionally punished. Any trace of an accent when speaking English would be pointed out and sarcastically mocked. This mocking persisted even though, and maybe because, some of the nuns were also "Spanish."[3]

By the age of seven, I was keenly aware that I lived in a society that had little room for those who were poor, brown, or female. I was all three. I moved between dualized worlds: private/public, Catholic/secular, poverty/privilege, Latina/Anglo. My *trenzas* and school uniform were a cultural disguise. They were also a precursor for the more elaborate mask I would later develop.

Presenting an acceptable face, speaking without a Spanish accent, hiding what we really felt—masking our inner selves—were defenses against racism passed on to us by our parents to help us get along in school and in society. We learned that it was safer to be inscrutable. We absorbed the necessity of constructing and maintaining a disguise for use in public. We struggled to be seen as Mexican but also wanted acceptance as Americans at a time when the mental image conjured up by that word included only Anglos.

Mine is the first generation of Latinas to be represented in colleges and universities in anything approaching significant numbers. We are now represented in virtually every college and university. But, for the most part, we find ourselves isolated. Rarely has another Latina gone before us. Rarely is there another Latina whom we can watch to try and figure out all the little questions about subtextual meaning, about how dress or speech or makeup are interpreted in this particular environment.

My participation in the Chicano student movement in college fundamentally changed me. My adoption of the ethnic label as a primary identifier gave me an ideological mask that serves to this day. This transformation of my public persona was psychically liberating. This nascent liberation was, however, reactive and inchoate. Even as I struggled to redefine myself, I was locked in a reluctant embrace with those whose definitions of me I was trying to shrug off.

When I arrived as a student at Harvard Law School, I dressed so as to proclaim my politics. During my first day of orientation, I wore a Mexican peasant blouse and cutoff jeans on which I had embroidered the Chicano symbol of the *águila* (a stylized eagle) on one seat pocket and the woman symbol on the other. The *águila* reminded me of the red and black flags of the United Farm Worker rallies; it reminded me that I had links to a particular community. I was never to finish the fill-in stitches in the woman symbol. My symbols, like my struggles, were ambiguous.

The separation of the two symbols reminds me today that my participation in the Chicano movement had been limited by my gender, while in the women's movement it had been limited by my ethnicity. I drew power from both movements—I identified with both—but I knew that I was at the margin of each one.

As time went on, my clothes lost their political distinctiveness. My clothes signified my ambivalence: perhaps if I dressed like a lawyer, eventually I would acquire more conventional ideas and ideals and fit in with my peers. Or perhaps if I dressed like a lawyer, I could harbor for some future use the disruptive and, at times, unwelcome thoughts that entered my head. My clothing would become protective coloration. Chameleon-like, I would dress to fade into the ideological, political and cultural background rather than proclaim my differences.

Máscaras and Latina Assimilation

For stigmatized groups, such as persons of color, the poor, women, gays and lesbians, assuming a mask is comparable to being "on stage." Being "on stage" is frequently experienced as being acutely aware of one's words, affect, tone of voice, movements and gestures because they seem out of sync with what one is feeling and thinking. At unexpected moments, we fear that we will be discovered to be someone or something other than who or what we pretend to be. Lurking just behind our carefully constructed disguises and lodged within us is the child whom no one would have mistaken for anything other than what she was. Her masking was yet imperfect, still in rehearsal, and at times unnecessary.

For Outsiders, being masked in the legal profession has psychological as well as ideological consequences. Not only do we perceive ourselves as being "on stage," but the experience of class-jumping—being born poor but later living on the privileged side of the economic divide as an adult—can also induce schizoid feelings. As first-year law students don their three-piece suits, they make manifest the class ascendancy implicit in legal education. Most Latinas/os in the legal profession now occupy an economic niche considerably higher than that of our parents, our relatives and frequently that of our students. Our speech, clothes, cars, homes and lifestyle emphasize this difference.

The masks we choose can impede our legal representation and advocacy by driving a wedge between self, our *familias,* and our communities. As our economic security increases, we escape the choicelessness and lack of control over vital decisions that afflict communities of color. To remain connected to the community requires one to be Janus-faced, able to present one face to the larger society and another among ourselves—Janus-faced not in the conventional meaning of being deceitful, but in that of having two faces simultaneously. One face is the adult face that allows us to make our way through the labyrinth of the dominant culture. The other, the face of the child, is one of difference, free of artifice. This image with its dichotomized character fails to capture the multiplicity, fluidity and interchangeability of faces, masks and identities upon which we rely.

Masking within the Legal Environment

The legal profession provides ample opportunity for role-playing, drama, storytelling and posturing. Researchers have studied the use of masks and other theatrical devices among practicing lawyers and in the law school environment. Mask imagery has been used repeatedly to describe different aspects of legal education, lawyering and law-making. One distinctive example is John T. Noonan, Jr.'s, analysis exposing the purposeful ambiguity and the duplicity of legal discourse.[4]

Some law students are undoubtedly attracted to the profession by the opportunity to disguise themselves and have no desire or need to look for their hidden selves. Some, however, may resent the role-playing they know to be necessary to succeed in their studies and in their relations with professors and peers. Understanding how and why we mask ourselves can help provide opportunities for students to explore their public and private personalities and to give expression to their feelings.

Un/masking Silence

My memories from law school begin with the first case I ever read in Criminal Law. I was assigned to seat number one in a room that held 175 students.

The case was entitled *The People of the State of California v. Josefina Chavez.*[5] It was the only case in which I remember encountering a Latina, and she was the defendant in a manslaughter prosecution. In *Chavez*, a young woman gave birth one night over the toilet in her mother's home without waking her child, brothers, sisters, or mother. The baby dropped into the toilet. Josefina cut the umbilical cord with a razor blade. She recovered the body of the baby, wrapped it in newspaper and hid it under the bathtub. She ran away, but later turned herself in to her probation officer.

The legal issue was whether the baby had been born alive for purposes of the California manslaughter statute: whether the baby had been born alive and was therefore subject to being killed. The class wrestled with what it meant to be alive in legal terms. Had the lungs filled with air? Had the heart pumped blood?

For two days I sat mute, transfixed while the professor and the students debated the issue. Finally, on the third day, I timidly raised my hand. I heard myself blurt out: What about the other facts? What about her youth, her poverty, her fear over the pregnancy, her delivery in silence? I spoke for perhaps two minutes, and, when I finished, my voice was high-pitched and anxious.

An African American student in the back of the room punctuated my comments with "Hear! Hear!" Later other students thanked me for speaking up and in other ways showed their support.

I sat there after class had ended, in seat number one on day number three, wondering why it had been so hard to speak. Only later would I begin to wonder whether I would ever develop the mental acuity, the logical clarity to be able to sort out the legally relevant facts from what others deemed sociological factoids. Why *did* the facts relating to the girl-woman's reality go unvoiced? Why were her life, her anguish, her fears rendered irrelevant? Engaging in analyses about The Law, her behavior and her guilt demanded that I disembody Josefina, that I silence her reality which screamed in my head.

A discussion raising questions about the gender-, class-, and ethnicity-based interpretations in the opinion, however, would have run counter to traditional legal discourse. Interjecting information about the material realities and cultural context of a poor Latina's life introduces taboo information into the classroom. Such information would transgress the prevalent ideological discourse. The puritanical and elitist protocol governing the classroom, especially during the 1970s, supported the notion that one's right to a seat in the law school classroom could be brought into question if one were to admit knowing about the details of pregnancies and self-abortions, or the hidden motivations of a *pachuca* (or a *chola*, a "homegirl" in today's Latino gang parlance). By overtly linking oneself to the life experiences of poor women, especially *pachucas*, one would emphasize one's differences from those who seemed to have been admitted to law school by right.

Information about the cultural context of Josephine Chavez's life would also transgress the linguistic discourse within the classroom. One would find it useful, and perhaps necessary, to use Spanish words and concepts to describe accurately and to contextualize Josephine Chavez's experience. In the 1970s, however, Spanish was still the language of Speedy Gonzales, José Jimenez and other racist parodies.

To this day, I have dozens of questions about this episode in Josephine Chavez's life. I yearn to read an appellate opinion which reflects a sensitivity to her story, told in her own words. What did it take to conceal her pregnancy from her *familia?* With whom did she share her secret? How could she have given birth with "the doors open and no lights . . . turned on?" How did she do so without waking the others who were asleep? How did she brace herself as she delivered the baby into the toilet? Did she shake as she cut the umbilical cord?

I long to hear Josephine Chavez's story told in what I will call Mothertalk and Latina-Daughtertalk. Mothertalk is about the blood and mess of menstruation, about the every month-ness of periods or about the fear in the pit of the stomach and the fear in the heart when there is no period. Mothertalk is about the blood and mess of pregnancy, about placentas, umbilical cords and stitches. Mothertalk is about sex and its effects. Mothertalk helps make sense of our questions: How does one give birth in darkness and in silence? How does one clean oneself after giving birth? How does one heal oneself? Where does one hide from oneself after seeing one's dead baby in a toilet?

Latina-Daughtertalk is about feelings reflecting the deeply ingrained cultural values of Latino families: in this context, feelings of *vergüenza de sexualidad* ("sexual shame"). Sexual experience comes enshrouded in sexual shame; have sex and you risk being known as *sinvergüenza,* shameless. Another Latina-Daughtertalk value is *respeto a la mamá y respeto a la familia. Familias* are not nuclear or limited by blood ties; they are extended, often including foster siblings and *comadres y compadres, madrinas y padrinos* (godmothers, godfathers and other religion-linked relatives).

Josephine Chavez's need to hide her pregnancy (with her head-to-toe mask) can be explained by a concern about the legal consequences as well as by the *vergüenza* within and of her *familia* that would accompany the discovery of the pregnancy, a pregnancy that was at once proof and reproof of her sexuality. Josephine's unwanted pregnancy would likely have been interpreted within her community and her *familia* and by her mother as a lack of *respeto.*

I sense that students still feel vulnerable when they reveal explicitly gendered or class-based knowledge, such as information about illicit sexuality and its effects, or personal knowledge about the lives of the poor and the subordinated. Even today there is little opportunity to use Spanish words or concepts within the legal academy. Students respond to their feelings of vulnerability by remaining silent about these taboo areas of knowledge.

The silence had profound consequences for me and presumably for others who identified with Josephine Chavez because she was Latina, or because she was female, or because she was poor. For me, the silence invalidated my experience. I reexperienced the longing I felt that day in Criminal Law many times. At the bottom of that longing was a desire to be recognized, a need to feel some reciprocity. As I engaged in His/Their reality, I needed to feel Him/Them engage in mine.

Embedded in Josephine Chavez's experience are various lessons about criminal law specifically and about the law and its effects more generally. The opinion's characteristic avoidance of context and obfuscation of important class- and gender-based assumptions is equally important to the ideological socialization and doctrinal development of law students. Maintaining a silence about Chavez's ethnic and socio-economic context lends credence to the prevailing perception that there is only one relevant reality.

Over time, I figured out that my interpretations of the facts in legal opinions were at odds with the prevailing discourse in the classroom, regardless of the subject matter. Much of the discussion assumed that we all shared common life experiences. I remember sitting in the last row and being called on in tax class, questioned about a case involving the liability of a father for a gift of detached and negotiable bond coupons to his son. It was clear that I was befuddled by the facts of the case. Looking at his notes on the table, the professor asked with annoyance whether I had ever seen a bond. My voice quivering, I answered that I had not. His head shot up in surprise. He focused on who I was; I waited, unmasked. He became visibly flustered as he carefully described the bond with its tear-off coupons to me. Finally, he tossed me an easy question, and I choked out the answer.

This was one instance of feeling publicly unmasked. In this case, it was class-based ignorance which caused my mask(s) to slip. Other students may also have lacked knowledge about bonds. Maybe other students, especially those from families with little money and certainly no trust funds, stocks or bonds, also would have felt unmasked by the questioning. But I felt isolated and different because I could be exposed in so many ways: through class, ethnicity, race, gender, and the subtleties of language, dress, make-up, voice and accent.

For multiple and overlapping reasons I felt excluded from the experiences of others, experiences that provided them with knowledge that better equipped them for the study of The Law, especially within the upper-class domain that is Harvard. Not knowing about bonds linked the complexities of class-jumping with the fearful certainty that, in the eyes of some, and most painfully in my own/my mother's eyes, I would be seen as *greñuda:* dirty, ugly, dumb and uncombed.

It was not possible for me to guard against the unexpected visibility—or, paradoxically, the invisibility—caused by class, gender or ethnic differences that lurked in the materials we studied. Such issues were, after all, pervasive, and I was very sensitive to them.

Sitting in the cavernous classrooms at Harvard under the stern gaze of patrician jurists[6] was an emotionally wrenching experience. I remember the day one of the students was called on to explain *Erie v. Tompkins*.[7] His identification of the salient facts, his articulation of the major and minor issues and his synopsis of the Court's reasoning were so precise and concise that it left a hush in the room. He had already achieved and were able to model for the rest of us the objectivity, clarity and mental acuity that we/I aspired to.

The respect shown for this type of analysis was qualitatively different from that shown for contextual or cultural analysis. Such occurrences in the classroom were memorable because they were defining: rational objectivity trumped emotional subjectivity. What They had to say trumped what I wanted to say but rarely did.

I have no memory of ever speaking out again to explain facts from my perspective as I had done that one day in Criminal Law. There was to be only one Latina in any of my cases, only one Josefina. While I was at Harvard, my voice was not heard again in the classroom examining, exploring or explaining the life situations of either defendants or victims. Silence accommodated the ideological uniformity, but also revealed the inauthenticity implicit in discursive assimilation.

As time went on, I felt diminished and irrelevant. It wasn't any one discussion, any one class or any one professor. The pervasiveness of the ideology marginalized me, and others; its efficacy depended upon its subtextual nature, and this masked quality made it difficult to pinpoint.

I had arrived at Harvard feeling different. I understood difference to be ineluctably linked with, and limited to, race, class and gender.[8] The kernel of that feeling I first associated with Josephine Chavez, that scrim of silence, remains within me. It is still my experience that issues of race, ethnicity, gender or class are invisible to most of my white and/or male colleagues. Issues of sexual orientation, able-bodiedness and sometimes class privilege can be invisible to me. I still make conscious choices about when to connect such issues to the topic at hand and when to remain silent. I'm still unclear about strategies and tactics, about being frontal or oblique.

Issues of race or gender are never trivial or banal from my perspective. Knowing how or when to assert them effectively as others react with hostility, boredom or weariness can be a "crazy-making" endeavor. Sometimes it seems that every interaction requires that I overlook the terms of the discourse or that I affirmatively redefine them. My truths require that I say unconventional things in unconventional ways.

Speaking out assumes prerogative. Speaking out is an exercise of privilege. Speaking out takes practice.

Silence ensures invisibility. Silence provides protection. Silence masks.

Trenzas: Braiding Latina Narrative

The law and its practice are grounded in the telling of stories. Pleadings and judicial orders can be characterized as stylized stories. Legal persuasion in the form of opening statements and closing arguments is routinely taught as an exercise in storytelling. Client interviews are storytelling and story-listening events. Traditionally, legal culture within law firms, law schools and courthouses has been transmitted through the "war stories" told by seasoned attorneys. Narrative laces through all aspects of legal education, legal practice and legal culture. In these various ways the use of narrative is not new to the legal academy.

Only recently, however, has storytelling begun to play a significant role in academic legal writing. In the hands of Outsiders, storytelling seeks to subvert the dominant ideology. Stories told by those on the bottom, told from the "subversive-subaltern" perspective, challenge and expose the hierarchical and patriarchal order that exists within the legal academy and pervades the larger society.[9] Narrative that focuses on the experiences of Outsiders thus empowers both the storyteller and the story-listener by virtue of its opposition to the traditional forms of discourse.

Understanding stories told from different cultural perspectives requires that we suspend our notions of temporal and spatial continuity, plot, climax, and the interplay of narrator and protagonists. The telling of and listening to stories in a multicultural environment requires a fundamental re-examination of the text, the subtext and the context of stories. The emphasis of critical scholarship (critical race theory, feminist jurisprudence, critical legal studies) on narrative affirms those of us who are Outsiders working within the objectivist orientation of the legal academy and validates our experimentation with innovative formats and themes in our teaching and in our scholarship.

Greñas: Un/braiding Latina Narrative

The Euro-American conquest of the Southwest and Puerto Rico resulted in informal and formal prohibitions against the use of Spanish for public purposes. So by situating myself in legal scholarship as *mestiza*, I seek to occupy common ground with Latinas/os in this hemisphere and others, wherever located, who are challenging "Western bourgeois ideology and hegemonic racialism with the metaphor of transculturation."[10]

As Latinas/os we, like many colonized peoples around the globe, are the biological descendants of both indigenous and European ancestors, as well as the intellectual progeny of Western and indigenous thinkers and writers. As evidenced by my names, I am the result of Mexican-Indian-Irish-French relations. I am also the product of English-speaking schools and a Spanish-speaking community. Making manifest our mixed intellectual and linguistic heritage can counteract the subordinating forces implicit in the monolinguality and homogeneity of the dominant culture. While I reject the idea that personal narratives can or should be generalized into grand or universalistic theories, our stories can help us search for unifying identifiers and mutual objectives. For example, the deracination of language purges words of their embedded racism, sexism and other biases.

Using Spanish (or other outlaw languages, dialects or patois) in legal scholarship could be seen as an attempt to erect linguistic barriers or create exclusionary discursive spaces, even among Outsiders with whom Latinas share mutual ideological, political and pedagogical objectives. Personal accounts of humiliation, bias or deprivation told from within the academy may sound to some like whining or may be perceived as excessive involvement with the self rather than with the real needs of the Outsider communities. As I have argued, this view would be seriously wrong. Instead, linguistic diversity should be recognized as enhancing the dialogue within the academy by bringing in new voices and fresh perspectives. Incorporating Spanish words, sayings, literature and wisdom can have positive ramifications for those in the academy and in the profession, and for those to whom we render legal services.

NOTES

1. My mother, like most bilingual Latinas or Latinos, moved between English and Spanish in the same sentence. This type of language-mixing has been dismissed as Tex-Mex or Spanglish. Analyses of this code-switching have revealed that it is linguistically competent. *See* Rodolfo Jacobson, *The Social Implications of Intra-Sentential Code-Switching, in* NEW DIRECTIONS IN CHICANO SCHOLARSHIP 227, 240–41 (Richard Romo & Raymond Paredes eds., 1978) (observing that such code-mixing is linked to psychological and sociological cues; for instance, some speakers switch to the stronger language when the topic relates to emotional issues and back to the other language when the conversation returns to general topics).

2. George Sanchez, "Go After the Women": Americanization and the Mexican Immigrant Woman 1915–1929 (1984) (unpublished manuscript, SCCR Working Paper No. 6, on file with the Stanford Center for Chicano Research), describes programs aimed at Mexican women established during the period 1915–1929 for the purpose of changing the cultural values of immigrant families. Two particular areas of focus were diet and health.

> In the eyes of reformers, the typical noon lunch of the Mexican child, thought to consist of a "folded tortilla with no filling," became the first step in a life of crime. With "no milk or fruit to whet the appetite" the child would become lazy and subsequently "take food from the lunch boxes of more fortunate children" in order to appease his/her hunger. "Thus," reformers alleged, "the initial step in a life of thieving is taken." Teaching immigrant women proper food values would keep the head of the family out of jail, the rest of the family off the charity lists, and save the taxpayers a great amount of money.

Id. at 17 (quoting PEARL IDELIA ELLIS, AMERICANIZATION THROUGH HOMEMAKING 19–29 (1929)).

3. For analyses of the internalization of colonization, *see, e.g.,* FRANTZ FANON, BLACK SKIN, WHITE MASKS (1967); ANTONIO GRAMSCI, *IN* 2 LETTERS FROM PRISON (Frank Rosengarten ed. & Raymond Rosenthal trans., 1994); ALBERT MEMMI, THE COLONIZER AND THE COLONIZED (1965).

4. In 1971, John T. Noonan, Jr., criticized law's emphasis on rationalized rules and the duplicity of legal language; he described the fictions employed by

Holmes, Cardozo and other famous judges and lawyers to suppress the humanity of those acting (e.g., "sovereign") or those being acted upon (e.g., "property" for slaves). Noonan's purposes were to show the dangers inherent in a system which fails to acknowledge human identity and to free the language of law from the masks and legal fictions which deny the humanity of different groups in society. *See* JOHN T. NOONAN, JR., PERSONS AND MASKS OF THE LAW (1976).

5. People v. Josephine Chavez, 176 P.2d 92 (Cal. App. 1947).

6. The classrooms at Harvard Law School feature large portraits of famous judges. Until fairly recently all the paintings were of white men.

7. Erie Railroad Co. v. Tompkins, 304 U.S. 64 (1938).

8. Learning about the varied experiences of students who had initially seemed to fit neatly into Us and Them categories was one of the profound lessons of law school. My life eventually was transformed by students of color from economically privileged backgrounds, self-described "poor farm boys" from Minnesota, the Irish daughters of Dorchester, the courage of a student with cerebral palsy. These and other students challenged the categories into which I forced my world.

9. By displacing the more usual forms of academic writing on which the dominant order relies, Outsider stories work a formal as well as a substantive subversion. *Cf.* ANNE DiPARDO, NARRATIVE KNOWERS, EXPOSITORY KNOWLEDGE: DISCOURSE AS A DIALECTIC 7 (Center for the Study of Writing, Occasional Paper No. 6, 1989) (reference omitted):

> While classical tradition bestowed preeminence on logical thought and the scientific revolution brought new prestige to empirically discerned fact, a different tradition sees storytelling as a vehicle for an equally rich, distinctly valuable sort of knowledge—indeed, the word "narrative" is derived from the Latin gnarus, denoting "knowing" or "expert."

10. FRANCOISE LIONNET, AUTOBIOGRAPHICAL VOICES: RACE, GENDER, SELF-PORTRAITURE 15–16 (1989) (translating the Cuban poet Nancy Morejaeon).

From the Editor:
Issues and Comments

W H Y should women (of any color) be the focus of special concern, of intrusive medical interventions, or of court orders simply on account of their pregnancy, when men are not subject to such interferences? You might say, "But only women can get pregnant," but Professor Ikemoto rejects that easy answer. Do you agree with her reasons? Intuitively, Professor Russell's treatment at the hands of the anonymous gorilla-pusher is much more serious than other forms of words ("You are the worst teacher I have had"; "Why do you always wear those dowdy dresses?"; "She just doesn't know how to explain things") that disparage professors, white or black. But why is it more serious? And is adopting the outlaw role that Monica Evans suggests a healthy means of survival for women and societies of color who are subject to daily assaults on their persons and self-esteem? Should outsider women insist on bringing their backgrounds and ethnicities to the fore in their teaching, scholarship, and interactions with colleagues? If so, is this bravery, or is it foolhardy, suicidal, and calculated to interfere with assimilation, acceptance, and learning? Is it, as Professor Montoya suggests, a source of strength and jurisprudential richness? Do you agree with Adrien Wing and Sylke Merchán that armies and colonizing nations throughout history have used rape as an instrument of terror and absolute control? If so, what is the remedy?

Suggested Readings

Davis, Peggy Cooper, *Contested Images of Family Values: The Role of the State*, 107 HARV. L. REV. 1348 (1994).

Roberts, Dorothy E., *Crime, Race and Reproduction*, 67 TULANE L. REV. 1945 (1993).

Roberts, Dorothy E., *Punishing Drug Addicts Who Have Babies*, 104 HARV. L. REV. 1419 (1991).

Roberts, Dorothy E., Rust v. Sullivan *and the Control of Knowledge*, 61 GEO. WASH. L. REV. 587 (1993).

Scales-Trent, Judy, *Black Women and the Constitution: Finding Our Place, Asserting Our Rights*, 24 HARV. C.R.-C.L. L. REV. 9 (1989).

PART XII

CRITICAL WHITE STUDIES

A N E M E R G I N G strain within Critical Race Theory focuses not so much on the way minority coloration functions as a social organizing principle as on the way whiteness does. In Part XII, Ian Haney López examines how the Supreme Court constructs and interprets whiteness under statutes that make this relevant. Thomas Ross analyzes the way in which whiteness is often equated with innocence. Trina Grillo and Stephanie Wildman discuss the use of metaphor in conversations about race, showing that people often make comparisons to an event that happened to them and that they believe is comparable to suffering racial discrimination. Finally, Stephanie Wildman and Adrienne Davis examine how privilege, especially the privilege of being white—of appearing to have no race—works in our society. Those comparisons end up minimizing racism, essentializing it, and turning the discussion from one of race to one of, say, the plight of short outfielders who want to play Little League baseball.

47 White by Law

IAN F. HANEY LÓPEZ

Then, what is white?[1]

IN ITS first words on the subject of citizenship, Congress in 1790 limited naturalization to "white persons."[2] Though the requirements for naturalization changed frequently thereafter, this racial prerequisite to citizenship endured for over a century-and-a-half, remaining in force until 1952.[3] From the earliest years of this country until just a short time ago, being a "white person" was a condition for acquiring citizenship.

Whether one was "white," however, was often no easy question. Thus, as immigration reached record highs at the turn of this century, countless people found themselves arguing their racial identity in order to naturalize. From 1907, when the federal government began collecting data on naturalization, until 1920, over a million people gained citizenship under the racially restrictive naturalization laws.[4] Many more sought to naturalize and were denied. Records regarding more than the simple decision in most of these cases do not exist, as naturalization often took place with a minimum of formal court proceedings, and so produced few if any written decisions. However, a number of cases construing the "white person" prerequisite reached the highest state and federal judicial circles, including in the early 1920s two cases argued before the United States Supreme Court, and these cases resulted in illuminating published decisions. These cases document the efforts of would-be citizens from around the world to establish that as a legal matter they were "white." Applicants from Hawaii, China, Japan, Burma, and the Philippines, as well as all mixed-race applicants, failed in their arguments. On the other hand, courts ruled that the applicants from Mexico and Armenia were "white," and on alternate occasions deemed petitioners from Syria, India, and Arabia to be either "white" or not "white." As a taxonomy of Whiteness, these cases are instructive because of the imprecision and contradiction they reveal in the establishment of racial divisions between Whites and non-Whites.

It is on the level of taxonomical *practice*, however, that they are most intriguing. The petitioners for naturalization forced the courts into a case-by-case struggle to define who was a "white person." More importantly, the courts were required in these prerequisite cases to articulate rationales for the divisions they were promulgating. It was not enough simply to declare in favor of or against a particular applicant; the courts, as exponents of the applicable law, faced the ne-

542

cessity of explaining the basis on which they drew the boundaries of Whiteness. They had to establish in law whether, for example, a petitioner's race was to be measured by skin color, facial features, national origin, language, culture, ancestry, the speculations of scientists, popular opinion, or some combination of the above, and which of these or other factors would govern in those inevitable cases where the various indices of race contradicted each other. In short, the courts were responsible not only for deciding who was White, but *why* someone was White. Thus, the courts had to wrestle in their written decisions with the nature of race in general, and of White racial identity in particular. Their categorical practices provide the empirical basis for this chapter.

How did the courts define who was White? What reasons did they offer, and what do those rationalizations tell us about the nature of Whiteness? Do these cases also afford insights into White race-consciousness as it exists today? What, finally, *is* White? This chapter examines these and related questions, offering an exploration of contemporary White identity. It arrives at the conclusion that Whiteness exists at the vortex of race in U.S. law and society, and that Whiteness as it is currently constituted should be dismantled.

The Racial Prerequisite Cases

Although not widely remembered, the prerequisite cases were at the center of racial debates in the United States for the fifty years following the Civil War, when immigration and nativism ran at record highs. Figuring prominently in the furor on the appropriate status of the newcomers, naturalization laws were heatedly discussed by the most respected public figures of the day, as well as in the swirl of popular politics. Debates about racial prerequisites to citizenship arose at the end of the Civil War as part of the effort to expunge *Dred Scott*, the Supreme Court decision that had held that Blacks were not citizens. Because of racial animosity in Congress towards Asians and Native Americans, the racial bar on citizenship was maintained, though in 1870 the right to naturalize was extended to African Americans. Continuing into the early 1900s, anti-Asian agitation kept the prerequisite laws at the forefront of national and even international attention. Anti-immigrant groups such as the Asiatic Exclusion League formulated arguments to address the "white person" prerequisite, arguing in 1910 that Asian Indians were not "white" but were rather an "effeminate, caste-ridden, and degraded" race who did not qualify for citizenship.[5] For their part, immigrants also mobilized to participate as individuals and through civic groups in the debates on naturalization, writing for popular periodicals and lobbying government.[6]

The principal locus of the debate, however, was in the courts. Beginning with the first prerequisite case in 1878, until racial restrictions were removed in 1952, forty-four racial prerequisite cases were reported, including two heard by the United States Supreme Court. Raising fundamental questions about who could join the polity as a citizen in terms of who was and who was not White, these cases attracted some of the most renowned jurists of the times, such as John Wigmore, as well as some of the greatest experts on race, including Franz Boas. Wigmore, now more famous for his legal-treatise writing, published a law review article in 1894 advocating the admission of Japanese immigrants to citizenship on the grounds that the Japanese people were anthropologically and culturally White.[7] Boas, today commonly regarded as the founder of modern anthropology, participated in at least one of the prerequisite cases as an expert witness on behalf of an Armenian applicant, arguing he was White.[8] Despite these accomplished participants, however, the courts themselves struggled not only with the narrow question of whom to naturalize but more fundamentally with the categorical question of how to determine racial identity.

Though the courts offered many different rationales to justify the various racial divisions they advanced, two predominated: common knowledge and scientific evidence. Both of these rationales are apparent in the first prerequisite case, *In re Ah Yup*.[9] "Common knowledge" refers to those rationales that appealed to popular, widely held conceptions of races and racial divisions. For example, the *Ah Yup* court based its negative decision regarding a Chinese applicant in part on the popular understanding of the term "white person": "The words 'white person' . . . in this country, at least, have undoubtedly acquired a well settled meaning in common popular speech, and they are constantly used in the sense so acquired in the literature of the country, as well as in common parlance."[10] Under a common knowledge approach, courts justified the assignment of petitioners to one race or another by reference to what was commonly believed about race. This type of rationale is distinct from reasoning that relied on knowledge of a reputedly objective, technical, and specialized sort. Such rationales, which justified racial divisions by reference to the naturalistic studies of humankind, can be labeled appeals to scientific evidence. A longer excerpt from *Ah Yup* exemplifies this second sort of rationale:

> In speaking of the various classifications of races, Webster in his dictionary says, "The common classification is that of Blumbach, who makes five. 1. The Caucasian, or white race, to which belong the greater part of European nations and those of Western Asia; 2. The Mongolian, or yellow race, occupying Tartary, China, Japan, etc.; 3. The Ethiopian or Negro (black) race, occupying all of Africa, except the north; 4. The American, or red race, containing the Indians of North and South America; and, 5. The Malay, or Brown race, occupying the islands of the Indian Archipelago," etc. This division was adopted from Buffon, with some changes in names, and is founded on the combined characteristics of complexion, hair and skull. . . . [N]o one includes the white, or Caucasian, with the Mongolian or yellow race, . . .[11]

These rationales, one appealing to common knowledge and the other to scientific evidence, were the two core approaches used by courts to explain the assignment of an individual to one race or another.

As *Ah Yup* illustrates, at least initially the courts deciding racial prerequisite cases relied simultaneously on both rationales to justify their decisions. However, after 1909, a schism appeared among the courts over whether common knowledge or scientific evidence was the appropriate standard. After that year, the lower courts divided almost evenly on the proper test for Whiteness: five courts relied exclusively on common knowledge, while six decisions turned only on scientific evidence. No court drew on both rationales. In 1922 and 1923, the Supreme Court intervened in the prerequisite cases to resolve this impasse between science and popular knowledge, securing common sense as the appropriate legal meter of race. Though the courts did not see their decisions in this light, the early congruence and subsequent contradiction of common knowledge and scientific evidence set the terms of a debate about whether race is social or natural. In these terms, the Supreme Court's elevation of common knowledge as the legal meter of race convincingly illustrates the social basis for racial categorization.

The early prerequisite courts assumed that common knowledge and scientific evidence both measured the same thing, the natural physical differences that marked humankind into disparate races. Any difference between the two would be found in levels of exactitude, in terms of how accurately these existing differences were measured, and not in substantive disagreements about the nature of racial difference itself. This position seemed tenable so long as science and popular beliefs jibed in the construction of racial categories. However, by 1909, changes in immigrant demographics and evolution in anthropological thinking combined to create contradictions between science and common knowledge. These contradictions surfaced most acutely in cases concerning immigrants from western and southern Asia, notably Syrians and Asian Indians, arrivals from countries inhabited by dark-skinned peoples nevertheless uniformly classified as Caucasians by the leading anthropologists of the times. The inability of science to confirm through empirical evidence the popular racial beliefs that held Syrians and Asian Indians to be non-Whites should have drawn into question for the courts the notion that race was a natural phenomenon. So deeply held was this belief, however, that instead the courts disparaged science.

Over the course of two decisions, the Supreme Court resolved the conflict between common knowledge and scientific evidence in favor of the former, although not without some initial confusion. In *United States v. Ozawa*, the Court relied on both rationales to exclude a Japanese petitioner, holding that he was not of the type "*popularly* known as the Caucasian race," thereby invoking both common knowledge ("popularly known") and science ("the Caucasian race").[12] Here, as in the early prerequisite cases, both science and popular knowledge worked hand in hand to exclude the applicant from citizenship. Within a few months of its decision in *Ozawa*, however, the Court heard a case brought by an Asian Indian, Bhagat Singh Thind, who relied on the Court's recent equation of "Caucasian" and "white" to argue for his own naturalization. In Thind's case, science and common knowledge diverged. In a stunning reversal of its holding in *Ozawa*, the Court in *United States v. Thind* repudiated its earlier equation, rejecting any role for science in racial assignments.[13] The Court decried the "scientific manipulation" it believed had eroded racial differences by including as Caucasian "far more [people] than the unscientific mind suspects," even some persons the Court described as ranging "in color . . . from brown to black."[14] "We venture to think," the Court said, "that the average well informed white American would learn with some degree of astonishment that the race to which he belongs is made up of such heterogenous elements."[15] The Court held instead that "the words 'free white persons' are words of common speech, to be interpreted in accordance with the understanding of the common man."[16] In the Court's opinion, science had failed as an arbiter of human difference; common knowledge succeeded it as the touchstone of racial division.

In elevating common knowledge, the Court no doubt remained convinced that racial divisions followed real, natural, physical differences. This explains the Court's frustration with science, which to the Court's mind was curiously and suspiciously unable to identify and quantify those racial differences so readily apparent to it. This frustration is understandable, given the promise of early anthropology to definitively establish racial differences, and more, a racial hierarchy that placed Whites at the top. Yet, this was a promise science could not keep. Despite their strained efforts, students of race could not measure the boundaries of Whiteness because such boundaries are socially fashioned and cannot be measured, or found, in nature. The Court resented the failure of science to fulfil an impossible vow; we might better resent that science ever undertook such a promise. The early congruence between scientific evidence and common knowledge reflected, not the accuracy of popular understandings of race, but the embeddedness of scientific inquiry. Neither common knowledge nor science measured human variation. Both only reported social beliefs about races.

The reliance on scientific evidence to justify racial assignments implied that races exist on a physical plane, that they reflect biological fact that is humanly knowable but not dependent on human knowledge or human relations. The Court's ultimate reliance on common knowledge says otherwise. The use of common knowledge to justify racial assignments demonstrates that racial taxonomies dissolve upon inspection into mere social demarcations. Common knowledge as a racial test shows that race is something that must be measured in terms of what people believe, that it is a socially mediated idea. The social construction of Whiteness (and race generally) is manifest in the Court's repudiation of science and its installation of popular knowledge as the appropriate racial meter.

It is worthwhile here to return to the question that opened this chapter, a question originally posed by a district court deciding a prerequisite case. The court asked: "Then, what is white?"[17] The above discussion suggests some answers to this question. Whiteness is a social construct, a legal artifact, a function of what people believe, a mutable category tied to particular historical moments. Other answers are also possible. "White" is: an idea; an evolving social group; an unstable identity subject to expansion and contraction; a trope for welcome immigrant groups; a mechanism for excluding those of unfamiliar origin; an artifice of social prejudice. Indeed, Whiteness can be one, all, or any combination of these, depending on the local setting in which it is used. On the other hand, in light of the prerequisite cases, some answers are no longer acceptable. "White" is not: a biologically defined group; a static taxonomy; a neutral designation of difference; an objective description of immutable traits; a scientifically defensible division of humankind; an accident of nature unmolded by the hands of people. No, it is none of these. In the end, the prerequisite cases leave us with this: "white" is common knowledge.

White Race-Consciousness

The racial prerequisite cases demonstrate that Whiteness is socially constructed. They thus serve as a convenient point of departure for a discussion of White identity as it exists today, particularly regarding the content of Whiteness.

As a category, "white" was constructed by the prerequisite courts in a two-step process that ultimately defined not just the boundaries of that group but its identity as well. First, note that the courts constructed the bounds of Whiteness by deciding on a case by case basis who was *not* White. Though the prerequisite courts were charged with defining the term "white person," they did so not through an appeal to a freestanding notion of Whiteness, but instead negatively, by identifying who was non-White. Thus, from *Ah Yup* to *Thind*, the courts did not establish the parameters of Whiteness so much as the non-Whiteness of Chinese, South Asians, and so on. This comports with an understanding of races, not as absolute categories, but as comparative taxonomies of relative difference. Races do not exist as abstract categories, but only as amalgamations of people standing in complex relationships with each other. In this relational system, the prerequisite cases show that Whites are those not constructed as non-White. That is, Whites exist as a category of people subject to a double negative: they are those who are not non-White.

The second step in the construction of Whiteness more directly contributes to the content of the White character. In the second step, the prerequisite courts distinguished Whites not only by declaring certain peoples non-White but also by denigrating those so described. For example, the Court in *Thind* wrote not only that common knowledge held South Asians to be non-White but that in addition the racial identity of South Asians "is of such character and extent that the great body of our people recognize and reject it."[18] The prerequisite courts in effect labeled those who were excluded from citizenship (those who were non-White) as inferior; by implication, those who were admitted (White persons) were superior. In this way, the prerequisite cases show that Whites exist not just as the antonym of non-Whites but as the *superior* antonym. This point is confirmed by the close connection between the negative characteristics of Blacks and the opposite, positive attributes of Whites. Blacks have been constructed as lazy, ignorant, lascivious, and criminal, Whites as industrious, knowledgeable, virtuous, and law abiding.[19] For each negative characteristic ascribed to people of color, an equal but opposite and positive characteristic is imputed to Whites. To this list, the prerequisite cases add Whites as citizens and others as aliens.[20] These cases show that Whites fashion an identity for themselves that is the positive mirror image of the negative identity imposed on people of color.

This relational construction of the content of White identity points towards a programmatic practice of dismantling Whiteness as it is currently constituted. Certainly, in a setting in which White identity exists as the superior antonym to the identity of non-Whites, elaborating a positive White racial identity is a dangerous proposition. It ignores the reality that Whiteness is already defined almost exclusively in terms of positive attributes. Further, it disregards the extent to which positive White attributes seem to require the negative traits that supposedly define minorities. Recognizing that White identity is a self-fashioned, hierarchical fantasy, Whites should attempt to dismantle Whiteness as it currently exists. Whites should renounce their privileged racial character, though not simply out of guilt or any sense of self-deprecation. Rather, they should dismantle the edifice of Whiteness because this mythological construct stands at the vortex of racial inequality in America. The persistence of Whiteness in its current incarnation perpetuates and necessitates patterns of superiority and inferiority. In both structure and content, Whiteness stands squarely between this society's present injustices and any future of racial equality. Whites must consciously repudiate Whiteness as it is currently constituted in the systems of meaning which are races.

Careful examination of the prerequisite cases as a study in the construction of Whiteness leads to the argument for a self-deconstructive White race-consciousness. This examination suggests as well, however, a facet of Whiteness that will certainly forestall its easy disassembly: the value of White identity to Whites. The racial prerequisite cases are, in one possible reading, an extended essay on the great value Whites place on their racial identity, and on their willingness to protect that value, even at the cost of basic justice. In their applications for citizenship, petitioners from around the world challenged the courts to define the phrase "white person" in a consistent, rational manner, a challenge that the courts could not meet except through resort to the common knowledge of those already considered White. Even though incapable of meeting this challenge, virtually no court owned up to the falsity of race, each court preferring instead to formulate fictions. To be sure, the courts were caught within the contemporary understandings of race, rendering a complete break with the prevalent ideology of racial difference unlikely, though not out of the question. Nevertheless, this does not fully explain the extraordinary lengths to which the courts went, the absurd and self-contradictory positions they assumed, or the seeming anger that colored the courts' opinions in proclaiming that certain applicants were not White. These disturbing facets of judicial inquietude, clearly evident in *Ozawa* and

Thind, arguably belie not simple uncertainty in judicial interpretation but the deep personal significance to the judges of what they had been called upon to interpret, the terms of their own existence. Wedded to their own sense of self, they demonstrated themselves to be loyal defenders of Whiteness, even to the extent of defining this identity in manners that arbitrarily excluded fully qualified persons from citizenship. Confronted by powerful challenges to the meaning of Whiteness, judges, in particular those on the Supreme Court, fully embraced this identity, in utter disregard of the costs of their actions to immigrants across the country. This perhaps is the most important lesson to be taken from the prerequisite cases. When confronted by the falsity of White identity, Whites tend not to abandon Whiteness, but to embrace and protect it. The value of Whiteness to Whites probably insures the continuation of a White self-regard predicated on racial superiority.

NOTES

1. Ex parte Shahid, 205 F. 812, 813 (E.D. S.C. 1913).
2. Act of March 26, 1790, Ch. 3, 1 Stat. 103. Naturalization involves the conferring of the nationality of a state upon a person after birth, by whatever means. *See* Immigration and Nationality Act § 101(a)(23), 8 U.S.C. § 1101(a)(23) (1952).
3. Immigration and Nationality Act § 311, 8 U.S.C. § 1422 (1952).
4. Louis DeSipio and Harry Pachon, *Making Americans: Administrative Discretion and Americanization*, 12 CHICANO-LATINO L. REV. 52, 54 (1992) (giving the figure as 1,240,700 persons).
5. *Proceedings of the Asiatic Exclusion League* 8 (1910), *quoted in* RONALD TAKAKI, STRANGERS FROM A DIFFERENT SHORE: A HISTORY OF ASIAN AMERICANS 298 (1989).
6. YUJI ICHIOKA, THE ISSEI: THE WORLD OF THE FIRST GENERATION JAPANESE IMMIGRANTS, 1885–1924, at 176–226 (1988).
7. John Wigmore, *American Naturalization and the Japanese*, 28 AMER. L. REV. 818 (1894).
8. United States v. Cartozian, 6. F.2d 919 (D.Ore. 1925). The contribution of Boas to anthropology is discussed in AUDREY SMEDLEY, RACE IN NORTH AMERICA: ORIGIN AND EVOLUTION OF A WORLDVIEW 274–282 (1993).
9. In re Ah Yup, 1 F. 223, 224 (D. Cal. 1878).
10. *Id.* at 223.
11. *Id.* at 223–24.
12. 260 U.S. 178, 198 (1922).
13. 261 U.S. 204, 211 (1922).
14. *Id.*
15. *Id.*
16. *Id.* at 214–15.
17. *Shahid, supra*, note 1, 205 Fed. at 813.
18. *Thind, supra*, note 13, 261 U.S. at 215.
19. Kimberlé Crenshaw, Race, *Reform and Retrenchment: Transformation*

and Legitimation in Antidiscrimination Law, 101 HARV. L. REV. 1331, 1373 (1988).

20. Drawing on a wider range of cases, Neil Gotanda also notes the close linkage of non-Black minorities with foreignness. Neil Gotanda, *"Other Non-Whites" in American Legal History: A Review* of Justice at War, 85 COLUM. L. REV. 1186, 1190–92 (1985).

48 Innocence and Affirmative Action

THOMAS ROSS

WHEN we create arguments, we reveal ourselves by the words and ideas we choose to employ. Verbal structures that are used widely and persistently are especially worth examination. Arguments made with repeated, almost formulaic, sets of words suggest a second argument flowing beneath the apparent argument. Beneath the apparently abstract language and the syllogistic form of these arguments, we may discover the deeper currents that explain, at least in part, why we seem so attached to these verbal structures.

Argument about affirmative action is particularly wrenching and divisive, especially among people who agree, formally speaking, on the immorality of racism. In a world where the dominant public ideology is one of nonracism, where the charge of racism is about as explosive as one can make, disagreement about affirmative action often divides us in an angry and tragic manner.

I shall examine a recurring element of the rhetoric of affirmative action. This element, the "rhetoric of innocence," relies on invocation of the "innocent white victim" of affirmative action. The rhetoric of innocence is a rich source of the deeper currents of our affirmative action debate. By revealing those deeper currents, we may gain a clearer sense of why the issue of affirmative action so divides good people, white and of color. Getting clearer about ourselves often is painful and disturbing. And the reason is simple—the rhetoric of innocence is connected to racism. It is connected in several ways, but, most disturbingly, the rhetoric embodies and reveals the unconscious racism in each of us. This unconscious racism embedded in our rhetoric accounts, at least in part, for the tragic impasse we reach in our conversations about affirmative action. My hope is that by dragging out these deeper and darker parts of our rhetoric we may have a better chance of continuing our conversation. If we each can acknowledge the racism that we cannot entirely slough off, we may be able to move past that painful impasse and talk of what we ought to do.

43 VAND. L. REV. 297 (1990). Originally published in the Vanderbilt Law Review. Reprinted by permission.

The Rhetoric of Innocence

A persistent and apparently important part of the affirmative action dialogue, both judicial and academic, is what can be termed the "rhetoric of innocence." The rhetoric of innocence is used most powerfully by those who seek to deny or severely to limit affirmative action, the "white rhetoricians."[1] This rhetoric has two related forms.

First, the white rhetorician may argue the plight of the "innocent white victims" of the affirmative action plan. The white applicant to medical school, the white contractor seeking city construction contracts, and so on are each "innocent" in a particular sense of the word. Their "innocence" is a presumed feature, not the product of any actual and particular inquiry. It is presumed that the white victim is not guilty of a racist act that has denied the minority applicant the job or other position she seeks; in that particular sense of the word, the white person is "innocent." The white rhetorician usually avoids altogether questions that suggest a different and more complex conception of innocence. In particular, the rhetoric of innocence avoids the argument that white people generally have benefited from the oppression of people of color, that white people have been advantaged by this oppression in a myriad of obvious and less obvious ways. Thus, the rhetoric of innocence obscures this question: What white person is "innocent," if innocence is defined as the absence of advantage at the expense of others?

The second and related part of the rhetoric of innocence is the questioning of the "actual victim" status of the black beneficiary of the affirmative action plan. Because an affirmative action plan does not require particular and individualized proof of discrimination, the rhetorician is able to question or deny the "victim" status of the minority beneficiary of the plan. "Victim" status thereby is recognized only for those who have been subjected to particular and proven racial discrimination with regard to the job or other interest at stake. As with the first part of the rhetoric, the argument avoided is the one that derives from societal discrimination: if discrimination against people of color is pervasive, what black person is not an "actual victim"?

These two parts work as a unitary rhetoric. Within this rhetoric, affirmative action plans have two important effects. They hurt innocent white people, and they advantage undeserving black people. The unjust suffering of the white person becomes the source of the black person's windfall. These conjoined effects give the rhetoric power. Affirmative action does not merely do bad things to good ("innocent") people nor merely do good things for bad ("undeserving") people; affirmative action does both at once and in coordination. Given the obvious power of the rhetoric of innocence, its use and persistence in the opinions of those Justices who seek to deny or severely to limit affirmative action is not surprising.

The Supreme Court's affirmative action jurisprudence essentially began with *Regents of the University of California v. Bakke*.[2] From *Bakke* through the most recently decided cases, the Court has splintered again and again, the Justices authoring opinions that constitute a bitter and divisive dialogue.[3] Within that dialogue the rhetoric of innocence is a persistent and powerful presence. In *Bakke* a majority of the Court struck down a medical school admissions program that set aside a specific number of places for minorities only.[4] The majority concluded that, although the admissions process might take account of race, the quota system employed by the state medical school either violated Title VI or denied the white applicants their constitutional right to equal protection under the fourteenth amendment.[5]

Justice Lewis Powell introduced the rhetoric of innocence to the Court's affirmative action discourse while announcing the judgment for the Court in *Bakke*. He used the rhetoric several times in the course of the opinion. Powell wrote of the patent unfairness of "innocent persons . . . asked to endure . . . [deprivation as] the price of membership in the dominant majority."[6] He wrote of "forcing innocent persons . . . to bear the burdens of redressing grievances not of their making."[7] In a passage that embodies both the assumption of white innocence and the questioning of black victimization, Powell distinguished the school desegregation cases and other precedents in which racially drawn remedies were endorsed.

> The State certainly has a legitimate and substantial interest in ameliorating, or eliminating where feasible, the disabling effects of identified discrimination. . . . In the school cases, the States were required by court order to redress the wrongs worked by specific instances of racial discrimination. That goal was far more focused than the remedying of the effects of "societal discrimination," an amorphous concept of injury that may be ageless in its reach into the past.
>
> We have never approved a classification that aids persons perceived as members of relatively victimized groups at the expense of other innocent individuals in the absence of judicial, legislative, or administrative findings of constitutional or statutory violations. . . . Without such findings of constitutional or statutory violations, it cannot be said that the government has any greater interest in helping one individual than in refraining from harming another. Thus, the government has no compelling justification for inflicting such harm.[8]

Thus Powell, who sought to circumscribe tightly the ambit of affirmative action, relied on the rhetoric of innocence.

In contrast to Powell's opinion, the dissenting opinions by Justices William Brennan and Thurgood Marshall each challenged the premises of the rhetoric. Justice Brennan rejected the idea of requiring proof of individual and specific discrimination as a prerequisite to affirmative action.[9] Marshall attacked directly the rhetoric of white innocence and the questioning of black victimization: "It is unnecessary in 20th-century America to have individual Negroes demonstrate that they have been victims of racial discrimination; the racism of our society has been so pervasive that none, regardless of wealth or position, has managed to escape its impact."[10]

The rhetoric of innocence continued in the cases following *Bakke*. In *Fullilove v. Klutznik*[11] a majority of the Court upheld a federal statute mandating a ten percent set-aside for minority contractors in federally supported public works projects. Justice Warren Burger made use of the rhetoric of innocence, even while writing to uphold the set-aside: "When effectuating a limited and properly tailored remedy to cure the effects of prior discrimination . . . 'a sharing of the burden' by innocent parties is not impermissible."[12] He proceeded to emphasize the "relatively light" burden imposed on the white contractors and the flexible nature of the set-aside provisions. Thus, although Justice Burger wrote an opinion that upholds a particular affirmative action program, he used the rhetoric of innocence to emphasize the limitations of his endorsement. Burger thereby implied that a heavier burden on the innocent white parties might have made the plan unconstitutional.

Justice Potter Stewart, dissenting, expressed the rhetoric in both its "innocence" and "actual victimization" parts:

> [The federal statute's characteristics] are not the characteristics of a racially conscious remedial decree that is closely tailored to the evil to be corrected. In today's society, it constitutes far too gross an oversimplification to assume that every single Negro, Spanish-speaking citizen, Oriental, Indian, Eskimo, and Aleut potentially interested in construction contracting currently suffers from the effects of past or present racial discrimination. Since the MBE set-aside must be viewed as resting upon such an assumption, it necessarily paints with too broad a brush. Except to make whole the identified victims of racial discrimination, the guarantee of equal protection prohibits the government from taking detrimental action against innocent people on the basis of the sins of others of their own race.[13]

Powell again invoked the rhetoric in his majority opinion in *Wygant v. Jackson Board of Education*.[14] In *Wygant* the majority struck down the provisions of a collective bargaining agreement that gave blacks greater protection from layoffs than that accorded white teachers with more seniority. The agreement was a product of prior litigation seeking to provide meaningful integration of the school faculties in the county. Without the special protection for the newly hired black teachers, the layoffs essentially would have undone the previous integration efforts. The majority nonetheless concluded that the agreement violated the constitutional rights of the laid-off white teachers:

> Societal discrimination, without more, is too amorphous a basis for imposing a racially classified remedy. . . . No one doubts that there has been serious racial discrimination in this country. But as the basis for imposing discriminatory *legal* remedies that work against innocent people, societal discrimination is insufficient and over-expansive. In the absence of particularized findings, a court could uphold remedies that are ageless in their reach into the past, and timeless in their ability to affect the future.[15]

Thus, mere societal discrimination is an insufficient predicate for the disadvantaging of innocent white teachers. This "societal discrimination" point is an important variant of the rhetoric of innocence. The black teachers are not real victims; they are subject merely to societal discrimination, a phenomenon that seems weak and abstract, practiced by no one in particular against no one in particular.[16]

Justice Byron White wrote separately in *Wygant*. For him the case was simple. White reasoned: The firing of white teachers to make room for blacks in order to integrate the faculty would be patently unconstitutional; laying off whites to keep blacks on the job is the same thing; therefore, the layoff provision is unconstitutional. In White's pithy one paragraph opinion he used the "actual victimization" part of the rhetoric, referring to "blacks, none of whom has been shown to be a victim of any racial discrimination."[17]

City of Richmond v. J. A. Croson Co.,[18] continues the uninterrupted use of the rhetoric of innocence in affirmative action dialogue within the Court. Justice Sandra Day O'Connor's opinion for the Court struck down Richmond's ordinance setting aside thirty percent of the dollar amount of city construction contract work for minority contractors. Her opinion relied on the essential premises and conclusion of the rhetoric without using the usual phrases. Justice O'Connor wrote of the "generalized assertion" and "amorphous claim" of racism in the Richmond construction industry, thereby denying the actual victimization of the black beneficiaries."[19] Other justices followed suit.

As we have seen, from *Bakke* through *Richmond* the Court has splintered on the issue of affirmative action. Through the splintering and uncertainty, the rhetoric of innocence persists as an important tool in the hands of those who seek to limit the use of affirmative action. I now explore the deeper nature and special power of this important rhetorical tool.

Innocence and Racism

It is hard to know whether, and how, rhetoric works. We do know, however, that both judges and academicians often use the rhetoric of innocence. Those who use the rhetoric presumably find it persuasive or at least useful. What then could be the sources and nature of its apparent power?

INNOCENCE

The power of the rhetoric of innocence comes in part from that of the conception of "innocence" in our culture. The idea of innocent victims, particularly when coupled with the specter of those who victimize them, is a pervasive and potent story in our culture. "Innocence" is connected to the powerful cultural forces and ideas of religion, good and evil, and sex. "Innocence" is defined typically as "freedom from guilt or sin" or, in the sexual sense, as "chastity."

The centrality of the conception of "innocence" to the Christian religion is obvious. Christ is the paradigmatic "innocent victim." Mary is the perfect embodiment of innocence as chaste. Although the concept of "original sin" complicates the notion of innocence in Christian theology, the striving toward innocence and the veneration of those who come closest to achieving it and thereby suffer are important ideas in modern Christian practice.[20] "Blessed are those who are persecuted for righteousness' sake, for theirs is the kingdom of heaven."[21] The idea of innocence also is connected to the myths and symbols of evil. For example, Paul Ricoeur in *The Symbolism of Evil* demonstrates the cultural significance of the "dread of the impure" and the terror of "defilement."[22] The contrasting state for "impure," or the state to which the rites of purification might return us, is "innocence," freedom from guilt or sin. Ricoeur's thesis spans the modern and classical cultures. He makes clear the persistence and power of the symbolism of evil and its always present contrast, the state of innocence.

What is central within the modern culture surely will be reflected in its literature. And in literature the innocent victim is everywhere. In *Innocent Victims—Poetic Injustice in Shakespearean Tragedy*, R. S. White argued "that Shakespeare was constantly and uniquely concerned with the fate of the innocent victim."[23] White observed, "In every tragedy by Shakespeare, alongside the tragic protagonist who is proclaimed by himself and others as a suffering centre, stands, sometimes silently, the figure of pathos who is a lamb of goodness: Lavinia, Ophelia, Desdemona, Cordelia, the children."[24] Shakespeare was not alone in the use of women and children drawn as innocent victims. In the work of Dickens, Hugo, Melville, and others, the suffering innocent is a central character.

The innocent victim is part of sexual practice and mythology. The recurring myth of the "demon lover" and its innocent victim is one example.[25] Moreover, we are preoccupied with innocence in the female partner as part of the mythological background of rape and prostitution and in our prerequisites in the chosen marriage partner.[26] The idea of the innocent victim always conjures the one who takes away her innocence and who thereby himself becomes both the "defiler" and the "defiled." In literature and in life the innocent victim is used as a means of conjuring the notion of defilement. In fact, it is impossible to make sense of the significance of either the "innocent victim" or the "defiler" without imagining the other. Each conception is given real significance by its implicit contrast with the other. Thus, the invocation of innocence is also the invocation of sin, guilt, and defilement.

The rhetoric of innocence in affirmative action discourse thus invokes one of the most powerful symbols of our culture, that of innocence and its always present opposite, the defiled taker. When the white person is called the innocent victim of affirmative action, the rhetorician is invoking not just the idea of innocence but also that of the not innocent, the defiled taker. The idea of the defiled taker is given a particular name in one of two ways. First, merely invoking the "innocent white victim" triggers at some level its rhetorically natural opposite, the "defiled black taker." This implicit personification is made explicit by the second part of the rhetoric, the questioning of the "actual victim" status of the black person who benefits from the affirmative action plan. The contrast is between the innocent white victim and the undeserving black taker. The cultural significance of the ideas of innocence and defilement thus gives the rhetoric of innocence a special sort of power.

UNCONSCIOUS RACISM

The rhetoric of innocence draws its power not only from the cultural significance of its basic terms but also from its connection with "unconscious racism." Professor Charles Lawrence explored the concept of "unconscious racism" and its implications for equal protection:[27]

> Americans share a common historical and cultural heritage in which racism has played and still plays a dominant role. Because of this shared experience, we also inevitably share many ideas, attitudes, and beliefs that attach significance to an individual's race and induce negative feelings and opinions about nonwhites. To the extent that this cultural belief system has influenced all of us, we are all racists. At the same time, most of us are unaware of our racism. We do not recognize the ways in which our cultural experience has influenced our beliefs about race or the occasions on which those beliefs affect our actions. In other words, a large part of the behavior that produces racial discrimination is influenced by unconscious racial motivation.[28]

We are each, in this sense of the word, racists.

Lawrence's thesis is disturbing especially to the white liberal who can think of a no more offensive label than that of "racist." Moreover, the white intellectual, whether politically liberal or conservative, typically expresses only disgust for the words and behavior of the white supremacists and neo-Nazis he connects with the label "racist." The dominant public ideology has become nonracist. Use of racial epithets, expressions of white genetic superiority, and avowal of formal segregation are not part of the mainstream of public discourse. These ways of speaking, which were part of the public discourse several decades ago, are deemed by most today as irrational utterances emanating from the few remaining pockets of racism.

Notwithstanding that the public ideology has become nonracist, the culture continues to teach racism. The manifestations of racial stereotypes pervade our media and language. Racism is reflected in the complex set of individual and collective choices that make our schools, our neighborhoods, our work places, and our lives racially segregated.[29] Racism today paradoxically is both "irrational and normal,"[30] at once inconsistent with the dominant public ideology and embraced by each of us, albeit for most of us at the unconscious level. This paradox of irrationality and normalcy is part of the reason for the unconscious nature of the racism. When our culture teaches us to be racist and our ideology teaches us that racism is evil, we respond by excluding the forbidden lesson from our consciousness.

The repression of our racism is a crucial piece of the rhetoric of innocence. First, we sensibly can claim the mantle of innocence only by denying the charge of racism. We as white persons and nonracists are innocent; we have done no harm and do not deserve to suffer for the sins of those other white people who were racists. If we accept unconscious racism, this self-conception is unraveled. Second, the black beneficiaries of affirmative action can be denied "actual victim" status only so long as racists are thought of as either historical figures or aberrational and isolated characters in contemporary culture. By thinking of racists in this way we deny the presence and power of racism today, relegating the ugly term primarily to the past. Thus, by repressing our unconscious racism we make coherent our self-conception of innocence and make sensible the question of the actual victimization of blacks.

The existence of unconscious racism undermines the rhetoric of innocence. The "innocent white victim" is no longer quite so innocent. Furthermore, the idea of unconscious racism makes problematic the "victim" part of the characterization. The victim is one who suffers an undeserved loss. If the white person who is disadvantaged by an affirmative action plan is also a racist, albeit at an unconscious level, the question of desert becomes more complicated.

The implications of unconscious racism for the societal distribution of burdens and benefits also undermine the "innocent" status of the white man. As blacks are burdened in a myriad of ways because of the persistence of unconscious racism, the white man thereby is benefited. On a racially integrated law faculty, for example, a black law professor must overcome widespread assumptions of inferiority held by students and colleagues, while white colleagues enjoy the benefit of the positive presumption and of the contrast with their black colleague.[31]

The historical manifestations of racism have worked to the advantage of whites in every era. Just as slavery provided the resources to make possible the genteel life of the plantation owner and his white family in early-nineteenth-century Virginia, more than a century later the state system of public school segregation diverted the State's resources to me and not to my black peers in Virginia. The lesson of unconscious racism, however, is that the obvious advantages of state sponsored racism, the effects of which still are being reaped by whites today, are not the only basis for skewing the societal balance sheet. Even after the abolition of state racism, the cultural teachings persist. The presence and power of unconscious racism is apparent in job interviews, in social encounters, in courtrooms and conference rooms, and on the streets. In our culture whites are necessarily advantaged, because blacks are presumed at the unconscious level by most as lazy, dumb, and criminally prone. Because the white person is advantaged by assumptions that consequently hurt blacks, the rhetorical appeal of the unfairness to the "innocent white victim" in the affirmative action contest is undermined.

Moreover, the "actual victim" status of the black person who benefits from affirmative action is much harder to question once unconscious racism is acknowledged. Because racial discrimination is part of the cultural structure, each person of color is subject to it, everywhere and at all times.[32] The recognition of unconscious racism makes odd the question whether this person is an "actual victim." The white rhetorician often seeks to acknowledge and, at the same time, to blunt the power of unconscious racism by declaring that "societal discrimination" is an insufficient predicate for affirmative action.[33] "Societal discrimination" never is defined with any precision in the white rhetoric, but it suggests an ephemeral, abstract kind of discrimination, committed by no one in particular and committed against no one in particular, a kind of amorphous inconvenience for persons of color. By this term the white rhetorician at once can acknowledge the idea of unconscious racism while giving it a different name and therefore a different and trivial connotation.

The rhetoric of innocence coupled with the idea of "societal discrimination" thus obscures unconscious racism and keeps rhetorically alive the innocence of the white person and the question of actual victimization of the black person. Unconscious racism meets that rhetoric on its own terms. Once one accepts some version of the idea of unconscious racism, the rhetoric of innocence is weakened analytically, if not defeated.

The rhetoric of innocence and unconscious racism connect in yet another way. Through the lens of unconscious racism the rhetoric itself can be seen to embody racism. Professor Lawrence described the two types of beliefs about the out-group held by racists:

> [S]tudies have found that racists hold two types of stereotyped beliefs: They believe the out-group is dirty, lazy, oversexed, and without control of their instincts (a typical accusation against blacks), or they believe the out-group is pushy, ambitious, conniving, and in control of business, money, and industry (a typical accusation against Jews).[34]

The stereotype of lazy and oversexed is abundant in our culture's characterization of the black person.[35]

The two parts of the rhetoric of innocence connect to and trigger at some level the stereotypical racist beliefs about blacks. The assertion of the innocent white victim draws power from the implicit contrast with the "defiled taker." The defiled taker is the black person who undeservedly reaps the advantages of affirmative action. The use of the idea of innocence and its opposite, defilement, coalesces with the unconscious racist belief that the black person is not innocent in a sexual sense, that the black person is sexually defiled by promiscuity.[36] The "over-sexed" black person of the racist stereotype becomes the perfect implicit, and unconsciously embraced, contrast to the innocent white person.

A similar analysis applies to the second part of the rhetoric of innocence. The question whether the black person is an actual victim implies that the black person does not deserve what the black person gets. This question draws power from the stereotypical racist belief that the black person is lazy. The lazy black seeks and takes the unearned advantages of affirmative action.

My point is not that the white rhetorician is consciously drawing on the stereotypical racist beliefs. Nor is the white audience consciously embracing those beliefs when they experience the rhetoric of innocence in affirmative action discourse. Both the rhetoricians and their audience are likely to reject the stereotypes at the conscious level. Moreover, they would be offended at the very suggestion that they might hold such beliefs. The great lesson of Professor Lawrence's work is that the beliefs are still there, even in the white liberal. The beliefs are there because the teacher is our culture; any person who is part of the culture has been taught the lesson of racism. While most of us have struggled to unlearn the lesson and have succeeded at the conscious level, none of us can slough off altogether the lesson at the unconscious level.

If we see the rhetoric of innocence as just another part of the debate, we get nowhere. If instead we push past the apparently simple forms of the rhetoric and struggle to understand the deeper currents, perhaps we can acknowledge and then move beyond the question of our own unconscious racism and start talking, in a hopeful and productive way, of what we might do about it.

Examination of the rhetoric of innocence may teach us that "innocence" is a powerful and very dangerous idea which simply does not belong in the affirmative action debate. Real and good people certainly will suffer as a result of the use of affirmative action. Yet, we will be much further along in our efforts to deal with that painful fact if we put aside the loaded conception of innocence. The question for us is not whether we shall make innocent people suffer or not; it is how do we get to a world where good people, white and of color, no longer suffer because of the accidental circumstances of their race. We cannot get from here to there if we refuse to examine the words we use and deny the unconscious racism that surrounds those words.

NOTES

1. I do not use the term "white rhetorician" to designate the race of the rhetorician. It is the white perspective, or the "whiteness" of the rhetoric, that makes the label appropriate, whatever the race of the rhetorician. The power of rhetorical perspective of course is not limited to the discourse of affirmative action. *See, e.g.,* Martha Minow, *The Supreme Court, 1986 Term—Foreword: Justice Engendered,* 101 HARV. L. REV. 10 (1987). In her thoughtful exploration of the "dilemmas of difference," Professor Minow reminds us: "Court judgments endow some perspectives, rather than others, with power." *Id.* at 94.
2. 438 U.S. 265 (1978).
3. *See* L. TRIBE, AMERICAN CONSTITUTIONAL LAW 1530–44 (1988).
4. The admissions scheme in *Bakke* was a special program completely separate from the regular one. If an applicant indicated on the regular application form a desire to be considered as a member of a "minority group," the application was forwarded to a special admissions committee. This committee then reviewed these candidates and rated them according to interview summaries, grade point averages, and test scores. Unlike the regular candidates, the special candidates did not have to meet the minimum grade point average of 2.5. The special candidates also were not compared to the general applicants; rather, they were compared only among themselves. The special committee then recommended candidates for admission until the number prescribed by the faculty was admitted. In 1974 this number was 16 out of a class of 100. *Bakke,* 438 U.S. at 272–75.
5. *Id.* at 421 (opinion of Stevens, J.); *id.* at 319–20 (opinion of Powell, J.).
6. *Id.* at 294 n.34 (opinion of Powell, J.).
7. *Id.* at 298.
8. *Id.* at 307–09 (citations and footnote omitted).

9. "Such relief does not require as a predicate proof that recipients of preferential advancement have been individually discriminated against; it is enough that each recipient is within a general class of persons likely to have been the victims of discrimination." *Id.* at 363 (opinion of Brennan, White, Marshall, and Blackmun, JJ.).

10. *Id.* at 400 (opinion of Marshall, J.).

11. 448 U.S. 448 (1980).

12. *Id.* at 484 (quoting Franks v. Bowman Transp. Co., 424 U.S. 747, 777 (1976)).

13. *Id.* at 530 n.12 (Stewart, J., dissenting). In a rather odd extension of the rhetoric, Stewart labeled affirmative action as a form of modern nobility, "the creation once again by government of privileges based on birth." *Id.* at 531. By this analogy the black beneficiaries of affirmative action are like the European noblemen of the Old World, enjoying great and utterly unearned advantage at the expense of the whites, who are like the feudal serfs.

14. 476 U.S. 267 (1986).

15. *Id.* at 276 (emphasis in original).

16. Powell again revealed his commitment to the conception of innocence when he used the term "innocent" to describe the disadvantaged white repeatedly in a brief two-paragraph passage contrasting *Wygant* with the Court's precedents:

> We have recognized, however, that in order to remedy the effects of prior discrimination, it may be necessary to take race into account. As part of this Nation's dedication to eradicating racial discrimination, innocent persons may be called upon to bear some of the burden of the remedy. "When effectuating a limited and properly tailored remedy to cure the effects of prior discrimination, such a 'sharing of the burden' by *innocent* parties is not impermissible. In *Fullilove,* the challenged statute required at least 10 percent of federal public works funds to be used in contracts with minority-owned business enterprises. This requirement was found to be within the remedial powers of Congress in part because the "actual 'burden' shouldered by nonminority firms is relatively light."

17. *Id.* at 295 (White, J., concurring).

18. 109 S. Ct. 706 (1989).

19. O'Connor stated:

> [A] generalized assertion that there has been past discrimination in an entire industry provides no guidance for a legislative body to determine the precise scope of the injury it seeks to remedy. . . .
>
> . . . .
>
> . . . [A]n amorphous claim that there has been past discrimination in a particular industry cannot justify the use of an unyielding racial quota.

Id. at 723–24.

20. "[U]nless persons are vulnerable to injury, pain, and suffering as possible consequences of choice, choice would have no meaning. . . . [T]he *necessity* that moral evil be possible seems implied in the possibility of good." R. MONK & J. STAMEN, EXPLORING CHRISTIANITY: AN INTRODUCTION 144 (1984) (emphasis in original). Professor Charles H. Long explored the power of religious symbolism,

particularly as it relates to questions of race. *See* C. LONG, SIGNIFICATIONS: SIGNS, SYMBOLS AND IMAGES IN THE INTERPRETATION OF RELIGION (1986).

21. *Matthew* 5:10 (New King James).

22. P. RICOEUR, THE SYMBOLISM OF EVIL 25 (1969).

23. R. WHITE, INNOCENT VICTIMS: POETIC INJUSTICE IN SHAKESPEAREAN TRAGEDY 5 (1986).

24. *Id.* at 6.

25. *See generally* T. REED, DEMON-LOVERS AND THEIR VICTIMS IN BRITISH FICTION (1988).

26. *See* H. LIPS & N. COLWILL, THE PSYCHOLOGY OF SEX DIFFERENCES 112–13 (1978) (observing that "[i]n our culture young and adolescent girls are not expected to engage in overt sexual activity, although it is more permissible for boys to do so," and that "[s]ociologically, it has been explained in terms of parents' differential expectations of appropriate behavior for boys and girls").

During the early times of Christianity, a woman thought to have become pregnant by a man other than her husband was humiliated publicly by a priest. Her hair was untied and her dress torn, and she was made to drink a potion consisting of holy water, dust, and ink. "If she suffers no physical damage from that terrifying psychological ordeal, her innocence is presumed to have protected her." W. PHIPPS, GENESIS AND GENDER: BIBLICAL MYTHS OF SEXUALITY AND THEIR CULTURAL IMPACT 71 (1989).

27. Lawrence, *The Id, the Ego, and Equal Protection: Reckoning with Unconscious Racism*, 39 STAN. L. REV. 317 (1987); *see also* J. KOVEL, WHITE RACISM: A PSYCHOHISTORY (1970).

28. Lawrence, *supra*, note 27, at 322 (footnotes omitted). "Simply put, while most Americans avow and genuinely believe in the principle of equality, most white Americans still consider black people as such to be obnoxious and socially inferior." G. Hazard, *Permissive Affirmative Action for the Benefit of Blacks*, 1987 U. ILL. L. REV. 379, 385.

29. A process known as the tipping phenomenon occurs when white families abandon a neighborhood after the black percentage of the population exceeds a certain amount, usually between 30 and 50 percent black. Bruce Ackerman, *Integration for Subsidized Housing and the Question of Racial Occupancy Controls*, 26 STAN. L. REV. 245, 251 (1974); *see also* Reynolds Farley, *Residential Segregation and Its Implications for School Integration*, 39 LAW & CONTEMP. PROBS. 164 (1975). In 1970 a study of 109 cities was conducted to determine the degree of racial integration. In every one of those cities, at least 60 percent of either the white or the black population would have had to shift their places of residence to achieve complete residential integration. In all but three of those cities, the figure was increased to at least 70 percent. *Id.* at 165. "Where neighborhoods are highly segregated, schools tend also to be highly segregated." *Id.* at 187. In some Northern districts where the courts and HEW had not integrated schools, school segregation was even higher than would be expected based on residential segregation levels. *Id.*

30. Lawrence, *supra* note 27, at 331.

31. *See* Kennedy, *Racial Critiques of Legal Academia*, 102 HARV. L REV. 1745 (1989); *see also* D. Bell, *Strangers in Academic Paradise: Law Teachers of*

Color in Still White Law Schools, 20 U.S.F. L REV. 385 (1986); A. Haines, *Minority Law Professors and the Myth of Sisyphus: Consciousness and Praxis Within the Special Teaching Challenge in American Law Schools,* 10 NAT'L BLACK L.J. 247 (1988).

32. "The battle against pernicious racial discrimination or its effects is nowhere near won." *Richmond,* 109 S. Ct. at 757 (Marshall, J., dissenting).

33. *See, e.g.,* Wygant v. Jackson Bd. of Educ., 476 U.S. 267, 274 (1986).

34. Lawrence, *supra,* note 27, at 333 (footnotes omitted).

35. William Brink and Louis Harris asserted that "[t]he stereotyped beliefs about Negroes are firmly rooted in less-privileged, less-well-educated white society: the beliefs that Negroes smell different, have looser morals, are lazy, and laugh a lot." W. BRINK & L. HARRIS, BLACK & WHITE 137 (1976).

36. *See* KOVEL, *supra,* note 27, at 67, 79. The miscegenation laws finally ruled unconstitutional in Loving v. Virginia, 388 U.S. 1 (1967), are a testament to the connection between racism and sex.

49 Obscuring the Importance of Race: The Implication of Making Comparisons between Racism and Sexism (or Other -isms)

TRINA GRILLO and STEPHANIE M. WILDMAN

W H I L E this chapter was being written, Trina Grillo, who is of Afro-Cuban and Italian descent, was diagnosed as having Hodgkin's Disease (a form of cancer) and underwent several courses of radiation therapy. In talking about this experience she said that "cancer has become the first filter through which I see the world. It used to be race, but now it is cancer. My neighbor just became pregnant, and all I could think was 'How could she get pregnant? What if she gets cancer?' "

Stephanie Wildman, her co-author, who is Jewish and white, heard this remark and thought, "I understand how she feels; I worry about getting cancer too. I probably worry about it more than most people, because I am such a worrier."

But Stephanie's worry is not the same as Trina's. Someone with cancer can think of nothing else. She cannot watch the World Series without wondering which players have had cancer or who in the players' families might have the disease. This world-view with cancer as a filter is different from just thinking or even worrying often about cancer. The worrier has the privilege of forgetting the worry sometimes, even much of the time. The worry can be turned off. The cancer patient does not have the privilege of forgetting about her cancer; even when it is not in the forefront of her thoughts, it remains in the background, coloring her world.

This dialogue about cancer illustrates a principal problem with comparing one's situation to another's. The "analogizer" often believes that her situation is the same as another's. Nothing in the comparison process challenges this belief, and the analogizer may think that she understands the other's situation fully. The analogy makes the analogizer forget the difference and allows her to stay focused on her own situation without grappling with the other person's reality.

Yet analogies are necessary tools to teach and to explain, so that we can bet-

1991 DUKE L.J. 397. Originally published in the Duke Law Journal. Reprinted by permission.

ter understand each other's experiences and realities. We have no other way to understand others' lives, except by making analogies to our own experience. Thus, the use of analogies provides both the key to greater comprehension and the danger of false understanding.

Introduction

Like cancer, racism/white supremacy is an illness. To people of color, who are the victims of racism/white supremacy, race is a filter through which they see the world. Whites do not look at the world through this filter of racial awareness, even though they also comprise a race. This privilege to ignore their race gives whites a societal advantage distinct from any received from the existence of discriminatory racism. Throughout this chapter we use the term racism/white supremacy to emphasize the link between the privilege held by whites to ignore their own race and discriminatory racism.

Author bell hooks describes her realization of the connection between these two concepts: "The word racism ceased to be the term which best expressed for me exploitation of black people and other people of color in this society and . . . I began to understand that the most useful term was white supremacy."[1] She recounts how liberal whites do not see themselves as prejudiced or interested in domination through coercion, yet "they cannot recognize the ways their actions support and affirm the very structure of racist domination and oppression that they profess to wish to see eradicated."[2] For these reasons, "white supremacy" is an important term, descriptive of American social reality. This chapter originated when the authors noticed that several identifiable phenomena occurred without fail in any racially mixed group whenever sex discrimination was analogized (implicitly or explicitly) to race discrimination. Repeatedly, at the annual meeting of the Association of American Law Schools (AALS), at meetings of feminist legal scholars, in classes on Sex Discrimination and the Law, and in law school women's caucus meetings, the pattern was the same. In each setting, although the analogy was made for the purpose of illumination, to explain sexism and sex discrimination, another unintended result ensued—the perpetuation of racism/white supremacy.

When a speaker compared sexism and racism, the significance of race was marginalized and obscured, and the different role that race plays in the lives of people of color and of whites was overlooked. The concerns of whites became the focus of discussion, even when the conversation supposedly had been centered on race discrimination. Essentialist presumptions became implicit in the discussion; it would be assumed, for example, that all women are white and all African-Americans are men. Finally, people with little experience in thinking about racism/white supremacy, but who had a hard-won understanding of the allegedly analogous oppression, assumed that they comprehended the experience of people of color and thus had standing to speak on their behalf.

No matter how carefully a setting was structured to address the question of racism/white supremacy, these problems always arose. Each of the authors has unwittingly participated in creating these problems on many occasions, yet when we have tried to avoid them, we have found ourselves accused of making others uncomfortable. Even after we had identified these patterns, we found ourselves watching in amazement as they appeared again and again, and we were unable to keep ourselves from contributing to them.

We began to question why this pattern persisted. We concluded that these phenomena have much to do with the dangers inherent in what had previously seemed to us to be a creative and solidarity-producing process—analogizing sex discrimination to race discrimination. These dangers were obscured by the promise that to discuss and compare oppressions might lead to coalition-building and understanding. On an individual psychological level, the way we empathize with and understand others is by comparing their situations with some aspects of our own. Yet, comparing sexism to racism perpetuates patterns of racial domination by marginalizing and obscuring the different roles that race plays in the lives of people of color and of whites. The comparison minimizes the impact of racism, rendering it an insignificant phenomenon—one of a laundry list of -isms or oppressions that society must suffer. This marginalization and obfuscation is evident in three recognizable patterns: (1) the taking back of center-stage from people of color, even in discussions of racism, so that white issues remain or become central in the dialogue; (2) the fostering of essentialism, so that women and people of color are implicitly viewed as belonging to mutually exclusive categories, rendering women of color invisible; and (3) the appropriation of pain or the rejection of its existence that results when whites who have compared other oppressions to race discrimination believe that they understand the experience of racism.

TAKING BACK THE CENTER

White supremacy creates in whites the expectation that issues of concern to them will be central in every discourse. Analogies serve to perpetuate this expectation of centrality. The center-stage problem occurs because dominant group members are already accustomed to being on center-stage. They have been treated that way by society; it feels natural, comfortable, and in the order of things.

The harms of discrimination include not only the easily identified disadvantages of the victims (such as exclusion from housing and jobs) and the stigma imposed by the dominant culture but also the advantages given to those who are not its victims. The white, male, heterosexual societal norm is privileged in such a way that its privilege is rendered invisible.

Because whiteness is the norm, it is easy to forget that it is not the only perspective. Thus, members of dominant groups assume that their perceptions are the pertinent ones, that their problems are the ones that need to be addressed, and that in discourse they should be the speaker rather than the listener. Part of being a member of a privileged group is being the center and the subject of all inquiry in which people of color or other non-privileged groups are the objects.

So strong is this expectation of holding center-stage that even when a time and place are specifically designated for members of a non-privileged group to be central, members of the dominant group will often attempt to take back the pivotal focus. They are stealing the center[3]—often with a complete lack of self-consciousness.

One such theft occurred at the annual meeting of a legal society, where three scholars, all people of color, were invited to speak to the plenary session about how universities might become truly multicultural. Even before the dialogue began, the views of many members of the organization were apparent by their presence or absence at the session. The audience included nearly every person of color who was attending the meeting, yet many whites chose not to attend.

When people who are not regarded as entitled to the center move into it, however briefly, they are viewed as usurpers. One reaction of the group temporarily deprived of the center is to make sure that nothing remains for the perceived usurpers to be in the center of. Thus, the whites who did not attend the plenary session, but who would have attended had there been more traditional (i.e., white) speakers, did so in part because they were exercising their privilege not to think in terms of race, and in part because they resented the "out groups" having the center.

Another tactic used by the dominant group is to steal back the center, using guerilla tactics where necessary. For example, during a talk devoted to the integration of multicultural materials into the core curriculum, a white man got up from the front row and walked noisily to the rear of the room. He then paced the room in a distracting fashion and finally returned to his seat. During the question period he was the first to rise, leaping to his feet to ask a lengthy, rambling question about how multicultural materials could be added to university curricula without disturbing the "canon"—the exact subject of the talk he had just, apparently, not listened to.

The speaker answered politely and explained how he had assigned a Navajo creation myth to accompany St. Augustine, which highlighted Augustine's paganism and resulted in each reading enriching the other. He refrained, however, from calling attention to the questioner's rude behavior during the meeting, to his asking the already-answered question, or to his presumption that the material the questioner saw as most relevant to his own life was central and "canonized," while all other reading was peripheral and, hence, dispensable.

Analogies offer protection for the traditional center. At another gathering of law professors, issues of racism, sexism, and homophobia were the focus of the plenary session for the first time in the organization's history. Again at this session, the number of white males present was far fewer than would ordinarily attend such a session. After moving presentations by an African-American woman, a Hispanic man, and a gay white man who each opened their hearts on these subjects, a question and dialogue period began.

The first speaker to rise was a white woman, who, after saying that she did not mean to change the topic, said that she wanted to discuss another sort of oppression—that of law professors in the less elite schools. As professors from what is perceived by some as a less-than-elite school, we agree that the topic is important and it would have interested us at another time. But this questioner had succeeded in depriving the other issues of time devoted (after much struggle) specifically to them, and turned the spotlight once again onto her own concerns. She did this, we believe, not out of malice, but because she too had become a victim of analogical thinking.

The problem of taking back the center exists apart from the issue of analogies; it will be with us as long as any group expects, and is led to expect, to be constantly the center of attention. But the use of analogies exacerbates this problem, for once an analogy is taken to heart it seems to the center-stealer that she is not stealing the center, but rather is continuing the discussion on the same topic, and one that she knows well.[4] So when the format of the program implicitly analogized gender and sexual preference to race, the center-stealer was encouraged to think "why not go further to another perceived oppression?"

When socially subordinated groups are lumped together, oppression begins to look like a uniform problem and one may neglect the varying and complex contexts of the different groups being addressed. If oppression is all the same, then we are all equally able to discuss each oppression, and there is no felt need for us to listen to and learn from other socially subordinated groups.

FOSTERING ESSENTIALISM

Essentialism is implicit in analogies between sex and race. Angela Harris explains gender essentialism as "[t]he notion that there is a monolithic 'women's experience' that can be described independent of other facets of experience like race, class, and sexual orientation. . . ."[5] She continues: "A corollary to gender essentialism is 'racial essentialism'—the belief that there is a monolithic 'Black Experience,' or 'Chicano Experience.' "[6]

To analogize gender to race, one must assume that each is a distinct category, the impact of which can be neatly separated, one from the other.[7] The essentialist critique shows that this division is not possible. Whenever it is attempted, the experience of women of color, who are at the intersection of these categories and cannot divide themselves to compare their own experiences, is rendered invisible. Analogizing sex discrimination to race discrimination makes it seem that all the women are white and all the men African-American. The experiential reality of women of color disappears. "Moreover, feminist essentialism represents not just an insult to black women, but a broken promise—the promise to listen to women's stories, the promise of feminist method."[8]

Many whites think that people of color are obsessed with race and find it hard to understand the emotional and intellectual energy that people of color devote to the subject. But whites are privileged in that they do not have to think about race, even though they have one. White supremacy makes whiteness the normative model. Being the norm allows whites to ignore race, except when they perceive race (usually someone else's) as intruding upon their lives.

THE APPROPRIATION OF PAIN OR THE REJECTION
OF ITS EXISTENCE

Part of the privilege of whiteness is the freedom not to think about race. Whites need to reject this privilege and to recognize and speak about their role in the racial hierarchy. Yet whites cannot speak validly for people of color, but only about their own experiences as whites. Comparing other oppressions to race gives whites a false sense that they fully understand the experience of people of color. Sometimes the profession of understanding by members of a privileged group may even be a guise for a rejection of the existence of the pain of the unprivileged. For people of color, listening to whites who profess to represent the experience of racism feels like an appropriation of the pain of living in a world of racism/white supremacy.

The privileging of some groups in society over others is a fact of contemporary American life.[9] This privileging is identifiable in the ordering of societal power between whites and people of color; men and women; heterosexuals and gays and lesbians; and able-bodied and physically challenged people. This societal ordering is clear to children as early as kindergarten.[10]

Judy Scales-Trent has written about her own experience as an African-American woman, of "being black and looking white," a woman who thereby inhabits both sides of the privilege dichotomy.[11] As one who was used to being on the unprivileged side of the race dichotomy in some aspects of her life, she discusses how the privilege of being able-bodied allowed her to ignore the pain of an unprivileged woman in a wheelchair, humiliated in seeking access to a meeting place. She realized that her role as the privileged one in that pairing likened her to whites in the racial pairing. The analogy helped her see the role of privilege and how it affects us, presenting another example of how comparisons are useful for promoting understanding. But this insight did not lead her to assume that she could speak for those who are physically challenged; rather, she realized that she needed to listen more carefully.

Not all people who learn about others' oppressions through analogy are blessed with an increased commitment to listening. White people who grasp an analogy between an oppression they have suffered and race discrimination may think that they understand the phenomenon of racism/white supremacy in all its aspects. They may believe that their opinions and judgments about race are as fully informed and cogent as those of victims of racism. In this circumstance, something approximating a lack of standing to speak exists because the insight gained by personal experience cannot easily be duplicated—certainly not without careful study of the oppression under scrutiny.[12] The power of comparisons undermines this lack of standing, because by emphasizing similarity and obscuring difference it permits the speaker implicitly to demonstrate authority about both forms of oppression. If we are members of the privileged halves of the social pairs, then what we say about the dichotomy will be listened to by the dominant culture. Thus, when we employ analogies to teach and to show oppression in a particular situation, we should be careful that in borrowing the acknowledged and clear oppression we do not neutralize it, or make it appear fungible with the oppression under discussion.

Conclusion

Given the problems that analogies create and perpetuate, should we ever use them? Analogies can be helpful. They are part of legal discourse, as well as common conversation. Consciousness raising may be the beginning of knowledge. Starting with ourselves is important, and analogies may enable us to understand the oppression of another in a way we could not without making the comparison. Instead of drawing false inferences of similarities from analogies, it is important for whites to talk about white supremacy, rather than leaving all the work for people of color. Questions remain regarding whether analogies to race can be used, particularly in legal argument, without reinforcing racism/white supremacy. There are no simple answers to this thorny problem. We will have to continue to struggle with it, and accept that our progress will be slow and tentative.

Epilogue

Today, the Sunday before Yom Kippur, I [Stephanie] go with my parents to my children's Sunday School for the closing service. The Rabbi is explaining to the children the meaning of Yom Kippur, the holiest Jewish day, the Day of Atonement. "It is the day," he explains, "when we think of how we could have been better and what we did that wasn't wonderful."

He tells a story of two men who came to the Rabbi before Yom Kippur. The first man said he felt very guilty and unclean and could never be cleansed because he had once raised a stick and hurt someone. The second man said he could not think of anything very terrible he had done and that he felt pretty good. The Rabbi told the first man to go to the field and bring back to the synagogue the largest rock that he could find. He told the second man to fill his pockets with pebbles and to bring them back to the synagogue, too.

The first man found a boulder and with much difficulty carried it to the Rabbi. The second man filled his pockets with pebbles, brought them to the Rabbi, and emptied his pockets. Pebbles scattered everywhere.

Then the Rabbi said to the first man, "Now you must carry the rock back and put it back where you found it." To the second man he said, "And you too must gather up all the pebbles and return them to where you found them."

"But how can I do that? That is impossible," said the second man.

The Rabbi telling the story says that the pebbles are like all of the things you have done for which you should wish forgiveness—you have not noticed them, nor kept track.

And so the Rabbi reminds the children that they should consider when they had ever done things that they should not have done.

He then asks them what looks different in the synagogue. The covering of the dais had been changed to white, which he explains is for purity and cleanliness. He asks the children to stand to see the special torah covers, also white to symbolize atonement and cleanliness.

My mother leans over to me at this point and says, "Can you imagine how someone black feels, hearing a story like this?"

Although no one in the temple was intending to be racist/white supremacist, the conversation could have had that effect, privileging whiteness in a society that is already racist/white supremacist. Is that racism the large rock, the boulder? It must seem truly that large and intractable to people of color. It seems like a boulder to me, when I think consciously about it. Yet it seems that as whites we treat our own racism like so many little pebbles; part of our privilege is that it may seem unimportant to us. So many times we are racist and do not even realize it, and so cannot acknowledge nor atone for it, or even attempt to change our behavior. Like the second man, we say we are not racist, because it is our wish not to be. But wishing cannot make it so. The sooner we can see the boulder *and* the pebbles, the sooner we can try to remove them.

NOTES

1. b. hooks, *Overcoming White Supremacy: A Comment, in* TALKING BACK: THINKING FEMINIST, THINKING BLACK 112 (1989).

2. *Id.* at 113.

3. Parents of young children who try to have a telephone conversation will easily recognize this phenomenon. At the sound of the parent's voice on the phone, the child materializes from the far reaches of the house to demand attention.

4. In one sex discrimination class, the assigned reading consisted of three articles by black women. In the discussion, many white women focused on sexism and how they understood the women of color by seeing the sexism in their own lives. The use of analogy allowed the white women to avoid the implications of white privilege and made the women of color feel that their distinct experience was rendered invisible.

Additionally, for the first time that semester, many members of the class had evidently not done the reading. Although the end of the semester was near, was this a guerilla tactic to retake the center or simply a lack of interest by the dominant group in the perceptions of the non-dominant group (another form of manifesting entitlement to centrality?).

5. A. Harris, chapter 22, this volume.

6. *Id.*

7. *See* ELIZABETH V. SPELMAN, INESSENTIAL WOMAN (1988) (criticizing the

way that gender essentialism ignores or effaces the experiences of women perceived as different from the white norm). For further discussion of the essentialist critique, see Kimberlé Crenshaw, *Demarginalizing the Intersection of Race and Sex: A Black Feminist Critique of Antidiscrimination Doctrine, Feminist Theory and Antiracist Politics*, 1989 U. CHI. LEGAL F. 139; and Harris, *supra* note 5; *see also* R. Delgado & J. Stefancic, *Why Do We Tell the Same Stories?* 42 STAN. L. REV. 207 (1989) (describing the role of categorization, broad or narrow, in channeling thought).

8. Harris, *supra* note 5, at 601.

9. *See, e.g.*, S. Wildman, *Integration in the 1980s: The Dream of Diversity and the Cycle of Exclusion*, 64 TULANE L. REV. 1625, 1629 (1990) (discussing the privileging of white males in the legal profession).

10. *See* F. KENDALL, DIVERSITY IN THE CLASSROOM: A MULTICULTURAL APPROACH TO THE EDUCATION OF YOUNG CHILDREN 19–21 (1983) (describing the development of racial awareness and racial attitudes in young children). Although the prevalent view would state that children are "oblivious to differences in color or culture," *id.* at 19, children's racial awareness and their positive and negative feelings about race appear by age three or four. *Id.* at 20.

11. Scales-Trent, *Commonalities: On Being Black and White, Different and the Same*, 2 YALE J. L. & FEMINISM 305, 305 (1990).

12. Standing to talk about the harm of racism has received attention in legal academic circles recently. Randall Kennedy argues that people of color should not receive particular legitimacy within the academy simply because they are of color. R. Kennedy, *Racial Critiques of Legal Academia*, 102 HARV. L. REV. 1745 (1989). Kennedy takes issue with the writings of several scholars of color whom he characterizes as proponents of a "racial distinctiveness thesis," which holds that the perspective of a scholar who has experienced racial oppression is different and valuable because of this awareness. *Id.* at 1746.

Replying to Kennedy, Leslie Espinoza argues that it is precisely Kennedy's standing as a person of color that gives special voice and power to his message: "Because Kennedy is black, his article relieves those in power in legal academia of concern about the merits of race-focused critiques of their stewardship, and it does so on the 'objective' basis of scholarly methodology." L. Espinoza, *Masks and Other Disguises: Exposing Legal Academia*, 103 HARV. L. REV. 1878 (1990). Espinoza discusses the "hidden barriers," *id.* at 1879, to participation by people of color in the legal academy; these "[s]ubtle barriers create a cycle of exclusion." *Id.* at 1881. The dominant discourse within the legal academy provides an identity to the privileged group as well as "a form of shared reality in which its own superior position is seen as natural." R. Delgado, *Storytelling for Oppositionists and Others: A Plea for Narrative*, 87 MICH. L. REV. 2411, 2412 (1989).

50 Language and Silence: Making Systems of Privilege Visible

STEPHANIE M. WILDMAN
with ADRIENNE D. DAVIS

T H E American Heritage Dictionary of the English Language defines privilege as "a special advantage, immunity, permission, right, or benefit granted to or enjoyed by an individual, class, or caste." The word is derived from the Latin *privilegium*, a law affecting an individual, *privus* meaning single or individual and *lex* meaning law. This definition touched a chord for me, because the root of the word recognizes the legal, systemic nature of the term privilege that has become lost in its modern meaning. And it is the systemic nature of these power systems that we must begin to examine.

Consider the use of terms like racism and sexism. Increasingly, people use -isms language as a way to describe discriminatory treatment. Yet this approach creates several serious problems. First, calling someone racist individualizes the behavior, ignoring the larger system within which the person is situated. To label an individual a racist conceals that racism can only occur where it is culturally, socially, and legally supported. It lays the blame on the individual rather than the forces that have shaped that individual and the society that the individual inhabits. For white people this means that they know they do not want to be labeled racist. They become concerned with how to avoid that label, rather than worrying about systemic racism and how to change it.

Second, the -isms language focuses on the larger category such as race, gender, sexual preference. -Isms language suggests that within these larger categories two seemingly neutral halves exist, equal parts in a mirror. Thus black and white, male and female, heterosexual and gay/lesbian appear as equivalent sub-parts. In fact, although the category does not take note of it, blacks and whites, men and women, heterosexuals and gays/lesbians are not equivalently situated in society. Thus the way we think and talk about the categories and sub-categories that underlie the -isms obscures the pattern of domination and subordination within each classification.

Similarly, the phrase *-isms* itself gives the illusion that all patterns of domination and subordination are the same and interchangeable. The language suggests that someone subordinated under one form of oppression would be similarly situated to another person subordinated under another system or form. Thus, someone subordinated under one form may feel no need to view himself/herself as a possible oppressor, or beneficiary of oppression, within a different form. For example, white women, having an -ism that defines their condition—sexism—may not look at the way they are privileged by racism. They have defined themselves as one of the oppressed.

Finally, the focus on individual behavior, seemingly neutral sub-parts of categories, and the apparent interchangeability underlying the vocabulary of -isms mask the existence of systems of power. It is difficult to see and talk about how oppression operates when the vocabulary itself makes those power systems invisible. The vocabulary allows us to talk about discrimination and oppression, but hides the mechanism that makes that oppression possible and efficient. It also hides the existence of specific, identifiable beneficiaries of oppression (who are not always the actual perpetrators of discrimination). The use of -isms language masks the privileging that is created by these systems of power.

The very vocabulary that we use to talk about discrimination obscures these power systems and the privilege that is their natural companion. To remedy discrimination effectively we must make the power systems and privileges which they create visible and part of discourse. So this is our problem with talking about race, sex, and sexual orientation: each needs to be described as a power system that creates privileges in some, as well as disadvantages in others. Most civil rights writing and advocacy have focused on disadvantage or discrimination, ignoring the element of privilege. To really talk about these issues, privilege must be made visible.

Law plays an important role in the perpetuation of privilege by ignoring that privilege exists. And by ignoring its existence, law, with help from our language, ensures the perpetuation of privilege.

What is privilege? We all recognize its most blatant forms. Men only admitted to this club. We won't allow African-Americans into that school. Blatant exercises of privilege certainly exist, but are not the heartbeat of what most people will say they believe belongs as part of our way of life. They are also only the tip of the iceberg in examining privilege.

When we look at privilege we see several things. First, the characteristics of the privileged group define the societal norm, often benefiting those in the privileged group. Second, privileged group members can rely on their privilege and avoid objecting to oppression. And third, privilege is rarely seen by the holder of the privilege.

Examining privilege reveals that the characteristics and attributes of those who are privileged group members are described as societal norms—as the way things are and as what is normal in society.[1] This normalization of privilege means that members of society are measured against characteristics held by those privileged. The privileged characteristic comes to define the norm. Those who stand outside are the aberrant or "alternative."

I had a powerful example of being outside the norm recently when I was called to jury service. Jurors are expected to serve until 5 P.M. During this year, my family's life has been set up so that I pick up my children after school at 2:40 and see that they get to various activities. If courtroom life were designed to privilege my needs, then there would be an afternoon recess to honor children. But in this culture children's lives, and the lives of their caretakers are the alternative (or "other") and we must conform to the norm.

Members of the privileged group gain many benefits by their affiliation with the dominant side of the power system. This power affiliation is not identified as such. It may be transformed into and presented as individual merit. This is how legacy admissions at elite colleges and professional schools are perceived to be merit-based. Achievements by members of the privileged group are viewed as meritorious and the result of individual effort, rather than as privileged. Another example is my privilege to pick up my children at 2:40.

Many feminist theorists have described the male tilt of normative standards in law, including the gendered nature of legal reasoning, the male bias inherent in the reasonable person standard, and the gender bias in classrooms. Looking more broadly at male privilege in society, definitions based on male models delineate many societal norms. As Catharine MacKinnon has observed:

> Men's physiology defines most sports, their health needs largely define insurance coverage, their socially designed biographies define workplace expectations and successful career patterns, their perspectives and concerns define quality in scholarship, their experiences and obsessions define merit, their military service defines citizenship, their presence defines family, their inability to get along with each other—their wars and rulerships—defines history, their image defines god, and their genitals define sex.[2]

Male privilege thus defines many vital aspects of American culture from a male point of view. The maleness of that view becomes masked as that view is generalized as the societal norm, the measure for us all.

Another characteristic of privilege is that members of privileged groups experience the comfort of opting out of struggles against oppression if they choose. It may be the privilege of silence. At the same time that I was the outsider in jury service, I was also a privileged insider. During voir dire, each prospective juror was asked to introduce herself or himself. The plaintiff's and defendant's attorneys then asked supplementary questions. I watched the defense attorney, during voir dire, ask each Asian-looking male prospective juror if he spoke English. No one else was asked. The judge did nothing. The Asian-American man sitting next to me smiled and recoiled as he was asked the question. I wondered how many times in his life he had been made to answer questions such as that one. I considered beginning my own questioning by saying, "I'm Stephanie Wildman, I'm a professor of law, and yes, I speak English." But I did not. I feared there would be repercussions if I did. But I exercised my white privilege by my silence. I exercised my privilege to opt out of engagement, even though this choice may not always be made consciously by someone with privilege.

Depending on the number of privileges someone has, she or he may experience the power of choosing the types of struggles in which to engage. Even this choice may be masked as an identification with oppression, thereby making the privilege that renders the choice invisible. For example, privilege based on race and class power systems may temper or alleviate gender bias or subordination based on gender. In spite of the common characteristics of normativeness, ability to choose whether to object to the power system, and invisibility, which different privileges share, the form of privilege may vary based on the type of power relationship which produces it. Within each power system, privilege manifests itself and operates in a manner shaped by the power relationship from which it results. White privilege derives from the system of white supremacy. Male privilege and heterosexual privilege result from the gender hierarchy.[3]

Examining white privilege, Peggy McIntosh has found it "an elusive and fugitive subject. The pressure to avoid it is great,"[4] she observes, as a white person who benefits from the privileges. She defines white privilege as

> an invisible package of unearned assets which [she] can count on cashing in each day, but about which [she] was "meant" to remain oblivious. White privilege is like an invisible weightless knapsack of special provisions, assurance, tools, maps, guides, codebooks, passports, visas, clothes, compass, emergency gear, and blank checks.[5]

McIntosh identified 46 conditions available to her as a white person that her African-American co-workers, friends, and acquaintances could not count on.[6] Some of these include: being told that people of her color made American heritage or civilization what it is; not needing to educate her children to be aware of systemic racism for their own daily protection; and never being asked to speak for all people of her racial group.[7]

Privilege also exists based on sexual orientation. Society presumes heterosexuality, generally constituting gay and lesbian relations as invisible.[8] Professor Marc Fajer describes what he calls three societal pre-understandings about gay men and lesbians: the sex-as-lifestyle assumption, the cross-gender assumption, and the idea that gay issues are inappropriate for public discussion. According to Professor Fajer the sex-as-lifestyle assumption means that there is a "common non-gay belief that gay people experience sexual activity differently from non-gays" in a way that is "all-encompassing, obsessive and completely divorced from love, long-term relationships, and family structure."[9] As to the cross-gender assumption, Professor Fajer explains that many non-gay people believe that gay men and lesbians exhibit "behavior stereotypically associated with the other gender."[10] The idea that gay issues are inappropriate for public discussion has received prominent press coverage recently as "Don't ask; don't tell" concerning the military. Thus, even if being gay is acceptable, "talking about being gay is not," according to Professor Fajer.[11]

Professor Fajer does not discuss these pre-understandings in terms of privilege. Nevertheless he is describing aspects of the sexual orientation power system which allow heterosexuals to function in a world where similar assumptions are not made about their sexuality. Not only are these assumptions not made about heterosexuals, but also their sexuality may be discussed and even advertised in public.

In spite of the pervasiveness of privilege, anti-discrimination practice and theory has generally not examined it and its role in perpetuating discrimination. Anti-discrimination advocates focus only on one half of the power system dyad, the subordinated characteristic, rather than seeing the essential companionship between domination that accompanies subordination and privilege that accompanies discrimination.

Professor Adrienne Davis has written:

> Anti-discrimination activists are attacking the visible half of the domination/subordination dyad, trying bravely to chop it up into little pieces. These anti-discrimination activists fail to realize that the subordination will grow back from the ignored half of the dyad of privilege. Like a mythic double-headed hydra, which will inevitably grow a second head if both heads are not slain, discrimination cannot be ended by focusing only on subordination.[12]

Yet the descriptive vocabulary and conceptualization of discrimination hinders our ability to see the hydra-head of privilege. This invisibility is serious because that which is not seen cannot be discussed or changed. Thus, to end subordination, one must first recognize privilege. Seeing privilege means articulating a new vocabulary and structure for anti-subordination theory. Only by visualizing this privilege and incorporating it into discourse can people of good faith combat discrimination.

For me the struggle to visualize privilege most often has taken the form of the struggle to see my own white privilege. Even as I write about this struggle, I fear that my racism will make things worse, causing me to do more harm than good. Some readers may be shocked to see a white person contritely acknowledge that she is racist. Understand I do not say this with pride. I simply believe that no matter how hard I work at not being racist, I still am. Because part of racism is systemic, I benefit from the privilege that I am struggling to see.

Whites do not look at the world through a filter of racial awareness, even though whites are, of course, a race. The power to ignore race, when white is the race, is a privilege, a societal advantage. Yet whites spend a lot of time trying to convince ourselves and each other that we are not racist. I think a big step would be for whites to admit that we are racist and then to consider what to do about it.[13] I also work on not being sexist. This work is different from my work on my racism, because I am a woman and I experience gender subordination. But it is important to realize that even when we are not privileged by a particular power system, we are products of the culture that instills its attitudes in us. I have to make sure that I am calling on women students and listening to them as carefully as I listen to men.

While we work at seeing privilege, it is also important to remember that each of us is much more complex than simply our race and gender. Professor Kimberlé

Crenshaw and others introduced the idea of the intersection into feminist jurisprudence. Her work examines the intersection of race, as African-American, with
gender, as female. Thus, Crenshaw's intersectionality analysis focused on intersections of subordination.

Intersectionality can help reveal privilege, especially when we remember that
the intersection is multi-dimensional, including intersections of both subordination and privilege. Imagine intersections in three dimensions, where multiple
lines intersect. From the center one can see in many different directions. Every
individual exists at the center of these multiple intersections, where many strands
meet, similar to a Koosh ball.[14]

The Koosh ball is a popular children's toy. Although it is called a ball and that
category leads one to imagine a firm, round surface used for catching and throwing, the Koosh is neither hard nor firm. Picture hundreds of rubber bands, tied in
the center. Mentally cut the end of each band. The wriggling, unfirm mass in your
hand is a Koosh ball, still usable for throwing and catching, but changing shape
as it sails through the air or as the wind blows through its rubbery limbs when it
is at rest. It is a dynamic ball.

The Koosh is the perfect post-modern ball. Its image "highlights that each
person is embedded in a matrix of . . . [categories] that interact in different contexts" taking different shapes.[15] In some contexts we are privileged and in some
subordinated, and these contexts interact.

Societal efforts at categorization are dynamic in the same way as the Koosh
is, changing, yet keeping a central mass. When society categorizes someone on
the basis of race, as either white or of color, it picks up a strand of the Koosh, a
piece of rubber band, and says, "See this strand, this is defining and central. It
matters." And it might be a highly important strand, but looking at one strand
does not really help anyone to see the shape of the whole ball or the whole person. And race may be a whole cluster of strands including color, culture, identification, and experience. Even naming the experience "race" veils its many facets.

Categorical thinking obscures our vision of the whole, in which multiple
strands interrelate with each other, as well as our vision of its individual strands.
No individual really fits into any one category; rather, everyone resides at the intersection of many categories. Yet categorical thinking makes it hard or impossible to conceptualize the complexity of an individual. The cultural push has long
been to choose a category.[16] Yet forcing a choice results in a hollow vision that
cannot do justice. Justice requires seeing the whole person in her or his social context.

Complex, difficult situations that are in reality discrimination cannot be adequately described using ordinary language, because that language masks privilege. Language masks privilege by making the bases of subordination themselves
appear linguistically neutral, so that the cultural hierarchy implicit in words such
as race, gender, and sexual orientation is banished from the language. Once the
hierarchy is made visible the problems remain no less complex, but it becomes
possible to discuss them in a more revealing and useful fashion.

NOTES

Note: I acknowledge my intellectual debt to two colleagues, Adrienne Davis and Trina Grillo, both professors at my school. The three of us worked together for almost two years, writing several working papers examining privilege and subordination. The "with" designation for authorship reflects Davis's contribution in paragraphs concerning "-isms" language and categories which we wrote together for the working papers. [S.M.W.]

1. Richard Delgado & Jean Stefancic, *Pornography and Harm to Women: "No Empirical Evidence?"*, 53 OHIO ST. L.J. 1037 (1992) (describing this "way things are." Because the norm or reality is perceived as including these benefits, the privileges are not visible.)

2. CATHARINE A. MACKINNON, TOWARD A FEMINIST THEORY OF THE STATE 224 (1989).

3. Sylvia Law, *Homosexuality and the Social Meaning of Gender*, 1988 WIS. L. REV. 187, 197 (1988); Marc Fajer, *Can Two Real Men Eat Quiche Together? Storytelling, Gender-Role Stereotypes, and Legal Protection for Lesbians and Gay Men*, 46 U. MIAMI L. REV. 511, 617 (1992). Both articles describe heterosexism as a form of gender oppression.

4. Peggy McIntosh, *Unpacking the Invisible Knapsack: White Privilege*, CREATION SPIRITUALITY, Jan./Feb. 1992, at 33. Marnie Mahoney has also described aspects of white privilege. Martha Mahoney, *Whiteness and Women, In Practice and Theory: A Reply to Catharine MacKinnon*, 5 YALE J. L. & FEMINISM 217 (1993).

5. McIntosh, *supra* note 4, at 33.

6. *Id.* at 34.

7. *Id.*

8. Adrienne Rich, *Compulsory Heterosexuality and Lesbian Existence, in* BLOOD, BREAD, AND POETRY, SELECTED PROSE 1979–1985 (1986)

9. *Id.* at 514.

10. *Id.* at 515.

11. *Id.*

12. Adrienne D. Davis, *Toward a Post-Essentialist Methodology; or, A Call to Countercategorical Practices* (unpublished, 1994).

13. See also Jerome McCristal Culp, Jr., *Water Buffalos and Diversity: Naming Names and Reclaiming the Racial Discourse*, 26 CONN. L. REV. 209 (1993) (urging people to name racism as racism).

14. The image of the koosh ball to describe the individual at the center of many intersections evolved during a working session between Adrienne Davis, Trina Grillo, and me.

15. Joan C. Williams, *Dissolving the Sameness/Difference Debate: A Post-Modern Path Beyond Essentialism in Feminist and Critical Race Theory*, 1991 DUKE L.J. 296, 307.

16. Thus in 1916 Harold Laski wrote: "Whether we will or no, we are bundles of hyphens. When the central linkages conflict, a choice must be made." Harold Laski, *The Personality of Associations*, 29 HARV. L. REV. 404, 425 (1916).

From the Editor:
Issues and Comments

I S M I N O R I T Y racial status only possible in a society that has formed the category of whiteness as a preferred condition? That is, are whiteness and blackness (or brownness, etc.) mutually dependent notions, such that without the one the other would not exist? If so, should it be a first order of business for any society bent on achieving racial justice to come to grips with the meaning of its own dominant coloration, namely whiteness? Do you agree that in our own society whiteness is equated with innocence, as Thomas Ross says; is the basis for extrapolation and metaphor, as Grillo and Wildman say; and is the baseline for determining privilege, as Wildman and Davis suggest? When it comes to deciding who can intermarry and who can naturalize, is even a drop of nonwhite blood tantamount to contamination, as Haney López implies, based on his assessment of Supreme Court jurisprudence?

The reader intrigued by recent Critical attention to the idea of whiteness may well wonder what is next, in particular whether masculinity, another category freighted by power and privilege, will not come in for examination. In the past few years, novels (e.g., Alice Walker, *The Color Purple*) and book-essays (e.g., Ishmael Reed, *Airing Dirty Laundry*) have called attention to issues of misogyny and divisions between men and women of color. Recently a few race-Crits have begun to address these issues as well. Derrick Bell's *And We Are Not Saved* contains a pungent—and controversial—Chronicle concerning black professional women's marriage chances. Through a fictional interlocutor, Bell raises the possibility that black men who date or marry white women, get themselves arrested, or otherwise make themselves unmarriageable are responsible for the predicament of black women faced with a lonely future (Derrick Bell, AND WE ARE NOT SAVED 193–214 (1987)).

Kevin Brown continues the interrogation of traditional notions of black masculinity. In a recent article (THE SOCIAL CONSTRUCTION OF A RAPE VICTIM, 1992 U. Ill. L. Rev. 997) he uses conversations with African American males in Indianapolis to show how belief systems operating in the black community constructed heavyweight boxing champion Mike Tyson as a victim of white justice, even though he was accused and convicted of raping Desiree Washington. Brown, an African American, points out how loyalty to the black community demands that racism trump sexism as the first struggle to be won, due to the ingrained belief that justice is white and sexism mainly a white issue. Brown argues that this view victimizes African-American women, leaving them exposed, perhaps indefinitely, because the racial problem will never be solved. It also victimizes black men by reinforcing stereotypes of them as violent and oversexed.

Jerome Culp, writing about the Rodney King case (NOTES FROM CALIFORNIA: RODNEY KING AND THE RACE QUESTION, 70 Denver U. L. Rev. 199 (1993)) argues that white insecurities play a large part in the predicament of black men. White police officers view uppity African-American men as sexual and political competitors and make sure that they remain in their place. Culp details the "rules of engagement" by which many African-American males are taught to survive during encounters with the police and urges that not acknowledging the role of race in criminal justice simply increases racial subordination.

Will Critical Race Masculinism be the next area of inquiry for civil rights scholarship and activism? Will we see a tide of writing reexamining the dynamics of sex from within the civil rights community? And if so, will this be a welcome tendency or a needless distraction? Developments move quickly in Critical thought, especially during times of ferment like the present. Only a few years ago, essentialism and antiessentialism, and intersectionality, were only beginning to be written about. Today, they are on the front burner. Critical white studies is an even more recent development; some books on Critical Race Theory do not even mention it. Although making predictions is always hazardous, it seems likely that a reexamination of the role of gender in communities of color, and of the construction of femininity and masculinity in general, is very much in order.

Suggested Readings

Bell, Derrick, *White Superiority in America: Its Legacy, Its Economic Costs*, Part II, this volume.

Flagg, Barbara, *"Was Blind, But Now I See": White Race Consciousness and the Requirement of Discriminators Intent*, 91 MICH. L. REV. 953 (1993).

Gordon, James W., *Did the First Justice Harlan Have a Black Brother?*, Part III, this volume.

Harris, Cheryl, *Whiteness as Property*, 106 HARV. L. REV. 1707 (1993).

Peller, Gary, *Notes Toward a Postmodern Nationalism*, 1992 U. ILL. L. REV. 1095.

Russell, Margaret M., *Race and the Dominant Gaze: Narratives of Law and Inequality in Popular Film*, Part II, this volume.

Scales-Trent, Judy, *Commonalities: On Being Black and White, Different, and the Same*, 2 YALE J.L. & FEMINISM 305 (1990).

Thomas, Kendall, *A House Divided Against Itself: A Comment on "Mastery, Slavery, and Emancipation,"* 10 CARDOZO L. REV. 1481 (1989).

Williams, Patricia, *Alchemical Notes: Reconstructing Ideals from Deconstructed Rights*, 22 HARV. C.R.-C.L. L. REV. 401 (1987).

About the Contributors

REGINA AUSTIN, professor of law at the University of Pennsylvania, writes and teaches in the areas of torts, products liability, and civil rights. She recently served as visiting professor of law at Harvard University School of Law.

ROBIN BARNES, professor of law at the University of Connecticut, teaches and writes in the area of constitutional law and Critical Race Theory.

DERRICK BELL, professor of law at New York University Law School, is considered the founder of Critical Race Theory. A prolific author, he has also served as dean at the University of Oregon Law School and as the first tenured African-American professor at Harvard Law School.

KEVIN D. BROWN, professor of law at Indiana-Bloomington School of Law, is a specialist in juvenile law, education law, and civil rights.

PAULETTE M. CALDWELL, professor of law at New York University Law School, teaches and writes in the areas of property, real-estate transactions, and civil rights.

ROBERT S. CHANG, professor of law at California Western School of Law, teaches contracts and Critical Race Theory and is a prime architect of Asian-American legal studies.

ROBERT J. COTTROL is a legal historian and constitutional-law scholar teaching at Rutgers-Camden School of Law.

JEROME McCRISTAL CULP, JR., teaches Black jurisprudence, law and economics, and labor law at Duke University Law School. A leading contributor to Critical Race Theory, he is currently serving as visiting professor of law at the University of California, Berkeley.

ADRIENNE D. DAVIS, professor of law at USF School of Law and visiting professor at the American University School of Law, writes and teaches about race, feminist theory, and property.

PEGGY C. DAVIS is professor of law at New York University Law School, where she teaches and writes on domestic relations, clinical teaching, and law and social science. Before entering law teaching in 1983, she served as judge of the Family Court of the State of New York.

RICHARD DELGADO, professor of law at the University of Colorado Law School, writes about Critical Race Theory, legal narratives, and hate speech.

RAYMOND T. DIAMOND, professor of law, teaches constitutional law, civil rights, and legal history at Tulane Law School.

MARY L. DUDZIAK is professor of law at the University of Iowa School of Law, where she writes and teaches about legal history, immigration law, and civil rights.

LESLIE G. ESPINOZA, professor of law at Boston College Law School, teaches clinical law, health-care law, trusts and estates, and women and the law. She writes about health law and Critical theory.

MONICA J. EVANS, professor of law at Santa Clara University, and visiting professor of law at Quinnipiac School of Law, teaches courses on business planning, torts, and constitutional law. She also writes in the area of Critical Race Feminism.

DANIEL A. FARBER, professor of law and associate dean at the University of Minnesota Law School, is one of the nation's most prolific legal writers. He is principally interested in the areas of jurisprudence, constitutional law, and civil rights.

ALAN D. FREEMAN teaches at SUNY—Buffalo School of Law, where he writes and teaches courses on nature and ecology, the First Amendment, and jurisprudence. One of the earliest contributors to the Critical Race Theory genre, he also writes about abortion and animal rights.

JAMES W. GORDON teaches law at Western New England College School of Law. He writes and teaches in the areas of legal history, the legal profession, and the role of lawyers in politics.

TRINA GRILLO, professor of law at the University of San Francisco Law School, writes and teaches in the areas of constitutional law, mediation, and alternative dispute resolution.

IAN F. HANEY LÓPEZ, Rockefeller Fellow in Legal Humanities, Stanford University, 1994–95, teaches law at the University of Wisconsin, where he specializes in Critical Race Theory, civil rights, and jurisprudence. His recent work has focused on understanding how our society constructs notions of race and nonrace.

ANGELA P. HARRIS teaches legal theory, civil rights, and criminal law at the University of California Law School at Berkeley (Boalt Hall).

LISA C. IKEMOTO, professor of law at Loyola University of Los Angeles, is an expert on reproductive law, legal narrative, and civil rights.

ALEX M. JOHNSON, JR., professor of law at the University of Virginia Law School, teaches and writes in the areas of trusts and estates, civil rights, and property law.

SHERI LYNN JOHNSON, professor of law at Cornell University School of Law, is a leading expert on the social science of race and racism. In recent years, her scholarship has focused on issues of conscious and unconscious prejudice in trials.

RANDALL L. KENNEDY teaches civil rights and contracts at Harvard. He has published numerous articles about civil rights in leading reviews and is the editor of *Reconstruction* magazine.

SYLKE MERCHÁN holds her B.A. from Grinnell, M.A. from Northwestern, and J.D. from the University of Iowa. A native of Germany, she is currently a clerk with the U.S. Immigration Service in Chicago.

KATHRYN MILUN is professor of anthropology at Rice University, where she specializes in critical theory and indigenous rights.

MARGARET E. MONTOYA, professor of law at the University of New Mexico Law School, writes on legal narratives and storytelling and on the intersection of feminism and civil rights.

MICHAEL A. OLIVAS, professor of law at the University of Houston Law School and director of the Institute of Higher Education Law and Governance, is an expert on immigration law, higher education law, and civil rights.

DEBORAH WAIRE POST, professor of law at Touro law school and visiting professor of law at Syracuse University School of Law, teaches courses in the areas of contracts law, securities regulation, and the sociology of law. She also writes about civil rights and feminist theory.

THOMAS ROSS writes about narrative theory, Supreme Court rhetoric, and civil rights. He teaches law at the University of Pittsburgh Law School.

JENNIFER M. RUSSELL, professor of law at Case-Western Reserve University School of Law, teaches civil procedure, feminist jurisprudence, and law and inequality.

MARGARET M. RUSSELL, professor of law at Santa Clara University Law School, teaches and writes about public-interest and constitutional law. As convenor of the 1993 Critical Race Theory workshop, she played a central role in the decision to produce this book.

SUZANNA SHERRY is professor of law at the University of Minnesota. She teaches and writes on constitutional law and history, the foundations of communitarianism, and feminist legal theory.

GIRARDEAU A. SPANN, professor of law at Georgetown Law Center, is an expert on civil rights and the courts.

JEAN STEFANCIC, research associate at the University of Colorado Law School, writes about Critical Race Theory and legal scholarship and bibliography.

GERALD TORRES is professor of law at the University of Texas, where he specializes in political theory and civil rights. He recently served as special assistant to U.S. Attorney General Janet Reno, with responsibilities in environmental and Native American affairs.

STEPHANIE M. WILDMAN teaches at the University of San Francisco School of Law, where she is a specialist in feminist legal theory and jurisprudence. She also teaches torts and employment discrimination and has served as visiting professor at Stanford and Santa Clara Law Schools.

PATRICIA J. WILLIAMS has written about race, civil rights, and constitutional law in leading law reviews and in books. She teaches law at Columbia University School of Law.

ROBERT A. WILLIAMS, JR., professor of law at the University of Arizona, is a prolific author and leading scholar on indigenous peoples' rights. He has served as a tribal judge, an expert witness in Indian litigation, and has testified before U.N. commissions investigating the status of indigenous peoples.

ADRIEN KATHERINE WING is professor of law at the University of Iowa School of Law, where she teaches and writes in the areas of comparative and international law and civil rights.

Index